DATE DUE

| | | | |
|---|---|---|---|
| | | | |
| | | | |
| | | | |
| | | | |
| | | | |
| | | | |
| | | | |
| | | | |

DEMCO 128-5046

# Children's
# Literature
# Review

# Guide to Gale Literary Criticism Series

**When you need to review criticism of literary works, these are the Gale series to use:**

| If the author's death date is: | You should turn to: |
|---|---|

After Dec. 31, 1959 (or author is still living)

### *CONTEMPORARY LITERARY CRITICISM*

for example: Jorge Luis Borges, Anthony Burgess, William Faulkner, Mary Gordon, Ernest Hemingway, Iris Murdoch

1900 through 1959

### *TWENTIETH-CENTURY LITERARY CRITICISM*

for example: Willa Cather, F. Scott Fitzgerald, Henry James, Mark Twain, Virginia Woolf

1800 through 1899

### *NINETEENTH-CENTURY LITERATURE CRITICISM*

for example: Fyodor Dostoevsky, Nathaniel Hawthorne, George Sand, William Wordsworth

1400 through 1799

### *LITERATURE CRITICISM FROM 1400 TO 1800 (excluding Shakespeare)*

for example: Anne Bradstreet, Daniel Defoe, Alexander Pope, François Rabelais, Jonathan Swift, Phillis Wheatley

### *SHAKESPEAREAN CRITICISM*

Shakespeare's plays and poetry

Antiquity through 1399

### *CLASSICAL AND MEDIEVAL LITERATURE CRITICISM*

for example: Dante, Homer, Plato, Sophocles, Vergil, the Beowulf Poet

---

## Gale also publishes related criticism series:

### *CHILDREN'S LITERATURE REVIEW*

This series covers authors of all eras who have written for the preschool through high school audience.

### *SHORT STORY CRITICISM*

This series covers the major short fiction writers of all nationalities and periods of literary history.

### *POETRY CRITICISM*

This series covers poets of all nationalities and periods of literary history.

ISSN 0362-4145

volume 26

# Children's Literature Review

Excerpts from Reviews,
Criticism, and Commentary
on Books for Children
and Young People

**Gerard J. Senick**
Editor

**Sharon R. Gunton**
Associate Editor

**Gale Research Inc.** • DETROIT • LONDON

## STAFF

Gerard J. Senick, *Editor*

Sharon R. Gunton, *Associate Editor*

Jeanne A. Gough, *Permissions & Production Manager*
Linda M. Pugliese, *Production Supervisor*
Paul Lewon, Lorna Mabunda, Maureen A. Puhl, Camille Robinson,
Jennifer VanSickle, *Editorial Associates*
Donna Craft, Brandy C. Johnson, Sheila Walencewicz, *Editorial Assistants*

Maureen Richards, *Research Supervisor*
Mary Beth McElmeel, *Editorial Associate*
Kathleen Jowiak, Amy Kaechele, Julie Karmazin, Tamara C. Nott, Julie
Synkonis, *Editorial Assistants*

Sandra C. Davis, *Permissions Supervisor (Text)*
Maria Franklin, Josephine M. Keene, Denise M. Singleton, Kimberly F.
Smilay, *Permissions Associates*
Rebecca A. Hartford, Michele M. Lonoconus, Shelly Rakcozy, Shalice
Shah, *Permissions Assistants*

Margaret A. Chamberlain, *Permissions Supervisor (Pictures)*
Pamela A. Hayes, *Permissions Associate*
Karla Kulkis, Nancy Rattenbury, Keith Reed, *Permissions Assistants*

Mary Beth Trimper, *Production Manager*
Mary Winterhalter, *Production Assistant*

Arthur Chartow, *Art Director*
C. J. Jonik, *Keyliner*

# Contents

# Preface

Children's literature has evolved into both a respected branch of creative writing and a successful industry. Currently, books for young readers are considered the most popular segment of publishing, while criticism of juvenile literature is instrumental in recording the literary or artistic development of the creators of children's books as well as the trends and controversies that result from changing values or attitudes about young people and their literature. Designed to provide a permanent, accessible record of this ongoing scholarship, *Children's Literature Review* (*CLR*) presents parents, teachers, and librarians—those responsible for bringing children and books together—with the opportunity to make informed choices when selecting reading materials for the young. This audience will find balanced overviews of the careers of the authors and illustrators of the books that they and their children are reading; these entries, which contain excerpts from published criticism in books and periodicals, assist users by sparking ideas for papers and assignments and suggesting supplementary and classroom reading. Ann L. Kalkhoff, president and editor of *Children's Book Review Service Inc.*, writes that "*CLR* has filled a gap in the field of children's books, and it is one series that will never lose its validity or importance."

## Scope of the Series

Each volume of *CLR* profiles the careers of authors and illustrators of books for children from preschool through high school. Author lists in each volume reflect these elements:

- author lists are international in scope.

- approximately fifteen authors of all eras are represented.

- author lists represent the variety of genres covered by children's literature: picture books, fiction, nonfiction, poetry, folklore, and drama.

Although earlier volumes of *CLR* emphasized critical material published after 1960, successive volumes have expanded their coverage to encompass important criticism written before 1960. Since many of the authors included in *CLR* are living and continue to write, it is necessary to update their entries periodically. Thus, future volumes will supplement the entries of selected authors covered in earlier volumes as well as include criticism on the works of authors new to the series.

## Organization of This Book

An author section consists of the following elements: author heading, author portrait, author introduction, excerpts of criticism (each followed by a bibliographical citation), and illustrations, when available.

- The **author heading** consists of the author's name followed by birth and death dates. The portion of the name outside the parentheses denotes the form under which the author is most frequently published. If the majority of the author's works for children were written under a pseudonym, the pseudonym will be listed in the author heading and the real name given on the first line of the author introduction. Also located at the beginning of the introduction are any other pseudonyms used by the author in writing for children and any name variations, including transliterated forms for authors whose languages use nonroman alphabets. Uncertainty as to a birth or death date is indicated by question marks.

- An **author portrait** is included when available.

- The **author introduction** contains information designed to introduce an author to *CLR* users by presenting an overview of the author's themes and styles, occasional biographical facts that relate to the author's literary career or critical responses to the author's works, and information about major awards and prizes the author has received. Introductions also list a group of representative titles for which the author or illustrator being profiled is best known; this section, which begins with the words "major works include," follows the genre line of the introduction. Where applicable, introductions conclude with references to additional entries in biographical and critical reference series published by Gale Research Inc. These sources include past volumes of *CLR* as well as *Authors & Artists for Young Adults, Contemporary Authors, Contemporary Literary Criticism, Dictionary of Literary Biography, Nineteenth-Century Literature Criticism, Short Story Criti-*

*cism, Something about the Author, Something about the Author Autobiography Series, Twentieth-Century Literary Criticism,* and *Yesterday's Authors of Books for Children.*

• **Criticism** is located in three sections: **author's commentary** (when available), **general commentary** (when available), and **title commentary** (in which commentary on specific titles appears). Centered headings introduce each section, in which criticism is arranged chronologically. Titles by authors being profiled are highlighted in boldface type within the text for easier access by readers.

The **author's commentary** presents background material written by the author or by an interviewer. This commentary may cover a specific work or several works. Author's commentary on more than one work appears after the author introduction, while commentary on an individual book follows the title entry heading.

The **general commentary** consists of critical excerpts that consider more than one work by the author or illustrator being profiled. General commentary is preceded by the critic's name in boldface type or, in the case of unsigned criticism, by the title of the journal. Occasionally, *CLR* features entries that emphasize general criticism on the overall career of an author or illustrator. When appropriate, a selection of reviews is included to supplement the general commentary.

The **title commentary** begins with title entry headings, which precede the criticism on a title and cite publication information on the work being reviewed. Title headings list the title of the work as it appeared in its first English-language edition. The first English-language publication date of each work is listed in parentheses following the title. Differing U.S. and British titles follow the publication date within the parentheses.

Entries in each title commentary section consist of critical excerpts on the author's individual works, arranged chronologically by publication date. The entries generally contain two to six reviews per title, depending on the stature of the book and the amount of criticism it has generated. The editors select titles that reflect the entire scope of the author's literary contribution, covering each genre and subject. An effort is made to reprint criticism that represents the full range of each title's reception—from the year of its initial publication to current assessments. Thus, the reader is provided with a record of the author's critical history. Publication information (such as publisher names and book prices) and parenthetical numerical references (such as footnotes or page and line references to specific editions of works) have been deleted at the editor's discretion to provide smoother reading of the text.

• Selected excerpts are preceded by **explanatory notes,** which provide information on the critic or work of criticism to enhance the reader's understanding of the excerpt.

• A complete **bibliographical citation** designed to facilitate the location of the original book or article follows each piece of criticism.

• Numerous **illustrations** are featured in *CLR.* For entries on illustrators, an effort has been made to include illustrations that reflect the characteristics discussed in the criticism. Entries on major authors who do not illustrate their own works may also include photographs and other illustrative material pertinent to the authors' careers.

### Special Features

Entries on authors who are also illustrators will occasionally feature commentary on selected works illustrated but not written by the author being profiled. These works are strongly associated with the illustrator and have received critical acclaim for their art. By including critical comment on works of this type, the editors wish to provide a more complete representation of the author's total career. Criticism on these works has been chosen to stress artistic, rather than literary, contributions. Title entry headings for works illustrated by the author being profiled are arranged chronologically within the entry by date of publication and include notes identifying the author of the illustrated work. In order to provide easier access for users, all titles illustrated by the subject of the entry will be boldfaced.

*CLR* also includes entries on prominent illustrators who have contributed to the field of children's literature. These entries are designed to represent the development of the illustrator as an artist rather than as a literary stylist. The illustrator's section is organized like that of an author, with two exceptions: the introduction presents an overview of the illustrator's styles and techniques rather than outlining his or her literary background, and the commentary written by the illustrator on his or her works is called illustrator's commentary rather than author's commentary. Title entry headings are followed by explanatory notes identifying the author of the illustrated work. All titles of books containing illustrations by the artist being profiled as well as individual illustrations from these books are highlighted in boldface type.

## Other Features

• An **acknowledgments,** which immediately follows the preface, lists the sources from which material has been reprinted in the volume. It does not, however, list every book or periodical consulted for the volume.

• The **cumulative index to authors** lists authors who have appeared in *CLR* and includes cross-references to *Authors & Artists for Young Adults, Contemporary Authors, Contemporary Literary Criticism, Dictionary of Literary Biography, Nineteenth-Century Literature Criticism, Short Story Criticism, Something about the Author, Something about the Author Autobiography Series, Twentieth-Century Literary Criticism,* and *Yesterday's Authors of Books for Children.*

• The **cumulative nationality index** lists authors alphabetically under their respective nationalities. Author names are followed by the volume number(s) in which they appear. Authors who have changed citizenship or whose current citizenship is not reflected in biographical sources appear under both their original nationality and that of their current residence.

• The **cumulative title index** lists titles covered in *CLR* followed by the volume and page number where criticism begins.

## A Note to the Reader

When writing papers, students who quote directly from any volume in the Literature Criticism Series may use the following general forms to footnote reprinted criticism. The first example pertains to material drawn from periodicals, the second to material reprinted from books.

¹ T. S. Eliot, "John Donne," *The Nation and the Athenaeum,* 33 (9 June 1923), 321-32; excerpted and reprinted in *Literature Criticism from 1400 to 1800,* Vol. 10, ed. James E. Person, Jr. (Detroit: Gale Research, 1989), pp. 28-9.

¹ Henry Brooke, *Leslie Brooke and Johnny Crow* (Frederick Warne, 1982); excerpted and reprinted in *Children's Literature Review,* Vol. 20, ed. Gerard J. Senick (Detroit: Gale Research, 1990), p. 47.

## Suggestions Are Welcome

In response to various suggestions, several features have been added to *CLR* since the series began, including author entries on retellers of traditional literature as well as those who have been the first to record oral tales and other folklore; entries on prominent illustrators featuring commentary on their styles and techniques; entries on authors whose works are considered controversial or have been challenged; occasional entries devoted to criticism on a single work by a major author; sections in author introductions that list major works by the author or illustrator being profiled; explanatory notes that provide information on the critic or work of criticism to enhance the usefulness of the excerpt; more extensive illustrative material, such as holographs of manuscript pages and photographs of people and places pertinent to the authors' careers; a cumulative nationality index for easy access to authors by nationality; and occasional guest essays written specifically for *CLR* by prominent critics on subjects of their choice.

Readers who wish to suggest authors to appear in future volumes, or who have other suggestions, are cordially invited to write the editor.

# Acknowledgments

The editors wish to thank the copyright holders of the excerpted criticism included in this volume, the permissions managers of many book and magazine publishing companies for assisting us in securing reprint rights, and Anthony Bogucki for assistance with copyright research. We are also grateful to the staffs of the Detroit Public Library, the Library of Congress, the University of Detroit Library, Wayne State University Purdy/Kresge Library Complex, and the University of Michigan Libraries for making their resources available to us. Following is a list of the copyright holders who have granted us permission to reprint material in this volume of CLR. Every effort has been made to trace copyright, but if omissions have been made, please let us know.

**COPYRIGHTED EXCERPTS IN *CLR,* VOLUME 26, WERE REPRINTED FROM THE FOLLOWING PERIODICALS:**

***The Alan Review,*** v. 12, Winter, 1985. Reprinted by permission of the publisher.—***Appraisal: Children's Science Books,*** v.4, Spring, 1971; v. 5, Winter, 1972; v. 6, Winter, 1973; v. 7, Winter, 1974. Copyright © 1971, 1972, 1973, 1974 by the Children's Science Book Review Committee. All reprinted by permission of the publisher.—***Appraisal: Science Books for Young People,*** v. 19, Fall, 1986; v. 23, Winter, 1990. Copyright © 1986, 1990 by the Children's Science Book Review Committee. Both reprinted by permission of the publisher.—***The Atlantic Monthly,*** v. 188, December, 1951. Copyright 1951, renewed 1979 by The Atlantic Monthly Company, Boston, MA. Reprinted by permission of the publisher.—***Best Sellers,*** v. 42, February, 1983. Copyright © 1983 Helen Dwight Reid Educational Foundation. Reprinted by permission of the publisher.—***The Book Report,*** v. 4, March-April, 1986. © copyright 1986 by Linworth Publishing Co. Reprinted by permission of the publisher.—***Book Week—World Journal Tribune,*** October 30, 1966. © 1966, *The Washington Post.* Reprinted by permission of the publisher.—***Book World—The Washington Post,*** October 29, 1967. © 1967 Postrib Corp./ March 3, 1968 for "To Be a Logger" by Helen Renthal; November 8, 1970 for "A Child's Wonder" by Julian May. © 1968, 1970 Postrib Corp. Both reprinted by courtesy of *The Washington Post* and the respective authors./ November 5, 1973; January 13, 1985; November 10, 1985; February 9, 1986; October 9, 1988. © 1973, 1985, 1986, 1988, *The Washington Post.* All reprinted with permission of the publisher.—***Bookbird,*** v. XI, June 15, 1973. Reprinted by permission of the publisher.—***Booklist,*** v. 74, May 1, 1978; v. 80, May 15, 1984; v. 82, October 1, 1985; v. 82, June 15, 1986; v. 83, January 1, 1987; v. 83, May 1, 1987; v. 86, October 15, 1989; v. 86, December 1, 1989; v. 86, May 15, 1990; v. 86, June 1, 1990. Copyright © 1978, 1984, 1985, 1986, 1987, 1989, 1990 by the American Library Association. All reprinted by publisher.—***The Booklist,*** v. 72, December 15, 1975. Copyright © 1975 by The American Library Association. Reprinted by permission of the publisher.—***The Booklist and Subscription Books Bulletin,*** v. 62, March 1, 1966; v. 62, April 1, 1966. Copyright © 1966 by the American Library Association. Both reprinted by permission of the publisher.—***Books,*** London, n. 13, 1988. © Gradegate Ltd. 1988. Reprinted by permission of the publisher.—***Books and Bookmen,*** v. 21, January, 1975. © copyright the author 1975.—***Books for keeps,*** n. 41, November, 1986; n. 57, July, 1989. © School Bookshop Association 1986, 1989. Both reprinted by permission of the publisher.—***Books for Young People,*** v. 1, April, 1987 for a review of "A Handful of Time" by Annette Goldsmith. All rights reserved. Reprinted by permission of the publisher and the author.—***Books in Canada,*** v. 16, June-July, 1987 for "Living in the Past" by Mary Ainslie Smith. Reprinted by permission of the author.—***Bulletin of the Center for Children's Books,*** v. XV, July-August, 1962; v. XVI, April, 1963; v. XVII, May, 1964; v. XVIII, September, 1964; v. XVIII, May, 1965; v. 19, September, 1965; v. 19, February, 1966; v. 20, September, 1966; v. 20, February, 1967; v. 20, April, 1967; v. 21, November, 1967; v. 23, June, 1970; v. 24, July-August, 1971; v. 27, October, 1973; v. 31, October, 1977; v. 32, July-August, 1979; v. 33, December, 1979; v. 35, May, 1982; v. 37, November, 1983; v. 38, September, 1984; v. 39, October, 1985; v. 40, January, 1987; v. 40, April, 1987; v. 41, December, 1987, v. 41, February, 1988; v. 41, May, 1988; v. 42, September, 1988; v. 43, September, 1989; v. 44, September, 1990. Copyright © 1962, 1963, 1964, 1965, 1966, 1967, 1970, 1971, 1973, 1977, 1979, 1982, 1983, 1984, 1985, 1987, 1988, 1989, 1990 by The University of Chicago. All reprinted by permission of the publisher./ v. XV, June, 1962; v. XXI, September, 1962; v. XVI, November, 1962. Copyright © 1962, renewed 1990. All reprinted by permission of The University of Chicago Press.—***Canadian Children's Literature,*** n. 26, 1982; n. 46, 1987; n. 49, 1988. Copyright © 1982, 1987, 1988 Canadian Children's Press. All reprinted by permission of the publisher.—***Chicago Sunday Tribune,*** part 4, September 30, 1956. © copyrighted 1956, renewed 1984 by Chicago Tribune Company. All rights reserved. Used with permission.—***Chicago Sunday Tribune Magazine of Books,*** October 22, 1950; May 22, 1955. Renewed 1978, 1983 by the Chicago Tribune./ June 12, 1960. Renewed 1988 by the Chicago Tribune. Reprinted by courtesy of the *Chicago Tribune.*—***Children's Book News,*** London, July-August, 1968; November-December, 1968; v. 5. May-June, 1970. Copyright © 1968, 1970 by Baker Book Service Ltd. All reprinted by permission of the publisher.—***Children's Book Review,*** v. IV, Autumn, 1974 for "Some Ingredients of 'Watership Down'" by Richard Adams. © 1974 by Five Owls Press Ltd. All rights reserved. Reprinted by permission of the author./ v. II, June, 1972; v. II, October, 1972; v. III, October, 1973. © 1972, 1973 by Five Owls Press Ltd. All rights reserved. All reprinted by permission

February, 1972; v. 18, May, 1972; v. 19, September, 1972; v. 19, February, 1973; v. 19, March, 1973; v. 20, December, 1973; v. 20, March, 1974; v. 20, April, 1974; v. 21, March, 1975; v. 21, April, 1975; v. 22, October, 1975; v. 23, May, 1977; v. 24, September, 1977; v. 24, February, 1978; v. 25, April, 1979; v. 26, November, 1979; v. 27, September, 1980; v. 27, October, 1980; v. 27, February, 1981; v. 28, October, 1981; v. 28, December, 1981; v. 28, April, 1982; v. 28, August, 1982; v. 29, March, 1983; v. 30, August, 1984; v. 32, October, 1985; v. 32, November, 1985; v. 32, January, 1986; v. 32, May, 1986; v. 33, February, 1987; v. 33, June-July, 1987; v. 34, October, 1987; v. 34, February, 1988; v. 25, May, 1988; v. 34, August, 1988; v. 35, October, 1988; v. 35, September, 1989; v. 36, February, 1990; v. 36, May, 1990; v. 36, June, 1990; v. 37, February, 1991. Copyright © 1963, 1965, 1966, 1967, 1968, 1969, 1970, 1971, 1972, 1973, 1974, 1975, 1977, 1978, 1979, 1980, 1981, 1982, 1983, 1984, 1985, 1986, 1987, 1988, 1989, 1990, 1991. All reprinted from *School Library Journal,* a Cahners/R. R. Bowker Publication, by permission.—*Science Books: A Quarterly Review,* v. 7, September, 1971. Copyright 1971 by AAAS. Reprinted by permission of the publisher.—*Science Books & Films,* v. V, September, 1969; v. XIII, March, 1978; v. XIV, May, 1978; v. XIV, March, 1979; v. 16, March, 1981. Copyright 1969, 1978, 1979, 1981 by AAAS. All reprinted by permission of the publisher.—*Science Fiction & Fantasy Book Review,* n. 19, November, 1983. Copyright © 1983 by Science Fiction Research Association. Reprinted by permission of the publisher.—*The Social Studies,* v. LXVIII, May-June, 1977. Copyright © 1977 Helen Dwight Reid Educational Foundation. Reprinted with permission of the Helen Dwight Reid Educational Foundation, published by Heldref Publications, 4000 Albemarle Street, N. W., Washington, DC 20016.—*The Spectator,* n. 7168, November 12, 1965; v. 225, December 5, 1970. © 1965, 1970 by *The Spectator.* Both reprinted by permission of *The Spectator.*—*The Times Educational Supplement,* n. 3562, October 5, 1984; n. 3649, June 6, 1986; n. 3858, June 8, 1990. © The Times Supplements Limited 1984, 1986, 1990. All reproduced from *The Times Educational Supplement* by permission.—*The Times Literary Supplement,* n. 3222, November 28, 1963; n. 3306, July 8, 1965; n. 3328, December 9, 1965; n. 3404, May 25, 1967; n. 3475, October 3, 1968; n. 3529, October 16, 1969; n. 3536, December 4, 1969; n. 3566, July 2, 1970; n. 3879, July 16, 1976; n. 3966, April 7, 1978; n. 4138, July 23, 1982; n. 4231, May 4, 1984; n. 4278, March 29, 1985; n. 4310, November 8, 1985; n. 4405, September 4-7, 1987. © The Times Supplements Limited 1963, 1965, 1967, 1968, 1969, 1970, 1976, 1978, 1982, 1984, 1985, 1987. All reproduced from *The Times Literary Supplement* by permission.—*The Use of English,* v. 30, Spring, 1979. Reprinted by permission of Scottish Academic Press, 139 Leith Walk, Edinburgh EH6 8NS.—*Virginia Kirkus' Bookshop Service,* v. XVIII, August 15, 1980. Reprinted by permission of the publisher. *Virginia Kirkus' Service,* v. XXXI, February 5, 1963; v. XXXII, March 15, 1964; v. XXXIII, January 1, 1965; v. XXXIII, July 15, 1965; v. XXXIII, November 1, 1965; v. XXXIV, August 1, 1966; v. XXXIV, December 15, 1966. Copyright © 1963, 1964, 1965, 1966 Virginia Kirkus' Service, Inc. All reprinted by permission of the publisher.—*Voice of Youth Advocates,* v. 5, October, 1982; v. 10, June, 1987. Copyrighted 1982, 1987 by *Voice of Youth Advocates.* Both reprinted by permission of the publisher.

## COPYRIGHTED EXCERPTS IN *CLR,* VOLUME 26, WERE REPRINTED FROM THE FOLLOWING BOOKS:

Arbuthnot, May Hill. From *Children and Books.* Scott, Foresman, 1947. Copyright 1947, renewed 1974 by Scott, Foresman and Company. Reprinted by permission of the publisher.—Arbuthnot, May Hill. From *Children's Reading in the Home.* Scott, Foresman, 1969. Copyright © 1969 by Scott, Foresman and Company. All rights reserved. Reprinted by permission of the publisher.—Bader, Barbara. From *American Picturebooks from Noah's Ark to the Beast Within.* Macmillan, 1976. Copyright © 1976 by Barbara Bader. All rights reserved. Reprinted with permission of Macmillan Publishing Company.—Blount, Margaret. From *Animal Land: The Creatures of Children's Fiction.* William Morrow & Company, Inc., 1975. Copyright © 1974 by Margaret Ingle-Finch. Reprinted by permission of the author.—Carpenter, Humphrey. From *Secret Gardens: A Study of the Golden Age of Children's Literature.* Houghton Mifflin, 1985, Unwin Hyman, 1985. Copyright © 1985 by Humphrey Carpenter. All right reserved. Reprinted by permission of Houghton Mifflin Company. In Canada by Unwin Hyman Ltd.—Crouch, Marcus. From *Treasure Seekers and Borrowers: Children's Books in Britain 1900-1960.* The Library Association, 1962. © Marcus Crouch, 1962. Reprinted by permission of the publisher.—Dannett, Sylvia G. L. From *Profiles of Negro Womanhood: 20th Century, Vol. II.* Educational Heritage, 1966. Copyright © 1966 by Educational Heritage, Incorporated. All rights reserved. Reprinted by permission of Emanuel Dannett.—Eyre, Frank. From *British Children's Books in the Twentieth Century.* Revised edition. Longman Books, 1971, Dutton, 1973. Copyright © 1971 by Frank Eyre. All rights reserved. Reprinted by permission of the publisher, E. P. Dutton, a division of Penguin Books USA Inc. In Canada by Penguin Books Ltd.—Green, Roger Lancelyn. From *Tellers of Tales.* Revised edition. Franklin Watts, Inc., 1965, Kaye and Ward, 1969. Copyright 1946, 1953, 1956, © 1965 by Edmund Ward (Publishers) Ltd. Reprinted by permission of William Heinemann Limited.—Grigson, Geoffrey. From *The Contrary View: Glimpses of Fudge and Gold.* Macmillan, 1974. © Geoffrey Grigson 1974. All rights reserved. Reprinted by permission of the author.—Helbig, Alethea K. and Agnes Regan Perkins. From *Dictionary of American Children's Fiction, 1859-1959: Books of Recognized Merit.* Greenwood Press, 1985. Copyright © 1985 by Alethea K. Helbig and Agnes Regan Perkins. All rights reserved. Reprinted by permission of Greenwood Publishing Group, Inc., Westport, CT.—Huck, Charlotte S., and Doris Young Kuhn. From *Children's Literature in the Elementary School.* Second edition. Holt, Rinehart and Winston, 1968. Copyright © 1961, 1968 by Holt, Rinehart and Winston, Inc. All rights reserved. Reprinted by permission of Holt, Rinehart and Winston.—Hürlimann, Bettina. From *Picture-Book World.* Edited and translated by Brian W. Alderson. Oxford University Press, London, 1968. English

## PERMISSION TO REPRODUCE ILLUSTRATIONS APPEARING IN *CLR*, VOLUME 26, WAS RECEIVED FROM THE FOLLOWING SOURCES:

Don Wood. Text copyright © 1985 by Audrey Wood. Reprinted by permission of Harcourt Brace Jovanovich, Inc.

# Children's
# Literature
# Review

# Vivien Alcock

## 1924-

English author of fiction and short stories.

Major works include *The Haunting of Cassie Palmer* (1980), *The Stonewalkers* (1983), *Ghostly Companions* (1984; U. S. edition as *Ghostly Companions: A Feast of Chilling Tales*), *The Cuckoo Sister* (1985), *The Monster Garden* (1988).

Called "one of England's most original spinners of tales" by *Kirkus Reviews,* Alcock is celebrated as a masterful and imaginative writer of contemporary realistic fiction for middle graders and young adults that characteristically incorporates strong elements of fantasy and the supernatural into suspenseful and thought-provoking stories. Often acknowledged for her sensitive characterizations of children and adults, her literary craftsmanship and fluid use of language, and her evocative delineation of the occult, Alcock is well known for using elements of genres such as the ghost story and the mystery to explore character and social issues in works noted for their depth of feeling, deftness, and wit. Her books usually feature preadolescent or adolescent female protagonists whose daily lives are changed through their relationship with the supernatural. Portraying a world of well-meaning but ineffectual adults, Alcock portrays the growth of her characters as they learn to accept their parents, each other, and themselves through their experiences. Usually addressing the theme that love, kindness, and trust are powerful antidotes to evil and help to develop self-confidence and communication, Alcock often portrays her characters as caretakers of vulnerable creatures such as ghosts, monsters, or aliens; she also underscores her works with the sentiment that true affection conquers differences in class and background, and consistently provides happy endings for her books despite their often nightmarish situations. Alcock is also the author of realistic fiction without supernatural elements that continues to define the journeys of her characters toward self-knowledge, two stories for primary graders which she writes in an easy reader format, and a collection of ten short stories, *Ghostly Companions,* for which she is compared to M. R. James.

A former commercial artist who is married to the writer Leon Garfield, Alcock began her literary career in response to their daughter's request for stories. As a child, Alcock's mother was often absent due to illness and her relationship with her father was weak; at the age of ten, she and her two older sisters were sent to live with family friends during her mother's terminal illness, an experience which she often reflects in her portrayals of family life. "I like to write about strange happenings—ghosts or secrets or misunderstandings—in an everyday setting," Alcock has said; she adds that since ghosts are often pitiful objects, a child can learn compassion through them. Her first books, *The Haunting of Cassie Palmer* and *The Stonewalkers,* include both psychic experiences and strained re-

lationships between mothers and daughters. In the first novel, twelve-year old Cassie, whose mother has been arrested on charges of fraud for pretending to be a medium, summons a ghost in a graveyard and goes into the past to put it to rest, while the second story describes how twelve-year-old Poppy, a compulsive liar who has been raised partially by foster parents due to her mother's poor health, becomes involved with a statue—first friendly but ultimately malevolent—that comes to life when it is hit by lightning; in both works, the protagonists begin to understand their mothers by the end of their adventures. Among Alcock's most distinctive works is *The Monster Garden:* in this story, Frances (Frankie) Stein, a motherless young girl whose father, a genetic engineer, is so preoccupied with his work that he neglects his family, discovers some stolen waste tissue from the lab and secretly grows a lovable dolphin-like creature. Realizing that she must part with the mutant for its safety, Frankie releases it in the sea after it saves her life, leading her father to realize how much he is needed by his children. Noted for going beyond its parallels to Mary Shelley's *Frankenstein, The Monster Garden* is acknowledged as an original and tender novel that raises questions about the ethics and direction of scientific experimentation. Three of Alcock's works have been named Notable Books of the Year by the American Library Association: *Travellers by Night* in 1985, *The Cuckoo Sister* in 1986, and *The Monster Garden* in 1988.

(See also *Something about the Author,* Vols. 38, 45, and *Contemporary Authors,* Vol. 110.)

---

## TITLE COMMENTARY

### The Haunting of Cassie Palmer (1980)

Isn't it stimulating, after watching all those brilliant young writers moving into middle age, to discover a really genuine new talent waiting in the wings. A very warm welcome to Vivien Alcock who, in her first novel, shows that she has what we are looking for in the way of originality, vitality and social relevance; what is much more, she can tell an excellent tale with humour and animation.

Poor Cassie, in her early teens, is saddled with a much-loved but embarrassing mum. 'Madame Palmer' is a professional medium, one who ekes out her fading gifts with a little harmless trickery. At intervals the family has to move on to another town where the Palmer reputation is unknown. Mum knows well that her professional days are numbered. All her hopes are fixed on Cassie who, as the seventh child of a seventh child, is bound to have exceptional psychic gifts. Cassie knows that she has nothing of the sort, until, in a desperate adventure in the local graveyard, she manages to raise a spirit—the wrong one as it happens! Deverill—a most unprepossessing ghost—has been called from his unquiet grave, and he follows Cassie around the town in a disconcerting way. When the story ends, most satisfyingly, Cassie is on the way to resolving her personal problems, and Deverill's grave has been embellished with the addition, from an amateur but loving hand, of the consoling letters: "R.I.P.".

Where Mrs. Alcock scores is in putting her excellent story into an authentic setting, presented without exaggeration. Cassie is an ordinary child among very ordinary people. The seedy gentility of her home is convincingly portrayed and so are her family and friends. Even Mum, who might have been a caricature, appears recognisable in her rather splendid awfulness. The writer knows how to fill in the social background and to match her characters with lively and clearly differentiated dialogue. Altogether a most impressive debut. It is such a relaxed, competent job that we can look forward with justifiable confidence to Mrs. Alcock's next. A new writer has arrived!

> *M. Crouch, in a review of "The Haunting of Cassie Palmer," in* The Junior Bookshelf, *Vol. 44, No. 5, October, 1980, p. 243.*

Cassie Palmer is a 13-year-old British girl who struggles with family, friends, the gift of second sight and ghost Deverill in this novel. . . . While there is a sense of excitement and a rapid pace to the final chapters, the earlier pages bog down in sibling rivalries, petty jealousies and other unresolved family conflicts stemming from Mum's charlatanism. These elements, which in themselves could have greatly enriched the full story, are neatly and conve-

niently explained away in the last few pages of the novel. All in all, a good story idea handled disappointingly.

> *Jerry Spiegler, in a review of "The Haunting of Cassie Palmer," in* School Library Journal, *Vol. 28, No. 8, April 15, 1982, p. 78.*

Seventh child of a seventh child, thirteen-year-old Cassie is expected by her mother, a medium, to have psychic powers. Cassie doesn't have the heart to tell Mum that she abhors the idea, and she's stunned with dismay when, on a dare, she attempts to raise a ghost and is successful. Homely and shabby, Deverill appears, announces his friendship and his gratitude at being brought back from limbo, and proceeds to make Cassie's life miserable. There is a quickening tempo to the relationship and its impact on family affairs; within the parameters of the fantasy's logic, there is a perfectly logical and touching conclusion. This is an impressive first novel from a British writer, with a fusion of realism and fantasy that are remarkably smooth. The characterization adds depth to the story, particularly in the depiction of Cassie's mother, big and blowsy, a psychic past her prime and repeatedly exposed as fraudulent, but a loving and garrulous woman.

> *Zena Sutherland, in a review of "The Haunting of Cassie Palmer," in* Bulletin of the Center for Children's Books, *Vol. 35, No. 9, May, 1982, p. 161.*

---

### The Stonewalkers (1981)

"Her name was Poppy Brown, and she was a liar. It was the only remarkable thing about her." Twelve-year-old Poppy, whose father had died when she was three and whose hard-working mother was frequently ill, had never enjoyed the security of a stable family. Rather, her life was a series of assignments to foster homes punctuated by intervals when her mother could find a live-in job where the child was tolerated. Now, living with her mother but virtually friendless, Poppy makes a confidante of a statue she names Belladonna and which she adorns with a bracelet fashioned from an old chain. A sudden bolt of lightning, attracted by the metal, somehow brings the statue to life. To Poppy's horror, it quickly loses its friendly innocence, becoming instead a destructive force. The girl enlists the aid of a schoolmate in an effort to impede the statue's progress as the now malevolent Belladonna recruits an army of stone figures from churchyards and gardens. After several harrowing hours as helpless playthings for the figures, the girls escape. Through skillful building of character and evocation of setting the author has created an absorbing tale of terror in the manner of Robert Westall. Poppy is basically an ordinary child, so her experiences are both chilling and credible—an intrusion of nightmares into the mundane.

> *Mary M. Burns, in a review of "The Stonewalkers," in* The Horn Book Magazine, *Vol. LIX, No. 3, June, 1983, p. 299.*

Take one lonely and imaginative child. Place her in the servants' quarters of an underpopulated English manor house. Throw in a down-to-earth friend. Add some thunder and lightning and a beautiful statue that comes to life, and you have a mixture sure to provoke delicious chills.

This second fantasy from Vivien Alcock gets off to a rousing and promising start. The opening description of the heroine, Poppy Brown, is splendid. . . .

The account of the coming to life of the statue, Belladonna, is even better: "Very slowly the statue got to its feet, moving its limbs with effort as if through deep water, and cracks running everywhere before they were smoothed out by the rain. It groaned again and began coming toward her, rocking slightly on stiff legs and sinking into the wet grass at every step."

Subsequent events take the action onto the moors, and new characters appear at every turn. These characters are not developed fully enough to sustain the early promise, and as a result the plot suffers. There are some fine Gothic shivers, though, and many beautiful images. . . . Readers can enjoy these virtues now and hope for fuller development in the author's next book.

> *Kathleen Leverich, in a review of "The Stonewalkers," in* The New York Times Book Review, *September 11, 1983, p. 57.*

Poppy Brown is twelve, or thirteen, lonely, friendless, and alienated. A compulsive liar, she has spent most of her life in foster homes because of her mother's frequent and extended illnesses. Lying is her means of gaining the attention and affection she so desperately needs.

The statues symbolically represent both Poppy and her mother, who have built shells around themselves and have thus become hard and unfeeling. But Poppy's adventures on the moors—getting lost with her newfound friend Emma and a boy named Rob, being held captive overnight in a cave by the statues, and almost being killed by a cave-in that does destroy her kidnappers—teach the girl to communicate, to care, and to trust and bring her together with her mother. They learn that love requires the time and effort of both parties if it is to be of value.

While *The Stonewalkers* is a charming and neatly-crafted book which reprises the archetypal journey from childhood to maturity, it does seem, on a few occasions, to be overly simplistic for its audience. This is a minor flaw, however, in a book that is well-worth the reading.

> *Carl B. Yoke, in a review of "The Stonewalkers," in* Science Fiction & Fantasy Book Review, *No. 19, November, 1983, p. 46.*

---

### The Sylvia Game  (1982)

[Vivien Alcock,] adept at evoking the uncanny, as she demonstrated last year in that strange, uncomfortably unforgettable nightmare, *The Stonewalkers,* has this time preferred to end with a rational explanation for all the odd incidents she has woven into her story. What, one constantly wonders, explains the fascination for children of the well-chilled spine? Is it because, as is often suggested, their own lives are so full of fears and insecurities that they find reassurance in fictitious horrors which the characters

survive? . . . In *The Sylvia Game* we have Emily, child of a feckless painter, haunted first by her dread of bills and bailiffs, and then by a new fear that her unsuccessful father is turning to art forgery. Equally insecure are her two holiday acquaintances, Oliver at the big house with his own bullying father, and Kevin the boy at her hotel, with other complicated uncertainties.

This book . . . opens with great vitality. It has gusto and humour to provide welcome relief from the sombre recurrent hints of the paranormal. Miss Alcock is unsentimental, but there is an unmistakable depth of feeling in her deft handling of her very human and imperfect characters. She is writing of fear and courage, exploring the ambivalent relationships of parent and child, boy and girl, boy and boy. The contemporary juvenile dialogue rings true, and there is felicity in the descriptive phrasing.

> *Geoffrey Trease, "Curdling the Blood," in* The Times Literary Supplement, *No. 4138, July 23, 1982, p. 788.*

This adolescent novel with only a hint of the supernatural offers nothing new. It is a capably written novel whose adolescent characters are fairly engaging, but characters and plot are very much stock equipment: the spunky young heroine, the tough young punk with the heart of gold, and the sniveling young aristocrat who learns bravery from his pals. The novel's mystery concerns whether an art forgery has taken place and is resolved with very little danger or tension. A slight whiff of the supernatural is wafted on the heroine's resemblance to the subject of a nineteenth-century portrait.

This novel can fill an hour for a voracious reader, more appropriately preadolescent than adolescent because of its lack of suspense, but libraries can ignore.

> *Joan Gordon, "Stock Pot with Whiff of Supernatural," in* Fantasy Review, *Vol. 8, No. 2, February, 1985, p. 34.*

The strength of Alcock's novel lies not only in the comfortable suspense of a British mystery, in the surprising twists and turns of plot; Alcock has also paid careful attention to relationships. The children's friendship and the family portraits cut across class lines and reveal a lot about social position. Only a shocking confession allows Oliver to free himself from his father's expectations. As for Emily, she finally sees that money cannot buy the self-respect and integrity her father so values. In the end, each child has developed a stronger sense of self and a fresh view of the future, and the reader feels satisfied and well entertained.

> *Susan Faust, "Four Novels That Deal in Danger," in* The Christian Science Monitor, *February 1, 1985, p. B5.*

---

### Travellers by Night  (1983)

Belle and Charlie are circus children, he an orphan who'd been taken in by her parents (his aunt and uncle) and she a once-flamboyant tightrope walker who had lost her courage and garnered a facial scar in an accident. Now the

*Alcock with her husband, writer Leon Garfield.*

circus has failed financially, Belle's parents have gone to America, and the two children are having a farm vacation before the school term and a new life with a hospitable aunt begin. The crisis that changes their plans is the discovery that Tessie, an old elephant they both love, is destined for the slaughter-house because her owner is old and ill. That's when Belle conceives the idea of stealing Tessie and, traveling by night and hiding by day, taking her to a safari park and sneaking her in. The situation and successful conclusion are improbable, but Alcock makes them believable and enjoyable, as Belle and Charlie have a series of adventures and encounters en route. They spend the money they have been hoarding to pay for plastic surgery for Belle, but she considers it spent in a good cause and indeed she finds, after inevitable publicity, that she has adjusted to having a scarred face. The pace is brisk, the children appealing, the mission one with which most readers will sympathize, and the book substantial in structure and style. (pp. 21-2)

> *A review of "Travelers by Night," in* Bulletin of the Center for Children's Books, *Vol. 39, No. 2, October, 1985, pp. 21-2.*

Both children are most realistically portrayed in terms of emotions and character. Their seemingly improbable adventure, that of spiriting an elephant by night to a safari game farm, becomes more believable and suspenseful as the journey progresses. The modern-day aspects of the story are creatively contrasted with the rather romantic setting of Yald Forest. The gang of fugitive drop-outs whom the children meet in the woods are a strongly original and realistic addition to the story that keeps readers from viewing the plot too romantically. Alcock's portrayal of self-sufficient children overcoming disadvantages while living in a world of well meaning but selfish and misguided adults is similar to Cassie Palmer's situation in Alcock's earlier *The Haunting of Cassie Palmer.* The author's writing is distinguished by clarity of intent and unusual sensitivity while maintaining unflagging interest in the unfolding story.

> *Karen P. Smith, in a review of "Travelers by*

*Night," in* School Library Journal, *Vol. 32, No. 2, October, 1985, p. 178.*

Circus performers live in a world apart from daily routine, yet underneath the glitter and painted smiles their basic emotions, needs, and attitudes are no different from those of the folk whom they entertain. It is this intersection of the exotic and the ordinary from which conflict is derived and great stories—like Ferenc Molnár's *Liliom*—are evolved. Vivien Alcock's superbly crafted novel belongs in that tradition. Like an *artiste* on a high wire, she builds her story delicately and surely, maintaining tension without faltering and leaving the reader breathless until the final moment, when the only right response is a standing ovation. Summarized, the plot is disarmingly simple. . . . But the story lingers in the memory, not just because of its clear, carefully paced plot line but because of the author's ability to develop characters with real personalities; to use language fluently, vividly, and unself-consciously; and to evoke genuine emotion—not merely a maudlin response. The result is a lovely tale, ideal for reading aloud, which is poignant and funny, suspenseful and satisfying. (pp. 54-5)

> *Mary M. Burns, in a review of "Travelers by Night," in* The Horn Book Magazine, *Vol. LXII, No. 1, January-February, 1986, pp. 54-5.*

---

***Ghostly Companions*** (1984; U. S. edition as *Ghostly Companions: A Feast of Chilling Tales*)

Some of the ten stories in ***Ghostly Companions*** show Vivien Alcock a true successor to M. R. James for younger readers. In particular, **'A Change of Aunt'**, in which Aunt Gertrude's insistence on taking the unwilling children at sunset past a haunted pool where a young nursemaid drowned herself ironically brings them the happiness of which she wants to deprive them, and **'The Whisperer'**, a beautiful eery tale of a shut-out child, are built on time-honoured ghostly traditions yet firmly rooted in believable children of today. Among the rest are such delights as the ancient figurehead bought by a very young antique dealer which creates seastorms around the house till returned to its own element, the patchwork quilt made by a ghost, the man whose reflection haunts him, the boy followed by Echo from Greece, the sinister village where all but one of the children are ghosts, and a dance of death in carnival Venice. The styles as well as the themes and backgrounds are varied and there is a nice humorous vein (an inept student is wished good luck by the Principal of her typing school "in the tone of voice of someone wishing a snowman a happy summer").

> *M. Hobbs, in a review of "Ghostly Companions," in* The Junior Bookshelf, *Vol. 48, No. 6, December, 1984, p. 260.*

From one of England's most original spinners of tales, ten new encounters with the supernatural.

Alcock deftly grounds each story with telling details, giving characters a next-door reality and settings a familiarity that makes the spooky happenings more enthralling. Her turns of plot are boundlessly inventive—a figurehead yearning to return to its sealove; a mean nursemaid whose body is captured by a ghost that longs to care for children; a Venetian masked ball where the mask itself seems to cause the emptiness of death within; the ghost of a child set to rest when another child responds to her piteous plea to "play with me"; a rogue typewriter, scissors comically administering retributive justice, and a beneficent fall of snow—there's plenty of variety to keep the pages turning.

Sometimes witty, often scary or suspenseful, always wise, these stories should be welcome wherever ghosts are popular reading companions. (pp. 789-90)

> *A review of "Ghostly Companions: A Feast of Chilling Tales," in* Kirkus Reviews, *Vol. LV, No. 9, May 15, 1987, pp. 789-90.*

With her deft use of words, Alcock creates vivid images that breathe life into her scenes and characters. When the ghost of a long-dead nursemaid brings happiness to two lonely children by rising out of a haunted pond and possessing the body of their abusive housekeeper, we see that "green mud clung like flesh to its washed bones." The combination of such terrifying images with happy resolutions will make the book popular for reading aloud; listeners with a taste for more macabre material could create alternative endings. The collection truly lives up to its subtitle. (p. 461)

> *Hanna B. Zeiger, in a review of "Ghostly Companions: A Feast of Chilling Tales," in* The Horn Book Magazine, *Vol. LXIII, No. 4, July-August, 1987, pp. 460-61.*

---

### The Cuckoo Sister (1985)

[*The Cuckoo Sister* explores] the idea that missing family members may be crucial to the individual identity—especially if they do not turn out as expected.

Kate Seton's conditions are firmly marked out. She lives in Hampstead with her father, a barrister, inquisitorial on duty and off; her sensitive mother, who defends herself against reality with migraines; and Mrs Trapp, the cook, a zealot for the superiority of the upper middle class. Kate aged fifteen narrates the story of when she was eleven, a difficult, secretive child since learning accidentally about Emma. On the first of August, Emma's birthday, up the gravel drive comes Rosie Martin, a hard-eyed thirteen-year-old, bearing a note from her mum: "i am sending her back to you better later than never yours faithful Louise". Rosie has not read the note, denies its claim with violent indignation, as does Kate. Louise has disappeared.

*The Cuckoo Sister* is partly a mystery novel, partly an examination of the securities and insecurities of class; more than either, it is a study of growing up, or at least of Kate's coming to terms with herself and her status. Each level poses problems for the author and Alcock has not dealt with any of them wholly successfully. As a mystery, the story suffers from a dearth of clues; it oscillates in uncertainty, and does not impel us to a resolution. As a description of society, it is handicapped by its portrait of Rosie. Rather than depicting adolescence in turmoil, the abrupt

discontinuities of her mood, disposition, education and language seem to be inconsistent characterization by an author who thinks that the dustbins of London's working class still have kipper heads in them. As Kate's memoir of her ordeal, *The Cuckoo Sister* is a more satisfactory book, well constructed, cleverly deploying the kind of symbols an intelligent but isolated child does use to interpret the world. Yet, oddly, the primitive conflict it purports to present is over too quickly. Rosie's arrival is something of a relief to Kate. She was far more threatened by the empty space. The title, and hence the whole psychological thrust of the book, seem quite wrong.

> *Colin Greenland, "Ritual Dismembering," in* The Times Literary Supplement, *No. 4310, November 8, 1985, p. 1274.*

The cuckoo sister is a tough slum kid who turns up on the doorstep with a misspelt note identifying her as stolen Emma. The emotional drama into which the family is now plunged makes a fascinating and moving tale. The contrasting backgrounds are handled with assurance and understanding, the dawning friendship between the girls allows both to change and grow, and the plot unwinds with the excitement of a detective story. Vivien Alcock's skilful use of an extraordinary situation, combined with her humane and compassionate eye for character, make this book a valuable addition to the secondary school library. Some upper juniors will enjoy it too.

> *Jane Inglis, in a review of "The Cuckoo Sister," in* The School Librarian, *Vol. 33, No. 4, December, 1985, p. 349.*

Vivien Alcock has written a powerful and poignant suspense story that is equally strong in character and plot. The author has a wonderfully sensitive ear and the ability to translate what she hears into brilliant dialogue. Words, speech patterns, and cadence vary appropriately with each character. . . . [In *The Cuckoo Sister,* the] author has created an intriguing situation and peopled it with characters that work both as individuals and as members of a family. The writing is tight, building the suspense right to the end. As the setting shifts from Kate's comfortable neighborhood to inner-city London, scenes—effectively drawn with care and economy of language—emerge colorful and complete. The best book to date from this skillful, imaginative author.

> *Elizabeth S. Watson, in a review of "The Cuckoo Sister," in* The Horn Book Magazine, *Vol. LXII, No. 4, July-August, 1986, p. 447.*

---

### The Mysterious Mr. Ross (1987)

Vivien Alcock's first book was the most original offering of its year, and now, six titles later, she continues to surprise as much as she delights.

In *The Mysterious Mr. Ross* it is the quality of the writing rather than the novelty of the theme which matters most. Mr. Ross appears, formally dressed and with brief-case in hand, on the dangerous shore of the Grey Gulls, and is rescued by Felicity, a girl who has hitherto been distinguished by her excessive clumsiness. Briefly she achieves fame, and so does Mr. Ross who seems content to sit back and enjoy being fussed by all the ladies of Gull Bay. Only Felicity's friend Bony remains sceptical about the mysterious man of the sea, scenting a phoney and trying to catch him out in his many and contradictory stories. Then Mr. Ross goes away as he came, walking down the cliffs on his way, so he says, to Gullington. He disappears from sight and—was it coincidence?—a great bird flies, 'its wings now catching the light, now dark against the sun.' He leaves behind him the people of Gull Bay, their problems strangely lessened by his stay.

Allegory? Maybe. I fancy that we may be wasting our energy hunting for hidden meanings. Better to take the story just as it is, enjoying the mastery of its telling and the richness of the character-drawing. The seediness of a downmarket seaside resort and the Fairweather Guest House, run by Fliss' mother while Dad looks for work, are touched in with delicate strokes, and the 'inmates'—it seems the only word for them—are drawn with equal skill. Perhaps some readers will look for more action, more suspense, but this is not that kind of book. Readers—and I don't mean only children—who care for how their stories are told will savour this one, from any page of which a happily devised image can be culled. 'The sea was on its long way in, licking at abandoned sandcastles as if they were so many ice-creams.'

> *M. Crouch, in a review of "The Mysterious Mr. Ross," in* The Junior Bookshelf, *Vol. 51, No. 4, August, 1987, p. 175.*

There are lands where fables hold sway, where mermaids emerge from the water with the ease and naturalness of a child who has had its swim and comes out to dry off and play in the sand. There is also everyday reality, a world more complicated than the phrase allows, but still arguably one most adults and children are familiar with. And there is a land in between, which is where many stories are set. This often looks deceptively like the everyday world, but with an inexplicable something more to it, such as the mysterious Mr Ross of Vivien Alcock's latest novel, who is fished out of a dangerous sea by an ordinary little girl, Felicity, in an ordinary seaside town that could easily lie on the Sussex coast. Mr Ross may simply be a rootless young man whose past, if only he revealed it, would answer the questions that hover around him. On the other hand, he could be an embodiment of the fantastic, the spirit in human form of the wandering albatross whose skull Felicity and her friend Bony find when they return at low tide to the place where he first appeared.

The question-marks have not been entirely shaken off when, at the satisfying, mildly tantalizing end of the story, Mr Ross turns down Felicity's mother's offer of a home and a job in her holiday guesthouse and sets off to continue his wanderer's life. In the mean time, the few weeks' recuperative stay with Felicity's family has brought much excited speculation to the guesthouse and the town; it has made a bit of a heroine of gangly Felicity and tested her friendship with clever, fat-boy Bony. It has of course given Vivien Alcock the opportunity to fill out her portrait of these two appealing child characters, but equally to explore the give and take of family relationships. She does

this with sensitivity and humour, charting the visitor's catalytic effect on the smooth running of the Fairweather Guesthouse. The new turns the outsider brings to its life allow Felicity to challenge her mother's unflagging efficiency and to bring about a renewal of her mother's warmth towards her and her father, a nice man who understandably keeps out of the way and close to a bottle.

> *Nicole Irving, "Everyday Mysteries," in* The Times Literary Supplement, *No. 4405, September 4-7, 1987, p. 964.*

Vivien Alcock never repeats herself. Each story is unique not only in plot and subject but also in style. The single common thread is excellence, for she blends suspense and characterization with uncanny and uncommon skill, creating a situation that is both immediate and compelling. Told from the perspective of the protagonist, twelve-year-old Felicity Tait, Alcock's latest book engages the reader's attention and sustains interest through a concentrated focus. Awkward, imaginative, poised between childhood and adolescence, Felicity is a dreamer, fond of spinning romantic tales about the inhabitants of her mother's summer guest house. On a particularly difficult day, she rescues a mysterious young man from the treacherous waters near her home. Suddenly, she is a heroine; more important, as the savior of the charming Albert Ross, she senses a special bond between them and resents his accepting attention from others in the community. . . . The contest between doubt and devotion, exacerbated by preadolescent angst, provides the central conflict in a stunning story of suspense, which is resolved logically and satisfactorily. Whether or not Albert Ross has adopted his name from an illustration of an albatross becomes less important than the joyful changes his presence brings to the Tait family in general and to Felicity in particular. Allusions to the albatross in literature and folklore are smoothly integrated into the narrative, adding dimension without detracting from rhythm and pacing. The author tells a good story; what makes it noteworthy is her ability to extend the elements of the suspense genre into a subtle exploration of character. Like the best of Hitchcock's films, the book is as unforgettable as it is riveting. (pp. 200-01)

> *Mary M. Burns, in a review of "The Mysterious Mr. Ross," in* The Horn Book Magazine, *Vol. LXIV, No. 2, March-April, 1988, pp. 200-01.*

---

### The Monster Garden (1988)

Vivien Alcock is well established, and there is nobody quite like her. She is a very funny writer, but her comedy is produced by wit, not by fooling. We know some of what will happen in *The Monster Garden* as soon as we find ourselves in company with a heroine whose name is Frances Stein (Frankie for short) and whose father is a genetic engineer running a not-entirely burglar proof laboratory; but in the hands of this author the story yields at once a fantasy of tenderness as well as amazement, and considerable light on family affection, on contemporary real-life. All this without a moment of lumpen-seriousness, or a single slow-moving phrase. Worth every penny of the selfish parent's outlay.

*Jill Paton Walsh, in a review of "The Monster Garden," in* Books, *London, No. 13, April, 1988, p. 14.*

I must admit to a feeling of disappointment in these books [**The Monster Garden** and Mollie Hunter's *The Mermaid Summer*], both by distinguished and sensitive purveyors of mystery for whose work I am usually enthusiastic. Vivien Alcock's heroine, whose father works in an experimental laboratory—her name is appropriately corrupted by schoolmates to Frankenstein—is at the beginning a rather irritating schoolgirl who talks too much: one sympathises with her older brother and her father, so preoccupied with his work that he seems unaware of his motherless children, and particularly of his daughter. David—the other two brothers are abroad—steals some waste tissue from a lab, and reluctantly has to share it with Frankie, who discovers him. She has the necessary patience: her part grows, he throws his away. The scientific explanations, even in her chatty style, become a little heavy-going, but Frankie's experience suggests the book intends a warning about the dangers of animal experimentation and genetic engineering. The weird mutant frightens her at first, but then he is made as lovable as any other young pet, and as vulnerable as a handicapped human. Her adventures in concealing him from David and their housekeeper with the help of three friends, one of whom turns traitor, and the gardener, an old countryman, become as gripping as one would expect from Vivien Alcock, and at the same time full of humour and genuinely moving, as girl and somewhat dolphin-like monster have to part for his safety. For good measure, he later saves her life, at which point her father realises how selfishly he has excluded his children from his existence, and as *he* only experiments with plants, anyway, all is set fair. Something of the moral situation is conveyed, but it is in any case only one side of the picture, and there is suggestion of the painful conflict involved.

*M. Hobbs, in a review of "The Monster Garden," in* The Junior Bookshelf, *Vol. 52, No. 4, August, 1988, p. 193.*

Alcock has created a sensitive portrait of the alienated Frankie and her attempts to reach out and protect a similarly alienated monster. Initially, the story may remind readers of *E. T.* in the portrayal of an alien creature of benign nature and the attempt of children to protect it, as well as conjure up ideas regarding the more intentional references to Shelley's novel *Frankenstein*. However, Alcock goes beyond obvious parallels and creates a strikingly original story which explores contemporary relationships and societal issues regarding future directions in scientific experimentation. The issue of trust also arises as a key factor, and is one with which young people will readily identify. The conclusion of the story is both unexpected and yet believable. Alcock has once again shown her ability to create a realistic situation through exploration of the fantastic. The smoothly written book will hold the attention of readers through to its touching conclusion.

*Karen P. Smith, in a review of "The Monster Garden," in* School Library Journal, *Vol. 35, No. 2, October, 1988, p. 138.*

---

## The Thing in the Woods (1989)

Antelope Books continue to attract outstanding writers who are prepared to work within the strict (but not too strict) confines of the 'easy reader.' In their new format the books represent good value both for physical presentation and imaginative treatment.

Vivien Alcock's contribution is a light-hearted fantasy. Jenny and Bill encounter a 'Thing' in the woods. It looks 'a bit like a tree on legs', and, after the initial fright, the children are as much intrigued as scared and more than anything moved by its plight. The Thing is suffering from shock and concussion and cannot remember its name. Even the phrase-book which it carries is unhelpful. Thank goodness its Mippa and Dappa turn up and take their child away in their 'luminous melon'. The fun is gentle and kindly, the observation of child behaviour shrewd.

*M. Crouch, in a review of "The Thing in the Woods," in* The Junior Bookshelf, *Vol. 53, No. 2, April, 1989, p. 65.*

The setting of **The Thing in the Woods** is far from being idealised. The atmosphere of mystery and magic inseparable from woodland is used selectively in the story without any exaggeration to support a tale of two children whose meeting with a strange being gives unexpected colour to their lives. Here is a writer whose judicious use of words and lack of padding is a positive virtue in a short 'Antelope', a writer skilful in introducing an element of fancy into an everyday scene. The 'Thing' could be the stuff of any predictable Martian invader:

> It stood on the path in front of them. Very tall. Very thin. Its eyes were a dusty purple, like plums. Its hair was green and sharp, like holly leaves. Its skin was grey—it wore a green fur coat. Each bare foot had four toes, three in front and one at the back, like a bird's.

But is this so predictable? Here is a real suffering person, as it were a child lost in a terrifying unfamiliar world, and Bill and Jenny are at once sorry for it and as ready to accept its oddness as its obvious fear. At first they find it hard to know how they can help it. The yellow book it shows them 'made of some thin, slippery stuff like silk' and containing 'squiggles, as if an inky spider had danced a jig', contains matched English sentences like 'Hurt. Where is doctor, hospital, ambulance?', sentences which hardly seem practical in the circumstances. Then there is the problem of bullying Johnny Connor, who pours scorn on their theory that this is a Martian tourist. They are right, of course, and when sad little Toz, desperately hungry in spite of the food they have purloined for it, is reclaimed by his parents, they are warmed by the brief but genuine affection generated between the three of them. Significant in the book is the pathos, the underlying theme of the sadness of differences—between individuals, between races—which adds the colour of feeling to a story exciting for its action and pleasing in the view of children coping with the unusual situation. (pp. 5153-54)

*Margery Fisher, in a review of "The Thing in the Woods," in* Growing Point, *Vol. 28, No. 1, May, 1989, pp. 5153-54.*

---

### The Trial of Anna Cotman (1989)

Of all the major children's writers of the day (and unquestionably Vivien Alcock is of that company) she is the least set in her ways. Each book is a new experience. So it is with **The Trial of Anna Cotman.** The author knows that in any community some children—a minority but a potent one—trail, not Wordsworthian clouds of glory but clouds of nastiness. In this disturbing story the SOM (Society of Masks) comes into being for partly good motives, to put up a united front against bullying. In the event children whose true identities are protected by masks soon begin to act out of (or perhaps in) character. It is a small step from nonentity to tyrant. One of the first victims is Anna Cotman, 'a poor little rabbit' of a new girl who cannot resist Lindy Miller's offer of friendship. Lindy has run out of friends, for very good reasons; she is a clever and insidiously nasty child. As Anna gets more deeply caught up in the web of the SOM she begins to think for herself, and to resist the pressures of the masked 'Lords', not so much for her own sake but because she resents their victimization of a small and feeble boy. The stage is set inevitably for a showdown and for Anna's trial on a charge of treason.

The implications of Vivien Alcock's story are to be taken very seriously. Adult readers will ask what the school and the parents were up to. The parents introduced into the story—Anna's Gran, loving but preoccupied with her business affairs, Lindy's shallow vain mother and her stepfather—are perhaps untypical. We see nothing much of the school. These 'Lords' and their wretched slaves of 'Companions' operate without restriction on the basis of fear. The resistance, when it comes, comes from within, although the despised stepfather serves to clear up the mess.

Excellent and scrupulously fair as Ms Alcock's characterisation is, her story is really one of atmosphere. She develops the feeling of dread that threatens to destroy her sturdy and likable heroine with very great skill. Ultimately it is literary professionalism that makes the book so powerful and so difficult to forget. I hope that parents will read it and accept its message. Eternal vigilance is no great price to pay for one's child's peace of mind. Children, I have no doubt, will read it for the exciting story and for the honest representation of their situation.

*M. Crouch, in a review of "The Trial of Anna Cotman," in* The Junior Bookshelf, *Vol. 53, No. 4, August, 1989, p. 183.*

Alcock, who delights in introducing the unusual into the ordinary lives of her characters, can be relied on to create a story that is both exciting and thoughtful. Building up atmosphere through action rather than description, she rounds out her characters in swift, telling phrases touched with wry humor. Readers will, of course, be attracted by the strangeness of the masks and rituals, but what they will remember above all is unlikable Lindy standing up for Anna when she needs her most. (p. 88)

*Ruth S. Vose, in a review of "The Trial of Anna Cotman," in* School Library Journal, *Vol. 36, No. 2, February, 1990, pp. 86, 88.*

Like her compatriot Gillian Cross, Alcock is a master of suspense tales that explore complex moral issues through the actions of well-developed characters in unusual situations. From the first gripping page till the final scene, when Lindy tells Anna that "Harry says there's a time to break promises and a time to keep them," a thoughtful, enthralling, perfectly structured novel. (p. 176)

*A review of "The Trial of Anna Cotman," in* Kirkus Reviews, *Vol. LVIII, No. 3, February 1, 1990, pp. 175-76.*

# Sylvia Cassedy

## 1930-1989

American author of fiction, poetry, and nonfiction; editor; and translator.

Major works include *In Your Own Words: A Beginner's Guide to Writing* (1979), *Behind the Attic Wall* (1983), *M. E. and Morton* (1987), *Roomrimes: Poems* (1987), and *Lucie Babbidge's House* (1989).

Praised as a writer of fiction for middle graders whose works blend fantasy and reality in an ambitious and distinctive fashion, Cassedy is celebrated for exploring the inner world of children with thoroughness, understanding, and insight. Acknowledged for creating especially memorable characters in works noted both for their power and their complexity, Cassedy describes how her protagonists, preadolescent girls who are withdrawn, unpopular, or fearful, learn self-awareness and self-confidence through creativity, play, and the imagination as well as through the discovery of their innate love and tenderness. Cassedy depicts the interplay between the harsh reality of the daily lives of the girls at home or in school and the healing properties of their imaginary worlds in a literary style considered notable for its precision, control, vigor, and inventive use of language and plot. In addition to her fiction, Cassedy is well regarded as a poet: as the author of *Roomrimes,* an alphabetical tour of rooms and spaces which includes rhymed, unrhymed, and haiku poetry, she favors varied rhythms and internal rhymes as well as vivid images and surprising humor; she is also well known for translating and compiling two acclaimed collections of poetry from India and Japan for primary graders. A teacher of creative writing in both primary and secondary schools as well as an instructor in the teaching of creative writing to children, Cassedy is the author of a work of nonfiction for middle and upper graders, *In Your Own Words: A Beginner's Guide to Writing,* in which she uses an informal, direct style to provide information on the writing of prose, poetry, and nonfiction.

Cassedy has written, "I spent a lot of my childhood time suffering. I *remembered* all that suffering, in what only can be described as loving detail. . . . All those troubled eleven- and twelve-year-old girls in my novels are, in their way, recreations . . . of how I perceived [my childhood] at the time and remember those perceptions now." Beginning her career with fantasies for younger children written in poetic prose, Cassedy created what is considered her first major novel with *Behind the Attic Wall.* The story describes how orphaned Maggie, a cynical twelve-year-old who has been expelled from nine boarding schools, goes to live with two great aunts in their stately home; in a secret part of the attic, she finds two old china dolls with a life of their own that is tied directly to the house. As Maggie cares for the dolls, she develops a sense of loving responsibility; the story is framed by an episode that suggests that Maggie finds happiness with another set of fos-

ter parents after her great aunts give her away. In her next story, *M. E. and Morton,* Cassedy outlines how bright but unpopular Mary Ella (M. E.), a seventh-grader with an admiring retarded brother, fourteen-year-old Morton, changes her self-perception after she meets Polly, a new girl who moves into the neighborhood and teaches M. E. how to find herself through fantasy and play. Cassedy's last novel, *Lucie Babbidge's House,* was published posthumously; in this work, which again features an orphaned girl and a family of magical dolls, Lucie Babbidge is a scapegoat at school but beloved at home, which is a dollhouse in the cellar of an orphanage. When she gets an English penpal, Delia, who is a descendant of the original owner of the house, Lucie discovers that the events of Delia's life are beginning to parallel those of the dollhouse; through her imagination, Lucie realizes her personal strength, is able to help Delia, and stands up to the taunts of her teachers. *Behind the Attic Wall* was named a Notable Book by the American Library Association in 1983, a designation received by *M. E. and Morton* in 1987; *Behind the Attic Wall* was also named a Children's Choice Book in 1983.

(See also *Something about the Author,* Vols. 27, 61 [obituary]; *Contemporary Authors New Revision Series,* Vol. 22; and *Contemporary Authors,* Vol. 105.)

---

## GENERAL COMMENTARY

**Christine McDonnell**

Sylvia Cassedy died on April 6, 1989, leaving a body of work crowned by three ambitious, unusual children's novels—*Behind the Attic Wall, M. E. and Morton,* and the posthumously published *Lucie Babbidge's House*—novels that explore the depth of children's inner lives, the intensity of their suffering, and the healing power of their imaginations.

Ignoring traditional boundaries between fantasy and realism, these novels trust the reader to travel with the characters back and forth between imaginary inner worlds and concrete, everyday reality. These are not, in fact, fantasies at all. In each, the child's inner world is created by her imagination to fill an emotional need, and this inner world is as real and as important as the external, concrete world she suffers through. Other children's authors have given us glimpses of children's inner lives—Marilyn Sachs in *The Bears' House,* Paula Fox in *The Stone-Faced Boy*—but in Sylvia Cassedy's novels, the children's inner worlds are developed so fully that readers, like the central characters themselves, can inhabit them and explore the interplay between these inner and outer realities.

*Behind the Attic Wall* was Sylvia Cassedy's first novel, noteworthy for its originality, detail, and consistency. It convincingly depicts the orphan Maggie's pain and defiance, draws us into her fantasy, and reveals her gradual healing. After nine unsuccessful placements, Maggie comes to live with her great-aunts, longing for a welcome and a home.

> "Great Aunt" had a kind of fairy-tale ring to it, and she thought of two great women in great billowing dresses with great white aprons and smiling great white smiles. . . . They would kiss her and say, "What a lovely face" and then they would tell her how happy they were to have her with them because they always wanted a girl of their own just like her.

But the aunts could not be more disappointing. " 'Skin and bones,' " is their first judgment, followed by other remarks about the physical Maggie: " 'Her hair is in strings' "; " 'She could do with a scrubbing from top to bottom.' " Only Uncle Morris, mysterious occasional visitor, welcomes her wholeheartedly, values her, and recognizes from the first her inner life. " 'What do you wonder about?' " he asks her, and " 'Do you keep a diary?' " When the aunts find her " 'disgusting,' " Morris finds her " 'enchanting.' " But Uncle Morris visits infrequently, leaving Maggie alone with the dreary, disapproving aunts.

In response to the bleakness of her life, Maggie creates an inner world for companionship. This imaginary world shows Sylvia Cassedy's greatest skill. Above all, it is convincing. Not only does it make sense for Maggie to create the characters and scenes, but they are described so accu-

rately that we accept them as real for Maggie. But beyond that, the inner life that Cassedy portrays rings true for all children, in varying degrees. Having imaginary friends, giving voices and histories to toys, imbuing objects with life, creating scenes, families, towns—these are central parts of children's play. Cassedy steps into the middle of these rich fantasy worlds and describes them as carefully as other authors describe the physical world of children.

> She played games in her head. She played caretaker. Caretaker was a game she had made up long ago, and she played it almost every day. . . . She was a caretaker in her game, a caretaker of five imaginary girls, the Backwoods Girls she called them, all poorer, younger, dirtier, and uglier than she was herself. And dumber. . . . It was Maggie's job to explain things to them.

The Backwoods Girls prove Maggie's superiority; she controls them and levels at them the insults she receives in the outside world. But in the attic of the aunts' house, Maggie discovers two dolls, and their voices, histories, and actions are independent of her, although her presence and participation is needed for them to come to life. When Maggie accepts her role in the lives of these dolls, as she fixes them and helps them, she becomes happier. (pp. 101-02)

In a letter to her editor, Marilyn Kriney, Sylvia Cassedy described her notion of the caretaker, a relationship central to all three novels:

> Throughout the book I have emphasized the main character's need not only to be cherished, but to cherish in return—to fix, to heal, to look after, to be what she calls a "caretaker"—and insofar as the story has a theme at all, it can be characterized as the power of such cherishing to alter the life of a troubled human being. As her need to cherish is fulfilled by the two dolls, Maggie develops from a withdrawn, emotionally crippled twelve-year-old, incapable of dealing with anyone except in the most hostile terms, into a girl who can for the first time sing a song, join in a game, cry over a death, and, finally, say "I love you."

What is most provocative about Sylvia Cassedy's work is her refusal to judge the imaginary worlds of her characters; within her portrayal is a thorough acceptance. Can dolls talk? Who is more real, the aunts or the dolls? Is Morton stupid? Is M. E. smart? Is Polly magic or is she crazy? Does Delia exist? Cassedy spins imagination and reality, the two halves of her characters' lives, so fast that, like an optical illusion, they merge and we no longer know—or care!—which is which. The core of her fiction's power is this acceptance of the validity and reality of imagination. The inner life is not a lesser world, nor a paler place, nor a poor substitute. Rather, it is a rich world, preferable by far to the bleakness of home, schoolroom, and neighborhood. (p. 103)

[One] example of shining fantasy is the box of paints in *M. E. and Morton,* transformed by Mary Ella into a play orphanage:

. . . twenty-four little girls dressed in beautiful gowns and marching two by two across my windowsill.

They weren't real little girls. They weren't even dolls. They were the little glass bottles from the paint set I got two Christmases ago and never painted with. In fact, I never thought of them as paints at all. They had white metal heads and smooth shiny bodies and they stood side by side in their cardboard box like a row of little girls in colored gowns.

I took them out one by one that Christmas Day and arranged them in little clusters—in families, really—of purple sisters and red sisters and blue sisters, and I called them by their names. They all had beautiful names printed on labels across their stomachs: Marigold, Ecru, Heliotrope, Mauve. . . . They lived in the cardboard box, standing waist high in separate round holes, and I let them out each morning just before I went to school.

Mary Ella's game with paint dolls includes school, dances, adventures, walks to town—all far more interesting than merely painting with the contents of the bottles.

In all three novels, reality and imagination become intertwined, and Cassedy relishes the ambiguity and overlap.

Against the warmth and color and infinite possibilities of the inner worlds of her characters, Sylvia Cassedy sets their painful realities. Maggie, orphaned and rejected; Mary Ella, friendless, isolated, and lonely; Lucie, ridiculed in her boarding school/orphanage, piecing together the memory of her parents' death. This backdrop of pain is so intense and unrelenting that, were it not for the reprieve of inner worlds, neither characters nor readers could endure it.

In a wry autobiographical sketch, Sylvia Cassedy explained the roots of this pain:

On the whole, I was not an unpopular kid. I had some good friends. I got invited to birthday parties. When I was eleven, a boy asked me to dance. But I *felt* unpopular. My good friends had better friends of their own, or seemed to. My place card at those birthday parties was somehow always at the end of the table, farthest from the hostess. The boy who asked me to dance was the shortest boy in the class; I was the shortest girl. He picked me for my size.

. . . I spent much of my time suffering. I collected hurts. I nurtured them, almost, relishing their details in a way that most people reserve for 4th of July parades. I took excruciating notice, for example, of how somebody's eyes would shift ever so slightly or her fingers curl into her palm as she explained why she couldn't play with me after school that day. They were hurts that I savored.

And remembered. Not only then, but now. Except that now I don't suffer over them; I write about them. All those troubled 11- and 12-year-old girls in my novels are, in their way, recreations not of my actual childhood but of how

I perceived it at the time and remember those perceptions now.

. . . So that, I suppose, is why I write: I spent a lot of childhood time suffering. I *remembered* all that suffering, in what can only be described as loving detail.

Sylvia Cassedy respected children's pain, just as she accepted the reality of their inner worlds, and these two forces balance each other in her novels. She shows us the complex relationship between isolation, however painful, and creativity—isolation breeding creativity, which in turn, helps to alleviate or fill the void of isolation. Perhaps in the same way, her writing balanced her memories. Her books, products of the solitary work of writing, reach out to us; they speak not only of pain but of the power of imagination to transform and heal.

A writer of great skill, originality, insight, and compassion, Sylvia Cassedy believed in the healing power of creativity and love. Sadly, we can only wonder what other stories she would have shared with us had her life not been shortened by cancer. Wonder, and be thankful for the daring books she left us. (pp. 104-05)

> *Christine McDonnell, "Sylvia Cassedy: Valuing the Child's Inner Life," in* The Horn Book Magazine, *Vol. LXVII, No. 1, January-February, 1991, pp. 101-05.*

---

## TITLE COMMENTARY

### *Little Chameleon* (1966)

A quiet little springtime book, in which a mother chameleon tries to explain to her small offspring why he changes color. There is no scientific explanation here, but simply a poetic mother and child situation, which small children will understand. . . . [The] prose, with its heavy reliance on onomatopoeia, recalls the poetry of Gerard Manley Hopkins. Fun to read aloud.

> *Elsie T. Dobbins, in a review of "Little Chameleon," in* School Library Journal, *Vol. 12, No. 9, May, 1966, p. 138.*

A very small book with a slight but pleasant theme; the rhythm and cadence of the text are appealing. . . . A small chameleon, sent out into the spring world by its mother, discovers that it adapts to the background color. The plot is weak in that it is based on a single idea, repeated; the style is better than the plot. Little Chameleon steps first into the yellow sand. "Yellow. Yellow is the pollen on the belly of a bee; willow-yellow; lily-yellow; lemon-yellow; yellow as the daffodil/ below the hollow tree. Yellow."

> *Zena Sutherland, in a review of "Little Chameleon," in* Bulletin of the Center for Children's Books, *Vol. 20, No. 1, September, 1966, p. 5.*

---

### *Pierino and the Bell* (1966)

The well-known and widely admired illustrations of Evaline Ness fail to save a manufactured story of old Tuscany. The author employs two conventions more common to opera and ballet than to present day storytelling for children: the peasants are addicted to acting in concert (laughing, dancing, hurrahing) and Pierino bursts into odd lyrics at odd moments. The story concerns the festival San Colombino Day on which the pigeons lay eggs with absentminded abandon all over the village square. Pierino, who rings the bell that he thinks summons all the pigeons to daily flight, finds a silver colored egg at the festival and, as is the custom with the children, takes it to hatch. Instead of releasing the resultant silver fledgling, he caged it. Next S.C. Day he released the silver pigeon. All the birds wheeled in pursuit of the freed silver bird. It looked as if it were all up for the pigeon egg collection until Pierino rang the bell. The birds flew back and laid eggs like crazy. They *all* turned out to be silver—"one thousand silver eggs in all." As usual, Miss Ness provides stunning illustrations. The silver pigeon's performance is stunning, too, considering he accomplished it all in one morning.

> *A review of "Pierino and the Bell," in* Virginia Kirkus' Service, *Vol. XXXIV, No. 15, August 1, 1966, p. 752.*

I found Sylvia Cassedy and Evaline Ness's **Pierino and the Bell** disheartening, if only for the thick, convoluted verbiage employed in telling a fairly simple tale of a little Italian boy's belief in a feast day and in a church bell's sound that attracts thousands of pigeons. . . .

Miss Cassedy, for all the care she takes in telling her story, clutters it with endless, unnecessary details, and one is left with words, words, words, as insistent as a buzz-saw. Evaline Ness's illustrations are in the fine style of her own *Sam, Bangs & Moonshine.* . . . They are direct, clear and to the point—elements her collaborator could profitably look into.

> *John Gruen, "Fancy Free," in* Book Week— World Journal Tribune, *October 30, 1966, p. 5.*

**Pierino and the Bell** has its setting in a lovingly-described Tuscan hill village but its true location is a quiet corner of dreamland. This gentle story of children and birds will be best appreciated and understood by those with artistic sensibility and a religious background.

> *Aileen Pippett, in a review of "Pierino and the Bell," in* The New York Times Book Review, *November 6, 1966, p. 60.*

---

**Birds, Frogs, and Moonlight** (with Kunihiro Suetake, 1967)

[Haiku] for young children, . . . with a triple-threat text: in Japanese characters, in transliteration to Roman letters, in translation to English. Some of the poems bring a quick smile—"A discovery!/ On my frog's smooth, green belly/ there sits no button;" others suggest a strange image— "Above the chorus,/ listen! A single cricket/ shakes a golden bell"—or call for contemplation. The selections generally have a nice easy relation to children's responses, and

should succeed. . . . The added attraction, of course, is the chance to *see and say* Japanese.

> *A review of "Birds, Frogs, and Moonlight," in* Kirkus Service, *Vol. XXXV, No. 15, August 1, 1967, p. 875.*

[I] wish I could praise Sylvia Cassedy & Kunihiro Suetake's **Birds, Frogs, and Moonlight** as an integrated work. For every separate ingredient is in excellent taste. Their translations of a set of Japanese haiku are sensitive, and it is a pleasure to see each poem printed next to its ideogram. The art work of Vo-Dinh is lovely. In one instance, a spare black-and-white crow wonderfully balances Basho's text ("Detestable crow! Today alone you please me—black against the snow"). Yet with this superb exception, drawings always overwhelm poems. You really can't keep your eyes off them, and the effect is one of lopsided pages, the poems on the right acting as a thin accompaniment to the art. Nevertheless, this is distinguished work; if it does not quite come off as a book, it is vastly superior to another collection of haiku, Doris Johnson's *A Cloud of Summer.* For Mrs. Cassedy's translations are always poems, Mrs. Johnson's original haiku—at their best—bland imitations.

> *John Unterecker, in a review of "Birds, Frogs, and Moonlight," in* The New York Times Book Review, *November 5, 1967, p. 61.*

---

**Moon-Uncle, Moon-Uncle: Rhymes from India** (with Parvathi Thampi, 1972)

The rhymes from India of which **Moon-Uncle, Moon-Uncle** . . . is composed make a delightful book. The choice is catholic, with plenty of surprises, and no tendency to regard unhappy endings, thefts, quarrels or non-sequiturs as unsuitable material. Without seeming to try, it gives the reader a sense of the country in which the ancient rhymes originated, and its explanation of the approach to translation is persuasive.

> *Josephine Jacobson, "Holy Halibut! It's Poetry," in* Book World—The Washington Post, *November 5, 1972, p. 4.*

According to the editors' notes these rhymes are the Indian equivalents of Mother Goose, which have "never before appeared in print, either in their native tongue or in translation," and therefore they should be of some interest to folklore enthusiasts. Only a few, however, are likely to strike the fancy of young children. "A crow from Cochin came to me/ built his house in the banyan tree" has a musical lilt, and "There was an old woman/ as I've heard tell,/ who sailed away/ in a walnut shell" requires no knowledge of Indian culture. On the other hand the verse "Dry, little patti, dry, dry, dry!" requires an explanatory footnote (a patti is a slate used in school). Some lines— such as the question asked the owl: "Have you a swelling beneath your coat?" or "Oh, twinkling stars,/ who was it stole/ the pearls from / Aunty's jewelry box"—don't survive the translation, while a little lesson on "Disobedience" ("Father built a sturdy fence,/ mother scrambled out./ Father gave her several whacks;/ Listen to her shout.") won't be a favorite with many moms. A selective adult could make the collection pull its own weight in the nursery. . . . (pp. 1428-29)

> *A review of "Moon-Uncle, Moon-Uncle: Rhymes from India," in* Kirkus Reviews, *Vol. XL, No. 24, December 15, 1972, pp. 1428-29.*

Pretend, if you can, that you don't know what the words "moon" and "uncle" mean and just listen to the sound of "moon uncle, moon uncle." That's what this book is about—sounds.

Sounds that take you to India. Nursery rhymes translated . . . into English, but sprinkled with syllables from foreign tongues. It makes you realize the variety of sounds possible: that a rooster need not say only cockadoodle-doo. In India it's "kuku-doo-croo." **Moon Uncle** is simple melodic escape. . . .

> *June Goodwin, "Magical Sights and Sounds," in* The Christian Science Monitor, *May 2, 1973, p. B4.*

---

### *In Your Own Words: A Beginner's Guide to Writing* (1979)

Cassedy's too-general guide covers everything from the proper form for a business letter to imagery and metrics in poetry. "Your own words" are the only contribution of your own that "you" will make to the mechanical exercises she assigns. They include rewriting the Phaethon myth with a modern setting, simulating a hero tale, building a story around a description of an object, and simply filling in a prescribed outline of a ghost story. ("Write about a stranger whose mysterious dress and behavior are explained only at the very end when it is revealed that he is paying an annual call at the scene of his death.") To Cassedy, it seems, "using your imagination" means adding the fanciful details. Her advice on letters, book reports, and other mundane projects is unobjectionable but commonplace, and if the sections on poetry are the most valuable in the book, that is due chiefly to the quality and aptness of the examples she cites.

> *A review of "In Your Own Words: A Beginner's Guide to Writing," in* Kirkus Reviews, *Vol. XLVII, No. 18, September 15, 1979, p. 1073.*

To be sure, library shelves are full of books on this subject, such as Jerome H. Perlmutter's *A Practical Guide to Effective Writing* (Random, 1965) and Charles W. Ferguson's *Say It with Words* (Univ. of Nebraska Pr, 1959). But whether one believes that writers are born and not made or vice versa, there is always room for one more guide, especially one as good as this. In a style that is lively, direct, and never condescending, Cassedy combines creative inspiration with down-to-earth information and advice. The section on prose covers both fiction (myth, fantasy, fairy tales, science fiction, etc.) and nonfiction (essays, editorials, school and book reports, letters). The section on poetry is especially attractive with its wealth of selections from Shakespeare, Emily Dickinson, William Butler Yeats, and many others, classic and modern. In sum, a title that is not only a useful tool, particularly for youngsters in gifted En-

glish programs, but one that, being lots of fun to peruse, may well encourage slow learners to embark on new, untold adventures in the second R. (pp. 85-6)

> *Daisy Kouzel, in a review of "In Your Own Words: A Beginner's Guide to Writing," in* School Library Journal, *Vol. 26, No. 3, November, 1979, pp. 85-6.*

Cassedy gives examples in each genre she discusses, and provides some information about each genre, but the focus throughout the text is on observing, recording, and experimenting through writing with those details and reactions experienced through all the senses. Helpful advice on organizing and preparing school reports and book reports is also given. While this book covers much of the same material as is provided in other books intended to help young would-be writers, it has a cheerful and encouraging tone, and the advice is sensible, if occasionally generalized. The writing style is not outstanding, but it is informal and casual, and the reader can learn a good bit about figures of speech, poetic forms, and such facets of fictional writing as plot, viewpoint, characterization, and dialogue.

> *Zena Sutherland, in a review of "In Your Own Words: A Beginner's Guide to Writing," in* Bulletin of the Center for Children's Books, *Vol. 33, No. 4, December, 1979, p. 68.*

[*The following excerpt is from a review of the revised edition, published in 1990.*]

It is difficult to conceive of children picking up this hefty tome on their own to discover the secrets of successful creative writing. The emphasis on the process approach to teaching writing; the growing acceptance by educators of the connection between reading and writing for all students is apparent in the subjects included. Cassedy discusses several types of fiction; more than a third of the book is devoted to explaining poetry, with a separate chapter on haiku. There is also an excellent chapter on letter writing. A caveat: in the chapter on school reports, Cassedy proposes that students go immediately to encyclopedias. This method is antithetical to the process approach, which suggests that students acquire a basic background on subjects from both fiction and nonfiction books before taking notes from encyclopedia articles. Because of the variety of topics covered, however, the book might be used by teachers and librarians who are exploring different literary genres with their students. Libraries owning the first edition definitely would not need to add this one.

> *Martha Rosen, in a review of "In Your Own Words: A Beginner's Guide to Writing," in* School Library Journal, *Vol. 37, No. 2, February, 1991, p. 85.*

---

### *Behind the Attic Wall* (1983)

A deftly-crafted fantasy has a twelve-year-old protagonist who is an incorrigible rebel; Maggie, an orphan, had been ejected from every boarding school she'd attended. Now she is sent to stay with two elderly great-aunts; like other guardians, they are horrified by the behavior of the thin, pale, hostile child who comes to live with them and who throws away the doll ("Dolls are dumb.") they have bought her. That is the realistic matrix for a fantasy world behind the attic wall, where Maggie finds two dolls who are articulate and who draw her into their world so that she becomes engaged and protective. The story is framed by episodes that show that Maggie has at last found a happy home (presumably as a foster child) after the rigid great-aunts have sent her away. What Cassedy achieves is the creation of a situation in which the stark characters are believable, in which the fantasy segment is both touching and comic, and in which the conversion of Maggie from a suspicious cynic to a concerned participant is made credible. A memorable story.

> *Zena Sutherland, in a review of "Behind the Attic Wall," in* Bulletin of the Center for Children's Books, *Vol. 37, No. 3, November, 1983, p. 45.*

Sylvia Cassedy's writing is clean, precise and vigorous. She depicts the tedium and routine of students' experiences in class, Maggie's fury and the lyrical, richly imaginative flights of Uncle Morris's fancy with equal skill and persuasiveness. At once satire, fantasy and tragedy, this strange novel keeps the reader off-balance. But the web of the story is intricately woven. Nothing is extra. If there are missing pieces, well, that's life, and, after all, this is a fantasy. Though young readers may be confused at times, they won't be bored. (p. 40)

> *Cynthia King, in a review of "Behind the Attic Wall," in* The New York Times Book Review, *November 20, 1983, pp. 39-40.*

**Behind the Attic Wall** dissolves the boundary between fantasy and reality. Down-to-earth Maggie spins her internal fairy story of the Backwoods Girls while the external tale of the ghost-dolls follows hard-headed rules. We know from the structure of the book however that her future is kinder and that she is destined for something like family life: her experiences at Adelphi Hills Academy are interleaved as flashbacks from a more settled existence, with adopted sisters dispossessing the Backwoods Girls.

Sylvia Cassedy's novel is neither the familiar rough-times-at-school story, nor the inner-life-as-refuge variant. Her prose is both comfortable and striking: it creates a satisfying exploration of a contemporary setting in which magical elements play a natural and integrated part. She is deft in presenting both the hidden life in the attic and the bleaker downstairs world. Her portrait of the well-meaning school, which goes in for such horrors as the "class wish", is chillingly credible: "The wish was full of words like 'peace' and 'brotherhood' and 'no more pollution', when what everyone really wished for was new clothes and maybe a stereo".

> *Joanna Motion, "The Backwoods Girls," in* The Times Literary Supplement, *No. 4231, May 4, 1984, p. 506.*

---

### M. E. and Morton (1987)

Mary Ella is a bright, precocious seventh grader who attends a private school for academically gifted students on a full scholarship. Most of the other students are from wealthy families and avoid Mary Ella because she is not wealthy, and the neighborhood children avoid her because she is different. She tells each group that she is popular with the other, but spends most of her time in her room with imaginary friends waiting for a best friend to appear.

Mary Ella's brother, Morton, is dumb—a term used repeatedly and annoyingly throughout the book. Morton has been left back three times but gets good grades in behavior. His parents are embarrassed by him and wish he would misbehave as it would be more normal; they completely fail to see his good qualities. When a new girl moves into the neighborhood, Mary Ella is excited about making a friend, but Polly turns out to be "dumb" too, and prefers Morton's company. Mary Ella becomes M. E. and begins to dress, talk and act like a "dumb" kid so Polly will be her best friend.

None of the children presented in this book are likable except Morton, and he is continually ridiculed and rejected by his peers and parents. The term "dumb" is offensive in its frequent use and seems to fit M. E. better than Morton who is, at least, nice to people. We know that children can be cruel to each other, but no good qualities of children are exemplified here. The adults are portrayed in an even worse light and his parents only realize the worth of Morton as a human being after tragedy almost kills him: feelings the reader sees as brought on more by guilt than affection. Children will not relate to the characters in this book and we should be grateful for that.

> *Susan Ackler, in a review of "M. E. and Morton," in* Voice of Youth Advocates, *Vol. 10, No. 2, June, 1987, p. 76.*

Like Cassedy's Maggie in **Behind the Attic Wall** Mary Ella (M. E.) survives on her imagination. . . . What M. E. wants is a friend to admire her; what she has, instead, is an admiring older brother, painfully awkward, painfully slow, an embarrassment to M. E., and an impediment to friendship. Or so he seems until Polly barges in, turning M. E. and Morton's lives upside down, browbeating them, loving them, changing them, then leaving them as suddenly (and magically?) as she had come. Cassedy enriches her story with engaging detail, so much so that readers may find the narrative moves too slowly. Still, this is a novel to be savored, and the delights to be found here are many. Cassedy's prose is simple and sure and leisurely paced, her structure neat, if not at all straightforward. (Elements of plot are often introduced only to be dropped, then expanded upon later, a technique that adds texture and aids momentum.) Cassedy's images are vivid and telling. But best of all are her characterizations, lovingly wrought, achingly real, and unforgettable. A beautifully crafted novel, one to be lingered over and shared.

> *Marcia Hupp, in a review of "M. E. and Morton," in* School Library Journal, *Vol. 33, No. 10, June-July, 1987, p. 93.*

**Behind the Attic Wall** was the debut of this highly imaginative writer who made readers love a despicable little girl. Now Cassedy writes a more realistic story of childhood heartbreaks and solutions. . . . Cassedy's story unfolds deliberately, interspersed with stories about Mary Ella's own creativity, which reveal her growing ability to cherish Morton. This novel is a canvas of wistful moods and a loner's yearning to belong, of complicated emotions that arise from a simple need to be loved; the strokes are broad and textured, and unutterably intense.

> *A review of "M. E. and Morton," in* Publishers Weekly, *Vol. 231, No. 27, July 10, 1987, p. 70.*

---

### Roomrimes: Poems   (1987)

In this appealing collection of 26 poems about rooms or spaces, each letter of the alphabet is represented from attic to loft to zoo via unrhymed, rhymed, and even haiku poetry. Many of the poems bring to mind Valerie Worth's poetic celebration of ordinary things (*Small Poems* [1972], *More Small Poems* [1976] and *Small Poems Again* [1985, all Farrar]) and will be enjoyed by the same audience. Particularly enchanting are the poet's description of **"Shell"** as "parlor to the clam"; **"Upstairs"** "is where you left your pen, your ballet shoes . . . when you're playing in the basement"; and her use of a long string of verbs with internal "z" sounds in imagining what might be in a **"Closet."** [Michele] Chessare's black-and-white illustrations match the mood each poem evokes whether it be comic, frightening, or simply reflective. Be sure to hold a space on juvenile poetry shelves for this welcome addition.

> *Barbara S. McGinn, in a review of "Room-rimes," in* School Library Journal, *Vol. 34, No. 2, October, 1987, p. 120.*

Most of the poems have many lines (sometimes too many) of just a few words each, and if Cassedy occasionally displays an overfondness for easy alliteration, her best verse combines strong rhythms with metrical (and metaphorical) surprise. In **"Imaginary Room,"** for example, she asks us to clasp our hands "hollow to hollow,/ as though/ you were holding/ a bird—" and then to "*let him go./* Don't follow his flight;/ it's the space left behind/ that we want." Most of the poems are illustrated, not badly, but unnecessarily—Cassedy's own humor and descriptive powers stand better on their own.

> *Roger Sutton, in a review of "Roomrimes," in* Bulletin of the Center for Children's Books, *Vol. 41, No. 6, February, 1988, p. 112.*

An alphabet of poems about rooms, some expected and some unexpected, runs the gamut of moods, styles, and subjects. . . . There is a variety of length in the lines, but most are very short, and the poems are easily accessible for younger readers. The poet is alive with new ideas, adept with original use of images and words, and skilled with internal rhymes and changing rhythms. . . . An outstanding collection—fresh, simple, and diverse.

> *Ann A. Flowers, in a review of "Roomrimes: Poems," in* The Horn Book Magazine, *Vol. LXIV, No. 2, March-April, 1988, p. 217.*

### Lucie Babbidge's House   (1989)

Lucie Babbidge, class scapegoat, has little more to say at school than "I don't know, Miss Pimm," but at home she is the center of a loving, eccentric family. Readers will be well into this book before they discover that Lucie is an orphan, living in "a place for girls who are neither this nor that," and her "family" exists in a forgotten dollhouse in the cellar of the orphanage. As in the late author's previous books, *Behind the Attic Wall* and *M. E. and Morton,* the setting here is realistic, but its most intensely detailed landscape is drawn within the mind of a silent outsider. Lucie's games with her dolls are refuge and triumph (she can tell Mumma and Dada all about how she won the game that in reality the other girls wouldn't even let her play) and, she eventually realizes, powerful, as the events in the dollhouse begin to happen in the life of Lucie's English pen pal Delia. While the first part of the novel is somewhat static, readers will be caught by the gothic mood, and Lucie's brave rescue of Delia's family (one of the other girls steals the dolls) has an eccentric suspense. Without ever resorting to superficial psychologizing, Cassedy always showed a deep understanding of the imaginative obsessions behind children's most ordinary games, where a paintbox could become a boarding school (in *M. E. and Morton*), or here, where a dollhouse can become a home that brings the world to a girl left too long alone.

> *Roger Sutton, in a review of "Lucie Babbidge's House," in* Bulletin of the Center for Children's Books, *Vol. 43, No. 1, September, 1989, p. 5.*

In Lucie, Cassedy has created another unforgettable, vivid character in the tradition of Maggie from *Behind the Attic Wall.* Her ability to make the extremely literate and imaginative Lucie appear dull and stupid in the company of her insensitive teacher and horrid classmates is a *tour de force.* But the book suffers in not being able to explain the mysterious link between the activities of Lucie's dolls and their seeming control over the lives of an English girl and her family with whom Lucie corresponds; this is the only weak and unbelievable element in an ambitious and highly satisfying novel for readers who delight in complex characterization, and the inventive use of language and plotting.

> *Ellen Fader, in a review of "Lucie Babbidge's House," in* School Library Journal, *Vol. 35, No. 13, September, 1989, p. 272.*

Describing a novel by Sylvia Cassedy is not easy; her works are as elusive as moonlight—and insistently memorable. Nowhere is this more evident than in her latest book. *Lucie Babbidge's House* draws much of its tension from its similarity to theater. Like a play, it is divided into three parts, each ending on a dramatic note linking one to the other. Part One portrays Lucie as the unkempt, withdrawn Goosey-Loosey, tormented by her classmates at Norwood Hall—a school about as appealing as a Dickensian orphanage—and dismissed by her teacher as uncooperative and stupid. However, when she enters her house after school, she is the beloved, admired daughter of a closely knit—if somewhat eccentric—family. At the end of Part One the reader becomes aware that Lucie Babbidge's house is a doll house, hidden in a basement storeroom at Norwood Hall, and that Lucie has created an imaginary retreat from the sad realities of her environment. In Part Two, further elements of Lucie's background are revealed, as details she inserts into the lives of her doll house companions indicate that her imagined world is grounded in the memories of a small child. Lucie also begins an extensive correspondence with a girl named Delia, who is a descendant of the original owner of the house; strangely enough, events in Delia's life seem suddenly to parallel events in Lucie's house. In the end, through the process of imaging, eleven-year-old Lucie achieves an integrated personality, recognizes the doll house for what it is, and draws on the inner strength, wit, and talent previously revealed only to her "family" to assert herself on the grim playing fields of Norwood Hall. The book ends on a note of triumph as she stands tall, responding clearly and distinctly to her teacher's taunts. For Lucie, there will be no sentimental ending, but she will survive—a satisfying note on which to conclude a truly remarkable novel, as complex and as tightly woven as a Jacquard fabric. Reading this book brings only one regret: that it is a posthumous publication. Sylvia Cassedy's unique voice and rare imagination will be sorely missed. (pp. 768-69)

> *Mary M. Burns, in a review of "Lucie Babbidge's House," in* The Horn Book Magazine, *Vol. LXV, No. 6, November-December, 1989, pp. 768-69.*

# Eilís Dillon

## 1920-

Irish author of fiction, nonfiction, and picture books, reteller, playwright, and editor.

Major works include *The Coriander* (1963), *The Sea Wall* (1965), *The Seals* (1968), *A Herd of Deer* (1969), *Living in Imperial Rome* (1974).

Celebrated as a writer whose works have increased the depth of the adventure story, Dillon is often considered the most important contemporary Irish author of literature for children and young adults. Praised as a natural storyteller and an exceptional creator of character as well as for her skillful evocation of the landscape and atmosphere of her characteristically Irish settings, she is noted for writing adventure stories and mysteries which address mature themes in a nondidactic fashion while entertaining young readers with exciting narratives written in clear, lyrical language. Dillon most frequently weaves her tales around the lands and people of the rugged western coast of Ireland, especially Connemara and the islands of Galway Bay; she is often recognized for her accurate and sympathetic descriptions of the traditions, superstitions, humor, and close-knit community life of the Irish people. Placing her books in both historical and recent times, she characteristically depicts adolescent male protagonists who face moral and social decisions as part of their maturation processes while dealing with the isolation and economic struggle of their physical world. Dillon often treats the consequences of adult mistrust and misunderstanding as she explores conflicts within family groups, between islanders and mainlanders, and between locals and newcomers. The problems in her novels are often caused by the obstinacy of the community males; notably, it is the tough, resourceful young adults and older women drawn into these situations who bring about their final reconciliation and healing.

Born in Galway, Dillon claims she received her understanding of the Irish people from her childhood experiences in a small village a few miles west of Galway as well as from the time she spent in the Aran islands and in the wild parts of Connemara; she has also lived in Italy, a setting that figures in several of her works. Dillon began her career as a children's writer with fantasies written in the Irish language. Her early books written in English reflect Dillon's use of the familiar characteristics of the adventure story: shipwrecks, deserted islands, stolen treasure, and kidnappings; she also includes local Irish animals such as horses, deer, and foxes as focal points. In her more recent works, Dillon often reaches into the past for her subjects. One or her most well-received titles, *The Seals,* addresses the fight for Irish independence in the 1920s; inspired by the experiences of Dillon's politically active parents, the novel describes how three boys and an elderly man outwit the Black and Tans and rescue the fugitive Irish champion of the islanders. In the award-winning *A Herd of Deer,* fif-

teen-year-old Peter Regan helps to restore the understanding between an expatriate gentleman farmer and his neighbors after he discovers the motives behind the theft of the farmer's Scottish deer. In addition to her adventure stories and mysteries, Dillon is the author of *Living in Imperial Rome,* an nonfiction title for young adults which describes the lives of a Roman senator, businessman, farmer, and stallholder in 110 A.D.; by depicting the lives of each of these figures and interrelating them with each other, Dillon provides information about both period and culture. Dillon is also the creator of several stories for younger children and retellings of traditional folktales, and is well known as the author of mysteries, novels, and nonfiction for adults; in addition, she is the translator of adult poetry from the Irish, French, and Italian and has translated the Latin liturgy into English. She also adapted her juvenile fantasy *The Cats' Opera* (1962) into a play and composed her own music for it. Named a Fellow of the Royal Society of Literature, Dillon received the Lewis Carroll Shelf Award for *A Herd of Deer* in 1970.

(See also *Contemporary Literary Criticism,* Vol. 17; *Something about the Author,* Vol. 2; *Contemporary Authors New Revision Series,* Vol. 4; *Contemporary Authors,* Vols. 9-10, rev. ed.; and *Contemporary Authors Autobiography Series,* Vol. 3.)

---

## GENERAL COMMENTARY

### Margery Fisher

What Allan McLean has done for Skye, Eilís Dillon is doing for remote Irish seaboards. Here are no crooks in the story-book sense, but people gone wrong. In *The Island of Horses* it is a local dealer who has turned thief to bolster up his self-importance. In *The Singing Cave* it is an egotistical recluse who covets the Viking found in the sand. In *The House on the Shore* it is an old man warped by his wife's death. With the free emotional swing of Irish tales, the motives of these very individual criminals are laid bare to us. . . . To find crime in everyday life, to find real motives for it, and to fuse detail into an imaginative whole—Eilís Dillon has done this, and has raised the standard of the adventure story in doing it. (pp. 261-62)

> *Margery Fisher, "Innocents in the Underworld: 'The Island of Horses', 'The Singing Cave', and 'The House on the Shore',"* in her Intent Upon Reading: A Critical Appraisal of Modern Fiction for Children, *Brockhampton Press, 1961, pp. 261-62.*

### Marcus Crouch

Apart from William Mayne and Philippa Pearce the 'fifties produced few new writers of unquestionable quality. The Irish writer Eilis Dillon wrote beautifully, notably in *The House on the shore* and *The Singing Cave,* and hovered rather disconcertingly on the edge of the Celtic twilight.

> *Marcus Crouch, "Widening Horizons: 'The House on the Shore' and 'The Singing Cave',"* in his Treasure Seekers and Borrowers: Children's Books in Britain 1900-1960, *The Library Association, 1962, p. 122.*

### Ruth Hill Viguers

[Eilís Dillon] can tell a suspense story so rich in atmosphere and stout Irish humor, and peopled with such diverse and well realized characters that the books are long remembered and often invite rereading. Eilis Dillon is an Irish woman, steeped in Irish legends and superstitions, so well acquainted with the rugged coast of Ireland and its proud little islands, that her books are vivid experiences. She has such eloquence in the portrayal of people that her characters, from small boys to the crones and patriarchs, are individual and authentic. (p. 491)

> *Ruth Hill Viguers, "Quests, Survival, and the Romance of History: Adventure Tales and Historical Fiction,"* in A Critical History of Children's Literature *by Cornelia Meigs and others, edited by Cornelia Meigs, revised edition, Macmillan Publishing Company, 1969, pp. 484-510.*

### Frank Eyre

It is not quite true to say that the traditional story of adventure has completely disappeared, because a few authors have produced books that are infinitely more realistic although they approximate to the older pattern in the concessions they make to the demands for excitement and thrills. The best of these are Allan Campbell McLean, with his John Buchan-ish stories of villainy of various kinds on the Island of Skye; . . . and Eilís Dillon with her very much better equivalents set on the west coast of Ireland, *The House on the Shore, The Island of Horses, The Singing Cave* and others. Eilís Dillon is an experienced novelist, so it is not surprising that her wide range of characters should all be fully drawn—the adults as well as the children. Both these authors succeed in communicating a real sense of setting and atmosphere and their characters, unlike their puppet equivalents in [W. E. Johns's] Biggles and his kind, are real people acting from believable motives. If the traditional adventure story has any future this is how it should be written. (pp. 96-7)

> *Frank Eyre, "Fiction for Children: 'The House on the Shore', 'The Island of Horses', and 'The Singing Cave',"* in his British Children's Books in the Twentieth Century, *revised edition, Longman Books, 1979, pp. 96-7.*

### Winifred Whitehead

All writers select, rigorously, that portion of the world they wish to present, but in so doing some writers for children make a curious and partial offering—a child's world from which the rest of the community, adults in particular, have been almost wholly excluded. In such a world the children . . . conduct their affairs with a freedom from adult control of their actions and movement that is rarely accorded to children in real life. . . . [In Arthur Ransome's work,] a striking and essential element of each story is the relative absence of adult control or interference: the children are on their own in a self-directed, self-enclosed community.

The Irish writer Eilís Dillon has an outstandingly vivid sense of the child's place *within* the larger community. Her books are remarkable for their distinctive recreation of rural Ireland; the men living close to the land or sea, as farmworkers or fishermen; the women working equally hard in their small houses, caring for their menfolk and their children; and the children themselves, seen essentially as part of the community, with their own place in it and their own chores to carry out at home, having only so much liberty to range the countryside, with its rich wildlife and its possibilities of adventure. Eilís Dillon does devise situations in which her heroes can escape from adult supervision, but always within a firm context of parents and neighbours, and with a constant reference to the ethos and expectations of the community in which they live.

In *A Family of Foxes,* for instance, four boys unite to hide away a family of silver foxes from the rest of the people on Inishownan, knowing well that if discovered the foxes would at once be killed. This involves the boys in a long conspiracy to evade the adults on the island while they scrounge or steal enough food to keep the foxes alive. In this way the boys are both separated off from the community by their activities, and yet are closely in touch with it. Adult attitudes are of crucial importance to the whole situation: their fear and distrust of foxes; their plans to exterminate all they can find on the island; their shamefaced superstition and their expectations of the young people themselves. At the crisis point, when the men discover what the boys have been up to, and the lives of the foxes hang in the balance, it is the carefully accumulated understanding built up in the earlier part of the story that creates the tense awareness of the extreme delicacy of the situation.

> Suddenly Patsy was out in the middle of the floor. He never knew how he got there. If he had taken time to think, it's certain that he would never have faced all the men with such courage.

At the end of his impassioned defence of the foxes:

> There was a long silence. Patsy still stood there with his fists clenched, feeling more and more every minute the awfulness of what he had done. For a boy to take part in the men's conversation was a terrible thing. But they did not look angry. He could hardly see their faces because their eyes were turned down to the floor. [No one seemed to want to look at him, not even his father, Seán Mór.]
>
> Then gradually he began to understand why. They were afraid, every man of them. Not one of them had the courage to undertake to kill those strange, powerful foxes, lest the man who did it, and his family, should suffer some terrible misfortune.

This central crisis point has been prepared for throughout the preceding story, in all the encounters with the boys' parents, in the discussions which had taken place round the fireside or amongst the boys themselves. In this way a living picture of the Irish community has been built up, and the boys are seen as acting within it, not cut off from it as though in some miraculous way they could exist, for however brief a time, in a vacuum. In this way Eilís Dillon's stories are more than tales of adventure: they are stories of real life.

Of course adventure stories, even stories that are pure fantasy, are often still related to the real life concerns of children. But the dimension added to Eilís Dillon's books, by her inclusion of the community in this way, offers a unique area in relation to which children can be invited to see themselves. Within *A Family of Foxes,* for instance, can be seen a particularly close, cooperative and interacting way of living which is now less easily observable in our towns and high rise flats, and which is certainly not often revealed in modern stories. Her close, detailed and loving observation of the countryside, and of the animals such as the horses, deer, seals and foxes which provide a focal point for many of her stories, is obviously attractive: a less obvious but valuable element is the vivid portrayal of the people, whose individual characteristics and foibles are so amusingly and compassionately detailed. This leads the young reader to a heightened awareness of the possibilities of community living: its complexity, in the mixture of motives—greed and selfishness alongside generosity and disinterestedness; and the failure of understanding and communication which can bedevil people living apparently close together—but also in the richness of a life in which some degree of mutual interdependence can foster virtues of concern and tolerance. This awareness provides a growing point for the young reader, who is led repeatedly to look behind the surface, and to see—in a way not often fostered in our fragmented and self-seeking modern society—how his natural egocentricity can be subordinated to the common good. This 'message' is the more valid in Eilís Dillon's stories in that it is not presented in any priggish moralistic fashion as 'the lesson' to be taken from the books: it is implicitly there as part of the greater tolerance and understanding of themselves and their neighbours achieved by the characters in the course of their adventures.

This awareness of 'community' which has been seen to be important in *A Family of Foxes* is the focal point of *A Herd of Deer.* . . . In this story, fifteen-year-old Peter Regan is sent to spend the summer working on his cousin's farm: instead he decides to look for a job on his own. He finds one unexpectedly with Michael Joyce, a man who has recently come from Argentina to his father's native Ireland. With a profound ignorance of Irish ways and attitudes, he has bought a house and land and established on it, in the expansive Argentinian manner, a herd of deer. Peter can immediately sense the nature of the outrage; the villagers' resentment of the rich foreigner, 'with his herd of deer and his huge kingdom of land, while they struggled to make a living out of twenty or thirty acres and a fishing boat, with perhaps a Government pension to keep off the worst of the winter's hunger'. They also deeply resent the Scottish herdsman, imported with the outlandish deer, and the affront he gives to their assumptions of hospitality and easy access to any land within their neighbourhood. So they have stolen some of the deer, intending at first merely to warn Michael Joyce off. Unfortunately, as is the way of things, the situation escalates, and Peter, having initially agreed to try to trace the deer and help a peaceable restoration, eventually finds himself in an ugly position between the warring parties. He has a foot uneasily in both camps, liking both parties and seeing both sides, but helplessly and exasperatedly unable to bring them together. What he most admires in the stubborn community of deer-stealers is their loyalty, interdependence and compassion for each other, their ability to work together, discussing, planning and tolerating the weaker, more eccentric and less creditable amongst them. But these very qualities, combined with their united hostility to the 'outsider', make the situation the more dangerous for Peter should he be found to have dealings with Joyce.

It can be seen that there are many points of discussion arising from this novel: the escalation from an initial misunderstanding into violence and even murder; the group hostility to an 'intruder' who unwittingly offends against accepted codes of behaviour; these are both problems which can be seen in our present society with its variety of urban tensions, but problems which here can be discussed on the neutral third ground offered by the novel. *The Seals,* a story set in an island off County Clare in 1920, can also be used as neutral ground for the discussion of important current political problems. This time the intruders are the Black and Tans active in Ireland two years before the creation of Eire as a separate state, when the fight for independence was at its height. The story begins quickly, with an approaching storm; and even as Pat and his friend Mike are busily helping to gather in the lobster pots they see the hooker which is bringing news of Pat's Uncle Roddy. The boys set off on a wild chase to rescue him from imminent capture and death at the hands of the Black and Tans. . . . This is not only an exciting story, but one which suggests a different perspective in viewing the 'troubles' in Ulster, while at the same time, by setting them at an historical distance, providing the more suitable 'third ground' on which both personal problems and social and national problems can be discussed. The point here is that such a discussion can firmly be anchored to the events of the books themselves, and in this context can become specific and informed; a very different matter from some of the large, abstract, uninformed, prejudiced—and often self-righteous and cliché-ridden—moralising which too often passes for 'debate' and 'discussion' in our schools.

It would be wrong, however, to leave an impression that Eilís Dillon's books are merely a springboard for discussion, however valuable socially this may seem. The discussion is to be seen essentially as a way to a deeper understanding and enjoyment of the books, and through them to a deeper understanding and enrichment of life. The stories are, indeed, enthralling: full of fun and humour, of vivid character sketches, drama and incident, with always a strong sense of the Irish landscape, a freshness of observation and a simple directness which are a delight. *The Coriander,* in which two boys kidnap a doctor whom they have rescued from a wrecked ship and hold him captive in an attempt to force him to stay on the island which is desperate for his services, and *The Cruise of the Santa Maria,* a story of two boys who sail a hooker to Spain on their own, and help to reconcile a fierce eccentric old man with his two daughters, would be good adventure stories at the Junior Secondary level. Like *A Family of Foxes, The Island of Horses* would probably appeal more at the top Middle School age range. This last is an exciting story in which two boys sail to a deserted island, and find, hidden amongst a herd of wild horses, a number of stolen animals, a discovery which brings its own perils. The most exciting incidents involve a wild stallion and a hair-raising sail through a storm with kidnappers who would obviously be glad to see the boys drown 'by accident'; and the outstanding characters, apart from the boys themselves, are a valiant old grandmother who leaves the fireside to take part in the final adventure, and Luke the Cats, an eccentric old man with a house literally bestrewn with cats, whose shrewd help is crucial at the climax of the story.

It is in these Irish stories that Eilís Dillon is most at home: she has tried writing stories of other lands and other times, but it is her first-hand knowledge of Ireland, her humour and her compassion, and her vivid and delightful recreation of the highly individual Irish communities of smallholders and fishermen that give her books their uniquely satisfying flavour. (pp. 58-62)

> *Winifred Whitehead, "Eilís Dillon and the Sense of Community," in* The Use of English, *Vol. 30, No. 2, Spring, 1979, pp. 58-62.*

## TITLE COMMENTARY

### *Midsummer Magic* (1950)

A new Irish writer contributes *Midsummer Magic* and is heartily welcome to the lists. The tale is told with natural ease and firm belief in faery, and has an added mystery to make the story more in tune with the taste of this modern age.

> *P. H. in a review of "Midsummer Magic," in* The School Librarian and School Library Review, *Vol. 5, No. 2, July, 1950, p. 138.*

### *The Lost Island* (1952)

This tale is a strange but likeable mixture of fantasy and adventure, which both charms and irritates; irritates because it never seems to quite make up its mind whether it is going to live in the world where things of this kind just *might* happen, or whether it really is dealing with the Never-Never Land. The result is that though the book is finely written about those enthralling subjects of small boats and islands as seen through the eyes of a boy, and an unusually delightful boy at that, it is as though the author's leap of imagination had somehow landed short. The plot is preposterous, if it is to be judged by everyday standards; and if it is not to be so judged, then the world of imaginative adventure into which we are led should be true to its own logic. It is asking a great deal of any author that he shall be able to persuade his readers to accept a magical enclosure in which the wildly improbable shall be more real than the life that we know. This does not quite happen here, yet Miss Dillon has written a book of real distinction, and at least one reader will look with anticipation to its successor. It is indeed a most 'buyable' book. . . . (pp. 216-17)

> *A review of "The Lost Island," in* The Junior Bookshelf, *Vol. 16, No. 4, November, 1952, pp. 216-17.*

[Eilís Dillon] has concocted an A-1 adventure story. The ingredients are familiar, but the final product has the fresh charm of a fine, spring morn in Galway.

> *Howard Boston, "Off to Inishmanann," in* The New York Times Book Review, *June 6, 1954, p. 31.*

This exciting young novel by a Galway author is unique in many ways. With an authentic background of town and country living and Irish belief in the supernatural, Mrs. Dillon starts Michael Farrell and a friend off on a rugged search for Michael's father, believed missing on the "lost island" of Inishmanann, "lost stronghold of Manannan, the old god of the sea," where a treasure was supposed to lie. The story is not one of fantasy, however, but wholly real as the boys under great odds succeed in getting to sea and find both Mr. Farrell and a rare living treasure. Beginning quietly with an ordinary market day, the book gathers speed and holds the reader enthralled to its conclusion.

> *Virginia Haviland, in a review of "The Lost Is-*

land," in The Horn Book Magazine, *Vol. XXX, No. 4, August, 1954, p. 251.*

## The San Sebastian (1953)

The opening situation of Miss Dillon's story of (mainly) gentle villainy is promising. When Pat Harnon finds and salvages a drifting brig on the shore of his Connemara home mystery amply fills the air. A drifting castaway brought in on the same current turns out to be a mysterious foreigner who seeks a ship of the same description but fears some other mysterious foreigners who turn out to be trawlermen out for his blood. His disappearance and the subsequent kidnapping of Pat are the prelude to a prolonged battle of wits—and even to physical combat—after which all is peace and contentment and generous reward all round. Miss Dillon writes well enough to make an unlikely story at least plausible and Richard Kennedy's drawings have the right touch of unreality to match the faint fantasy of the story. Suspense is well maintained and the characters, though elliptical rather than round, are real enough to give the book some distinction among the more material kinds of story.

*A review of "The San Sebastian," in The Junior Bookshelf, Vol. 17, No. 5, November, 1953, p. 238.*

In **The San Sebastian** perception of the exterior world is never lulled asleep, the landscapes are no longer those of the imagination but lie geographically vivid in Ireland and Brittany; the people are differentiated, and are felt to live of themselves even when the narrative is not concerned with them. Yet, perhaps because its setting is a fishing village hardly changed for centuries, it has the strength of legend as well as the stamp of life. The San Sebastian is a sailing brig blown ashore in a gale and towed as "wrack" to shelter in a tidal cave by Pat Hernan, a boy of 15 who tells his own story. His adventures with the Spaniards who come (without legal claim) to look for the brig, his kidnapping, his escape with another boy, the kindness of Michael Mór, the solitary who hides them in his hole in the hill and lends them a horse belonging to his skinflint brother, their lonely ride by night through miles of mountainside and bog back to Pat's home, the fight, the accidental discovery within the San Sebastian of treasure ultimately spent on a fleet of trawlers for the village; all these are sound, solid, actual, as well as strange and wild.

*"Could It Really Happen?," in The Times Literary Supplement, No. 2704, November 27, 1953, p. xvi.*

Miss Dillon's story is in an altogether older tradition of children's adventure books [than Richard Church's *Dog Toby*]: behind it one may dimly perceive a far-off vista of *Treasure Island.* . . . I thought it well done; the fights are good, the mystery of the ship is sustained, and it is very nicely written.

*Walter Allen, "Crusoes and Cruisers," in The New Statesman & Nation, Vol. XLVI, No. 1187, December 5, 1953, p. 730.*

## The House on the Shore (1955)

The best story of the yarn-spinning, come-gather-round-and-listen kind [of the books reviewed], is **The House on the Shore.** It is told in the first person by the boy to whom it all happens. The setting is the west coast of Ireland where almost anything could happen, and indeed does. From the time when Jim comes walking barefoot down the mountain to the strange village by the sea to find his uncle, to the final life and death chase in sailing boats across the night sea, there is no let-up of the tension. It is fine story-telling, by a writer who never fails to record just the sort of details that children want from each scene; whose every character is lively and round. There are several authors producing good, well-worked-out adventure stories today. Eilis Dillon should be noticed for being, imaginatively, a jump ahead of the rest of them.

*Pamela Whitlock, "No Common Place or Play," in The Spectator, Vol. 195, No. 6628, July 8, 1955, p. 51.*

**The House on the Shore** is full of suspense, exciting, often melodramatic. Boys of the hero's age (sixteen) or somewhat younger should delight in the adventurous deeds of Jim O'Malley, especially those who have already discovered Miss Dillon's **Lost Island.** From the moment Jim finds his Uncle's house empty and strangers with foreign accents lurking in the dark woods nearby you follow his exploits breathlessly. The plot is good, with unexpected twists and reversals, and sure-fire elements such as stolen treasure, a tree hideaway, a secret chimney-room, vengeful villagers and a grim sea race. The atmosphere of the Irish sea-coast village and its people dominates and gives depth to this sturdy tale, quite in the *Kidnapped* tradition.

*Margaret Sherwood Libby, in a review of "The House on the Shore," in New York Herald Tribune Book Review, June 17, 1956, p. 8.*

In her third highly successful book for young people to be published in this country, Mrs. Dillon weaves a timeless tale of mystery in an Irish coastal village near the Aran Islands. Her young heroes, Jim and Roddy, with the courage and enterprise necessary for apprehending villains, overtake their elders in a danger-filled search to get the villagers' stolen money back from Jim's hated uncle. However, in their entanglements with the tricky sailors from abroad who have led Uncle Martin into wickedness, they do not always take the right step, committing errors that make the boys the more convincing and their story more and more full of suspense. Every detail in description and speech counts, to give exactness and flavor to a book that both boys and girls will find absorbing. (pp. 262-63)

*Virginia Haviland, in a review of "The House on the Shore," in The Horn Book Magazine, Vol. XXXI, No. 4, August, 1956, pp. 262-63.*

## The Wild Little House (1955)

It must be every writer of fantasy's dream to be illustrated by Violet Drummond. Miss Dillon's dream has come true and she deserves her good fortune. Her story of the little house which yearned for the sea is gay, stylish and individual; it has just the right kind of topsy-turvy seriousness for picture book treatment, and, if the story is a little long, its words and phrases have an inevitable quality which defeats pruning. I liked the story immensely and believe that children will take it straight to their hearts.

> *A review of "The Wild Little House," in* The Junior Bookshelf, *Vol. 19, No. 4, October, 1955, p. 211.*

A happy fantasy about a little wooden house which stood on four stout posts like legs and which had a hankering for the seashore. One night it discovered it could walk, and from that moment its adventures and those of the shoemaker and his wife and their son John, who lived in it began. The story is charmingly told and Miss Dillon manages to make the impossible quite credible. V. H. Drummond's illustrations ably reflect the humor and liveliness of the story and add to the appeal this book will have to many young readers.

> *G. Taylor, in a review of "The Wild Little House," in* The School Librarian and School Library Review, *Vol. 8, No. 3, December, 1956, p. 229.*

### The Island of Horses (1956)

Two boys who live on an island off the coast of Connemara decide to explore the mysterious Island of Horses, long deserted by its inhabitants and believed to be haunted by the ghosts of Spanish horses. They find a herd of wild horses, bring home a colt—"the finest colt that ever walked the soil of Ireland"—and are thereby involved in more sinister adventures, including kidnapping and shipwreck. Miss Dillon is a fine writer, and she has here a story to match her gifts—fast-moving, with plenty of action which never exceeds the bounds of credibility. The characterization is particularly good: Pat and Danny emerge as distinct and likeable boys.

> *A review of "The Island of Horses," in* The Times Literary Supplement, *No. 2856, November 23, 1956, p. xxiii.*

The final scene of the mystery is splendid, the sudden savage attack of the black stallion and Pat's plucky grandmother, who has insisted on seeing the island once again, brought face to face with the enemy.

This tale is more closely knit, more believable and more exciting than the excellent *House on the Shore,* with a vivid sense of the place and the people. It is superior fare for adventure-loving boys and girls. A good story, beautifully told.

> *A review of "The Island of Horses," in* New York Herald Tribune Book Review, *November 17, 1957, p. 12.*

The familiar ingredients used here might have made a trite yarn, but Eilis Dillon weaves a magic Irish spell and an A-1 mystery-adventure story, taut with action and suspense, results. Characters like Luke the Cat and Granny Conroy are distinctively drawn. The tale sparkles with the

atmosphere of the sea and of small-town life along Ireland's west coast.

> *Howard Boston, "An Unlucky Place," in* The New York Times Book Review, *November 17, 1957, p. 30.*

### The Singing Cave (1959)

Miss Dillon comes time and again within reach of success. Once more she just fails to grasp it.

*The Singing Cave* is another story of Connemara. Pat is living with his grandfather on the island when a freak storm opens up the singing cave, disclosing its wonderful contents. Many of the adventures that follow are frankly improbable, but they are narrated with style and passion and most readers will readily suspend belief. Certainly one would not, for the sake of probability, forego the superb story of the voyage to Brittany on the lobster boat. Fine story-telling with some colourful characters. Unfortunately the whole story turns on the character of Mr. Allen, the local gentleman, and his is a fundamentally unsatisfactory portrait.

It is tantalising that so good a book, which has its full share of fun and excitement and a serious theme, should not be just a little better. (pp. 142-43)

> *A review of "The Singing Cave," in* The Junior Bookshelf, *Vol. 23, No. 3, July, 1959, pp. 142-43.*

As good as Eilis Dillon's earlier stories were, none of them can top *The Singing Cave* for narrative pace, atmosphere, or suspense. The villagers are all sharply and distinctively sketched. Ever present in the background are the restless sea, the shrilling winds and the wild splendor of the Irish coast.

> *Howard Boston, "Found and Lost," in* The New York Times Book Review, *May 8, 1960, p. 8.*

In other books for teen-agers Miss Dillon has shown she can spin a tale in the best romantic tradition of a Buchan or a Stevenson. But never has she written one as stirring as this one, in which an exciting plot vies for interest with a dramatic Irish setting. . . .

A chase thru turbulent seas, a cattle stampede on a high cliff's edge, the recovery of the treasure and its strange fate provide many a thrill. Pat, his grandfather, and their hardy, individualistic neighbors, are skillfully portrayed. And the sea girt, wind swept island exerts a fascination not soon forgotten.

> *Polly Goodwin, in a review of "The Singing Cave," in* Chicago Sunday Tribune Magazine of Books, *June 12, 1960, p. 6.*

### The Fort of Gold (1961)

No writer today comes nearer to greatness, without quite getting there, than Eilis Dillon. This new book is characteristic. The scene again is an island which is not one of the Arans but much like it. The men of the island are busy with their horse breeding. The children too work hard, but they have time for play, and time to find the ages-old treasure of the Fort of Gold. Because of this they fall foul of a gang of ruffians. The denouement is not quite satisfactory.

There is much good character-drawing, and the narrative moves briskly. It is perhaps in writing that the book falls short of excellence. There is not quite a broad enough sweep in the story, and the author does not make us hear the thunder of the surf as we should. For all that, this is a very good book, with illustrations, by Richard Kennedy, which extend its emotional range.

> *A review of "The Fort of Gold," in* The Junior Bookshelf, *Vol. 25, No. 4, October, 1961, p. 219.*

[**The Fort of Gold** starts] with an island called Inishdara off Galway, with a place called the Fort of Gold or the Fort of Sorrow, where the Spaniards had been killed to a man, "buried there among the old stones, and their gold with them, so the saying went. . . ." Disbelief is too willingly suspended as the boys find and hide the treasure before ever the yellow-faced Mr. Kelly or the yellow-livered Mr. Crann can lay their thieving hands on it. Eilís Dillon is an enchanter. Tension mounts as the boys find themselves forced to work for Kelly and Crann and at the same time spy on them for their fellow islanders' sake. Both adults and adolescents are entirely credible, events grow more and more thrilling yet never seem improbable or melodramatic, and such incidents as the removal of the gold to another island in bad weather are of an excitement rare in children's books today.

> *"After Buchan," in* The Times Literary Supplement, *No. 3118, December 1, 1961, p. xxiv.*

The plot is melodramatic, but the book is otherwise excellent: the atmosphere and background are evocative, the characters beautifully developed, and the Irish humor (especially in conversation) pervasive and sly.

> *Zena Sutherland, in a review of "The Fort of Gold," in* Bulletin of the Center for Children's Books, *Vol. XV, No. 11, July-August, 1962, p. 175.*

---

### The Cats' Opera   (1962)

Eilis Dillon is one of the most interesting of contemporary writers for children but not one of the most successful. Again and again she seems to come almost within grasp of success. **The Cats' Opera** is a good example; it has an excellent idea, very fine writing, sharpness of characterisation—yet I doubt if it will be enjoyed greatly or remembered long. There is perhaps too much calculation in Miss Dillon's writing; some of her best passages come, one thinks, more from the head than the eye or the heart.

This is the story of the Mulligans who live in an opera-house, presumably in Ireland, and of their cat Simon who, when the theatre is closed for the night, calls in his feline artistes and rehearses an opera. On Saint John's Eve, when all the animals talk human, the opera is presented before an audience of cats, Mulligans and scene-shifters. There is plenty of good observation here of operatic oddities, but this surely is for the adult reader. All the time one feels that this is a children's book for adults, and the clever-ugly illustrations [by Kveta Vanecek] reinforce this impression. If a children's book, it is one for adults to read aloud; the difficulties are formidable for the children who might be attracted by the fantasy.

> *A review of "The Cats' Opera," in* The Junior Bookshelf, *Vol. 26, No. 2, March, 1962, p. 61.*

[**The Cats' Opera**], for readers of seven or eight and upwards, has just that edge of outrageousness which seems to be needed to make us grip a book, but is otherwise in a courtly and honoured convention. The Opera House has a caretaker, the caretaker has a son, the son has a cat, the cat is one of a nation of cats, and the cats stage an opera. Opera is the cats' art-form, if ever they had one, even more than religious ceremony or the signallings of destiny. It is not so much that opera is stylized, by force of art, to just that degree, as that cats can mimic man no closer. So this book has an elusive, teasing reality about it, like marionettish opera music.

> *Ted Hughes, in a review of "The Cats' Opera," in* New Statesman, *Vol. LXIII, No. 1627, May 18, 1962, p. 726.*

In this witty tale the lumpish humans just begin to realise the richness of cat's lives after dark, while the cats, in a splendid traditional opera ( . . . reminiscent of [the books by Hugh Lofting about Dr.] Dolittle) take off human affectations. The spidery drawings, in the Searle manner, add the final touch to a book a little sophisticated for most children under nine, but with a special appeal to imaginative and adventurous readers.

> *Margery Fisher, in a review of "The Cats' Opera," in* Growing Point, *Vol. 1, No. 3, September, 1962, p. 42.*

---

### A Pony and a Trap   (1962)

A good story, like stills from a film, freezes moments of activity so that you scarcely believe you are not actually seeing movement, hearing voices. This is something more than realism. Accumulated detail will not do the job unless the spark of imagination is there to light it. Such a spark Eilís Dillon certainly has. In barely ten thousand words she draws an Irish village, with the church, the walled farmyard and big barn of old Mr. Callan, the field with two horses in it, the road to Miss Durand's house, the lanes and alleys where boys gather. The death of Michael's grandfather has left the village without a choirmaster. There is Miss Durand, once renowned as a conductor—but she lives outside the village and must be transported. The enthusiastic small boys have the answer ready—a pony and trap. Someone in the village must have a spare one. Of course someone has, and they get it; and in the getting they find new friends, improvise a play (a good one) and cheer a lonely visitor.

The author selects her details so carefully that her narrative seems leisured, when it is really very compressed. Her vocabulary is varied, and the sentences have a pleasant Irish lilt, as well as a delightful humour. The large print and generally pleasant look of the book makes it well suited to children between five and seven, whether capable readers or eager listeners. The illustrator [Monica Brasier-Creagh] has caught from the author the prevailing mood of the story—the busy activity of small boys. Children will feel absolutely at home here, for text and pictures embody dreams and ambitions which belong to all of them.

> *Margery Fisher, in a review of "A Pony and Trap," in* Growing Point, *Vol. 1, No. 3, September, 1962, p. 33.*

---

### The Coriander (1963)

Eilis Dillon has a wicked knowledge of how to evade revenue men and how to conceal ships that have been happily wrecked on the shore of your tiny island home. If I lived on the tiny island of Inishgillan, apparently as far west as Europe goes, I should know that too. And if I were a quick-witted lad I should no doubt know that if I found a shipwrecked doctor with a broken leg, I should keep him on the island, because he was a necessity of life. It is a pleasant conceit, to hold on to him and make him work at his trade. I smiled a little, and expected badgers to come to surgery when the lad who tells the story drops into a Tommy Stubbins-John Dolittle mood and goes round helping the doctor with his cases. There is a good sweep of story, all centred on the island. There are characters who are full without being overstuffed with richness, a community that works out its hardships without having a boast made of them. There is a documentary quality to the whole book. Wherever we go on the island we are shown little snapshots to realise for us the feel of the place, explanations of why things are done in such a way, why someone said what he did, how some natural event had affected the landscape or the activities of men. I liked this fresh book very much.

> *William Mayne, "Water Salt and Water Cold," in* New Statesman, *Vol. LXVI, No. 1704, November 8, 1963, p. 670.*

Eilís Dillon's **The Coriander** is totally unlike anything else in this collection [of books reviewed], and outshines them all, good as some of them are. Here children are not artificially segregated from adults, the "gang" comprises a whole community, the inhabitants of a small island off the Galway coast. They have always needed a doctor, and when a ship is wrecked off their shores they send back the survivors to the mainland, but keep the doctor who was among them. Eilís Dillon is not noticeably writing for children at all, though the narration is put into the mouth of a young boy who watches his elders discussing, deciding, and then finally setting out to murder the doctor because they think he has betrayed them. The people and the island are beautifully depicted; Eilís Dillon never strikes a false note, she can handle the darker and the lighter moment with equal felicity, and her plot moves with dexterous ease.

> *A review of "The Coriander," in* The Times

Literary Supplement, *No. 3222, November 28, 1963, p. 979.*

An adventure story needs to be straight, strong and direct, with no fumling in the narrative and no moment when the reader can draw breath to say 'I don't believe it.' Eilís Dillon has never written a more credible or more fascinating story than this. The scene is the usual small island off the Galway coast, a community almost self-sufficient, living more by its own traditions than by mainland law. Wrecking is against the code, but a man may take what his ingenuity can win from the waves. Can he kidnap a survivor from a wreck? Young Pat and his friend Roddy believe this is right, when the doctor is washed up at their very feet—for hasn't the island needed a doctor? His enforced stay on the island brings good at first but when the feud with the nearby island of Inishthorav breaks out again he shows he was not entirely to be trusted. Two points of action—kidnapping and sheep-stealing—are neatly combined, and the unusual motives and characters add interest to a forceful story. Above all, there is a ruminative note all through that contrasts with the violence of storms and human feelings. We see at once that Pat, the narrator, is a thoughtful boy, and become really concerned with him, with his anxiety to learn the doctor's work and with his growing understanding of the people he has known all his life.

In many of Eilís Dillon's tales, a boy stands in the forefront of the action and seems to grow in experience before our eyes. She has never let this become a mechanical story-telling device. She is genuinely interested in character, as she is in the ever-changing Irish seascape she describes so brilliantly. This is a fine book from a very fine writer.

> *Margery Fisher, in a review of "The Coriander," in* Growing Point, *Vol. 2, No. 8, March, 1964, p. 273.*

The attitudes and viewpoints of the islanders, often at variance with the law, and the subtle distinctions between right and wrong add fascinating complexities to the plot and show the author's remarkable understanding of the people. The unusual overtones, the convincing atmosphere, and the superb storytelling make this the most exciting of all Miss Dillon's books.

> *Ruth Hill Viguers, in a review of "The Coriander," in* The Horn Book Magazine, *Vol. XL, No. 4, August, 1964, pp. 379-80.*

---

### A Family of Foxes (1964)

Patsy, Seámus, Michael and Colm are four boys living on Innishowan, a tiny island in Galway Bay. The people of the Island are very superstitious and of all the animals they dread most the fox. Patsy, however, secretly feels sorry for the poor hunted animals. One day whilst he and his three friends are playing on the sea shore, they find two silver foxes who have been washed ashore after a storm at sea. The animals are half dead, but the boys manage to revive them and hide them in an old disused sheep shed. The next morning they discover their family has been increased to six, four cubs having been born during the

*Dillon at boarding school, age eighteen.*

night. Now their problem is how to get food for them and keep their whereabouts concealed from the Islanders, who would certainly want to kill them, until they can contact their owner and he comes to claim them. The boys are very resourceful and all ends happily. This is an enchanting book, told very simply and yet movingly. The picture of life on this remote island, where superstition goes hand-in-hand with religion and the greatest event is the arrival of the Post Boat, is excellent. The people are portrayed as dignified, polite and generous, as indeed they are. There are some very good descriptive passages of the sea both during and after the storms. Eilís Dillon is a fine, creative writer who seems to establish, quite effortlessly, a bond of sympathy between herself, the reader and the subject. Like most good books this one will appeal to children of all ages who love animals.

> *A review of "A Family of Foxes," in* The Junior Bookshelf, *Vol. 28, No. 5, November, 1964, p. 308.*

[*A Family of Foxes* is] a must for every school library. Discriminating top juniors should enjoy it as much as thirteen-year-olds, and teachers who care for children's literacy will take heart at this publication. . . .

The vivid yet unusually gentle account of [the strategems of the four boys], set against the atmosphere of island life—the wild sea wind, the clannishness, and the Irish

folk-lore coupled with the harsh reality of living—mark this as another fine book by a first-rate writer.

> *Laurence Adkins, in a review of "A Family of Foxes," in* The School Librarian and School Library Review, *Vol. 13, No. 1, March, 1965, p. 115.*

Although the animals' passive acceptance of their captivity and the success in hiding them in so watchful a community seem a bit unlikely, the boys, their efforts and their anxieties, are real and vivid. For younger readers than Dillon's *The Coriander* or *The Island of Horses,* it lacks their breathless pace but is a well developed, tender animal story and a memorable re-creation of an island world shaped by isolation, superstition, and ceaseless economic struggle. Highly recommended.

> *Elva Harmon, in a review of "A Family of Foxes," in* School Library Journal, *Vol. 11, No. 5, May, 1965, p. 100.*

---

### Bold John Henebry (1965)

The bold John Henebry is a self-made Irish rebel and industrialist whose career from the time he becomes station master at a village on a tiny branch line in County Mayo in 1904, to the present day when he is an often bemused father and grandfather of a large brood and head of the great firm of John Henebry & Son, is the subject of Eilís Dillon's likable but uncertainly composed new novel.

Fortunately John Henebry's own astute but honest nature is firmly and cheerfully delineated in the first few pages and it remains constant and interesting to the end. This firmness of character drawing makes his business career, which is referred to every now and then but never described in any great detail, at least credible, and the same applies to his politics and social attitudes, which are also rather vaguely sketched in. The character of his first son Daniel, a guileful countryman born of a marriage to a tubercular and soon dead bride in the little Mayo village before the move to Dublin, is also of interest in its accurate delineation of country wiles overlaid by the sophistication of an ambitious pedagogue. It is with the other children and their own numerous offspring that the trouble commences. The novel is after all only of average length and the attempt to pack an Irish *Forsyte Saga* into 250-odd pages soon becomes a cruel test of the reader's memory for names as well as of the author's power to memorably imprint character and relationships in a few phrases. Since the main interest is not so much John Henebry's rise to power as his perturbed speculations about what sort of a dynasty he has begotten author and reader are inclined to part company, the reader being every bit as bemused as John Henebry himself, though in a different way. This is a pity, after a bold and vigorous opening, and because flashes of rather wasted illumination remain to the end.

> *"Irish Saga," in* The Times Literary Supplement, *No. 3306, July 8, 1965, p. 581.*

John Henebry, born in County Cork, at work at fourteen, inspired a revolutionary ballad when as a young stationmaster he showed the submissive villagers how to stand up to the local landowner. Though implicated in the troubles of 1915, John was never a rebel so much as a liberal, with a curious benevolent innocence which stayed with him all his life; a country boy at heart, he was happiest when he spent his acquired wealth on restoring the Big House at Gorestown (so making a circle of his life). Bold John's character is one of the pillars on which this interesting novel rests. Another is the sequence of the generations. Through John's family (and especially through the vigorous and selfish Daniel with his twelve neglected children) the author shows that John, lavishing on them the material advantages he never had, made them soft and self-seeking instead of ambitious like himself. The constant changes in the family pattern are delineated with great skill. Because Eilís Dillon knows her characters so well we can see this really as a *family*, with all that this implies of continuity and tension. Above all (as in her stories for children) she sets action and character firmly in their habitat—in this case the bars and ballrooms of Dublin, Paris in the '20's, and, by contrast, the Gorestown cottage where Daniel's old grandmother ekes out her days. This is a vivid novel expressing honestly and strongly much that is important about the Irish, and about people everywhere, their ways with each other. As such, for a girl, particularly, of sixteen or so, it should have plenty of interest.

> *Margery Fisher, in a review of "Bold John*

> *Henebry," in* Growing Point, *Vol. 4, No. 3, September, 1965, p. 569.*

The gradual maturing of the young rebel, the passing of the bitterness with the years, and the development of the revolutionary fervour into a compassionate nobility are traced in a most masterly way, and establish the author more firmly than ever in the virtuoso class. Highly recommended for fifth and sixth forms.

> *Robert Bell, in a review of "Bold John Henebry," in* The School Librarian and School Library Review, *Vol. 13, No. 3, December, 1965, p. 329.*

---

### The Sea Wall (1965)

Eilís Dillon is perfectly at home with the old, simple life on a remote island off the west coast of Ireland. In *The Sea Wall* she describes the tiny green islands criss-crossed by stone walls, the little white cottages, and the sturdy independent people who live there. It is a straightforward story of a tidal wave, which sweeps over the ruined sea wall and spoils the low-lying houses. One old woman is determined to get the wall repaired, before another wave comes and washes away half the island. The other islanders are stubborn and suspicious and her only sympathizers are two boys. They manage to cross to Galway and make the County Council listen to them, and the story ends happily as the islanders' reluctance to have the new wall built is gradually overcome, and the engineer in charge captivates them by singing all their favourite songs. The big wave is described too prosaically: it has none of the menace and excitement it ought to have; but the boys' trip to the mainland is full of absorbing details.

> *"Firm of Purpose," in* The Times Literary Supplement, *No. 3328, December 9, 1965, p. 1133.*

Old Sally foretells that "The Big Wave" will come again and wash over the sea wall, which is falling down, as it did twenty-nine years ago. No one on the island takes any notice of her, in spite of the fact that she gets her grandson's friend, John, to write to the County Council in Galway about it. Two "strangers" from the mainland come to inspect the wall, but the islanders will not let them land.

Then the wave does come again, carrying destruction in its path. But yet no one will listen to Sally, so she sends her grandson Pat, and John to Galway to a County Council meeting to explain the whole situation.

Eilis Dillon is a past master at writing about the islands off the Connemara coast. She has an understanding of the people and a respect for their dignity and traditions which is rare among contemporary writers. She never laughs at them, nor does he allow his characters to appear in comic situations. Her prose is wonderfully clear and simple. On page sixty-four there is a perfect description of an Island shop. Because of its sincerity and style this could be one of the best novels of 1965. Teenagers and adults alike will enjoy it and admire the integrity of its author.

> *A review of "The Sea Wall," in* The Junior

Bookshelf, *Vol. 30, No. 1, February, 1966, p. 42.*

Eilís Dillon likes to direct two young characters right into the middle of a community problem and let them solve it in their own way. . . . With a classically simple story, apt choice of episodes and the broad effects of landscape and weather, here is a book right up to the standard of a consistently excellent writer.

*Margery Fisher, in a review of "The Sea Wall," in* Growing Point, *Vol. 4, No. 8, March, 1966, p. 668.*

The author's particular and near-magical skill in evoking the atmosphere of Ireland and the attitudes and way of life of its people are nowhere more in evidence than in this superb story.

Interest is caught from the first page and held firmly throughout. Description and character drawing are beautifully done, and the island will be a very real place to young readers. (pp. 119-20)

*Robert Bell, in a review of "The Sea Wall," in* The School Librarian and School Library Review, *Vol. 14, No. 1, March, 1966, pp. 119-20.*

## The Lion Cub (1966)

Compared to the author's usually excellent stories about Ireland, **The Lion Cub** is just a runt. A mild, very contrived little daydream, it deals with eight year old Mark who is taken to the zoo, and snitches a lion cub on the way out. He and his older sister Catherine try to bring up the cub on their farm and keep it completely secret. Eventually all the neighbors find out and only Mark's parents are ignorant until the day that the townspeople unite to demand the eviction of the cub. That the parents should be so unwitting, that Mark should return the cub with complete lack of concern, and that the keeper should have been confident all along that the animal would be brought back—all seem to push logic too far with too little compensation from the uneventful story.

*A review of "The Lion Cub," in* Kirkus Reviews, *Vol. XXXIV, No. 18, September 15, 1966, p. 976.*

Although reminiscent of Miss Dillon's fine **Family of Foxes,** this pallid boy-loves-animal story shows little of the author's marked talent for developing strong place orientation or sustained pace. (p. 125)

*Elva Harmon, in a review of "The Lion Cub," in* School Library Journal, *Vol. 13, No. 7, March, 1967, pp. 124-25.*

## The Road to Dunmore (1966)

When John was given a violin for his fifth birthday, his mother said to his father: " 'Augustus, this is a terrible thing you have done.' 'Keep calm,' said his father. 'No need to be alarmed. I'll teach him to play on it.' " And so he did. So that when John and his little brother Andy were left behind on their way to holiday at Dunmore, John was able to play his way along the road, befriended by first one traveller and then another.

The story is written with all Eilis Dillon's usual charm, beautifully simple and effective.

*A review of "The Road to Dunmore," in* The Junior Bookshelf, *Vol. 30, No. 6, December, 1966, p. 370.*

## The Cruise of the Santa Maria (1967)

In the best adventure stories, the exploits and excitements seem to arise quite naturally from what people are; the characters are not mere cogs in the machinery of the plot. Eilis Dillon again and again achieves this sort of excellence; and it is tempting to suggest that she is helped by her setting. In the little Irish islands she writes of, people take to the sea, and have the natural adventures of the sea farer, as part of their daily existence. Again, there is not that severe articulation of life into the juvenile and the adult that is a feature of larger communities; and where handfuls of people live closely together, in isolation and according to restricted patterns of living, their characters ripen and grow rich. But having said all that—having made, as it were, a gesture of envy towards Miss Dillon's subject matter—one has to say that she is simply a good writer, loving and understanding people, and concerned to tell stories that are as exciting as adventure stories should be but in which the events are tied firmly to human probability.

**The Cruise of the Santa Maria** is one of her best. The *Santa Maria* is the last boat built by John's grandfather, unpopular because he makes no secret of his belief that he can build better than the other islanders. Even worse for the boat's reputation, she is finished by John's aunt, who is red-headed and so unlucky. John and a friend take the boat for its first sail, and a storm blows them ashore on a lonely island. Here lives an old man who has succeeded in driving his whole family away, including a beloved daughter who twenty years before had eloped with a Spanish fisherman. To prove their boat, but also moved by compassion, the boys sail to Spain with a message for the lost daughter. The account of the journey and of the excitements that follow when they bring the daughter home with them is beautifully done, but under the narrative thrills there is the constant and more enduring excitement of language well used, of character sympathetically examined.

*"Oh Boys! Oh Boys!" in* The Times Literary Supplement, *No. 3404, May 25, 1967, p. 443.*

The *Santa Maria* was ten years in the building and meant to be the finest boat ever made. Her first voyage, manned by John and Jim, lands the boys on an apparently deserted island where they meet a very odd old man whose story sets them off on a voyage to Spain and back. The people are more than the story. Maggie, John's aunt, is a fascinating character; the portrait of old Colman is painstakingly and critically drawn; and the Spanish interlude is gay and enlightening. The writing is some of Eilis Dillon's best.

*A review of "The Cruise of Santa Maria," in* The Junior Bookshelf, *Vol. 31, No. 3, June, 1967, p. 181.*

Like the Irishmen she writes about, Eilís Dillon is a natural storyteller. Her new yarn is ostensibly about three boys, but the plot focuses primarily on a feud between an old man and his offspring.. . . . The lives of Irishmen and Spaniards are honestly and effectively described and characterized here. For all that, though, only the mature reader can be comfortable with a story of gossipy intent, in which the teenagers are, for the most part, spectators of the affairs of adults.

*Jean C. Thomson, in a review of "The Cruise of the Santa Maria," in* School Library Journal, *Vol. 14, No. 1, September, 1967, p. 128.*

---

## The Key   (1967)

[**The Key** is set in a Basque village and describes] the perplexities of young Paco on an important day in his life. For the first time he is to go to town with his father to sell the melon crop; but a visit to Aunt Maria brings unexpected adventures, in which a lost key, a thoughtless landlord and a poor widow have their part. Through the ramifications of Paco's day we can see the place, the people and the unexpected problems which help boys to take a step forward in their growing-up.

*Margery Fisher, in a review of "The Key," in* Growing Point, *Vol. 6, No. 8, March, 1968, p. 1072.*

For me Eilís Dillon could not write a bad book. The plot may be thin and the characters stereotyped, as these present ones are, but somehow the style, the verve, the descriptive powers are such that this becomes a good, simple book. . . . Children who have just mastered the art of reading should find this an entrancing book, while fathers who read a bedtime story will find the chapters the right length and the plot exciting enough to carry on to the next night.

*Joan M. Murphy, in a review of "The Key," in* The School Librarian and School Library Review, *Vol. 16, No. 1, March, 1968, p. 111.*

---

## Two Stories: "The Road to Dunmore" and "The Key" (1967)

**"The Road to Dunmore"** and **"The Key"** are linked by common authorship, little else. The first's a sly sportive anecdote: a boy urged by his father to keep his violin handy at all times finds it comes in handy in cadging cart rides (and prompting a recalcitrant donkey). That one is set in the presumptive past, ostensibly in England; the second is longer, slower and locale-colored, a Basque peasant-landlord scuffle. Because Don Manuel has decided to close his well to the local women, Paco's Aunt Maria steals the key to the cabinet containing the robes for his investiture in the Great Order of the Winegrowers. Paco hides the key in a melon which disappears, has all sorts of trouble recovering it, finally reproaches Don Manuel

for his perfidy and offers to trade key for continued use of the well. Don Manuel; abashed admits that he was misled by his overseer and determines to do better. Raise glassess . . . In the genre, pleasant and relaxed, but no match for the first: the difficulty of selling two separate stories is compounded by the improbability of finding a common audience. (pp. 897-98)

*A review of "Two Stories: 'The Road to Dunmore' and 'The Key',"* in Kirkus Service, *Vol. XXXVI, No. 16, August 15, 1968, pp. 897-98.*

The mildly zany characters and bubbling conversation [in **The Road to Dunmore**"] are Dillon at her best. The second and longer story is more serious and not quite as effective. . . . The style is good and the characterization apt, but the plot has some notes of contrivance.

*Zena Sutherland, in a review of "Two Stories: 'The Road to Dunmore' and 'The Key',"* in Saturday Review, *Vol. LI, No. 45, November 9, 1968, p. 66.*

---

## The Seals   (1968)

Irish authors have not far to look for stories of tension and conspiracy that realistically involve young people in matters of life and death. In **The Seals** Eilís Dillon draws on the immediacy that the Irish-English conflicts still have in Ireland to write a simple stirring story of rescue, courage, loyalty and noble cunning. To outwit the Black and Tans and to save a much sought-after fugitive, three boys and an old man brave a stormy crossing to the mainland. Drawn into the web of Irish resistance in Connemara, the young islanders have their first encounter with the hated English soldiery and taste the frightening reality of the struggles. Unequivocally partisan, the author rounds out a good narrative with the kind of incident, characterization and dialogue that evolves out of complete familiarity with her source—which makes the difference between her stories and those superficially imposed on conveniently colourful backgrounds.

*J. S. Jenkins, in a review of "The Seals," in* Children's Book News, *London, Vol. 3, No. 4, July-August, 1968, p. 204.*

One might say that all Eilis Dillon's earlier books, splendid in their own right, were in some way a preparation for this one. The loving portrayal of the islands off Connemara in their many moods and colours, her deep understanding of people, meet here in a historical plot of the time of the Black and Tans worthy of her style. . . . The book conveys a wonderful sense of the continuity of history to the Irish, with the memory of oppressors like Cromwell as fresh as if they lived yesterday. Miss Dillon's unrivalled observation of detail creates a vivid sense of place: the interior of a cottage, a storm at sea or a ride over a barren hillside, and everything unites to make this an unforgettable tale. (pp. 306-07)

*A review of "The Seals," in* The Junior Bookshelf, *Vol. 32, No. 5, October, 1968, pp. 306-07.*

Adventure stories for boys don't *have* to strain for excitement or put incredibly young and inexperienced people into appalling situations which they surmount with extraordinary coolness and expertise. Eilís Dillon's new novel, *The Seals,* seems almost to be avoiding opportunities for garishly dramatic moments—keeping its quota of suspenseful incidents, but relying much more upon modestly straightforward and believable storytelling. . . . There are only one or two examples of unlikely resourcefulness or fortunate coincidence in a simply told story which catches with some skill the atmosphere of remote island and village life during the Irish troubles. Eilís Dillon knows her people well—their sense of historical grievance, their superstition, their quiet and implacable unity— and weaves them into a narrative as effective in its restraint as many tales are in a more superficially exciting fashion.

> *"Back to Eirin," in* The Times Literary Supplement, *No. 3475, October 3, 1968, p. 1118.*

ONE OF THE chief virtues of this story is its restrained and controlled excitement. Eilis Dillon is a gifted and consistent writer who never descends to sensationalism but who holds the reader through the skilled pacing and the probability of her stories. Outstanding too in this story, set in a small island off the coast of County Clare during the 'troubles' of the 'twenties, is the author's insight into the minds and hearts of adolescent boys. The book portrays the ambivalence of their relationships with adults—they need adults to prop up their idealism, but they are also critics of adult society when they see village gossip for what it is. Adolescent boys will enjoy the delectable bits of detail in the story—see for example the description of boys lighting a fire—and the more sensitive among them will enjoy the perceptive portrait of island community life.

Highly commended for the secondary school library.

> *Colin Field, in a review of "The Seals," in* The School Librarian, *Vol. 17, No. 1, March, 1969, p. 89.*

---

### Under the Orange Grove   (1968)

The grove [in *Under the Orange Grove*] has belonged to Nino's family for several generations. When his father grows old it will belong to him, and "when you are old you'll make it over to your son, and so it will go on for ever and ever". But will it? For an important Roman villa is discovered under the orange grove. Nino is a modern child, who has been on a school outing to Pompeii, and he understands the longing look with which his teacher views the orange grove; but he is still enough of the peasant to want it to go on for ever and ever. A not entirely convincing solution is found to the dilemma, by which the villa is excavated without disturbing the orange grove, and everybody is happy.

The author has a gift for bringing her scene and characters vividly to life. One can almost feel the sun on the hillside, smell the oranges, and share Nino's pleasure in the view from his roof. The characters, too, are very real, especially

Nino himself, the grandfather whom he understands so well, and the lazy, mean neighbour.

> *"The Good Earth," in* The Times Literary Supplement, *No. 3475, October 3, 1968, p. 1118.*

Here is the simple life—a pleasant Italian idyll about a boy who discovers a Roman villa beneath his grandfather's most cherished possession, the orange grove that has belonged to his family for generations. The way in which Peppino solves the problem is neatly contrived the style impeccable, but the over-all impression is one of self-indulgence on the part of the author which has little relevance to the eight- to ten-year-old readers.

> *V. C. Alderson, in a review of "Under the Orange Grove," in* Children's Book News, *London, Vol. 3, No. 6, November-December, 1968, p. 314.*

This is another very successful story by Eilis Dillon for younger children. It is refreshingly and authentically set in Italy with a background of archaeology which becomes a fascination to Nino, the boy chief character.. . . .

> *A review of "Under the Orange Grove," in* The Junior Bookshelf, *Vol. 32, No. 6, December, 1968, p. 374.*

---

### The Wise Men on the Mountain   (1969)

Without being in the least didactic, this tale of how a man discontented with his lot journeys three times to consult a wise man only to find that his solution, and his happiness, lie within himself, has something really worthwhile to say.

> *"Shaggy-dog Story," in* The Times Literary Supplement, *No. 3536, December 4, 1969, p. 1387.*

Although nothing in the book or on the dust jacket indicates that the story is merely another retelling of a universally familiar folk tale, so many versions have been available that even children will likely recognize the theme. . . . Brilliant full-color illustrations emphasizing the fun in the foolishness [by Gaynor Chapman] make an inviting picture book. (pp. 154-55)

> *Ethel L. Heins, in a review of "The Wise Man on the Mountain,"in* The Horn Book Magazine, *Vol. XLVI, No. 2, April, 1970, pp. 154-55.*

---

### The Voyage of Mael Dúin   (1969)

The eleventh-century legend of Mael Dúin is material so appropriate for a picture-story book that it is surprising that it has not been retold before. The hero heads for an island to avenge his murdered father but, because he has disregarded a druid's advice, he is driven off course by a storm: he comes with his followers to many strange islands of beauty and terror—home of fair maidens and youths who bathe in a lake of regeneration, home of teeth-grinding ants as large as foals, fiery demons, howling horses and red hot creatures resembling pigs. And eventually he comes to the island of the holy hermit from whom he learns forgiveness; thus Mael Dúin journeys home, spared by God, sparing of his enemies. The new Christian spirit of love has replaced the old heroic code of vengeance. Miss Dillon's version is graceful and astringent; conscious of the colour and drama of her material, she allows it largely to speak for itself.

> *"Shaggy-dog Story," in* The Times Literary Supplement, *No. 3536, December 4, 1969, p. 1387.*

**The Voyage of Mael Duin** brings together for the first time two distinguished and underrated artists. Eilis Dillon's text is based on a Celtic legend, one which is so confusing that it must be authentic. Mael Duin seeks revenge, but after great hardships he finds a deeper satisfaction in forgiveness. The difficult story prompts Alan Howard to some of his finest as well as some of his least satisfactory drawings. He is magnificent with stormy seas and blazing ruins. Some of the haunted creatures which Mael Duin meets on his travels seem more comic than fearsome and that could hardly have been the intention. A handsome and immaculately produced book, it must nevertheless count as a near miss.

> *A review of "The Voyage of Mael Duin," in* The Junior Bookshelf, *Vol. 34, No. 1, February, 1970, p. 18.*

**The voyage of Maelduin** has still about it the quintessence of ancient terror; author and illustrator in this version have done their best to keep this feeling alive. In the circuitous, surprising journey which young Maelduin makes to avenge his murdered father, accidents and tragedies happen because he has ignored the Druid's advice and taken the King's three sons with him. The cycle of stories as told here takes its shape from the successive fates of the Princes—one enchanted by a cat in a strange palace, the second turned into a perpetual mourner, the third caught in eternal youth. Beyond mere symmetry of action, Maelduin's mistake brings to the story a feeling of doom, and Eilís Dillon's incantatory prose enhances this feeling, as symbols—the cat, sea-horses, jewels—take their place in the sequence of event. Alan Howard's emphatic, mannered style adapts itself well to the book. His rich colour lightens the gravity of the story but the curious, intertwined designs that he makes out of Maelduin's adventures go a long way to echo its ancient terror.

> *Margery Fisher, in a review of "The Voyage of Maelduin," in* Growing Point, *Vol. 8, No. 8, March, 1970, p. 1478.*

-----

### A Herd of Deer (1969)

A pale but steady glow grows on you as you grow into [a **Herd of Deer**]—with Peter Regan, come from Leitrim in Ireland to Connemara country for the summer. Hungry when robbed on the road by ostensibly hospitable tinkers, the Burkes, he is spotted by a gentleman farmer and hired to spy for him. Mr. Joyce owns the largest property in the area: all about him are luckless sheep and cattle raisers who resent his intrusion, his land, and his thriving herd of Scottish deer; part of the herd has been stolen and Peter, fifteen, is to camp along the countryside, mouth closed and ears open to clues. He impresses the local people with his fine new tent, his skill in a shark hunt, his solitary fortitude, and he tracks down the deer, the thieves, and their motives—these last so singularly Connemaresque that Mr. Joyce is at a loss to fathom them. Action is episodic— the hunt, the conspiracies, a re-encounter with the Burkes and subsequent retribution—as Peter balances his allegiance to his employer with his own increasing empathy for native folkways. Not a swift story, but a dusky, timeless, tranquil, boyishly rugged experience.

> *A review of "A Herd of Deer," in* Kirkus Reviews, *Vol. XXXVIII, No. 7, April 1, 1970, p. 389.*

It is always a pleasure to read Eilis Dillon, who tells her stories in enchanting language. This one, **A Herd of Deer,** is about a rich expatriate who stocks his Irish acres with an imported herd of deer. Some of the herd disappear and the neighbours stop being friendly. Peter Regan, on an illicit holiday in the vicinity, finds out where the missing deer have been taken and helps to restore understanding between the landowner and his neighbours. This is a beautifully paced book which, without being outstanding, is memorable for the appreciation of every human relationship it touches on with surety and warmth.

> *Catherine Storr, "Dream Meanings," in* New Statesman, *Vol. 79, No. 2044, May 15, 1970, pp. 702, 704.*

This is Eilís Dillon at her best. The story . . . is full of excitement and tension. The writing is atmospheric and the description poetic in its feeling for the Irish countryside. But it is the sympathetic insight into the Irish character that marks the book as outstanding. Miss Dillon brilliantly conveys the men who are a mass of superstitions and contradictions; passionate in their hatreds and ready to do violence one minute, yet won over to friendship the next, for no better reason than that is how the feeling takes them. This is for teenagers or younger readers who can appreciate a mature talent in storytelling.

> *D. Huddy, in a review of "A Herd of Deer," in* Children's Book News, *London, Vol. 5, No. 3, May-June, 1970, p. 130.*

The people are so real that they almost walk out from the pages, and there is a wealth of exciting incident, particularly a thrilling account of shark fishing from a currach in Galway Bay. The book must be regarded as among the very best that this splendid author has given us.

> *Robert Bell, in a review of "A Herd of Deer," in* The School Librarian, *Vol. 18, No. 2, June, 1970, p. 212.*

-----

### The King's Room (1970)

There is an ancient treasure to be discovered in this book and perhaps another treasure as well, for Pipo learns something about people when he goes to stay in a remote village and gets to know old Maria, caretaker at the derelict villa, who has kept its secret so well that it has become indistinct in her mind. The Italian landscape and people are lively and attractive in this neatly contrived mystery. (pp. 1627-28)

> *Margery Fisher, in a review of "The King's Room," in* Growing Point, *Vol. 9, No. 5, November, 1970, pp. 1627-28.*

**The King's Room** is a deceptively simple-looking little book. The flyleaf of the jacket announces. 'This is a Hamish Hamilton Reindeer Book for children to read to themselves.' For this purpose it seems exactly right and the reader should be about the age of the young hero Pipo, who in his striped jersey and shorts accompanies us from the cover design to the last moment of his search for hidden treasure in the King's Room. The book is of manageable size, has large print; the five chapters are not exhaustingly long. The illustrations are evocative for those who well know the countryside around Rome and inspiring for those for whom it is a pleasure to come. I can well see a proprietary ten-year-old stumping away with 'My Book' under his arm.

The ingenious appearance of **The King's Room** is quite a joke. It is a little polished gem. It is impossible to fault for accuracy either of the past or the modern Italian scene. It reads like a true story, though perhaps the last wonderful incident sounds almost too good to be true. Pipo, standing on her shoulders, and held up by old Maria, at last discovers her source of fortune and salvation left her by her old employer, the Princess, and hidden for her by the faithful shepherd Dino before the Germans arrived to take over the beautiful but now mouldering and cat-ridden villa near Frascati. It has been well hidden and Maria is now so senile, she cannot remember clearly things that happened so long ago and in such a moment of terror. 'I didn't hide it there', Maria said slowly, 'because in a hall, people are always passing through'. They try the salon in vain. Maria hammers on her forehead with her closed fist, as Pipo had seen his father do with the telephone box when his metal token had got stuck inside. 'I can't remember. I can't remember.' At last 'I would hide it in the King's Room', Maria said softly. 'That's where I would hide it, in the special room that was always ready for the King. It's on the top of the mirror, in the King's Room, a silver and gold crucifix, made in Florence, by someone called Cellini. . . . Can you get it down?' 'I don't know yet. I wish I were six inches taller!' 'We can't wait for you to grow . . . ' (pp. v-vi)

> *Carola Oman, "Two from Italy," in* The Spectator, *Vol. 225, No. 7432, December 5, 1970, pp. v-vii.*

### The Five Hundred (1972)

It is a very special day for Luca and his family when at last they can afford to buy a Fiat Five Hundred car, so useful to Luca in bringing goods to his market stall in Rome. When it is stolen Luca's son, Pierino, manages to track down the thieves, and the family recovers the car with the help of a friendly policeman. This simple story is woven around the main thread of the market itself, which comes to life so vividly that the book is full of the sound and colour of it. The family relationships come over very strongly, making this a very happy little book.

> *Sheila Pinder, in a review of "The Five Hundred," in* Children's Book Review, *Vol. II, No. 5, October, 1972, p. 147.*

The title of this book is rather dull which is a pity because the story is a good one and should appeal to children of all age groups. . . . The author has caught the atmosphere of Italy and the Italians exactly, and managed to convey all this in vocabulary which will not strain the youngest reader.

> *G. L. Hughes, in a review of "The Five Hundred," in* The Junior Bookshelf, *Vol. 36, No. 5, October, 1972, p. 315.*

---

### *Living in Imperial Rome* (1974; U.S. edition as *Rome under the Emperors*)

The author describes in detail, and in turn, the life of a Roman senator, business man, farmer, and stallholder, all living in Rome in A.D. 110, at the time of the Emperor Trajan. Each one's life and the circumstances surrounding it are interlinked with the others so that the whole book presents a vivid and lively panorama of life in Rome at that time. All kinds of people enter the scene—adults and children, freemen and slaves—and in discussing the life and work of each of these four central people the author is able to convey a sound and fascinating knowledge of the religion, politics, law, medicine, philosophy and military procedure of that period. It is an erudite book, but probably because the author usually writes novels, the presentation in a series of four family stories is endowed with very real characters who bring history into close proximity in an entertaining as well as an enlightening manner. As each of the four pictures are linked there tends at times to be a little confusion, but on the whole the interlacing of the four families and their views regarding each other is cleverly and harmoniously done. The author gives evidence of research and scholarship which is illuminated by her knowledge of human nature, and her interest in present-day Rome which obviously and rightly she feels is still strongly coloured by its history. The author should be commended for producing a book of individual and distinctive character which will provide for more than merely background material to the study of the history of that time and place. The illustrations by Richard Kennedy have the same animation as the text but not quite the same attention to detail. They emphasise the very lively human story aspect but not so much the scholarly one. This accent, however, is perhaps a good one, calculated to imbue a piece of history with a due sense of strong reality. (pp. 116-17)

> *E. A. Astbury, in a review of "Living in Imperial Rome," in* The Junior Bookshelf, *Vol. 39, No. 2, April, 1975, pp. 116-17.*

Arguably, children may find Roman history more palatable when peopled by assorted cardboard characters with 'suitable', if arbitrary, names such as Quintus, Octavian and Julia. My own feeling is that such attempts as this fall rather painfully between two stools: neither history nor historical novel, they tend to lack precise, authentic detail, and imaginative colouring. This may be a personal prejudice: Eilís Dillon has written several children's books, and may have judged her audience better than I. But there are other irritants, too: a fair sprinkling of printing errors, and plausible generalisations masquerading as facts; Pliny the Younger, worthy man, elevated to almost supernatural grandeur (no doubt because of his claims as chief witness); a moralising coyness about the games; and a rather disjointed narrative style. However, there is some real Roman atmosphere, and at least the writer has got away from the temptation to assume that all boys were senators' sons—there is a cross-section of society. Also there are several delightful glimpses of rural and urban life—and for these alone the book merits consideration. But I still feel that readers will be left with a confused miscellany of scraps.

> *D. W. Taylor, in a review of "Living in Imperial Rome," in* The School Librarian, *Vol. 23, No. 2, June, 1975, p. 155.*

This analysis of life in Imperial Rome from four different but inter-related points of view is cleverly conceived and immaculately carried through. Often in books on this subject, Rome—so formidable, so military—seems cold and calculating. Eilís Dillon's Romans are hot-blooded Latins in an Imperial phase—living on the fruits of Empire, fearful of any new ideas (like Christianity) that might sow the seeds of disintegration. By taking first a Senator's family, then a businessman's (the Senator's lawyer), then a farmer's (the lawyer's brother), then a stallholder's (a freed slave who had once belonged to the Senator) the author gives the reader a lively all-round view of a complete society.

> *Elaine Moss, "People and Places: 'Living in Imperial Rome',"* in her Children's Books of the Year: 1974, *Hamish Hamilton, 1975, p. 94.*

Eilis Dillon's book is an enjoyable introduction to the study of Roman history. . . . Although the accounts are written in the fictionalized manner of a novelist, Miss Dillon writes with a historian's regard for accuracy: I found almost no errors of historical fact and few of historical interpretation, other than the usual one which ascribes to Greeks of the second century AD the values of Athenians of the fifth century BC. Even this may be intentional, for the Greek slaves and paedagogues serve largely to comment on the defects of Roman society, which Miss Dillon's Romans could not do without stepping out of character—and she is careful not to allow them to do so. Many aspects of ancient civilization which we now regard as very bad—slavery, imperial tribute, the terrible overcrowding of the urban plebs—are accepted with the matter-of-factness that must have been standard in the days of the Emperor Trajan.

Another virtue of Miss Dillon's book is that her characters, although intended to represent types of Roman soci-

ety, are individuals, not simply stereotypes, and are interesting in themselves. It is this that will make her book so appealing to young readers and hopefully will sustain their interest in classical antiquity until they can graduate to Carcopino's *Daily Life in Ancient Rome* and other books of the same level. In the meantime, Miss Dillon's book is highly recommended.

> *Lee R. Johnson, in a review of "Rome Under the Emperors," in* The Social Studies, *Vol. LXVIII, No. 3, May-June, 1977, p. 132.*

---

### *The Shadow of Vesuvius*   (1977)

**The Shadow of Vesuvius** is a slight tale about a Greek boy, Timon, who has been captured and sold as a slave to the dotty but lovable painter, Scrofa. The two of them are working on the paintings for the house of the Vettii and a complicated plot involving a runaway marriage, an escaping gladiator and perfidious pirates reaches its conclusion as the volcanic ash begins to rain down.

Eilís Dillon tries hard to create a picture of the busy, heartless, commercially minded and materialistic city, but she is only intermittently successful. Her characters, too, lack conviction and their dialogue is frequently wooden. Yet there is something in the book, for all that: a sense, perhaps, of a fundamental decency which, though its standards differ from our own, is none the less genuine.

> *Anne Carter, "Gift of the Gods," in* The Times Literary Supplement, *No. 3966, April 7, 1978, p. 382.*

Ellis Dillon seems more at home in the offbeat poetry of Ireland than in the harsh commercial world of Pompeii on the eve. But she is above everything a story-teller and she has a good one to tell here. . . . (p. 152)

Miss Dillon has done her homework well and Pompeii, which we know as well as any place in the ancient world, shows crisp and clear in all its tawdriness. There are thrills aplenty but no contrivance. Even the villains are villains by circumstance. Some of the portraits, especially Scrofa the old painter, are beautifully done, but psychology never gets in the way of the narrative which drives forward at a fine pace—a good read. (pp. 151-52)

> *M. Crouch, in a review of "The Shadow of Vesuvius," in* The Junior Bookshelf, *Vol. 42, No. 3, June, 1978, pp. 151-52.*

The romantic sub-plot of Cornelia the merchant's niece, destined for an old man and in love with a dashing young aristocrat, broadens into an adventure of escape and disguise in which the suffocating atmosphere of impending eruption doubles the tension and brings the story to a strong climax. The earlier part of the book gains enormously by the way old Scrofa the mural artist is developed but the colour and vivacity lent by technical details (and by a certain sardonic humour in Scrofa's attitude to his rich patron) does not last long; nor does his Greek slave-apprentice, Timon, seem interesting enough to give readers of eleven or so a strong personal interest in this tale of the distant past.

*Margery Fisher, in a review of "The Shadow of Vesuvius," in* Growing Point, *Vol. 17, No. 2, July, 1978, p. 3366.*

---

### The Seekers (1986)

In 1632, lovestruck Edward Deane leaves Yorkshire, England, his family, and his livelihood as a shepherd to follow beloved Rebecca, her aunt and her n'er-do-well father to America. Edward's departure from home is secretive; the voyage on *The Swallow* is at times stormy and debilitating; his glimpse of life in New Plymouth persuades him that there's no place like home. Although passion supposedly drives Edward after Rebecca, the account of his journey is a passionless, lackluster chronicle of people and places. Edward's first-person narration gives a sense of immediacy to setting and events, but characters and relationships seem inconsequential, and the story never builds to a climax. Historical tidbits and descriptions are presented throughout the novel, but Dillon fails to convey the excitement and anxiety of leaving home, crossing a forbidding ocean and beginning life in the New World. Edward's observations of sickness aboard ship, the hardships of daily colonial life and the strict religious practices of the colonists lack poignancy and tension. After one winter in New Plymouth, he announces that he and Rebecca are returning to England. Their decision is neither traumatic nor ironic nor climactic. Although junior high readers will have no trouble with the text, they will need the pressure of an assignment on early America to seek out this novel. In contrast, Patricia Clapp's *Constance: a Story of Early Plymouth* (Lothrop, 1968), is a much more compelling account, tracing almost identical events and imbuing historical people and places with a spirit and vitality of their own.

*Gerry Larson, in a review of "The Seekers," in* School Library Journal, *Vol. 32, No. 9, May, 1986, p 101.*

In this smoothly written historical novel, the author departs from her usual settings in Ireland and Italy to trace the journey of five Yorkshire villagers to the New World. Life in Plymouth Colony in 1632 will be a familiar subject, but this account is fresh in its limpid style and in showing two unadventurous teens: Edward, who tells the story, and Rebecca, whom he loves. The middle-aged members of the party exhibit the true colonial spirit, changing in surprising and positive ways. Though the story lacks a strong emotional focus (Edward and Rebecca's love affair grows curiously placid), it provides a convincing, engaging portrait of the period.

*A review of "The Seekers," in* Publishers Weekly, *Vol. 229, No. 22, May 30, 1986, p. 68.*

Dillon's writing style is smooth and professional; she makes the seventeenth-century setting believable. Oddly, however, the only vivid characters are the middle-aged Moses and Abigail. The young protagonists, in whom one might expect to see some conflict or development, are virtuous and dull, devoid of any spark of life that might have made them memorable. This limits the book's appeal, particularly to children. Perhaps the most convincing por-

trayal is that of the colony itself, full of unspoken tension between those who came with high religious ideals and those who did not and overshadowed by the specters of sickness, starvation, and death that haunted all comers.

*Carolyn Phelan, in a review of "The Seekers," in* Booklist, *Vol. 82, No. 20, June 15, 1986, p. 1538.*

---

### The Island of Ghosts (1990)

This is an odd story, and its credibility depends upon how well one believes its evocation of the social milieu on the remote Irish island of Inishglass. The tale is told by Dara Faherity, who recounts how he and his best friend, Brendan Conneeley, become captives of their tutor, an eccentric American recluse who wants to form a perfect society on a supposedly haunted nearby island. Though this sounds like the stuff of an escapist thriller, the novel is, instead, a vehicle for exploring a boy's self-understanding and how he makes a crucial decision that sets the course for the rest of his life. On a broader scale, Dillon also toys with questions that involve methods and uses of education as well as the lines between eccentricity, creative genius, and madness. Though the plot has a couple of unbelievable twists, Dillon still preserves her story's essential thoughtfulness. Absorbing.

*Denise Wilms, in a review of "The Island of Ghosts," in* Booklist, *Vol. 86, No. 4, October 15, 1989, p. 455.*

The strength of Eilís Dillon's novels lies in evocation of place and delineation of character as well as structure. Her latest book is no exception. Suspenseful, well paced, it suggests the duality of modern day Ireland, where the lives of isolated villagers do not differ much from those of their ancestors despite their awareness of changes in the outside world. . . .

The resolution is remarkable, for it not only brings the story to a satisfactory conclusion but also reveals much about the Irish character. Unusual both in theme and in execution, this novel is one of those rare tales that read quickly but are not easily forgotten. (pp. 67-8)

*Mary M. Burns, in a review of "The Island of Ghosts," in* The Horn Book Magazine, *Vol. LXVI, No. 1, January-February, 1990, pp. 67-8.*

The setting of Eilís Dillon's latest novel—the storm-tossed island of Inishglass off the coast of Galway—is familiar Dillon territory and is recreated with a compassion and authenticity strongly reminiscent of the Synge of *Riders to the Sea*. . . . The unfolding of the relationship between the boys and their captor, Bárdal, is fascinatingly portrayed: it is the principal means through which the writer raises the novel's moral issues, the most significant of which has to do with the disparity between mere schooling and real knowledge.

Bárdal, the romantic outsider, a visionary who has clearly assimilated Thoreau and Defoe, establishes for a brief time a self-sufficient kingdom of three, thereby transforming the Island of Ghosts into the legendary paradise of Hy-Brasil. It is a domain to which Dara—though not the less imaginative Brendan—becomes increasingly attached, to the extent that as a married adult he will return there to settle. Before such time, however, the insular idyll has to be shattered. The eventual reunion of all parties provides an excellent concluding chapter which clearly demonstrates that conflicting dreams and ideals can be resolved without loss of dignity or integrity.

*Robert Dunbar "Island Idyll," in* The Times Educational Supplement, *No. 3858, June 8, 1990, p. B12.*

# Sam(uel) Epstein
## 1909-
# Beryl (Williams) Epstein
## 1910-

(Have also written as Adam Allen, Douglas Coe, Martin Colt, Charles Strong, and Samuel Epstein and Beryl Williams; Sam Epstein has also written as Bruce Campbell and Beryl Epstein as Beryl Williams) American authors of nonfiction and fiction.

Major works include *The Great Houdini: Magician Extraordinary* (1950), *William Crawford Gorgas: Tropic Fever Fighter* (1953), *Who Needs Holes?* (1970), *Dr. Beaumont and the Man with the Hole in His Stomach* (1978), *Kids in Court: The ACLU Defends Their Rights* (1987), the "Ken Holt" series (by Sam Epstein as Bruce Campbell), the "Real Book about . . . " series, the "First Book of . . . " series.

The creators of approximately one hundred and fifty books on a variety of subjects for children and young people in grade school through high school, the husband and wife team of the Epsteins are praised for providing their audience with lively works which are both informative and entertaining. Although they have written several works of fiction, including adventure stories, mysteries, and contemporary realistic and historical fiction, the Epsteins are perhaps best known for their nonfiction, especially for "The Real Book about . . . " series, which treats topics in the natural and social sciences, and "The First Book of . . . " series, which helps young readers to develop a scientific outlook towards their world, as well as for their biographies of both famous and less well known but influential people in science, politics, and sports. In their informational books, the Epsteins address subjects in the natural and biological sciences, including animals, the environment, and electricity; cities, states, and countries, including Mexico, North Africa, Italy, Alaska, Hawaii, Boston, and Washington, D. C.; the history of language; inventions and inventors; baseball; cartography and measurement; historical events, holidays, and festivals; tools; astronomy; prehistoric man and animals; the World Health Organization, the Red Cross, and the American Civil Liberties Union; and romantic figures such as spies and pirates; noted illustrator Tomie dePaola has provided pictures for several of the volumes in "The First Book of . . . " series. Often recognized for their skill in delineating personalities, the Epsteins profile both national and international figures in their biographies, including Houdini, Paul Revere, Franklin Delano Roosevelt, Harriet Tubman, Benjamin Franklin, Winston Churchill, and Jackie Robinson. The Epsteins are also the creators of several biographies of scientists, researchers, explorers, and other pioneers such as Dr. Charles Beaumont, Margaret Mead, Enrico Fermi, Michael Faraday, and Charles Willson Peale, as well as titles which demonstrate how scientific discoveries have affected historical events. Several of the team's books combine fiction and nonfiction to present factual material in a fictional framework. In their fiction, the Epsteins explain such concepts as farming, journalism and printing, and building a car and a dam; often setting their works on farms or within the newspaper industry, they underscore the stories with such values as cooperation, tolerance, resourcefulness, and determination. The team also uses literary devices such as fictional narrators and created dialogue to introduce the topics in their informational books and biographies. In addition to their collaborations, the Epsteins have worked successfully as individuals; as Bruce Campbell, Sam Epstein is well known as the creator of the "Ken Holt" mystery series, eighteen volumes published over fifteen years about the adventures of a teenage photographer who solves crimes and escapes from danger through creativity and logic. For this series, which is considered especially innovative for its promotion of tolerance as well as for its superior development of character and plot, Sam Epstein is called "one of the most distinguished authors of juvenile series literature" by critic Henri Achee; Epstein is also the creator of the "Roger Baxter" mystery series about a young detective and his brother that incorporates scientific information within exciting narratives. Beryl Epstein is the author of fiction and nonfiction which is often set in the fashion industry; she is also the creator of *Lucky, Lucky White Horse* (1965), an autobiographical story in which young Ellen gains independence and confidence during the three weeks when she is separated from her bossy cousin, and the picture book *Two Sisters and Some Hornets* (with Dorrit Davis, 1973), in which two sisters present humorously different versions of the same experience.

Sam, who was formerly a science editor and editorial consultant in the department of microbiology at Rutgers University, and Beryl, who had been a journalist and editor, collaborated on their first book for young people before they were married. Beginning their career by writing at the rate of three books per year, the team initially used a variety of pseudonyms and have also collaborated with such authors as John Gunther. Traveling widely to gain ideas and background for their books, the Epsteins often write their nonfiction about friends and professional contacts. For example, Sam's work with Selman Waksman, the discover of streptomycin, prompted the Epstein's only adult work *Miracles from Microbes: The Road to Streptomycin* (1946), which in turn led to the creation of

*Medicine from Microbes: The Story of Antibiotics* (1964), a nonfiction title for young people which traces the development of antibiotics from prehistory. While writing these works, the Epsteins met scientist Lazarro Spallanzani, a pioneer in the study of bacteriology whose research is the subject of *Secret in a Sealed Bottle: Lazarro Spallanzani's Work with Microbes* (1979). The team currently works together on the planning and research of their nonfiction and then writes each section of their books individually, with Sam taking the more technical parts; the Epsteins then trade sections and edit each other's work. For their biographies, the collaborators vary this approach: one member usually writes the early life of the subject while the other covers the later life. In all of their works, the Epsteins are acknowledged for the thoroughness of their coverage, the clarity of their writing style, their lack of condescension, and the enthusiastic, balanced treatment which they provide. Several of the team's books are also acknowledged for promoting respect for other cultures; for example, their fiction and nonfiction about Mexico is often credited for its positive representation of the country and its people. *William Crawford Gorgas: Tropic Fever Fighter* was named an honor book by the New York Academy of Science in 1953, a designation also received by *Dr. Beaumont and the Man with a Hole in His Stomach* in 1979.

(See also *Something about the Author,* Vols. 1, 31; *Contemporary Authors New Revision Series,* Vols. 2, 18; and *Contemporary Authors,* Vols. 5-8, rev. ed.)

---

## AUTHORS' COMMENTARY

[*The following excerpt is from an interview by Catherine E. Studier.*]

The respect which the Epsteins have for their young readers is one significant aspect of the high standards exemplified in their books. This respect is apparent in both their books and their conversation. Writing down to children is not a problem for these two authors:

> We had one or two publishers ask us to write using some vocabulary list, but we won't do that. We don't believe in it. If you're going to limit children in their reading to what they already know, how are they ever going to learn anything else? We're careful to use a new word with no definition and then, very shortly after, use it in a frame of reference in which the meaning is unmistakable. It is a little bit more trouble writing, but well worth it, we think.

While the Epsteins have no children of their own, they do remember what it was like to be children, and they still have a "child-like interest" in new things: "If we do have any particular qualifications to write for children, it's our own spongelike desire for information. We just get fascinated."

Ideas for books seem to come to the Epsteins from everywhere. One source was Sam's part-time job in a lab at Rutgers University in the early forties. He worked with Selman Waksman, the scientist who discovered streptomycin. This experiment led to the writing of *Miracles from Microbes: The Road to Streptomycin* (1946), their only adult book, and, quite a bit later, to *Medicine from Mi-*

*crobes: The Story of Antibiotics* (1964), a similar book written for the young adult reader. Both books trace the history of antibiotics from prehistoric times. While researching and writing those books, Sam and Beryl ran across a scientist, Lazzaro Spallanzini, whose discovery that there is no such thing as spontaneous generation was the basis for the study of bacteriology. "A few years ago, when we were thinking about a subject for a new book, we thought about our friend Spallanzini, and we wrote a children's book about how he made his discovery" (*Secret in a Sealed Bottle*).

Will this information lead to a fourth book? "It may. Whatever you learn is not lost, even though you think you'll forget it."

Sam and Beryl collaborate on the initial planning and research of a book, but not on the actual writing: "We make a flexible outline, and we both do all the basic research because that's the part we enjoy the most. Then, when it comes to the writing, we each bury ourselves in our own sections."

How the "sections" are divided depends upon the genre of the book. When writing a biography, the Epsteins decide how much of the person's life they want to cover and then divide the time period roughly in half. For example, one may take the first twenty-one years, the other, the years after age twenty-one. The person who writes the second half has a more difficult job beginning; however, after both sections are written, they smooth out the transition section.

When writing informational books, the work is divided differently. Beryl explains, "Some chapters are more technical than others. Sam does the technical chapters, and I do the 'blah' ones in between."

Occasionally, Sam and Beryl write books of their own, but they prefer to work together. Either way, having a "built-in editor" around at all times is most efficient. "It's hard to judge one's own writing unless it's put away for awhile. But having an editor in the house provides an 'instant reaction,' and the book doesn't have to be put away. We are each told off very fast!"

In addition to the benefits, writing together can have its problems. The Epsteins do have their disagreements. They try not to argue in the editing stages, however, the person who has not written a particular section has the final word on that section. Sam is likely to argue about that rule because, "She always cuts out my best sentences!"

Both Sam and Beryl find it more difficult to work together on fiction:

> We get an idea in our heads which has no basis. Neither of us can say to the other, "but look, this is what we know to be the fact!"
>
> We had one terrific argument one time. It was a book of historical fiction set here on Long Island when it was held by the British (*Jacknife for a Penny*). We figured out a plot and divided the writing into two sections. We had a little boy character and his grandfather. The boy's older brother had gone to Connecticut to fight with the Patriots, so the boy and the grandfather were left. So we had this idea, and we each wrote something, and we read each other's first productions. The grandfather was not the same person in both sections. We had just said, "a nice old grandfather." Neither of us wanted to give up the man we had; we liked him.
>
> We finally called the editor and said, "We give up. We can't write this book." So our editor came out and beat us over the head all weekend and said, "Yes, you can. Yes, you can." And so we finally changed the grandfather to an elderly cousin. This time we sat down at the table and evolved a character so that we each knew the same Aunt Bess before we started.

Since they each write their own sections of a book, it isn't necessary for both to be working at the same time. Beryl settles in and works for a long period of time. Sam is more likely to take a walk down to the dock and talk to the clams for awhile when he gets stuck on something.

They work in a small room with two desks and two windows overlooking the bay. They cover the floor with piles of paper; usually a pile constitutes a chapter. The housekeeper has been instructed never to open the window! Sam pointed out the wastebasket, where "most of my best writing winds up." (pp. 61-3)

Would the Epsteins write children's books if they had it to do all over again? "Oh yes. I don't know what else we'd do! We enjoy what we do. We've been fantastically lucky, really." So have the children and young adults who have enjoyed and learned from the books of Sam and Beryl Epstein. (p. 64)

> *Catherine E. Studier, "Profile: Sam and Beryl Epstein," in* Language Arts, *Vol. 59, No. 1, January, 1982, pp. 60-4.*

## GENERAL COMMENTARY

**Henri Achee**

One of the staples of the juvenile series book is the mystery. For this genre to succeed with young readers, it must not only bond the reader to the character, but also hold his attention while the threads of the mystery are woven slowly together to reveal the story's ultimate secret. One series that was very successful at doing this, while maintaining a depth of detail and description unusual for a series aimed at a juvenile audience was **"The Ken Holt Mystery Stories."**

It made its first appearance in 1949; by 1963, when the last volume was issued, eighteen volumes had been published. The man responsible for this fifteen year reign was Sam Epstein, writing under the pseudonym Bruce Campbell. Epstein was no stranger to the mystery genre. Between 1946 and 1948, he co-wrote with his wife, Beryl, **"The Roger Baxter Mysteries"** . . . . This three volume series foreshadowed later developments in the Ken Holt series and served to sharpen the author's mystery writing skills.

In 1948, Grosset and Dunlap, publishers of the Hardy Boys and Nancy Drew series, asked the Epsteins if they would be interested in developing and writing a new juvenile series. At this time, juvenile series were reemerging from the depression and the paper shortage of World War II. . . . The time was ripe and the Epsteins carefully considered their options. If the series was to succeed, they felt the central character needed to be grounded in the real world where intelligence and logic often have to cope with human fallibilities before problems can be resolved. They also wanted the characters to be associated with the newspaper business because they had some knowledge of the field and it would allow the stories to shift locations from time to time. . . . (p. 182)

If a mystery adventure series is to succeed, it must be able to develop and sustain long scenes of action and suspense. This was an area in which Sam Epstein excelled. Ken's intelligence, determination, and resourcefulness were continually challenged with each twist of the plot. Readers knew that Ken and Sandy would find a way out of each predicament, but the question of how kept them involved. It was like a series of knots: as soon as one was untied, another would appear. If Ken was to unravel and escape the mystery's many secrets and traps, he would have to be a young Houdini.

This Houdini theme was first explored in Fred Woodworth's review article on Ken Holt in his *Mystery & Adventure Series Review* periodical. Woodworth noted that Epstein wrote a nonfiction juvenile book on Houdini in 1950 and *The Mystery of the Vanishing Magician* in the Ken Holt series had some allusions to Houdini in it. Woodworth suggested that the author drew some of his inspiration for the series from Houdini. In a letter to Woodworth, Epstein did not directly comment on the Houdini reference, but he did mention his "own inflexible rule that Ken and Sandy had to be smart, intelligent, ingenious, and inquisitive, and yet had to get themselves into difficult and dangerous situations" without recognizing their implications until it was too late to seek assistance.

How the author accomplished this without resorting to abnormal contrivances and frequent human assistance is readily apparent when we closely examine the first volume in the series, *The Secret of Skeleton Island.* Ken, concerned about his father, the famous newspaper correspondent Richard Holt, takes a chance and finds himself in the hands of criminals who wish to discover how much he knows about his father's recent investigations. Epstein uses this moment quickly to establish the young man's ability calmly and rationally to analyze a dangerous situation:

> For an instant panic took control and Ken almost reached out for the door handle, but again he was able to fight down the impulse. What was the best course to take? What should he answer Turner? If he denied knowing anything about the story, these men would feel free to do anything they wanted to him and his father. If he admitted knowing about it, they would feel compelled to silence them one way or another. The situation looked hopeless until a flash of inspiration crossed his racing thoughts. Suppose he admitted knowing about the story, but said he had kept the letters? Then they would be afraid to

touch either him or his father until they were sure they had all the evidence that could be used against the gang.

Biding his time, Ken shrewdly discards an incriminating letter from his father and escapes at a food stop by tossing salt and pepper into the eyes of his captors. By the conclusion of the sequence, the writer has cemented the reader's identification with Ken and laid the groundwork for future traps and escapes.

The reader can identify with Ken's concern for his father and can rationalize his mistake in accepting a ride from the criminals. Everyone makes mistakes. The character of a person grows by what he learns from others. By allowing the reader to enter Ken's thought patterns, the author makes him a participant in the puzzle. By limiting the puzzle's resolution to the hero's abilities alone, Epstein fulfills the young reader's own yearning to control his destiny and resolve his own problems with as little adult intervention as possible. By emphasizing the mental resolution of the problem over the physical one, Epstein enhances the resemblances between the character, the reader, and the real world. The author's success in creating this empathy is evident in the successful fifteen year run of the series.

However, this empathy would never have developed without the complicated, unpredictable, and life-threatening situations the author created for his hero. These situations ranged from the simple to the more complex. One of the simplest examples is found in a scene shortly following Ken's first escape in *The Secret of Skeleton Island.* Having found refugee with the Allen family, Ken, accompanied by the youngest Allen, Sandy, visits his father's apartment in New York where they are captured by the criminals. Tied securely with tape and their own belts to two chairs, Ken and Sandy are left alone while the gang tends to business. With their mouths taped and knowing that when the gang returned they would be taken to the gang's hideout, Ken and Sandy struggle to escape. Toppling his chair, Ken drags himself to Sandy who removes the tape from his mouth. Able to communicate now, they search for something to cut the tape. Hoping for a potential cutting tool on the bureau dresser, Ken walks his chair to the bureau and pulls the cloth cover from the dresser. Holding glass from a broken alarm clock between his teeth, Ken struggles back to Sandy and begins cutting his bonds. With the bonds cut over halfway, Ken, his mouth bleeding, drops the glass and is too tired to recover it. Sandy strains against the sliced tape and it finally gives. Moments after they are free, a member of the gang returns and Ken knocks him out. Just before other members of the gang return, Ken and Sandy flee out the window and up the fire escape to safety.

One can see from this single scene the care and detail with which the author builds each action sequence. By allowing this scene to unfold slowly over ten pages of text, Epstein makes the reader feel each torturous movement and cut; he uses time to bring realism to the fictional world.

Because he involves the reader in his story, Epstein is able to use variations of his tied up scene in other stories without losing the reader's attention. The finest example of this is found in *The Mystery of the Invisible Enemy.* After an assault, Ken awakes in the dark with his limbs bound and his mouth covered. After the initial shock of discovering Sandy's inert body, he revives him and hums lines from songs to indicate that he has a flashlight. However, when Sandy manages to turn it on, they discover they are trapped in a fanhouse soon to be filled with the deadly fumes and heat of a foundry company's furnace. It takes all of Ken's wits and Sandy's physical strength to escape the deadly trap and eventually unmask the unknown enemy.

What makes these escape sequences exciting and effective for the reader is the refusal of the author to make them episodical. The writer maintains a smooth narrative from one action sequence to the next and introduces complicated twists and turns that build from one scene to the next. Thus he is able to avoid the high and low peaks between scenes that sometime occur with cliff-hanger chapter endings. The remaining scenes in *The Secret of Skeleton Island* aptly illustrate this. Ken and Sandy, pursuing one of the gang from the apartment, are trapped in a pier warehouse. As the gang closes in, they climb the mooring of a ship used by the gang, only to have the ship set sail. When the ship rendezvous with a ferry carrying stolen automobiles, the duo transfers to the ferry, but just as the ferry reaches the gang's island haven they are discovered and forced to jump overboard. After a desperate underwater swim to evade their potential captors, they seek refuge in an automobile garage, only to have the car they are hiding in transferred to the ferry. Fleeing the ferry before it can be fully loaded, Ken and Sandy borrow bellhop uniforms from their sleeping owners and enter the gang's hotel headquarters. Discovering Bert, Sandy's older brother, they overpower one criminal only to have Ken captured by the boss when his inept handling of the telephone switchboard draws the attention of the gang leader. United with his father and aware of Sandy's presence outside their captor's door, Ken signals Sandy and they quickly subdue the boss and one of his henchmen. With the rest of the gang converging on the hotel, they mingle with them in the dark, then slip away to the dock and escape by boat.

While not all books in the series have as many twists and turns as *The Secret of Skeleton Island,* each has enough unique scenes that the reader can't help admiring Epstein's creative and inventive mind. What gives these scenes their sharp edge is the danger that continually surrounds the heroes. By placing Ken and Sandy in life threatening situations, the author reinforces their mental and human qualities in the mind of the reader. While the reader knows they will survive, the author's depictions are so vivid that small doubts are created in his mind and mystery and suspense are heightened. (pp. 182-83)

What makes these dangers even more real are the portraits Epstein draws of their creators, the villains. As Woodworth points out, they are not your typical stereotypes. For the most part, they are not sinister in appearance, but rather "ordinary". In *The Secret of Skeleton Island,* the old, overweight man in a bathrobe and pajamas who asks Ken for help in fixing his lamp turns out to be the boss of the automobile theft gang. This is the author's subtle way of reminding the reader that appearances can be deceptive. One's outward appearance is seldom an accurate guide to the belief system that operates below the surface. Like Ken and Sandy, the criminal masterminds in the series are clever, shrewd, and smart. What separates them from our young heroes is their value systems, not their appearance or social position. The author reinforces this in *The Mystery of the Invisible Enemy* when the culprit who is trying to bring down the Brentwood Foundry and Casting Company turns out to be its building superintendent.

While villains provide the traditional counterpoints to the stories, there are other supporting characters that add depth and emotion to Ken's world. The most notable is the Allen family. With Ken's mother dead and his father always away on assignment, the Allens become Ken's surrogate family at the end of *The Secret of Skeleton Island.* This was a necessary development. By giving Ken a family identity, the author not only preserved the main character's juvenile status, but gave him a set of recurring characters with which to interact.

In early portions of the stories set in Brentwood, the Allen's hometown, the Allen clan often served as a sounding board for Ken's speculations. The questions of Pop Allen and the skepticism of Sandy's older brother, Bert, served to refine Ken's deductions and expose their early flaws. In this way, Epstein was able to build his story slowly while showing Ken's human fallibilities. The author also used the Allen family to add some realistic touches to Ken's daily experiences. In *The Mystery of the Iron Box,* we see Ken washing dishes and Mom Allen carefully disguising her curiosity about Richard Holt's Christmas present. In other stories, Ken and Sandy perform maintenance on their car, eat breakfast under Mom Allen's watchful eye, and engage in the routine tasks associated with publishing Pop Allen's newspaper, the *Brentwood Advance.* In such ways, the author suggests that it is only life's little accidents that separate the reader from the character. (pp. 183-84)

However, the most significant contribution of the Allen family to the series is their youngest son, Sandy. In providing Ken with a partner and friend, the author fulfills one of the requirements for a successful juvenile series. The presence of this feature in such long running juvenile series as the Hardy Boys, Rick Brant, and Tom Swift Jr. attest to this fact. A companion gives the writer a counterbalance to the main character. It allows the author to alternate points of view and gives the main character a sounding board for his ideas. The partner can be used to complement or compensate for the strengths and weaknesses of the main character. It also provides the author with a way to introduce different personality traits without making the main character too perfect. Finally, it also allows the writer to shift the focus of attention occasionally to the partner so the emphasis on the central character does not become overbearing for the reader.

Sandy Allen meets all these requirements. By allowing Sandy to display both superior physical and photographic skills, the author escapes the one dimensional physical presence that has occasionally limited the range of supporting characters in other juvenile series. In a series where the central character's chief asset was his reasoning power, the author recognized the importance of having the main supporting character show some mental aptitude of his own. This the writer quickly establishes in volume two of the series, *The Riddle of the Stone Elephant,* where Sandy's photograph of the Elephant Rock plays a key role in resolving an old boundary dispute. It is further enhanced in *The Clue of the Marked Claw,* where Sandy dupes a criminal into believing that important photographic evidence has been destroyed. Even Ken believes the photograph has been destroyed until Sandy informs him that he had suspected the photographic solution had been tampered with and had substituted pictures of the light bulb in the developing room for the important photograph. If any more evidence of Sandy's complementary role is needed, one can simply turn to the exciting conclusion of *The Mystery of the Green Flame,* where Sandy's radio transmitter, constructed from miscellaneous items in their garage hideout, saves both of them from a dangerous foe. This scene is also significant because it is a reworking of a similar scene in *Stranger at the Inlet,* the first book in the Roger Baxter series. The scene in the Ken Holt volume is more developed and believable than the one in the Roger Baxter book and shows how far Epstein's writing craft had evolved.

Epstein's writing skill was also apparent in the way Ken and Sandy related to one another. The reader could almost feel the warmth, friendship, and trust the two shared. The author projected this in many different ways. By having Ken and Sandy share late night discussions, he reminded the reader of similar experiences with their relatives or friends and how special those relationships were. In each escape, the writer had both boys work together to free themselves. (p. 184)

One form of relationship that the author was very adroit at handling throughout the series was the one between the young detectives and the adult supporting characters. In any juvenile series, it is important that adults do not upstage the young heroes. When the young characters are not allowed to be the central focus of the action or the final resolvers of the mystery, the juvenile nature of the work is changed and the interest of the young reader is weakened or lost. This was the main problem with the Roger Baxter series. [In an essay on the Ken Holt books in the *Mystery & Adventure Series Review,* I. R. Ybarra] has suggested that the very young age of the central character played an important role in the short life of the series. Allowing the adults to dominate too much of the action reduced the amount of identification the reader had with Roger. This was particularly acute in *The Riddle of the Hidden Pesos* and probably reduced reader interest in the series.

The fact that this never became a problem in the Ken Holt series shows the marks of a good writer, the ability to grow and mature. In the series, Ken and to a lesser extent Sandy are center stage. The adult supporting characters are not allowed to dominate the action. . . . While the police are involved in several stories, the author carefully avoids giving them the key role in solving the mystery or capturing the criminals. In this manner, Epstein preserves the adult side of the juvenile world without allowing it to compromise the integrity of the young detectives or the plot.

At the same time, the author uses a variety of plot devices to challenge Ken's reasoning power and keep the reader involved in the story and the series. They range from a lobster's claw in *The Clue of the Marked Claw* to a broken thermos bottle in *The Mystery of the Shattered Glass.* Whether it is headlight reflections or the penetration of a sealed room, the reader can always participate in the reasoning process. Epstein even allows the devices to have humorous sides. In *The Black Thumb Mystery,* Ken convinces a criminal that he has been exposed to radiation when actually his black thumb is the result of Sandy's photographic developing chemicals.

The author further enhances these plot devices and the series by changing the locales from time to time. By doing this, he introduces the reader to new surroundings and characters while creating new situations for Ken and Sandy to find their way out of. The stories are not only travelogues, but also learning experiences for the reader. By the time the reader finishes *The Clue of the Marked Claw* and *The Mystery of the Shattered Glass* he has a thorough knowledge of the lobster fishing industry and the internal workings of an ocean-going freighter, respectively. At the same time, the reader is treated to vivid descriptions of the landscapes of Colorado and Southern Europe in *The Riddle of the Stone Elephant* and *The Mystery of the Sultan's Scimitar,* respectively. These depictions add not only depth and detail to the stories, but they also provide the reader with a realistic frame of reference.

One point of reference that is singled out for repeated use is Mexico. One reason for this is that the Epsteins vacationed there. Another more subtle reason may have been an attempt to introduce some social commentary into the series. Ethnic and racial groups had received little attention in the major boys' juvenile series published since World War II. So it was significant that Mexicans were given prominent supporting roles in *The Mystery of the Green Flame, The Mystery of Gallows Cliff,* and *The Mystery of the Plumed Serpent.* What is also important is the positive image the writer creates. The characters are given varying social backgrounds. There is a distinguished police officer, a young man studying in the United States, and a young boy. Each, particularly the police officer, actively participates in resolving the mysteries. This effort to introduce the reader to other cultures is rivaled only by Hal Goodwin's Chahda in the Rick Brant series in terms of post World War II juvenile series fiction.

This was not the author's first attempt at promoting ethnic harmony in juvenile series literature. As Ybarra has pointed out, more overt attempts were made in the Roger Baxter series. In *The Secret of Baldhead Mountain,* criminals use local prejudices against Mexicans to convict a Mexican of causing a cave-in. *The Riddle of the Hidden Pesos* featured not only scenes that appeared in *The Mystery of the Green Flame* and *The Mystery of the Plumed Serpent,* but also a rather detailed look at Mexican village life. When one realizes that these books appeared in the late 1940s, it is easy to recognize the author's role as one of the groundbreakers in this area of juvenile series fiction.

In other areas, however, he followed the traditions of boys' juvenile series fiction. Guns are not used by Ken and Sandy. Villains or other characters are not killed. Finally, the series is dominated by male characters. (pp. 184-85)

The most significant of these characteristics for the Ken Holt stories was the absence of both strong and young female characters. Ken's and Sandy's young friends are males. Unlike other series of the time, the Ken Holt series does not even include passive girlfriends. Adult female characters were present, but were largely limited to traditional roles. While Mom Allen was the head of the household, her area of expertise was the home and the family. While a woman hotel owner and a female criminal can be found in *The Riddle of the Stone Elephant* and *The Mystery of the Sultan's Scimitar,* respectively, the other women that appear in the series are fairly traditional and passive. While an argument can be made that the series reflected the climate of the times and the passive female was the norm in most boys' juvenile series, the author's efforts in creating a realistic fictional world for the reader were hampered by the absence of young female characters.

This small criticism is not meant to undermine Samuel Epstein's position as one of the most distinguished authors of juvenile series literature. That distinction is not in doubt, particularly after we examine two of his finest works, *The Mystery of the Iron Box* and *The Mystery of the Grinning Tiger.* In *The Mystery of the Iron Box,* Mom Allen's gift, an intruder, a fire in a jewelry shop, and a lighter iron box lead Ken and Sandy on a twisting trail of a suspect in New York. Stalked themselves and eventually captured, they leave a trail of counterfeit bills and escape their captor only to discover they are trapped on a sinking barge on a stormy sea. Their condition is vividly portrayed in the following passage:

> Outside, they found themselves in an angry world. All around them rose huge combers that seemed to be racing toward the barge or away from it with express-train speed. The foam-flecked water reflected the dirty gray of the sky. There was no land in sight, and no other craft. There was nothing but water—steep vicious mountains of it that seemed at every moment in danger of tumbling down upon the wallowing barge.

As the above passage indicates, Epstein was at his best when he was creating a mood. (pp. 185-86)

Interestingly, these skills were not Epstein's alone. While he "did the plotting and most of the writing," his wife, Beryl, reviewed the stories and pointed out problems. They also worked together collecting materials for the books and outlining them.

Nevertheless, this cooperative effort was unable to prevent the demise of the mystery series in 1963. There were several factors that brought this about. The major one was the reduction in pages. . . . Beginning with volume 13, the number of pages dropped substantially. The series ranged from a high of 184 pages for volumes 13 and 15 to a low of 176 and 177 pages for volumes 17 and 18, respectively . . . Woodworth attributes this to rising prices and economic problems in the late 1950s. . . . The reduction

in pages hurt Ken Holt because it compressed the plot reducing the scale and number of action scenes. The reduced number of pages did not allow the story to evolve slowly and build. The "pauses" that added realism to the stories were reduced. The elements that had made the series a success were being undermined. . . .

Even Epstein's plotting was not on the same level. Both *The Mystery of Gallows Cliff* and *The Mystery of the Plumed Serpent* have concluding underground sequences that do not compare to similar ones in *The Mystery of the Vanishing Magician* and *The Clue of the Coiled Cobra. . . .* The problem was that the author had raised the series to such a high level that the inevitable settling was more apparent to the reader than it would have been with a lesser series. There were still good scenes such as the steps sequence in *The Mystery of the Sultan's Scimitar* and the marketplace in *The Mystery of the Plumed Serpent.* There just were not as many sparks.

These factors, coupled with changing reading habits, higher prices, and more emphasis by Grosset and Dunlap salespersons on the Stratemeyer Syndicate books, helped bring the series to a close in 1963. Of the boys' series published since World War II, only Tom Swift Jr., Rick Brant, Chip Hilton, and Bronc Burnett had longer runs and more volumes than Ken Holt. However, quantity was not what made the series special. It was Samuel Epstein's literary gift for transporting a young reader's mind into a maze where intelligence, courage, and determination were the keys to an evening of mystery and suspense. For those special moments, the series deserves to be recognized as one of the finest juvenile mystery series ever written. (p. 186)

*Henri Achee, "Ken Holt: Epstein's Houdini,"*
*in* Children's Literature Association Quarterly, *Vol. 14, No. 4, Winter, 1989, pp. 182-87.*

---

## TITLE COMMENTARY

### *Tin Lizzy, and How She Ran*   (as Adam Allen, 1937)

If there exists a boy who doesn't enjoy tinkering with a car, then he's not the one for *Tin Lizzy,* by Adam Allen, whose numerous photographs combined with the text give such simple explanations of an engine and its difficulties that it may inspire other boys to follow Tod's example. When he found he couldn't go to camp, he spent the summer assisting in a garage and bought a car out of his earnings. Tod and Bill really get more than that but we won't give away their secret.

*Euphemia Van Rensslaer Wyatt, in a review of*
*"Tin Lizzy, and How She Ran," in* The Catholic World, *Vol. 146, December, 1937, p. 380.*

The appearance of this book does not do the story justice: a title page so clumsy does not lead any one accustomed to good book making to give proper attention to what follows, or is the look of the page likely to lend it dignity. But the story itself is well worth a boy's attention if he is in the least interested in what makes things go, and not beneath that of his parents if they are not altogether at ease with the inside of the family car. In short, it is a family find in its own field.

Tod at thirteen finds he cannot go to camp, makes the usual first protest against a family that won't give him what he wants, and then the usual determination to get it for himself as easily as possible. At this point many a boy has gone wrong. But Tod's plan of washing cars for the near-by filling station leads him, largely by accident, into a summer's work that is not only informative but formative. He gets as interested in the care and repair of motors as a mechanically-minded small boy is likely to be, and when a derelict car is offered to him and his friend if they will put it in order, throws himself into the business with lasting enthusiasm. The filling-station man, a youth not enough older than Tod to have lost touch with the ambitions of boys, shows him how to deal with his problems one by one, and large clear photographs show the parts concerned. By the time the car runs, and the town turns out to celebrate, Tod's character has developed in the direction of manliness and the cheerful acceptance of responsibility. He has learned by doing.

> *May Lamberton Becker, in a review of "Tin Lizzy," in* New York Herald Tribune Books, *January 2, 1938, p. 7.*

---

### Printer's Devil (as Adam Allen, 1939)

*Printer's Devil* sets out to do just one thing, and does it. It answers all the questions a ten-year-old boy, fascinated by printer's ink, will ask when he gets inside a printing office. This is higher praise than may at first meet the eye. The questions of an intelligent small boy are direct and searching; they aim at basic facts and cannot be evaded. You can often deal with an inquiring adult after the method of the cuttlefish, which is to let out a flood of darkness and escape before things clear up. But under the cold, candid eye of a small boy, you must either answer precisely, or tell him to shut up. Mr. Allen answers with such precision that any one who wants to know the elementary facts about type and how it is set, and about the workings of a small-town printing establishment, with few to work it, will find himself satisfied.

The young proprietor of the "Advance" likes Bob from the moment he answers the sign in the window, "Boy Wanted." So do the others on the staff. He knows nothing about anything; they tell him. The editor even encourages him to write a short news story about a baseball game, then takes it to pieces under his eyes and re-writes it in the professional manner. Before the summer is gone, the sandlot teams of Mason are organized by the "Advance" into a local league, of which one leading citizen says, "When you get a whole town interested in something—not just the mothers and fathers, and not just the kids, but all of them—why, you've done something."

> *May Lamberton Becker, in a review of "Printer's Devil," in* New York Herald Tribune Books, *March 12, 1939, p. 8.*

There is nothing spectacular about this story of a boy's initiation into the newspaper game. Bob Mason neither scoops a rival paper nor distinguishes himself as an amateur detective, but his experiences as office boy, printer's devil and general factotum on a country weekly parallel the early training of many a successful newspaper man. . . .

Neither very bright nor dull, as he frankly admitted to the friendly young editor, [Bob has] such a keen interest in whatever he was doing that the entire staff of *The Advance*, consisting of editor, society reporter, pressman, compositor and linotype operator, was glad to explain the whole process of getting out the paper. In a series of conversations which are so clear that they are understandable even to the non-mechanically minded and yet have nothing of the stilted quality of exposition, Bob learned everything from folding the sheets as they came from the press to the reasons for advertising and the importance of circulation. He learned about such technicalities as galleys, sticks and rules, how type is set and illustrations reproduced and in between times he was busy organizing a baseball league sponsored by the paper and learning the principles of sports writing.

The progress of the baseball championship series gives a thread of continuity to the story, but its main interest is the amazing amount of information on newspaper production which it conveys in a singularly painless manner to would-be reporters and serious-minded editors of school papers.

> *Ellen Lewis Buell, "Newspaper Work," in* The New York Times Book Review, *April 9, 1939, p. 11.*

Obviously, the author knows printing and newspaper work. This book is far more plausible than the average quick success story of the cub reporter. However, the long pages of description, clear and comprehensible though they are, drag the reader too far from the story. Bob is unusually childish for a boy about to enter high school, for he acts and speaks like a fifth grader . . . We wish the author had written this book without the coating of fiction, or had centered on the story. Perhaps in his next work he will not make this mistake.

> *Eleanor Kidder, in a review of "Printer's Devil," in* Library Journal, *Vol. LXIV, April 15, 1939, p. 332.*

---

### Dynamo Farm (as Adam Allen, 1942)

Significant and timely story of present-day American youth. . . . Fifteen-year-old Terry Dunham and his widowed mother leave security of their city life and go to run-down farm. There Terry learns full meaning of cooperation through friendship and help given by 4-H group in community. The 4-H principles are admirably presented in story that is worthwhile and convincing, though not outstanding in style.

> *Elizabeth A. Groves, in a review of "Dynamo Farm," in* Library Journal, *Vol. 67, May 1, 1942, p. 534.*

It does not take long to learn that this man knows what

he is talking about. You share the sensation of country cold—so much colder than anywhere else and coldest in a house that has been shut up for a year. You recognize a button-pusher's bafflement when he wonders just where the kerosene goes into the lamp. In short, you are made partaker of the feelings of a fifteen-year-old city boy and his mother, entering for the first time the farmhouse where they must live, with their only cash income what Sister Anne can send from a schoolteacher's salary.

This atmosphere soon changes. The 4-H Club takes a hand. They show the city slickers how to manage. Because the 4-H young people so plainly enjoy themselves, Terry begins to get farming fever. Because he has a gift for mechanics and electricity, he finds a place in the rural world for his gift. School is better than he had expected. Girls are more sensible: Janey has as much sense as a boy—in her own line, of course, but somehow her line and a boy's work together better than they would in town. Working together, co-operation: that is the point of this 4-H business. It carries a farm story of the modern kind through modern complications to the point where Old Ed, whom everybody likes, is saying: "This rural electrification business is getting to be a pretty big thing. I want to get into farm modernization. But much as I hate to admit it, a young lad like you knows more about it than I do. Want to loan me your books and go into business with me?"

> *"Facts Are Fascinating," in* New York Herald Tribune Books, *May 10, 1942, p. 20.*

---

### Dollar a Share   (as Adam Allen, 1943)

The Kent Junior Cooperative was started by Ted Morgan and his friends to raise money for sports equipment for their junior high school. Parents and teachers furthered scheme with helpful advice and encouraging interest, and the young people, though faced with difficulties and setbacks, made a success of their Cooperative Sporting Goods Store. Stresses important lessons of working together and of assuming responsibility. Not outstanding in plot or style and has type characters and situations, but it does give clear idea of working of a co-operative.

> *Helen Y. Long, in a review of "Dollar a Share," in* Library Journal, *Vol. 68, May 15, 1943, p. 434.*

Led by his earlier stories to expect the maximum of information and the minimum of frills in fiction for twelve-year-old boys, I found the best example of this that Adam Allen has yet produced, in the present story of a small-town junior high school's "co-op shop" to sell sporting goods. A new teacher could double as football or baseball coach and Kent Junior High had taken this as proof that a team would take the field. But there was no town money for equipment. Their first reaction was to write a stinging editorial for the school paper. The editor of the local newspaper asks a cogent question: just what do they want the School Board to do when it hasn't got the money? The boys suggest pooling their allowances ($17 all told for the season); then selling ads in the school paper: on the latter their advisers have a sensible word to say. The local rich boy is willing to start the team overnight, his father financ-

ing it, but their growing self-reliance stands in the way. Then the coach tells them about the co-operative movement that started at Rochdale. The enterprise gets going, and before the baseball season starts, snags in the way of consumer co-operation as put into practice by intelligent and opinionated American kids, have been successfully negotiated. If that sounds like a sermonizing story, it isn't: most of the snags in co-operation's course are purely human, not to say emotional.

> *May Lamberton Becker, in a review of "Dollar a Share," in* New York Herald Tribune Weekly Book Review, *June 27, 1943, p. 7.*

---

### Marconi: Pioneer of Radio   (as Douglas Coe, 1943)

If all the boys who have tinkered with radio—including those who now have boys of their own—read this book for boys, it will have the audience it has earned. For they will read with a sense of living through the years when wireless was coming into being, and even those who begin it with no more knowledge of that subject than any intelligent modern boy is bound to have will emerge with a clear idea of the sort of mind that could, as a youth, take all discoveries, theories and practices of men who had preceded him in this field and add the element of genius that made them all work together.

The first part of the book presents the boyhood of a genius, not one who fights against heavy odds of poverty, but one who chooses the difficult road of science when that of pleasure lies open to him. When the experiments young Guglielmo had been carrying on in two big rooms on the third floor of the Marconi villa had reached, after months of heartbreaking work, the point where he could call his mother to hear a bell ring thirty feet away from the switch, and he needed money to go on, his father, an astute business man, had to be shown, practically in words of one syllable, what all this was about and just how it worked, before he would invest. The effect of this on the book is that by listening in to this interview the reader gets a basic explanation that could scarcely be clearer, and all along young Marconi's career he had to explain each new development to people so suspicious that they began their reports "Marconi says.". . .

This is the sort of history to which a boy takes kindly if he has the engineering turn possessed by so many boys.

> *May Lamberton Becker, in a review of "Marconi, Pioneer of Radio," in* New York Herald Tribune Weekly Book Review, *July 25, 1943, p. 6.*

Unusually interesting biography of a man about whom little has been written for young people. Marconi's interest in science, his experiments with wireless, his failures and successes until transatlantic communication was established, the wonders he accomplished, all this will hold attention of scientifically minded boys and girls. Diagrams by Kreigh Collins add considerably to understanding of text, and the excellent index will make book even more useful. Should be included in all library collections.

> *Judith E. Stromdahl, in a review of "Marconi:*

Pioneer of Radio," *in* Library Journal, *Vol. 68, September 1, 1943, p. 672.*

### Water to Burn  (as Adam Allen, 1943)

When the Marsden family acquired a longed-for farm, young Sandy decided to dam the brook running through their land and use it as swimming pool. His enterprise brought unexpected opposition from some of his neighbors and lasting friendships with others. In addition, he acquired considerable knowledge of dam building on small scale. Well told, offering same good characterization and well-incorporated technical detail found in author's **Dynamo Farm.** Should be of special interest to boys in rural areas and those who are "construction-minded."

Margaret M. Clark, *in a review of "Water to Burn," in* Library Journal, *Vol. 68, October 15, 1943, p. 847.*

### Road to Alaska: The Story of the Alaska Highway  (as Douglas Coe, 1943)

The United States Army Engineers are the heroes of this thrilling tale of the war between the Northern wilderness and men and machines. The engineers were told to build the foundations of the Alaska Road in a year. Attacking at three points, they built it in a little over eight months. Only an army made up of resourceful individuals could have done it, and an American sense of humor certainly helped! They called one of the trucks "Susie," and treated her as though she were a temperamental woman instead of a machine. When the pet deer, carefully brought up on a baby's bottle, and known as "Moosevelt," ate five pounds of dehydrated eggs—and died—the Army cooks all the way from Dawson Creek to Fairbanks were teased unmercifully. Hadn't the men *told* them about those eggs?

When the Spring thaw slowed them up, they were bored to death, although they remained cheerful. When they could go on with the muddy, cold, difficult job they yelled loudly and attacked the forest with such vigor that, long, long before the head engineers expected it, the two corps met—and the Road was through. . . .

Every event, great and small, since that day in November, 1942, when the ribbon across the Alaska Highway was cut, confirms the importance of what the Secretary of the Interior called "the Little Man's Road, where Mr. Jones and Mr. Ivanovich and Mr. Chang will help each other fix a flat."

The saga of its building will become a North American legend.

Mary Gould Davis, *"War against Wilderness," in* The Saturday Review of Literature, *Vol. XVII, No. 5, January 29, 1944, p. 29.*

### New Broome Experiment  (as Adam Allen, 1944)

Another first rate story against a modern farm background from the author of **Dynamo Farm.** Two city boys,

Mark Berman and Wes Marshall, come for the summer work to the Broome's farm. Then trouble brews, when Nick Broome builds up an active antagonism towards Mark, fearing that Mark will reveal an experience that Nick has hidden and that dates back to a camp both boys has attended. When he discovers that Mark is a Jew, he allows that to intensify his dislike—and almost costs his father the much-needed aid of the two boys. It takes a serious epidemic among the cattle—a wise and deeply respected Doctor and his experimental work in antibiotics; a completely understanding Mr. and Mrs. Broome, and a handful of other adults to straighten out two fine boys, tangled because of hurts in the past for which neither was to blame. Good farm story—spiced with interest in scientific experiment—and keyed by problems of racial prejudice. A book for thoughtful teen age boys.

A review of "New Broome Experiment," *in* Virginia Kirkus' Bookshop Service, *Vol. XII, No. 17, September 1, 1944, p. 407.*

**New Broome Experiment,** in the course of showing scientific experiment now involved in progressive farming, introduces a problem at once social and personal. Two college students come to the modern mechanized farm of Nick Broome's father to work for the summer. Nick likes one at sight: the other rubs him the wrong way. Nick, a visitor at a near-by boys' camp, has had a nerve-racking experience there; Mark Berman says darkly that "they had a very good technique for getting rid of undesirables." To Nick this means that Mark must have been in the crowd that ran Nick off the place by singing "Nick the Hick." That Berman might be speaking of his own trials never occurs to him. The name means nothing, and he has never met a Jew; but when some one else says that "all Jews are" various unpleasant things it gives him reason for personal dislike. The story presents, with justice to both sides and in a spirit of understanding, one inferiority complex in collision with another. Before the effect has worn away the story has gone through experiments in cattle-raising and bacteria-fighting discoveries in the nature of penicillin that will deal with deadly bovine diseases. [This book dramatizes], without overdoing it, the stern but grateful struggle of the farm.

"Our New Farms," *in* New York Herald Tribune Weekly Book Review, *November 12, 1944, p. 24.*

### Fashion Is Our Business  (1945)

[Fashion Is Our Business *was written by Beryl Williams.*]

The devotee of the bobby-sock and the out-size sweater might possibly pass this book by, but it's more than an even bet that she won't, because it is addressed to those who find clothes exciting—and what girl in her 'teens doesn't? It will be of special interest to those who are thinking of a career as a fashion designer, since it shows by the examples of twelve American designers what success in that field is made of—mainly, apparently, of originality, taste and, especially, hard work. Some of them couldn't sew much, some of them couldn't sketch very well, but they all had ideas, good ones, too, about the kind of clothes that American women and children need and like. The accent is upon simplicity and suitability to the occasion and to the individual. The inculcation of these standards of dress are well worth risking any possible increase in feminine vanity which might result from reading this entertaining book.

> *Ellen Lewis Buell, "American Stylists," in* The New York Times Book Review, *March 11, 1945, p. 290.*

Bessie Beatty introduced this book with a radio fashion show, preceded by interviews with a number of the designers who are described in its pages. How they chose their careers, what their basic philosophy of clothes consists of, and what they are like as people makes this a unique book for women as well as girls—readers of fashion magazines, and those who'd like to read them. The names include many familiar ones in the field,—Clare Potter, Hattie Carnegie, Jo Copeland, Mabs and others. Good vocational or career shelf material—spot biography—spot fashion notes.

> *A review of "Fashion Is Our Business," in* Virginia Kirkus' Bookshop Service, *Vol. XIII, No. 5, March 15, 1945, p. 137.*

One reads these twelve short biographies of outstanding designers of clothes for women with a sense of refreshment. There have been so many fictionized "career" stories that lack reality and humor. These have both, because these are true stories reported by a writer with an eye for the points that are important to girls who need to make their own living and want to do it through creative art. Some of these designers are men and some are women. They all work in a "commercial" atmosphere. They are all artists and are recognized as such. Disappointment and a sense of frustration probably came to most of them before they found the ladder to success. The variety in their background and experience is responsible, perhaps, for the book's vitality.

> *M. G. D., "True Career Stories," in* The Saturday Review of Literature, *Vol. XXVIII, No. 16, April 21, 1945, p. 31.*

---

### *Stranger at the Inlet*   (as Charles Strong, 1946; British edition as Martin Colt)

A Roger Baxter mystery (This is the start of a series.) in which Roger and his younger brother Bill, work with a secret service agent to help capture some diamond smugglers. Straight adventure appeal with sound if rough character sketches. The setting is a New England fishing village—and addicts of the "comics" will find the Baxters thoroughly satisfying. Independent, quick, resourceful, alert to mechanical and electrical problems, the boys help rig an electric system which helps trap the dishonest men.

> *A review of "Stranger at the Inlet," in* Virginia Kirkus' Bookshop Service, *Vol. XIV, No. 2, January 15, 1946, p. 37.*

### *The Burma Road*   (as Douglas Coe, 1946)

This is the thrilling, factual story of the famed Burma Road, built against overwhelming obstacles so that China might have a supply route to the outside world in her long, bitter struggle against Japan.

Blockaded by sea, China knew that without an overland route to her "back door" she could not get even the small trickle of weapons and supplies she so desperately needed in order to hold off the enemy.

The millions of native workers who tackled the job of building the long road had only the most primitive tools. They literally scratched the highway out of the towering mountains with their fingernails. Thousands of them died of malaria, and hunger, or were crushed in mountain landslides, drowned in the swollen streams, or fell to their deaths over the precipitous cliffs. But the road went through!

Finally trucks laden with precious supplies began to crawl along it to the besieged armies in China's interior. Then, in 1941, the Japanese hordes suddenly broke through and overran the road. Once again China was cut off.

But by now China had allies. Together they set about the task of building a new road, this time starting from Ledo, in India. American bulldozer crews pushed ahead, foot by foot, while soldiers held off the Japs. Once again a link with the outside world was opened. Over it, once more, moved trucks laden with troops, weapons and supplies.

The saga of the Burma Road, related in this book with skill, sympathy and a painstaking regard for fact, is a story that will live long in the memory of man.

> *Henry B. Lent, in a review of "The Burma Road," in* The New York Times Book Review, *July 14, 1946, p. 28.*

The Burma Road and the Stilwell Road loomed large in the strategy of the war in southwest Asia. Douglas Coe, author of *Road to Alaska,* has told the dramatic story of their building and has woven into his story the historic significance of the two roads and their meaning for the future. Replete with the detail and colorful background which appeal to young people, . . . it is a book that should interest older boys and girls.

The first thirty pages provide a background sketch of Chinese history up to the commencement of work on the Burma Road in the fall of 1937. The building of this road, almost entirely by hand with the aid of small primitive tools—hammers, crowbars, rakes, crude stone-rollers, and gun-powder in place of dynamite—is a fascinating story of courage and sacrifice. So also is the account of how the operation of the road was put on an efficient basis—with the aid of Danny Arnstein, a former New York taxi driver. Then the Japanese army surged forward, in overwhelming superiority. Burma fell—and the Burma Road became useless to its builders. Far different, but no less dramatic, was the building of the branch road from Ledo, later named the Stilwell Road, which was built to the slow tempo of the return of the Allied forces.

At a moment when, as seldom before, the future of the

world seems to depend upon the establishment of understanding between all peoples, this book is especially timely. Young people will probably read it for its description and its drama. But as they read they will learn much about southeastern Asia and its people. They will discover that courage and devotion are not the exclusive characteristics of any one race or nation. They will sense the interrelatedness of the modern world. And some, perhaps, will catch a vision of a future in which education, health, and security are the birthright of all peoples.

> *Ralph Adams Brown, "Burma Road," in* The Saturday Review of Literature, *Vol. XXIX, No. 39, September 28, 1946, p. 42.*

---

### *People Are Our Business* (1947)

[People Are Our Business *was written by Beryl Williams.*]

To young career seekers interested in working with people this book will give much inspiration and information. The author has made each kind of job sound vital and dramatic, but she has done it without glamorizing it. Besides giving her readers an idea about the kind and amount of education needed and the type of work entailed she has introduced 10 people who are worth knowing. These are Margaret Scoggin, young people's librarian; Charlotte Hayman, psychiatric social worker; Clyde Murray, settlement house worker; Evelyn Murray, employment placement consultant; Elinore Herrick and Robert Metcalf, industrial relations directors; Ruth Young, industrial union secretary and Mark Starr, union educational director; Marjorie Fish, occupational therapist; George Lawton, psychologist.

> *A review of "People Are Our Business," in* The Booklist, *Vol. 44, No. 4, October 15, 1947, p. 73.*

---

### *Lillian Wald: Angel of Henry Street* (1948)

[Lillian Wald: Angel of Henry Street *was written by Beryl Williams.*]

Biography of Lillian Wald, daughter of well-to-do German-Jewish and Polish-Jewish parents, born in Rochester about 1867. Neither her background nor her finishing school education seemed to indicate the great work she was to do. She lied about her age in order to gain admittance into the New York Hospital as a student nurse. Then she studied medicine. During these years she lectured East Side women on hygiene and cleanliness, and gained her first glimpse of conditions among immigrants. Shocked and moved, she persuaded Mrs. Loeb and Jacob Schiff into letting her, along with another nurse, move into the area to help better the conditions. It proved a colossal task, which became the basis of the Henry St. Settlement, the Visiting Nurse service, and the power behind the effort to abolish sweat shops, pass child labor legislation, bills for slum clearance, better housing, and so on. A bit slow in spots, but interesting. Double value on career book shelf.

> *A review of "Lillian Wald: Angel of Henry*

*Street," in* Virginia Kirkus' Bookshop Service, *Vol. XVI, No. 17, September 1, 1948, p. 442.*

What a good story the life of Lillian Wald and her nursing and her settlement and her part in many national movements makes, and how simply and dramatically the author has told it. What strikes one about the impulsive girl who socialized so many phases of our life is that she was no less an individual with private life and feelings though the style of her good works and noble living was joined to mass movements and professional organizations. She was personal, she was imaginative, she knew what a great many people have never understood, that a democratic society, a broad-based and sharing society, has to proceed by fits and starts of fashion, a general aristocratic manner, inclusive, not exclusive. The book teems with well-delineated characters,—other nurses like Lavinia Dock, a great deal about Jane Addams, and Teddy Roosevelt and Oswald Villard; lots about how Henry Street Settlement grew and Theater prospered there, and the many East Side children whom the Settlement sent on their way to careers; about housing and slums; about, not one, but two Russian Revolutions, and what they meant to immigrant New York, about the founding of the federal Children's Bureau, a lot about the writing of books. This is a first rate introduction to social work in the contemporary scene. A girl's book, anybody's book, to be grateful for. (pp. 154-55)

> *A review of "Lillian Wald," in* The Commonweal, *Vol. XLIX, No. 6, November 19, 1948, pp. 154-55.*

A warm, sympathetic, readable biography of a great woman. Realistic portrayal of Lillian Wald and the lower East side where she worked. Although this is but an outline of her work, the highlights are there, and it is a fine picture for young people. Highly recommended for all older boys and girls and for young people's collections.

> *Mary Dodge Read, in a review of "Lillian Wald: Angel of Henry Street," in* Library Journal, *Vol. 74, No. 1, January 1, 1949, p. 69.*

---

### *The Great Houdini: Magician Extraordinary* (as Beryl Williams and Samuel Epstein, 1950)

A mature and intelligent biography of one of the most fabulous personalities in the history of the stage—the greatest escape artist of all time and specialist in mass illusion. Houdini, born Ehrich Weiss in Appleton, Wisconsin, performer in traveling shows at the age of twelve, apprentice to a locksmith, and handcuff "escape artist" in the days of "museum" shows and beer halls, finally hit the big time with his wife as a partner in 1899. Then came a series of European tours, return to the States and fame. Audiences gasped as Houdini extricated himself from padlocked milk cans submerged in water, the most baffling strait jackets, handcuffs and fetters made by the finest craftsmen in Europe and America, and the vaults and cells of any prison accepting Houdini's dramatic challenge. The vaudeville audiences watched spellbound while this humorless, arrogant man made elephants disappear into thin air, passed himself though brick walls, and repeatedly achieved the impossible. Through this life story the personality of Houdini emerges as a cool, brilliant technician with remarkable physical and intellectual courage, but no supernatural being as he was believed by some to be. Young people and adults will race to the end of the book where some of Houdini's escape tricks are explained. The whole family will want to read this one.

> *A review of "The Great Houdini, Magician Extraordinary," in* Virginia Kirkus' Bookshop Service, *Vol. XVIII, No. 4, February 15, 1950, p. 106.*

Although Houdini died in 1926, his name is still a synonym for escape artist and even to this day there has been no one to rival his almost incredible escapes from handcuffs, strait jackets, and boxes of all sorts. Since Kellock's *Houdini: His Life Story* has long been out of print this is most welcome and will be read with avidity by those from eleven or twelve up who hope to find explanations of Houdini's secrets.

As a matter of fact, the most interesting part of the book for any reader will probably be the last section which does describe some of the more spectacular escapes. For the most part, this is a conscientious though somewhat fictionized (at least, I assume that most of the frequent conversations are imaginary) record of Houdini's bitter struggle to win the recognition to which he thought himself entitled. His constant practice for perfection, his lifelong devotion to his mother and to his wife, his European tours, his triumphant return in 1905 to the United States as a star, his unmasking of spiritualists—are interesting. Houdini is revealed as a vain, humorless, irascible and overbearing man but still a magnificent escape artist and showman. There is a good index. I should have liked a few photographs to set Houdini in his time.

> *Margaret Scoggin, in a review of "The Great Houdini: Magician Extraordinary," in* New York Herald Tribune Book Review, *May 7, 1950, p. 17.*

The many boys fascinated by magic—and the general reader as well—will enjoy this biography of the twentieth century's great magician, Harry Houdini. . . .

[His] escapes—from hundreds of jails in Europe and America, from the handcuffs of Scotland Yard, from chains and locks while hanging head down under water—his research in the history of magic, and the chapter revealing some of his secrets are all interesting. There may be more significant subjects for new biographies for young people, but few could offer more possibility for interest than does this fabulous, paradoxical personality, and the authors have done well with it.

> *F. C. Smith, "Escapist," in* The New York Times Book Review, *June 18, 1950, p. 16.*

---

## No Pattern for Love (1951)

[No Pattern for Love *was written by Beryl Williams.*]

Another career story in which the vocational information

is slighted and the emphasis is on quick success both in work and love. Tracy sets out to learn dress designing and to win the love of Steve Dovato. She divides her time and thought almost equally between the two for the major portion of the book. Then Jo Hunt appears on the scene and she realizes that he is her true love. In typical career book style she ends up with a job and Jo. The characters are all types, with no reality in either actions or speech. Not recommended.

> *A review of "No Pattern for Love," in* Bulletin of the Children's Book Center, *Vol. IV, No. 8, July, 1951, p. 57.*

---

### The Real Book about Inventions   (as Samuel Epstein and Beryl Williams, 1951)

[Children] start studying prehistoric man in the very early grades, so are ready for the first steps in invention, as weapons were crudely made with sticks and stones, dugout canoes provide early water travel, the first wheel is invented. Step by step, the text approaches the complexities of modern life, by taking up those key inventions that have made this industrial age possible. Lots of fascinating answers to questions every child asks, done in very readable fashion.

> *A review of "The Real Book about Inventions," in* Virginia Kirkus' Bookshop Service, *Vol. XIX, No. 13, July 1, 1951, p. 321.*

---

### The Real Book about Alaska   (as Samuel Epstein and Beryl Williams, 1952)

One of the best of the ["Real Books"] series, in a long needed exploration of the lively potentials of the Alaska story. Here is our new frontier, echoing even today the glamor of the Old West, and in this book these frontier elements are competently dealt with. In the process of spinning the lively history of Alaska in which explorers, exploiters, prospectors, pioneers and "natives" played a tumultuous role, the authors have included a vast amount of information about people, places and institutions; the native Aleuts, Tlingets, Athabascans and Eskimos, their lives and cultures; the great explorers, from the Dane, Bering, who sailed for Peter the Great, on down; the despised "icebox purchase"; the discovery of gold, in the Yukon, the Klondike; fishermen and fisheries; cities grown from starvation-ridden mining camps; the government pioneer farming project, Matanuska; Alaskan railroads and airports; her strategic position in the war. Alaska is a country for youth. This will bring them under the spell of the Yukon. A Must for schools as supplementary reading.

> *A review of "The Real Book about Alaska," in* Virginia Kirkus' Bookshop Service, *Vol. XIX, No. 24, December 15, 1951, p. 704.*

Readable, informative, up-to-date book on "sourdoughs and prospectors, Indians and Eskimos, gold rushes and explorations on America's last frontier." Compares favorably with others on this subject, though Stefansson's *Here is Alaska* is preferred for illustrations and material on the

Eskimos and Pilgrim's *Alaska* is more detailed on government and animal life.

> *Sonja Wennerblad, in a review of "The Real Book about Alaska," in* Library Journal, *Vol. 77, April 1, 1952, p. 602.*

---

### The Real Book about Benjamin Franklin   (as Samuel Epstein and Beryl Williams, 1952)

[*The following excerpt is from an advance review of* The Real Book of Benjamin Franklin.]

A serviceable, but not particularly inspired, biography of that most remarkable citizen, whose many skills and interests, canny ingenuity and bluff, withhold appeal for all ages. Franklin's "firsts" hold recurrent interest. Among his lesser known inventions was a musical instrument called the "armonica", composed of revolving drinking glasses, and sufficiently accepted in his time for Beethoven and Mozart to write music for it. There was a chimney damper, a ladder chair, a gadget (precursor to today's grocery shelf tongs?) designed for lifting books down from upper shelves. His unfamiliar exploits are given due emphasis along with his contributions to the cause of revolution and the new republic:—his work as deputy postmaster to all British North America; negotiations for peaceful Indian relations; direction of volunteers sent to disperse the blood-thirsty "Paxton boys"; diplomatic manoeuverings on behalf of the Pennsylvania Assembly in regard to the demands of Penn's sons. Useful supplementary reading in history.

> *A review of "The Real Book about Benjamin Franklin," in* Virginia Kirkus' Bookshop Service, *Vol. XIX, No. 24, December 15, 1951, p. 704.*

[*The Real Book about Benjamin Franklin*] weaves the life of the good, inventive Franklin into the background of colonial history in a pattern that is necessarily gentler, more softly hued. More of Franklin as a person, foolish, wise, grey eyed, with a love of books, the sea and making things with his hands—emerges in the reflective rather than dramatic account. But in its leisurely style, it is faithful to the man and does not lose strength in the recounting of Franklin's struggles for the freedom of the colonies.

> *A review of "The Real Book about Benjamin Franklin," in* Virginia Kirkus' Bookshop Service, *Vol. XX, No. 6, March 15, 1952, p. 190.*

A straightforward, unfictioned presentation of the many-sided Franklin—printer, inventor, author, postmaster, and statesman—with a clear background of eighteenth-century colonial life, the Revolution, and international affairs in which he played so important a part. Less lively reading than the Eaton story-biography but an interesting and comprehensive account that has value for upper elementary grade use. Chronology, selection of sayings, and index.

> *Virginia Haviland, in a review of "The Real Book about Benjamin Franklin," in* Library Journal, *Vol. 77, April 15, 1952, p. 727.*

### The Real Book about Pirates   (as Samuel Epstein and Beryl Williams, 1952)

Henry Morgan sailed the Caribbean; Horuk Barbarossa sailed the Barbary coast; Mrs. Hon-Cho Lo the China Seas; and by the time you've finished his book you know pretty much about the world's lot of buccaneers, corsairs and odd Jolly Rogers. A once over lightly about types and periods of piracy and the customs of the pirates' own societies, precedes an account of the career of the Barbarossa brothers who terrorized Algiers and its surroundings from pre-Columbus days to 1520. Following, are wave after wave of the derring do of Drake, Kidd, the gentle pirates Mission and Tew, Blackbeard, and three Pirates in petticoats—Rachel Zamprano, Mary Read and Anne Bonney. The lesser knowns, Mrs. Hon-Cho Lo, Jean Lafitte, Alexander Selkirk, Exquemelin and the rest, are fitted into a neatly annotated listing of more personages in piracy's hall of fame. All material well gounded in history. (pp. 372-73)

> *A review of "The Real Book about Pirates," in* Virginia Kirkus' Bookshop Service, *Vol. XX, No. 13, July 1, 1952, pp. 372-73.*

Brief accounts of some of the major pirates of the past. Contents include the Barbarossa brothers, Sir Francis Drake, Henry Morgan, Misson and Tew, Captain Kidd, Blackbeard, and a chapter on women pirates. A well-written and accurate telling that does full justice to the subject without resorting to exaggeration or sensationalism.

> *A review of "The Real Book about Pirates," in* Bulletin of the Children's Book Center, *Vol. VI, No. 10, June, 1953, p. 75.*

---

### The Real Book about Spies   (as Samuel Epstein and Beryl Williams, 1953)

A familiar writing team that is especially good when at work on personalities, does a rather bang up job on the greats of espionage. Nathan Hale, Karl Shulmeister, Wilhelm Stieber, Mata Hari, the Churchill Club and Klaus Fuchs are some of the dozen or so agents and groups of agents who have gone to bat for country or for name—that the authors portray with zest and in a way that warns of spying's unglamourous side and the spy's often ignoble end. But there's plenty of thrill to offset the morals and John Pfiffner's drawings have a cloak and dagger air to them. (pp. 42-3)

> *A review of "The Real Book about Spies," in* Virginia Kirkus' Bookshop Service, *Vol. XXI, No. 2, January 15, 1953, pp. 42-3.*

Real stories of real spies from the Israelites who went into Palestine during the time of Moses to modern atomic spies. The author has managed to de-glamorize his subject without having it lose any of its appeal for young readers. He makes clear the place of espionage in the modern world without creating the atmosphere of fear and suspicion that too often accompanies discussions of spies and spying.

*A review of "The Real Book about Spies," in* Bulletin of the Children's Book Center, *Vol. VI, No. 7, March, 1953, p. 50.*

Some of the best examples of modern reporting are found in books of facts for children and young people. This one on spies, another in the Real Books series, reveals the reporter's art at work on a befogged and romanticized subject. What are spies? What do they do? Who are some of the famous or notorious spies? Here are the facts, authors Epstein and Williams say. And the facts make the kind of exciting, understandable reading that boys and girls demand. Accounts of spies, such as Mata Hari and "Cicero" (of World War II) are given. Not many of the others, however, are so well known. Trading in secrets seldom brings wealth or fame. Spies generally are soon forgotten. Armed with the facts, the reader knows why this is so.

*Iris Vinton, "Under Cover," in* The New York Times Book Review, *May 24, 1953, p. 26.*

---

***William Crawford Gorgas: Tropic Fever Fighter*** **(as Beryl Williams and Samuel Epstein, 1953)**

Williams' and Epstein's knack for writing exciting, factual narratives about real people and events comes to the fore in this clean cut biography of the man who fought yellow fever. There is good pace and the right amount of scientific detail as Gorgas' career is followed—student days at New York's Bellevue Hospital; his first army post job in the southwest where he met and fell in love with Marie Dougherty; Havana, the Spanish American war and his work with Carlos Finlay and Walter Reed; the struggle in the Canal Zone; later work among the miners at Kimberley in South Africa. Historical awareness too, present in the examination of wars and political issues, rounds out a good volume.

*A review of "William Crawford Gorgas," in* Virginia Kirkus' Bookshop Service, *Vol. XXI, No. 3, February 1, 1953, p. 73.*

Here is a biography that will introduce teen-agers to a phase of the world of medicine which they may not yet have considered, and to the international aspects of several dread diseases. Besides conquering yellow fever in Panama and thus making possible the building of the Canal, Gorgas fought this horrible menace first in Havana, and later in South America. He advised on anti-pneumonia measures in Rhodesia, and reorganized the U. S. Army Medical Corps and hospitals in the first world war. After receiving many honors, here and abroad, he was stricken by paralysis in London in 1920, at the age of sixty-six. "The battle he fought was gallant—and it changed the face of the earth." His life-long dream, to prove that tropical cities could be safe habitations, had been achieved.

Mr. and Mrs. Epstein present his story in easily readable, though undistinguished, style. More use of Gorgas' own words would have given us a better picture of the man, and more direct quotation from sources would have given the book more dignity. The imagined scenes are less impressive than the mere facts about Gorgas' uphill struggle for sanitary reform. A summary of progress in the battle

against yellow fever after his death makes a valuable final chapter, and gives the young reader a sense of the growing unity of the world of medical discovery, and of the necessity for a world-wide fight against tropical disease.

*A review of "William Crawford Gorgas: Tropic Fever Fighter," in* New York Herald Tribune Book Review, *May 17, 1953, p. 7.*

Lives of pioneers in medicine have a strong appeal for young people, as they do for adults. These require an ability on the part of the writer to present scientific facts in easily understandable terms. Beryl Williams and Samuel Epstein have done this skillfully in ***William Crawford Gorgas: Tropic Fever Fighter***. Characterization of the doctor is done in broad, simple outlines; the finer shadings of personality are omitted, but his long fight against yellow fever, his conflict with ignorance, superstition and indifference are told with dramatic intensity and without sentimentality.

*Ellen Lewis Buell, in a review of "William Crawford Gorgas: Tropic Fever Fighter," in* The New York Times, *Section 7, August 2, 1953, p. 14.*

---

***The First Book of Electricity*** **(1953)**

Clear, succinct simplifications about practically every main aspect of electricity chalk up another "first" for the explicit Epsteins. For budding scientists or engineers, or for any housekeeper in distress, here are the elements of theory—of household appliances—and of the power sources. Measurement, famous events in electrical history and instructions for a few basic experiments are equally well covered.

*A review of "The First Book of Electricity," in* Virginia Kirkus' Bookshop Service, *Vol. XXI, No. 17, September 1, 1953, p. 584.*

An unusually clear presentation, with many helpful diagrams [by Robin King], of the ways in which electricity works, particularly in our homes. Children are cautioned Never to experiment with electric current, but several safe and informative experiments with inexpensive batteries are suggested. Included also are a list of books for further reading; and, perhaps most fun of all, directions for making, with very little equipment, a telegraph set on which children can tap out messages in Morse code.

*Jennie D. Lindquist, in a review of "The First Book of Electricity," in* The Horn Book Magazine, *Vol. XXX, No. 2, April, 1954, p. 100.*

*[The following excerpts are from reviews of the revised edition published in 1977.]*

This extremely well-written book throws much light on the nature of electricity and applications of its everyday use. . . . Although the authors explain electricity succinctly and clearly, emphasis is on description of familiar electrical uses: house wiring, meter reading, fuses, wall switches, toasters, TV, etc. Three simple experiments are given, including directions for making a telegraph set.

Definitely a first choice for elementary science collections. (pp. 60-1)

*Shirley A. Smith, in a review of "The First Book of Electricity," in* School Library Journal, *Vol. 23, No. 9, May, 1977, pp. 60-1.*

As a child's introduction to electricity, this book has in its favor good pictures [by Rod Slater], pleasant writing, some suggestions for experiments, and even a glossary and bibliography. Generation, measurement, transmission and household use of electric power are explained. Power from nuclear fission and from unconventional sources such as fuel cells and solar cells is mentioned. A brief discussion of static electricity and Franklin's experiments come last. More mention of safety precautions in use of electric circuits might have been included. It seems unfortunate that this little book, now in its third edition, should still be marred by easily correctable blunders of terminology: "the *force* we call electricity;" "electricity is *made* only if the electrons start moving;" "generators are starters;" "*pressure* (volts), *amount* (amperes);" "the meter measures how much electric *power* you use . . . to charge for the electric *current* you use . . . in *kilowatt-hours;*" "magnetic poles: the two *ends* of a magnet out of which its *power* flows;" and more.

*R. L. Weber, in a review of "The First Book of Electricity," in* Science Books & Films, *Vol. XIV, No. 1, May, 1978, p. 38.*

### The Real Book about Submarines (as Samuel Epstein and Beryl Williams, 1954)

An addition to the *Real Books* that meets a definite need, a factual text on modern submarines,—their history, the men who strove to achieve them, their operation today. It's a honey, one of the best in a succession of sound fact books from the inexhaustibly ambitious Epstein couple. There's a lively sense of sound reporting, keen observation, extensive research; there's an appreciation of the kinds of questions that demand answers. There is, too, an awareness of human values, from the groping inventors, to the closely knit, mutually responsible crews. And never is the sense of magic generated by Jules Verne many generations ago lost in the miracle of the modern submarine.

*A review of "The Real Book about Submarines," in* Virginia Kirkus' Bookshop Service, *Vol. XXII, No. 3, February 1, 1954, p. 67.*

### The First Book of Words: Their Family Histories (1954)

An excellent first text on the origins of speech and writing and the fascinating ways they have changed through the ages. In simplified form here is word history written with accuracy and a zest that should pull the shortest of the "short hairs". That "hello" was invented with the telephone sets up the principle that words follow on needs—and the stage for a look at early wordless man. From then on it's smooth sailing into many branches of philology—language development, divisions of the Indo-European trunk, how one language can influence many others

*Sam Epstein at his desk.*

(Latin, for example), linguistic similarities, word roots, the gap between spelling and pronunciation, grammar lags, changes in word meanings, how slang is made and so on. Very good going. (pp. 710-711)

*A review of "The First Book of Words," in* Virginia Kirkus' Bookshop Service, *Vol. XXII, No. 20, October 15, 1954, pp. 710-11.*

[This] book recounts in easy-to-understand text . . . the history of language, the development of word families, the spread of oral and written speech, the influence of communication. Though brief in its treatment for such a subject it gives a fine feeling for the etymology of English words and the contributions made by other languages. Listings of words derived from people's names, of brand names, of trick words, of slang expressions, of Christian names and their meanings; a diagram of word families; a chart of the evolution of the alphabet; and the table of contents in the back make this book useful for reference as well as fascinating for reading.

*Frances Lander Spain, in a review of "The First Book of Words: Their Family Histories," in* The Saturday Review, *New York, Vol. 37, No. 46, November 13, 1954, p. 85.*

This is a history of words rather than a dictionary, as the title would lead one to think. The approach is somewhat different from *Picturesque Word Origins,* the text more simple. Although upper elementary and junior high school pupils will make more extensive use of the book, senior high school students in speech classes will find in it interesting information for talks. The history fills a long felt need in junior high library collections.

> *Lois Anderson, in a review of "The First Book of Words: Their Family Histories," in* Junior Libraries, *Vol. 79, No. 4, December 15, 1954, p. 27.*

### The Real Book about the Sea　(1954)

> [*The British edition of* The Real Book about the Sea *was edited by Helen Hoke and Patrick Pringle.*]

This able writing team has produced another very readable and accurate book that reads smoothly and clearly, with no talking down, for ages 10-16. It covers tides, ocean currents, what lives in the sea, etc. . . . Recommended for all science collections for upper elementary and junior high, since this is not an over-worked area; this competent book serves as a good junior *The Sea Around Us.*

> *Lois Anderson, in review of "The Real Book about the Sea," in* Junior Libraries, *Vol. 1, No. 4, December, 1954, p. 27.*

An interestingly written account of the oceans, how they were formed, what is known about the life to be found in various parts of the ocean, and how the ocean affects our everyday life. Some of the potential future uses of the ocean and its products are also discussed. In one or two instances a tendency toward over-simplification could lead to misunderstandings, but on the whole the material is well-handled and should have wide appeal. (pp. 50-1)

> *A review of "The Real Book about the Sea," in* Bulletin of the Children's Book Center, *Vol. VIII, No. 6, February, 1955, pp. 50-1.*

The sea, vast and variable, may be regarded from many points of view. In the contrast between these [*The Real Book about the Sea* and Ley Kenyon's *Discovering the Undersea World* ] we see this. While *The Sea* deals widely with its subject: from waves to the ocean bed, from land climate to sea food, from movement *on* the sea to movement *of* the sea; *Undersea World* deals more restrictively with one exploration and gives a lot of information about diving. Here we have a section on how to recognize by fins and tails fishes you would meet while diving, while *The Sea* talks generally about marine animals.

Mr. Kenyon's narrative of the exploration around Akra in the Aegean is enthralling and should capture the imagination of most children; perhaps even encouraging some to join a 'Sub-aqua' club, a list of these being included in the book. Even the factual sections like those on sunken treasure, modern diving and the history of diving are entertainingly written. By contrast *The Sea* seems both didactic and pedestrian. Battles between giant squid and whales are used to describe the natural history of the species rather more than for the sake of the fight itself.

For the child who wants a general book about the sea and doesn't mind references to the North American coastline

then *The Sea* would be for him. *Undersea World* is for the aqua-lung and snorkel divers. Both books have bibliographies, and although *The Sea* is American the booklist has been modified for English readers. Both are well worthy of being included in the school library, but if I had to choose one it would be *Undersea World.*

> *J. D. Bloom, in a review of "The Sea," in* The School Librarian and School Library Review, *Vol. 11, No. 2, July, 1962, p. 202.*

### The First Book of Hawaii　(1954)

An introduction to the Hawaiian Islands and the people who live there today, with some information about the history and economic development of the islands. The straightforward information is broken up by the thread of a slight story about a family who live in Hawaii and entertain some mainland guests for a vacation. Despite the often confusing organization, the book will serve as a general picture of the Islands. Families about to make a trip to the Islands will be interested in the suggestions of things to see on each island.

> *A review of "The First Book of Hawaii," in* Bulletin of the Children's Book Center, *Vol. IX, No. 2, October, 1955, p. 22.*

### The Rocket Pioneers: On the Road to Space　(as Beryl Williams and Samuel Epstein, 1955)

Prolific writers for the juvenile market place—on this subject as well as a host of others—Beryl Williams and Samuel Epstein have all the qualifications for turning out this competent, lively survey of the men and organizations who have paved the way towards coming space flight. First on their list is William Congreve. He thought of using rockets for weapons in the early 19th century and had to go to the toymakers for his supplies, but his name became a legend in Napoleonic times. Jules Verne follows with the imagination that was the spur of future space ship designers. Working in Russia in the late 19th century, Ziolkovsky was a pioneer theorist, but an obscure school teacher who might have received more notice under different circumstances. Robert Hutchings Goddard was the father of U.S. rocketeering and his inventions startled the inhabitants of Worcester, Mass. Hermann Oberth, the German rocket society VfR, the American Rocket Society, and Hitler's organization at Peenemunde—these round out the contributory list. And biography has been combined with scientific detail for a maximum of interest to the ever dedicated audience.

> *A review of "The Rocket Pioneers," in* Virginia Kirkus' Service, *Vol. XXIII, No. 3, February 1, 1955, p. 112.*

Although our present-day high-altitude rockets are a development of the last 10 or 15 years, man's interest in and knowledge of rocket power dates back at least four centuries. This volume traces the highlights in this long history in terms which will be understood and enjoyed by the layman. It concentrates on the work of Congreve, Ziolovsky,

Goddard, and Oberth, and shows how the early experimentations were encouraged and popularized by the novels of Jules Verne, Kurt Lasswitz and others. The pioneering work of the American Rocket Society, its German counterpart, the Verein für Raumshiffahrt, and the Peenemünde Group, are described at length. The authors have leaned heavily on the writings of Ley, Pendray, and Dornberger, but they have also introduced much new material not readily found in other books on the subject. Recommended for general purchase.

> *Jack E. Brown, in a review of "The Rocket Pioneers," in* Library Journal, *Vol. 80, March 1, 1955, p. 560.*

**The Rocket Pioneers on the Road to Space** is a history of actual rocket developments. It includes biographies of nineteenth and twentieth century men who devoted their lives to rocket projection. The development of rockets in Europe and the United States is carefully traced and the story behind the big V-2's the Germans used in World War II is quite complete. The authors largely keep away from space travel because their purpose is to show what has been achieved so far: their interest is in the pioneering of rockets. With this book done so well, it is hoped they will soon tackle the future.

> *Bliss K. Thorne, "Into the Blue," in* The New York Times Book Review, *August 28, 1955, p. 16.*

---

### The First Book of Glass   (1955)

A fascinating subject is covered well by the Epsteins' text. Contrasting first the rarity of glass in ancient times with its commonness today, the text then tells how glass is made by nature and by man. Amplifying its man-made aspects, there is a brief history of glass blowing—in Egypt, in Venice, in the United States—and this sets the stage for the many modern uses of glass—in building, as decoration, in optical instruments and so forth. Each of the operations and uses is explained in detail sufficient to answer all the sharpest of incipient curiosities.

> *A review of "The First Book of Glass," in* Virginia Kirkus' Service, *Vol. XXIII, No. 14, July 15, 1955, p. 494.*

A brief history of glass making from very early to modern times. The importance of glass in the progress of civilization and its use both as an object of ornamentation and for more practical purposes are discussed. The illustrations [by Bette Davis], showing the tools and some of the processes of glass making are of as much, or greater, value as the text, although in one sequence, showing the making of a pitcher, the illustrations do not match the accompanying text. Not as detailed an account or as attractive a book as Diamond's *The Story of Glass* (Harcourt, 1953), but written at a somewhat lower level of reading difficulty.

> *A review of "The First Book of Glass," in* Bulletin of the Children's Book Center, *Vol. IX, No. 6, February, 1956, p. 67.*

Excellent layout, well chosen photographs, some illumi-

nating black and white drawings, help out a survey which, within the tight limit of wordage, is very thorough, starting with the oldest Egyptian moulded glass and ending with John Piper's Coventry window. Plate-glass and glass-fibre, mosaic and stained glass, the possible origin and practice of glass-blowing, the most famous manufactured goods (Venetian and Syrian)—on these and other subjects there is much information that will be new and useful, presented simply and with no condescension.

> *Margery Fisher, in a review of "The First Book of Glass," in* Growing Point, *Vol. 3, No. 2, July, 1964, p. 350.*

---

### The First Book of Printing   (1955)

The mysteries of printing are explained with imagination in this successful attempt to cover its history from Gutenberg to the present. Excellent illustrations [by Lazlo Roth] and understandable use of technical language give necessary specific detail for typesetting, various kinds of presses, color and picture printing. A well-planned, well-designed book that will interest school classes and, especially, those individual children with a desire to cultivate a printing hobby.

> *Virginia Haviland, in a review of "The First Book of Printing," in* The Horn Book Magazine, *Vol. XXXII, No. 2, April, 1956, p. 117.*

[**The First Book of Printing**] is very well done, and fills a definite need. It would interest any one over twelve as a brief introduction to this fascinating field. Beginning cleverly with your own thumbprint and the seals of ancient kings, it leaps to facts about a great city paper and about the United States Printing Office. The history of typemaking is quickly surveyed. Modern machines and methods are clearly described, and we meet a few great printers by the way. The many pictures are explicit and often amusing. One must admit that the typography is far from distinguished, yet the general effect is lively and alluring to the reader.

Anyway, it is not a book about typography, but about all kinds of printing. It should have a wide sale both for general reading and as a school library book.

> *Louise S. Bechtel, in a review of "The First Book of Printing," in* New York Herald Tribune Book Review, *July 22, 1956, p. 8.*

*[The following excerpt is from a review of the revised edition published in 1975.]*

Updated illustrations [by Lesley Logue] lend new appeal to this revised edition. The text, however, is virtually unchanged, except for a few inconsequential deletions—e.g., a brief sketch of the *New York Times* and the GPO at work and a few "Did you know" questions about John Newbery, the Braille system, United States currency, etc. As thorough but more elementary than Simon's *The Story of Printing* (Harvey, 1965), this is a good information source which children will find interesting to look at as well as to read.

> *Deborah Shulman Karesh, in a review of "The*

First Book of Printing," in School Library Journal, *Vol. 22, No. 2, October, 1975, p. 98.*

### The First Book of Mexico   (1955; revised edition as Mexico)

A semi-fictionalized introduction to Mexico. Through the activities of Juan, a young boy living in Mexico City, the reader is given a brief view of typical Mexican family life in the city and in a small village where Juan visits. Bits of Mexican history, places of interest, culture, and religion are also woven into the account as Juan visits famous monuments and takes part in festivals and holidays. Interestingly presented, although somewhat superficial.

> *A review of "The First Book of Mexico," in* Bulletin of the Children's Book Center, *Vol. IX, No. 9, May, 1956, p. 93.*

*[The following excerpts are from reviews of the revised edition published in 1967.]*

Revised from the 1955 edition, reillustrated with photographs instead of drawings, rewritten, but with only summary treatment of the conditions in Mexico in the last few years. The text offers a brief rundown of political change in the country since ancient times and some superficial coverage of the cultural background and mores of the people—a chronological outline and an encyclopedia extract would be as informative. The book begins and ends with fiesta time ("there are holidays all the year around in Mexico," is how the country is typified) but it all seems as colorless as the small, unimaginative, black-and-white photographs.

> *A review of "The First Book of Mexico," in* Virginia Kirkus' Service, *Vol. XXXIV, No. 24, December 15, 1966, p. 1286.*

This revised edition gives a picture of Mexico that is amazingly good for so brief a book. It is definitely preferable to the first edition. With no fictionizing, it is more mature and quite up to date. Drawings have been discarded in favor of photographs; the glossary has been omitted but is not missed since unfamiliar words are explained in the text, with pronunciation given for some. Emphasis is on the political and social life of Mexico rather than the topography of this Latin American country.

> *Laurie Dudley, in a review of "The First Book of Mexico," in* School Library Journal, *Vol. 13, No. 5, January 15, 1967, p. 66.*

*[The following excerpt is from a review of* Mexico, *published in 1983.]*

In an easy-to-understand manner, the Epsteins introduce readers to basic historical, political and economical aspects of Mexico. The book tells about Mexico's pre-Columbian past, the Spanish conquest and colonial periods, Mexico's fight for independence, Mexico's agricultural and oil problems, tourist attractions and unique government. In contrast to other books that either patronize or misrepresent Mexico, this is indeed a straightforward, simple introduction to what Mexico was and is. It brings up to date information contained in the 1967 edition. Un-

fortunately, the black-and-white photographs do not do justice to Mexico's many and varied attractions.

> *Isabel Schon, in a review of "Mexico," in* School Library Journal, *Vol. 29, No. 7, March, 1983, p. 174.*

### Young Faces in Fashion   (1956)

*[*Young Faces in Fashion *was written by Beryl Williams.]*

A group of vividly written biographies captures all the glamour and excitement of the fashion world that any clothes conscious youngster could wish for. Here the accent is on young designers and as the success stories of Anne Fogarty, Jeanne Campbell, James Galanos, Helen Lee, John Moore and others are unfolded, there is the comforting if mistaken supposition that it is good for women to be preoccupied with clothes. Personal opinions, colorful anecdotes and a succinct general survey of New York's Seventh Avenue will add up to must reading for anyone who regards costuming as a basic part of life.

> *A review of "Young Faces in Fashion," in* Virginia Kirkus' Service, *Vol. XXIV, No. 1, January 1, 1956, p. 9.*

This is a collection of "success" stories featuring eight prominent modern fashion designers who are decidedly on the youthful side. One of them is a husband-and-wife team, Lorraine and Bard Budney. The others are Anne Fogarty, identified with the small-waist-full-skirt styles; Jeanne Campbell, noted for her versatile "separates"; James Galanos, only recently a winner against great odds; the Frankfurt sisters of Dallas, who pioneered in the modern maternity styles; Helen Lee, caterer to the six-to-fourteen-year-olds; John Moore, who calls himself plain "lucky"; and Bonnie Cashin, whose specialty is theater costumes.

The one who seemed to face the most discouragements is Galanos; the most "lucky," John Moore. But every one of them had a dedicated willingness to work, wait, and do anything at all to inch toward the goal. Their stories make fascinating reading, and will be an inspiration to career-minded young women and men.

> *Silence Buck Bellows, in a review of "Young Faces in Fashion," in* The Christian Science Monitor, *July 5, 1956, p. 13.*

The information is interesting, although presented in a somewhat over-enthusiastic tone and, taken as a whole, the book seems to put a disproportionate value on clothes. However, there is much good material here for vocational guidance classes.

> *A review of "Young Faces in Fashion," in* Bulletin of the Children's Book Center, *Vol. X, No. 4, December, 1956, p. 59.*

### The Andrews Raid: Or, the Great Locomotive Chase, April 12, 1862 (1956)

The zest the Epsteins have shown in their account of the famous Northern attempt to capture a locomotive and destroy the Southern supply line in the early part of the Civil War is evident in their careful research and reconstruction of the raid. Working from contemporary accounts and from conversations with people whose railroad and Civil War connections have given them authority to speak, the authors have put together a narrative that makes touch and go reading all the way. From the moment we meet James Andrews, the man known as a Confederate sympathizer who came to General Mitchel and the Ohio Volunteers with his daring plan, we enter fully into the pinpoint timing and planning of a fantastic bit of derring-do. Andrews asked for volunteers and we get to know some of the men who went into the South with him; in Atlanta, we are switched to the activities of William Fuller, the young Southern engineer most responsible for the raid's failure. With the capture of the locomotive running north to Chattanooga events fall thick and fast and with the build up of men's characters as well as their endeavors, the narrative becomes the best sort of reading adventure.

> A review of "The Andrews Raid," in Virginia Kirkus' Service, Vol. XXIV, No. 13, July 1, 1956, p. 444.

The Epsteins have done an outstanding job in retelling this true story of one of the Civil War's most dramatic adventures. By alternately switching the action from pursued to pursuers the authors give the viewpoints of Northerners and Southerners alike and still maintain a full head of steam and suspense. The numerous maps drawn by R. M. Powers are a great help in following this classic chase. Either as competitor with or complement to the current motion picture on the same subject, this book is excellent.

> George A. Woods, "The General," in The New York Times Book Review, August 19, 1956, p. 24.

Where could you find such a perfect example of truth, that is stranger than fiction. The actual theft of a Confederate locomotive by James Andrews and his small band of young raiders' presents a spectacular race that was a natural for the films.

The authors have told the story from the viewpoint of both Northerners and Southerners by alternating chapters throughout most of the tale, portraying it so fairly that the reader is torn between loyalties. Continuous suspense, old-time railroad atmosphere, and authentic history are skillfully blended.

Richard Powers' illustrations point up the drama of the chase and provide charts and maps by which to follow it. An exciting experience for any young history student.

> Olive Deane Hormel, in a review of "The Andrews Raid," in The Christian Science Monitor, May 2, 1957, p. 11.

### The First Book of Codes and Ciphers (1956)

The two principal methods of secret writing plus several ways to make invisible ink are engagingly and entertainingly revealed by the Epsteins. In the first section of the book they show the difference between codes (which use symbols for whole words) and ciphers (which use symbols for different letters of the alphabet) and follow this up with famous examples of cryptic messages from Caesar's day to the discovery of the Rosetta Stone. Problems in encoding and decoding accompany the material and should engross the myriad young spies and undercover agents around us.

> A review of "The First Book of Codes and Ciphers," in Virginia Kirkus' Service, Vol. XXIV, No. 14, July 15, 1956, p. 479.

A welcome addition to any children's room. Directions and explanations are clear, concise, and easy to interpret. The black-and-white illustrations [by Lazlo Roth] show exactly how to set up your chosen system for encoding and decoding messages. Alphabet ciphers, number ciphers, a semiphone code, and making invisible inks are all included. Range of difficulty in the types of codes discussed makes this volume usable by ages 9 through junior high.

> Alice Hagar, in a review of "The First Book of Codes and Ciphers," in Junior Libraries, Vol. 3, No. 4, December, 1956, p. 24.

---

### Prehistoric Animals (1956)

Often as the story has been told, the Epsteins have done it again with a clarity that makes their book definitive enough to give young interests a well rounded amplification of the subject. The statement that there are two branches to the study of paleontology—learning of the animals themselves and how man has found out about them—sets the stage for following material. Starting with the "how", the Epsteins tell us that the Greeks voiced suspicions of a prehistoric life 2000 years ago. They then bring us up to the beginnings of modern paleontology in the work of William Smith, whose study of stratified rocks in England led to the naming of the different periods of animal development. The periods themselves—500,000,000 ago and the age of trilobites, the age of fish, landward migration, early reptiles and so on up to mammals and man—are freshly described with a clarity to make them memorable. And as evolutionary theories, most brilliantly transmitted by Darwin, came to have meaning for the transitions, they too are enumerated.

> A review of "Prehistoric Animals," in Virginia Kirkus' Service, Vol. XXIV, No. 19, October 1, 1956, p. 757.

Prehistoric animals have certainly captured the imagination of modern young people. Well-illustrated books of description of these (to us) eccentric creatures abound, of which Scheele's Prehistoric Animals is the finest. The youngest have Marie Bloch's Dinosaurs, and there is The First Book of Prehistoric Animals by Alice Dickinson and All About Strange Beasts of the Past by Roy Chapman Andrews, for slightly older children. There is also the very decorative *The Earth Changes* by Jannette Lucas, filled with picture maps by Helene Carter showing the geologic changes in the earth from archaeozoic times until now with the different inhabitants of land and water in each era. Now the older ones, whose interest has been whetted, have a fine book by the versatile Epsteins emphasizing the way man came to discover the details of the development of various forms of life on this earth and describing the dominant species of each geologic era. The text moves swiftly and interestingly, much as a good teacher would tell the story, from "five hundred million years ago" on to the drama of the ice age, referring constantly to the geologic timetable. . . . The jacket is eye-catching, while the book itself is a handsome, dignified green cloth with a natural colored back strip printed boldly in brown. The format will not cause it to be tossed aside as a "young" book by the teens who are really readers. They will quickly see what an excellent simple introduction to paleontology this is.

> *Margaret Sherwood Libby, in a review of "Prehistoric Animals," in* New York Herald Tribune Book Review, *March 17, 1957, p. 10.*

The authors have here written a lively as well as informative account of the detective work which has accompanied the piecing together of the known details of prehistoric creatures. The description of these creatures from rock formation to Ice Age holds one spellbound and the multifarious illustrations [by W. R. Lohse] in bold line make the account convincing. The great mystery of living creatures is unfolded with continuous wonder on every page and there is absolutely no writing down. An admirable book for the school library or for an individual gift. (pp. 289-90)

> *A review of "Prehistoric Animals," in* The Junior Bookshelf, *Vol. 22, No. 5, November, 1958, pp. 289-90.*

---

### All about the Desert   (1957)

Comprehensive information about deserts the world around. Straightforward style and good print make the book useful for almost any age from fourth grade up. Information appears to be accurate, although there are no indications of sources. Fritz Kredel's illustrations and maps and charts amplify the text. Unfortunately, lack of an index will limit usefulness as a reference tool. Not as beautiful as Walt Disney's *Living Desert* nor as lively as Hiser's *Desert Drama,* both of which cover only the American Southwest. Much fuller than Goetz's *Deserts* which is useful as an introduction to the subject.

> *Allie Beth Martin, in a review of "All about the Desert," in* Junior Libraries, *Vol. 4, No. 2, October 15, 1957, p. 146.*

Concentrating on dry deserts, with only a brief description of cold, salt and wet deserts, the authors discuss the characteristics of deserts in general, the kinds of plants and animals to be found in them and some of the uses that mankind has made of deserts. At the end, the major deserts of Africa, Asia, Australia, North and South America are described in some detail. The material is interesting and

well-handled both for reference and for general reading purposes.

> *A review of "All about the Desert," in* Bulletin of the Children's Book Center, *Vol. XI, No. 3, November, 1957, p. 35.*

---

### The First Book of Italy   (1958)

While an enormous amount of information is packed into these pages, the end result is surprisingly colorless, almost synthetic. One knows the facts; but one loses the pulsing color, vitality, provocative quality that is Italy. The historical and geographical aspects have been whittled down to bare essentials. One learns something of the new factors operating to bring a new Italy into being. One is told of the terraced farms, the modern orchards and grain fields and vineyards of the river valleys. But somehow one does not see the sun-drenched, vibrantly green hills and vineyards, and the families at work. One learns of the new industries in Italy's towns and cities; but one gets only bare bone pictures of the streets and piazzas and parks, while emphasis is put on the tenements and slums. The sporting events are here, and the high holidays and holy days, the schools, and the opera houses and the galleries. But there seems more space given to Vatican City than to the ancient ruins shouldering the modern Rome built around them. The other cities—Florence, Milan, Venice—are snapshots only. Enough, perhaps, to titivate the appetite if the appetite was already there. But somehow not enough to create the drive that makes Italy a goal.

> *A review of "The First Book of Italy," in* Virginia Kirkus' Service, *Vol. XXVI, No. 20, October 15, 1958, p. 804.*

Italy, ancient and modern, the birthplace of much of Western civilization, is glimpsed in these pages. This brief survey of her history, climate, customs, occupations and cultural contributions of her energetic, hard-working people can be a stepping-stone to further study along more specialized lines of interest. The drawings [by Lili Réthi], in full-page size and smaller, printed in tones of brown ranging from light to almost black, give the proper feeling of antiquity and of the centuries-old beauty of Italy's famous cities, buildings, sculptures, paintings and processions. A list of "some famous Italians" with their dates and an index suggest possibilities for further study.

> *Norma R. Fryatt, in a review of "The First Book of Italy," in* The Horn Book Magazine, *Vol. XXXV, No. 2, April, 1959, p. 137.*

[*The following excerpt is from a review of the revised edition published in 1972.*]

This revision replaces the drawings in the previous edition with clear photographs which reflect Italy's culture as well as its sights. The sections on the Arno River, Venice, and the Port of Pozzuoli include more information on the people, and, in some cases, sentences have been reworded to read more clearly. Changes in format include a slightly larger size and clearer print. Also, a new map has been added, the cover design changed, and the index enlarged. Nevertheless, the book remains a simple, concise description of the religion, art, education, crafts, living conditions, and politics of the Italian people, with geographical and historical facts interwoven throughout.

> *Ruth F. Sauerteig, in a review of "The First Book of Italy," in* School Library Journal, *Vol. 19, No. 7, March 15, 1973, p. 106.*

### Jackknife for a Penny (1958)

[*The following excerpt is from an advance review of* Jackknife for a Penny.]

The Hopkins homestead was in Mattituck, Long Island, and the British were in control. Though Cousin Bess and pretty Parny, her daughter, already sheltered Gideon, Tim's elder brother, they made newcomer Tim welcome too. Tim's heart was set on a knife. Gideon—too busy arranging to join the Patriot army—could not supply it. When he left, he cautioned Tim to help the cause. For a time Tim thought Cousin Bess and Parny were Tories, for outwardly they sympathized with Lieutenant Green and Captain Scott, the British soldiers who confiscated their crops and were quartered at the Hopkins house. Neighbor Peter Bell, son of a hoarding opportunist who alleged fealty to the King, almost thwarted Tim's concealment of a sabotage fire set by the Patriots. But Tim had discovered the culvert in which Mr. Bell hid his cattle. When Tim later learns that a raid planned by the Patriots on a British sloop will be ambushed by the British—who used the vessel as a decoy—he warns them in time to prevent capture. Tim is rewarded with the jackknife of Nathan Hale. Thwacking action, good plot, adventure, this is a characterful adventure story with a hero who invokes both sympathy and admiration.

> *A review of "Jackknife for a Penny," in* Virginia Kirkus' Service, *Vol. XXV, No. 22, November 15, 1957, p. 841.*

The Epsteins, who lately gave us that vigorous recreation of a Civil War incident, **The Andrews Raid,** have now written a fine novel of the Revolutionary period. Outstanding in this book are the details of the Colonial intelligence network established between Long Island and Connecticut and the drama and excitement of the clash between Tory and Colonial sympathies in the fateful days of 1776.

> *George A. Woods, "The Lobsterbacks Came," in* The New York Times Book Review, *February 2, 1958, p. 28.*

### The First Book of Maps and Globes (1959)

A much needed book and one which approaches the subject of maps and mapping by way of situations applicable to any child's experience. How would one child tell another child how to get from school to his house? By drawing a plan, showing streets and identifiable objects. So with this simple type of diagram making, the Epsteins take their young map makers step by step to the proper way to read maps in atlases, to read road maps, to understand globes. The many ways in which maps are used; the value

of maps; the signs and terminology; all this adds up to an excellent introduction to cartography. An impressive amount of factual information is presented with a contagious enthusiasm and a sense of discovery. The Epsteins have made another valuable contribution to this series, in which they have published numerous books.

> *A review of "The First Book of Maps and Globes," in* Virginia Kirkus' Service, *Vol. XXVII, No. 7, April 1, 1959, p. 266.*

This is a workmanlike introduction to maps and globes for nine- to eleven-year-olds. The black and white pictures [by Lazlo Roth] brighten it up for the children but add little otherwise and are not in harmony with the sketches and maps. The red end papers with white "legends" are suitable and attractive. The text wastes no words and supplies a splendid amount of information briefly on the principles on which maps are made, how to read sketch maps, road maps, global maps and maps of the sea, the way maps indicate direction, distance, depth and height, how symbols are used and how scale is indicated. In addition to all this there is a glossary, something about map-makers and references to several books, especially Hammond's *Illustrated Atlas for Young America* and *Down to Earth: Mapping for Everybody,* by David Greenhood, which go more deeply into the subject. A most useful book for schools, for scouts or for alert children who are curious.

> *Margaret Sherwood Libby, in a review of "The First Book of Maps and Globes," in* New York Herald Tribune Book Review, *September 6, 1959, p. 9.*

### Change for a Penny (1959)

A further adventure of Timothy Penny this is the story of a Long Island teen-ager and his daring role in the revolutionary war. Strategically located, Tim's home faces Connecticut, a stronghold of Patriot soldiers. Tim's ardent admiration of his older brother makes him wish frantically for an active role in the war against the Crown. And his wish is amply gratified when he acts as a guide for the raiding troops of Colonel Meig, using his familiarity of the terrain as effectively as any soldier might use a musket. Strategy, history, and familiar adventure make this an acceptable addition to the list of historical novels for the not too precocious high school student.

> *A review of "Change for a Penny," in* Virginia Kirkus' Service, *Vol. XXVII, No. 16, August 15, 1959, p. 602.*

Timothy Penny, introduced in **Jackknife for a Penny,** continues as a loyal Patriot on Long Island during the Revolution. His most important mission is to guide Patriot raiders in whaleboats through the treacherous marsh for an attack on Sag Harbor. The well-constructed plot is full of action and suspense. Characters and situations are credible, and style is adequate. Recommended.

> *Barbara M. Doh, in a review of "Change for a Penny," in* Junior Libraries, *Vol. 6, No. 6, February 15, 1960, p. 47.*

## All about Prehistoric Cave Men (1959)

Aside from the fascination that cave life holds for many people, caves provide definitive clues as to what life was like in the days before recorded history. Taking into consideration caves everywhere from Spain to China, the Epsteins reconstruct the history of man by means of evidence found in cave excavations. Anecdotes of spectacular findings, analyses of cave exploration technique, and descriptions of actual caves fill this text which is distinguished by its lucidity and enthusiasm.

> *A review of "All about Prehistoric Cavemen," in* Virginia Kirkus' Service, *Vol. XXVII, No. 18, September 15, 1959, p. 702.*

The Epsteins have themselves explored the caves of France and Spain and they have written a book that is both informative in its content as well as descriptive of the methods used by scientists as they explore and interpret their findings. They deal in a most readable manner with Peking and Neanderthal Man and others who inhabited these early caves; the life and times of the cave dwellers is described to the limit of known facts. Tools are described in considerable detail. Maps, geological diagrams and other pertinent drawings [by Will Huntington] add to the interest and understanding.

> *Glenn O. Blough, "The Old, Old Days," in* The New York Times Book Review, *November 15, 1959, p. 58.*

## The First Book of Measurement (1960)

A good introduction to the topic, with a simple explanation of the need for systems of measurement and a description of the kinds of systems we have: some for measuring capacity, some for weight, some for time, etc. The authors discuss the development of metric systems, the establishment of standards, and some of the tools used for different kinds of measurement.

> *Zena Sutherland, in a review of "The First Book of Measurement," in* Bulletin of the Center for Children's Books, *Vol. XV, No. 4, December, 1961, p. 58.*

## The First Book of Washington, D.C.: The Nation's Capital (1961; revised edition as Washington, D.C.: The Nation's Capital )

Combining three elements with varying emphasis, historical information, physical description and modern day functioning, the important landmarks of Washington, D. C., are outlined with accompanying black and white photographs. Although there is much useful information here (even tidbits on how to get around in the oft-confusing network of Washington's layout) the overall impression is unbalanced with "L'Enfant and his Plan" the heading of one chapter, and "The White House Lawn", another.

> *A review of "The First Book of Washington,*

*D. C.," in* Virginia Kirkus' Service, *Vol. XXIX, No. 5, March 1, 1961, p. 216.*

A book that gives a considerable amount of information about Washington but is so weakened by the rambling arrangement of the continuous text that its value is diminished. This is all the more regrettable because the authors have a pleasant, light style and they have included many odd and interesting bits of information. Photographs are clear, but not always well-placed; an index is appended.

> *Zena Sutherland, in a review of "The First Book of Washington, D.C.: The Nation's Capital," in* Bulletin of the Center for Children's Books, *Vol. XV, No. 10, June, 1962, p. 157.*

[*The following excerpt is from a review of a revised edition of* Washington, D.C.: The Nation's Capital *published in 1981.*]

This is an up-to-date guidebook to the District of Columbia, presenting an interesting blend of statistics, history and landmarks. The activities of various government agencies are accompanied with bits of local legend as readers are introduced to federal buildings and museums. The text is brisk and upbeat and has easily accessible information. The Epsteins have arranged their material in a more logical and orderly fashion than have Carol Bluestein and Susan Irwin in their *Washington D.C.: a Guidebook for Kids* (Noodle Pr, 1976), which, in addition to the straight information, also presents a series of quizzes and puzzles for readers of the same age group. Allan Carpenter's *District of Columbia* (Childrens Pr, 1967) is for older readers, and antiquated by now.

> *Phyllis Ingram, in a review of "Washington, D.C.: The Nation's Capital," in* School Library Journal, *Vol. 28, No. 4, December, 1981, p. 62.*

## The First Book of the Ocean (1961)

If this really were the first book published about the ocean and its life, it would be more necessary on the library shelves, but, since so many such books have been added to our collections recently, this hardly seems essential. Uniform with others in this famous series, it covers tides, currents, slopes, and the ocean floor, and plant and animal life, with a final chapter on the future, which includes desalting and further depth exploring.

> *Elsie T. Dobbins, in a review of "The First Book of the Ocean," in* Junior Libraries, *Vol. 7, No. 8, April 15, 1961, p. 51.*

After noting what can be learned about the sea from a walk along the beach the authors discuss briefly the ocean's waves, tides, and currents, the continental shelves and slopes, the ocean floor, and plants and animals that live in the sea; they also talk about underwater exploration, the mapping of the ocean floor, and the ocean in man's future. Despite its brevity this readable description compares favorably in content with existing fuller accounts.

> *A review of "The First Book of the Ocean," in*

The Booklist and Subscription Books Bulletin, *Vol. 57, No. 22, July 15, 1961, p. 702.*

### The First Book of Teaching Machines  (1961)

A useful book, with competent handling of material and good organization, but rather dry and sedate in style. Approximately a third of the book is devoted to photographs of machines, old and new, or parts of machines; each page also carries a few lines of text in quite small print. The explanation of the way in which a machine is programmed is clear; the author's analysis of the relative merits of teaching machines is objective; a brief index is appended.

> *Zena Sutherland, in a review of "The First Book of Teaching Machines," in* Bulletin of the Center for Children's Books, *Vol. XXI, No. 1, September, 1962, p. 6.*

### Plant Explorer: David Fairchild  (as Beryl Williams and Samuel Epstein, 1961)

A most interesting biography, written with informality and enthusiasm. Fairchild's experiences and experiments in discovering and bringing to this country plants from tropical countries were varied and original. His work took him to exotic places that are vividly described, so that his story is a romantic one. Mr. Fairchild is an appealing personality, and his patron, Barbour Lathrop, is—in crisp contrast—acidulous and impatient as he is generous. A lengthy index is appended. A book that will also be useful for slow high school readers.

> *Zena Sutherland, in a review of "Plant Explorer: David Fairchild," in* Bulletin of the Center for Children's Books, *Vol. XVI, No. 3, November, 1962, p. 51.*

### Grandpa's Wonderful Glass  (1962)

For beginning independent readers, an introduction to the use of a magnifying glass. Johnny and Jessie, seeing their grandfather use a glass for reading, try it and are enchanted; they keep interrupting the reading to borrow the glass. Grandpa gives up and goes for a walk. The writing is just a bit stilted, but much less so than in most books for beginning readers, and there is some humor in the story—as well as a few interesting facts about what the children see when they use the magnifying glass.

> *Zena Sutherland, in a review of "Grandpa's Wonderful Glass," in* Bulletin of the Center for Children's Books, *Vol. XVI, No. 8, April, 1963, p. 125.*

### Pioneer Oceanographer: Alexander Agassiz  (as Beryl Williams and Samuel Epstein, 1963)

A very readable biography of Alexander Agassiz complements those about his famous father, Louis, by Peare and Tharp. Written from Alex' viewpoint, the story tells how he and his mother helped to solve the human and financial problems of impractical Louis. Alex emerges as a stronger, more self-reliant person than his father and a scientist in his own right. Alex is important for his world-wide research on marine life and coral reefs and his amazingly varied activities as mining industrialist, designer of sea-dredging machinery, and one of the world's first oceanographers. Fascinating reading for the student interested in zoology and oceanography. Recommended.

> *Helen M. Kovar, in a review of "Pioneer Oceanographer: Alexander Agassiz," in* School Library Journal, *Vol. 10, No. 1, September, 1963, p. 2564.*

Particularly interesting in this biography is the picture of the difficult, intricate relationship between father and son, and of the warm, deep friendship that developed between Alexander and his stepmother, who became the first president of Radcliffe College. The authors have rescued from obscurity a person of great integrity, charm, and accomplishment.

> *Margaret Warren Brown, in a review of "Pioneer Oceanographer: Alexander Agassiz," in* The Horn Book Magazine, *Vol. XXXIX, No. 4, August, 1963, p. 394.*

Louis Agassiz, father of Alexander, had such a remarkable career as a scientist that the son's reputation has, to a considerable extent, been overshadowed. Although this book focuses on Alexander's life and work, the authors make good use of the contrasts between father and son in bringing alive their controversy about the merits of Darwin's theory of evolution.

Alexander Agassiz provides good copy. Owing to financial difficulties he interrupted his career as a scientist to become a millionaire. Returning to his scientific career, Agassiz brought with him not only money to finance his work (and that of others) but also engineering skill that enabled him to make important advances in equipment for exploring the ocean depths. Agassiz' career thus illustrates the important point that science is an activity requiring not only intellectual skills but also adequate financial resources and proper equipment. (pp. 12-13)

> *John Imbrie, "Geography, Geology and Paleontology," in* Natural History, *Vol. 72, No. 10, December, 1963, pp. 12-14.*

### The Story of the International Red Cross  (1963)

To honor the centennial of the IRC, here is a glowing history of the organization, from the original idea of Henri Dunant through all the birth-pangs and tremulous adolescence to maturity in World War I; its role in peacetime disasters, its multifarious and efficient activities during World War II right on to its work in Hungary and the Congo. A good, although uncritical, journalistic account.

> *Alibeth M. Howell, in a review of "The Story of the International Red Cross," in* School Library Journal, *Vol. 10, No. 1, September, 1963, p. 127.*

An interesting and useful book, carefully compiled and

written in a succinct and straightforward style. The authors describe first a dramatic large-scale emergency program; they then trace the history of the organization beginning with the work of Dunant, the role of Clara Barton, the operation of the Red Cross in two world wars, and the cooperation with United Nations agencies. Some of the programs described are intensely moving and impressive; one of the most valuable aspects of the text is the information given about the organizational structure and operation—the training, the tracing methods, the extension of Red Cross activities both in quantity and variety. A list of suggested readings and an index are appended.

> *Zena Sutherland, in a review of "The Story of the International Red Cross," in* Bulletin of the Center for Children's Books, *Vol. XVII, No. 9, May, 1964, p. 138.*

---

### Hurricane Guest  (1964)

A hurricane descends on the Davis family at the worst possible time. Mr. Davis is away while Mike, Tess and their mother are entertaining Peter, Mike's English pen-pal. It had been a carefully planned and long awaited visit. Everything had been centered on outdoor activities and cook-out meals. Plays on words are not the usual fare of easy readers, but Peter thinks that his hurricane visit is "smashing" as he and the Davis family hurl themselves into a scramble of activity to safeguard the house and the supplies from the rising waters of the creek. The text, while simply worded, does not suffer from the rigid structure and banal conversation so often encountered in books of this category.

> *A review of "Hurricane Guest," in* Virginia Kirkus' Service, *Vol. XXXII, No. 6, March 15, 1964, p. 292.*

A very good story for the middle grades: good length, good story-line, especially good dialogue, and realistic treatment of two unusual events. The reaction of a family to a hurricane, and the reaction of children to a child visitor are skilfully depicted. The two Davis children are excited at the prospect of a visit from Mike's English pen-pal, but they find him a bit odd when he arrives, and it takes the excitement of the hurricane to break down the barriers of difference, although it is clear that the rapport would have been established anyway, albeit more slowly.

> *Zena Sutherland, in a review of "Hurricane Guest," in* Bulletin of the Center for Children's Books, *Vol. XVIII, No. 1, September, 1964, p. 7.*

---

### Spring Holidays  (1964)

Although containing many bits and pieces of information, this is a book for which there seems only limited use, since it compiles in somewhat random fashion facts about some holidays in the United States ("May Day in America" deals with the United States, not all of America) for the most part, but in some sections gives a few facts about other countries. The holidays covered are Groundhog

Day, Arbor Day, Audubon Day, May Day, April Fools' Day, and the First Day of Spring. Memorial Day and Easter are not included. Some of the lesser-known customs or variants are interesting, but the book is not well-organized or comprehensive.

> *Zena Sutherland, in a review of "Spring Holidays," in* Bulletin of the Center for Children's Books, *Vol. XVIII, No. 1, September, 1964, p. 7.*

---

### The First Book of the World Health Organization  (1964)

'This book, intended for children, will certainly also interest many grown-ups' (the Director of the World Health Organization in the Foreword). Of how many well-written and well-informed school books can this be said!

The first two chapters introduce 'human interest stories' designed to show the WHO in action (against smallpox and against yaws). The book then goes on to a quite straightforward account of the organization, how it was set up, and how it works, with many specific instances of programmes and campaigns. It includes too a useful, if short, retrospective chapter on the historical background, on medieval quarantine, the work of Edwin Chadwick, etc.

The phrase, 'intended for children', is in fact too modest. It would be a very useful book for study in the middle and upper forms of secondary schools of all kinds, clear, sensible, informative. It certainly deserves a place in school libraries. (pp. 99-100)

> *Anthony McLean, in a review of "The First Book of the World Health Organization," in* The School Librarian and School Library Review, *Vol. 15, No. 1, March, 1967, pp. 99-100.*

---

### Lucky, Lucky White Horse  (1965)

[*Lucky, Lucky White Horse was written by Beryl Epstein.*]

When Ellen's family moved to Columbus in 1916 she knew that her cousin Hetty's family would move next door three weeks later. That was the way it had always been and Ellen had grown up in bossy Hetty's shadow. The story moves through the three short weeks in which Ellen starts to establish a personality of her own in a new neighborhood. The incidents are unified by Ellen's determined efforts at an easily adapted and amusing wish game. Every time she sees a white horse, it has to be counted along with a ritual chant. When the figure reaches 100, she is to walk around the block without stopping and find something. Just before the advent of Hetty, Ellen finds Mindy. The pace is easy, the story warmly real in its household and neighborhood detail, and a natural for girls at this age level who are consciously making their first step into the world when they make their first friend outside the family.

> *A review of "Lucky, Lucky White Horse," in* Virginia Kirkus' Service, *Vol. XXXIII, No. 1, January 1, 1965, p. 5.*

Although set in 1916, this pleasant story for girls is embellished with period details in the illustrations [by Mia Carpenter] more than in the text. . . . The theme of the child who gains courage or achieves self-reliance while working for a specific goal is not rare, but it is always appealing—especially when it is, as here, given a realistic setting with warm personal relationships.

> *Zena Sutherland, in a review of "Lucky, Lucky White Horse," in* Bulletin of the Center for Children's Books, *Vol. 19, No. 1, September, 1965, p. 7.*

### The Game of Baseball   (1965)

Simply written, this fills the need of the young reader who desires to know the history of his favorite sport. Bits of imagined conversation enliven the narrative describing the evolution of the game with reasons for its growth, accounts of important games and of the recognized stars. Large type, brief sentences, lucid explanations, and appealing drawings [by Hobe Hays] and photographs make this an excellent book for young fans.

> *Herbert Deutsch, in a review of "The Game of Baseball," in* School Library Journal, *Vol. 11, No. 8, April, 1965, p. 66.*

A book that gives the history of baseball in this country, skimming the highlights and giving a small amount of information about the way the game is played. . . . . The writing style is stilted and awkward: "The men with George Washington at Valley Forge lived in huts. They couldn't keep warm. They almost starved. Then spring came. A soldier took a ball out of his knapsack and tossed it. 'Let's have a game!' someone shouted. 'Here's a shovel handle to use as a bat!' " The endpapers show identical diagrams of a baseball diamond, giving a few paragraphs of explanatory text. The treatment is superficial, but the book may be useful for slow readers in the upper grades. (pp. 127-28)

> *Zena Sutherland, in a review of "The Game of Baseball," in* Bulletin of the Center for Children's Books, *Vol. XVIII, No. 9, May, 1965, pp. 127-28.*

### Medicine from Microbes: The Story of Antibiotics   (as Beryl Williams and Samuel Epstein, 1965)

Adequately researched and written by the prolific Epsteins, this nevertheless lacks the drama and excitement of de Kruif's classic *Microbe Hunters* (1926, 1953) which it supplements (but surprisingly omits from the brief, adult oriented list of additional reading). While a short history of medicine introduces the subject, the microbes themselves are never well defined. The romance of early work is of course included, but most valuable is the inclusion of the later work with penicillin and streptomycin. The relatively brief final chapter includes the past 10 years and discusses present and future matters: mutation, vitamin production, application to cancer and arthritis.

> *A review of "Medicine from Microbes: The*

Story of Antibiotics," in Virginia Kirkus' Service, Vol. XXXIII, No. 14, July 15, 1965, p. 686.

After sketching the contributions of ancient and medieval scientists, the authors present fuller accounts of the careers of Pasteur and Koch. Building on this foundation, they carefully develop the interrelationships among the contributions of such men as Fleming, Florey, Heatley, and Waksman. "In science," Pasteur is quoted as having said, "chance favors only the prepared mind." The authors demonstrate the importance of this maxim in the history of antibiotics, where several important discoveries were the result of accidents. A minor flaw is the attempt in the very brief final chapter to generalize about some aspects of medical treatment. The authors are more competent in their roles as historians and biographers and tend to oversimplify in discussing a subject of myriad subtle distinctions. However, this is, otherwise, an accurate, often absorbing book which will interest young people with or without much science background.

> *David M. Paige, in a review of "Medicine from Microbes: The Story of Antibiotics," in* School Library Journal, *Vol. 12, No. 2, October, 1965, p. 242.*

A well-written account of microbiological research and the development of antibiotics with major emphasis on the discovery of penicillin. Though much of the material is available in other books, the enlightening commentary on research methods together with historical and biographical information makes a stimulating and useful addition to books on medical science. A glossary and short list of adult books for further reading are included.

> *A review of "Medicine from Microbes: The Story of Antibiotics," in* The Booklist and Subscription Books Bulletin, *Vol. 62, No. 15, April 1, 1966, p. 775.*

### The First Book of News   (1965)

The latest book in this familiar series provides a thorough explanation of news as covered by the newspaper, radio, and television media. Beginning with Greek and Roman times, the authors trace the earliest means of communication to the development of printing and the growth of a free press. Good historical background and orientation and explanation of the importance of fast, accurate communication of major historical events. Will be helpful to elementary social studies classes. Written in crisp, graphic fashion. More detailed than Sootin's *Let's Take a Trip to a Newspaper* (Putnam, 1965). Well supplemented by contemporary photographs and historical material from the Library of Congress, New York Public Library, the Bettman Archive, and historical societies.

> *Jeraline Nerney, in a review of "The First Book of News," in* School Library Journal, *Vol. 12, No. 4, December, 1965, p. 74.*

More general in treatment than Bradley's *The newspaper, its place in a democracy,* . . . this historical survey of the gathering and dissemination of news from the time of the ancient Greeks to the present provides an excellent introduction to the importance of news in keeping people informed about the world in which they live. The authors explain what news is, the relationship of news to concurrent politics, business, and daily life, and the development of modern news coverage by press, radio, and television.

> *A review of "The First Book of News," in* The Booklist and Subscription Books Bulletin, *Vol. 62, No. 13, March 1, 1966, p. 662.*

### Young Paul Revere's Boston　(1966)

A simply written book, with . . . an attractive endsheet reproduction of an old print. The text is rather loosely organized and occasionally stilted in style, but it gives adequate coverage in describing the port of Boston in 1747. The fact that the activities, foods, dress, educational patterns, et cetera, are tied to the Revere family is a bit artificial, yet it is useful in those parts of the book where the authors distinguish between the ordinary family, such as the Reveres, and a wealthier family like the Hancocks. A glossary and an index are appended, the former giving definitions for quite a few words that have already been explained in the text. (pp. 119-20)

> *Zena Sutherland, in a review of "Young Paul Revere's Boston," in* Bulletin of the Center for Children's Books, *Vol. 20, No. 8, April, 1967, pp. 119-20.*

### The Sacramento: Golden River of California　(1968)

The authors have used the Sacramento River as a peg on which to hang a brief, brisk history of California. Beginning with the Gold Rush, the book travels backwards in time to discuss the Indians who once inhabited the country (including Ishi, the remarkable Stone Age Indian who one day stepped into the 20th Century). Spanish, Mexican, and American settlements are detailed. A chapter on California water problems, past, present and future, is included. The book will be most useful, of course, to California school and public libraries but can also provide material of some value on this region for other libraries across the country.

> *Phyllis L. Shumberger, in a review of "The Sacramento: Golden River of California," in* School Library Journal, *Vol. 14, No. 9, April, 1968, p. 126.*

### The Picture Life of Franklin Delano Roosevelt　(1968)

FDR in photos, mostly from the Hyde Park archives, some quite fresh, quite unofficial, with a brief text that similarly holds nothing sacred. The young Franklin is sheltered in boyhood, at loose ends after Harvard graduation, indebted to Eleanor for direction; shy Eleanor is dominated initially, as Franklin has been, by his mother (see the adjacent brownstones she built for herself and the newlyweds). Cocky and headstrong, Franklin antagonizes his political elders; after his attack of polio, he learns to laugh at himself. His career and his achievements are merely outlined, with acknowledgement that he "made mistakes" and "made enemies, too." Probably that's all a second grader needs to know beyond knowing Roosevelt himself, which is accomplished better here (because of the photos and the absence of puerilities) than in the otherwise comparable Wise.

> *A review of "The Picture Life of Franklin Delano Roosevelt," in* Kirkus Reviews, *Vol. XXXVII, No. 1, January 1, 1969, p. 5.*

### Harriet Tubman: Guide to Freedom　(1968)

This clearly written, fictionized biography traces the life of Harriet Tubman, her early brutal treatment at the hands of slaveholders, her two marriages, her role in the Underground Railroad as the Moses of her people, her Civil War activities as Union Army scout and nurse, and her founding of the John Brown Home for ill and impoverished Negroes. High in interest level, this is valuable material for remedial reading and will provide an introduction to a subject well treated in more comprehensive books for older readers: Petry's *Harriet Tubman* (T.Y. Crowell, 1955) and Sterling's *Freedom Train* (Doubleday, 1954).

> *Ann L. Sarver, in a review of "Harriet Tubman: Guide to Freedom," in* School Library Journal, *Vol. 15, No. 6, February, 1969, p. 75.*

### Who Says You Can't?　(1969)

. . . fight City Hall! Seven case studies of individuals or groups bucking not only official bureaucracies but also public lethargy, private interests and professional incompetence prove otherwise—and each one is a prescription for change, not a placebo. The Great Swamp in New Jersey, eyed as a metropolitan jetport site, is saved by a small group of conservationists, birdwatchers turned bird-doggers as they learn the techniques of raising funds: now it is a National Wildlife Refuge. Ralph Nader wins a public apology from the President of General Motors for harassment; meanwhile he's spurred auto safety legislation, started scrutinizing other industries and, perhaps most important, conceived of an ACLU counterpart for consumers. The brief biography of Nader is a demonstration of what makes a crusader click, and so is the chapter on Daniel Fader. Prototype of the local editor vs. the entrenched politicos is Gene Wirges in Conway County, Arkansas, who continues to earn his 1963 Elijah Lovejoy Award by sticking it out in a precarious situation. Also included are Dr. Frances Kelsey, whose insistence on proof kept thalidomide from being precipitously licensed, and Dr. Helen B. Taussig, who publicized its danger and caused supplies to be destroyed; Joseph Papp, the people's impresario; Reverend Leon Sullivan, originator of Philadelphia's innovative job training program with its provision for fundamental education. Each account is thorough, direct and highly informative; the assumption is that to do good you have to know what you're doing, whether it be Dr. Kelsey drawing on previous fetus study or the ladies in New Jersey learning to write a news release. A booster rocket for any age.

> *A review of "Who Says You Can't," in* Kirkus Reviews, *Vol. XXXVII, No. 2, January 15, 1969, p. 59.*

Sharp "profiles in courage" of seven contemporary private citizens who have sponsored worthy causes and, in so doing, successfully opposed the Establishment. . . . Because of the detailed nature of the accounts, the book is not completely suited for recreational reading; nor will it readily fit into a rigid curriculum. However, the timeliness of the theme—effective individual protest—has high-interest potential for today's socially and politically aware high-schoolers.

> *Sister Gabriel Marie, C.S.J., in a review of "Who Says You Can't?" in* School Library Journal, *Vol. 15, No. 8, April, 1969, p. 126.*

### Take This Hammer   (1969)

The familiar hammer as a common tool is explained in this beginner book with the aid of Tomie de Paola's clever drawings, some of which are in color. Various kinds of hammers, each adapted to a special use are described: clawhammer, watchmaker's hammer, sledge hammer, the wrecker's steel ball swung by a crane, hammers in musical instruments, the pile driver, the croquet mallet, etc. It's a good book for adults to discuss with youngsters to teach them basic principles of mechanics. The lever, energy, force, density, are terms not used in the text, but probably could have been since they are indirectly explained. At any rate the objective of explaining the "how and why" of familiar objects is achieved in a minor way.

> *A review of "Take This Hammer," in* Science Books & Films, *Vol. V, No. 2, September, 1969, p. 123.*

### Who Needs Holes?   (1970)

Holes in your clothes? Of course—armholes, buttonholes, holes to put shoelaces through. Out of the holes you take for granted comes an in*form*al lesson—a paper punched full of holes becomes a filter for sunlight and a source of confetti, other perforations produce a colander and a shower head. Then there are spatial applications: a hole dug down (one opening) could be an oil well, a hole dug through (two openings) is a tunnel—for a train or for prairie dogs. Ranging widely, the authors fill holes with interest . . . and put forth one with nothing inside (a clay snake bent into a circle). They've missed a chance to tell youngsters how to cut "a neat round circle" by not telling them to start in the center, but they haven't missed much: **Who Needs Holes?** can't be pigeonholed but it's peppered with 500('s) possibilities. . . .

> *A review of "Who Needs Holes?" in* Kirkus Reviews, *Vol. XXXVIII, No. 7, April 1, 1970, p. 386.*

[**Who Needs Holes?**] grabs the reader with a seemingly idiotic question, then teaches some surprisingly abstract notions of space and topology. Holes seem downright lovable when the Epsteins have finished. Illustrator Tomie de Paola contributes to the fun by drawing a sprightly collection of them. Who needs holes? The reader will soon find out; and doughnuts, confetti, and showerheads need never go their way unsung again.

> *Julian May, "A Child's Wonder," in* Book World—The Washington Post, *November 8, 1970, p. 4.*

**Who Needs Holes?** is a delightful book . . . it is well written and nicely illustrated. Starting with a discussion of holes in clothes, the book proceeds to a series of activities in which children examine holes and make holes in a variety of materials. The importance of holes in nature becomes very apparent as the book proceeds. The only hole in the book is the fact that prairie dogs dig holes with their feet not their teeth.

> *Harry O. Haakonsen, in a review of "Who Needs Holes?" in* Appraisal: Children's Science Books, *Vol. 5, No. 1, Winter, 1972, p. 16.*

### Enrico Fermi: Father of Atomic Power   (1970)

This biography of a notable atomic age scientist is marred by frequent fictionizing—recreated dialogues between Fermi and his brother and school friends. The fact that Fermi's wife was consulted by the authors may lend some authenticity to these imagined conversations, but except for statements made by Fermi during the latter part of his career, no verification is given. The book concentrates on the scientist's personality rather than on the technical aspects of his work, but enough explanation of his research is provided to enable readers to understand what he did achieve. Nevertheless, the authors' onesided, flattering view and frequent fictionizing make this book an undesirable choice.

> *Penelope M. Mitchell, in a review of "Enrico Fermi: Father of Atomic Power," in* School Library Journal, *Vol. 17, No. 7, March, 1971, p. 144.*

Told in a rather stilted textbook style for the younger reader, here is the life of Enrico Fermi, the atomic scientist. Beginning with Fermi's childhood in Italy, when he showed an unusual aptitude in mathematics, through his education at the University of Pisa, we follow his career in Rome and the United States. Simply explained are the years of work on radioactive substances which ushered in the atomic age. Fermi emerges as a quiet, dedicated but colorless man. A useful but uninspiring book.

> *Elizabeth Gillis, in a review of "Enrico Fermi: Father of Atomic Power," in* Appraisal: Children's Science Books, *Vol. 4, No. 2, Spring, 1971, p. 13.*

A brief biography with very little science. Fine for the age group. My objections are, I suppose, quibbles. I realize that one should not try to teach wave mechanics to fourth graders, but it might have been better on the bottom of page 25 to say that physicists *believed,* rather than that they *knew,* electrons went around the atomic nucleus "like planets." On page 39 reference to Fermi's paper on the "particles in a perfect gas" should, I think, either have been amplified in language appropriate to the reader's age or simply referred to as a "scientific paper." I may be wrong; it may stimulate the more curious and active minded youngsters to probe more deeply.

*Harry C. Stubbs, in a review of "Enrico Fermi: Father of Atomic Power," in* Appraisal: Children's Science Books, *Vol. 4, No. 2, Spring, 1971, p. 14.*

---

## Michael Faraday: Apprentice to Science　(1971)

**Michael Faraday** is an excellent biography for upper elementary students for outside reading. An advanced sixth grader found it interesting, easy reading, but complained that a lot of material must have been left out. The book is charmingly written and has fine illustrations, both drawings [by Raymond Burns] and photographic reproductions of portraits. It covers the entire span of Faraday's personal and scientific life. It also gives a good deal about Faraday's relation to Sir Humphry Davy and the difficult Lady Davy. The book also provides good, brief accounts of the related scientific work of Ampère, Franklin, Maxwell, Oersted, and others. It describes Faraday's amateur experiments while he was an unhappy bookbinder—apprentice and craftsman; his unsuccessful attempts to find work in the field of science; his final employment by Sir Humphry Davy, first as a clerk, then as laboratory assistant; his gradual assumption of increasingly important roles as demonstrator, lecturer, and director of the Royal Institution in London; his famous Christmas lecture; his researches and contributions in chemistry, electricity, and magnetism; his election to the Royal Society; his deteriorating health; his death at the age of 75; and "the electric magic which today's world takes for granted" as the monument to his memory. The treatment of the various aspects of science, although simplified, is valid and interestingly presented. The index is a great convenience.

*A review of "Michael Faraday: Apprentice to Science," in* Science Books: A quarterly Review, *Vol. 7, No. 2, September, 1971, p. 110.*

[*Michael Faraday: Apprentice to Science* and *Albert Schweitzer: Great Humanitarian* by Elizabeth Rider Montgomery are] Two highly fictionized accounts of famous men. Faraday is portrayed as a poor boy who worked very hard and took advantage of the opportunities that came his way. The treatment of the scientific material presented stresses theory, testing and retesting, with failures as well as successes noted. When an experiment is discussed, a simple diagram is included for further clarification. . . . Unfortunately, no sources are given for any material presented in either title. The characteristics of the series which contribute to the low cost of these books (identical number of pages, uniform size and style, etc.) give each volume the look of a textbook. Adequate line drawings and photographs are included; however, although photo credits are listed on the verso of the title page, no credit is given for a picture on the page on which it appears. Children who can read at fifth grade level or above will probably be more attracted to, and better off with John Tyndall's *Faraday As a Discoverer* (Crowell, 1961) . . . . (pp. 113-14)

*Marian L. Strickland, in a review of "Michael Faraday: Apprentice to Science," in* School Library Journal, *Vol. 18, No. 2, November 15, 1971, pp. 113-14.*

Michael Faraday is an especially good choice for a children's biography. His self-made career in science, culminating in revolutionary discoveries in electricity and magnetism, is educational and inspirational for the young would-be scientist. The Epsteins have recorded the progress of Faraday's research clearly and accurately, contributing to the reader's knowledge both of Faraday and of the science of electro-magnetism. I recommend this book highly.

*Shirley Roe, in a review of "Michael Faraday: Apprentice to Science," in* Appraisal: Children's Science Books, *Vol. 6, No. 1, Winter, 1973, p. 14.*

---

## Pick It Up　(1971)

Scooping, sucking, grasping, hooking—they're all ways of picking things up, and each is illustrated here with examples using the human body (mostly hands), animal parts (teeth, trunk, tail), and machines. Thus, for sucking, sprightly pictures [by Tomie de Paola] and a sparing text that is largely questions ("Do you know about any machine that picks up things by sucking?") reveal a boy and girl drinking from the same oversized glass with soda straws, a bee and a butterfly sucking honey from a flower, and a water pump, which "sucks up water from the ground." Like the same team's **Who Needs Holes,** this fits no curricular niche, but it sets young minds to noticing in a scientific way and that's the best kind of start.

*A review of "Pick It Up," in* Kirkus Reviews, *Vol. XXXIX, No. 17, September 1, 1971, p. 948.*

The authors have taken the simple concept of how things are picked up and developed it into an attention-holding exploration for younger readers. Covered are grasping, hooking, sticking or stabbing, scooping, magnetism, etc.—all used by people, animals and machines in varying ways. The informative, easy-to-read text is illustrated with black, green, brown and blue drawings that are both amusing and very informative. There are no comparable titles available, so this one will be useful, especially in school libraries.

*Linda Lawson Clark, in a review of "Pick It Up," in* School Library Journal, *Vol. 18, No. 6, February, 1972, p. 55.*

---

## Winston Churchill: Lion of Britain　(1971)

Churchill was indeed the "Lion of Britain" but his character and charm are unfortunately absent from this otherwise sound volume. . . . The boyhood of the politician is well-drawn and relevant to young readers, but the albeit excellent military outlines and political descriptions overshadow the man. Nevertheless, the coverage is balanced and informative and there is a useful index. The writing is clear and accurate quotes from writings and remembrances are incorporated along with fictionalized dialogue. Black-and-white photographs are large and well placed in the text but comprise mainly portraits. Reynolds' *Winston Churchill* (Random, 1963) more successfully treats the many facets of Churchill's personality without any fictionizing; however, the Epsteins cover events through his death in 1965 whereas Reynolds' book ends with Churchill's resignation as prime minister in 1955.

> *Ken Haycock, in a review of "Winston Churchill: Lion of Britain," in* School Library Journal, *Vol. 19, No. 1, September, 1972, p. 130.*

### Two Sisters and Some Hornets  (with Dorrit Davis, 1973)

[Two Sisters and Some Hornets *was written by Beryl Epstein and Dorrit Davis.*]

A hornet buzzing around two old ladies on a porch stirs up long-standing resentments as each reviews her version of the events that transpired one long-ago afternoon at Aunt Hattie's farm. Conflicting cameo memories dominate facing pages as the sisters, revising the record from their rocking chairs above, argue with waning gentility (regressing at the end to repeated "she did not!" / "She did so!") about just how deliberate was Gertrude's speed in rescuing the younger, unbuttoned Agnes from a hornet-infested outhouse, and whether Aunt Hattie really had to cut the hornets out of Agnes' hair. [Illustrator] Rosemary Wells' oblique projection makes the most of the contradictory reconstructions, so that though you're bound to sympathize with touseled Agnes against her prim, complacent sister (coiffed as an adult in bee-hive elegance), you're never sure of anything—except the off-beat, on-target precision of the execution.

> *A review of "Two Sisters and Some Hornets," in* Kirkus Reviews, *Vol. XL, No. 17, September 1, 1972, p. 1020.*

In this clever picture book, two elderly sisters recall a disastrous trip to an outhouse during a visit to their aunt's farm at the turn of the century. . . . In each double-page spread, the younger sister as an old lady is shown in a small pen-and-ink sketch at the top of the left-hand page, the elder opposite her on the right page. Pencil-and-wash drawings in oval frames are set below them, juxtaposing each sister's conflicting recollection of the events. Both the narrative and the illustrations are fresh and engaging, but it seems unlikely that most six- to eight-year-old picture-book patrons will fully appreciate subtle contradictions in the accusing/defensive variant interpretations. (pp. 57-8)

> *Janet D. French, in a review of "Two Sisters and Some Hornets," in* School Library Journal, *Vol. 19, No. 6, February, 1973, pp. 57-8.*

### Hold Everything  (1973)

Sewing, glue, iron-on-patches, welding, hooks, zippers are ways of holding things together . . . and then there are teams and clubs for holding people together and the word "and" for holding words together. It's hard to imagine what children really learn from this kind of once-over except a way of observing and generalizing, but if the Epsteins' *Who Needs Holes* and *Pick It Up* were found to work as classroom conversation starters, then perhaps *Hold Everything* will be similarly functional.

> *A review of "Hold Everything," in* Kirkus Reviews, *Vol. XLI, No. 3, February 1, 1973, p. 119.*

What holds things together? Glue, thread, pins, staples, rivets, heat, etc. The cartoon-like pictures [by Tomie de Paola] illustrate the text clearly and have an ingenuous appeal, and the concept of the book is intriguing. The text is written simply, with statements and questions that are intended to lead the reader to closer investigation, "If you wanted to build a doghouse, would you use staples to hold the pieces of wood together? No, you would probably use nails or screws. Do you know the difference between them?" The text goes on to explain that difference; few of the topics are given this much attention, most being very brief. The book is weakened somewhat by the fact that the last few pages move to an area so different that it is jarring: people are held together by friendship, words are held together by the word "and." These are both unlike the major part of the book and unlike each other, and are given short shrift.

> *Zena Sutherland, in a review of "Hold Everything," in* Bulletin of the Center for Children's Books, *Vol. 27, No. 2, October, 1973, p. 26.*

*Hold Everything* is an interestingly written book on the way things are held together. Examples are chosen from a very broad range of areas (from birds' nests to human groups), and although the explanations are necessarily oversimplified, the book has substance and verve. The illustrations are delightful, and the authors provide some refreshing examples of projects and questions to be answered—some, in fact, where they have even resisted the temptation to provide ready answers.

> *Richard H. Weller, in a review of "Hold Everything," in* Appraisal: Children's Science Books, *Vol. 7, No. 1, Winter, 1974, p. 16.*

### Look in the Mirror  (1973)

In the same question-studded format as their *Pick It Up* and *Hold Everything* but less likely to spark further inquiry, the Epsteins cast a casual glance at different kinds of mirrors—curved, magnifying, double—and their different uses—for a rear view in a car, a tooth inspection by a dentist, a submarine's periscope, or to "collect" and "aim" light in a flashlight or telescope. But it's hard to imagine that directives such as "hold a mirror up in front of you, but off to one side. Does it show you what is happening behind your back?"—will sharpen anyone's habits of observation, or that the Epsteins' closing questions will stimulate investigation: "How many real mirrors do you have in your house? How many times a day do you look at yourself?" The authors conclude that "a mirror gives you a better image of yourself than a sheet of clear glass because you can't look through the mirror and see other things mixed up with your own mirror-image," but they offer neither a hint of the optics involved nor any inducement to independent reflection.

> *A review of "Look in the Mirror," in* Kirkus Reviews, *Vol. XLI, No. 20, October 15, 1973, p. 1164.*

An introduction to the mirror, its uses and methods of construction. Simple experiments deal with the mirror image, the concave, convex and magnifying mirrors. The uses of the rear-view mirror, the mirror in a flashlight, and the mirrors of a periscope are imaginatively explained. . . . Although the Epsteins offer an engaging concept book, Philip B. Carona's *Mirror on the Wall: How It Works* (Prentice-Hall, 1964) includes the relationship between light and the mirror and is more useful overall.

> *Sandra Weir, in a review of "Look in the Mirror," in* School Library Journal, *Vol. 20, No. 4, December, 1973, p. 42.*

### More Stories of Baseball Champions: In the Hall of Fame (1973)

Fans may be familiar with the Cy Young awards for pitching in each league but they're not likely to know that Denton ("Cy" was short for Cyclone) Young won over 500 games between 1890 and 1911. The other two Hall of Famers treated in short biographies here are better known: Napoleon Lajoie, the most graceful and effective second baseman of his era, and Tris Speaker, a great centerfield player. This title, a follow-up to the authors' **Baseball Hall of Fame: Stories of Champions,** includes too much fictional dialogue, but the brisk text, photographs (though some are now familiar), and three-color action drawings [by Victor Mays] help hold attention.

> *Robert Unsworth, in a review of "More Stories of Baseball Champions: In the Hall of Fame," in* School Library Journal, *Vol. 20, No. 7, March, 1974, p. 104.*

### A Year of Japanese Festivals   (1974)

Representative Japanese festivals, arbitrarily divided into five categories, are described in short, simple sentences with special attention to the fascinating mechanics of preparing floats, etc. However, the piecemeal treatment of the religious elements in the festivals results in a confusing and misleading picture of the Japanese as primitive and superstitious people. Although it lacks some of the enticing details, Vaughan's *Land and People of Japan* (Lippincott, rev. ed. 1972) is a much clearer view of Japanese life and customs.

> *Dora Jean Young, in a review of "A Year of*

*Japanese Festivals," in* School Library Journal, *Vol. 21, No. 7, March, 1975, p. 95.*

### Jackie Robinson: Baseball's Gallant Fighter   (1974)

An easy-to-read, fictionalized biography of the man whose successful baseball career paved the way for the admission of other Black players into the major leagues. The account focuses on the hardships Robinson endured as the first Black Major Leaguer, highlighting the key games of his career, but the authors do not neglect Robinson's personal life—e.g., his son's drug addiction, cure, and accidental auto death. This updates Rudeen's *Jackie Robinson* (Crowell, 1971), an easier biography for the same age group, and gives a more insightful picture of Robinson's feelings and aspirations.

> *Judith Silverman, in a review of "Jackie Robinson: Baseball's Gallant Fighter," in* School Library Journal, *Vol. 21, No. 8, April, 1975, p. 52.*

### Henry Aaron: Home-Run King   (1975)

A better-than-average Aaron biography. The subject is realistically portrayed, action scenes are effective, and the prose is basically smooth and unpretentious. If another book on Hank is needed to satisfy demand, this title fills the bill. Black-and-white photographs, most of them action shots, illustrate the work.

> *Judith Goldberger, in a review of "Henry Aaron: Home-Run King," in* The Booklist, *Vol. 72, No. 8, December 15, 1975, p. 577.*

### Mister Peale's Mammoth   (1977)

Canny folks, the Epsteins (as if we hadn't known before). Here's Charles Wilson Peale, who "took for granted that his children . . . would be interested in everything that interested him," inviting young Rembrandt and Raphael and Angelica ("each named after a famous painter") to watch him unpack and draw—bones, big bones. "Trying something new" is his greatest pleasure; besides, his drawings are going to be paid for, and celebrated painter that he is, "he was still regularly out of blast, as he put it." Another few pages, and you've learned that the new natural scientists, having rejected divine creation, "were coming close to discovering the idea of a constantly changing world" 75 years before Darwin's formulation of the theory of evolution. You know, too, that Mr. Peale is hoping that an American mammoth will turn up with bones at least as large as those of the recently disinterred Siberian mammoth: "He had been annoyed when a French scientist, the Count Buffon, declared that all animals in America were smaller than the animals of other continents." There follows, in time, the difficult, dogged search for the bones of the Great American Natural Wonder, and its reconstruction—spirited along by the reader's appreciation of its import and the host of motifs (literary, anecdotal, factual) introduced at the outset. . . . The stylish fancy of Margaret Cooper's *Great Bone Hunt* (1967) is not to be dismissed;

*Beryl Epstein at her desk.*

this, however, will capture the imagination of children with a more down-to-earth bent. It instructs as it delights.

*A review of "Mister Peale's Mammoth," in* Kirkus Reviews, *Vol. XLV, No. 9, May 1, 1977, p. 488.*

Charles Willson Peale was an American patriot and famous portrait artist. This is a passable account of how his interest in the new science of natural history drove him to make part of his home into the first museum in America and then to launch the country's first scientific expedition—to unearth the skeleton of an American mammoth. Several black-and-white illustrations [by Martin Avillez] add to the story, which moves along at a fast pace but, unfortunately, is unnecessarily fictionalized.

*Diane Holzheimer, in a review of "Mister Peale's Mammoth," in* School Library Journal, *Vol. 24, No. 1, September, 1977, p. 126.*

---

### Saving Electricity (1977)

A fictionalized beginning book on what electricity is and how it is harnessed for productive work, all centered around why a blackout occurs. Sources of electrical power and their relative effectiveness are discussed. Energy-saving tips are given for school, home, and industry. For ecology consciousness-raising aimed at the youngest readers, this book is a logical forerunner to the authors' more advanced *First Book of Electricity*.

*Shirley A. Smith, in a review of "Saving Electricity," in* School Library Journal, *Vol. 24, No. 6, February, 1978, p. 46.*

Since conservation of energy is necessary, teaching children to conserve is a good idea. By means of drawings [by Jeanne Bendick] and a simple text which tells about a utility blackout in a small town, the authors describe how electric energy is produced, distributed and used. The short, concise book will be of interest to very young children who have a beginning curiosity about nature and science. Older children, who perhaps have been frightened by the apparent complexities of science, will find the book instructive and helpful. The Epsteins illustrate some easy ways to save electricity, such as wearing a sweater to compensate for lowering a thermostat; running a dishwasher or washing machine only with a full load; avoiding opening a refrigerator frequently and for long periods of time. Alternate energy sources for the future are also discussed.

> *S. Reid Warren, Jr., in a review of "Saving Electricity," in* Science Books & Films, *Vol. XIII, No. 4, March, 1978, p. 224.*

---

### Dr. Beaumont and the Man with the Hole in His Stomach (1978)

Anyone with reservations about Dr. Beaumont as a children's book hero will be reassured by the Epsteins' very first words—introducing their "strange-but-true story" of two men whom "only an accident could have brought together." Army surgeon Beaumont's lust for fame is emphasized from the start, as is his snobbishness; and his French-Canadian patient/guinea pig-to-be is first seen racing his voyageur's bateau onto Mackinac Island and into a seasonal celebration which, as the Epsteins describe it, offers a vivid picture of the lusty voyageurs and a poignant one of what Alexis is soon to lose when an accidental gunshot wound leaves him near death. After he has healed, the hole in his stomach remains, "rather like a mouth pursed up, ready to whistle." And the doctor sees his opportunity—starving and stuffing, tricking, bullying, displaying, and virtually imprisoning Alexis as he dips bits of food into the hole to time their disintegration, removes gastric juices for test-tube digestion and analysis in Europe, lectures and writes of his findings, and achieves his fame. The experiments made spectacular news in the early 1800s and they are fascinating yet; and the Epsteins don't play up the exploitation angle but simply slip in well-chosen bits of evidence: when Alexis escapes to Canada, for example, Dr. Beaumont sets fur company agents to watching for the "ungrateful wretch"; later, having lured him back, he signs Alexis into the army so he can hold him with warnings of the fate of deserters. Alexis perhaps has the last laugh, outliving the doctor by 27 years, during which time he continues to be studied—but with "great courtesy" and "generous fees," for now he too is famous. From the pair who charmed us last year with **Mr. Peale's Mammoth,** another coup.

> *A review of "Dr. Beaumont and the Man with the Hole in His Stomach," in* Kirkus Reviews, *Vol. XLVI, No. 6, March 15, 1978, p. 308.*

A combination of accurate history, interesting science, and vivid storytelling, this is the account of a pioneer researcher and the man upon whom he based his discoveries. . . . The situation reveals much about earlier medicine, frontier life, class distinctions, and the conceits of human nature. Pen-and-ink drawings [by Joseph Scrofani] spark the text, and a selected bibliography attests to reliable sources. It is just such quirks of fate that do not appear in textbooks and that can addict readers to further inquiry.

> *Betsy Hearne, in a review of "Dr. Beaumont and the Man with the Hole in His Stomach," in* Booklist, *Vol. 74, No. 17, May 1, 1978, p. 1430.*

Most appropriate for fifth and sixth graders. **Dr. Beau-**

**mont** is a worthwhile effort. The medical information is presented clearly and accurately. The discussions of Alexis St. Martin's injury, and of the subsequent use that Beaumont made of his experiments with St. Martin, are tactfully handled. Readers should understand the nature, purpose and significance of the experiments. The authors use a narrative style which is quite satisfactory for the age group. Unfortunately, the illustrations are not as good as the text: On the map in the beginning of the book, the exact location of Mackinac Island is confusing. The picture of St. Martin on page 20 is poor; if the illustration had shown him from the side, the reader would be able to understand exactly where the injury was and where the stomach is in relation to the visible external parts of the body. The illustration of Beaumont sitting with his feet up, holding an implied alcoholic beverage and with his hand on a statue of some unidentified person (apparently a scientist), is both confusing and in poor taste. In spite of these criticisms, the overall impact of the book is good. Recommended as a reliable source of information on a fascinating topic, for collateral reading for youngsters interested in the medical field, and as a discussion starter in the classroom.

> *David T. Mininberg, in a review of "Dr. Beaumont and the Man with the Hole in His Stomach," in* Science Books & Films, *Vol. XIV, No. 4, March, 1979, p. 232.*

---

### What's Behind the Word   (1978)

After a brief history of English emphasizing where specific words have come from, the authors discuss the origin and development of writing and the sources of and rules for forming modern English words. The book ends with a brief dictionary of word and name origins and a collection of the names for groups of animals. The Epsteins' book is easy reading and is light on theory and heavy on the sources of individual words. It is suitable for the student just beginning to develop an interest in words and might serve as the next step after one of the very simple, elementary-school-level books on this list.

> *Robert Small, in a review of "What's Behind the Word," in* English Journal, *Vol. 67, No. 9, December, 1978, p. 64.*

---

### Secret in a Sealed Bottle: Lazarro Spallanzani's Work with Microbes   (1979)

Lazzaro Spallanzani, who falls between Van Leeuwenhoek and Pasteur, spent many years trying to disprove the popular theory that microbes were generated by spontaneous combustion. This is the tortuous central premise of the Epsteins' fictionalized account of his experiments. The slim series format with soft pen-and-wash illustrations [by Jane Sterret] is deceiving in this instance since the text is more difficult than it appears. Although containing more information on Spallanzani's contributions to science than most sources this does not measure up to other books by the authors nor other titles in the series. Both Isaac Asimov's *How Did We Find Out About Germs?* (Walker,

1973) and Paul De Kruif's *Microbe Hunters* (HBJ, 1932) offer livelier reading.

> *Margaret Bush, in a review of "Secret in a Sealed Bottle: Lazzaro Spallanzani's Work with Microbes," in* School Library Journal, *Vol. 25, No. 8, April, 1979, p. 54.*

The title refers to the challenge Spallanzani assumed in order to prove that microorganisms—animalcules to him—could certainly not arise in broth unless living progenitors were present. The book is mainly a biography of Spallanzani, one which also discusses spontaneous generation and the state of science in the eighteenth century. . . . A comparison of the book with an encyclopedia article revealed no essential facts to be missing. It is hard to say with certainty, however, which parts of the book are factual and which are fictionalized. Obviously, the authors intended readers to absorb the essence rather than the detail of carefully worked out descriptions and conversations. The book is worthwhile for its setting, for its demonstration of Spallanzani's reasoning, and for giving a sense of how a prodigious scientist worked. . . . A glossary, a bibliography, and a list of scientists are included; but a list of primary sources would have been interesting and helpful.

> *A review of "Secret in a Sealed Bottle: Lazzaro Spallanzani's Work with Microbes," in* The Horn Book Magazine, *Vol. LV, No. 3, June, 1979, p. 340.*

It says much about Lazzaro Spallanzani that, having finished his studies in natural history, he was able to continue them and support himself by taking a post as a professor of Latin, Greek, and mathematics. One of the great scientists of the 18th century, Spallanzani was the first to prove, by his research, that the microbes known to the scientific world since the invention of the microscope did not appear through spontaneous generation. The authors give a dramatic account of his repeated tests, improvised and repeatedly improved procedures, and his elation when he could finally announce to fellow scientists that the "little beasties" came from their own kind, not—as one group held—from nowhere but borne by air. The book covers other research done by Spallanzani, focusing on his scientific achievements rather than his personal life; it is written with vitality in a narrative but not unduly fictionalized style, and it shows clearly how scientists build a body of knowledge by trial, error, exchange of opinions, and objective evaluation of their own research findings. (pp. 189-90)

> *Zena Sutherland, in a review of "Secret in a Sealed Bottle: Lazzaro Spallanzani's Work with Microbes," in* Bulletin of the Center for Children's Books, *Vol. 32, No. 11, July-August, 1979, pp. 189-90.*

---

### *She Never Looked Back: Margaret Mead in Samoa* (1980)

As you'd expect from the Epsteins, this is no birth-to-death biography but a very close and human portrait of 23-year-old Margaret (or, as the Samoans called her, Ma-

kelita) on her first visit to Samoa. The book begins, astutely, with Makelita's ordeal: the young woman, who "earlier that same year . . . had faced a difficult exam for her doctorate degree," must demonstrate her new serving skills at the village *kava*-drinking ceremony. (Can she handle the inflections of the language? Will she stumble? Or miss one of the men's cup names? Would she shame the chief who has given her a princess title?) After that opening, there are only a few pages on Mead's education and choice of career before we are back with her in Samoa, learning with her about the little girls' babysitting responsibilities and their older sisters' happy freedom, and experiencing with her the fierce New Year's Day hurricane that necessitated the rebuilding of the entire village. The Epsteins don't lecture or summarize, but through homey detail they convey a sense of the young anthropologist's seriousness, the already changing culture she studied, and above all the friendly relationship that grew up between Makelita and the villagers of all ages. Following a loving goodby to the island, one short chapter rounds out the life. Then, after pointing up what we have all learned from Mead's observations of another way of life, the book skips to the 1970s for her "joyous return" to Samoa, her new preface to the 1928 book, and the five-day 75th birthday party celebrated by the American Museum—an event that says all that's needed about the guest of honor's fame, success, and beloved status in her own community. (pp. 290-91)

> *A review of "She Never Looked Back: Margaret Mead in Samoa," in* Kirkus Reviews, *Vol. XLVIII, No. 5, March 1, 1980, pp. 290-91.*

Most of this book describes Mead's experiences in Samoa, although the second chapter tells about her life leading up to those experiences and the ninth chapter very briefly describes the rest of her life. The authors use a story format, with dialogues, to tell about events that took place. The experience of anthropological field work is well depicted, and the results of Mead's study of Samoan life are presented simply. The authors obviously have some anthropological background and combine this with simple writing to produce a neat little book for young people.

> *William H. Anderson, Jr., in a review of "She Never Looked Back: Margaret Mead in Samoa," in* Science Books & Films, *Vol. 16, No. 4, March, 1981, p. 217.*

The book is not a biography. Mead's life, other than the time spent in Samoa, is given very little attention, and the complexities and contradictions that were Margaret Mead are rarely even hinted at. In addition, little is included about the field of anthropology other than a short definition and occasional references to the dedication and sincerity of the anthropologist.

What the book does cover and cover very well is *Coming of Age in Samoa*. Taking a view which is primarily nonjudgmental, the author uses Mead's experiences as a basis for discussing cultural differences and the need to respect cultures different from one's own. The book also describes the problems of living and working in a different culture and the effort that an outsider must make to be accepted.

A few stereotypes and patronizing conversations about "primitive people" are included in the book, although generally Mead either refutes these comments or is upset and embarrassed by them. In general, Samoa is portrayed as an idyllic place. This unfortunately weakens what could have been a very valuable aspect of the book. The book discusses the differences between female adolescent experiences in Samoa and in the U.S., explaining why the experience is so much less painful and less traumatic in Samoa. Unfortunately, the Samoa of Mead's study seems so far removed from the U.S. that it will be very hard for the young reader to relate to much of the information.

The book is an interesting tale of other lives, other places and other times; it attempts to teach readers respect for other cultures and to provide insight into the powers of environment in forming "human nature." . . . *She Never Looked Back* deserves to be read.

> *Patricia B. Campbell, in a review of "She Never Looked Back: Margaret Mead in Samoa," in* Interracial Books for Children Bulletin, *Vol. 12, Nos. 4 & 5, 1981, p. 35.*

---

### Kids in Court: The ACLU Defends Their Rights   (1982)

Ten meaty and riveting accounts of court cases, many ending up in Supreme Court, in which the American Civil Liberties Union defended the rights of minors. The cases are preceded by an enlightening introductory chapter on the ACLU's history, founder, principles, and criteria for taking on a case. Most of the cases pit students against representatives of their public schools, which the ACLU recognizes as, while in session, "closed institutions" (like prisons and mental hospitals) in which the inmates are confined by force and have little or no control over their lives. Adults will recognize several cases from newspaper accounts: the free-speech victory of high school Vietnam War protesters who wore black armbands to school; the "right to privacy" ruling against a "potential drug abuse" test that would classify eighth graders on the basis of family, social, and personal qualities; the New Jersey girl investigated by the FBI for writing to the Socialist Labor Party on a class assignment. (An address mixup sent the letter to the Socialist Workers' party, which was under mail surveillance.) A heartening aspect of this last case is that the school officials were the first to recognize the violation of her rights. Most moving and outrageous is the obviously racially tinged strip-search of a Bayside, New York, high school girl who was not told the object of the search (nothing was found, though the searcher claimed in court that she had spotted a marijuana pipe) and who cried whenever she had to recall the offense. This case was complicated by the jury's inconsistency and clear misunderstanding of the issues. Without seeming to digress from the narrative, the Epsteins keep the issues clearly in sight throughout the accounts, so that irrelevant considerations which often cloud such controversies don't intrude. (The searched girl *was* guilty of staying inside during a fire drill, and she had been caught smoking marijuana on a previous occasion; two boys denied due process *had* made the obscene phone call that got them arrested; the off-campus kids' newspaper that high school authorities tried to kill had no literary

or journalistic value.) Another important point the Epsteins make clear is that these battles are never won once and for all. Appropriately, the Epsteins end by affirming that it is important for young people to know their rights and protest their violation. This book should contribute to that awareness, and getting kids to read it won't be a problem.

> *A review of "Kids in Court: The ACLU Defends Their Rights," in* Kirkus Reviews, *Vol. L, No. 9, May 1, 1982, p. 561.*

This well-documented study of the American Civil Liberties Union as champion of minors begins with a history of the ACLU and then describes 11 significant test cases in which the organization helped young people claim their constitutional rights. These include the 1969 Tinker case, in which students wearing black armbands to protest U.S. involvement in Vietnam were suspended from their high school; the "strip search" in 1978 of a 15-year-old girl suspected of carrying a marijuana pipe; an "invasion of privacy" case involving a proposed project designed by a psychiatrist to determine "potential drug abusers" among eighth graders; and the suspension of four energetic high-school students who published a satirical newspaper (a case similar to the one fictionalized in Susan Beth Pfeffer's *A Matter of Principle,* Delacorte, 1982). The seven other cases are also clearly and unemotionally described by the authors, who believe that all citizens (especially minors) should know their rights and be prepared to fight for them if necessary. The Epsteins' presentation is far more logical and effective than Peter Sgroi's in *Blue Jeans and Black Robes* (Messner, 1979), which covers some of the same cases, but in an overly detailed and confusing manner. *Kids in Court* is a valuable addition to Robert Loeb's excellent *Your Legal Rights as a Minor* (Watts, 1974), a legal handbook that defines the specific rights of minors in a straightforward way but does not describe the cases that led to each court decision. The Epsteins' useful book shows how the U.S. courts work to provide justice for all. (pp. 124-25)

> *Wendy Dellett, in a review of "Kids in Court: The ACLU Defends Their Rights," in* School Library Journal, *Vol. 28, No. 10, August, 1982, pp. 124-25.*

A very informative and readable survey of juvenile rights based on ACLU case histories. Starting appropriately with the Gault decision in 1967 which guarantees juvenile due process, the Epsteins vividly and clearly present eleven landmark cases that have made significant impact on interpretation of the Constitution. A useful bonus is a historical overview of the ACLU and while not totally unbiased, it is an excellent primer chapter on this controversial organization.

Not a book to hand to a kid checking his legal rights at the local level, this will be tremendously useful in school and public libraries and should be required reading for every volunteer, caseworker and custodial staff working in juvenile corrections. It should also act as a nudge to the ACLU to update their guides to the rights of young people and students (Avon, 1977 & 1973).

*Susan B. Madden, in a review of "Kids in Court: The ACLU Defends Their Rights," in* Voice of Youth Advocates, *Vol. 5, No. 4, October, 1982, p. 53.*

## What's for Lunch? The Eating Habits of Seashore Creatures  (1985)

Even though there are numerous books on seashore and marine animals which include the same information as **What's for Lunch?,** this book is a unique and fascinating discussion of the eating habits of these animals and of the tactics they employ to keep from being eaten. From 1 to 4 pages are devoted to each of 20 creatures including various birds, crustaceans, jellyfish and mollusks. The clear, succinct writing style describing the sometimes bizarre behavior patterns of these animals (the reddish egret spreads its wings while standing in shallow water to attract schools of small fish mistaking the shadow as a safe hiding spot; the sea squirt pumps as much as 45 gallons of water through its body to collect plankton to feed on) makes this book useful as well as entertaining.

*Cynthia M. Sturgis, in a review of "What's for Lunch? The Eating Habits of Seashore Creatures," in* School Library Journal, *Vol. 32, No. 3, November, 1985, p. 84.*

A useful introduction to the feeding behaviors of organisms commonly encountered in seashore visits. Twenty creatures from worms to ospreys are highlighted with a lively, informative style. . . . (pp. 38-9)

The book does not take a false step until the last sentence inquiring if readers will look for food as these shore animals do "or will you stick to the usual habit of human beings, and take sandwiches with you." The usual habits of human beings is to forage and fish along margins, and a brief chapter devoted to our seashore harvesting habits would have made a more appropriate conclusion. (p. 39)

*Don Lessem, in a review of "What's for Lunch?: The Eating Habits of Seashore Creatures," in* Appraisal: Science Books for Young People, *Vol. 19, No. 4, Fall, 1986, pp. 38-9.*

## Tunnels  (1985)

Nearly every 10-year-old, at one time or another, constructs a tunnel into a hillside, or digs a cave, or plans a secret underground fort. For such burrowers this is an ideal book for days off on account of rain. The Epsteins detail the problems and solutions to some of the world's great engineering feats: Greek and Roman aqueducts, the Mont Frejus tunnel through the Alps, Brunel's "shield" for digging in silt and sand, the Hoosac tunnel, and more. Period pictures enliven an already imaginative text, and the result makes this a particularly fine book for any would-be engineer.

*Michael Dirda, in a review of "Tunnels," in* Book World—The Washington Post, *February 9, 1986, p. 10.*

Tunnels are at once a bit scary, mysterious, and intriguing. In them we are under the earth or sea, traveling through what was once impenetrable. How is this possible? Are we safe? The Epsteins' interesting book clearly explains the how of tunnels but goes further to show us the why, when, and who. The authors are able to simplify the various tunnel-building methods so that they are easily understood; yet the reader never loses sight of the real feats of engineering necessary for tunneling. The dangers of tunnel construction are clearly outlined but not overly emphasized, and the authors maintain a balance in presenting historical, technical, and biographical information. The text is arranged by type of tunnel: aqueduct, canal, railroad, underwater, subway, and escape. Illustrative material both enhances the appearance of the book and is helpful in showing construction technique and machinery. Glossary and index.

*Elizabeth S. Watson, in a review of "Tunnels," in* The Horn Book Magazine, *Vol. LXII, No. 2, March-April, 1986, p. 219.*

A good book should enrich and deepen the reader's experience. This, I believe, is as true for books on technology as for any other kind of book. **Tunnels** is such a book. The reader will admire the ingenuity and persistence of the tunnel builders in the face of obstacles that almost always require novel and imaginative solutions. The reader will also learn to respect the laborers, many of whom gave their lives in the building of tunnels, we now consider among the ordinary artifacts of our time. They will be ordinary no longer. Turning the tap to draw water, traveling under a river, through a mountain, or under the city, will become a new, a more significant experience. . . .

I wish that the book could have been a little longer. There would then have been room for more than just two maps. We could have even more photographs, especially from the collection at the Hoosac Tunnel Museum. Most important, we could learn something about the science related to this work: geology, the pressure of water and air, human physiology, mechanics. Perhaps the authors will write another book to illuminate the science of tunneling as well as they have illuminated its history and technology.

*Lazer Goldberg, in a review of "Tunnels," in* Appraisal: Science Books for Young People, *Vol. 19, No. 4, Fall, 1986, p. 38.*

## Jackpot of the Beagle Brigade  (1987)

The authors introduce Jackpot, a diminutive beagle whose job is to sniff out agricultural products entering the country illegally through the customs area at JFK International Airport. Photographs [by George Ancona] feature Jackpot weaving his way through the customs crowds with his handler, Hal Fingerman. It's all in a day's work for Jackpot to nab contraband items such as deliberately hidden fruit, innocently carried gifts from relatives, or a can of perfectly legal lime-scented shaving cream. . . . This book is likely to be a popular browsing item; Jackpot makes an appealing sleuth whose specialty will be news to most readers.

*CHILDREN'S LITERATURE REVIEW, Vol. 26*                    EPSTEIN

*Denise M. Wilms, in a review of "Jackpot of the Beagle Brigade," in* Booklist, *Vol. 83, No. 17, May 1, 1987, p. 1366.*

---

## Bugs for Dinner? The Eating Habits of Neighborhood Creatures  (1989)

Realistic black-and-white drawings [by Walter Gaffney-Kessell] reveal a frog with tongue outstretched to seize a passing fly; a praying mantis defending itself against an intimidating snake; a diagram of an ant's internal organs. These and other illuminating illustrations attractively space the highly readable and informative descriptions of how backyard and neighborhood critters gather their food. As the Epsteins note a squirrel's industriousness, detail the honeybees' complex food-gathering and sharing techniques, and outline mosquitoes' multistaged development, they also remark on the human sport and pest control that interfere with nature's order. A first-rate addition to science collections.

*Ellen Mandel, in a review of "Bugs for Dinner? The Eating Habits of Neighborhood Creatures," in* Booklist, *Vol. 86, No. 7, December 1, 1989, p. 742.*

The natural science information in this book is clearly laid out, accurately stated and surprisingly comprehensive. Each familiar animal is covered in three to four easily read pages, but the amount of information contained therein rivals many a science text. This is possible because the focus of the book is limited to food preferences and food gathering, as the title suggests. Even young children will know most of the thirteen "neighborhood creatures" presented, and this is another plus. As every teacher knows, a chance encounter with a squirrel, mosquito, pigeon or worm can become a real learning moment for children. The authors have made it easy to take such a moment and delve a little deeper without dampening the excitement of a new discovery. **Bugs for Dinner** gives answers that will satisfy early elementary school students. This book deserves to be in every classroom and will serve nicely as a reference for teachers, too. (pp. 23-4)

*Jonah Roll, in a review of "Bugs for Dinner?: The Eating Habits of Neighborhood Creatures," in* Appraisal: Science Books for Young People, *Vol. 23, No. 1, Winter, 1990, pp. 23-4.*

After admirably describing the ways in which seashore creatures find food in **What's for Lunch?,** the Epsteins demonstrate equal success in this companion volume by focusing on such common animals as squirrels, sparrows, spiders, and ants. Managing to telescope a wide range of information into each chapter, the Epsteins' breezy survey helps children understand an important principle of nature: every creature, if it is not vigilant, can be another creature's meal. Always entertaining, presenting an astounding variety of intriguing facts—for instance, dragonflies can hold more than one hundred mosquitoes in their mouths at a given time—this readable overview of the food-finding methods of familiar animals will enrich all future encounters with them.

*Ellen Fader, in a review of "Bugs for Dinner?: The Eating Habits of Neighborhood Creatures," in* The Horn Book Magazine, *Vol. LXVI, No. 1, January-February, 1990, p. 87.*

# Janosch

## 1931-

(Pseudonym of Horst Eckert) Polish-born German author and illustrator of fiction, picture books, poetry, and short stories, and reteller.

Major works include *Bollerbam* (1969), *The Magic Auto* (1971), *Not Quite as Grimm* (1975), *The Trip to Panama* (1978), *The Big Janosch Book of Fun and Verse* (1980).

Regarded as one of Germany's most prominent writers and artists for young readers, Janosch is considered an especially imaginative creator of fantasies and satires which range from gently humorous to darkly parodic and reflect his pacifistic philosophy; critic Horst Künnemann writes of Janosch, "In his very own area, his domain of children's and picture books, he remains without competition." A prolific author who is internationally popular, Janosch writes stories, verses, and rhymes—both as individual works and in collections—which feature human characters, anthropomorphic animals and objects, anecdotal texts, and childlike drawings and paintings; often writing as a traditional moralist whose lessons, both overt and implicit, are presented in updated folktales, he is acknowledged as the author of the first German antiwar book with a negative ending, *Bollerbam*. Janosch is also well known as a parodist, adding his distinctive stamp to such familiar literary works as Aesop's fables, the fairy tales of Jakob and Wilhelm Grimm, and Daniel Defoe's *Robinson Crusoe*. Although some of his books depict sadness, cruelty, and death and are considered overly sophisticated for the young, Janosch is noted for stressing his belief in the benefits of creativity and play as well as for including such attributes as love, friendship, bravery, and security in his works.

Several of Janosch's first books to have been published in English are moral fables with themes of antiviolence; perhaps the most well known is *Bollerbam*. In this story, the cross-eyed title character, who is the only straight-shooter in his kingdom's army, desires to have his eyes uncrossed; when his wish is granted by a magical pacifistic bird during a war, Bollerbam, who can no longer shoot, is captured by the enemy and eventually dies. Janosch often utilizes a variety of animals, such as bears, rabbits, and mice, as protagonists in his stories; among his most popular works are the picture books about Little Bear and Little Tiger, lovable companions who live in a riverside community and have a series of adventures that lead them back home or show their affection for each other; throughout the books, Janosch includes a pull-toy duck that lightly parodies the actions of his characters. He also blends his stories and fables with verse, jingles, and rhymes in several collections which feature his characteristic animal characters and irreverent humor. As an illustrator, Janosch is often lauded for his exuberant black and white drawings and paintings in double-page spreads, works noted both for their naive quality and the artist's skillful use of color

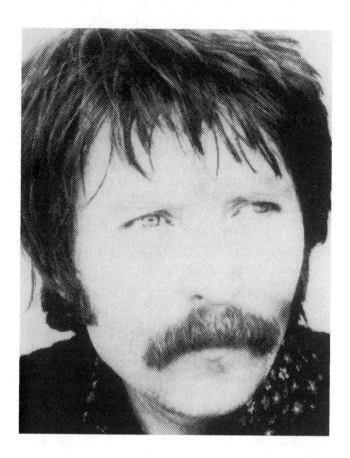

and design; Janosch has also provided the pictures for books by such authors as Hans Baumann, James Krüss, Beverly Cleary, Jack Prelutsky, and Walter D. Edmonds. In addition to creating his juvenile literature, Janosch is an adult novelist and painter who has been exhibited frequently. He was named a highly commended illustrator for the Hans Christian Andersen Medal for his body of work in 1972, won the Deutscher Jungendliteraurpreis for *Oh, wie schön ist Panama* (*The Trip to Panama*) in 1979, and received both a Gold Medal for *The Big Janosch Book of Fun and Verse* and a plaque for his art at the Biennale of Illustrations Bratislava.

(See also *Something about the Author*, Vol. 8 and *Contemporary Authors*, Vols. 37-40, rev. ed.)

---

## GENERAL COMMENTARY

**Bettina Hürlimann**

A naïvety in the interpretation of stories through pen-drawing is . . . found in the work of Janosch who has produced a quantity of picture-stories which look almost like sketch-books but which have great charm. There is a genuineness about the simplicity of his drawing which attests the directness of experience or of childhood memories. On the whole his work appeals more to grown-ups than to children, but this is not to deny that he has the talents to create good picture-books for children. (p. 12)

> *Bettina Hürlimann, "Picture Books in German-Speaking Countries," in her* Picture-Book World, *edited and translated by Brian W. Alderson, Oxford University Press, London, 1968, pp. 8-17.*

## Horst Künnemann

Author and artist Horst Eckert, whose approximately 50 picture books have been published since 1960 under the name "Janosch", has a special place among the picture book makers in the German Federal Republic. This special position: Janosch is extraordinarily imaginative and productive; Janosch is very successful and has been met with considerable international resonance in both the East and the West; Janosch's name has appeared several times on the "honour list" of the "German Juvenile Book Prize". . . . What are Janosch's particularities in particular, what characterizes his picture book fantasy? Janosch paints with pretended naiveté. His coloured pictures seem naive, almost primitive and like those of a Sunday painter. As the child looks at *Heute um neune hinter der Scheune* (Tonight at Nine) *Onkel Poppoff kann auf Bäume fliegen* (Uncle Poppoff can fly on trees) or the most successful *Das Auto hier heißt Ferdinand* (This auto's name is Ferdinand), he has the impression that he too can paint like this!

The same is true of the pen-and-ink drawings Janosch has sketched for his own stories *Poppoff und Piezke, Leo Zauberfloh* (Leo-magic-flea) and the tragi-comical horse story *Valek.* This technique too is closely related to many features of the child's creations and is like the broad bristle-brush technique of the coloured pictures. Only when his paintings for adults are viewed does one see that Janosch produces his work for children with deliberation, that he holds his fantasy under control and that he only uses his repertory of montage, built-in bubbles and letters and numbers as alienation effects for adults.

How manifold Janosch's talents are—both materially and formally—is also proved by the fact that he published an extremely vital novel for adults three years ago at the Bitter publishing house in Recklinghausen—*Cholonek oder; Der liebe Gott aus Lehm* (Cholonek or: God of clay). . . . (pp. 18-19)

Janosch's fantasy: the artist's imagination has drawn partially upon his Upper Silesian home; the Polish and Slav sounding names are reminiscent of it. The names of the towns and countryside, usually fictitious, could easily be found on an imaginary map of the Beskids and the Carpathian Mountains, of the eastern industrial area behind Beuthen and Kattowitz. In his novel *Cholonek* he attempted to create a novel like the Danzig *Tin Drum* by Günter Grass from the southeastern point of view. In his very own area, his domain of children's and picture books, he remains without competition.

It is not enough for Janosch's fantasy to make up a new place and the people who live there, which are exclusively

the product of the artist's imagination. Janosch has also discovered a great many mad stories and escapades, original counting verses and humorous rhymes. If it is characteristic for creative fantasy that it be original and singular in nature, "balanced" and humorous, full of jokes and tricks, then Janosch has discovered an immense wealth of new, often comical and absurd stories and made them a part of contemporary German children's literature. The fact that the world shines out of his pictures and texts is probably due to the extent to which his work is known on an international scale. Janosch books and Janosch pictures are seen by children in Czechoslovakia and in Japan, in the Soviet Union and in South Africa. Janosch belongs among the few German picture book artists who are able to live and exist from the returns of their work for children. To date Janosch's books have been published throughout the world in an edition of more than half a million. (p. 19)

What kind of stories does Janosch write? Children land among several showbooths, are given dark glasses and led into the land of their desires (*Herr Wuzzel und sein Zauberkarussel—Mr. Wuzzel*). In a little village two rascals spread the rumour that a lion has escaped. The frightened inhabitants hide in a tunnel system they have dug. Only one sceptic stays outside and is promptly devoured by an escaped lion (*Leo Zauberfloh*). City children of dreary surroundings encounter a strange magician in a garbage dump. He helps them fly away into the realm of fantasy where they tame lions and sharks with magic tricks (**Flieg Vogel Flieg**—Fly bird fly).

Whoever has followed the discussions and arguments which have been smouldering the German Federal Republic for several years between children's literature and the social sciences—a discussion which has also been led in other countries with similar questions—is able to ask: where is the reference to the child's reality and the everyday experiences of young people in such flights of the imagination? Where are the child's interests perceived and solidarity, readiness to take part in conflict, critical consciousness and individuality awakened?

Janosch has never written a book which can be said to be of a primarily political or indoctrinating nature. What he has attained however—and this is the reason for his unequivocal success—is to have brought the child's imagination and fancy into motion. Not only have many children throughout the world received possibilities for "climbing out" of their dreary environment, but new opportunities for living, unfamiliar places for playing and being free are also opened up for them. Creative fantasy and imagination, mobility and creativity doubtlessly belong among the virtues of the democratic way of life. And in this sphere Janosch has attained a great deal and will continue to do so, since his imaginative and creative power have by no means run out!

In the past years Janosch has worked in the most varying areas and in very many different ways. . . . He has illustrated text books, readers and poetry collections, has drawn book-covers and posters, has created a calendar and paperback and record covers with his own picture book themes. His main theme of the eastern eccentric has never been enough for him, but rather he constantly seeks and finds new subjects and motifs. For instance, he dared to write the first German anti-war book with a negative ending—the death of the hero (**Böllerbam und der Vogel—Bollerbam**). His variation on an original German theme, **Janosch erzählt Grimms Märchen** (Janosch tells Grimms' fairy tales), belongs to the most contested and most successful books of 1972. Here the step into "critical consciousness" was doubtlessly made. The hermetic garment of power and suppression, of old fashioned, vindictive administration of justice and inflexible fixation of roles in the fairy tales was perforated. Janosch succeeded at least in irritating the believing fairy tale listener and destroying his faithful identification with his "electrified" Little Red Riding Hood and his utilization of modern themes of full motorization and technical ballast. Janosch brought here something of that which began to appear in his newest picture books: nothing is inflexible and established forever. Everything must be doubted and critically examined. Much in life is a game. Things and problems must also be seen from the lighter side. The wonderful and difficult sphere of the creative is opened up for children over this position. Here books, tones, texts and sounds are only the reason for creating one's self, for painting one's pictures, for singing songs and poems one has made up one's self, for making one's own laws, which are only given up when they collide with the interests of others. Here Janosch has given children a new place to play with their own initiative and spontaneity and to live together in friendship. (pp. 19-21)

> *Horst Künnemann, "Janosch; or, An Excursion into Fantasy in the Modern Picture Book," in* Bookbird, *Vol. XI, No. 2, June 15, 1973, pp. 18-23.*

## TITLE COMMENTARY

### Just One Apple   (1966)

A poor peasant wishes for "just one apple" to grow on his tree. Finally, one grows so large that no one wants to buy it. He is relieved of this curious burden only when the king confiscates the apple in order to bribe a dragon who is harrassing his subjects. Although the dragon succumbs, after the fashion of Snow White, there is no fanfare for the little peasant, who simply makes an even more modest wish for next year. The somewhat enigmatic ending and the complex plot may appeal only to the more mature child, but the drawings are a delight. The paintings of cold purple nights and blue windy days have the bright freshness of children's drawings, and are so well reproduced the brush strokes are almost tangible.

> *Jean C. Thomson, in a review of "Just One Apple," in* School Library Journal, *Vol. 12, No. 9, May, 1966, p. 144.*

Poor Walter wished for just one apple on his bare apple tree and then nurtured it so that it grew into a monster apple so big that nobody at the market wanted it. This rare phenomenon makes a good modern fairy tale, complete with king and dragon (which is slain by choking on the giant apple). There are some charming anachronisms: The

king's detectives in their black suits are like gangsters from the thirties. The illustrations set a model example for application of the principles of modern painting to book illustration.

> *Barbara Novak O'Doherty, in a review of "Just One Apple," in* The New York Times Book Review, *May 22, 1966, p. 26.*

### Tonight at Nine   (1967)

One by one the animals, and Farmer Freidel, assemble for the evening concert: Bruno the dog barks and drums, Greta Goat trumpets clear, Katie the pig can only grunt "Queek, queek," etc. Announcing each entrance is a jingle jangle rhyme and, on the facing page, a full-color drawing, deliberately childlike, of the animal disporting himself. The illustrations have some verve; the verses are vapid; the concept is vacuous.

> *A review of "Tonight at Nine," in* Kirkus Service, *Vol. XXXV, No. 13, July 1, 1967, p. 735.*

Full of joy, the illustrations combine the directness of children's art with sophisticated design, humor, and sparkling color. Although the text is light-weight, Janosch's art makes it a better choice than many picture books for reading aloud.

> *Barbara Gibson, in a review of "Tonight at Nine," in* School Library Journal, *Vol. 14, No. 1, September, 1967, p. 110.*

### Bollerbam   (1969)

Because he's cross-eyed, Bollerbam is the only straight-shooting gunner in the bodyguard of King Bimbam of Margarine. But the story doesn't play straight with him or with the reader when it switches from papier mache farce to moral fable: in the intermittent, unprovoked war on Buttercupland, Bollerbam is the key combatant until a peace-loving bird, failing to dissuade him, grants him the one wish— to uncross his eyes—that will make him vincible. No longer a sure shot and weighted down by his medals, Bollerbam is captured by the Buttercuppers, imprisoned, and fed on bread and water until he dies. "No flowers grew on his grave, no birds sang to him, and it served him right." A scurvy trick, and hardly a peaceful settlement.

> *A review of "Bollerbam," in* Kirkus Reviews, *Vol. XXXVII, No. 16, August 15, 1969, p. 851.*

The latest offering of Janosch is, as always, noteworthy for the exuberance of the illustrations which are similar in technique and freshness to his other offerings: **Just One Apple; Tonight at Nine.** Unfortunately, this anti-war story is neither gay, logical nor sufficiently magical to promote a "willing suspension of disbelief." . . .

Unmistakably reminiscent of Cowley's The Duck in the Gun, published earlier this year, this has more weight because of the color and flamboyance of the illustrations. The tools of war look so beautiful that they are bound to

*From* Dear Snowman, *written and illustrated by Janosch.*

attract gun-conscious little boys, thus visually contradicting the story's intent. (pp. 71-2)

*Margaret Riddell, in a review of "Bollerbam,"
in* School Library Journal, *Vol. 17, No. 6, February, 1970, pp. 71-2.*

[*Bollerbam*] has a pleasing verbal style, an honourable theme, and pictures in a deceivingly childlike manner: swirling paint lines, trees that are thick round blobs on bright pink trunks, birds with paintbox stripes, expressive guileless faces of men and sheep (and an odd tiger in the undergrowth). Bollerbam is a "small blue soldier" with a curly moustache, in charge of a small cannon in the army of King Bimbam of Margarine.

> The noise was very loud and unpleasant, but King Bimbam, like all kings, was vain and stupid, so the thunder of the cannon was like music to him, and he loved it.

Because he loves the noises so much, he orders a war, and the Margariners launch an attack on their pastoral neighbours the Buttercuppers. It is an anti-war tract, of course—though it could just be that the bang-bang of the wicked guns, and even the all-fall-down mortalities, have a lure of their own for the young. To be sure, the gun-happy Bollerbam comes to a real bad end. And, as the book firmly states, "it served him right". (p. 716)

*"Failed Magicians and Flying Baths," in* The Times Literary Supplement, *No. 3566, July 2, 1970, pp. 716-17.*

### Mr. Wuzzel (1969)

**Mr. Wuzzel** is the owner of a little, old roundabout. Janosch describes the excitement his arrival arouses in one small village, and paints imaginary scenes to match four

children's dreams as they ride in turn on the carousel. A nice idea, ploddingly executed: one is reminded of Bottom among the fairies.

*"Picture Parade," in* The Times Literary Supplement, *No. 3536, December 4, 1969, p. 1392.*

### The Thieves and the Raven (1970)

More amusing than the robbers' increasingly audacious crimes (even than their offkey singing that keeps the animals awake) are the futile attempts of the populace to capture them. Slickest of all is their undoing, stemming from their appetite for ravens' eggs "and sometimes even a baby raven": Wenzel, king of the ravens, steals the watch of one, which sets them to fighting, then caw-caws, which makes them think "Cops, cops" and sets them to running. There's a jauntiness about the whole, names (namely Fobrokel, Spobrokel and Lefty) that rate a separate laugh, and a sly last line; also Janosch's typically brash, cheerful pictures. Hardly distinctive but certainly entertaining.

*A review of "The Thieves and the Raven," in* Kirkus Reviews, *Vol. XXXVIII, No. 2, January 15, 1970, p. 54.*

The themes of the weak triumphing over the strong and thieves falling out are not new, and this picture book plods through the classic folk-tale pattern. Three rough thieves move into the forest, plundering the countryside and neatly eluding all efforts to capture them. When they discover how good ravens' eggs are to eat, the King of the Ravens devises and carries out a plan to make the thieves angry with and frightened of each other, whereupon they each run off in a separate direction. This exploit is limited to the final quarter of the book, with the first three quarters devoted to a less than exciting list of the robbers' activities in terrorizing the villagers, stealing food, drinking, and carrying off maidens. The vivid illustrations have a child-like quality that appeals, but they are not enough to offset the stiffness of the telling or the dullness of the thieves.

> *Elizabeth Haynes, in a review of "The Thieves and the Raven," in* School Library Journal, *Vol. 17, No. 1, September, 1970, p. 94.*

### Dear Snowman   (1970)

Janosch obviously let himself go in this story. He threw all plausibility out the window and had himself a picnic describing and illustrating this history of a snowman who liked people. The result is a warm and lively book that will delight all snow-bound children.

> *A review of "Dear Snowman," in* Publishers Weekly, *Vol. 198, No. 21, November 23, 1970, p. 39.*

Striking color illustrations on wide, glossy paper give this picture book immediate appeal. Johnny, a very engaging snowman, is pictured in surroundings which convey a real feeling for winter. The illustrator's East European background is effectively revealed in his pictures of people and houses. One might wish, however, that his pen were as skillful as his paint brush, for the text (telling of Johnny's visit with a little girl on her birthday and how he mysteriously disappears in the night) is only mildly interesting and overlong considering the scant incident. Nevertheless, this will not detract from the enjoyment which the book will provide for small children.

> *Mary B. Mason, in a review of "Dear Snowman," in* School Library Journal, *Vol. 17, No. 7, March, 1971, p. 121.*

### The Crocodile Who Wouldn't Be King   (1971)

Slapdash, childlike splashes decorate a namby-pamby fable in which a clean, polite crocodile rejects the ways of his fierce and greedy father (a king) and finds happiness in a city zoo where everyone lives in peace. There he sleeps every night on "a thousand flowers" while "butterflies covered him, and pants kept him warm." If this bland and docile domestication is indeed the only alternative, most crocodiles and children are bound to opt for tyranny.

> *A review of "The Crocodile Who Wouldn't Be King," in* Kirkus Reviews, *Vol. XXXIX, No. 13, July 1, 1971, p. 673.*

As in the author's *Joshua and the Magic Fiddle* the first page is written in script but the story is continued in print. In general, the brightly colored child-like illustrations are stronger than the text which includes such unrelated statements as "Three men were riding to Portugal. Is Portugal a foreign country?"; however, the little crocodile can hardly be seen on some of the busy full-page spreads while on others he is incongruously large.

> *Patricia Vervoort, in a review of "The Crocodile Who Wouldn't Be King," in* School Library Journal, *Vol. 18, No. 5, January, 1972, p. 51.*

### The Magic Auto   (1971; British edition as The Rain Car)

A boy who longs for a real auto receives a tiny hand carved one from Grandfather for his seventh birthday. But on the first rainy day the auto grows and takes Wasti for a ride to a city, a circus (to perform on a tightrope), the site of a robbery (where it scares off the robbers), across an ocean, and finally home—where the auto shrinks and Wasti goes inside for supper. Janosch's typically gay, childlike pictures sustain the fantasy for the brief duration of the reading, but the magic auto won't take anyone very far.

> *A review of "The Magic Auto," in* Kirkus Reviews, *Vol. XL, No. 1, January 1, 1972, p. 1.*

One rainy day the wooden auto carved by grandfather for Wasti's seventh birthday swells to traveling size and the lad is off on a series of improbable adventures. The magic auto scales and descends a skyscraper, performs on a circus tightrope, foils a gang of robbers, and adapts itself to ocean travel by sprouting twin smokestacks. Balancing a trip around the world against the lure of grandmother's potato pancakes, Wasti returns home, where the toy auto shrinks to its original size. There is little or no transition from one unlikely event to another, but Janosch's illustrations—beautifully reproduced color spreads alternating with black-and-white sketches—effectively extend across the pages in a series of vivid visual encounters.

> *Mary Lou McGrew, in a review of "The Magic Auto," in* School Library Journal, *Vol. 18, No. 9, May, 1972, p. 67.*

The artist's distinctive use of colour, crazy perspective and his stiff childlike figures, make this very much a child's picture book. Every small boy will sympathise with Toby's disappointment when his grandfather gives him a car carved out of wood instead of a *real* car. But this car is magic and when it is wet with rain it grows into such a car as Toby wanted. . . .

Most young boys dream of a car like this. Here is the dream's fulfilment.

> *E. Colwell, in a review of "The Rain Car," in* The Junior Bookshelf, *Vol. 43, No. 1, February, 1979, p. 19.*

### The Yellow Auto Named Ferdinand   (1973)

Machine-loving youngsters will be disappointed by this series of unrelated adventures involving a yellow convertible named Ferdinand. It is Ferdinand—not the little man with a mustache sitting in the automobile's single seat—who decides to climb a mountain, to visit Africa, to rescue a lion princess, and who braves the rifle shots of a robber gang and accepts the gratitude of the Lion King. Humorous, action-filled pictures done in bright colors cannot make up for the story's lack of cohesiveness and unity.

> *Virginia Lee Gleason, in a review of "The Yellow Auto Named Ferdinand," in* School Library Journal, *Vol. 20, No. 8, April, 1974, p. 50.*

### The Mouse Sheriff (1975)

*The Mouse Sheriff* is a hilarious take-off of cowboys and the Wild West, especially as the characters in it are all mice. A small mouse with extra large whiskers, wearing a Stetson with five bullet holes in it, leather jeans and cowboy boots with spurs, walks into Mouseburgh with an exaggerated bow-legged swagger as if he had just got off a horse. He *had* been merely a poor Church mouse called Joe Brown, but now he calls himself Yippee Brown and tells the tallest of tall tales. In fact his thoroughly incredible stories about his adventures in the Wild West form the rest of the book, and hold his credulous audience spellbound. The more they enjoy his tales the more absurd they become, so that he is knocking billions of Indians off their horses with his miracle whiskers. 'Some of 'em were two on a horse—some were even three. To tell you the truth, some of 'em were riding thirty on a horse, and that's a fact.' His adventures reach the height of absurdity when he has to improvise a tightrope out of his own whiskers during a circus performance. "So there was I, in the ring, with the big top above me—but no tightrope. There weren't any tightrope walkers in this show. Now what? Well, I put my head on one side—like this, see?—and stuck my whiskers upright in the air. Then I climbed up my own whiskers and down again, once, twice three times. The third time I stayed at the top, laid my whiskers sideways again, and walked along them and back a few times. Yes, sir, I walked the tightrope along my own whiskers! And that was the end of my act.' But as wise old Bartholomew Mouse says, 'Lies have a way of coming home to roost, and at the end Yippee Brown's imagination is nearly the death of him, for the sentries have left their posts to listen to his increasingly exciting stories, and the town cat grabs him in its jaws. Incredibly enough, Yippee really *is* saved by his much vaunted whiskers, which make the cat sneeze and momentarily release him. Again the illustrations, this time rumbustious and humourous, perfectly capture the flavour of the story.

> *Lavinia Marina Learmont, in a review of "The Mouse Sheriff," in* Books and Bookmen, *Vol. 21, No. 4, January, 1975, p. 76.*

### Not Quite as Grimm (1975)

Janosch has done a thorough anti-establishment job in *Not quite as Grimm,* a book whose layers of double-takes leave the reader somewhat dizzy. A disingenuous introduction asks "how much of a sacred cow should we make of the book as we know it" and points out how much Wilhelm Grimm altered the stories he collected to make them "truly educational"; it goes on to praise Janosch for taking the stories "from the deep-freeze in which they have lain for a century" and thawing them out. The chosen stories lend themselves to satire pretty readily. There is **"Mother Holle,"** whose activities cause economic chaos because "There was too little of everything and too much of everything". There is **"The brave little tailor,"** who is given increasingly powerful weapons by the Government until one day "when he was feeling really brave, he linked every single wire together, fired all the weapons at once from his

sofa with one finger and destroyed the world." There is the **"Rumblestiltskin,"** a stool which rejects every bottom that rests on it except that of the king's daughter. There are the **"Musicians of Bremen,"** who are taken up by a record company and die from over-promotion. With black and white pictures to match the insistent humour, some of them actually telling the story over again in strip-form, the book is an interesting exercise in black humour; it is unlikely to make the Grimms so much as stir in their graves. (pp. 2552-53)

> *Margery Fisher, in a review of "Not Quite as Grimm," in* Growing Point, *Vol. 13, No. 7, January, 1975, pp. 2552-53.*

There are justifications advanced for this twentieth century version of some thirty-five fairy tales by the Brothers Grimm: the originals are read and forgotten, many are ignored, they rest on out-dated assumptions and defunct social structures, they preach false standards.

Janosch has taken the stories "because he did not like them as they were and considered them unsuitable for children" and has created his own modern fairy tales. Purists will be relieved that he has not tampered with such favourites as Snow White and Cinderella but has selected less hackneyed tales to retell for today's readers.

Take, for example, The Princess and the Frog. In Janosch's version, the frog is a prince who plays with his golden air-bubble in a pond one metre seventy-six deep. One day he loses his air-ball; "a girl stuck her head through the reeds" and promises to catch the bubble if the frog will marry her. The frog is not keen: the girl is tiresome, "legs too short, bottom too fat, nothing to commend her from head to toe", but father frog insists that she is admitted into the water-palace. They feed on fly and gnat salad, and make for bed: the frog determines to be rid of this unwanted creature and sets about drowning her—instead she is transformed into a beautiful green frog princess.

It certainly is not Grimm; for many older readers it will definitely be grim. Remember childhood and being surprised by the joy of fairyland—and this collection is likely to nauseate. Treat it as a zany modern potpourri of off-beat tales, amusingly illustrated, and it could click.

> *G. Bott, in a review of "Not Quite as Grimm," in* The Junior Bookshelf, *Vol. 39, No. 1, February, 1975, p. 40.*

### Zampano's Performing Bear (1976)

Not since *Horace* has there been such a bear. Janosch is the supreme master of the naive style, painting pictures which look at first like the work of a six-year-old of genius, but which turn out to be full of subtleties of design, colour and characterisation. No artist has such a dead-pan humour. The audience may be rolling in the aisles, but not a flicker disturbs Janosch's gravity.

When the mighty Zampano arrives in the village he puts his bear through a sequence of humiliating tricks. But a fly tickles the bear's nose and his professional concentration is shattered and with it Zampano's mastery. How beautifully the bear takes to freedom, while the mighty Zampano flies endlessly in orbit. A joyous book. (pp. 263, 266)

> *M. Crouch, in a review of "Zampano's Performing Bear," in* The Junior Bookshelf, *Vol. 40, No. 5, October, 1976, pp. 263, 266.*

---

## *Hey Presto! You're a Bear!* (1977)

"And don't forget you're a bear—a real bear! A bear can do his work with one hand tied behind him and can shout at the boss. He really is a bear and that's thanks to me". A glorious fantasy picture book for every child under five who has believed his father to be invincible. Witty, amusing and wholly child-centred, a superb picture book not to be missed; the illustrations are full of glorious details like the mouse trying to hammer the cats' tails to the floor.

> *J. Russell, in a review of "Hey Presto! You're a Bear!" in* The Junior Bookshelf, *Vol. 42, No. 1, February, 1978, p. 17.*

[Translator Klaus] Flugge's exclamatory English reads like a literal transaltion from the German, nonstop dialogue telling a tale probably intended as madly comic. Many, however, will find Janosch's ranting boy "hero" distasteful rather than funny. He likes to change his little brother and friends into animals, a warm-up for feats he brings off when his tired father returns from work. The hypermagician turns his father into a big bear and forces the man into carrying out destructive play adventures. Mother is merely the figure who complains about the mess and is left behind when the cruel child takes the father out to perform as a trained bear and obey other orders, never given a moment's rest. The full-color illustrations are expert but hardly cheery illustrations of the fantasy's unsubtle Freudian theme.

> *A review of "Hey Presto! You're a Bear!" in* Publishers Weekly, *Vol. 218, No. 3, July 18, 1980, p. 62.*

Any child covetous of a parent's time and attention has his fantasies played to the hilt here. Father does everything little Philip says; sort of a child-instigated *Cat in the Hat* (Beginner, 1957), with parent participating. Janosch's homely pen-and-wash drawings use muted colors, yet the pictures have an intensity that augments the action and adds to the frenzy. The drawings contrast the fantasy with the family's drab, spare real-life environment and suggest that play is an escape for parent and child alike. (p. 58)

> *Corinne Camarata, in a review of "Hey Presto! You're a Bear!" in* School Library Journal, *Vol. 27, No. 6, February, 1981, pp. 57-8.*

---

## *The Trip to Panama* (1978)

Little Bear and Little Tiger live together in a house on the riverside. Little Bear finds a crate of bananas with the word "Panama" marked on the outside. Little Bear decides that Panama is the land of dreams. Little Bear and Little Tiger set off on a humorous adventure. The illustrations and text are beautiful. They show the affection and kindness of Little Bear and Little Tiger toward one another. This is a truly delightful picture book that children will love.

> *Christine Boutross, in a review of "The Trip to Panama," in* Children's Book Review Service, *Vol. 9, No. 13, July, 1981, p. 112.*

Little Bear and Little Tiger live in a cozy house by a river where they happily spend their days fishing and hunting mushrooms. One day Little Bear discovers a banana crate labeled "Panama" and from that moment ceases to be satisfied with his life by the river. The two set off after making a signpost to show the way; they meet various animals on their journey, all of whom try to direct them but none of whom really know the way. When they again reach the signpost they believe they've reached their destination; they are, of course, back home and are satisfied. There is a lot for children to like in this story. They will no doubt catch on immediately to where the animals end up, but no matter. The characters are endearing in a stuffed-animal-like way, as is their friendship. The detail of the inside of their little house will appeal to children as will Little Tiger's constant companion—a tiger-striped pull toy that he drags everywhere. Illustrations are in subdued watercolor with outlines in ink, and the length of the book makes it a good choice for reading aloud.

> *Patricia Homer, in a review of "The Trip to Panama," in* School Library Journal, *Vol. 28, No. 2, October, 1981, p. 130.*

---

## *The Treasure-Hunting Trip* (1980)

Pictures well suited to small children, toylike and appealing, are married to an over-long and over-metaphysical text which will need some paraphrasing if the book is to be enjoyed as it deserves to be. This second adventure of Little Bear and Little Tiger is, like *A Trip to Panama*, the account of an unsuccessful quest that ends at home with unexpected rewards. Children who follow the various excavations should especially delight in the insertion in each of the softly dramatic wash and line scenes of a small frog with a toy pull-along duck; his actions mirror or parody those of the heroic travellers, with quaint effect.

> *Margery Fisher, in a review of "The Treasure-Hunting Trip," in* Growing Point, *Vol. 19, No. 1, May, 1980, p. 3710.*

---

## *Crafty Caspar and His Good Old Granny* (1980)

There is no doubt however that Janosch's naivety speaks directly to the child. Here is an author-artist who has not lost his fairyland. And a right earthy, tough, rumbustious fairyland it is too. There is something of Punch and Judy in this ruthless tale of cunning rewarded. I yield to no one in my loving admiration for this highly individual Polish-German artist, but I wish he had exercised more economy in his text, which goes on far too long for the young reader's patience.

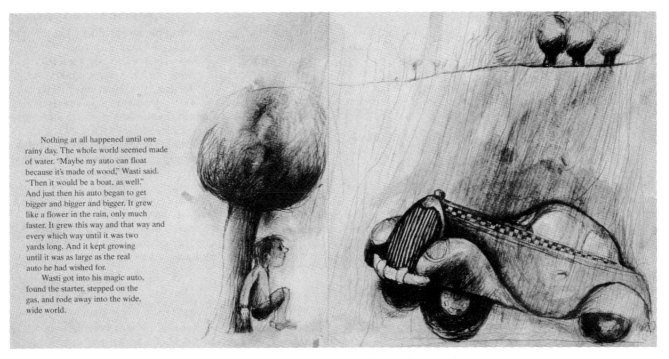

Nothing at all happened until one rainy day. The whole world seemed made of water. "Maybe my auto can float because it's made of wood," Wasti said. "Then it would be a boat, as well." And just then his auto began to get bigger and bigger and bigger. It grew like a flower in the rain, only much faster. It grew this way and that way and every which way until it was two yards long. And it kept growing until it was as large as the real auto he had wished for.

Wasti got into his magic auto, found the starter, stepped on the gas, and rode away into the wide, wide world.

*From* The Magic Auto, *written and illustrated by Janosch.*

*M. Crouch, in a review of "Crafty Caspar and His Good Old Granny," in* The Junior Bookshelf, *Vol. 44, No. 5, October, 1980, p. 232.*

### The Big Janosch Book of Fun and Verse (1980)

Well worth the price for its hundreds of delectable pictures (vivid line and wash); its nursery rhymes, all new, but with the wild tang of the old; its two or three mini-novels—notably one about a mouse boy and girl who are not as their parents fondly (if conventionally) hoped; its fables nicely relooked at; its abiding logical dottiness. The nursery book of the season.

*Naomi Lewis, "Poetry, Fable, Song," in* The Observer, *December 7, 1980, p. 31.*

Janosch's characteristic little animals—bears, rabbits, tigers, mice and so on—make forays into the human world with parachutes, quill pens, cauldrons and toy boats and human figures are involved now and then, as well, in tales and rhymes about congenial subjects like treasure-seeking, the seasons and musical gatherings. A lively, idiosyncratic bundle of nursery ditties, strip adventures and mini-stories, all decked with energetically expressive wash and line pictures; a box of delights for the very young to rustle through.

*Margery Fisher, in a review of "The Big Janosch Book of Fun and Verse," in* Growing Point, *Vol. 19, No. 5, January, 1981, p. 3822.*

### A Letter for Tiger (1981)

Two lovable little characters, Little Bear and Little Tiger,

have another adventure. Their loneliness when separated makes them devise a way of sending letters.

A well-produced book which will become a firm favourite with young readers, the brightly coloured, simple pictures are joyously alive. Even the tiny creatures in the background, like the mouse playing with the tiger striped duck, are quite enchanting. There is plenty of action, a crisp text with short sentences using descriptive language and natural dialogue. It could be as successful as the other books about Little Bear and Little Tiger—the prize winning **Trip to Panama** and **The Treasure Hunting Trip.**

*A. Thatcher, in a review of "A Letter for Tiger," in* The Junior Bookshelf, *Vol. 45, No. 6, December, 1981, p. 243.*

### The Cricket and the Mole (1982)

**The Mole And The Cricket** is an off-beat rendition of the old cautionary fable: but *this* time, the cricket fiddles the summer away, and then has a perfectly super winter with her good friend Mole. The moral of the story has been somewhat obscured, and the final illustration of an unlikely duo cosily ensconced for a long winter's nap is more than a little ambiguous. Writers with a tongue-in-cheek style, however amusing, should save this kind of humour for adult readers. Those who write for very young children must keep their audience and its needs firmly in focus, at whatever cost to their own jeu d'esprit. . . .

*Joan McGrath, in a review of "The Mole and the Cricket," in* Canadian Children's Literature, *No. 26, 1982, p. 94.*

A neat, elegant, enchanting miniature containing tiny fables and minuscule adventures, with Janosch's unmistakeable cuddly little animals (fox, lion, hare, mole and a superbly personalised cricket) as actors in dramatic situations of danger and surprise. The sly element of parody sharpens the softness of the humour, and the illustrations make a virtue of smallness with their soft wash colour and idiosyncratic details. A perfect gift for a small girl or boy of three or four.

> *Margery Fisher, in a review of "The Cricket and the Mole," in* Growing Point, *Vol. 22, No. 2, July, 1983, p. 4109.*

Each page of this little book has a line and wash illustration of great charm and delicacy, featuring small appealing or comic animals. There are four short fables. The first, a simple tale about kind mole and improvident cricket.

**"The Goose Opera"** is interspersed with parodies of well-known rhymes, as a group of geese outwit a hunting fox, chase and dance him to death, and then use his clothes to keep warm and cosy. In the third, **"Jack the Lion"** simple rhymed couplets caption a series of unrelated pictures. **"Robinson Hare"** is a short, simply written version of Robinson Crusoe, including Hare Friday.

The choice of story is not particularly suitable for the young children for whom this book is intended, and there are few original ideas, but the quality and attractiveness of the illustrations, and the variety of the type used in the presentation of this slim volume give it a rather old-fashioned appeal as a gift to be enjoyed.

> *A. Thatcher, in a review of "The Cricket and the Mole," in* The Junior Bookshelf, *Vol. 47, No. 5, October, 1983, p. 208.*

---

## *Animal Antics* (1982)

Much as I admire Janosch—and at his best he has scarcely an equal in Europe as author-illustrator—I cannot feel happy about this fat and expensive book. It consists of short stories and rhymes, all lavishly illustrated with Janosch's characteristic faux naif drawings in colour. The tales are modern fables with morals, written or implicit, which deliberately mock the old conventions. The poems are mostly crude in technique and not very funny, at least to adult eyes. It is difficult to see for whom the whole book is intended. Very small children at the picture-book stage are likely to miss the irony, without which most of the stories are pointless. Children, say, of nine or ten would get some fun out of the stories if they could bring themselves to read what appears to be a baby's book. It is not an uncommon dilemma. (pp. 26-7)

> *M. Crouch, in a review of "Animal Antics," in* The Junior Bookshelf, *Vol. 47, No. 1, February, 1983, pp. 26-7.*

Comic fantasy tilts the balance of everyday towards impossibility in degrees that will vary according to the intended readership and the literary tact and skill of the author and artist concerned. It is a long step from the gentle frolics designed for small children, who are well able to believe that animals are people while knowing perfectly well that they are not, to satirical pieces for older children who enjoy spying on the vagaries of their elders through some kind of animal guise. Janosch sustains the gentler type of fantasy in **Animal Antics,** in his wash-pictures, where small animals, not too far from their natural forms, often look as much like toys as living creatures. His texts are less consistent, in that there is an element of satire and moral instruction behind the simple, comic incongruity of the fables. For instance, Valerian the peaceful hare institutes a campaign against a bullying dog and mice similarly join forces against a predatory owl. The oddity of these rhymed and prose anecdotes is not unlike that of Donald Bisset, but the tales are less original and inventive, and less sprightly, than Bisset's nonsense-pieces, and the small children for whom Janosch's book seems intended will probably read the pictures in their own way and regard the sometimes tendentious texts as secondary.

> *Margery Fisher, in a review of "Animal Antics," in* Growing Point, *Vol. 21, No. 6, March, 1983, p. 4033.*

The noted German author/illustrator collects snippets of his poetry and prose into a book which will find most currency amongst students of his work.

Most of the stories here are short, fable-like concoctions, many with cynical endings (e.g., a father hare gives advice to his three children as they go out into the world; the only one who survives is the one who ignores him; conclusion: "Such things do happen"). The poems are mostly doggerel and seem produced to match the many colorful illustrations, which are funny, earthy, and charming. The whole is tied together with the animal theme, though the final, most entertaining sequence involves imaginary creatures called "snoddles."

Anthea Bell's translation is, as usual, excellent and smooth, serving the author's intent in language and style, but it cannot conceal the fact that this is really a collection of odds and ends cobbled together to make a book which, in style and sentiment, is inaccessible to most American children. Collectors of Janosch's art, however, will have a field day.

> *A review of "Animal Antics," in* Kirkus Reviews, *Vol. LIV, No. 24, December 15, 1986, p. 1861.*

---

## *The Curious Tale of Hare and Hedgehog* (1985)

Janosch has given a new twist to the fable. Hare, as challenger, runs to Lands End and back, is caught in a trap but released by an old man who looks askance at his exhaustion; after 145 miles he collapses, while Hedgehog and his family, with their friends, are enjoying a placid row on the lake and a fish-picnic. No winner is announced, for Hare is never seen again. The wash and ink scribble pictures vigorously suggest the moods and actions of the animals and the domestic and country details are entrancingly miniature and pointed.

> *Margery Fisher, in a review of "The Curious*

Tale of Hare and Hedgehog," in Growing Point, *Vol. 24, No. 1, May, 1985, p. 4448.*

Janosch, almost my favourite artist in the great European tradition, has no such illustrious literary prototype [as does Val Biro with Robert Browning in his *The Pied Piper of Hamelin*] for his cheerful free version of the fable of the hare and the tortoise. Dim athletic Hare is no match for Hedgehog. The latter in fact gives not a thought to the race, and while Hare is wearing himself out with speed, accident and anxiety Hedgehog takes his little wife for a picnic, with their frog-dog on a leash, beside the Wide Water. After that they go to bed. And who won the race? It was H. . . . There's a moral somewhere in these genial pages, but the reader won't worry too much about it. Sufficient to the day is the humour thereof, and Janosch is not far off his best in these soft landscapes with their teeming and relevant detail. Anthea Bell's translation is, as always, faithful to the spirit of the story and a gentle and homely accompaniment to the master's pictures.

> *M. Crouch, in a review of "The Curious Tale of Hare and Hedgehog," in* The Junior Bookshelf, *Vol. 49, No. 4, August, 1985, p. 171.*

---

### Harum Scarum: The Little Hare Book   (1985)

Janosch's appealing little animals, with their entirely human moods and expressions superimposed on quasi-natural behaviour, appear once more in this assemblage of poems, anecdotes, nonsense-jingles, counting-out rhymes and fables. Father Hare, a doddering and irresponsible animal, reduces all the accepted conventions of children's stories to nonsense, while Uncle Badger offers his own sardonic view of life. The wash and pen pictures are, as always, comical and active, adding a very personal touch to the traditional humanising of animals.

> *Margery Fisher, in a review of "Harum Scarum: The Little Hare Book," in* Growing Point, *Vol. 24, No. 3, September, 1985, p. 4505.*

---

### Little Tiger, Get Well Soon!   (1986)

[*Little Tiger, Get Well Soon*] focuses on the desired childhood privilege of invalid status—nothing too serious, but enough to gain attention. Little Tiger isn't well. Little Bear must carry him home, then bandage him, then provide his favourite dish. (Problem: it can't be done.) More events occur in the Animals' Hospital (a happy place, parents note). "Next year", says Bear, "it will be my turn to be ill and you can make me better, all right?" "Of course," says Tiger. Plenty of text; delectable Janosch pictures. A canny under-six year old could have the pleasure of sharing Little T's recovery while seeing through his wiles.

> *Naomi Lewis, "The Right Mixture," in* The Times Educational Supplement, *No. 3649, June 6, 1986, p. 54.*

When Little Tiger is taken to hospital by his anxious friends the doctors discover he has a stripe missing; once this has been replaced he is conducted home again by a cheerful throng. Cosy scenes with humanised animals—bear, goose and others—offer to the young viewer that familiar Janosch device of the small pullalong duck which has to be located in each picture. A happy tale likely to reassure children who fear a visit to hospital; bandages, injections and other sources of apprehension are encountered very cheerfully by endearing Little Tiger. (pp. 4689-90)

> *Margery Fisher, in a review of "Little Tiger, Get Well Soon!" in* Growing Point, *Vol. 25, No. 3, September, 1986, pp. 4689-90.*

---

### The Old Man and the Bear   (1987)

This allegory may appeal to religious families, but it is very bleak for the average reader. A poor old man who has so little food one winter that he takes a sick bird he is caring for and appeals to a bear for help. The bear takes them in, but the old man dies of exposure. The bear runs out of food, and he and the bird walk to town to appeal to the humans there for help. The bear collapses, outside the church, cradling the bird in his hands to keep it warm. When the people pour out of the church, the children want to help the bear, arguing that he might be an enchanted prince, but their parents hurry away. Before the sun rises again, an angel has carried the bear and the bird to the stars. To adults, this story, with its moody illustrations, is quite lovely. But the sad mood of the piece is overwhelming, and for some children, the behavior of the people toward the bear and bird may seem cruel and frightening. (pp. 92-3)

> *A review of "The Old Man and the Bear," in* Publishers Weekly, *Vol. 232, No. 11, September 11, 1987, pp. 92-3.*

If a plot summary of this book seems disjointed, it's probably because there are just too many disparate elements in the plot. Many details lead nowhere: Why do the group of animals, pied-piper-like, follow the Old Man to the Bear's house? Why do they never appear again? What purpose does the narrator serve? A picture book, like a poem, demands unity and conciseness; anything unnecessary detracts considerably from the whole. And the deaths of the two main characters seem pointless or didactic or maudlin. Janosch's artwork deserves a better story. The watercolor and ink illustrations are effectively composed and attractive. His use of color and feeling for texture are excellent. But there are so many wholly wonderful Christmas picture books available that it's not necessary to buy one that relies on the art to carry the story.

> *Lauralyn Persson, in a review of "The Old Man and the Bear," in* School Library Journal, *Vol. 34, No. 6, February, 1988, p. 62.*

---

### Hello, Little Pig   (1988)

Janosch's endearing toy/miniature animal friends Tiger and Bear are not as comradely as they used to be, for Tiger has been persuaded by idle Pig to play hide-and-seek instead of gathering mushrooms for supper. Worse still, he goes home with Pig but soon finds that the chores he is expected to do while Pig lies abed are heavier than those allotted to him by Bear and, besides, Pig's taste in food is sloppy and sickly and makes him feel ill. The happy ending is predictable but welcome to those who enjoy Janosch's spry little tales and his splendidly slapdash scenes with, as usual, a striped pull-along duck acting as a recurring footnote to the jaunty little comedy). (pp. 5019-20)

> *Margery Fisher, in a review of "Hello, Little Pig," in* Growing Point, *Vol. 27, No. 2, July, 1988, pp. 5019-20.*

A highly moral tale about how Little Tiger is seduced away from his nice, ordered life with Little Bear by the loose living of Little Pig. But, alas, all is a snare and a delusion! Once in Little Pig's house, Little Tiger has to do all the work; he decides to go back home, but where is Little Bear? Looking for Little Tiger, of course, and all ends happily when they find each other.

I liked the style of the prose; it has a rather child-like 'and then, and then' feel and the dialogue is much like the sort young children write for themselves. Whether this is due to the original or to the translation I don't know. The illustrations are, of course, the original and are typically Janosch, awkward but charming. Liked by all the children I read it to, or with, but especially by middle infants.

> *Liz Waterland, in a review of "Hello, Little Pig," in* Books for Keeps, *No. 57, July, 1989, p. 9.*

# William Joyce

## 1957-

(Also illustrates as Bill Joyce) American author and illustrator of picture books.

Major works include *George Shrinks* (1985), *Dinosaur Bob and His Adventures with the Family Lazardo* (1988), *A Day with Wilbur Robinson* (1990).

Considered one of the most original creators of picture books to have emerged in recent years, Joyce is recognized as a writer and artist of exuberant works which use succinct, matter-of-fact narratives to introduce wildly colorful, often outrageous plots and illustrations. Praised for his skill as an artist as well as for his cleverness and wit, Joyce is often acknowledged for his inventiveness in creating stories that combine the real and the surreal; in the words of critic Heather Vogel Frederick, "[Joyce's] wild imagination knows no limits." Observers regard his works, which are usually structured around American families and often feature shock-headed small boys as characters, as especially distinctive for their stylized reflection of American culture from the 1930s through the 1950s, a characteristic which is most obvious in the nostalgic style and details of Joyce's illustrations. Filled with allusions to literature, film, and popular culture, the stories include episodes ranging from hilarious to hair-raising that Joyce presents to young readers in a cinematic fashion.

Joyce's first picture book, *George Shrinks,* depicts the dream of a responsible young boy who ingeniously performs the household chores outlined for him by his parents after he finds himself reduced to a tiny size. In his next work, the popular *Dinosaur Bob and His Adventures with the Family Lazardo,* Joyce introduces an engaging brontosaurus who is adopted by a well-to-do family on a trip to Africa; back in suburbia, Bob is jailed for chasing cars but redeems himself when he becomes the hero of the Pimlico Pirates baseball team. When the bespectacled young narrator of *A Day with Wilbur Robinson* goes to visit his friend Wilbur and his family, he is greeted by an incredible array of eccentric parents, grandparents, siblings, aunts, uncles, and cousins as well as by several animals, both real and anthropomorphic, a lifesize train set, an antigravity machine, and a robot. Described as "a thinly disguised account of William Joyce's childhood," *Wilbur Robinson* calmly describes the events of the day while illustrating the bizarre lifestyle of the extraordinary household in bold pictures filled with light, shadow, motion, and surprising details. As an illustrator, Joyce provides imaginative expansions of his texts with paintings that are overtly realistic but filled with otherworldly elements in color and content; the pictures also feature the artist's unusual use of scale and perspective. Influenced by cartoons and comic books, science fiction and horror movies, and classic works of literature for both children and adults, Joyce was working on illustration assignments before complet-

ing his degree in filmmaking and illustrating; he has since provided pictures in black and white and color for such authors as Marianna Mayer, Jan Wahl, Joyce Maxner, and Stephen Manes.

(See also *Something about the Author,* Vol. 46 and *Contemporary Authors,* Vol. 124.)

---

## TITLE COMMENTARY

### *George Shrinks* (1985)

In his parents' absence, George dreams that he's small, and he awakens to find himself about three inches high. The understated text (largely the words of a note left to remind George to make his bed, brush his teeth, take out the garbage, etc.) is counterpointed by paintings with realistic detail in cartoon colors and—outstandingly—by their perspective: a mouse-eye view of the high adventure such boring chores become under the unusual circumstances. George's high-handed treatment of a malevolent cat, and the cat's near-revenge (thwarted when the shock-headed hero, under the bedcovers, pops back to normal size just in time for Mom and Dad's return) provides a little narrative line for the fun and excitement. Some witty touches and '50s nostalgia should please parents, who will root along with their kids for this updated and unflappable Tom Thumb. Treehorn, move over!

> *Patricia Dooley, in a review of "George Shrinks," in* School Library Journal, *Vol. 32, No. 2, October, 1985, p. 156.*

[*George Shrinks*] takes us inside the fantasy of shrinking from the child's point of view. In a dream (which we don't know is a dream until the book's end) George becomes the lilliputian inhabitant of his otherwise unchanged world. He is a good little lad (most of the time), and does what his parents tell him to do in the note that they leave him while they're out. He brushes his teeth, takes a bath, eats his breakfast and does his chores—but each of these simple events takes on a grand, (and at times quite scary) adventurous scale for a two-inch tall little boy.

Joyce sets his story in what seems to be the 1940s, which makes all those everyday objects of George's life—from the toothbrush to the telephone, the dishes to the doorknobs—familiar and yet foreign, distant, dreamlike. Joyce gives this well-worn fantasy situation new wrinkles through illustrations that are generous in their sense of humor, character and clever pace. Together, they hold the reader in the spell of young George's adventures. Joyce does not overwork his plot by laboriously constructing detailed narrative bridges to link the moments in this episodic story. He leaves room for a little mystery and for the reader's own imagination to join George in his often hilarious and hair-raising exploits. (p. 19)

> *John Cech, "A Palette of Picture Books," in* Book World—The Washington Post, *November 10, 1985, pp. 19, 22.*

In William Joyce's illustrated story, a young boy named George awakes from his nap to discover he has become as small as a mouse. His blanket engulfs him like a collapsed parachute. His once-cuddly teddy bear now resembles a benign grizzly. Resting against the alarm clock is a piece of poster-size paper on which parental instructions are written telling George all that he should do after getting up.

Because most of the book's text consists of this note's contents, the story of *George Shrinks* belongs to a minimalist preschool. Yet its meager prose is a perfect foil for Mr. Joyce's whimsical, perceptive illustrations of a world filled with tigerlike cats, jungles of garden plants and the toy airplane in which George flies about obeying his parents' admonition to get some "fresh air."

The flat, rather stern tone of their note is what makes Mr. Joyce's colorful modern-day Lilliput so alluring by contrast. Told to "wash the dishes," George does so by sliding down plates on a sponge. At his new size, he finds that the fish are best fed by riding one like a horse. And his younger brother is the perfect beast of burden to haul out the trash in a wagon with George on his back like a pasha. *George Shrinks* is a thoroughly charming piece of work. The shortest critic in my house calls it "a funny book."

> *Ralph Keyes, in a review of "George Shrinks," in* The New York Times Book Review, *December 29, 1985, p. 23.*

[*George Shrinks*] is an endearing oddity. . . . The drawings which accompany this alarming story treat each situation with fitting gravity. Nicely economical in word and line, the book squeezes the last thrill out of its situation. (pp. 141-42)

> *M. Crouch, in a review of "George Shrinks," in* The Junior Bookshelf, *Vol. 50, No. 4, August 4, 1986, pp. 141-42.*

---

**Dinosaur Bob and His Adventures with the Family Lazardo** (1988)

From the creator of *George Shrinks* and illustrator of other books comes a campy extravaganza about the savvy Lazardo family, which, while on vacation in Africa, acquires a dinosaur. Scotty and his sisters, Zelda and Velma, plead to keep him, and their parents agree. Bob, named after Scotty's great-uncle, is happy with the Lazardos—he swims in the morning, plays baseball in the afternoon and sings songs around the campfire at night. But it is soon time to go home to Pimlico Hills, and while Bob is a hit

*From* Dinosaur Bob and His Adventures with the Family Lazardo, *written and illustrated by William Joyce.*

on the ocean liner, his popularity at home diminishes quickly when the police catch him chasing cars. How the Lazardos rescue him incorporates mythic elements of the national pastime (Bob exhibits great skill at the plate) with a matter-of-fact telling. Joyce's dinosaur is gargantuan yet unthreatening, rendered in an illustrational style reminiscent of 1920s magazine advertising. Surprising juxtapositions of scale enliven the drawings, and many employ unorthodox aerial perspectives. Joyce's is a world of light-drenched, chiseled-edge landscapes and brooding night scenes in which active crosshatchings bring shadows to life.

> *A review of "Dinosaur Bob and His Adventures with the Family Lazardo," in* Publishers Weekly, *Vol. 233, No. 25, June 24, 1988, p. 111.*

**George Shrinks,** William Joyce's winsome variant on "The Incredible Shrinking Man" theme, displayed an original talent, less in its barebones prose than in its pictures—realistic but with an oddly dissonant palette favoring strange and slightly disorienting greens, blues, purples. In his new book, an appealing homage to the 1930s, a well-off family from Pimlico Hills discovers a brontosaurus in the African jungle, adopts it as a pet, and eventually brings it home to America.

Not quite tongue-in-cheek, the story nonetheless offers up a number of little touches of Depression-era culture. The book is dedicated, in part, to Nick and Nora Charles (as in Hammett), two of the Lazardo children are named Scotty and Zelda (as in Fitzgerald), and the third is named Velma (as in the femme fatale of Chandler's *Farewell, My Lovely*). The family's silent Indian bodyguard Jumbu bears more than a passing resemblance to that of Daddy Warbucks'. Bob, the dinosaur, acts rather like a more benign King Kong, as he travels down the Nile, crosses the Atlantic on board an elegant cruise liner, and travels from New York atop a sleek new train, just off the Raymond Loewy drawing board. (I wish I could think of a Jazz Age Lazardo, but the only character who comes to mind is Dr. Lizardo the alien villain of the film *Buckaroo Banzai.*)

Once in America, Dinosaur Bob enjoys picnics and baseball but, unfamiliar with our customs, eventually gets in trouble with the law. Dr. Lazardo helps him escape from jail, and things look grim, but wait—who, or what, is that in the outfield, wearing the uniform of the Pimlico Pirates, and ready to lead the perennial losers on to a stunning victory at home? Any dinosaur-loving kid will take to Joyce's story; it's as all-American as an Andy Hardy movie. (pp. 10-11)

> *Michael Dirda, in a review of "Dinosaur Bob and His Adventures with the Family Lazardo," in* Book World—The Washington Post, *October 9, 1988, pp. 10-11.*

---

### A Day with Wilbur Robinson (1990)

Modern children are hard to fool. Sit them down with *Randolph the Raccoon Learns About Responsibility* and within five minutes they'll be tugging at your sleeve, asking if it's Nintendo time yet. Such children will take more kindly to William Joyce's book **A Day With Wilbur Robinson,** in which there are no raccoons and no lessons about responsibility, though there is a giant sea squid named Lefty.

The story—according to the jacket "a thickly disguised account of William Joyce's childhood"—begins with the bespectacled young narrator going to spend the day with his shock-haired friend, Wilbur Robinson. "His house is the *greatest* place to visit," he remarks. On the next page the narrator says hello to Dmitri and Spike, "the twin uncles"; the aforementioned Lefty takes his bag.

Mr. Joyce's technique, most of the time, is to leave the best part unsaid; the picture provides the punch line for the text. Thus: " 'It's kind of dull around here today,' said Wilbur. I looked around. Aunt Billie was playing with her train set, Cousin Pete was walking the cats, and Uncle Gaston sat comfortably in the family cannon." The cats are tigers and the train is a locomotive. The cannon follows Chekhov's gun rule.

On the next page we are introduced to Mr. and Mrs. Robinson and their robot, Carl. Other family members include Cousin Laszlo, who has invented an antigravity device; Grandfather, who, along with "Mr. Ellington and Mr. Armstrong," is training frogs to play jazz; and Uncle Art, "newly arrived from abroad"—very far abroad, judging from his vehicle.

Like the cartoonist Glen Baxter, Mr. Joyce . . . enlivens an intentionally drab text with wild illustrations and paints in a nostalgic style. While Mr. Baxter's illustrations recall the cartoons of the 20's, however, Mr. Joyce's paintings have a decidedly 30's feel to them. His palette of deliciously artificial Necco-wafer colors brings Edward Hopper to mind, as well as the commercial art of the Depression—advertisements in which red-cheeked little boys happily guzzled Ovaltine or Coca-Cola. Painted in such a realistic way, the bizarre events in the pictures seem appealingly plausible.

The illustrations are full of motions and shadows; something odd and reptilian invariably extends a limb from the corner. And they contain as many details to which the text doesn't point as details to which it does: a giant goldfish; a turbaned frog feeding grapes to Wilbur's sister Tallulah; a frog on dogback (complete with saddle). There are also a mummy, some very large croquet sticks and a most extraordinary hat.

Finally, as the day draws to a close, all the members of the Robinson clan, like their Swiss namesakes, go to sleep in a tree; Uncle Art tells "hair-raising stories about his adventures in outer space"; the frogs play their violins. In the morning, as his family serenades our hero with "Yes, We Have No Bananas," Wilbur apologizes: "Sorry it was such a dull day."

There is a touch of "You Can't Take It With You" to this charming, new-fangled, old-fashioned book: Grandpa and Mr. DePinna in the basement, mother banging out her plays on an old typewriter in the living room—that crazy, wonderful other family everyone would like to abandon their own for and get adopted into, only this time with singing frogs and robots. In the end, however, our hero admits that he's "ready to go home for a while." Be forewarned: even with Nintendo in the offing, young readers may be more reluctant to leave.

*David Leavitt, "Can I Go Over to Wilbur's?,"
in* The New York Times Book Review, *November 11, 1990, p. 29.*

**Dinosaur Bob** fans should rejoice: in his latest work, Joyce pulls out all the stops and introduces the weirdest family since his Lazardo clan. A young narrator, going to see his best friend Wilbur, remarks, "His house is the *greatest* place to visit." Readers soon see why. Wilbur's large household includes an aunt whose train set is life-sized, an uncle who shares his "deep thoughts" ("Mississippi spelled with *o*'s . . . would be *Mossossoppo!*") and a grandfather who trains a dancing frog band. There's not much in the way of formal plot here—save a slight mystery involving Grandfather's missing false teeth—but Joyce's wonderfully strange paintings abound with hilari-

ous, surprising details and leave the impression that a *lot* has happened. A visit to the Robinsons' is a bit overwhelming (as the narrator says, "I was kind of sad to leave, but I was ready to go home for a while"), but it's a trip children will want to make again and again.

*A review of "A Day with Wilbur Robinson," in*
Publishers Weekly, *Vol. 237, No. 30, July 27,
1990, p. 232.*

Joyce is arguably the most original talent working in the children's-book field today. Who else could have created a family as endearingly wacky as the Robinsons—ranging from Uncle Judlow, who relaxes with his brain augmenter, to cousin Laszlo, who demonstrates his new anti-gravity device to the frogs who steal Grandpa's false teeth. Joyce's style as an artist is as exuberantly zany and distinctive as his writer's imagination. Buy two copies of this book: one for the kids and one for yourself. (p. 24)

*Michael Cart, "Picture Windows to the
World," in* Los Angeles Times Book Review,
*November 25, 1990, pp. 24-5.*

# Lois Lenski

## 1893-1974

American author and illustrator of fiction, picture books, poetry, nonfiction; playwright; and reteller.

Major works include *The Little Auto* (1934), *Phebe Fairchild: Her Book* (1936), *Indian Captive: The Story of Mary Jemison* (1941), *Strawberry Girl* (1945), *The Life I Live: Collected Poems* (1965), the "Roundabout America" series, the "We Live in . . ." series.

One of the most prominent and highly respected American writers and illustrators for children of the twentieth century, Lenski is lauded as a pioneer in the development of regional juvenile literature and as the author and artist of the informational picture books about the various careers of the toylike character Mr. Small. A versatile and prolific creator of books for children and young adults from preschool through high school, she is often credited with presenting accurate, well researched portrayals of American society, both contemporary and historical, and is often acknowledged for the realism of her writing and the variety of her artistic styles, for her cultural observation and understanding of children, and for her success in introducing young people both to their heritage and to the current American landscape. "No other author of children's literature," wrote critic Charlotte Huck of Lenski, "has so richly interpreted childhood and the American scene." Lenski set her works in all four corners of the United States, although she centered her regional books most frequently in the rural areas of the Southeast and North Central states; she also covered a number of periods in her historical fiction ranging from the seventeenth through the early twentieth centuries. In her regional novels, Lenski often concentrates on the lives of the underprivileged and the working class, and creates situations that draw upon the cultural milieu of each locale while outlining how her young male and female protagonists surmount personal problems. Although she often presents her readers with the harsh details of existence such as squalor, tragedy, and death, she describes her characters, their parents, and their communities without judgment and underscores her works with such values as hard work, education, and endurance. The books are also noted for Lenski's warmth and optimistic view and for her emphasis on the dignity of her subjects and the importance of love and family loyalty. In her historical novels, Lenski also demonstrates the courage, strength, and adaptability of her child and adult characters while outlining the background of each period that she addresses. In addition to showing ethnic, economic, and industrial patterns, Lenski fills her books with humor and the joy of everyday life.

The daughter of a Lutheran minister who wanted her to be a teacher, Lenski spent her youth in the small farming town of Anna, Ohio. After receiving her degree in education, she decided to follow her dream of becoming an artist and moved to New York to study at the Art Students

League; in 1920, she went to England to continue her studies at London's Westminster School of Art and received her first assignments as an illustrator, eventually providing the pictures for over fifty books by such authors as Kenneth Grahame, Padraic Colum, Cornelia Meigs, Hugh Lofting, Watty Piper, Maud Hart Lovelace, and Clyde Robert Bulla. Lenski lived most of her married life in a farmhouse built in 1790 near Torrington, Connecticut, an area that inspired her to write historical fiction. The first books she both wrote and illustrated, *Skipping Village* (1927) and *A Little Girl of 1900* (1928), are stories that draw upon Lenski's own experiences in growing up. The interests and exploits of her son Stephen prompted Lenski to create her picture books about Mr. Small, and she based the character of Davy, a small boy who is the central figure in six picture books for preschoolers, on the child who lived with her family while his mother was ill; she also created six picture books about a small girl, Debbie, and her siblings. Ordered south for the sake of her health, Lenski moved to Florida and created the first of her regional books, *Bayou Suzette* (1943), the story of ten-year-old Suzette Durand of Bayou Barataria in Louisiana and her extended family. In creating her regional stories, Lenski approached her subjects as an anthropologist would: operating as an outsider, she traveled to the regions she describes to live with families, basing her stories on their experiences and her drawings on their homes, clothes, and environment; notably, Lenski also included accurate regional dialect in her books as well as many examples of slang and colloquial language. After writing regional literature for twenty-five years, Lenski wrote poetry and verse with city and country settings, much of which had musical accompaniment by Clyde Robert Bulla, who also provided the music for three of Lenski's plays. Lenski is also the author of four picture books on the seasons, two picture books on Washington, D. C. and New York City, a collection of nursery rhymes, and retellings of folktales; she is also an author of nonfiction and verse for adults. As an illustrator, Lenski worked in a variety of styles: line drawings noted for portraying action, character, and humor with a minimum of detail, two color wash illustrations with line drawings in the Mr. Small series, and softly detailed pencil sketches in the regional books; she also exhibited her oil and watercolor paintings throughout the United States. Lenski was awarded the Newbery Medal for *Strawberry Girl* in 1946; two of her works were also named Newbery honor books, *Phebe Fairchild* in 1937 and *Indian Captive* in 1942. *Judy's Journey* won the Children's Book Award from the Child Study Association of America in 1947 as the best book dealing realistically with contemporary problems. For her body of work, Lenski received the Regina Medal and University of Southern Mississippi Medallion in 1969; she also received recognition from several American colleges and universities.

(See also *Something about the Author,* Vols. 1, 26; *Contemporary Authors,* Vols. 13-14 and 53-56 [obituary]; and *Dictionary of Literary Biography,* Vol. 22.)

## AUTHOR'S COMMENTARY

We are grateful to Wendell Willkie for giving us the phrase "One World." He meant, as we all know, that we must learn to live as brothers to make the world "one." We have now many separate worlds, little worlds with fences between, fences so high we cannot see over them. Each of us thinks that *our* world is the only one. We do not know or understand other people's worlds, beyond our own fence. Before we can hope to understand foreign nations and live at peace with them, we must understand our own country and the different kinds of people who live in it.

Regional art, painting, and literature, is, basically speaking, the presentation of a *way of life* in a certain region which has developed or preserved in itself a certain homogenous individuality. Because of the great diversity of setting and of types of people in our country, it is practically impossible to write of it as a whole, as a national entity. We have our New England, our South, our Middle West, our Far West, and under these divisions, many more subdivisions and groups. And so any sound understanding of our country as a whole becomes an understanding of its component parts. (p. 289)

The native son, who has his roots there, should be by all means the best interpreter of his own region. There are

many fine examples of authors who have done this. I think particularly of Sara Orne Jewett and her fine stories of New England and New England character. Among our juvenile books we have Marguerite de Angeli of Pennsylvania, May Justus of Tennessee, Will James of the Cow Country, Laura Ingalls Wilder of the Prairie Country, and many others.

But often the native son has limitations. He is too close to the scene, he "cannot see the forest for the trees." Sometimes too he is ashamed of his own background and beginnings. He wants to go *somewhere else* to find something to paint or write about. The native son may know the scene so well he cannot get outside of it and see it with perspective. (pp. 289-90)

The outsider, coming into a region new to him, has the great advantage of having "eyes to see," he has a greater receptivity because of the newness of the scene—it has never had a chance to grow stale to him.

It was, of course, as an outsider that I gathered the material for my three regional books, *Strawberry Girl, Bayou Suzette,* and *Blue Ridge Billy.* I did not deliberately set out to travel in search of book material, but I have always found material, crying out to be recorded. Those who have "eyes to see" never run out of subject matter for creative expression.

Some fifteen years ago, I, Ohio born and bred, went to live in Connecticut in an old 1790 farmhouse. Before I consciously realized what was happening, I was learning Connecticut history from my neighbors and I was starting a series of books for children with Connecticut and New England historical backgrounds.

Later, it so happened that because of ill health, my doctor advised my spending my winters in a warmer climate. I went first to Louisiana and spent a winter in New Orleans, where I was confronted with stories on all sides. There was the exciting history of old New Orleans, the charm of the French Quarter, the fascination of the colored children—a thing to be constantly resisted—and there was the real life I saw being lived by French speaking people in the rural regions along the bayous, especially the life of the children there. I had to put it into a book, I couldn't help myself. It was there waiting for me.

When I found out what an exciting life the Louisiana children live, I wanted to go right home to Connecticut and tell the children there about it. Then I went to Florida and learned that children live still different lives in that land of sunshine and orange trees and strawberries. Why don't we know more about our own country? Why shouldn't the children of Louisiana and Florida and Connecticut and other parts of the country get to know each other? Why haven't Louisiana writers told us how Louisiana people live? Why haven't Florida writers told us how Florida people live? If the native sons and daughters have not "eyes to see," why should not an outsider do it?

And so I found myself writing regional books for children, and through the process, I have developed an insatiable curiosity about how other people live.

To write these books, I went to live with the people in

these regions, to really get to know them firsthand. I talked with them, ate and drank with them, sat in their kitchens and on their porches, and always I listened as they told their experiences. The children told me a great deal and so did their parents. I took my sketchbook with me, and made drawings of the people, their houses, their furnishings, and many details of their surroundings. (p. 290)

Children often ask me if my stories are true, and my characters real. I call these regional books "true to life," because for most of the characters in them, I had living persons in mind. Birdie Boyer in **Strawberry Girl** is a real little girl I saw plowing in a sandy field in Florida. Little did I dream when I snapped her photograph and talked to her, that she would make friends for me all over the country and return to me nearly three years later, bearing the Newbery Medal in her hand! So when I am asked if my characters are real, I feel I can honestly say yes.

Because of its very nature, regional literature for children becomes a challenge, a challenge to authors to interpret our regions with insight and understanding, and a challenge to those of us who use books, to understand their fundamental purpose and thus help in the important task of widening understanding among different groups.

A regional book shows how a way of life is controlled by an environment. It shows how people live in a certain region and why they live as they do and how outward circumstances have made them live as they do. It will emphasize unimportant outward differences, but it will also emphasize the inward universal likenesses in behavior.

A book is always a vicarious experience. This is particularly true for a child, who identifies himself with the hero of a book in an astonishing way, because of the tremendous power of his imagination. In a book about a horse, the child *becomes* the horse. In a book about a dog, he *is* the dog. In the same way, an adult or child lives with the hero or heroine of a novel, thinks with him, suffers and rejoices with him, speaks and acts like him, understands and loves him.

Surely we all realize the inadequacy of personal experience. Two people, standing face to face, can be as remote as the north and south poles. How often, standing before him, you have not the slightest clue to what the other person is thinking. Faced with a strange person, a strange scene or situation, an unfamiliar experience, we are apt to be suspicious or to laugh defensively. After we get to know the strange person, we are surprised to learn that he has two eyes, two ears as we have. He has two arms, two legs, even a heart and a mind. He is no longer a misunderstood monster, but a human being like ourselves, with faults and frailties, similar to our own, but also with our feeble goodness, our own faith in the right, in justice, and in truth. How can this metamorphosis come about? How can this unfamiliar monster be changed into a human being?

One of the best ways is through books. This is about the only way that children—or adults—can get a vivid glimpse into the inner life and thought processes of a strange person—by sharing it in a book. This is made possible because the author has studied, sympathized with,

and loved these people, shared their life, become "one of them," and by his gifts of creation and imagination has laid the strange person's thoughts, emotions, motives, and intentions bare before the reader—*and they are not very different from the reader's own.*

I believe that children should be constructively taught a sympathetic approach to the strange person, and by the phrase "strange person" I mean any person different from themselves in race, color, creed, or background. Without such teaching, children are apt to follow the crowd like sheep; they think in herds, because they haven't the courage for independent thinking and action. They are thoughtless—they can torture a newcomer in their group who is different in speech, in clothing, or in habits. But I do not believe for a minute that they have basically cruel or barbaric tendencies. When they perpetrate cruelties, it is either the result of adult example, or they do it out of thoughtlessness or lack of imagination. They do not realize how it hurts the other person. They have never learned to put themselves in the other person's place. This shows their great need of guidance, of books which stress the inward thinking of different kinds of people. (p. 291)

We want to encourage a pride in our own locality, a pride in our own local, colorful use of the American language, and a pride in the particular cultural heritage which our group has contributed. Instead of emphasizing these differences between groups deliberately to separate and bring hostility between them, we want to look upon them as a valuable heritage. We want to encourage also a pride in those universal qualities which are common to all groups and which can help us to live harmoniously together. The magnificent thing is that out of so many backgrounds and heritages, there exist so many similarities and likenesses if we will only look for and acknowledge them.

We must never forget that among all men there exists a response to the beautiful, the love of home and family, the fear of insecurity, the appreciation of sacrifice, the desire for personal achievement, and the longing to be at one with the universe. These are universal experiences, these are the bonds which hold men together.

There used to be a time, not so long ago, when the little home, the little farm in this country was self-sufficient and self-contained, a safe little world in itself. But the automobile and enlarged means of communication have changed all that. People now leave their own back yards and, in the family car, travel thousands of miles into other regions than their own. They see people living in all sorts of different ways they never thought possible before. Southerners come north, northerners go south, easterners go west, westerners come east. The traveler comes home, and he remembers those other regions, those other homes so different from his own, that other people love just as dearly as he loves his own. He becomes a new person, a person with a wider vision. He come to only one conclusion: here is our great, wide, beautiful country, with room enough for all, for many kinds of people. We need not all be alike, we must not all be alike. We must hold fast to our individuality, but our local patriotisms can be cherished without any conflict between them. And so, loving my own little corner, where my roots are put down, becomes a part of loving the whole, a part of a true tolerance for all those other people in their back yards.

In regional books for children, then, we stress a particular environment and the way of life which it has brought into being. By understanding this environment, we learn *why* the people speak, think, and act as they do. We realize that under the same circumstances, we would speak, think, and act the same as they do. And so we come to understand a basic concept behind all experience—the universality of human behavior. The most important lesson that any child—or adult—has to learn is the ability to put himself in the other person's place.

And so we need to hold our banner high, the banner of unselfishness, of genuine love for others, and of faith in our fellow men. This may be a dark and a confused and a complicated age through which we are passing, but there are certain eternal verities as true today as they have always been. Let us hold them up as a lighted candle in a dark place. Fortunate indeed, are we who work with children. In their world, there is always joy, beauty, and hope. There is constant faith, trust, and respect for all. Work with and for children is always constructive, building for the future—building One World. (p. 292)

> Lois Lenski, "Regional Children's Literature," in Wilson Library Bulletin, *Vol. 21, No. 4, December, 1946, pp. 289-92.*

---

## GENERAL COMMENTARY

### Josiah Titzell

It is curious that all the books Miss Lenski has written or compiled for herself to illustrate are thoroughly American in flavor while a large number of the books which publishers have given her to illustrate call for the mediaeval pictures which she does so well. It may be that she had to do her American texts in order to do the delightfully sly, yet never malicious, pictorial commentary on life in this country both now and in the golden oak nineties. Certainly there is a far cry—and out of it a great hurrah for her abilities—from the embellished American interiors and ginger-bread architecture of *Skipping Village* to the middle-age tapestries of *A Book of Princess Stories.* Miss Lenski is not a lazy worker. She does much and she works hard over all of it to suit her illustrations and decorations to her text. (p. 1968)

Miss Lenski likes working quietly and unobtrusively. She does not expect to set the world on fire. She does her work because she enjoys it and when she has to give it up for a period of time is miserable until she can get back at it again. She likes, the freedom of this form of illustrating and she likes children and senses their point of view. This sympathy with the form and the audience for whom her books are intended complement her real ability as an artist and make her the distinguished illustrator she is. She has an honest love of order and beauty, a true feeling for pattern and above all she has a sense of humor that allows for much unspoken comment—a comment that is never cruel. (pp. 1968-69)

She is willing to compromise with the limitations of reproduction but she is not willing to make any allowances for the failings of a printer. When you admire the printed color in her illustrations, publishers will tell you with a quiet respect that Miss Lenski keeps calling for proofs until she has the color she originally asked for. In spite of the enthusiasm of the critics and the children of the country, she has no illusions about the literary importance of the books she has written, but considers them very satisfactory vehicles for her illustrating. (p. 1969)

> Josiah Titzell, "Lois Lenski: A Serious Artist with a Sense of Humor," in Publishers Weekly, *Vol. CXVIII, No. 17, October 25, 1930, pp. 1966-69.*

### May Hill Arbuthnot

Children's literature owes much to Lois Lenski, who sketches as cleverly as she writes. She has a sure knowledge of children and engages in meticulous research for everything she does, from little verses for the two-year-old to historical and regional fiction for the teen age. It is easy to account for the popularity of her gay pictures of *Susie Mariar* or the interest in her historical novels such as *Blueberry Corners,* or her regional *Strawberry Girl.* But apparently no grown-up fully understands the fascination of her *Little Auto* for the two- to five-year-olds. Librarians, teachers, and mothers who have to read this book aloud over and over, knowing full well that the child can recite every word of it, are baffled by its hypnotic power over their youngest.

It tells in pictures with the briefest possible captions a day in the life of Mr. Small and his little auto. He takes it out of the garage, drives downtown, obeys all the traffic laws, parks the little auto, and eventually drives it safely home. No plot, no problems, no conflict—a complete and docile obedience to all safety rules, rewarded by a shining and virtuous serenity or, perhaps, security. This story may sound priggish and tame, but somehow it isn't. A three-year-old digs into every detail, and Miss Lenski has not missed one. The child studies the pictures intently; he broods over them lovingly and repeats the captions, which by now seem fairly obvious. The adult closes the book at the end with a shamefaced sense of relief, but the youngest reopens it firmly and the grown-up finds himself beginning once more to intone the ritual of Mr. Small and the little auto.

Its great virtue is undoubtedly its unadorned simplicity. Here is honest writing, the attempt to tell a straightforward narrative so that a young child can understand every detail of something that is really complicated. Nothing important is omitted; nothing trivial or extraneous is included. It is more fact than fiction, more information than story. Yet Mr. Small is a real person to the young reader. Undoubtedly, the child identifies himself with the competent Mr. Small. Perils lie on all sides of Mr. Small, but with masterly presence of mind he always does the right thing. "That's just what I do when I drive," commented a four-year-old.

*The Little Sail Boat, The Little Airplane, The Little Farm, The Little Train,* and *The Little Fire Engine* follow

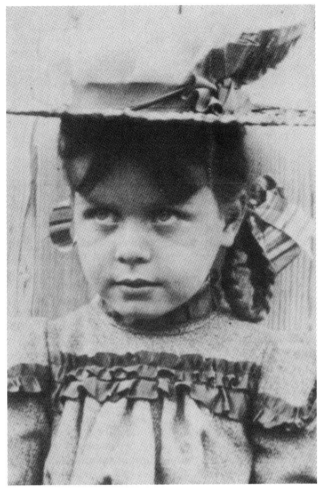

*Lenski in 1899.*

similar patterns, but the train book with Engineer Small comes next in popularity. It goes into more complicated details than *The Little Auto* and is appreciated by children of seven. They study it with profound seriousness. After all, learning a trade is no smiling matter, and apparently that is what the child is up to when he pores over these books. You see him later running his own train in Engineer Small's best manner, and his soliloquies reflect the influence of the Small terminology. To have written career books for the nursery is no mean achievement, and Miss Lenski has accomplished this task with honest competence and not a hint of affectation or pedantry.

The line drawings she makes for most of her own books are sparing of details but get the maximum characterization, action, and drollery into the fewest lines. The "Little" books are done with a soft crayon wash which gives Mr. Small and his machines a pleasant rotundity and depth. There is a blandness about the Small clan that is amusing to adults but properly grave to children. (pp. 364-65)

> *May Hill Arbuthnot, "Here and Now: 'The Little Auto and Other Stories'," in her* Children and Books, *Scott, Foresman and Company, 1947, pp. 364-65.*

**Leland B. Jacobs**

Lois Lenski has worked diligently in the interest of children through her writing. She has written delightfully for the young child in the doings of the Small family and in her short but perceptive seasonal interpretations. She has produced distinctive historical fiction for older children. But undoubtedly her most distinguished contribution to the field of children's literature has been her regional fiction, in which she has pioneered and has achieved a level of creative accomplishment that gives her the distinction of being the most widely known contributor in this genre today. Year by year an appreciative and eager audience of boys and girls look forward to exploring another vital American life situation with Lois Lenski, whose eye is clear, whose mind is sensitive, whose ear is atune to the tempo and overtones of child living in readily identified settings in our vast country.

For any writer who would work with integrity, regional literature poses unique problems and imposes spiritual obligations. If the writer works within the regional setting in which he is reared, he runs the risk of being so deeply involved personally that he is narrowly provincial. If the writer goes into a region new to him to gather his material, he runs the risk of being so charmed by the picturesque that he fails to comprehend the essential elements that are affecting the total behavioral patterns of life in the community.

Good regional fiction for children is neither subjectively sentimental nor objectively superficial. It has, rather, a neat balance of honest sentiment, accurate descriptive detail, and insight into the spirit and quality of mind of the people of whom the author would write. Its purpose is not to mirror the life of the region so much as it is to illuminate such living. Its aim is not to judge the patterns of regional mores and customs; it aims to explore regional behavior as insightfully and sympathetically as the talents of the writer permit. Its obligation to the reader is so to absorb him into the story that he lives as richly as possible in the family and peer groups, in the home and community of a child whose life is both like and different from his own. Good regional fiction assures the reader a high type of entertainment which is achieved because he has lived sympathetically for a moment in the lives of others whose cultural conditions are vitally involved in the story to be told. And in the larger sense, true regional fiction looks intimately inward upon life in a particular geographical locale at a given moment in time not to glorify locale or to promote sectionalism but rather to comprehend locale so intimately that a sense of the universality of man's quest for the good life emerges. Through the printed page, then, the young reader comes to see that, from "sea to shining sea," American children are all searching for ways to live healthfully, happily. That their questions and searchings must, of course, be conditioned by the environment in which they live makes a difference. And cultural differences must be respectfully treated, implies the competent writer in this field, for from diversity there can come national strength.

Few writers for children have been to articulate with regard to their philosophy about a genre in which they produce as has Lois Lenski. She has stated her values and beliefs and ideals concerning writing of child life within the culture unequivocally. (pp. 261-62)

[Hers] is a worthy credo for the writer of regional fiction who would genuinely meet the mind of the child. It is a credo that values children as a great national resource, that trusts children with important big ideas, that recognizes children's abilities to explore significant problems of living if these problems are geared to their level of maturity. Moreover, here is a writer who is explicit about her faith that literature for children must come to grips with philosophical and sociological matters that touch the hearts and minds of boys and girls intimately. In no sense does this imply, however, that Lois Lenski would approve indoctrination or didacticism in fiction. Such spurious ends would belie her criterion of "stories of real people as they really live."

For each of her own regional stories this writer has written a foreword which further clarifies her position. (p. 263)

In one way or another the forewords of all her recent books of regional fiction show Lois Lenski's concern that the American child should be well acquainted with "all the vividness and drama that the American scene holds."

When one turns more directly to the works of this author, one notes first the locales that have held her attention: the Cajun country of Louisiana; Ashe County, North Carolina; the Cracker country of Florida; the oil lands of Oklahoma; the Atlantic coastal plains; the cotton belt of Arkansas; the ranch territory of Texas; the Dakota prairies, for example. Here are rural settings and an agrarian viewpoint. They reflect, then, the influence that the country and small town still have upon a society that has become rapidly urbanized. They are actual, to be sure, as regional settings, and real in ideology, but they are skewed toward a concept of less urbane living than the totality that is our land today might suggest. Herein lies the significance of Lois Lenski's contribution to regional fiction, and also the limitation. Some other writer will have to supply the stories of urbanized locales and thus complement what this writer has so successfully achieved.

Lois Lenski's method of going into a locality and living and working there suggests how thoroughly she believes in the first-hand experience as a necessary ingredient for the development of serious regional fiction for children. By living and working with those about whom she writes, she is able to sensitize herself both to the obvious, material cultural environment and the psychological and spiritual motivations of those about whom she would write. Yet this author assiduously avoids the picturesque for its own sake. When, in *Strawberry Girl,* the Mt. Lebanon Church is described as a "long, boxlike structure" with "handmade benches with sloping backs," the reader is not looking at a rural oddity but rather he goes in to the church with a family. He knows that "the best thing about it was the organ music" because Birdie, the heroine, believed that to be true. (pp. 263-64)

On page after page, the reader lives with people whose food, clothing, and shelter, whose institutions, whose modes of entertainment may differ from those that the reader knows. And yet this writer is consistently considerate of the workaday customs and habits of the people who populate her stories. She creates the essence of the setting by involving the characters in situations that call forth the use of the artifacts of culture familiar to the locale. Without becoming provincial, the writer thus involves vicariously her young readers as participants in an environment that is, at one and the same time, typically individual and typically American.

Lois Lenski's plots have about them, from book to book, an episodic quality that implies, at first glance, a lack of inventiveness. However, stories that find their bearings in the daily life activities of a child as he lives in his family and his community must be couched in a pattern that is suggestive of the way life happenings do occur. Too tightly structured a plot might very well defeat the writer who would catch the colorings and flavors of ordinary, everyday events. Life is not that neat. In every one of Lois Lenski's regional stories, children are facing up to the developmental tasks of living. Their plots center not so much in actionful adventure as in vital solutions to personal problems. In *Strawberry Girl,* how does a child help her family establish itself in a new community? In *Boom Town Boy,* how does one live with new wealth? In *Prairie School,* how does one out-wit the villain, weather? In *Judy's Journey,* how does the child of the migrant worker make life good?

Sociologically rooted, these stories are not sociological treatises. They escape this pitfall because they are human documents, centering their attention on individual personalities that come to life on the printed page in human dramas of courage, faith, industry, and affections. These people are not abstractions, not stereotypes in the ordinary sense of such terms. They are, rather, symbols of American common folk who work and play in their own unique ways because their homes and communities have been so great an influence on their living and learning. Thus, in these regional stories, one moves with a character through his daily tasks as he works to solve a problem. This movement constitutes the essential plot of the story, episodic though it may appear at first glance. Certainly this type of plot is better handled in some books than in others. One might look to *Blue Ridge Billy, Strawberry Girl,* or *Prairie School* to observe Lois Lenski's plot patterns at their best.

Because her ear is tuned to the tempo and overtones of language, and because language itself is so humanizing a force, Miss Lenski has given astute attention to this matter in her regional stories. Of this matter she writes in her foreword to *Blue Ridge Billy:*

> We have as many different kinds of American speech as we have regions. It is interesting to consider in how many different ways the American language is used. Speech is so much more than words—it is poetry, beauty, character, emotion. To give the flavor of a region, to suggest the moods of the people, the atmosphere of the place, speech cannot be overlooked. When I remember the soft, velvety tones of the bayou-

French people, the way they transfer our English words into their native French rhythm, when I hear again the soft, lazy drawl of the Florida Crackers, or the mountain people with fine old forgotten Elizabethan phrases on their lips, it seems to me sacrilege to transfer their speech to correct, grammatical, School-Reader English, made easy enough for the dullest child to read. To me, this would be a travesty on all the beauty and character in the lives of these people.

Words become alive only with use. A coat takes on the character of a man, after he has worn it and shaped it to his person—it becomes truly his and reflects his personality. Until words are used they are dead and lifeless. Through use, words become living speech, echoing the spirit within. Words need to be "worn" to attain beauty.

It is not so much dialect that she uses to capture the language patterns of the peoples of whom she writes as it is the natural speech rhythms of the locales that more deeply show the sureness of her ear. What colloquialisms she uses have about them dignity and warmth. They are caught up naturally in the overtones of what seem, on the printed page, to be spoken words that come from the minds and hearts of real people.

In the introduction to **Peanuts for Billy Ben** Lois Lenski extends this invitation to children: "Come, let us look at the ways of life in our country. Let us go into out-of-the-way corners, upon the hills and down in the valleys, into city streets and village homes. Let us see and get to know the people. Here and there, round about America, are friends worth knowing." This is a fine invitation to young readers, and an honest one. But an invitation implies an obligation to those who accept and this author is up to her responsibility. Since the publication of **Bayou Suzette** in 1943 she has been entertaining audiences of preadolescent readers with reading fare of regional fiction that is well-seasoned, nourishing, and appealing. In retrospect, one can see that from the days of the publication of **Skipping Village** Lois Lenski has been getting ready to extend her invitation to children to "see beyond the rim of their own world." (pp. 264-66)

> *Leland B. Jacobs, "Lois Lenski's Regional Literature," in* Elementary English, *Vol. XXX, No. 5, May, 1953, pp. 261-66.*

### The Times Literary Supplement

What Dick Bruna is now doing for the under threes, Lois Lenski has been doing for years for the under fours. In her chosen field she reigns supreme. She is the least flashy, the least selfconscious of writers. The Small family's lives and activities are flatly recorded, with no attempt to quicken the pace or heighten the drama; it is astonishing how many interesting facts can be dug out of an ordinary day. **Davy and his Dog** and **A Dog Came to School** are both now published in England for the first time; Davy has not quite the holding power of Fireman Small, or Cowboy Small, but he is a very recognizable little boy.

> *"Pictures to the Point," in* The Times Literary Supplement, *No. 3328, December 9, 1965, p. 1149.*

### Charlotte S. Huck and Doris Young Kuhn

The name of Lois Lenski is closely associated with the term "regional fiction." Lenski goes to live in a community, observes as an anthropologist would observe, listens to the people, asks them to tell what has happened in their lives. Then she weaves the facts into an interesting plot centered upon one family. Lenski writes of the purposes of her books:

> I am trying to introduce the children of one region to another, thus widening their horizons. I want to tell how they live and why, to point out details in backgrounds, occupations and customs peculiar to each region. But along with these differences, I show also the inward likenesses—the same universal love of family and kinfolk, the same devotion to or longing for one's homeplace, the same universal struggle for the things we all hold dear—truth, security and happiness. My stories emphasize not the things that hold us apart, but all those things that bring and hold us together in the one great human family.

In **Strawberry Girl,** a Newbery Award book, she describes life in the central Florida backwoods early in the twentieth century. In **Coal Camp Girl,** the West Virginia family experiences hunger during a winter when there is no food; they know the agony of waiting for the rescue of men trapped in a mine and the hard economic lesson of being paid "scrip" in advance of the salary and buying at the high-cost company store.

**Texas Tomboy** is about a young girl who wants to become a ranchwoman. Riding over the plains with her father, "Charlie Boy" learns the lore of ranching. Strong and fearless, her imagination and energy sometimes cause problems. Charlie Boy is often thoughtless, sometimes cruel, and frequently disobedient. The child who reads this book learns about problems of ranch life; he also gains insight into the conflicting demands of society and the individual, as a little girl rebels against her expected sex role. In **Prairie School,** Lenski has written a modern story of prairie life. The trials of life on a snowbound prairie of South Dakota are arduous. Miss Lenski realistically portrays the snowbound days in the school, the dramatic episode when the teacher takes Dolores through the storm for an appendectomy, and the hay drop by helicopter to save the cattle. In these stories, children and adults face their problems and eke out a living, but characters seldom make value choices or grow up as a result of experience. Although the children show little character change, they do effect change. Frequently, it is the child who improves the lot of the family.

Lenski's observations have included language patterns that have been accurately recorded. For example, when Birdie Boyer, in **Strawberry Girl,** is accused of being a Yankee she explains:

Shucks, no! . . . We're shore 'nough Crackers. We was born in Marion County. We're just the same as you-all . . . I done tole you we ain't Yankees.

This may be one of Lenski's greatest contributions, for some regional dialects are being lost with the advent of television and greater mobility of population. In *Corn Farm Boy,* Dick says "He just don't like hogs, Dad," but these characters seldom use "yeah," "git," or omit the "g" sound in verbs as do many rural Iowans today. This illustrates the problem of attempting to portray an entire region with one book. Northern Iowa speech may be different from that of southern Iowa.

Teachers also need to help children who read these books to become aware of the time period. Lenski portrays changes coming to the region at the time she writes, but the reader needs to realize that the San Francisco of 1953 is not San Francisco in 1968. A further problem is that the people in these books are poor or from the lower middle class. Teachers need to remember that each book presents only one small aspect of life in a particular region. Children need to be reminded of the danger of generalizing about all people of a region, class, or occupation. (pp. 234-35)

> *Charlotte S. Huck and Doris Young Kuhn, "Realistic Fiction," in their* Children's Literature in the Elementary School, *second edition, Holt, Rinehart and Winston, Inc., 1968, pp. 215-37.*

**Charlotte S. Huck**

No other author of children's literature has so richly interpreted childhood and the American scene as has Lois Lenski. Her books reflect a perceptive understanding of children of all ages while they realistically present the diversity of background and culture which forms the strength and pattern of the American kaleidoscope.

Lois Lenski's **"Davy"** books are written for the pre-school child. These little books are deceptively simple in both text and illustrations as they portray the daily experiences of one child. It is this very simplicity which eludes most authors of books for the youngest. Miss Lenski understands what is important to the two- and three-year-old and she presents it in a direct manner without any tone of condescension or "cuteness." She can convey excitement in the commonplace as she identifies the satisfaction derived by a pre-schooler in learning to dress himself, or the anticipation of a birthday party. The young child's world is circumscribed by the sphere of his own activities. These simple events frequently appear insignificant and unimportant when they are compared to the busy concerns of adults. Lois Lenski's **"Davy"** books restore them to their proper place of magnitude in the child's small world.

Besides his own activities, the young child is always interested in the weather, the seasons and their effect upon his world. Lenski has provided four books, *Spring Is Here, Now It's Fall, I Like Winter* and *On a Summer Day,* which satisfy this interest. In cheerful rhymed text, she captures the spirit of each season and emphasizes its particular play opportunities. An added feature of each of these stories is the inclusion of music for the words of the text. (p. 346)

Books need to do more than reflect children's daily experiences, they should also extend them. Boys and girls of five, six and seven are naturally curious about their world and appreciate Lenski's straight-forward presentation of information in her stories of the activities of that eternal small boy in adult clothing, Mr. Small. In *Little Farm,* Mr. Small cares for his farm and uses his machinery in the cheerful, matter-of-fact way that characterizes his actions in *The Little Auto, The Little Sail Boat, The Little Fire Engine, The Little Train,* and *The Little Airplane.* In all these books, Miss Lenski presents a simple yet accurate explanation of the operation of each of these vehicles. Usually, in at least one illustration, the salient feature of the machine or equipment is clearly labeled. In *Cowboy Small* and *Policeman Small* all the tools of their occupation are pictured while the text emphasizes their vocational responsibilities. The technical terminology and detailed information in these books are frequently reflected in children's conversation and dramatic play. Young children do want answers to their questions but not complex ones. Lois Lenski's **"Mr. Small"** books satisfy the primary age child without overwhelming him.

Much as the **"Davy"** and **"Mr. Small"** books are beloved by children, Lois Lenski's regional stories are thoroughly enjoyed by children in the middle grades. And it is these stories of children from under-privileged families in various parts of our country which probably represent Lois Lenski's greatest contribution to the field of juvenile literature.

Her regional stories are written for two age groups, the Round about America Series which are easy-reading books for children in the third and fourth grades and her Regional Series which are for somewhat more mature readers. Her foreword to the Round-about America Series describes her purpose in writing these stories:

> Come, let us look at the ways of life
> in our country. Let us go into out-of-the-way
>     corners, up on the hills and down in the
> valleys, into city streets and village homes.
>     Let us see and get to know the people.
> Here and there, round about America, are
>     friends worth knowing.

Through the writings of Lois Lenski, hundreds of American children have come to know intimately the hardships, the joys, the disappointments, the hopes of other American boys and girls whom they would never have met or even knew existed. The horizons of children from sheltered homes are widened as they read of other American children who are too poor to own shoes or to go to a movie. Different ways of living are described in these books but none are judged better than others. Lois Lenski never judges but she helps the reader understand the reasons which necessitate a particular way of life. (pp. 346-47)

The plots of most of the Roundabout America Series are episodic but this is appropriate to the author's desire to show the everyday life of the children in a particular region or minority group. Four of the books, *We Live in the South, We Live By the River, We Live in the City, We Live in the Country* are collections of short stories which show the varying influence of a particular geographical location on the lives of people. The effect of an emergency government housing project on the lives of children is portrayed in *Project Boy* while the dominance of a particular crop is stressed in *Peanuts for Billy Ben* and *Berries in the Scoop.* Another of the series, *Little Sioux Girl* describes Indian reservation life of 1950. The mingling of the old and new, the need for better schools and more adequate medical care is made clear in this story of an Indian girl who faced prejudice, yet found pride in her heritage.

Lois Lenski's finest regional stories have been written for older children from nine to fourteen. There are some fourteen books in this Regional Series which depict the lives of American children in many different, often unheard of, places. Miss Lenski explains her purpose in writing these books in the foreword of *Strawberry Girl.*

> In this series of regional books for American children, I am trying to present vivid, sympathetic pictures of the real life of different localities. We need to know our country better; to know and understand people different from ourselves; so that we can say: "This then is the way these people live. Because I understand it, I admire and love them."

These books are authentic in every detail, for Miss Lenski gathers all the information for her stories through first hand experience with the section of the country about which she is currently writing. She lives among the people, sketching, talking and listening to their problems and concerns. This meticulous research is revealed in the accuracy with which she describes their homes, the food they eat, their work and their play. In *Cotton in My Sack,* her descriptions of the heat of the sun in the fields, the weight of a full cotton sack and the resulting weariness of body are based upon actual experiences in the cotton fields.

The ring of authenticity is heard clearly in the natural speech patterns of her characters. She has preserved the

*From* The Little Auto (*Collection:* More Mr. Small), *written and illustrated by Lois Lenski.*

rhythm of speech which is typical of the region while making judicious use of slang and colloquialisms. In *Strawberry Girl,* for example, children in the middle grades have an opportunity to hear the color and flavor of such idiomatic phrases as used by the Florida "Crackers" as "gettin biggity," "totin water," "right purty," and "plumb good." They can discuss the meanings and origins of such idioms and hopefully they will learn to appreciate the richness of our regional variations of language patterns.

This same respect for realism is revealed in Lenski's character descriptions. Her characters speak and act in accordance with their age, culture and educational backgrounds. She courageously portrays drunken fathers, improvident parents and objectionable neighbors as these are a part of the real life drama of the children in her stories. Her books are not without hope, however. They do more than mirror the despondent life of underprivileged families. There is warmth and family solidarity, there is love and joy along with despair and sadness. Frequently, the children in her books exhibit greater wisdom than their parents. . . . In her foreword to *Cotton in My Sack,* Miss Lenski expresses her admiration for the courage, stoicism and fortitude of the cotton children in these words:

> They had seen sorrow and so they were compassionate. They had seen meanness, and so they valued goodness. They had endured hardships, and so theirs was an attitude not of escape but acceptance. They were ready for whatever life might bring. And because sorrow, meanness and hardship were a part of their lives, they had a better understanding of the joy of living, which comes by a full sharing in human adventure.

While Miss Lenski is best known for her regional stories, her earliest writing was historical fiction for older children. Again her concern for accuracy and authenticity is clearly reflected in these fine historical novels. Even in these stories of the past the discerning reader can see the author's incipient interest in the problems of human relations. In her book *A-Going to the Westward,* she tellingly writes of the adjustments which Yankees from Connecticut, Pennsylvania Dutchmen and Kentucky southerners faced as they learned to live together in the wilderness of the Ohio country in the early 1800's. The theme of the exciting book, *Indian Captive: The Story of Mary Jemison,* is the basic conflict between the Indians' and early settlers' way of life. Based upon the actual accounts of the capture of a twelve-year-old girl by the Seneca Indians, the plot revolves around Mary's determination not to accept the Indian ways despite their kind treatment of her. Almost without her realizing it, when she begins to understand the Indians, she finds that she loves them. When the time comes for her to decide whether she will remain with them or go with the English, she elects to stay. Whether Lois Lenski writes of the hardships faced in the past or the present, she writes with compassion, understanding and respect for mankind.

Miss Lenski has illustrated all of her own books in a style which is uniquely her own and readily identifiable. Her knowledge of children extends to their preferences and appreciation for art. In her **"Davy"** books, for example, she has taken into consideration the very young child's inability to see perspective and has included little or no background in her illustrations. Her **"Mr. Small"** books reflect the same careful attention to essential detail as represented in the text. Her drawings for both these series are done in two colors in a simple almost childlike manner. She frequently includes the sun in her pictures, a characteristic feature of young children's drawings. Her figures are done in a soft crayon wash and have a rounded look. Mr. Small has the size and proportion of a four-year-old even though he is dressed as an adult. This helps the young child to identify with Mr. Small.

The illustrations for the Roundabout America Series are realistic black and white sketches. Her Regional Series show even more accurate detail in the soft pencil drawings of the interiors of homes and schools. Her pictures of people express more emotion than do those in her books for younger children. Realism is portrayed in the disheveled appearance of the children and their shabby homes. Interesting and detailed end papers summarize events of the story as in *Judy's Journey,* or portray the locale as in *San Francisco Boy,* or an important environmental aspect such as the company store in *Coal Camp Girl.* Lenski's art work is sketched on the spot and is as authentic as the incidences in her stories.

It is only as one views the writings and illustrations of Lois Lenski's in their entirety that one can comprehend her vast contribution to children's literature. She is a prolific writer producing many books of various types and for different age groups. She has never sacrificed quality for quantity and each of her books makes a distinctive contribution to the type of literature it represents. The essence of her greatness is in the versatility of her writing, for her work encompasses all of childhood. No author has interpreted American children more accurately or perceptively; no author has given more abundantly to children than has Lois Lenski. (pp. 347-50)

> *Charlotte S. Huck, "Lois Lenski: Children's Interpreter," in* Catholic Library World, *Vol. 40, No. 6, February, 1969, pp. 346-50.*

### May Hill Arbuthnot

In Lois Lenski's series of regional stories, young readers encounter families of sadly limited resources, economic and otherwise. In *Strawberry Girl,* Birdie Boyer's family belongs to Florida's small crop farmers. The Boyers are hard working, neat, and efficient, but they are pestered by mean, shiftless neighbors, Paul Slater and his slatternly wife. However, Shoestring Slater, their son, is intelligent and quick to learn better ways from the Boyers, even though his loyalty to his family keeps him on the defensive.

In Lois Lenski's *Cotton in My Sack,* everyone in the family works to the point of exhaustion cotton-picking all week, only to go on a Saturday spree of aimless, foolish spending. Other of the Lenski regional stories include *Boom Town Boy, Judy's Journey, Prairie School,* and *Coal Camp Girl.* These are grim stories, despite occasional flashes of humor. What lifts the characters out of the squalor in which they live is their patient endurance, courage, and a fierce family pride that binds them together with un-

shakeable loyalty. It is good for children of suburbia to discover that enduring family love at whatever level gives richness to life. (p. 116)

> *May Hill Arbuthnot, "Realism for the Middle Years, 9-10-11: 'Strawberry Girl'," in her* Children's Reading in the Home, *Scott, Foresman and Company, 1969, pp. 111-41.*

### Sam Leaton Sebesta and William J. Iverson

Certainly the regional stories by Lois Lenski continue to be good fare today. Lenski traveled to colorful regions of America, particularly the Southeast and North Central states. As evidenced by the ample conversation in her stories, she carefully recorded speech patterns typical of regional dialect and painstakingly attempted to transmit them through spelling and diction that dared to differ from standard English. In all her regional books the plots are heavily loaded with incidents highlighting ways of life peculiar to the regions. The title character in *Bayou Suzette* discovers alligator eggs and is discovered by an alligator, learns of a ghost that supposedly inhabits the bayou, and encounters regional attitudes toward Indians. Tina, the *Coal Camp Girl,* faces near tragedy when her father is trapped in the flooded mine. The events in *Prairie School* display the nobility and cheerfulness of children and their teacher during a bitter blizzard year in South Dakota.

The Lenski books contain the author's own illustrations and maps, the latter often in the form of picto-maps to aid the reader in following the story. In fact, nearly every attempt is made to clarify the reader's concept of each region. Less successful, however, is the attempt to create memorable characters. Despite the local color, Lenski heroes and heroines seem somewhat abstract. They react in stereotyped ways, and incidents that should be crucial to character development are glossed over. For instance, in *Coal Camp Girl* Tina is so depressed about the injury of her uncle that she leaves school; a couple of pages later this depression is dismissed and Tina worries instead about a colt with the colic; shortly thereafter she is exploring an empty house, trying to solve its mystery. The pattern in all these books is one of quickly solved problems. The optimistic tone is preserved perhaps at the expense of heavier involvement and more deeply felt characterization. Nevertheless, on most grounds these are good books of the regional type, simply enough written for the lower intermediate level. (p. 274)

> *Sam Leaton Sebesta and William J. Iverson, "Realistic Fiction," in their* Literature for Thursday's Child, *Science Research Associates, Inc., 1975, pp. 234-306.*

### Barbara Bader

Before she came to picturebooks Lois Lenski had done much illustrating and some writing and, reversing the balance, she would do a great deal more; but for a brief period, roughly 1927 to 1937, she produced one after another picturebook of distinctive charm. As for instance: *Jack Horner's Pie,* nursery rhymes with funny quaint figures, and its successor *Alphabet People; The Wonder City,* a panorama of New York, part social science, a large part enjoyment; **Benny and His Penny,** which has a coin set into its cover and delicate, fluttery cartoons that Mary Petty might almost have drawn. From this period, too, comes the snappy cloth book **Sing a Song of Sixpence.**

Nonetheless it is the Littles and Mr. Small—little and small for no logical but every good reason—who delighted children and tried the patience of their parents; fixed a form of expression and a sign-off ("and that's all . . . ") in young minds and old; and, setting the table, changing a tire, going to church, plowing with a tractor, roping a calf, piloting a plane, brought first the immediate and familiar, then the inaccessible and desirable, into what may well be every reading household.

The Littles are a model family saved from stuffiness by the prosaic sorts of things they do and the laconic matter-of-fact text. Similarly, what is chaste about the pictures is off-set by their compact cheerfulness and certain small, light touches—the steam corkscrewing up from Mrs. Little's washbasin, Mr. Little's flapping shoelace, the flying grass-clippings. As compositions, they have order, definition, above all equipoise; as illustrations, they come alive.

Mr. Small, going for an outing in the little Auto, is a cartoon figure, big of head and hat, always a little stiff, a little unreal—no-man, the better to be everyman (or, alternatively, a mannikin). The little Auto is disproportionately big too, most of the time, and for all the oiling and pumping and stopping for gas, it is his toy; he beats out a horse and buggy, plows up hill and speeds down hill, "scares the ducks and chickens". This irresponsible delight in playing with a car, a car that is still a novelty and not a high-powered mechanism, is part of what children enjoy; had the little Auto been a later model, it might have been sooner for the scrap heap.

Of the Mr. Small books, **The Little Sail Boat,** blue and white, crisp and finished, is the beauty. The gray tones and modeled forms stand out against the flat ground, and there is little of the formula drawing or the slack design found elsewhere. Shipshape it is, but it is also less a toy-book and, perhaps on account of its subject too, has less attraction for small children. At four, boats are not to sail but to watch chugging and puffing and making waves.

Tractors, however, are to ride and cowboys are to be, and the books to have, funny-looking or not, are **The Little Farm** and **Cowboy Small.** A day in the life of Farmer Small takes in the work of a year, with the tractor pulling a plow and a harrow in the spring, cutting hay in the summer, hauling apples in the fall. If he goes over a stone and loses a few, all the better—children will speak up and say so.

A dividend of a different sort is the paper-doll endpapers of **Cowboy Small;** indispensable as they (and the near-by glossary) may be to parents, children who have their own copy have been known to cut them up, the better to play cowboy with). In **Cowboy Small** they get not only directions, but also a script. Though it has no more plot than its predecessors, there is, in the windup, something of a story. "Next day, Cowboy Small rides a bucking bronco. '*Yip-pee!—Yip-pee! Ride'em, cowboy!*'/*Ker-plop!* Cowboy Small hits the dust!/But—he's a pretty good cowboy, after

all! Cactus is waiting, so—/ '*Giddap, Cactus!*' Cowboy Small rides again!"

Hi yo Silver it isn't, any more than Cactus is a proper name for a Wild West horse, and Cowboy Small hasn't any more business being as big as Cactus than Mr. Small has being as big as the little Auto; but any doubt as to who's in the saddle is dispelled by the endsheet, where he stands without his western togs on. (pp. 76-9)

> *Barbara Bader, "The Small Child's World,"* in her American Picturebooks from Noah's Ark to the Beast Within, *Macmillan Publishing Co., Inc., 1976, pp. 73-80.*

## Barbara Bader

The first American picture book of everyday family life is still with us—Lois Lenski's **The Little Family.** How prim, how conventionalized, how unreal it looks to us today! What it resembles, actually, is a catalogue of that era for Best & Company's swank Lilliputian Bazaar. Lenski was a commercial artist, so the resemblance is not strange. The book's appearance was determined also by the new process of color-offset printing, which called for strong outlines and flat colors. Thus, what we might be inclined to see as the embodiment of middle-class propriety—as a combination of class values, prescribed family roles, and rigid ideas of child rearing—must also be seen as the result of artistic conventions and technical considerations.

Still, the book is curiously and significantly unreal. Lenski made it for her own three-year-old, to whom it's dedicated. Yet the boy and the girl are the same size, though there's no suggestion they're twins. What distinguishes them throughout are the things they do. He has a wheelbarrow, to help his father in the garden; she waters the plants. While he tosses his ball, she looks at a book. The differentiation between the father's and mother's roles is absolute—and when the family goes for a ride, the relative positions of males and females couldn't be more plain. Yet Lenski was what we'd call today a working mother. We can safely say that **The Little Family** was an unconscious reflection of certain social conventions—a model or abstraction of family life; its realism lay in the very depiction of a father leaving for work and a mother keeping house.

In 1934 came the first of Lenski's stories of Mr. Small, **The Little Auto.** Working chiefly in black and white, Lenski could model and use shading; to our eyes today, the pictures look both naive and Art Deco. Mr. Small was a mannikin with a certain dash, a real little streamlined gent: the reason, perhaps, he's been imperishable. Lenski brought him back in **The Little Sail Boat,** of 1937; Engineer Small in **The Little Train,** of 1940; Farmer Small in **The Little Farm,** of 1942; and Cowboy Small, in the 1949 book of that title.

Finally, in 1951, be became Papa Small, and in this guise my children met him in the 1950s. Twenty years after **The Little Family,** Lenski's **Papa Small** was just about the only head-on depiction of ordinary recognizable family life doings. In content **Papa Small** is very similar to **The Little Family.** But the 1951 Smalls are a far cry from the 1932 Littles. The family is bigger, and so is the house. Family life is structured—Lenski chronicles first a day, then a week—but it's also informal and fluid, the image of conge-nial togetherness. When Papa Small shaves in the morn-ing, the small Smalls, half dressed, come in to watch. When Mama Small cleans, or fixes dinner, both Paul and Polly help. And on Monday when Mama does the laun-dry, Papa hangs the clothes on the line. On Saturday, of course, the Smalls do the week's marketing. The little roadster remains; it's Mr. Small's trademark. But the fam-ily arrangement is casual and practical. And the super-market scene—in which Mama carries the list, Papa push-es the wagon, Baby Small rides in the seat, and Paul and Polly pick out packages—is post-World War II suburbia incarnate.

These little books are artifacts—yet they are also hardy perennials. And the question of why they have survived is a complicated one. Lenski was in no sense a major tal-ent, either as artist or writer. Her subject matter, too, has had more skillful and imaginative treatment at the hands of others. In style, construed in its broadest sense, her work is dated; the information she purveys is often out-of-date. What is the appeal, then, of these curios?

The key may be the combination, in Lenski's work, of di-rectness, purposeful activity, and individuality. Mr. Small is the little man who can, the doer—whether as sailor, en-gineer, pilot, or cowboy. Then he is Papa: not an authority figure, not even an exalted personage—but everybody's dad. Just saying that is a reminder of the difference a word makes. Probably he became "Papa" as a parallel to "Pilot," "Engineer," and so on. In *Papa Small,* however, everybody does: The book is a beehive of family activity, not excluding periods of rest and relaxation.

So the books can be at once documents—social or voca-tional microcosms—and timeless mini-dramas, with per-sonalities of their own. (pp. 168-71)

> *Barbara Bader, "A Second Look: 'The Little Family',"* in The Horn Book Magazine, *Vol. LXI, No. 2, March-April, 1985, pp. 168-71.*

### Zena Sutherland and May Hill Arbuthnot

In 1946, when the Newbery Medal was given to Lois Len-ski's *Strawberry Girl,* attention was called to a unique se-ries of books about regional groups from all over the Unit-ed States.

Lois Lenski began her series with *Bayou Suzette,* a story about the French-speaking people in the bayou section of Louisiana. . . .

*Strawberry Girl* is typical of these books at their best. It is the story of Birdie Boyer's family, newly moved to Flori-da's backwoods for the purpose of raising small crops of "sweet 'taters," strawberries, oranges, and the like.

The values of this series are to be found in its objective re-alism and compassion. Young members of disadvantaged families meet families like their own in these regional sto-ries of Lois Lenski's. And they take heart, because always the ups and downs of these hardpressed, courageous peo-ple yield a ray of hope. Things are, or give promise of be-coming, better. And to the children of more affluent fami-lies, these books give a picture of a kind of family love and loyalty that may be new to them.

> *Zena Sutherland and May Hill Arbuthnot, "Books for the Middle Group: 'Strawberry Girl',"* in their Children and Books, *seventh edition, Scott, Foresman and Company, 1986, p. 343.*

---

## TITLE COMMENTARY

### *Jack Horner's Pie: A Book of Nursery Rhymes*   (1927)

All the old nursery favorites are here in this bright and al-luring book of yellow and shaded green, more than a hun-dred of them, with pages upon pages of pictures in gay col-ors in which numbers of the persons of the drama of the various poems appear busily engaged in their proper activ-ities. Even the smallest tots will enjoy picking out the vari-ous characters.

> *A review of "Jack Horner's Pie: A Book of Nur-sery Rhymes,"* in The New York Times Book Review, *December 4, 1927, p. 36.*

Many familiar rhymes are included in the hundred and fifty chosen for this collection. The delightful illustrations in line and flat color are childlike in conception, frequently employing a cross-section of a house and revealing the characters surrounded by just the right amount of minute and interesting detail. (pp. 286-87)

> *A review of "Jack Horner's Pie: A Book of Nur-sery Rhymes,"* in The Booklist, *Vol. 24, No. 7, April, 1928, pp. 286-87.*

---

### *Skipping Village*   (1927)

Some creative artists find their form of expression in color and line, some in words, some in clay or textiles or an in-definite number of other mediums. Few think in terms of two at once. But Miss Lois Lenski seems to have that spe-cial gift. Her pictures in this charming book are as cons-tant and spontaneous an expression of her thought as are the chapters and paragraphs in which normally one would expect to find it embodied. The two were obviously insepa-rable in her imagination. Lucky artist to have access to two modes of expression, each so charmingly supplement-ing the other! This must account, incidentally, for the gen-erous supply of illustrations. Small and large, sketch and full page picture, their number evidently was limited only by the author's impulse to express fully her own ideas. In the world of child literature we seem to have here a new ideal—pictures and text in equal values.

The text is one of delightful simplicity, of the kind which to a child presents a pleasant and interesting realism. An old-fashioned (but perennially existent) village lives through its round of months with their routine of charac-teristic homely happenings—school life, family life, play, in all four seasons—and the children of a typical family follow these outwardly simple events with the gusto and vivid interest and healthy enthusiasm of childhood. That is all of the book;—no plot, no thrills. But it is so genuine and so true that any adult reader who happens upon it will feel a real pull upon memories small but deep,—memories not often stirred; and children will find it full of what to them is the real stuff of life. Or if they are so limited mentally to apartment or city life that the book speaks an unfamiliar language—why, all the better for them to absorb it! It will let in fresh air upon their imaginations. They will not fail to pick out with satisfaction, also, the high spots of the village blocks on the delightful map within the book cover, just as they will enjoy at length every fine-drawn detail of the delightful people and animals and objects in the illustrations.

Finally a word should be said about the merry rhymes, each with its little drawing, with which this generous author begins and ends every chapter. They seem to complete the very full measure of this unusual book, whose quaint and attractive jacket is an appropriate sign-post for what awaits within.

> *Marian C. Dodd, "An Unusual Book," in* The Saturday Review of Literature, *Vol. 4, No. 20, December 10, 1927, p. 438.*

---

### A Little Girl of Nineteen Hundred (1928)

This ought to be a much more charming story for children than it is. Its period is the turn of the century, and we imagine that it will be more interesting to parents who were growing up in the 'nineties than to their 1928 children. Miss Lenski has made ingenious use of historical materials and we at least got a great deal of enjoyment out of remembering things that she calls to mind,—the black bands around the papers when President McKinley was shot, for instance, and one's mothers saying, "Poor Mrs. McKinley." We envied Flora Baxter, who was frightened almost to death by her first ride in a horseless carriage. We never rode in one until they had been made safe for democracy, and being frightened to death as an adult hasn't many thrills. It is rather a test of the quality of writing if a grown-up can read a book written, too obviously, for the young, with genuine emotion and pleasure. Our question is whether the audience for which it is written will not find it a slow moving chronicle of a pompous and somewhat stuffy decade.

> *A review of "A Little Girl of Nineteen Hundred," in* The Saturday Review of Literature, *Vol. 5, No. 16, November 10, 1928, p. 357.*

**A Little Girl of Nineteen Hundred,** . . .would be a very good book for some little girl to give to her mother, for it takes up all those pleasures her mother knew when she was young. It seems as though this material could have been put into more interesting shape. It is too stiff and tabulated in its present form.

> *Mark Graham Bonner, in a review of "A Little Girl of Nineteen Hundred," in* The New York Times Book Review, *December 16, 1928, p. 28.*

*Greenacres, Lenski's studio from 1935 to 1964.*

### The Wonder City: A Picture Book of New York (1929)

[The] charm of this book is in its decorative pattern of shifting scenes rendered in clear, soft green, pink, yellow in combination with black and white. Two lines of obvious verse accompany each of the drawings, picturing Jimmy and Joan on a visit to New York. They begin with the Grand Central Station, cross over Fifth Avenue at Forty-second Street, visit the Metropolitan Museum, the Zoo, the Children's Room of the Library, the Natural History Museum, Central Park (a very delightful double spread), the Aquarium, the Woolworth Tower, Orchard Street, etc. One of the most effective pages bears the most descriptive of the versified captions:

> A taxi man took them with jolts and with knocks,
> To see a big steamship just leaving the docks.

Miss Lenski has also pictured "the jolly old El" and has done an interesting pictorial map of Manhattan reminiscent of one drawn by Jay Van Everen for Nicholas, some years ago.

Since this is the first book of a projected series for children on the outstanding cities of the United States, the Owls await with interest the verdict of the children as to how they like to look at and think about great cities they have never seen. They are themselves of the opinion that New York needs more beauty, more life and more fun as a child sees and feels it than Miss Lenski has imparted in **The Wonder City.** Nor has it enough of the essential comic spirit to justify the publisher's statement that it would be a "boon to distressed parents of children who are devoted to the 'funnies.'" We have no idea that children will look upon it in that way. It is the grown-up who will so classify it. As a picture book introducing children of our own and of other countries to New York, it lacks depth and meaning. It is too much concerned with the commonplace to have any permanent value, but it does contribute as colorful a note as a nice bit of chintz to the new books of the summer.

> *Anne Carroll Moore, in a review of "The Wonder City: A Picture Book of New York," in* New York Herald Tribune Books, *August 4, 1929, p. 7.*

Here is a book of hardly more than thirty pages which should prove a source of endless diversion to the very young child, for it is a whole city, the city of New York, in microcosm. From the moment that Miss Lenski's engaging small boy and girl emerge from the waiting-room of the Grand Central station to that fleeting glimpse of them waving farewell as the observation car rolls out of it, the two little figures make their way through a series of scenes depicting various sections and features of the city and the men, women, and children who people it. As full page illustrations Miss Lenski's drawings produce an effect of confusion which results from the numbers of small figures that throng them, but reduced to their various incidents they are delightful, portraying both realistically and humorously the various points of interest in New York, such as the menagerie, the park, the library, the aquarium, and the Brooklyn Bridge.

Miss Lenski manages with a few lines to get remarkable expressiveness of attitude and countenance, and injects just enough of the burlesque into her delineation to lend something of the cartoon to her drawings. There are a dozen types on such a page as that picturing Orchard Street, a multiplicity of figures which will engage the interest of the child and call forth the admiration of his elders for Miss Lenski's cleverness. The end papers in black and white present a pictorial map of Manhattan and provide a pleasing contrast to the color of the rest of the illustrations.

> *Amy Loveman, in a review of "The Wonder City," in* The Saturday Review of Literature, *Vol. 6, No. 5, August 24, 1929, p. 78.*

### The Washington Picture Book   (1930)

In her *Washington Picture Book* Lois Lenski has made a delightful and very decorative double spread of the Easter Monday egg rolling on the White House lawn, which should be remembered in children's libraries when Easter comes next year. I find the whole book far more effective and amusing than the New York picture book of this artist—*The Wonder City.* The drive in the victoria on the way to call on the President and the dinner at the White House with President Hoover are two pictures children will especially enjoy. . . .

In neither of the two books—the Washington or the New York—is the color printing entirely successful. Both the Washington monument and the Lincoln Memorial would be far more effective without color. [We] wish that Miss Lenski would draw her Jimmy and Joan with more of a sense of life and fun. They are properties rather than personalities, and bear no intelligent relation to the sights they see, the adventures they have and the children they represent. Sharpness of characterization would work wonders and add measurably to the length and strength of the appeal of these picture books of American cities.

> *Anne Carroll Moore, "The Three Owls," in* New York Herald Tribune Books, *May 4, 1930, p. 8.*

The second of the series on American cities done in picture

by Lois Lenski. It takes Jimmy and Joan, two small children, through Washington on a sight-seeing tour of the capital in fifteen colored cartoons. In each one the two tots appear, Jimmy with his guide-book and toy horse, Joan with handbag and doll. They view the Capitol, the Monument, the Library of Congress, and many of the other regular features of a trip to Washington, and they manage to slide down the bannisters of the Library and sit in the forbidden chairs at Mount Vernon—two performances which would shock Washington beyond belief! Also they dine in state—and private—with President Hoover.

The drawing is pleasant and just sufficiently humorous, and the episodes are enough in number to whet the appetite without cloying it. The color reproductions in flat tints are excellent, simple and positive as a child's crayon work. The book will obviously not appeal to youngsters of the size of Jimmy and Joan, but a girl of thirteen, who picked up the book before I could get a chance to write this review, was entranced by it. She has never been to Washington, but it is nevertheless a real place to her, and she knew enough of the places delineated to appreciate the pictures. It is far better than photographs would be, and a pleasant book to look at—which is what a picture book should be.

> *Carl Rollins, in a review of "The Washington Picture Book," in* The Saturday Review of Literature, *Vol. VI, No. 44, May 24, 1930, p. 1078.*

The pictures are, on the whole, more attractive than those in Miss Lenski's *The Wonder City, A Picture Book of New York.* The children, however, are still pert and smug, and it is doubtful if the drawings of Jimmy and Joan sliding down the banisters in the Congressional Library, banging the piano at Mount Vernon and climbing ladders in the Arts and Industries Museum are really childlike in humor.

> *Anne T. Eaton, in a review of "The Washington Picture Book," in* The New York Times Book Review, *June 22, 1930, p. 17.*

### The Little Auto   (1934)

[*The Little Auto*] follows every step in taking care of and in running a car; oiling, pumping up the tires, driving with due attention to traffic rules, parking, washing and polishing. The illustrations have the amusing quality of toyland come to life and the slight thread of story which is, in effect, hardly more than captions for the pictures, will satisfy the 6 and 7 year olds who enjoy books about the everyday things with which they are familiar.

> *Anne T. Eaton, in a review of "The Little Auto," in* The New York Times Book Review, *October 7, 1934, p. 17.*

The age for Miss Lenski's *The Little Auto* is so early it all but collides with Mother Goose. It is a picture-book for children who still play with one-passenger foot-power automobiles and are more interested in how they go than why. The adventures of Mr. Small, who has a little auto, red and shiny, keeps it in a little garage and drives it through traffic, into filling stations and through the possibilities of a "baby" car, are not too far ahead of the possibilities of their own cars to make Mr. Small's machine seem out of their range. It is one of a series of picture books that cost little and show brains.

> *May Lamberton Becker, in a review of "The Little Auto," in* New York Herald Tribune Books, *December 30, 1934, p. 5.*

---

### *Phebe Fairchild: Her Book*   (1936)

#### AUTHOR'S COMMENTARY

Nine years ago we moved to the country. In the northwest corner of Connecticut we found a fine old house built in 1790, near a small village, with one hundred acres of woodlot, meadow land and pasture. (p. 395)

Some time later, while attending a country auction, I bought an armful of old books. Among them was a little book in green paper covers, called *Scenes in the Country.* The inscription on the fly-leaf was written in a stilted hand, in faded ink: *Kate Daniels Her Book—October 1825—from her Cousins in Litchfield.* And then the quotation:

> "This is a preshious Book, indeed,
> Happy the Child who Loves to Read."

That was the beginning. I began to search not only for early books, but for all the information I could collect about them. I found out that when our ancestors were chopping wood in the primeval forests of New England, fighting battles, building stone walls and driving stagecoaches through muddy, rutty roads, they had the time and also the inclination to prepare and publish special books for children. Children read books in 1776 and in 1800, and on through the nineteenth century. These tiny, frail, paper-covered books tell us more about their inner lives than any other source. They tell us about children's interests and occupations, the morals and religion of the day, parental ideals, opinions and discipline, and they give many details regarding the care and upbringing of children. They open up a brilliant vista of the child's world of the past.

You cannot live in New England without becoming acquainted with your neighbors. Most of mine are descendants of original settlers, fifth or sixth generation. From them I have heard many stories of the early history of the town. (pp. 395-96)

And so, without realizing it, through the two-hundred-year-old town and the old house and their associations, through the old books which the children read, through the lives of my neighbors and their ancestors, I have been studying New England history for nine years—no, not studying it, but feeling it and living it. The past has come alive for me in a way that it never did in the history books. I hated History in school; to me it was only a meaningless procession of dates and battles to be memorized. But when I decided to tell the story of our house, to fill it with people and describe the life they might have lived one hundred years ago, as soon as I looked at History from the human

standpoint, it became fascinating and absorbing and very much alive.

I wanted to describe the ordinary everyday life of a family in a house like ours, home-life as it affected child-life, and village-life as it affected both. For the children did not live lives of their own in those days—they lived in an adult world and were affected by everything that went on in that adult world. The very self-sufficiency of every farm, providing as it did everything necessary for living, in the way of shelter, food and clothing, gave the life of a child an inconspicuous place. Children were taught to be seen but not heard, you will remember—the home was such a busy plant there wasn't time to listen to what the children had to say. Thrown upon their own initiative, they developed inner resources of strength and vigor which enabled them to withstand the rigors of their harsh training and environment.

When Phebe Fairchild came from New Haven to Winton in 1828, the farmhouse was already old and had a past. Benjamin built his house in the new 1830 style because his father's house, built forty years before, was out-of-date. The illustrations in the book show actual views of this house, both interiors and exteriors.

As my story developed, the characters became very real to me and to the members of my family. (p. 397)

I spent many months in research. I read old numbers of the *Connecticut Courant;* I saw the millinery and hairdressing advertisements which caught Great-Aunt Pettifer's eye; the portrait painter's announcement which attracted Christopher. I studied account books from a local store and found out what purchases people made in 1830 and the "country pay" they gave in exchange; I saw invoices listing the actual stock carried; I found records of actual hauling of merchandise from Bristol Basin on the Farmington Canal. The story of the canal's opening is based on the actual account of an eye-witness. I held in my hand a stagecoach time-table, listing the various tavern stops from New Haven to Litchfield. In my collection of early American children's books I have a little brown morocco-covered *Mother Goose,* like Phebe's, which caused so much trouble; a *Ladies' Pocket Library,* with gloomy black covers, from which the two blackbirds read about conduct and behavior to while away the tedium of the stagecoach journey. I have a pink paper-covered Watts' *Divine Songs for Children,* with the hymns which Phebe had to learn; a soiled and worn *Memoirs of Miriam Warner,* whose forlorn appearance in itself would give any child the heartache. And I have a tiny little book, 1½ by 2½ inches, with only eight pages, which is simply bursting with eloquent objections to *Mother Goose* as "silly rhymes, unfit for children to read." Another small eight-page book is called *The Folly of Finery* or, *History of Mary Lawson;* it tells the sad fate of a little girl who loved pretty clothes and personal adornments. It was largely through this handful of little books that Phebe Fairchild came alive.

Phebe lived with me in spirit for many months, as real as any member of my family. Her ghost will, I haven't a doubt, continue to haunt my home and my heart forever. (pp. 398-99)

*Lois Lenski, "The Story of 'Phebe Fairchild Her Book',"* in The Horn Book Magazine, *Vol. XIII, No. 6, November-December, 1937, pp. 394-400.*

Miss Lenski's story of ten-year-old Phebe from New Haven, spending the year 1830 with her father's folks in the Connecticut country while her parents are on a voyage, is more than a pleasant tale of a child's ups and downs in hard living and no place to wear pretty clothes. It is the nearest to a complete reconstruction of child life in this place and period that has been offered to children so young. Helen Fuller Orton did this for northern New York in *The Treasure in the Little Trunk,* so well that books of this kind will be long compared with hers; Miss Lenski's story has been documented with the same devoted care. The songs they sing in **Phebe Fairchild** are contributions to a study of American balladry, the charming clothes the child's cousins think too fine are the real thing, and the objections to her reading-matter are in the spirit of the time, "the transition between the home industry period and the beginning of the small manufactures." I quote this from a preface that children, after their fashion, will not read; students of the time well may do so and see on what sympathetic research these many details are based. Mother Goose, for instance, figures largely in the plot; it has survived its early opposition by those who had no mind to see children reading books meant only for pleasure; the objections this family make to it are taken bodily from a child's guide to virtue popular at this period.

This, as much as the reliability of its incidents, distinguishes the book: its determination to be faithful to the time and show its differences between what one might call the coastal and the inland points of view. These differences began early in New England. Only a few miles on the map might make them. A child need not get this from the story, but the liveliness of the plot is kept up by it, and a reading child will find a lovable little heroine, homely incidents, and a happy ending—incidentally, a vindication of the right to happiness through reading "Mother Goose." The many quaint little pictures are at every point in the text, true, tidy and funny.

*May Lamberton Becker, in a review of "Phebe Fairchild: Her Book,"* in New York Herald Tribune Books, *November 8, 1936, p. 10.*

The incidents in the story are the everyday ones of a busy farm of that period, while Phebe herself is a child with considerable spunk and individuality. The distinction of this book lies in its excellent recreation of a period in New England life with great accuracy and consideration for detail. Rarely has this been done so successfully for younger readers, for the story never becomes over-weighted with this picturesque account "of the transition between the home industry and the beginnings of small manufacturing". The first volumes of *Mother Goose* were reaching children who had known, and were to know for many more years only the *Bible* and instructive books. Teachers will find much valuable material here.

*Pauline A. O'Melia, in a review of "Phebe Fairchild: Her Book,"* in Library Journal, *Vol. 61, December 1, 1936, p. 930.*

This is an excellent example of a book written for children with the same careful study of background and period, the same accuracy of detail, that would be considered necessary in a book for adults. It is combined with an imaginative understanding of childhood, with humor and a fine power of characterization, so that a Connecticut country community of a hundred years ago promptly comes to life before the reader's eyes.

The author tells us in the foreword that she has consulted contemporary records, and as we realize with what care Miss Lenski has assembled her material, we feel at the same time how vividly she has lived in imagination with her little heroine in the big Fairchild farmhouse, where pot hooks hung in the kitchen fireplace, and the cross beams of the ceiling were decorated with strings of dried apples, red peppers, pumpkin rings, crook necks and festoons of corn with braided husks. Phebe's dresses—her buff cassimere with bretelles, her green taffeta with leg-of-mutton sleeves, her embroidered India muslin with blue ribbons, and the rest of the wardrobe that she unpacks from her round-topped green morocco trunk—will delight any one interested in American period costumes. The description of the meals in the farmhouse kitchen shows the kind of food served in New England a hundred years ago.

The clockmaker and tinker stops by with his wares, the traveling artist, with his canvases on which he hopes to add portrait heads to the figures already painted, stays long enough to paint a landscape on the walls of the north parlor. Church on Sundays, lessons on weekdays and plenty of household tasks fill Phebe's time. The pig-butchering season comes around, candles are dipped, geese plucked and there is a house-raising. Thanksgiving Day is bountifully celebrated, though these descendants of the Puritans still look askance at Christmas festivities. The songs that the characters sing are authentic songs of the period and the speech has a Yankee flavor.

The puritanism that provided a rule of life for the family and caused them to think that Phebe's clothes were too fine and to question her reading matter is thoroughly in keeping with the period of which the author wrote and which she calls "the transition between the home-industry period and the beginning of small manufactures."

Some of these matters have figured before in books for children, but it has remained for Miss Lenski to describe, in entirely delightful fashion, the first "pleasure book" for children. Phebe's little paper-covered "Mother Goose's Quarto" in which her father had written, "Phebe Fairchild Her Book," travels safely in Phebe's muff to Winton, where the little girl is to stay with relatives while her sea-captain father takes her mother on a long sea voyage. Though Phebe knew the rhymes by heart, it was comforting during dark and trying moments to hold the little volume in her hand, and it was a very real grief to her when Aunt Hannah, shocked by what she considers its frivolity, confiscates her treasure. It is returned to her, however, for, like a prophecy of the golden future of books for children, grim Aunt Hannah herself is conquered by the gayety and homely wisdom of Mother Goose. Aunt Hannah's objections to Mother Goose are taken straight from one of the children's books of the period.

Miss Lenski's plot and incidents are fresh and interesting; we see the Connecticut country through the changing seasons, and not only Phebe but her relations are characterized with vigor. ***Phebe Fairchild Her Book*** is both a lively story and a complete, well-rounded picture of life in an inland Connecticut village a hundred years ago. The text, illustrations and design have a fine harmony and the result is a notable piece of book making. A book that girls from 10 to 12 will enjoy and one that adults interested in the history of books for children should on no account miss.

> *Anne T. Eaton, in a review of "Phebe Fairchild: Her Book," in* The New York Times Book Review, *December 27, 1936, p. 10.*

In her foreword, Lois Lenski states that she has attempted to picture a cross-section of New England life in 1830, a time of transition between the home industry period and the beginning of the small factory. Her research was thorough and included not only numerous reference books, but also "contemporary newspapers, store invoices, account books and church records." Her authenticity was praised over and over by contemporary reviewers. But, today, with careful research the rule, the reader is perhaps more inclined to observe and be critical of other elements. It appears that the author, absorbed in the study of her period, simply could not bring herself to omit interesting data, with the result that there is a plethora of facts, submerging the imaginative content of the story in an accumulation of irrelevant details. This may be the reason the author failed to create the living and memorable characters that appear in some of her later books. None of the children, not even Phebe, is a very real child. The adults are more memorable than the children, perhaps because they live for us in relation to their eccentricities. (p. 62)

> *Marilyn Leathers Solt, "The Newbery Medal and Honor Books, 1922-1981: 'Phebe Fairchild: Her Book'," in* Newbery and Caldecott Medal and Honor Books: An Annotated Bibliography, *by Linda Kauffman Peterson and Marilyn Leathers Solt, G. K. Hall & Co., 1982, pp. 61-2.*

---

### A-Going to the Westward (1937)

In 1811, the Bartletts in Connecticut had Ohio on their minds. When their story closes, the head of the family, having brought them the long journey by wagon and flatboat, has stocked the log-cabin store that is to become the center of a "town" on a branch of the Scioto River, with goods from Pittsburgh by way of Zanesville and Lancaster. Another stage in the process of pushing the frontier westward has been passed. It has been described in detail leaving no point in the process a matter of doubt. Miss Lenski has spared no pains in research; long as the book is—one of the longest historical stories we have offered to our children—the impression remains strong that she could find much more to say. She has given her readers

history as an American family and their many friends, fellow travelers and chance comrades helped to make it.

This is clearly as far as a review can go in outlining the plot. The value is less in plot than in cumulative detail. For instance, placing the story in time, on the first page, by Reuben's coming home with a new haircut, having at last sacrificed a life-long queue, ribbon and all, to the established vogue of short hair. Or the differences in the way of life of Germans along the Delaware, and the religious idea's appealing to Lutheran pilgrims, Puritan emigrants and Grandma Scuggs from Kentucky who decided that "these air prayin' people too; they've got religion same as weuns, fer all their queer notions." Or the songs every one sings—in this the author is expert—and the appearance of the bookshop of Zadok Cramer the Quaker, on Market Street in Pittsburgh, with the fitting sign of The Franklin Head. Many small, decorative, and usually funny woodcuts, type and tinted paper easy on the eyes, give the book an appearance that suits the story.

> *May Lamberton Becker, in a review of "A-Going to the Westward," in* New York Herald Tribune Books, *October 31, 1937, p. 9.*

Based on eye witness accounts left by travellers of the period, the story is well-told without undue heroics. The author weaves into her story the religious feeling, political sentiment and customs of the countryside along with a good deal of exciting incident, and her elfin illustrations in black and white add much to the book.

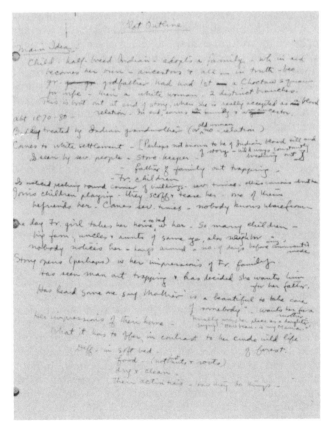

*Lenski's outline for her first regional novel,* Bayou Suzette.

*Sara E. MacPherson, in a review of "A-Going to the Westward," in* Library Journal, *Vol. 62, November 15, 1937, p. 882.*

Miss Lenski seems to have omitted no significant detail in presenting the many angles of her story; the various types of pioneers and their diverse viewpoints are well conceived and painstakingly drawn, yet she has, in portraying the sober Bartlett family, somehow missed the real spark of life and adventure. Piety was a very important factor in the life of such people, one too often overlooked in the literature of today, yet in this case it has been stressed to such a point that the record of the journey becomes in retrospect largely a succession of hardships borne with fortitude, but without zest, and nowhere does Betsy come to life with the engaging reality of a Phebe Fairchild. This is, in the final analysis, history seen with the knowledge of an adult, and not with the wondering enthusiasm of a child.

In appearance the book is delightfully suggestive of the age of linsey-woolsey and butternut dye, with its red-brown endpaper maps, its parchment colored paper and the lively decorations done in Miss Lenski's characteristic style.

*Ellen Lewis Buell, "Westward Bound," in* The New York Times Book Review, *November 21, 1937, p. 12.*

---

### Bound Girl of Cobble Hill   (1938)

This book resembles **Phebe Fairchild** in its excellent recreation of a period in our history. Miss Lenski presents a story of Mindwell Gibbs, who is bound out at the age of seven to work for the tavern-keeper of Cobble Hill until she is sixteen. The story opens in the year 1784 and we follow the fortunes of poor little Mindwell over a number of years. The custom of "binding out" boys and girls was common practice in our history and yet you seldom find a book dealing with this phase of childhood. On the manners and customs of village life in Connecticut, Miss Lenski must have spent endless time for she gives us a remarkable picture of the eighteenth century. Thoroughly complete in details of the period it is also a most readable book and will be enjoyed by anyone over thirteen. The author's own black and white illustrations add their share of quaint charm.

*Ruth Weeden Stewart, in a review of "Bound Girl of Cobble Hill," in* Library Journal, *Vol. 63, November 1, 1938, p. 847.*

**Bound Girl of Cobble Hill** tells the story of Mindwell Gibbs, indentured at 7 years of age to her uncle, a tavern keeper in a Connecticut town. Until she is 16 she is to help in the tavern, where she serves the guests, washes and cleans, learns to spin and weave, and does her best to follow her mother's farewell instructions, "Mind well, my child, and do your duty always whatever your lot in life." Though Mindwell's lot seems almost unbelievably hard, she is courageous enough to come through with her spirit unbroken, and finally, after many trials and vicissitudes, finds that she has made a real place for herself in her uncle's household and in the town itself.

In her skillful and interested search for the details of early New England life Lois Lenski shows the instinct of the true collector. She has taken infinite pains and it is plain to see that her explorations in old records and diaries have given her keen pleasure and satisfaction. Her historical stories **Phebe Fairchild Her Book, A-Going to the Westward,** and **Bound Girl of Cobble Hill**—are like her drawings, meticulous in detail, touched with human interest and in the spirit of the period. It is in her settings and backgrounds that Miss Lenski excels, rather than in her characterization. Mindwell Gibbs is Miss Lenski's most successfully realized heroine, but even she is not entirely convincing and the other characters of the story never come to life.

*Anne T. Eaton, "Early New England," in* The New York Times Book Review, *December 4, 1938, p. 11.*

---

### Ocean-Born Mary   (1939)

Miss Lenski is no beginner in historical fiction for children. She writes it lightly, but takes it seriously; **Phoebe Fairchild** and **Bound Girl of Cobble Hill** are based on sound documentation and give ten-year-olds participation in our past by means of real and lively details. Her new story, rising from her steady concentration on the New England of an older day, has more romance and color than its predecessors. Its heroine had one of those names, not infrequent in colonial records, showing the owner had been born at sea: Oceanus Hopkins, of the "Mayflower." John Cotton's son, Seaborn: Ocean-born Mary Wilson, who first saw the light on July 28, 1720 during a passage from Ireland to this country and was given her name and a green brocade dress pattern by a pirate who captured the vessel, but for love of the baby let the emigrants go free. History records she lived ninety-four honorable years, an ornament to Henniker, N. H. But because pirates kept coming into the rumors of her life, she attracts the attention of romance. In this story of her childhood Portsmouth takes back its old name of Strawberry Bank and Londonderry reverts to Nutfield, towns to which the pirate makes more or less veiled visits, keeping an eye on his grateful godchild and making things difficult for her.

The background has the bustle of fifty years before our Revolution. The Pine Tree Law and restrictions on wool weaving raise trouble. Ships coming and going from England keep coast settlements excited: every one has a hand in "ventures," private trading in some matter small or large. This is the part I like best now; were I ten it would be the appearances of Capt. Babb, the buccaneer, and his far-from-merry men. The pictures are little decorations, lively, but keeping close to facts.

*May Lamberton Becker, in a review of "Ocean-Born Mary," in* New York Herald Tribune Books, *October 29, 1939, p. 8.*

Of all her stories from history this is Lois Lenski's best. The legend of Ocean-Born Mary, who was christened on the high seas by a pirate, is one of New England's own. She is now a girl of eleven years, sent by her mother to help in the household of a cousin in old Portsmouth, where she meets again the pirate captain with all his bravado and outlaw daring. All seagoing persons and crafts are naturally attractive to the little backwoods girl with the romantic infancy and she becomes involved in some hazardous doings. Manners and customs in pre-Revolutionary New England make a fitting background for a story of fresh and genuine interest.

> *A review of "Ocean-Born Mary," in* The Horn Book Magazine, *Vol. XV, No. 6, November-December, 1939, p. 390.*

The book is crowded with characters, including Indians, rope makers, loggers, the town crier, the woman who keeps the village store, inhabitants of the almshouse, the daughter of a wealthy merchant, the parson—all the types whom careful research would reveal as having lived in a New England port of that period. It therefore gives a thorough picture of the time and place but gives the impression of being over-researched and suffers from lack of probability and poor motivation in its plot elements, as well as a didactic tone and slow pace. (p. 378)

> *Alethea K. Helbig and Agnes Regan Perkins, in a review of "Ocean-Born Mary," in their* Dictionary of American Children's Fiction, 1859-1959: Books of Recognized Merit, *Greenwood Press, 1985, pp. 377-78.*

---

### Blueberry Corners  (1940)

Two little New England girls living in a country parsonage one hundred years ago bring the humor and also the limitations of their daily experiences clearly before us. Through their eyes we share in the celebration over the coming of the first train to the Naugatuck Valley and pick blueberries in the Connecticut pastures. The kindly woman who gave the school children one of the best apple trees in her orchard well deserves to be remembered as we read of the rows of red apples on the battered desks. And Becky's determination to observe Christmas makes a memorable landmark in the home life of a strict Puritan household. Miss Lenski, writing with her informed historical background, will reach younger children than have usually read her books of this kind.

> *A review of "Blueberry Corners," in* The Horn Book Magazine, *Vol. XVI, No. 5, September-October, 1940, p. 349.*

---

### The Little Train  (1940)

Ever since these books were published some years ago, little children have found great satisfaction in following the doings of Mr. Small in *The Little Auto, The Little Airplane* and *The Little Sailboat.* Now the same Mr. Small is engineer on a train. In very simple language and aided by pictures on every page, Miss Lenski explains how a train works and what the signals mean. From one end of his run to the other, Mr. Small drives his train; it comes to a crossing where automobiles must wait until the gates swing up again, it passes cows and horses in the fields, hills and woods and streams, it slows down at a caution signal

and waits till the semaphore swings up to say "clear track ahead," it crosses a drawbridge, goes through a tunnel and comes at last to the city. Here, after the passengers have left and the baggage and mail have been taken off, the little engine goes to the roundhouse where it will spend the night and be made ready for the trip back.

*The Little Train* is more nearly picture book size than the earlier volumes. The drawings have action and humor and charm, they show details so plainly that the little child will find them eminently satisfying, and they are beautifully reproduced in clear, soft blacks and grays and a warm brown which delight the eye. A book that school and public libraries will want and one that the 4- to 7-year-old will take to his heart at once.

> *Anne T. Eaton, "How Trains Are Run," in* The New York Times Book Review, *October 6, 1940, p. 12.*

The "little" books in this series are for small children whose favorite toys are ships, automobiles, airplanes and so on, and who play that these are large, real ones. Thus Miss Lenski's pictures in these books combine the two, and are amusingly like both. The little train in this one—as usual, run by Mr. Small—has a strong likeness to the train you buy for a five-year-old, but it has also a close relationship to the one on a real track. The five-year-old likes it better for this double kinship; its mechanism, reduced to simplest terms, is easier for a very little person to take in.

> *"Pleasing Information," in* New York Herald Tribune Books, *November 10, 1940, p. 32.*

[Books] like Lois Lenski's *The Little Train* and Alice Dalgliesh's *The Little Wooden Farmer* . . . , skillfully blend simple facts and toy-town illustrations, never bothering to raise a ripple of doubt concerning the predictable workings of a bustling, perfectly ordered world. Though adults are likely to find them pedestrian and dull, particularly to read again and again, these tales fulfill the small child's need to acquire increasing bits of knowledge, as well as his craving for the world about him to be both purposeful and explicable. Such books are often requested for bedtime reading and remembered for years, occasionally forming the basis for a child's first real efforts at matching specific words with memorized text—the most magical beginning of reading for the lucky few. (pp. 181-83)

> *Selma G. Lanes, "Once Upon the Timeless: The Enduring Power of a Child's First Books," in her* Down the Rabbit Hole: Adventures & Misadventures in the Realm of Children's Literature, *Atheneum Publishers, 1971, pp. 179-203.*

---

### Indian Captive: The Story of Mary Jemison  (1941)

The fictionized story of a real little girl, famous later as "The White Woman of the Genesee," who in 1758 was captured by raiding Indians in eastern Pennsylvania and adopted by the Senecas. Her early years with the Indians are recounted in this most fascinating book. *Indian Captive* would be invaluable if considered only for its authentic picture of Indian life, customs, and ideas; the addition of the charming yet realistic illustrations and the thrilling story make this a book which all libraries can well afford to purchase. The heart-breaking fight of a small girl of about twelve years with homesickness and her rebellion against adopting Indian ways place this book in a class for older readers than **Ocean-Born Mary,** but the story will be enjoyed by girls especially, from eleven years upward. The make-up of the book is attractive and the pictures are particularly interesting.

> *Alice M. Wetherell, in a review of "Indian Captive: The Story of Mary Jemison," in* Library Journal, *Vol. 66, No. 19, November 1, 1941, p. 952.*

Lois Lenski gives twelve-year-olds not only her best work here, but a story more than one generation can read . . .

The Indian raid is breathlessly real, emphasizing not physical suffering, but the mental state of the family when doom bursts into the kitchen. The young reader shares the victims' sense that all this couldn't possibly be happening, the confusion of values that made Mary, silent through the wreckage of the house, cry because the corn pone had burned. The most convincing detail of the forced march is the look in the father's eyes—the look of utter humiliation at being not only a prisoner but prisoner of an Indian.

Mary's mother bids her go with her captors, not to forget to pray, to speak English and to remember that "It don't matter what happens if you're only strong and have great courage." The girl is scarcely out of sight before the parents are killed; this Mary does not learn till long after. Meanwhile she has done her best, first to get along with her captors, then to try to understand what they mean by what they do, and to do her part in the struggle they all share. She comes to be, not an Indian, but one who sees the Indian's side, appreciates the rough kindness she receives, and understands that cruelty often may be compelled by desperate conditions. Though she might have been rescued by English visitors, women of the tribe hide her because they think of her, and love her, as one of their own. She does become one of theirs; in history, very little changed for the exigencies of the early teens, she was respected and honored by both races, but buried with Indians at last. These pictures are Miss Lenski's most successful; the mannerisms of her style are absorbed in a richer, more sympathetic manner, and her accuracy has been guaranteed by experts.

> *May Lamberton Becker, in a review of "Indian Captive: The Story of Mary Jemison," in* New York Herald Tribune Books, *November 2, 1941, p. 10.*

Miss Lenski's fictional reconstruction of the facts is sensitive and well documented, both in the text and the drawings of life in a Seneca Indian village. The story of the little girl who gradually became so much an Indian that she refused to go back to the whites when she was "rescued" is necessarily a rather sombre one, but for readers over twelve it will give that pleasurable thrill and chill of coming on the real thing for once. (pp. 115-16)

> *K. S. W., in a review of "Indian Captive," in*

The New Yorker, *Vol. XVII, No. 43, December 6, 1941, pp. 115-16.*

After making the careful study of period and background which we have come to expect from her, Lois Lenski tells the story of the first two years which Mary Jemison, the 12-year-old white girl who was carried off by Seneca Indians, spent with her captors. . . .

Miss Lenski presents Indian life with accuracy and a fine detail. Nine to thirteen year olds are interested in the story, and because the author shows us, with imaginative sympathy, something of the inner conflict of a young person who succeeded in adjusting herself to a new and different way of life, though she did not forget her past or cease to feel herself a white girl, Mary Jemison emerges as a real and appealing personality. The attractive drawings portray Seneca Indian life with a fine authenticity.

> *Anne T. Eaton, "Mary Jemison," in* The New York Times Book Review, *December 28, 1941, p. 9.*

---

### Bayou Suzette *(1943)*

You cannot follow this story of ten-year-old Suzette Durand, of Bayou Barataria, in Louisiana, without making friends with most of the local population. Her family, large in itself, considered cousins, uncles, aunts as part of the immediate family circle. That circle, ever-widening, took so many Acadians that you get, in the course of these gayly illustrated pages, the illusion of having spent a good while along the bayou. It is a good place to spend time, of which there is a great deal, all good.

Perhaps resentment kept Suzette's papa from recovery from a gunshot; perhaps he had been waiting for an excuse to forgo violent exercise. Anyway, in spite of strong hints from everybody except the adoring Suzette, he left it to Maman and the others to get a living. The storekeeper's trust had just reached the breaking point; nobody worried, because the Durands just didn't worry, but it was no time to bring home a little Indian girl, which Suzette did. Marteel was like a lost puppy, living on the edge of the swamp, a kind, silent little savage: Suzette loved her at sight. Getting her into the house at all, keeping her there when Maman in well earned exasperation would cry "She gotta go, and this time never come back"—this provides ups and downs of lively action.

On the last page Marteel, looking up into a fat, good face, is saying "How beautiful is my Maman!" The droll pictures are as crowded as the cabins.

> *A review of "Bayou Suzette," in* New York Herald Tribune Weekly Book Review, *November 14, 1943, p. 30.*

Miss Lenski's new storysetting brings to children's books an unfamiliar American region which her readers will remember vividly. She gathered her material within the last two years, along the banks of the Bayou Barataria, once Jean Lafitte's domain. She expresses in both her story and pictures a deep affection for the friendly French people of the Louisiana bayou country. . . .

The friendship, amounting to sisterhood, between Suzette and Marteel, their adventures in the cypress swamps, Marteel's courage that won her a real home with the Durands, are story elements of sustained interest. Their plentiful drama is climaxed by the Mississippi flood and the healing of the Durand-Broussard feud.

Bayou scenes, strange customs of living, the memories of Lafitte and his treasure, the Mardi Gras, are local color details of rare individuality.

> *I. S., "Children on the Water," in* The New York Times Book Review, *November 14, 1943, p. 26.*

*Bayou Suzette* has an unfamiliar American setting, the bayou country of Louisiana. Suzette, a little French girl, is the heroine of this warm, human story. There is plenty of action in this story about generous, but daring Suzette. . . .

The book has the genuine feeling of the country and French-Bayou people. Lois Lenski's own pictures add atmosphere and charm to this outstanding book. . . .

> *Florence Bethune Sloan, "Let's Follow the Book Week Parade!" in* The Christian Science Monitor, *November 15, 1943, p. 12.*

---

### Puritan Adventure  (1944)

A composite New England village, for the story of god-fearing, but not in sympathy with Puritanical, harshly godly ways, Aunt Charity who comes to live with Partridges. In spite of warnings, she continues to share English traditions and customs with the children as their rightful heritage, and Christmas, shroving, May Day, all bring secret pleasure to her young relatives and their friends. She proves too that kindness has more power than rigorous negation, and helps to lighten the colony's grim life. An interesting subject—in which there is a definite sense of the way in which the early settlers thought, spoke and acted. Unaffectedly illustrated by the author.

> *A review of "Puritan Adventure," in* Virginia Kirkus' Bookshop Service, *Vol. XII, No. 15, August 1, 1944, p. 342.*

With her usual thoroughness Lois Lenski has gone to original sources to prepare this detailed picture of Puritan life in the Massachusetts Bay Colony. Since no study of Puritan life is complete unless it includes something of the background from which the first Massachusetts settlers came, the author has introduced a character freshly arrived from the Old World, Aunt Charity, who is unwilling to don the mantle of austerity and harshness so completely as the other settlers. Through Aunt Charity's natural gayety and love for the old English ways of celebrating holidays, a little mirth and liveliness are woven into the drabness of daily living. The chapter in which the Partridge family and Aunt Charity (and finally the neighbors) celebrate Christmas in the face of the Governor's proclamation of "A day of work and no cheer" is one that young readers will find particularly satisfying. Emphasis is on what the colonists did, how they dressed, what they ate,

how they built their houses and on their relations with the Indians rather than on characterization and plot. Miss Lenski's many drawings, full of action and as carefully authentic as the text, add to the appeal of the book.

> *Anne T. Eaton, "Aunt Charity," in* The New York Times Book Review, *September 17, 1944, p. 21.*

The time of this story is ten years after the landing at Plymouth. The Partridge family—father, mother, and five children—are living in the tiny settlement of Fairhaven. To them from England comes their mother's young sister, gay, pretty Aunt Charity. . . . But, with all her daintiness, Aunt Charity has strength and humor and courage. Her first act on the soil of the New World is to defend the bound girl, Patience Tucker, who has made a nuisance of herself on the voyage from England. To the sober Puritan children Aunt Charity brings warmth and a gracious happiness. But she definitely upsets the Pilgrim Fathers! Eventually she is called before the Magistrate's Court, where she not only defends herself and wins the support of the Puritan women for whom she has done much, but frees poor Patience who has, by this time, committed most of the minor sins on the Puritan calendar. This is an absorbing scene.

Miss Lenski has obviously done a piece of interesting and varied research for this story. All of its details sound authentic, and yet they never intrude on the action and the characters.

> *Mary Gould Davis, "Pilgrim Family," in* The Saturday Review of Literature, *Vol. XXVII, No. 43, October 21, 1944, p. 31.*

---

### Spring Is Here  (1945)

In this seasonable little volume Lois Lenski has caught the exhilaration and gaiety of the first spring days. In the pictures happy children roll their hoops, lose their hats in the March wind, fly their kites, greet birds and rabbits (including the Easter bunny), start their gardens and play ball, to the accompaniment of a simple, rhymed and rhythmical text. Small in size and as delicately gay in color as the first gold-green leaves, this is a book that three to five year olds will enjoy possessing—and one that will add a pleasant springlike touch to the picture-book collections in schools and libraries.

> *Anne T. Eaton, "Vernal Season," in* The New York Times Book Review, *April 15, 1945, p. 25.*

Such a moving little book you never saw—everything in it moves! Sister's hair and Brother's hat when the south wind blows, the milkman's horse prancing at the smell of spring, washing bobbing gayly on the line, baby calf and little lamb running before they can walk, and all the fat little children Lois Lenski can put into bright colors engaging in games and sports peculiar to the season. This is a tiny picturebook that brings out, better than any other I have seen, the fact that spring is the time when things and creatures move—especially little children who burst

*From* Strawberry Girl, *written and illustrated by Lois Lenski.*

out of winter into hop-scotch, skip rope, roll hoops and send swings and kites into the sky.

*A review of "Spring Is Here," in* New York Herald Tribune Weekly Book Review, *April 22, 1945, p. 6.*

*Strawberry Girl* (1945)

## AUTHOR'S COMMENTARY

[*The following excerpt is from Lenski's Newbery acceptance speech, orginally delivered on 18 June 1946.*]

As you doubtless know, I am working on a group of books for middle-aged children, with their settings in different parts of the United States—a regional American series.

The first, published in 1943, was *Bayou Suzette,* a story of the French-speaking bayou people of Louisiana. The second is *Strawberry Girl,* dealing with the Crackers of Florida. The third, to be published this fall, is *Blue Ridge Billy,* a story of the mountain people of North Carolina. You must forgive me if I find it impossible to talk about *Strawberry Girl* independently. I can think of these books only as small parts of a larger whole. In my mind they are indissolubly bound together.

For a number of years after moving into a small Connecticut village, I carried on a study of child life of the past, which I used for the background of my historical books for older boys and girls. The preparation of these books confined me to my isolated studio or to a quiet library alcove. The material in them was derived from books and from old documents and records left by the people themselves. Through them I became keenly interested in bringing alive for modern children the people of a past age.

Then suddenly my viewpoint shifted. I became dissatisfied. I had had enough of history and books—I felt a tremendous urge for a broader experience. I must get out and see people for myself, get to know and understand them. I wanted to put living people into my books.

My fundamental interest in both my historical and my regional books is always the same. It is an interest in *people*—especially children. I have a great curiosity to find out what people think, feel, say and do; to understand their behavior and the motives behind it; and in the case of these native-born regional groups, to learn how their thoughts and actions are bound up and controlled by the environment in which they live.

The exigencies of ill-health made it possible, some five years ago, for me to begin spending my winters in the South. I began a new lease on life; I began to see America with my own eyes—and heart and mind—for the first time. Being both writer and artist, the experience, absorbing all my faculties, has been rich and rewarding.

What a wonderful country ours is! Wherever you go, you can always find new scenes, people with new customs and habits and different ways of making a living from those you have seen in other regions.

I think the artist is a specially privileged person, because, always he sees the world spread out like a stage before him, a play being enacted for his own special benefit. He approaches it objectively, with all his senses sharpened, filled with "a great awareness"—a sensitivity like that of a human camera, to make a record of it. He looks not for those things which are the same or similar to his own past experience, but for differences; he forgets himself and identifies himself with the new scene and its activities.

The approach of the artist and the writer is not exactly the same, even when they are one and the same person. An artist looks at the outward surface of things. He is primarily interested in what meets the eye. He looks for beauty, character, action, design and pattern, but he rarely goes more than skin-deep. The writer, on the other hand, has to understand reasons and motives. With all the inquisitiveness of a four-year-old, he keeps asking, "Why? Why? Why?" He must find out the hidden meanings beneath all he sees and hears.

What fun it is to explore a new and unknown world, full of limitless possibilities—of drama, human character and conflict, all the things that go to make up storytelling. The writer is blest with a wonderful gift—the ability to enter a new world of people unlike any he has ever known, to bring to them an active sympathy, the outgrowth of his own past experience, to enter into their lives with understanding and to write of them *as if he were one of themselves.* (pp. 278-80)

We need to know our country better. We need to know not only our own region, where our roots are firmly put down, but other regions where live people different from ourselves—people of different races, faiths, cultures and backgrounds. We need to know native as well as foreign-born groups. I dislike the terms "minority groups" and "underprivileged peoples," because they imply superiority and condescension on the part of the person who uses them. I wish we could think of all men as people. When we know them, understand how they live and why, we will think of them as "people"—human beings like ourselves. Once we know them, we can say: "This is the way these people live. Because I understand it, I admire and love them." Even though they haven't bath-tubs and electric washers, there is a great deal to admire and love.

I have often wished for an invisible cloak to wear, or at least a disguise, when I have gone visiting the Cajuns of Louisiana, or the Crackers of Florida, so that I might become *one of them* and be accepted as such. But even then my speech and actions would betray me. It was very inconvenient, when gathering story material in the Deep South, to look so much like a "Dam-Yankee!" But no— there was no other way. I had to go as myself—as an "outsider."

In the bayou country, you are an "American;" in the Cracker country, you are a "Yankee"; in the Southern Appalachian Mountains, you are a "foreigner" or "from the outland;" and that is always a handicap. It is difficult for any "outsider" to be accepted and to share the deeper side of their lives. The surface, yes. They are all kind and curious and very human. But there is a barrier beyond which the outsider can rarely go—until he breaks it down.

A young Louisiana librarian, in advising me, said: "Well, if I wanted to get inside the Cajun homes, I'd go out and sell them something!" Strangely enough, although I wore no disguise, the children along the Louisiana bayous *did* ask me if I were selling something, because in one hand I carried a mysterious bag (containing lunch, purse, sketchbook, notebooks and camera) and in the other a campstool, without which no artist can ever travel. Always a crowd of children gathered, eager to watch a drawing grow on a sheet of paper—and eager to tell me many things I wanted to know. The children accepted me without question. Anyone who can draw pictures becomes their immediate friend. Wherever I went I always found a warm welcome because I drew pictures. My drawing helped, as nothing else could, to break down the barriers of suspicion. Drawing is a universal language which everybody understands.

Knowing the children was but a step toward knowing the adults. Soon their mothers were asking me to come and sit on the front gallery, or to come in the kitchen and have a cup of coffee. (pp. 280-82)

It is easy to see why a certain environment makes people

live as they do, and affects every phase of their life—why in watersoaked Louisiana, where it is too wet to raise crops, the people make a living by fishing; and how in the dry sandy soil of Florida a struggle is necessary to grow oranges and strawberries; and how the simple farm life on steep hillsides has kept the mountain people cut off from the world. When we understand their environment and see how their lives have been conditioned thereby, then we can understand their behavior. We can imagine ourselves in the same situation, and we wonder if we would be different.

My own experience in getting stories from people who have lived them has been so rich that I have felt a strong desire to pass them on to others. It is my hope that young people, reading my regional books, will share the life of these people as I shared it, and living it vicariously, through the means of a vivid, dramatic, authentic, real-life story, will learn something of tolerance toward people different from themselves.

I am trying to say to children that all people are flesh and blood and have feelings like themselves, no matter where they live or how simply they live or how little they have; that man's material comforts should not be the end and object of life. I am trying to point out that people of character, people who are guided by spiritual values, come often from simple surroundings, and are worthy of our admiration and even our emulation.

Just as recent American painters no longer go to Paris for painting material, but have found here on our own doorstep a vivid, dramatic America which they are portraying not romantically or sentimentally, but realistically and truthfully, just so accurate regional books for children should present all the vividness and drama that the American scene holds. We need not manufacture excitement—it is here, inherent in the scene itself. The way that Americans have struggled and fought and mastered their environment, in all its great variety, is an unending American saga.

Because these are true-to-life stories, I have included in my regional books certain incidents which we, as authors, following perhaps some unwritten taboos, have not often used in children's books. Our attitude, perhaps unconsciously, has been protective. We have felt that books for girls, at least, should be "nice," even though we have allowed somewhat stronger fare for boys. So, many of our girls' books have been pretty, sweet, and happy . . . and not much else.

I am writing for both boy and girl readers, and it has been my observation that our modern girls can take as strong fare as our boys. Children are getting exciting drama in many forms every day from other agencies, from the comics, the movies and the radio. Books must meet this competition, because anemic Pollyanna stories will only be shoved aside and not read at all.

We have not often put drunken fathers or malicious neighbors into a book for children. I have done this, and I would like to tell you why. These incidents are a direct outgrowth of the environment which I have described. They are true and authentic. They have happened not once but a hundred times in this particular locality, and have been experienced by the children as well as the adults. To leave them out and to pretend that such things never happen would be to present a false picture. (pp. 283-84)

I have always believed that children are strongly affected by their parents' way of life and by everything that happens to them. There are, unfortunately, many drunken fathers and objectionable neighbors in the world, and there are many children, whether we like to believe it or not, who have to face these facts and do something about it, as Birdie and Shoestring did.

There are also more fortunate children who have never come in contact with facts of this kind. I believe that it will do the latter no harm to widen their horizons a bit, and let them know that such conditions exist. Our present-day attitude toward children—that a child should live a completely sheltered life, have no cares, no responsibilities, no knowledge of the existence of pain, sorrow and trouble, may well be questioned.

After all, these boys and girls in the upper grades are now preparing to meet life as adults. In ten years they will be voters. Why shouldn't they know something about the country they live in? And the different kinds of people who live in it? Why shouldn't they begin now to think a little?

I have been dwelling at length on my purpose behind this series of regional books. My approach, however, is not that of the propagandist or even of the humanitarian. It is that of the artist. To enjoy a work of art is to live more intensely, to see, through the artist's interpretation, a deeper meaning in the commonplace. And so a book of this kind should need no explaining. I do not believe we need deliberately to preach or teach in a story book. Children are so quick to respond. If a book tells a vital human-interest story, children will quickly pick up the overtones. We need not ram it down their throats.

A book about a strange people should be as vital an experience as meeting these people face to face. It should do more than that—it should enable the reader to get beneath the skin of the strange person, to stand in the strange person's shoes, to *be* that person in imagination.

What better way, than through the reading of a book, to enter the minds and hearts of others and find them full of good things? What better way to learn to love our neighbor as ourself? Only when we truly *see others as ourselves* can we hope to have a world in which all men are brothers.

I cannot conclude without a word as to the speech or dialect used in these books. We have as many different kinds of American speech as we have regions. It is interesting to study the different ways the American language is used. Speech is so much more than words—it is poetry, beauty, character, emotion. To give the flavor of a region, to suggest the moods of the people, the atmosphere of the place, speech cannot be overlooked. (pp. 285-86)

The sound of a horse's hoofs pounding on a country road makes a beautiful and a satisfying rhythm. The noises of nature—the caw of the crow as it flies over the field, the buzz of the bee, the hum of the locust—all these have their rhythm. And so does the speech of the human being. In New England we hear one rhythm, in Louisiana another, in Florida and the mountains another. In the simplest words, with only a minimum of distortions in spelling, this is what I have tried to convey. There may be some children who will find it difficult reading. But I am willing to make that sacrifice, because of all that those who *do* read it will gain, in the way of understanding "the feel" of a different people, and the "flavor" of a life different from their own.

If these books should help only a few children to "see beyond the rim of their own world" and gain that "ultimate wisdom," I shall be rewarded. (pp. 286-87)

> *Lois Lenski, "Seeing Others as Ourselves," in* Newbery Medal Books: 1922-1955, *edited by Bertha Mahoney Miller and Elinor Whitney Field, The Horn Book, Inc., 1955, pp. 278-87.*

Another story in her regional series (last year's **Bayou Suzette** might be called a companion piece)—This time she has told a family story of life among the Florida Crackers, when Florida was just beginning to emerge as an agricultural and fruit growing state. Miss Lenski captures successfully the speech, customs, way of life with its trials, and joys, in the story of the feud between the ambitious, hard-working Boyers, and the violent, proud, lazy Slaters. It is a story for girls, chiefly—and the alert third and fourth graders will like it fully as well as their slightly older sisters. Mildly dramatic—and perhaps a shade too moralistic, but all in all good regional material. Authentic and charming quality to the black and whites by the author.

> *A review of "Strawberry Girl," in* Virginia Kirkus' Bookshop Service, *Vol. XIII, No. 11, June 1, 1945, p. 252.*

The two families in Lois Lenski's latest regional story might be taken as living examples of neighborliness—good and bad. . . .

The story is not only accurate in its picturesque details, it is realistic to a degree that may complicate matters in assigning its age level. The well sustained plot is unmistakably that of a tale for ten-year-olds: the local language is reproduced with such fidelity that those who fear to give young children examples of unorthodox spelling or grammar may be put off by it. But the same realism gives a young reader a lively sense of being present at cane grinding, going to a one-room school, racing gopher turtles, packing strawberries and adapting what was a little lost pocket of yesterday to the ideas of this age.

> *A review of "Strawberry Girl," in* New York Herald Tribune Weekly Book Review, *September 2, 1945, p. 4.*

Every incident, every attitude, every word of the dialogue helps to create a picture of the Cracker country and its people, of the pine woods and swamps, of the snakes and alligators, of the travelling preacher who holds a revival meeting and converts Pa Slater, of the homely little town and railroad station where the oranges and strawberries are loaded on freight trains for their long journey to Philadelphia and New York. This is the second of Miss Lenski's regional stories of America. The first was **Bayou Suzette.** They both picture a way of life in a specific part of America that has its own peculiar objectives, its own customs and speech. The speech in this one is particularly interesting. It is based on old English and has a distinctive flavor and rhythm. The illustrations, too, strengthen the feeling of locality. Miss Lenski does not give glamour to Birdie and her friends. They are drawn as they are. They look rather thin and badly nourished, but there is spirit and humor in them. They are exactly right as illustrations for a story that is obviously based on research and a true friendliness for its subject. (pp. 44-5)

> *Mary Gould Davis, "Florida Crackers," in* The Saturday Review of Literature, *Vol. XX-VIII, No. 42, October 20, 1945, pp. 44-5.*

As in her **Bayou Suzette,** there is a strong sense of a locality and the life that goes on there, in Lois Lenski's story of farming among the Crackers of Florida. She draws a revealing contrast between a certain thrifty family and an equally shiftless one, and enlists her readers' sympathy with the trials caused by lazy and indifferent neighbors. And she adds another spirited and lovable little girl to her already memorable gallery, in Birdie, with her cherished strawberry plants, subject to attack from many pests. The peculiar speech of the Florida backwoods, handed down from Anglo-Saxon origins, gives flavor to a vivid regional story, but does not obscure the humor and kindliness of an understanding writer.

> *A review of "Strawberry Girl," in* The Horn Book Magazine, *Vol. XXI, No. 6, November-December, 1945, p. 457.*

Miss Lenski has stated that she takes her books from life, and that most of her characters are real. She says that Birdie Boyer is a real little girl she saw plowing in a sandy field in Florida and that the incidents she uses are true as well. She stated that because her books were true-to-life stories she included certain characters like drunken fathers and malicious neighbors which had not often been used in children's books. She notes that after some of the worst fights, the quarreling neighbors would get together for a frolic; so she wrote it that way. The chapters that relate a merry making, cane-grinding with a candy-pulling and dance in the evening, for example, show the happier side of these people's lives, and they also provide relief from the tension that is built up in the other chapters.

The author's authenticity extends to reproducing with fidelity the peculiar speech of the Florida backwoods which has been handed down from Anglo-Saxon origins. In her illustrations, Miss Lenski does not glamorize Birdie and her friends, but draws them as she saw them at home and in the fields. Her illustrations, as well as her use of the native speech, strengthen the feeling of locality.

Although Lois Lenski began to write regional books because she wanted children to know the various areas of their own country better, she also wanted them to observe the ways in which people are alike as well as the ways in which they are different. Even though she had a definite purpose, she has avoided preaching and teaching while retaining her enthusiasm for her material. *Strawberry Girl* is regional literature at its best. (p. 97)

> *Marilyn Leathers Solt, "The Newbery Medal and Honor Books, 1922-1981: 'Strawberry Girl' " in* Newbery and Caldecott Medal and Honor Books: An Annotated Bibliography, *by Linda Kauffman Peterson and Marilyn Leathers Solt, G. K. Hall & Co., 1982, pp. 96-7.*

---

### *Judy's Journey* (1947)

Judy, ten years old, stringy hair around a pale face, in overalls, with bare feet, her voice a frightened whisper, on the first page of Miss Lenski's presentation of the seamy side of American childhood desperately defies fate in the form of an overseer for the company. Though cotton comes right up to their rickety shack in Alabama, so that no garden patch can add to a diet of fatback and cornbread, though they're plumb tard of movin' the bed every night to dodge the drip from rain, it's all the house they have and the overseer has been trying to get them out since settlement day. Papa is a sharecropper.

Then the heavens open. Papa drives up in a jalopy with a two-wheel trailer, for which he has traded their mule, wagon, plow and shovels. Mama adds to the trailer's load something seems like she couldn't live without—the bit of carpet from her mama's house, good quality, dollar sixty-nine a yard. They are off in search of a piece of land to make a crop of their own. They have joined the Great American trek. Judy's family is going anywhere. They have become migrant workers.

They begin with Florida, picking beans. Virginia means strawberries and beans; in Delaware they pick apples with Italians who used to work on pants in a factory but like it better where there is a little fresh air to blow. When peaches are over in New Jersey Mama has another baby and they head back to Florida. This time it's different. They have made friends all along the way. Judy has lost the acute shyness that takes the form of truculence; she smiles first and no longer thinks all strangers must be fought. The little house has begun to take shape, for Papa has bought a blown-down tourist cabin, mounted it on a truck and takes them back to Florida under a roof. Five acres can be retrieved from ruin; the house on wheels becomes the first unit of a home that will end "gallivantin' all over the country and puttin' your young uns in the crops to support you."

Hard, bitter hours have passed before this haven is reached; the story is as realistic as the sensibilities of young readers will permit an author to be. But if we are to tell children about our migrant workers at all, it isn't fair to strew sugar on the facts. Miss Lenski doesn't; her facts keep their harsh flavor. What sweetens her story is the way in which the family whose fortunes she follows develops in character in spite of—partly because of—what happens to them.

*May Lamberton Becker, in a review of "Judy's Journey," in* New York Herald Tribune Weekly Book Review, *September 14, 1947, p. 14.*

The people who follow the crops have been portrayed in several books, beginning with Lenski's *Judy's Journey* in 1947. Conditions were so bad for these sharecroppers that they had to sell some of their possessions and begin following the crops. Papa spends the money as he makes it; he does not want to work inside a factory:

> " . . . Machine's a big monster tryin' to gobble a feller up and break his spirit. . . . A little piece of land is all I want. . . . This country's always been a place where a man has a right to own a little piece of land."

Judy's more practical mother notes, "So many big companies buy it up, a lone man ain't got a chance." As the family works in Florida and up the coast, they learn there are few opportunities for the migrant. Too proud to accept help from the Salvation Army or the women's welfare society, they struggle on. "We're not destitute, and we don't take *charity* off nobody. We still got our pride." Lenski seldom uses metaphor in her writing; she builds detail upon detail until the reader receives the total impression of the scene. She describes Judy's work in the fields:

> Potatoes—potatoes—nothing but potatoes. . . .

The sun got hotter and hotter. Her ragged overalls stuck to her, and she was red with sunburn and prickly heat. Her back ached badly—she must rest for a minute. She stretched out full length in the dirt.

At school Judy fought the town kids, learned to read, and to care for the cuts and bruises of others. She learned from her parents: " 'People are what you think they are,' said Papa. 'If you think they're good and treat 'em right, they'll *be* good and treat *you* right. But first, you got to be plumb good your own self.' " No matter where they live, or what their economic status, children need to ponder this idea of life. (pp. 240-41)

*Charlotte S. Huck and Doris Young Kuhn, "Realistic Fiction: 'Judy's Journey'," in their* Children's Literature in the Elementary School, *second edition, Holt, Rinehart and Winston, Inc., 1968, pp. 240-41.*

In *Judy's Journey,* Lois Lenski has painted a great canvas of the lives of migrant workers. With sweeping brush strokes she creates one memorable character after another in a child's *Grapes of Wrath.* She moves easily from the general to the specific, and always there is the Drummond jalopy bouncing down the road, pursuing the will-o'-the-wisp of a better life just around the bend.

The heroine of the story is Judy, oldest daughter of irre-

*From* Mama Hattie's Girl, *written and illustrated by Lois Lenski.*

sponsible Jim Drummond and his long-suffering wife. Judy's dream is to be able to stay in one place and not have to move on "when the crop is finished."

The first tragic moment in the tragic symphony of Judy's life is the Drummonds' eviction from the shack that has been their temporary home. (p. 42)

Then upon the scene comes light-hearted Papa in his jalopy. Judy's spirits rise and she helps him load their "plunder" into the car as Jim Drummond promises good fortune in his own repetitious theme.

But the Drummonds' fortunes worsen. Like the Joads, they are constantly harassed by Reeves-like villains until the tragic moment when Judy suddenly finds herself. Up to this point, she has responded to the recurrent assaults upon her dignity by "sassing" people. Now, suddenly mature, she responds with true dignity to a cruel rebuff from her classmates, not seeming to be affected by their insulting behavior, but resolutely turning from them and putting the episode behind her, she goes home to see what can be done to help her mother.

Lois Lenski's theme is like Steinbeck's in substance, for despite trials and the daily crudity of existence, the human spirit is elastic.

Judy has found her identity, but with her new clarity of vision comes a realistic view of her father. Instead of the sunlight in her dark world, she understands that his irresponsibility is the cause of the darkness, and in the final tragic moment of the story, Judy enters the family camp, and failing to see her father standing in the shadows, pours out her disillusionment with him and his promises. Papa hears her and acknowledges soberly that she is right. The symphony has reached its climax and a final peaceful movement accompanies a turn in the tide of fortune for the Drummonds. A little house is made available for them with ten acres of land for Papa to farm.

In musical point and counterpoint, the author plays one character against another in her story. Jim Drummond is the happy-go-lucky soul always chasing rainbows, too easygoing to worry or display much backbone. Judy is the fighter of the family, although her spirit is often misdirected. At a carnival one day, Judy meets Madame Rosie, a mountainous fortune-teller, who is first to hold out hope to the starved little girl of a white house with a picket fence. Madame Rosie is the mystical element in the story, the reappearing catalyst who has real concern for Judy. She stiffens Papa's backbone by pointing out his shortcomings to him, and softens his daughter. The two kinds of catharsis are sharpened by contrast. Judy loses the ever-present chip on her shoulder and finds more attractiveness in those she meets. Conversely, her father at last shoulders his responsibilities. Both gain maturity and the ability to cope.

This is not a pretty story. The Drummonds move from rotting shacks to tents beside stinking drainage canals. They either suffer from cold or are baked by a merciless sun, always moving on, hoping for beauty and seeing ugliness, trying to keep alive some semblance of home. The author has not drawn back from depicting the misery of life. Yet the human spirit, although crushed and bruised, does go on, and in this story for children, there is a little white house waiting at the end of the journey for Judy. (pp. 42-4)

> *Carolyn T. Kingston, "The Tragic Moment: Rejection," in her* The Tragic Mode in Children's Literature, *New York:* Teachers College Press, 1974, pp. 5-56.

---

## *Surprise for Davy* (1947)

Davy, aged four, has a birthday such as any four year old would want. Among his gifts are books and trains and trucks, a sweater, a puzzle, a bubble pipe and so on. And then his friends turn up for a surprise party, and they play all the usual games and have crackers and caps, and eat ice cream and cake. And of course they sing Happy Birthday to you. The very commonplaceness of the details is its attraction.

> *A review of "Surprise for Davy," in* Virginia Kirkus' Bookshop Service, *Vol. XV, No. 18, September 15, 1947, p. 500*

The Davy of Miss Lenski's popular **Davy's Day** is growing up. This gay little book tells of his fourth birthday, his realization that he will never be three again, all the wonderful boxes full of presents, his big party. Three to six year olds will love having this read to them; and the simple wording and the repetition of the names of Davy's guests make it fun for the beginning reader.

> *Ruth A. Gordon, in a review of "Surprise for Davy," in* The New York Times Book Review, *November 16, 1947, p. 42.*

---

## *Mr. and Mrs. Noah* (1948)

Best-loved of the Old Testament tales by denizens of the nursery, the story of Noah's Ark is set forth here in a form perfectly adapted to that age. Reverence is implicit in the rhythmic prose in which Miss Lenski retells the story and at the same time there is a delightful sense of intimacy with Mr. and Mrs. Noah, their family and their animal charges. This latter feeling is strengthened by the illustrations. Resplendent with color, appealingly small in scale but clear in detail, these are patterned after the traditional wooden figures of old Noah's Arks. They have the endearing quality of those toys, yet manage to seem very much alive. This little book will undoubtedly be a favorite bedtime companion to many children.

> *Ellen Lewis Buell, in a review of "Mr. and Mrs. Noah," in* The New York Times Book Review, *March 14, 1948, p. 26.*

By the simple device of making the figures of a toy ark, reproduced in the bright colors they had when you bought them, act out the story of Noah and the flood, Lois Lenski produces a distinctive picture book for babies that has the charm of a traditional toy. Noah has the ulster, his wife the hourglass figure dear to our memories: his sons have joints, the pairs of animals disregard the hues of nature in the good old way, and when the waters go down the family lines up to salute a noble rainbow. All this appears also in large type and short words with a gentle chime.

> *May Lamberton Becker, in a review of "Mr. and Mrs. Noah," in* New York Herald Tribune Weekly Book Review, *March 28, 1948, p. 6.*

Since the toy Noah's arks made in recent years have shown signs of modernization, it is all the more satisfying to find in *Mr. and Mrs. Noah,* . . . an ark drawn according to the old-time pattern, and Mr. and Mrs. Noah and family as firmly cylindrical and simple in their anatomy as they were when the first toy ark was made. Children approve that simplicity, for them to look at the clear, brilliantly colored pictures, while they listen to the story told by Miss Lenski in a simple, rhythmic prose, will be a deeply satisfying experience. A book for every little child to own.

> *Anne Thaxter Eaton, "Reading Is Such Fun!" in* The Christian Science Monitor, *April 13, 1948, p. 14.*

---

### Now It's Fall   (1948)

Companion to *Spring Is Here*—stocking book size with predictable Lois Lenski drawings in two colors, and a simple text with occasional end rhymes and format suggesting verse which is patently limping at best. But the subject matter is well conceived for small reader observation,—falling leaves, ripe apples, nuts, birds going south, pumpkins and Halloween, Thanksgiving, and first days at school.

> *A review of "Now It's Fall," in* Virginia Kirkus' Bookshop Service, *Vol. XVI, No. 16, August 15, 1948, p. 394.*

Romping in the yellow leaves, walking through rain, picking apples, nutting, going to school (First Grade, of course) and making a Jack-o'-Lantern are parts of the theme of a bright little book called *Now It's Fall.* Printed in autumn's colors, told in short-line verses that the new reader will learn in half a minute, this book matches Lenski's earlier and equally beguiling *Spring Is Here.*

> *Sarah Chokla Gross, in a review of "Now It's Fall," in* The New York Times Book Review, *September 19, 1948, p. 29.*

---

### Cowboy Small   (1949)

Mr. Small has been variously a pilot, a fireman, an engineer and captain of a sailboat. Now he is a cowboy, and this is the first small boy cowboy book that has just the right amount of text information and pictures that four and five year olds care for. He is shown doing the things a cowboy does,—saddling his horse Cactus, riding the range, cooking his supper outdoors, rounding up cattle, and later—playing his banjo and singing songs made familiar to children through records. Equipment is identifiable in the end papers, and the pictures have a direct sim-

plicity that has realistic appeal. Sturdy cloth binding gives this a chance for affectionate rereading. (pp. 206-07)

> *A review of "Cowboy Small," in* Virginia Kirkus' Bookshop Service, *Vol. XVII, No. 8, April 15, 1949, pp. 206-07.*

Those who met Mr. Small on his little farm, or in his little fire engine or trains or airplane, when each book first appeared, must now be quite grown up. But they never will forget him, and treasure their well-worn copies, such merry introductions to the serious affairs of the grown-up world.

"Hi there!" calls Cowboy Small today, at the gate of the Bar S Ranch. He takes good care of his horse Cactus, so that you know exactly what your own make-believe horse needs to have done for him. He rides the range to fix his fences, sleeps in his bedroll under the stars, rides in the round-up, ropes a calf, rides a bucking bronco.

> *A review of "Cowboy Small," in* New York Herald Tribune Weekly Book Review, *May 8, 1949, p. 14.*

---

### Cotton in My Sack   (1949)

To write this book the author lived with, and worked with the "cotton children" of Arkansas. She deserves praise for putting down this unusual picture from the children's angle, and also for reflecting honestly the whole adult and economic picture, mixing the good with the bad, fun with sorrow, and bringing into the story, besides the work, the school, teachers, books, the boss, the store, the bank account—giving a rounded world, not a slanted view. She wrote at the request of the very children she tells about, who had heard a radio dramatization of *Strawberry Girl*. . . .

Joanda, who could pack eighteen pounds of cotton a day into her seven-foot bag, isn't even a "half-hand" yet. But every pound she and her brothers and sisters pick is important to her family and to their boss. She soon becomes a heroine most real and touching, with her love for the baby Lolly, her fondness for the miracle of reading, and her ability to make friends with the worried wife of the boss. The story traces the change from a shiftless family to an ambitious one, with daddy slowly cheered, through friendship and help, till he can become a tenant farmer, and they can move from a "shotgun house" to a five-room, permanent home. The children still will be cotton pickers, but life holds new hope and dignity, and Joanda sings her cotton-picking song with a new content in her heart.

It will please first the boys and girls in Arkansas who inspired it. Next, one hopes for even a larger audience of those around twelve who have liked Miss Lenski's other regional books. Younger readers might have difficulty with the dialect so cleverly reported and with the many regional words. But once caught into sympathy with Joanda, readers of various ages will follow this unusual, excellent story of a world of work which many do not know exists.

> *Louise S. Bechtel, in a review of "Cotton in My*

*Sack," in* New York Herald Tribune Weekly Book Review, *August 28, 1949, p. 8.*

Ten-year-old Joanda, the middle child in a family of seven, is the central figure of a series of events depicting the simple joys and all-too-frequent tragedies of the small cotton farmer's household. The hazards of cotton farming and the barrenness of sharecropper life are vividly seen through her eyes. As always, Miss Lenski makes her people and their work seem dignified and important, faithfully recording their courage and kindliness as well as their hardships and follies.

> *Elizabeth Hodges, "Arkansas Cotton-Pickers," in* The New York Times Book Review, *September 4, 1949, p. 13.*

The story is written to present facts about cotton growing and the life of the sharecropping poor whites. The didactic message is obvious and the characters predictable. Even though some of the hardships facing the family are detailed, the assumption that upward mobility is possible by hard work and will power is simplistic. (p. 112)

> *Alethea K. Helbig and Agnes Regan Perkins, in a review of "Cotton in My Sack," in their* Dictionary of American Children's Fiction, *1859-1959:* Books of Recognized Merit, *Greenwood Press, 1985, pp. 111-112.*

### Texas Tomboy  (1950)

Another stunning regional story about one of the sturdy breed of tomboys in Texas cattle country, distinguished by the author's sympathetic, lively and earth-warm imagination. Charlotte Clarissa, who insists on being called "Charlie Boy" at Triangle ranch, is jauntily tough, fiery-tempered and irrepressible as the Texas land of winds, storm and killing "droughts". Charlie is no blue-jeaned imitation of the real thing. She knows what to do with a starving tooth. Cocky Charlie Boy raises ructions in the schoolroom, makes a dead run through Duffy's farm, ruining the poor farmer's crop and teases her feminine sister, Grace. There is no magical transformation into ribbons and lace for Charlie—the skill, good sense, high spirits and courage of this Texas cowboy are never suppressed—but Charlie does learn tolerance of others and the fruits of kindness. Again the handsome, sturdy drawings by the author.

> *A review of "Texas Tomboy," in* Virginia Kirkus' Bookshop Service, *Vol. XVIII, No. 16, August 15, 1950, p. 466.*

At a time when glamorous cowboy stories are at a peak of popularity, Miss Lenski offers a realistic tale of a time of "drouth" on a big ranch in the semi-arid country of western Texas. The tough little ranch child "Charlie Boy," ruthless, selfish, spoiled by a hard-working father who makes her his pal, is the sort of heroine who has perennial appeal.

We have to laugh at this Charlie, with her love of excitement, bravery, willingness to work hard, and utter indif-

ference to her mother's dreams of an easier life in town and attempts to "civilize" her. Unlike her sickly small brother, and her conscientious older sister, Charlie really was born for life on a ranch. By the end, as she turns eleven, she has lived through several near tragedies, and developed a new spirit of co-operation. . . .

"It's a hard life, but Charlie's got what it takes," says a neighbor. "Will the next generation be hardier, or will softness win?" In her introduction, Miss Lenski says that softness has won, surprising news for children in the East, in their cowboy clothes. But they never have seen their father fall off a windmill, nor lived through a "twister," nor known small boys killed at round-ups.

This is a grand book full of clear morals and also human understanding.

> *Louise S. Bechtel, in a review of "Texas Tomboy," in* New York Herald Tribune Book Review, *October 29, 1950, p. 18.*

### I Like Winter  (1950)

Another endearing very little book, by the author-illustrator of the long-loved **"Mr. Small Books,"** gaily projects the joys of winter for the youngest children. The pictures are most successful, with their flat colors, and full of the very nip of snowy days. Small listeners will love a preview of Christmas joys, shared with these gay children. The happy little recital, in simple verses, ends with Valentine's Day. The first page offers an "I Like Winter" song, easy to sing and play. Thanks to Miss Lenski for a thoroughly satisfactory addition to the nursery shelf.

> *"For the Age That Looks and Listens," in* New York Herald Tribune Book Review, *November 12, 1950, p. 16.*

### Prairie School  (1951)

Eighth in Miss Lenski's regional series, this thrilling story of a year in the lives of school children of the Dakota plains, is, as the author herself declares in her preface "no synthetic, manufactured adventure". On the strength of letters received from the pupils and teacher in a tiny one-room schoolhouse in South Dakota, Miss Lenski spent some time living in the little school absorbing the "everyday" drama of their continuous battle with the elements. The story begins with the two-children welcoming committee, composed of Delores and Darrell Wagner, awaiting their teacher, Miss Martin, as she arrives for the school year in the midst of a prairie fire, and continues through the winter's adventures—terrible blizzards, when each day's decision as to whether the children should go home is literally a matter of life and death; nights spent in the schoolhouse with limited supplies in the midst of a paralyzing storm; and emergencies demanding quick thinking and courage, when the temperature is twenty-five below and the drifts are ten feet high. The children and the adults are very real people—some strong, some weak, but all living very close to the fierce elements they must face. Illustrated by the author, in her familiar style which though unfortunately creating some rather unattractive faces, makes its point.

*A review of "Prairie School," in* Virginia Kirkus' Bookshop Service, *Vol. XIX, No. 13, July 1, 1951, p. 319.*

In 1948 the children of a one-room school in South Dakota wrote to tell Lois Lenski how much they had enjoyed her *Strawberry Girl.* Thus began a correspondence culminating in Miss Lenski's visit to the school in the spring of 1950. Arriving by jeep in a blinding snowstorm, she immediately began gathering material about prairie life. . . .

This is a chronicle based on the actual experiences of real children, supplemented by drawings which bring the homely setting to life and emphasize the hardy, endearing qualities of the prairie people. It is one of the most graphic of Miss Lenski's regional stories.

*Elizabeth Hodges, "South Dakota Winter," in* The New York Times Book Review, *August 26, 1951, p. 18.*

For people who live in cities or even in country towns where the school bus promptly picks up mittened youngsters by their mailboxes, it is hard to imagine the almost Abe Lincoln primitiveness in this saga of contemporary education. The book gave me a thrill and I am inclined to think it might be a good thing to have around the house for those under-twelves who have to be bribed with television to do their homework and threatened with its withdrawal if they don't get a hustle on, school mornings. When they ask, "Did those kids really get frostbitten trying to make a geography class on time?" you can look them steadily in the eye and answer, "Yes. And it happened in the United States last year. And it's just as true as an A-bomb." (pp. 100-01)

*Margaret Ford Kieran, in a review of "Prairie School," in* The Atlantic Monthly, *Vol. 188, No. 6, December, 1951, pp. 100-01.*

### Papa Small   (1951)

The youngsters love them, so it is axiomatic by this time that the *Small Series* mean sales, and here at last the family of Mr. Small with the same simple text and shiny little pictures by the author. Papa Small, Mama Small, Baby Small and the small Smalls, Paul and Polly, live in a big house on a hill and this is the story of how the Smalls spend their week in work and play-ending with church on Sunday and a ride in the car. Easy identification, shared family activities, level of interest, and firm, realistic drawing establish the success of this series.

*A review of "Papa Small," in* Virginia Kirkus' Bookshop Service, *Vol. XIX, No. 18, September 15, 1951, p. 528.*

Lois Lenski's picture books are a delight to little children. The adventures of Mr. Small in *The Little Auto, The Little Airplane* and other books in this series satisfy them because the stories have a homely quality which speaks directly to a child and the pictures show exactly what is happening. Their enthusiasm is also due in part to the fact that children are fascinated by mechanical things and because Mr. Small seems to them a real and friendly character. They will, therefore, be charmed to meet him again in this new book and to meet his small son and daughter, the baby and Mama Small and to live with them for one week, keeping house and playing just like every other family.

*Frances Chrystie, "Mr. Small at Home," in* The New York Times Book Review, *September 30, 1951, p. 32.*

The "Small" family have become a nursery fixture. They were the first to introduce many a two or three-year-old to the translation to paper of simple images of train, auto, airplane, etc. *Papa Small* . . . has the same irresistible simplicity as all the others, telling about the Small home life and Papa's share in it. It is a happy first book about a family for the very youngest. The toy-like figures, the use of one bright color, the clear arrangement of details, the humor, all prove this artist's mastery of appeal to the seeing eyes of the nursery age.

*Louise S. Bechtel, in a review of "Papa Small," in* New York Herald Tribune Book Review, *October 7, 1951, p. 30.*

### Peanuts for Billy Ben; We Live in the South   (1952)

Noted for their realism, Miss Lenski's regional stories— *Strawberry Girl, Prairie School* and others—have won a special place for themselves among boys and girls of 8 to 12. Now in the Roundabout America stories she presents the same kind of material for younger readers, but shorter in form, simplified in structure and in vocabulary.

The first two books in the series portray life in various regions of the South today. *Peanuts for Billy Ben* is set in the peanut fields of southern Virginia. Here 6-year-old Billy Ben does his share of chores because he knows how important it is to the family to have a big crop—and also because, like a good many other youngsters, he "never et too many peanuts—yet." For all the hard work, it is a merry story, too, as the gay verses between chapters indicate. It is essentially a family story because everyone works together.

The four stories in *We Live in the South* have a strong sense of family life too. These are set in the piney woods of the Southeast, in the Negro quarter of a Southern town, on the Gulf Coast and in a Florida orange grove. The first is rather flat in tone and the second could have happened almost anywhere, but the other two are really lively and entertaining. The short story form ought to appeal to beginning readers.

*Ellen Lewis Buell, "In Dixie," in* The New York Times Book Review, *March 30, 1952, p. 30.*

As the first two volumes in a new series by this author-illustrator, called **"Roundabout America,"** these books will be welcomed by a wide audience. . . . [These] new books live up to expectations. They are sympathetic, simple stories which spotlight typical conditions in different sections of our country.

*From* We Live in the Country, *written and illustrated by Lois Lenski.*

As its title indicates, the story about Billy Ben concerns peanut growing. In a simple text and many illustrations the sights and sounds, joys and hardships of life on a share-crop plantation in Virginia come alive.

**We live in the South** pictures four localities. The first story tells of a "poor white" family in the piney woods of what is perhaps Mississippi. Each story is located on a hand-drawn map. Poignantly appealing is the second story of a little Negro girl with heart trouble who lives in South Carolina or Georgia, very poor but sheltered by family love and loyalty. Then come the problems of the little son of Louisiana fisherfolk. A brief episode in a slightly more prosperous home in a Florida orange plantation completes the quartette.

We keep referring to these stories in pictorial terms because the direct narrative and the many drawings by the author create the feeling that the reader has actually shared the life that she describes. (pp. 52-3)

> *Cornelia Ernst Zagat, in a review of "Peanuts for Billy Ben" and "We Live in the South," in* The Saturday Review, *New York, Vol. 35, No. 19, May 10, 1952, pp. 52-3.*

Billy Ben lives on a half-shares farm, somewhere in the peanut country, where Virginia meets North Carolina. His father's crop is peanuts and we first meet Billy shelling them for seed. The whole family helps: a neighborhood party helps. We go through the seasons on this farm, planting, picking and getting the "peas" to market. Each brief chapter has a bit of fun or adventure, with songs thrown in at the beginning and the end.

Here is the first of a new series called **"Roundabout America"** for readers of seven to nine years, in large type, with many pictures. Peanuts are grown in seven states, but all the youngsters who like to eat them will be interested in how they are grown and will like Billy Ben.

The second book is less interesting, with four unconnected stories and no verses. But the tales are good for this age reader. They are about a "piney woods girl" of the Southeast, a Negro child who has heart trouble, in a city tenement section, a boy who goes fishing in the Gulf of Mexico and an adventure with an alligator in an orange grove. All the families are hard-working people and the social intention of the stories is clear.

> *Louise S. Bechtel, in a review of "Peanuts for Billy Ben" and "We Live in the South," in* New York Herald Tribune Book Review, *May 18, 1952, p. 10.*

## On a Summer Day (1953)

A delightful come-on for all kinds of play—house, store, Indian, school, grown-up, train and animal. Lois Lenski's appetizingly rounded brother and sister pictures, one to a page, each have an accompanying quatrain, on the opposite page, about the game they are playing, and the end paper designs are a miniature parade of what's going on between. A gay book whose green and orange colors and hand-small size make it even more enticing.

> *A review of "On a Summer Day," in* Virginia Kirkus' Bookshop Service, *Vol. XXI, No. 4, February 15, 1953, p. 109.*

"Play," play, on a summer day—" so goes the little song that opens this gay little book. In the familiar, clear pictures, full of amusing details and ideas, we see all the play imaginings of two happy little children. The simple verses are gentle and, almost entirely factual: "And then we take turns swinging up in a tree; I push Brother and he pushes me." They are exactly right on the three- or four-year level, as are the three other books of seasons in this popular little series. Many a brother and sister will say, "Just like us," and want it read over and over again.

> *A review of "On a Summer Day," in* New York Herald Tribune Book Review, *May 17, 1953, p. 10.*

## Mama Hattie's Girl (1953)

The latest book in Lois Lenski's program of regional stories for young readers is a very authentic picture of Negro life in a small southern town. Along with the other active, bustling families on Hibiscus Street live Lula Bell, her mother Imogene and her grandmother, Mama Hattie. It is Mama Hattie who rules the roost like a queen and to whom Lula Bell really "belongs." There are the fun and the good times. But mostly, their days bring one serious problem after another—each one of which is followed through with the author's unerring feeling for these people and the kind of realism so often kept out of juvenile writing. Mama Hattie has heart trouble and is subject to disturbing attacks. When Imogene decides to go "up North" where her husband Joe has been working in New Jersey, she fights bitterly with Mama Hattie over the sale of the house. And once "up North", none of the family really thrives and there is the exodus back to Hibiscus Street where, without too much to go on, they at least have each other and hope. A book that has its depressing moments, but is a positive affirmation of a peoples' tenacity, gaiety and above all, humanity.

> *A review of "Mama Hattie's Girl," in* Virginia Kirkus' Bookshop Service, *Vol. XXI, No. 17, September 1, 1953, p. 580.*

The latest addition in Miss Lenski's regional series presents again an authentic, almost photographic picture of a way of life. Mama Hattie, her daughter and granddaughter in a small southern town, represent an economic group parallel to those of the other books in this series, and so the family is beset with all the problems created by poverty but with the added burden of racial discrimination. Their temporary move to the North does not solve their problems. There is unhappiness, frustration, and even cruelty here but also occasional rays of hope and gaiety. The book has a place as part of a large regional picture and has been done with sympathy and integrity, without caricature of stereotype. However, it is extremely important that other more positive books be in the collection to give a representative picture of the American Negro. Recommended with the above reservations.

> *Augusta Baker, in a review of "Mama Hattie's Girl," in* Library Journal, *Vol. 78, No. 18, October 15, 1953, p. 1858.*

Although [this] book presents a lively account of the small, everyday affairs of poverty-stricken Negroes, North and South, it cannot be recommended for purchase for general library collections. Its drama arises from the competitive spirit, the selfishness and the quarrelsome nature of the characters. There is not one warmhearted, unselfish, and in some way lovable character in the book. Perhaps Mama Hattie comes closest to the reader, but her whining, selfish, small-minded bickering nature cannot class her as anyone to whom a child would be drawn. In fact the one quality that unites the book is the acquisitive, selfish concern of each character to gain materially. For adults, as a sociological study of one section of the United States, the book could provide points for discussion. As a book for children, to represent for them a way of life either of Negroes or whites in these poverty-stricken circumstances, it is both harmful and unjust. A great deal of sociological knowledge is required to accept and understand such unrelievedly self-centeredness and intellectual backwardness in both adults and children living in the United States today. Children in the elementary grades do not have such a background for interpreting books of this kind and in their hands the book becomes a serious misrepresentation of the way of life among Negroes in both the North and South.

> *A review of "Mama Hattie's Girl," in* Bulletin of the Children's Book Center, *Vol. 7, No. 4, December, 1953, p. 31.*

## Project Boy (1954)

[The] story is laid in a veteran's housing project. Young Teddy Parker and his family are interested in fixing up their house and yard, but they get very little help or encouragement from their neighbors in the project. The other boys steal the pickets from the fence, the neighbors complain about Teddy's pumpkin vines, and Mrs. Parker has troubles with the other women over the use of the laundry facilities. In spite of all this, they have fun in their home and with their neighbors. The book gives a quite realistic picture of the difficulties of life in such a situation and should help youngsters understand some of the problems which their own and other families face in these days of inadequate housing.

> *A review of "Project Boy," in* Bulletin of the Children's Book Center, *Vol. VII, No. 9, May, 1954, p. 75.*

## Songs of Mr. Small (1954)

Mr. Small is such a beloved character to the small fry who have met him as farmer, engineer, fireman, sailor, cowboy, that there'll be a readymade market for these songs which sound as though children had made up the rickety verses. The music too is nondescript. But there is a kind of beat, and an activity suggestion in the words, that may fit right into pre-school programs. Certainly that is the outlet most likely to find this to their liking.

> *A review of "Songs of Mr. Small," in* Virginia Kirkus' Bookshop Service, *Vol. XXII, No. 21, November 1, 1954, p. 726.*

All who have enjoyed the various books about Mr. Small will be delighted by these rhythmic little songs written and illustrated by Miss Lenski. They tell about his life on the farm, in the air, or in his car and at the ranch and elsewhere. The catchy little tunes by Clyde Robert Bulla are simple to play and to sing. Recommended for children in nursery, kindergarten or primary grades and for all teachers of these ages.

> *Elsie T. Dobbins, in a review of "Songs of Mr. Small," in* Junior Libraries, *Vol. 79, No. 4, December 15, 1954, p. 24.*

## San Francisco Boy (1955)

An irresistible invitation to Lois Lenski from the fourth grade children of Commodore Stocksten School in San Francisco resulted in **San Francisco Boy,** a charming addition to her American Regional Series. "We are Chinese children and live in Chinatown. Would you like to know more about us? Then come and visit us . . . We wish you good luck and good health."

And Lois Lenski did visit them, in their homes, on the streets of Chinatown, in bakeries, poultry and fish markets, art shops and factories, sketching as she went. In a very understanding and exciting way she has traced the adjustment of Felix Fong to city life after his earlier happy years in the smaller town of Alameda. Younger Sister, Mei Gwen, knows only the city and is a happy, responsible child.

Their daily adventures, kite flying contests, fishing under the Hyde Street pier, flying down the roller coaster hills on soapbox scooters into almost serious consequences and the famous New Year parade with the Chinese Dragon are used to illustrate the racial pride of the parents and the philosophy of the grandparents.

Father Fong, seeing the children off on an expedition one day admonished them, "My children, you were born in America and have lived there all your lives. Therefore you are Americans. Although you are of the Chinese race, you feel like Americans. But remember, the tourists who come to San Francisco from all parts of the country think of you as Chinese. Many of them have never seen Chinese children before. So you must always be thoughtful, polite and courteous, for you are representing your race."

Through growing friendships with American and Italian children, happiness and contentment came to Felix Fong. "He had the heritage of age-old customs and traditions behind him and the exciting way of a newer world before him. The combination was a good one."

Lois Lenski's many sketches are full of action and true San Francisco flavor. *San Francisco Boy* is not only for the local audience but will widen the horizon of all children in the eight to twelve age group.

> *Dorothy Robertson, "From China Town," in*
> The Christian Science Monitor, *November 10,*
> *1955, p. 2B.*

Lois Lenski's regional stories are always welcome. They contribute to the social studies program through their interpretation of people and a way of life in many parts of our country. This one describes a Chinese family in the fascinating Chinatown of San Francisco. Their daily life, work, play, and adventure bring an appreciation of their culture and an understanding of the joys and sorrows of life in a crowded bustling community—in contrast to the country life they had known. . . . The tale is told in simple, direct narrative with Lois Lenski's interpretive pictures.

> *Elizabeth O. Williams, in a review of "San*
> *Francisco Boy," in* The Saturday Review, *New*
> *York, Vol. 38, No. 46, November 12, 1955, p.*
> *62.*

This latest of Lois Lenski's regional stories is laid in San Francisco's Chinatown and, like her other books, presents likable children living in a world of their own yet firmly established in their own community. Her *San Francisco Boy,* however, is not quite like the others, since he is sensitive and withdrawn, homesick for Alameda where he was born, and unwilling and unable to adjust to the bustle of city life or the activities of the other boys. Only his grandmother seems to understand and in the end gives him courage to face the world as it is rather than as he might

wish it to be. It is Felix's little sister Mei Gwen, however, who very nearly captures the attention of both Miss Lenski and the reader with her impulsive friendliness, her lively interest in every one and everything about her, her little girl jealousies and fears which are so childlike and bewitching that her poor brother seems, in contrast, a bit of a bore. One cannot but hope that Miss Lenski will some day give us more of Mei Gwen and her San Francisco Chinatown.

> *M. S., in a review of "San Francisco Boy," in*
> New York Herald Tribune Book Review, *No-*
> *vember 13, 1955, p. 24.*

---

**Berries in the Scoop: A Cape Cod Cranberry Story; We Live by the River** (1956)

To her **"Roundabout America"** Series, stories of contemporary regional life for quite young readers, Lois Lenski now adds two titles. *We Live by the River* contains three stories, each one divided into brief chapters. This form is ideal for children who are beginning to read beyond the primer stage but, in general, the execution here is disappointing. **"Sammy Joe Lives on the Bank"** is a well-knit story of an Ohio River mussel fisherman and his family which has something pertinent to say about the ephemeral benefits of sudden wealth. In the other two stories the details of life on an island in the Mississippi and near a dam on the Pearl never quite jell into an integrated whole. Too often the quite promising events are so under-played that they trail off into anti-climax.

**Berries in the Scoop** is a different matter, a good, easy-flowing story about the Portuguese cranberry pickers on Cape Cod and about one little girl, Kayla, in particular. Kayla is tempted to naughtiness early in the book and from then on, right through the summer picnic and the autumn cranberry harvesting any normal small girl will find plenty of emotional tension. And by the time Christmas rolls around, and with it a solution to Kayla's problems, the reader will have come to know and enjoy a gay, hardworking people.

> *Ellen Lewis Buell, "River and Bog," in* The
> New York Times Book Review, *August 12,*
> *1956, p. 24.*

[*We Live by the River* includes three] stories and five brief poems. The first story describes a lock-keeper's family on the Pearl River, the second tells of life on an island in the Mississippi River, and the third concerns a family earning a meager living by fishing and collecting mussel shells on the Ohio River. The first two, written in short jerky sentences, have little plot; the third is more exciting. The poems are mere rhymes. Material is unusual and probably authentic, but plot and literary style are poor. Ages 7-10. Not recommended.

> *Elizabeth Elliott, in a review of "We Live by*
> *the River," in* Junior Libraries, *Vol. 3, No. 1,*
> *September 15, 1956, p. 34.*

## Big Little Davy   (1956)

To the young child it is almost incomprehensible that he was once as small as his little brother and sometimes it seems almost as incredible that he will ever be really big. In this cozy, hand-sized book Lois Lenski offers proof of both these concepts. Twenty-two pictures, accompanied by succinct text, show Davy as he grows from a new baby to a 6-year-old, jauntily setting off for the first day at school. In each picture he is a little bigger and his activities a little more complicated, so that the whole is a fictional biography that should give confidence to younger children and understanding to older ones.

> Ellen Lewis Buell, "First Years," in The New York Times Book Review, *September 16, 1956, p. 38.*

What a pleasant surprise! A new book about that popular character, Davy, but this time a sort of streamlined biography. . . . A really clever lesson in growing up, in which a young child should find reassurance and an older one new understanding of and sympathy for a little brother.

> Polly Goodwin, in a review of "Big Little Davy," in Chicago Sunday Tribune, *Part 4, September 30, 1956, p. 7.*

---

## Houseboat Girl   (1957)

Another in the excellent regional series that is introducing young America to the factual data of ways of living in different parts of the country. This story spans a far reach of the Mississippi valley—from Paducah to Memphis, as it is familiar to the Fosters, a houseboat family. The pattern of the story, with its day by day details, give this a somewhat different flavor, but a more or less predictable development. To nine-year-old Patsy, the life was not as satisfactory as an established home—but they went through adventures and misadventures before the river floated them high and dry on a hilltop. If the Fosters leave something to be desired as people one would want as intimates, the story shares a philosophy of life that is worthwhile. Not perhaps a peak in the series, but a welcome addition.

> A review of "Houseboat Girl," in Virginia Kirkus' Service, *Vol. XXV, No. 18, September 15, 1957, p. 691.*

---

## Davy and His Dog   (1957)

A tiny book for Davy-fans, this gives the familiar interchanges of boy-and-puppy fun. Spot hides. He spats with a cat. He does tricks. The primer prose is very easy, with plenty of word-repetition to encourage eager readers with limited word recognition range. There's an original song by Lois Lenski about a little dog with illustrations characteristic of her books in brown and green. A little story reassuringly familiar in pleasant miniature form.

> A review of "Davy and His Dog," in Virginia

Kirkus' Service, *Vol. XXV, No. 21, November 1, 1957, p. 811.*

---

## I Went for a Walk   (1958)

Lois Lenski who writes successfully for children of varied age levels invites the youngest reader for a musical stroll around town. This particular peach and white town is bustling and energetic, but scaled with its jaunty tunes and diminutive illustrations for the most tender citizen. Through a series of little verses the reader is introduced to the elements of his town, city or village, learning as he sings the author's simple melodies, the names and nature of the objects which surround him. A happy introduction to community life. (pp. 801-02)

> A review of "I Went for a Walk," in Virginia Kirkus' Service, *Vol. XXVI, No. 20, October 15, 1958, pp. 801-02.*

---

## At Our House   (1959)

A nosegay of familiar events, toy-like illustrations, and simple tunes, this book by the author of *I Went For a Walk* once again revolves about the familiar. Presenting it in diminutive terms, the everyday world of the child becomes at once comfortably recognizable and newly charming. Easy rhymes and uncomplicated melodies serve to support the impression of the printed word in the mind of the child who stands at the threshold of books.

> A review of "At Our House," in Virginia Kirkus' Service, *Vol. XXVII, No. 15, August 1, 1959, p. 547.*

On each page, a brief poem about some small aspect of everyday life; below this is printed a simple tune to which the words are set; on the facing page, an illustration of the activity described. Drawings in blue, black and white are appropriate for the bland tone of the text. There is an appeal for children in reading of, or in singing about, familiar things; the poetry is, however, often colorless and occasionally labored. The use of elision ("deliv'ry boy") achieves rhythm, but creates difficulty for independent reading. (pp. 116-17)

> A review of "At Our House," in Bulletin of the Center for Children's Books, *Vol. XIII, No. 7, March, 1960, pp. 116-17.*

---

## Coal Camp Girl   (1959)

Nine-year-old Tina Wilson, a West Virginian, finds, within the mining community in which she is growing up, a rich, varied, and exciting life. The constant threat of disaster, the intense feeling of community, the caves which offer riches, adventure, and sometimes tragedy form an atmosphere of which the responsive Tina is keenly aware. Lois Lenski writes of the town, the company store, those men who are born with the love of coal in their blood and those who live to leave the mines with unusual feeling, embellishing her story with much factual information on the workings of a mine and the lives of its miners. Illustrated by the author in evocative black and white drawings, this is a story unique in the truthful portrayal it offers the readers of this age level. One of the best in this regional way of life series. (pp. 789-90)

> *A review of "Coal Camp Girl," in* Virginia Kirkus' Service, *Vol. XXVII, No. 20, October 15, 1959, pp. 789-90.*

Another in the series of regional studies of life in the United States. Tina Wilson lives in a West Virginia coal mining town; and the details of her family's life, the feeling of the miner for his work, the relationship of the small worker to the big company give a vivid picture, realistic but not oppressive. Conversation is realistic; this book conveys with fidelity the atmosphere of the bleak mining country and the resilience of its residents. The text is rather dull: it is certainly useful, it is interesting—but it reads like a fictionalized version of a documentary film or a case history from a social service textbook.

> *A review of "Coal Camp Girl," in* Bulletin of the Center for Children's Books, *Vol. XIII, No. 4, December, 1959, p. 63.*

As a story the narrative is unexciting reading, possibly because of the colorless, though realistic dialog and the dull tone of the writing; however, as an authentic picture of a

*Lenski at her desk in 1962.*

coal-mining community and an honest portrayal of the life, character, and philosophy of miners and their families the book is decidedly worthwhile.

> *A review of "Coal Camp Girl," in* The Booklist and Subscription Books Bulletin, *Vol. 56, No. 12, February 15, 1960, p. 358.*

---

## We Live in the Country   (1960)

To many children, there are two possible places in which to live: the city or the country. In this charming book of stories, Lois Lenski dramatizes the difference between four regions of this country by showing how rural life in four states—Connecticut, Arkansas, Texas, and Louisiana—determines the life of four children. Cathy lives on a New England chicken farm, Jinny on a cotton farm, Rosita, a lamb farm, and Jesse on a lumber farm. The various enterprises indigenous to the region bring about emotional consequences in the lives of these children, told in a simple and entertaining style by the author. Punctuated by drawings and poems, this is a warm portrayal of life in the United States.

> *A review of "We Live in the Country," in* Virginia Kirkus' Service, *Vol. XXVIII, No. 17, September 1, 1960, p. 753.*

This is country life as it is, unglamorized version. . . . Each of the four stories gives informative details about the industry—not in an obtrusive fashion, but in a way that shows how the lives of people are affected. Primarily, the stories are family stories, and their appeal lies in the meticulous realism of the writing: natural conversation, natural family relationships, natural small incidents, and minor problems, troubles, and pleasures.

> *Zena Sutherland, in a review of "We Live in the Country," in* Bulletin of the Center for Children's Books, *Vol. XV, No. 1, September, 1961, p. 11.*

Lois Lenski is the most purposeful of writers. In this, as in her many regional books, she pursues the entirely admirable aim of showing how other children live. In four stories she gives glimpses of life on a chicken farm, among share-croppers, on a sheep farm and in the timber forest. The writing has what one must assume to be a conscious lack of distinction, as if the author wants nothing to distract from the authentic ordinariness of her material.

The result is a book which is admirable in intention and much less enjoyable in performance. At first one thinks that here may be one of the answers to the reluctant reader, for the writing is simple and the material naturalistic, but reluctant readers will presumably be discouraged by the free use of dialect. The "corny" illustrations do not help much, and the poems which separate the stories serve only to indicate that Miss Lenski is no poet.

For all its admirable intentions, **We Live in the Country** is one of the American books which would best be left for home consumption. A British publisher might however very well steal the basic idea for a set of stories of country life in the British Isles.

*A review of "We Live in the Country," in* The Junior Bookshelf, *Vol. 25, No. 5, November, 1961, p. 271.*

### When I Grow Up (1960)

A very pleasant little book, with the lines of text repeated and set to music on each page, and with an illustration on the facing page. The music is simple, and the musical lines continuous. The first part of the book describes all the things a boy might be; the second part of the book is a similar song for a girl. The text can be read aloud without using the music and will stand by itself, but the simple and melodic tunes can be easily learned by a small child.

*Zena Sutherland, in a review of "When I Grow Up," in* Bulletin of the Center for Children's Books, *Vol. XIV, No. 7, March, 1961, p. 112.*

### Davy Goes Places (1961)

A small book that tells, in simple and rather dull text, the vehicles that Davy used at home and on a visit to Grandfather's farm. Cart, scooter, train, bus, car, truck, boat . . . even an airplane, which was the best of all. An adequate catalog of ways to get about, but presented in a rather pedestrian text.

*Zena Sutherland, in a review of "Davy Goes Places," in* Bulletin of the Center for Children's Books, *Vol. XV, No. 2, October, 1961, p. 31.*

### Policeman Small (1962)

A formula that never seems to fail has endeared the Mr. Small books to the picture book age. Add this factor to the unfailing interest in policemen and you have a sure candidate for another successful Lenski title. All the things a middle sized town policeman does day after day add up to his being a good friend for the small fry.

*A review of "Policeman Small," in* Virginia Kirkus' Service, *Vol. XXX, No. 14, July 15, 1962, p. 620.*

A day in the life of a policeman on traffic detail is told in simple text, with a few lines on each page being faced by a page of illustration. As Policeman Small greets children en route to school, stops traffic for an ambulance, hands out tickets to two drivers who have collided, or warns a speeding driver, the reader learns some aspect of a policeman's job. The chief appeal of the book, as of all the Small books, is in the familiarity of everyday experiences; here the text, despite the bland style of writing, is satisfying in its provision of a picture of the flow of community life.

*Zena Sutherland, in a review of "Policeman Small," in* Bulletin of the Center for Children's Books, *Vol. XVI, No. 3, November, 1962, p. 44.*

### We Live in the North (1965)

Three stories set in Michigan, giving—as do so many of Miss Lenski's stories—pictures of ethnic, industrial, or economic patterns that are seldom found in books for children. The writing is stilted, but the nature of the material, the honest treatment, and the large print make the book most useful. The first story describes a Polish-American family in Detroit: father is an assembly-line auto-worker; there are strong family ties, much ado about a relative who changes his name, and a constant reflection of the importance of the Roman Catholic Church. The second story presents a large, fatherless family of Finnish extraction who are migrant pickers; the last story concerns a family who own a Christmas tree farm.

*Zena Sutherland, in a review of "We Live in the North," in* Bulletin of the Center for Children's Books, *Vol. 19, No. 6, February, 1966, p. 101.*

### The Life I Live: Collected Poems (1965)

Lois Lenski has gathered together 368 selections, some previously unpublished, others from her books—from the **"Davy"** series to the regional. All are generously illustrated in the author's typical style. Not all are poems of high quality; Miss Lenski calls them verse and says that "verse is poetry in petticoats." They are very simple, deal with everyday things, and many of them have a city setting. Teachers in city schools and country schools for "disadvantaged" children may find them useful. To me they are really little rhyming or cadenced stories.

*Alice Dalgliesh, in a review of "The Life I Live: Collected Poems," in* Saturday Review, *Vol. 49, No. 12, March 19, 1966, p. 44.*

### High-Rise Secret (1966)

This is an attempt to give a realistic picture of life in a high-rise housing project for people with low incomes. The Murphy family come eagerly to their new home, but 10-year-old Peggy and eight-year-old Pete find their new life presents many problems. Pete steals; Peggy hides a stray cat in the apartment because pets are forbidden; there is tension between neighbors, and, most melodramatic of all, a tough street gang shoots at the project inhabitants landing both Peggy and Pete in the hospital. Of course there is a happy ending. Despite attempts to show the darker side of project living, this book fails to be convincing. The children are puppets and the plot is predictable.

*Johanna Hurwitz, in a review of "High-Rise Secret," in* Library Journal, *Vol. 91, No. 16, September 15, 1966, p. 4338.*

High-rise housing projects for low-income families are a part of modern living and thus a natural subject of Lois Lenski's latest book in the **"Roundabout America"** series. Many city children will recognize the problems: the "no pet" rule, the rival gang, the child on welfare who is the butt of jokes, the inadequate laundromat, the desirable and undesirable tenants and the human friction of too many people living too close together. Unfortunately, the changes for the good in this story come as a result of a sniper's bullets that wound two children—and all problems are too easily solved. Let's hope the resolution of the real-life difficulties in city living doesn't require gunshots to get action.

> *Anne Izard, in a review of "High-Rise Secret," in* The New York Times Book Review, *November 27, 1966, p. 42.*

A rather rambling but realistic story set in a high-rise housing project. The five Murphys find that their neighbors run the gamut from generous friendliness to hostility, that the space and light are fine, but the noise and the lack of community feeling are depressing. . . . When some of the women try to clean up the area, they are shot at by teen age snipers. The project then gets some bad publicity and some much-needed improvements, in a closing that is believable but abrupt. The style is simple, the print large, the story line uncohesive; the book is fairly interesting despite these weaknesses, since the setting is one that is familiar to increasing numbers of children.

> *Zena Sutherland, in a review of "High-Rise Secret," in* Bulletin of the Center for Children's Books, *Vol. 20, No. 6, February, 1967, p. 93.*

---

## To Be a Logger   (1967)

Little Joe's father is a logger and a compulsive tree-cutter, who cuts down all the trees on his own property making their small house slide toward the creek; his mother is a spendthrift who lets tin cans accumulate in the corners of the living room: in a one-store town they live the life of the rural poor. In a series of barely related episodes, their story is told: Joe's camping trip, the cock-crowing contest, the forest fire, Dad's serious accident. Although we're not aware that Joe is trying to decide on a profession, the last chapter is dialogue pro and con the scientific methods of the Forest Service, ending with his decision to join up and reject professional logging; this, and the sissy description will certainly seem tacked on. A disorganized and not very gripping introduction to a disorganized way of life.

> *A review of "To Be a Logger," in* Kirkus Service, *Vol. XXXV, No. 13, July 1, 1967, p. 741.*

Miss Lenski has managed to include a good deal of accurate information and an unbelievable amount of action in this regional book. The plot is just a vehicle to convey the facts, and the characters are not well developed. The list of definitions and the introduction in Miss Lenski's book give good background, but a more usable source of accurate information is *The First Book of Lumbering* by Louise Rich.

> *Eleanor S. Everett, in a review of "To Be a Logger," in* School Library Journal, *Vol. 14, No. 2, October 15, 1967, p. 176.*

In this newest addition to her regional series, Lois Lenski takes on the problem of America's disappearing wilder-

ness. The indifference if not the irresponsibility of logging operations, the man-made desolation along with that of fire and gale, are portrayed in her spare, simple, sometimes leisurely account. But more particularly, it is the story of a boy who finds himself torn between his love of the forest and his growing hatred and fear of it.

Seen through the boy's eyes, the question of whether nature is simply a commodity to be used up emerges with force and drama. The resolution is a bit pat, but Lois Lenski has a practiced hand with a didactic story, and this often engrossing one about logging has its place.

> *H. R., in a review of "To Be a Logger," in* Book World—The Washington Post, *March 3, 1968, p. 21.*

---

## Deer Valley Girl   (1968)

They're still feudin' up thar in Vermont (?): the Pecks claim the Otises are the *meanest* and the Otises think the Pecks are rotten for cutting off their water supply. Abby Peck (twelve) just loves animals, gets annoyed when the Otis boys chase away dogs (including hers) who would attack their visiting deer, and she gets really angry when her dog Hobo is shot by an unknown assailant. When sister Susan loses her buttons (from her new winter coat) to Cassie Otis' nimble scissors, the two retaliate by pushing the Otis girl into the nearest stream. And so it goes in round after round of sapless venom with a sprinkling of Grammy Peck's nostalgic refrains ("Why, I can remember when there warn't but one road through Deer Valley and it warn't no good, nothin' but a mess o' mud and ruts") and a plot as structured as popping corn. Mom (Peck) ends the feud by hiring a surveyor who discovers each family owns half of that disputed property—ha, ha, after all these years. Miss Lenski was invited up to Vermont by schoolchildren who asked for a "Regional" but this is neither the real McCoy nor a coat of local color.

> *A review of "Deer Valley Girl," in* Kirkus Service, *Vol. XXXVI, No. 4, February 15, 1968, p. 183.*

---

## Debbie and Her Grandma   (1967)

The rounded, naïve style which Lois Lenski has made especially her own (though it is carried on today also by Eleanor Schick) may not find as many devotees now as it did in the days of Papa Small; tastes change. But small children will always enjoy a description of familiar ploys and this artless sequence of dressing up, gardening, listening to a story, has its surely popular point—that Debbie is spending the day *on her own* with Grandma, in a happy relationship.

> *Margery Fisher, in a review of "Debbie and Her Grandma," in* Growing Point, *Vol. 7, No. 4, October, 1968, p. 1196.*

One's pleasure in finding a new Lois Lenski for beginner readers, illustrated with her delightful clarity of line, is for once dimmed a little by the more than usually sentimental text. Debbie goes to stay overnight with Grandma, helps her (they sing a little song about how they love each other), hears tales of Daddy as a child, plays with the children next door, falls and is comforted—at this point, the other children run off, leaving Debbie crying and the dressing-up clothes strewn over the floor! Next day, Grandma takes Debbie home and they say goodbye—no parents appear! It will nevertheless appeal to those for whom it was written.

> *A review of "Debbie and Her Grandma," in* The Junior Bookshelf, *Vol. 33, No. 1, February, 1969, p. 18.*

---

### Debbie Herself; Debbie and Her Family  (1969)

In the flat statements of **Papa Small** but drawn in color, [**Debbie and Her Family** describes] Who's Who in Debbie's large family from Great-Grandpa to tiny Cousin Betty. This might be as innocuous as it appears if it didn't type people by appearances: Great-Grandpa is deaf and needs to be shouted at; Great-Aunt Susan is a straight-backed old maid shunned by the children; Aunt Lily is "young and pretty" and everybody's playmate. A bad example.

> *A review of "Debbie and Her Family," in* Kirkus Reviews, *Vol. XXXVII, No. 21, November 1, 1969, p. 1145.*

Stiff drawings add little appeal to two books about a three-year-old girl. In **Debbie Herself** the child's everyday activities are described: "Debbie dresses up in funny clothes / And down the street prancing she goes / Sister comes running to bring her back / She says, 'Come home!' and gives her a smack." In **Debbie and Her Family,** which does not have a rhyming text, the various members of Debbie's family are introduced and briefly described. While the books have some usefulness as a starting-point for discussing familial relationships and some value in reflecting everyday activities, they are dull and humorless, and they do not always depict the most positive aspects of intra-family attitudes.

> *Zena Sutherland, in a review of "Debbie and Her Family," in* Bulletin of the Center for Children's Books, *Vol. 23, No. 10, June, 1970, p. 161.*

---

### Debbie and Her Dolls  (1970)

Debbie tends her many dolls, Debbie and neighbor Stevie play store and school with the dolls, big Brother and Sister don't play fair with the dolls—and it all looks as stiff as it sounds. With the added debit of Brother and Sister being just plain unmitigated, unmotivated mean and what they do to the dolls not being plain at all: is the yellow bucket brimming with suds, and if so why aren't the dolls wet? if the clothing Debbie takes out is dolls' clothing, why are they all fully dressed?

> *A review of "Debbie and Her Dolls," in* Kirkus Reviews, *Vol. XXXVIII, No. 5, March 1, 1970, p. 239.*

### Debbie Goes to Nursery School  (1970)

Striding unaccompanied to the door and comfortably fitting into the day's activities (which constitute the content here), Debbie conquers nursery school as if there were nothing to it. And, beyond a prospectus, there isn't. For the majority of children who have some apprehension, *Will I Have a Friend?* is more to the point.

> *A review of "Debbie Goes to Nursery School," in* Kirkus Reviews, *Vol. XXXVIII, No. 6, March 15, 1970, p. 316.*

**Debbie Goes to Nursery School** is a very slight story that presents a superficial treatment of nursery school and a too easy solution. There are many better books on the subject, such as Cohen's *Will I Have a Friend* (Macmillan, 1967).

> *Trevelyn Jones, in a review of "Debbie Goes to Nursery School," in* School Library Journal, *Vol. 16, No. 9, May, 1970, p. 89.*

---

### City Poems  (1971)

Docile, conventional, bland, the old fashion . . . but at least the rhyming is dependable—notably, in the wake of the current profusion of almost unscannable verse—except where it's forced to accede to the meters, themselves rarely varied (a few attempt calypso-like cadences). Ditto the schemata, description, vignette, exhortation, enumeration (catchier)—all of which *in*voke (not evoke) city themes. Typically, "Down in the subway under the ground. / The trains keep running all around; / Some go fast and some go slow, / They take you where you want to go." Crowdedly deployed in discouragingly small print among busy line-drawings, over 100 poems (mostly new) to memorize for recitation and promptly forget. (pp. 505-06)

> *A review of "City Poems," in* Kirkus Reviews, *Vol. XXXIX, No. 9, May 1, 1971, pp. 505-06.*

Some previously published poems are included here, but most of the selections are new, and the poems are grouped: places in the city, I like the city, fun in the city etc. The poems are short, one or two to a page, and their chief attraction is, for the urban child, the familiarity of the sights and activities they describe. The writing is pedestrian, and the rhyme occasionally falters: "The big cranes come / and knock the walls down / Bulldozers crawling / all over the ground," but the inclusion of such subjects as the local bully, buying things on credit, gangs, and riots reflects the way it is for many children, and the book has a balance of advantages and disadvantages in urban living.

> *Zena Sutherland, in a review of "City Poems," in* Bulletin of the Center for Children's Books, *Vol. 24, No. 11, July-August, 1971, p. 174.*

---

### Debbie and Her Pets  (1971)

To add to her pet collection Debbie finds a caterpillar (" 'I like pets!' said Debbie"), two worms (" 'I want a lot of pets,' said Debbie"), and a grasshopper (" 'See all my pets!' said Debbie"). Apparently unaware of the pleas of humane and conservation societies, she also gets two chicks for Easter and a baby alligator from Florida. Then brother and sister set all her pets free, but she soon cheers up, for she still has Pussy and Puppy, and they "were the best pets, after all!" All the names—Peek-a-Boo for the turtle, Jumper for the frog, Peep and Cheep for the chicks—are as unimaginative as the flat little narrative and the crudely unattractive pictures.

> *A review of "Debbie and Her Pets," in* Kirkus Reviews, *Vol. XXXIX, No. 15, August 1, 1971, p. 803.*

**Debbie and Her Pets** is a companion to the Davy series. The story, such as it is, centers on a pet show and concludes with the moral that tame pets are best, after all. The little, dot-eyed, pink, green and yellow stick-figured companions, Debbie and Davy, find a variety of worms, insects, spiders and frogs, plus Debbie receives rabbits and baby alligators from fond relatives while yearning for elephants. The animals all go into boxes until brother and sister finally let them out (good ecology). But mundane Puppy and Pussy win the pet show prize, anyway. Children who know the Daddy-Long-Legs would not recognize the flower-like multipled (10 legs—count 'em) on page 13.

> *Eleanor C. Trimble, in a review of "Debbie and Her Pets," in* School Library Journal, *Vol. 18, No. 4, December, 1971, p. 68.*

---

**Lois Lenski's Big Book of Mr. Small; More Mr. Small (1979)**

The word for Lenski's doll-like heroes is "timeless." Some of the author-illustrator's Mr. Small stories first appeared in the 1930s, and [in **Lois Lenski's Big Book of Mr. Small**] today's children are treated to the still fresh tales in a triple feature. The first is **"Policeman Small,"** about a hardworking public servant with a kind heart. Directing the busy traffic in a great city, he doesn't hesitate to stop the long line of cars while a stray kitten laps up spilled milk or to help a trembling puppy across the street. A song accompanies this story, followed by the adventures of **"Cowboy Small,"** and an account of doings on **"The Little Farm."** The book's color-washed drawings are simple and effective.

> *A review of "Lois Lenski's Big Book of Mr. Small," in* Publishers Weekly, *Vol. 217, No. 24, June 20, 1980, p. 86.*

Here, combined into two chunky volumes of three stories each, are Lois Lenski's Mr. Small books, some of the first ever aimed directly at preschoolers. *The Big Book of Mr. Small* (not larger, just thicker) contains *Policeman Small, Cowboy Small* and *The Little Farm. More Mr. Small* includes the transportation stories about *The Little Auto, The Little Sailboat* and *The Little Airplane.* These stories have bored generations of mothers to the point of fits while their enchanted toddlers demand "read it AGAIN, Mommy!" The episodes about everyday experiences, houses, jobs, and people still hit the mark with twos and threes. And, although they are not sized for a child's hands, these new editions will see lots of use.

> *Jane Bickel, in a review of "Lois Lenski's Big Book of Mr. Small," in* School Library Journal, *Vol. 27, No. 2, October, 1980, p. 136.*

# A(lan) A(lexander) Milne

## 1882-1956

English author of fiction, poetry, and plays.

Major works include *When We Were Very Young* (1924), *Winnie-the-Pooh* (1926), *Now We Are Six* (1927), *The House at Pooh Corner* (1928), *Toad of Toad Hall* (1929).

The following entry presents criticism of *When We Were Very Young, Now We Are Six, Winnie-the-Pooh,* and *The House at Pooh Corner.*

Often celebrated as the most gifted and popular poet of childhood for writing *When We Were Very Young* and *Now We Are Six,* the two books of verse inspired by his small son, Christopher Robin, Milne is best known as the creator of Winnie-the-Pooh, the endearing anthropomorphic bear who was Christopher's stuffed companion, is introduced in the verses, and becomes the central character of the fantasies *Winnie-the-Pooh* and *The House at Pooh Corner.* Although he was a prolific and successful playwright, essayist, novelist, and writer of light verse for adults as well as the author of other stories and a play for children, Milne is chiefly remembered today for these "four trifles for the young," as he called them. He is often lauded for his accurate observations of child behavior and for the sympathetic understanding of his audience which he reflects in his children's books. In addition, Milne is praised for his skill with language, especially wordplay and dialogue; for his imaginative characterizations; for his wit and craftsmanship; for the charm, warmth, and readability of his stories and verses; and for their universal appeal to both children and adults. As a poet, Milne is compared favorably to such writers as Lewis Carroll, Robert Louis Stevenson, and Walter de la Mare; what distinguishes the verses, which range in subject from the everyday activities of children to more profound themes such as the child's thoughts about God, is their portrayal of preschoolers as artless, often ruthless egoists. The verses are also notable for their variety: utilizing such forms as the nursery rhyme, the ballad, the cautionary tale, and the nonsense poem, they also reflect Milne's use of intricate rhythms and rhyme schemes as well as parenthetical asides and inventive capitalization and typographical patterns. In the Pooh books, Milne retains the intimate tone, playful wordplay, and capitalization technique of his verses to describe the humorous and occasionally touching adventures of Pooh and the other inhabitants of the Hundred Acre Wood; the books also include songs and verses, called "hums," composed by Pooh. The forest denizens include several additional toys—timid yet plucky Piglet, Pooh's closest companion; Eeyore, the sarcastic and self-deprecating donkey who, next to Pooh, is Milne's most popular creation; the maternal Kanga and her enthusiastic son, Roo; and the bouncy tiger, Tigger—as well as two woodland animals, the bossy organizer, Rabbit, and the pretentious, pompous Owl. Milne creates a self-contained world in which such activities as eating, explor-

ing, and games form the pattern for the lives of his characters, whose adventures often consist of their attempts to capture strange animals or to rescue each other from real or imagined dangers. Although the forest is threatened by floods and storms, it is ultimately a secure place due to the presence of Christopher Robin, who acts as a loving deus ex machina for the characters, as well as by the spirits of equality, cooperation, and kindness with which Milne underscores his books. At the end of *The House at Pooh Corner,* Christopher Robin tells Pooh that he can no longer return to the forest because he is being beckoned by adulthood; this chapter, considered among the most tender in all of juvenile literature, completes Milne's oeuvre for children. Both the stories and the verses are illustrated with lively black-and-white line drawings and decorations by Ernest H. Shepard, who used Christopher Robin and his toys as models for his pictures; Shepard is often credited both for his successful artistic collaboration with Milne and for the contribution of his illustrations to the success of the books.

Youngest of the three sons of schoolmaster John Vine Milne, Milne is often thought to have taken inspiration for many of his subjects, characters, and themes from his relationships with his father and his brother, Ken, from the memories of his own happy childhood, and from his professional contacts. After graduating from Cambridge with honors in mathematics, he became a freelance writer and was later appointed an assistant editor of the humor magazine *Punch,* to which he contributed weekly essays. Milne wrote the poems which became *When We Were Very Young* during a rainy vacation in North Wales; he later commented that "[*When We Were Very Young*] is the work of a light-verse writer taking his job seriously even though he is taking it into the nursery," a statement which observers acknowledge as true of all of his works for young readers. *When We Were Very Young* was immediately recognized as a new kind of children's book, one which moved away from the fairy fashion and overly didactic literature of the time to portray children realistically in an enjoyable, stylish manner. Achieving both critical and popular success with *When We Were Very Young* and the more sophisticated *Now We Are Six,* Milne wrote the Pooh stories after acquiring Cotchford Farm, a family vacation spot in rural Sussex, and watching the interaction of Christopher and his mother, Daphne, with the boy's beloved toys. In these books, which began as bedtime stories, Milne reveals both a fatherly benevolence and an incisive assessment of human eccentricities through his portrayal of his characters; although childlike, the animals often possess clearly adult foibles which Milne satirizes. With Winnie-the-Pooh, however, Milne presents children with a character with which they can readily identify. Pooh can be greedy, self-absorbed, and sometimes dim, but by the end of *Pooh Corner* he begins to realize his own competency after demonstrating bravery, quick thinking, and generosity. "Pooh [is] the most famous bear ever created," writes critic Margaret Blount, while critic Marcus Crouch notes of Milne, "In his creation of Pooh, [he] proved himself one of the supreme myth-makers." Both the verses and the stories became publishing phenomena and have since been accepted into popular culture; the character of Pooh has become a cult figure who has prompted a publishing industry featuring spinoff books, toys, calendars, and other merchandise as well as animated Walt Disney films and television programs. During his lifetime, Milne was criticized for writing overly sentimental and whimsical verses and stories that reflect a bourgeois lifestyle and attitude and are directed more to adults than to children; more recently, he has received a mixed reception both for his negative view of women and for creating an overly idealized, unsympathetic character in Christopher Robin. However, most observers confirm Milne's sincerity and literary skill while acknowledging that his books are classics of children's literature; May Hill Arbuthnot notes, "We shall never encounter a writer who understands more completely the curious composite of gravity and gaiety, of supreme egotism and occasional whimsy, that is the young child." *The World of Pooh,* a collected edition of the Pooh stories, received the Lewis Carroll Shelf Award in 1958, an honor received by *The World of Christopher Robin,* a collected edition of the verses, in 1962.

(See also *CLR,* Vol. 1; *Twentieth Century Literary Criticism,* Vol. 6; *Yesterday's Authors of Books for Children,* Vol. 1; *Contemporary Authors,* Vol. 104; and *Dictionary of Literary Biography,* Vols. 10, 77, and 100.)

## AUTHOR'S COMMENTARY

In August of [1920] my collaborator produced a more personal work [than the play *Mr. Pim Passes By*]. We had intended to call it *Rosemary,* but decided later that *Billy* would be more suitable. However, as you can't be christened William—at least, we didn't see why anybody should—we had to think of two other names, two initials being necessary to ensure him any sort of copyright in a cognomen as often plagiarized as Milne. One of us thought of Robin, the other of Christopher; names wasted on him who called himself Billy Moon as soon as he could talk, and has been Moon to his family and friends ever since. I mention this because it explains why the publicity which came to be attached to 'Christopher Robin' never seemed to affect us personally, but to concern either a character in a book or a horse which we hoped at one time would win the Derby.

When he was three, we took a house in North Wales for August with the Nigel Playfairs. It rained continuously. In the one living-room every morning there were assembled Five Playfairs, Three Milnes, Grace Lovat-Fraser, Joan Pitt-Chatham, Frederic Austin, and a selection of people to whom Nigel had issued casual invitations in London before starting north for what he supposed to be his Welsh castle. In a week I was screaming with agoraphobia. Somehow I must escape. I pleaded urgent inspiration, took a pencil and an exercise-book and escaped to the summer-house. It contained a chair and a table. I sat down on the chair, put my exercise-book on the table, and gazed ecstatically at a wall of mist which might have been hiding Snowdon or the Serpentine for all I saw or cared. I was alone. . . .

But sooner or later I should be asked what I was writing. What was I writing?

About six months earlier, while at work on a play, I had wasted a morning in writing a poem called '**Vespers.**' I gave it to Daphne, as one might give a photograph or a valentine, telling her that if she liked to get it published anywhere she could stick to the money. She sent it to Frank Crowninshield of *Vanity Fair* (N.Y.) and got fifty dollars. Later she lent it to me for the Queen's Doll's House Library, and later still collected one-forty-fourth of all the royalties of *When We Were Very Young,* together with her share of various musical and subsidiary rights. It turned out to be the most expensive present I had ever given her. A few months after this, Rose Fyleman was starting a magazine for children. She asked me, I have no idea why, to write some verses for it. I said that I didn't and couldn't, it wasn't in my line. As soon as I had posted my letter, I did what I always do after refusing to write anything: wondered how I would have written it if I hadn't refused. (pp. 278-79)

After another wasted morning I wrote to Miss Fyleman to say that perhaps after all I might write her some verses. A poem called "**The Dormouse and the Doctor**" was the result. It was illustrated by Harry Rountree; proofs had come to me in Wales; and with them came letters from both illustrator and editor saying: 'Why don't you write a whole book of verses like these?'

So there I was with an exercise-book and a pencil, and a fixed determination not to leave the heavenly solitude of that summer-house until it stopped raining . . . and there in London were two people telling me what to write . . . and there on the other side of the lawn was a child with whom I had lived for three years . . . and here within me were unforgettable memories of my own childhood . . . what was I writing? A child's book of verses obviously. Not a whole book, of course; but to write a few would be fun—until I was tired of it. Besides, my pencil had an india-rubber at the back; just the thing for poetry.

I had eleven wet days in that summer-house and wrote eleven sets of verses. Then we went back to London. A little apologetically: feeling that this wasn't really work: feeling that a man of stronger character would be writing that detective-story and making £2,000 for the family: a little as if I were slipping off to Lord's in the morning, or lying in a deck-chair at Osborne reading a novel, I went on writing verses. By the end of the year I had written enough for a book.

It was only after the book was in the publisher's hands that Owen Seaman heard about it. Probably Lucas, then chairman of Methuens, had mentioned it casually. Owen asked if *Punch* could print some of it, and I told him, reluctantly enough, that he could use what he liked, for I feared that as a 'reprint from *Punch*' it might not get the attention which would be given to a new book. However, the publication of some of the verses had two good results; it confirmed my opinion that Shepard was the right illustrator for the book, and, with the first appearance of ***The King's Breakfast,*** gave the publishers an idea of its ultimate reception. This was enthusiastic beyond all imagining, both in England and America. In the ten years before it went into a cheap edition half a million copies were sold.

It is inevitable that a book which has had very large sales should become an object of derision to critics and columnists. We all write books, we all want money; we who write want money from our books. If we fail to get money, we are not so humble, nor so foolish, as to admit that we have failed in our object. Our object, we maintain, was artistic success. It is easy to convince ourselves that the financial failure of the book is no proof of its artistic failure; and it is a short step from there to affirm that artistic success is, in fact, incompatible with financial success. It must be so: for how else could we be the artists we are and remain in our first editions? If any other artist goes into twenty editions, then he is a traitor to the cause, and we shall hasten to say that he is not one of Us.

All this is commonplace. What has been particularly irritating about the sales of Christopher Robin books (even though the irritation has produced no more intimidating retort than the writing of the name 'Kwistopher Wobin') is that the books were written for children. When, for instance, Dorothy Parker, as 'Constant Reader' in *The New Yorker,* delights the sophisticated by announcing that at page 5 of ***The House of Pooh Corner*** 'Tonstant Weader fwowed up' (*sic,* if I may), she leaves the book, oddly

enough, much where it was. However greatly indebted to Mrs Parker, no Alderney, at the approach of the milkmaid, thinks 'I hope this lot will turn out to be gin,' no writer of children's books says gaily to his publisher, 'Don't bother about the children, Mrs Parker will love it.' As an artist one might genuinely prefer that one's novel should be praised by a single critic, whose opinion one valued, rather than be bought by 'the mob'; For once, and how one hates to think it, *vox populi, vox Dei.* The position can only be saved by asserting that it isn't the genuine voice of the people. It is the illiterate mothers who speak. Even so, it might be held that mothers have their own particular qualifications for speaking.

In fact I know that a great many children did, and do, like ***When We Were Very Young.*** I think that such merit as attaches to the verses for this (as distinct from the illustrations to which the book is so obviously indebted) was won by taking pains: more pains, perhaps, than is usual. Whatever else they lack, the verses are technically good. The practice of no form of writing demands such a height of technical perfection as the writing of light verse in the Calverley and *Punch* tradition. ***When We Were Very Young*** is not the work of a poet becoming playful, nor of a lover of children expressing his love, nor of a prose-writer knocking together a few jingles for the little ones, it is the work of a light-verse writer taking his job seriously even though he is taking it into the nursery. It seems that the nursery, more than any other room in the house, likes to be approached seriously.

Whether I have added to technique that 'wonderful insight into a child's mind' of which publishers' advertisements talk so airily, I wouldn't know. I am not inordinately fond of or interested in children; their appeal to me is a physical appeal such as the young of other animals make. I have never felt in the least sentimental about them, or no more sentimental than one becomes for a moment over a puppy or a kitten. In as far as I understand their minds the understanding is based on the observation, casual enough and mostly unconscious, which I give to people generally: on memories of my own childhood: and on the imagination which every writer must bring to memory and observation. Again to avoid paraphrasing myself I shall quote here from a Preface to Parents, which I wrote for a particular edition of the verses.

> In real life very young children have an artless beauty, an innocent grace, an unstudied abandon of movement, which, taken together, make an appeal to our emotions similar in kind to that made by any other young and artless creatures: kittens, puppies, lambs: but greater in degree, for the reason that the beauty of childhood seems in some way to transcend the body. Heaven, that is, does really appear to lie about the child in its infancy, as it does not lie about even the most attractive kitten. But with this outstanding physical quality there is a natural lack of moral quality, which expresses itself, as Nature always insists on expressing herself, in an egotism entirely ruthless.
>
> Now it seems to me that the writer who is trying to put a child upon paper must keep these two

outstanding facts about children before him, and endeavour to preserve his sense of proportion. A sentimental painter might leave out the wart on Cromwell's face; but the biographer who, priding himself on his realism, calls attention to the wart every time he mentions the face, is just as falsely sentimental, since any small blemish on the face of one we know soon passes unnoticed. A pen-picture of a child which showed it as loving, grateful and full of thought for others would be false to the truth; but equally false would be a picture which insisted on the brutal egotism of the child, and ignored the physical beauty which softens it. Equally false and equally sentimental, for sentimentality is merely an appeal to emotions not warranted by the facts.

To avoid equally these two sentimentalities is the difficulty in front of the writer. It is easy (at least, I suppose it is easy, if one is a painter) to paint a beautiful child, but it is not easy to describe one. Any attempt to do so will become either conventional or indescriptive. But it is possible to give what one might call 'an air of charm,' particularly when writing in verse, to any account of a child's activities, and it seems to me that this 'charm,' if one can convey it, should have as much chance in the printed page as in real life of hiding from the sentimentalist the uncharming part of a child's nature: the egotism and the heartlessness.

I shall now expose my own egotism by giving one or two examples of how I have tried to do this.

The mother of a little boy of three has disappeared, and is never seen again. The child's reaction to the total loss of his mother is given in these lines:

> James James
> Morrison Morrison
> (Commonly known as Jim)
> Told his
> Other relations
> Not to go blaming him.

And that is all. It is the truth about a child: children are, indeed, as heartless as that: but only in one sense have I made a song about it.

In **"Buckingham Palace"** Christopher Robin is taken by his nurse to see the changing of the guard. She tells him about the soldiers and the Palace and the King, and at the end of it all he has only one question to ask: 'Do you think the King knows all about Me?' Could egotism be more gross? If you were to take an author up to your most admired friend—as it might be Lindbergh—and on the way were to whisper to him of all the wonderful things your hero had done, would you not be disgusted if his only remark were, 'Do you think Lindbergh knows all about Me?' But since a child of three can say these things, and be innocent and charming enough to make them sound innocent and charming, so then, in the poem, if a true picture is to be given, the egotism must be there for the unsentimental to find, but there must also be charm enough to give it at least a surface covering.

Finally, let me refer to the poem which has been more sentimentalized over than any other in the book: **"Vespers."**

Well, if mothers and aunts and hard-headed reviewers have been sentimental over it, I am glad; for the spectacle in real life of a child of three at its prayers is one over which thousands have been sentimental. It is indeed calculated to bring a lump to the throat. But, even so, one must tell the truth about the matter. Not 'God bless mummy, because I love her so', but 'God bless Mummy, I know that's right'; not 'God bless Daddy, because he buys me food and clothes,' but 'God bless Daddy, I quite forgot'; not even the egotism of 'God bless Me, because I'm the most important person in the house,' but the super-egotism of feeling so impregnable that the blessing of this mysterious god for Oneself is the very last thing for which it would seem necessary to ask. And since this is the Truth about a Child, let us get all these things into the poem, and the further truth that prayer means nothing to a child of three, whose thoughts are engaged with other, more exciting matters; but since the Truth about a Child is also that, fresh from its bath, newly powdered and curled, it is a lovely thing, God wot, why then, let us try, however inadequately, to get at least a hint of this upon paper, so that, if possible, the reader, no less than the spectator, may feel that Beauty is hovering. . . . For some day we may be describing a Scientist Shaving and calling it *Matins,* and then there will be no need to wait upon Beauty.

***Winnie-the-Pooh*** was written two years later, and was followed by a second book of verses and, in 1928, ***The House at Pooh Corner.*** The animals in the stories came for the most part from the nursery. My collaborator had already given them individual voices, their owner by constant affection had given them the twist in their features which denoted character, and Shepard drew them, as one might say, from the living model. They were what they are for anyone to see; I described rather than invented them. Only Rabbit and Owl were my own unaided work. These books also became popular. One day when Daphne went up to the nursery, Pooh was missing from the dinner-table which he always graced. She asked where he was. 'Behind the ottoman,' replied his owner coldly. 'Face downwards. He said he didn't like **When We Were Very Young.'** Pooh's jealousy was natural. He could never quite catch up with the verses.

It is easier in England to make a reputation than to lose one. I wrote four 'Children's books,' containing altogether, I suppose, 70,000 words—the number of words in the average-length novel. Having said good-bye to all that in 70,000 words, knowing that as far as I was concerned the mode was outmoded, I gave up writing children's books. I wanted to escape from them as I had once wanted to escape from *Punch;* as I have always wanted to escape. In vain. England expects the writer, like the cobbler, to stick to his last. As Arnold Bennett pointed out: if you begin painting policemen you must go on painting policemen, for then the public knows the answer—Policemen. If you stop painting policemen in order to paint windmills, criticism remains so overpoweringly policeman-conscious that even a windmill is seen as something with arms out, obviously directing the traffic. These last ten years in which I have been writing plays, novels and invocations against war are littered with affiliation orders on behalf of all the 'juveniles' born so lovingly and with such complete absence of labour into the bookworld. If I didn't put my name to them, 'that,' as the King of Hearts said, 'only makes the matter worse.' It proves that my spiritual home is still the nursery, that I am still thinking of policemen. As a discerning critic pointed out: the hero of my latest play, God help it, was 'just Christopher Robin grown up.' So that even when I stop writing about children, I still insist on writing about people who were children once. What an obsession with me children are become! (pp. 280-87)

> *A. A. Milne, in his* Autobiography, *E. P. Dutton & Co., Inc., 1939, 315 p.*

---

### John Drinkwater

[*The following excerpt is from a review of* When We Were Very Young *that originally appeared in the* Sunday Times *on 23 November 1924. According to critic Ann Thwaite in her* A. A. Milne: The Man Behind Winnie-the-Pooh, *Drinkwater "spoke out for the arrival of a 'new prophet,' somehow fit to be mentioned in the same breath as Lewis Carroll."*]

Mr Milne's deftness is not to be questioned, but the fortunate thing is that it is, apart from the few lapses, always at work, as Lewis Carroll's was, on a sound common sense foundation . . . Mr Milne treats his small companion as a sensible being who, indeed, wants to make up things, as is proper, but wants to make them up about real life and not about fairy doodleum. These two go about in the gayest and most whimsical of tempers, but the things that engage their attention are the soldiers at Buckingham Palace, the three little foxes who didn't wear stockings and didn't wear sockses, the gardener, the king who asked for no more than a little butter for the royal slice of bread . . . It is all great larks, but I wonder whether the Sterner Critics will realize that it also is a very wholesome contribution to serious literature.

> *John Drinkwater, in an excerpt in* A. A. Milne: The Man Behind Winnie-the-Pooh *by Ann Thwaite, Random House, 1990, p. 264.*

### Helen Cady Forbes

[**When We Were Very Young**] is that rare thing, a book about children which they may enjoy. The rhythm alone would hold them entranced, even without the absolute rightness of the sense and nonsense. The book has the vitality that children crave; there is nothing conventional between its covers, not an insipid line, either in the verses or in the drawings that so perfectly illustrate them. Nor is there a trace of condescension. While the poems frequently mention a certain Christopher Robin, that child will have no reason to reproach his father by and by when he looks at the book with older, colder eyes. . . .

**When We Were Very Young** is essentially different from other volumes of poetry about children. There is more variety of form and thought. The flying kites, the flying clouds, the tiresome rice pudding are taken more gayly, more tenderly, than usual. There are poems of quiet loveliness balanced by the most delightfully nonsensical stories. . . .

Animals figure largely in these verses, as they do in children's interest, but these are no ordinary beasts. They possess personalities far removed from the animals of bedtime lore.

Their elders may wish to read these poems aloud, but children will want to take the book away to read to themselves and to each other, to chant each rhyme as many times as they like before going on to the next. The very music of childhood is here, sung with a varied cadence peculiar to these poems, essentially and uniquely the dramatic expression of tenderness.

> *Helen Cady Forbes, "Delicious Sillies," in* New York Herald Tribune Books, *December 14, 1924, p. 6.*

### The New York Times Book Review

The man who can write really first-rate verses for children ought to be prevented forcibly from spending his time in any other way, for it will be a long time before the number of volumes which merit that rating will be sufficient to fill anything like a five-foot shelf. Yet that would be a harsh measure to apply to Mr. A. A. Milne, whose light touch in the drama has won him distinction, whose essays have a pleasant humor and whose versatility has also placed to his credit an excellent mystery story. He might be let off on the promise that he will write at least one other book of children's verse as good as **When We Were Very Young.** And the further stipulation might be made that the illustrations must be the work of Mr. Shepard, whose drawings contribute much to the charm and gayety of the present volume.

*Milne as a small boy.*

Aside from little matters like imagination and light-heartedness—a fancy that springs up as spontaneously as the child's own, and a buoyant spirit that isn't a grim adult determination to be amusing, verses for children are best when they have an easily caught rhythm and rhymes that seem to come without half trying. Children are awake to the pleasure of rhyme and rhythm long before they can read, and the poet who can't provide these essentials had best take his talents elsewhere. Mr. Milne has them all and in such degree that **When We Were Very Young** belongs in the company of the best, which is to say in the company of Lewis Carroll, Stevenson, Field and Walter de la Mare.

Mr. Milne understands, too, the games that children make up for themselves and which they enjoy much more thoroughly than those which are made for them. . . .

Mr. Milne doesn't try to slip in little moral lessons and admonitions concerning good behavior, after the fashion of the sugar-plum school. He is content, and able, to write from the child's point of view. . . .

And he is altogether willing, when the occasion calls for it, to brush the rules of grammar genially aside. . . .

So, too, when the right word is necessary, Mr. Milne is not above supplying it without regard to its claim to a place in the dictionary. . . .

Mr. Milne is at his best in the pieces that have a humorous turn. He writes of nature prettily, but without the magic that is Walter de la Mare's.

> *"Rhyme, Rhythm and Mr. Alexander A. Milne," in* The New York Times Book Review, *January 11, 1925, p. 16.*

**Anne Carroll Moore**

[**When We Were Very Young**] came over too late for our review of children's books of 1924. It was without question the book of the year and of many years. Its rhymes have now been said and sung—for fourteen of them have been set to music—from coast to coast. I have met only one young man who said he thought it "the silliest book" he had ever read; but there's hope for him, since his first child was but five months old. "Wait until he's five *years* old", said I. "You'll bless Christopher Robin then for having a father like Hoo and a friend like Ernest Shepard to make pictures for his book. If you don't enjoy the verses as the children do, for their rhythms and fun, then read them for their child psychology. I know of no book more penetrated with it." (p. 181)

> *Anne Carroll Moore, "Children's Books of 1925," in* The Bookman, *New York, Vol. LXII, No. 2, October, 1925, pp. 178-82.*

**Marcia Dalphin**

It is two years ago—that November day in 1924—when the reading world, happening to pick up in the shops a little red book entitled **When We Were Very Young,** sampled a page, rubbed its eyes, read a little further, and then without more ado reached out and took A. A. Milne gently but with unmistakable firmness to its capacious breast. There it has held him ever since. But while it is a fond

heart that beats there, there is such a thing as waistcoast buttons sticking into one, and it must be rather exhausting, not to mention warm in summer, something like being in the perpetual embrace of Mr. Edward Bear. Is Mr. Milne perhaps trying to ransom himself when he offers us a new Christopher Robin book this fall [**Winnie-the-Pooh**]?

Out of a sedate looking little green and gold book steps Winnie-the-Pooh, bashful and a bit out of breath (because of Stoutness), to make his bow to a waiting world. Winnie-the-Pooh is the name that Christopher Robin gave to Edward Bear when he demanded an exciting one all to himself, and of course when we stop to think of it we can all see that it is one of those indisputably right things.

Writers for children have done stories about bears often enough, but it has remained for Milne to discover to us in **Winnie-the-Pooh** the essential wistfulness of these great lumbering, blundering creatures. Others have shown their clumsiness, their heavy, halting intelligence, their occasional flashes of sly humor, their greediness. Pooh has all these; but he has something else as well—a disarming humility in the presence of his quicker-witted fellows, a longing for approval, a desire to be correct (did he not take Stoutness Exercises in front of the glass?), a—well, there's no word for it but wistfulness—that goes straight to your heart. . . .

As you read the conviction grows on you that Mr. Milne has done it again. There are not so very many books that, sitting reading all alone, you find yourself laughing aloud over. This is one of them. Here is nonsense in the best tradition; entirely plausible on the surface, as true nonsense always is, with good sense at its core, and the high seriousness about it that children and other wise people love. The illusion is perfect. You never forget that these are nursery animals, and that you exist as a reader only because you are allowed to see them through the eyes of a loving little child. Who could have done it except [A. A. Milne]?

> *Marcia Dalphin, "Mr. Edward Bear, His Book," in* New York Herald Tribune Books, *October 17, 1926, p. 8.*

**Margery Williams Bianco**

**Winnie-the-Pooh** is a joy; full of solemn idiocies and the sort of jokes one weeps over helplessly, not even knowing why they are so funny, and with it all the real wit and tenderness which alone could create such a priceless little masterpiece. Kanga and baby Roo, Piglet, and above all Pooh and Christopher Robin himself, are characters no one can afford to miss. It is even better than **When We Were Very Young,** which is saying much. (pp. 277-78)

> *Margery Williams Bianco, in a review of "Winnie-the-Pooh," in* The Saturday Review of Literature, *Vol. 3, No. 15, November 6, 1926, pp. 277-78.*

**The Nation and Athenaeum**

As soon as I brought home **Winnie-the-Pooh**, . . . the children seized it, and, ever since, they have been reading it, learning it by heart, quarrelling over it, and loving it. So far as I can judge, from the hurried glimpses they have allowed me, it is a real children's book, in the direct line of succession to *Alice in Wonderland, Uncle Remus,* and *The Wind in the Willows,* and worthy to rank with those immortal works. It is the gift book of the year. (p. 355)

> *P. I., in a review of "Winnie-the-Pooh," in* The Nation and the Athenaeum, *Vol. XL, No. 9, December 4, 1926, pp. 355-56.*

### The Saturday Review, London

[*The following excerpt is from a review of* Now We Are Six.]

Mr. Milne has become the laureate of the nursery. His Christopher has discovered a new continent rich in silver and gold and his Robin, piping songs of innocence, has become the prodigy of his time. It is useless for superior people to cry "Pooh!" to his Winnie and pretend that these brats haven't a way with them. They have become common conquerors on both sides of the Atlantic. Mr. Pim may stop passing by, but the children are likely to continue.

> But now I am six, I'm as clever as clever,
> So I think I'll be six now for ever and ever.

We agree. It is certain to happen.

Mr. Milne is "as clever as clever" because he knows that children are realists and applies a gentle versification to the realities of the nursery. Consider this statement of grievance and the apt rebuke:

> I go to a party, I go out to tea,
> I go to an aunt for a week at the sea,
> I come back from school or from playing a
>     game;
> Wherever I come from, it's always the same;
>     Well?
> Have you been a *good* girl, Jane?

To which Jane very reasonably replies:

> Well, what did they think that I went there to
>     do?
> *And why should I want to be bad at the Zoo?*
> *And should I be likely to say if I had?*
> So that's why it's funny of Mummy and Dad,
> This asking and asking, in case I was bad,
>     Well?
> Have you been a *good* girl, Jane?

What could be more actual? No children's book can succeed which does not satisfy the grown-ups and Mr. Milne includes **'King Hilary and the Beggar Man'** for the aunts and uncles and other people who have seven-and-sixpence to spare, and Mr. Shepard, we think, must be very popular with aunts. But the contemporaries of Christopher Robin need not be frightened; there are plenty of the things which really matter, such as toy-trains with string brakes ("It's a good sort of brake, but it hasn't worked yet") and fishing, and a beetle in a matchbox and other great possessions. So long as Mr. Milne concentrates on these he has the passport to all nurseries and school-rooms, and so long as he continues to be sentimental about the charcoal-burner ("He and the Forest close together") he has the parents in his pocket. (pp. 515-16)

> *"More Milne," in* The Saturday Review, *London, Vol. 144, No. 3755, October 15, 1927, pp. 515-16.*

### Helen Cady Forbes

Milne's is the freest and freshest light verse. It is impossible for him to be dull and it would seem that for him rhyming is as easy as breathing. *Now We Are Six,* if we had never seen *When We Were Very Young,* would be a landmark in books of verses about children that could be enjoyed by the children, too. But the book cannot stand alone. The first thought of most of the thousands and thousands who took delight in the earlier volume will be to compare this with that and ask, "Is it as good?" Physically it is much the same because of the Shepard drawings, but the slight difference in test begins with the lettering on the jacket, not quite as spontaneous as that other zigzagging, sprawling title. Within the covers there is nothing to touch **"The King's Breakfast,"** nothing to be chanted like James. James, no bliss comparable to John's joy in his waterproofs.

But Milne's fundamental characteristics are here, his whimsical humor, his intelligent sympathy and understanding of a small boy's problems, his honest affection for children; neither has he lost his powers of observation. And his rhymes are perfect still, the cadence falling on the ear with all the charm that variety and the unhackneyed can give. . . .

To the average adult the book will be another amusing lot of verses to read aloud, but children will be able to find matter for thought as well as rhythm, notions worth turning over. Now We Are Six, Milne's Christopher Robin and his Johns and Elizabeth Anns think for themselves with much simple and inquiring comment on the habits of their elders. . . .

The story of how Alexander Beetle was let out of his match-box cage by mistake and how he was found again is one of the best.

There is also an emperor with whom every arithmetic hater will have a fellow feeling:

> He would whisper and whisper.
> Until he felt crisper,
>     This odd little rhyme to the sky:
>
> Eight eights are eighty-one;
>     Multiply by seven.
> If it's more,
> Carry four,
>     And take away eleven.

Now and then there is a tendency toward sentimentality in *Now We Are Six,* a suspicion of the commonplace. It is not that Mr. Milne doesn't do the sentimental as well as any one could, but it interrupts. It has no place between the ballad of **"The Knight Whose Armour Didn't Squeak"** and the fresh simplicity of **"The Charcoal Burner,"** for it is completely out of key with either of them.

Mr. Milne and Christopher Robin seem to have chanced upon the old fairy tale, "All Good Things Must Come to an End." It is a wise man who knows when to stop, and a man of such originality as his can't be interested in doing the same thing over and over again. Moreover, seven or eight is not too young for an English boy to be going away to school, and Christopher Robin will find it easier to keep the secret that he is Christopher Robin if his father allows the public to become interested in something quite different. The preface sounds as if he were aware of this: "So we want you to know that the name of the book doesn't mean that this is us being six all the time, but that it is about as far as we've got at present, and we half think of stopping there." And the last rhyme of all is The End:

> But now I am Six, I'm as clever as clever. So I
> think I'll be Six now for ever and ever.

[Children] don't care very much of most of the verse that is written for them. They are serious-minded young things, many of them, with no time to waste and an ear for the music in poetry. They like sensible stuff, too, inclining toward the instructive. They like things that are direct and simple, but not so simple that it is imbecile. They like purest nonsense and well accented rhythm, they like to laugh at some absurd turn and twist, and all these things they got in Milne's verses.

> *Helen Cady Forbes, "The Milne School of Verse," in* New York Herald Tribune Books, *October 16, 1927, p. 8.*

**Constant Reader [pseudonym of Dorothy Parker]**

Every day, it becomes a little more difficult for me to keep from confusing Christopher Morley with Christopher Robin. I do try, honestly I do. Each morning that I wake—and I've waked every morning, sharp, so far—I say to myself, "I will be strong, I will be true, I will get this thing clear." But if I don't watch myself like an old mother hawk, I find that during those fretful hours when I am tossing and turning at my typewriter, during the mellow evenings, during the dim, drowsy watches of the night, my mind goes crooning:

> Christopher Morley goes hippetty, hoppetty,
> Hippetty, hippetty, hop.
> Whenever I ask him politely to stop it, he
> Says he can't possibly stop. . . .

The thing is too much for me. I am about to give it all up. I cannot get those two quaint kiddies straightened out.

Oh, how quaint Christopher Morley is! Whoops, how quaint Christopher Morley is! Judas, how quaint Christopher Morley is! In his latest book, *I Know a Secret,* he fairly out-whimsies himself. (p. 112)

While we are on the subject of whimsies, how about taking up Mr. A. A. Milne? There is a strong feeling, I know, that to speak against Mr. Milne puts one immediately in the ranks of those who set fire to orphanages, strike crippled newsboys, and lure little curly-heads off into corners to explain to them that Santa Claus is only Daddy making a fool of himself. But, I, too, have a strong feeling in the matter. I have a very strong feeling about the whimsicality of Milne. I'm having it right this minute. It's in my stomach.

Time was when A. A. Milne was my only hero. Weekly

I pounced on *Punch* for the bits signed "A. A. M." I kept *Once a Week* and *Half Hours* practically under my pillow. I read *The Red House Mystery* threadbare. I thought *The Truth About Blayds* a fine and merciless and honest play. But when Mr. Milne went quaint, all was over. Now he leads his life and I lead mine.

*Now We Are Six,* the successor to *When We Were Very Young,* is Mr. Milne gone completely Winnie-the-Pooh. Not since Fay Bainter played "East is West" have I seen such sedulous cuteness. I give you, for example, the post-script to the preface: "Pooh wants us to say that he thought it was a different book; and he hopes you won't mind, but he walked through it one day, looking for his friend Piglet, and sat down on some of the pages by mistake." That one sentence may well make Christopher Morley stamp on his pen in despair. A. A. Milne still remains the Master.

Of Milne's recent verse, I speak in a minority amounting to solitude. I think it is affected, commonplace, bad. I did so, too, say bad. And now I must stop, to get ready for being ridden out of town on a rail. (pp. 112-13)

> *Constant Reader [pseudonym of Dorothy Parker], "Mr. Morley Capers on a Toadstool— Mr. Milne Grows to be Six," in* The New Yorker, *November 12, 1927, pp. 112-13.*

**Dorothy Parker**

> The more it
> SNOWS-tiddely-pom.
> The more it
> GOES-tiddely-pom
> The more it
> GOES-tiddely pom
> On
> Snowing.
>
> And nobody
> KNOWS-tiddely pom,
> How cold my
> TOES-tiddely-pom
> How cold my
> TOES tiddely pom
> Are
> Growing.

The above lyric is culled from the fifth page of Mr. A. A. Milne's new book, *The House at Pooh Corner,* for, although the work is in prose, there are frequent droppings into more cadenced whimsy. This one is designated as a "Hum," that pops into the head of Winnie-the-Pooh as he is standing outside Piglet's house in the snow, jumping up and down to keep warm. It "seemed to him a Good Hum, such as is Hummed Hopefully to Others." In fact, so Good a Hum did it seem that he and Piglet started right out through the snow to Hum It Hopefully to Eeyore. Oh, darn—there I've gone and given away the plot. Oh, I could bite my tongue out.

As they are trotting along against the flakes, Piglet begins to weaken a bit.

" 'Pooh,' he said at last and a little timidly, because he didn't want Pooh to think he was Giving In, 'I was just wondering. How would it be if we went home now and *practised* your song, and then sang it to Eeyore tomorrow—or—or the next day, when we happen to see him.'

" 'That's a very good idea, Piglet,' said Pooh. 'We'll practise it now as we go along. But it's no good going home to practise it, because it's a special Outdoor Song which Has To Be Sung In The Snow.'

" 'Are you sure?' asked Piglet anxiously.

" 'Well, you'll see, Piglet, when you listen. Because this is how it begins. *The more it snows, tiddely-pom—*'

" 'Tiddely what?' said Piglet." (He took, as you might say, the very words out of your correspondent's mouth.)

" 'Pom,' said Pooh. 'I put that in to make it more hummy.' "

And it is that word "hummy," my darlings, that marks the first place in *The House at Pooh Corner* at which Tonstant Weader Fwowed up.

> *Dorothy Parker, "Far from Well," in* The New Yorker, *Vol. IV, No. 35, October 20, 1928, p. 98.*

### The New York Times Book Review

The first thing the children will want to be sure about in this sequel to *Winnie-the-Pooh The House at Pooh Corner*] is that it is actually about Pooh Bear, Piglet, Eeyore, Rabbit, Roo, and the other remarkable characters in Christopher Robin's play world. They will be immediately reassured by the first sentence, which begins, as might be expected, with the assertion that "One day when Pooh Bear had nothing else to do he thought he would do something." This, as every child knows, is true Milne. The young readers or listeners—for Milne is eminently an author to be read aloud—will sink back contentedly. . . .

[When the story ends for its childish auditors, strangely] enough even the adults who have been amusing the children by reading it aloud lay it down with a sigh of regret. A. A. Milne's fun is of a sort which is especially at home in a children's book. But every good children's book has something in it for adults, since children, to all intents and purposes, are adults. In Piglet, in Pooh Bear, and especially in Eeyore Milne has created characters which with very little dressing-up might be carried over into adult fiction. The world in miniature moves through Christopher Robin's forest—is, in fact, Christopher Robin's forest. When Christopher Robin grows up and recurs to the adventures of his childhood he will find that a number of things have not changed, and that the motivations of his infancy are also those in large measure of his grown-up life.

It is hard to tell what Pooh Bear and his friends would have been without the able assistance of Ernest H. Shepard to see them and picture them so cleverly. Shepard and Milne are as indispensable one to the other as Sir John Tenniel and Lewis Carroll. The highest praise one can give them is that they do not in this book fall appreciably below the level of *Winnie-the-Pooh.* They are, and should be, classics.

> *"Winnie-the-Pooh Is Back Again!" in* The New York Times Book Review, *November 11, 1928, p. 2.*

### The Times Literary Supplement

In *The House at Pooh Corner,* the bear Pooh closes those few episodes in his life which have been disclosed by Mr. Milne, for this is the last, he declares, of the Winnie-the-Pooh books. It is impossible not to recognize the wisdom of Mr. Milne's self-denying ordinance and equally impossible not to regret it. The series has won and deserved a unique place in nursery literature, and Mr. Milne is acting in Pooh's interests in safeguarding his reputation, for it is as true of bears as of men that they are in the end only written, or talked, down by themselves. There is an obvious danger lest the most charming and effective whimsical writing may become mechanical with success; and so many of Pooh's best remarks are of a nonsensical inconsequence that invites his inventor to indulge in a mechanical denial of logic, to try just writing the opposite of what logically follows to see if the effect is not funny. Another source of Pooh's definite and attractive character is his use of personal names; indeed, the few simple names of the simple people in his world are as a general rule repeated and used instead of pronouns wherever possible. "Sing Ho for Piglet-Piglet-Ho," is a line which not only appears in an important poem in the book one of the more ambitious and effective flights of Mr. Pooh's muse—but a line which expresses in itself one of the keynotes in which the whole work is written. But Pooh and all his companions are simple, or they would not be themselves, and the simple are soon understood, and once they have been sympathetically described no one can injure them save their creator. *The House at Pooh Corner* is a more finished piece of work than its companion story, and Mr. Milne has curbed himself more severely when there have been openings for those touches of sentiment which are so easily overdone. There is no talk of sending love to the reader, and Pooh's admirably good-tempered and altruistic disposition is the sturdy uprightness of a bear taking life as it comes; and the absence of any other characters beyond his animal world makes that world much more effective and its problems, like the question of securing a house for Eeyore, much more real.

> *"Pooh Corner," in* The Times Literary Supplement, *No. 1402, December 13, 1928, p. 985.*

### Eileen Squire

Mr. Milne's understanding of a child's mentality comes out much more in his prose than in his verse. The best test of what a child will appreciate is to try it on the grown-ups. When the reading aloud of any passage turns to tedium, and spiritless utterance sets in, it is pretty certain that that passage will be having the same effect upon the listener. What affects the reader as bright and entertaining will be the passages that interest the child also. Almost all the way through the charming stories about Winnie-the-Pooh, Pight and the rest, the sparkle of Irish interest and amusement never dies out. Mr. Milne is scarcely ever mechanical here, but lots of the verses are completely mechanical. One has only to read them aloud to demonstrate this—they drag and die, and fall like torn up pages to the ground, as the last words limp out. . . .[This is] lurid, easy, vapid rhyming. The tired voice runs out as the utter absence of any kind of meaning or sense runs out. But, of course, **"Buckingham Palace"** and **"The King's Breakfast"** are honourable exceptions. (pp. 188-89)

> *Eileen Squire, in a review of "Buckingham Palace" and "The King's Breakfast," in* The London Mercury, *Vol. XXI, No. 122, December, 1929, pp. 188-89.*

**Mary Ethel Nesmith**

There is little doubt that A. A. Milne . . . is the most famous of present day poets for children. His delightful child-verses have not been surpassed, in their marvelous appeal to children, by any writer of his generation. Few poets are gifted with the light, playful touch, the ingenious imagination, the humorous interpretation, and the perfect understanding of child life that pervades every page of these two volumes. In addition to Mr. Milne's inimitable style he seems to divine the very thoughts and language of the child.

Christopher Robin, Mr. Milne's little son, for whom and about whom he has written his verses, by his very presence in these matchless poems has added a charm of reality and an assurance of appeal to children. A stronger appeal, however, than the presence of Christopher Robin is the author's power of imagination in depicting his own experiences and imaginings as a child. In this respect Mr. Milne has no equal except perhaps Robert Louis Stevenson. (p. 172)

Mr. Milne has chosen to write almost all of his verses about the everyday doings of children. However, throughout these two volumes he inserts, now and then, a perfect little gem, usually a descriptive poem, totally unlike the verses dealing with the everyday experiences of children. After reading one of these little poems, one almost fancies that the author is impliedly saying to the little folks for whom he is writing, "Now, here is a little poem that is full of sheer beauty. It is put here to make you reach up a little and learn to enjoy the beautiful." **"Twinkletoes," "Water-Lilies," "Daffodowndilly," "Spring Morning," "The Island," "The Mirror,"** and **"Wind on the Hill"** belong to this group. One of the most attractive poems of this group is **"The Mirror,"** which is charming in its serene beauty and quiet images. (p. 173)

> *Mary Ethel Nesmith, "The Children's Milne," in* The Elementary English Review, *Vol. IX, No. 7, September, 1932, pp. 172-73, 192.*

**Compton Mackenzie**

> [*The following excerpt was originally published in Mackenzie's* Literature in My Time *(1933).*]

**When We Were Very Young** marks an epoch as positively as any children's book has ever marked one. It is not extravagant to surmise that a distant posterity may find in that volume of children's verse a key with which to unlock the present more easily than with any contemporary novel, poem or play.

> *Compton Mackenzie, in an excerpt in* A. A.

Milne: The Man Behind Winnie-the-Pooh *by Ann Thwaite, Random House, 1990, p. 266.*

**Frank Eyre**

A. A. Milne's books . . . owe much of their success to their readability. The curious adult passion for his four books which was one of the features of that supposedly sophisticated age the nineteen twenties, resulted for a time in prejudicing many people, especially intellectuals, against them. Now, twenty years later, it is possible to look at them objectively and realize how good they are. (p. 43)

Milne's best work for children is in the two volumes of stories, **Winnie The Pooh** and **The House At Pooh Corner,** about the lovable animals which he created from his own son's toys. . . . [There] is a stage in every child's development when these two books are exactly right. (p. 44)

> *Frank Eyre, "The In-Between Books," in his* 20th Century Children's Books, *Longmans, Green and Co., 1952, pp. 40-9.*

**May Hill Arbuthnot**

Although no hard and fast line divides humor from sheer nonsense, there is, nevertheless, a difference. Nonsense is more daft, more impossible, with Pobbles, Jumblies, potatoes that dance, chickens that go out to tea, gargoyles and griffins—a wild crew close kin to the "cow that jumped over the moon." Humorous verse, on the other hand, deals with the amusing things that befall real people, or might conceivably befall them. Edward Lear and Laura E. Richards sometimes wrote humorous verse, but for the most part their contributions are on the side of hilarious nonsense. In contrast, A. A. Milne writes occasional nonsense, but on the whole his poems involve people and situations that are amusingly possible, however improbable they may be. This distinction is not too important, and there is no reason for debating the classification of any particular poem on this score. It is mentioned only because nonsense verse is not an adequate description of the plausible fun of the English writer, A. A. Milne. (p. 90)

[In] the generations to come it is probable that Milne's reputation as a writer will rest more securely upon his two books of verse for children than upon any of his adult stories and dramas. Why are these light-hearted verses so unforgettable?

Milne's first charm is his ability to present small children as they are. He gives us their bemused absorption in their private inner world of make-believe, their blithe egotism, their liking for small animals, their toys and games, and the peculiar angle from which they view the odd behavior of those adults who move vaguely on the fringe of their private world.

Christopher Robin speaks for the make-believe of children around four to six years old. His imaginative world is not peopled with the fairies of the eight-year-old but is just the everyday sort of play of the nursery age. One chair is South America and another is a lion's cage. When walking with his nurse becomes just too stale, flat, and unprofitable to be endured, Christopher scares himself into a pleasant spinal chill by imagining that bears are skulking just around the corner and are watching his approach with a sinister smacking of the lips. Only he fools them, of course, and gets away. This is characteristic play for a solitary but well-cared-for child. So, too, are his imaginary companions. There is Binker, visible only to Christopher Robin, and there is the omnipresent Pooh, who appears in both the poems and the prose adventures.

Much has been written about the egocentricity of the young child's thought and language, but it has never been recorded more accurately than by A. A. Milne. Christopher Robin goes to the market looking for a rabbit and is naïvely astonished that the market men should be selling mackerel and fresh lavender when *he,* Christopher Robin, wants rabbits. He catalogues his articles of clothing, fascinating because they are his. You can hear the smug emphasis on the personal pronoun. Changing the guard at Buckingham may be very impressive, but the child's only concern is, "Do you think the King knows all about Me?" This is a typical four-year-old, thinking and speaking of everything in terms of himself—an amusing and endearing little egoist!

Knowing children's interests, Milne reflects them in his writing. There we find the child's love of small animals:

*Milne as a Westminster schoolboy with his father John Vine Milne.*

dormice, rabbits, puppies, snails, and goats, whose antics and vicissitudes enliven the verses. Toys are there, too—balls, tops, hoops, and the beloved teddy bear. The verses are full of the small child's activities, also. He walks, rolls, and plays. He gets sand between his toes. He stalks down the sidewalk missing all the lines. He sits on the stairs and meditates, or he goes hoppitty, hoppitty, hop. He enjoys complete happiness when he gets his mackintosh and waterproof boots on. He sometimes refuses rice pudding (or rather Mary Jane does), and he often resents foolish adult questions. On the whole, he is a busy, active child, immersed in his own affairs and oblivious of any world beyond his own horizon.

The self-sufficiency of children is also evident in these verses. We soon realize that Christopher Robin is an only child. "Mummy" and "Daddy" are there, and Nana, the nurse, chaperones his every walk, but where are the other children? There are Mary Jane, and John of the waterproof boots, and Emmeline, whose hands were "purfickly clean," but these, too, are lone children with only supervising adults in the offing. None of these children plays with other children. There are no brothers or sisters or even neighbors' children, but neither Christopher Robin nor the young readers of these verses seem to miss them in the least. Perhaps because the young child is so astonishingly egocentric and lives so completely within a world of his own, these verses that speak understandingly of one child speak adequately for all children alone or in groups.

[We find] a juggling with funny words: "sneezles and freezles," foxes who didn't wear "sockses," "biffalo-buffalo-bisons," "badgers and bidgers and bodgers," and a mouse with a "woffelly nose." The children seize upon them as their very own, for these words are exactly what they might have said. If you study Milne's funny words, you discover that they fall within the range of the child's own vocabulary. Here we find no "fatally fair flamingo" of the older child's level, but the measles and "sneezles" that "teasles" the funnybone of the little child because they are all close to words he recognizes. When words go rambunctious, they are funnier to us if we know them well in their prosaic workaday form. Hence the success of Mr. Milne's word-teasing with young children.

No one can tell a better tall tale for children than Alan Alexander Milne. For examples, read **"The King's Breakfast," "Disobedience," "Teddy Bear," "The Dormouse and the Doctor,"** and perhaps **"Bad Sir Brian Botany."** Some boys were convinced that they detested all "pomes," but, after listening to **"Disobedience"** read aloud several times, they were heard chanting it vociferously. After that, they wanted Milne and more Milne and progressed steadily in their respect and liking for "pomes."

Usually it is **"The King's Breakfast"** that is the favorite with most Milne addicts. This starts reasonably with the king asking for a little butter on the "Royal slice of bread," and it moves along smoothly until the sleepy Alderney upsets all royal regularity by suggesting "a little marmalade instead." From then on the dialogue becomes entirely daft, reaching a joyous climax when the king bounces out of bed and slides down the banisters. This is, of course, the essence of the fun—the incongruity of a king who is so deeply concerned with marmalade that he whimpers, sulks, bounces, and slides down banisters. The verse pattern of each episode reinforces the mood.

Read Mr. Milne's two little books, *When We Were Very Young* and *Now We Are Six,* and you will discover an author who knows how to write verse that dances, skips, meditates, and changes to reflect changing moods. We can analyze his tripping trochees, his iambics and dactyls, but those academic names do not seem to convey any idea of the fluid and flashing use Mr. Milne makes of words, rhyme, and rhythm to convey character, mood, and action. For example, read **"Buckingham Palace"** aloud and hear the marching of soldiers in the background throughout those brief descriptions and the whispered conversations of Alice and Christopher. The feet thud, thud, thud through every line. So, too, when Christopher Robin hops through the jingle called **"Hoppity,"** the lines go in exactly the pattern of a child's hop, ending with a big one and a rest, just as hopping always does. But best of all is that juvenile meditation, **"Halfway Down."** . . . Why [small children] like to clutter up stairs with their belongings and their persons only Mr. Milne knows, and he has told us with arresting monosyllables that block the way as effectually as Christopher Robin's small person blocks the stairs. (pp. 91-3)

Over and over again, Mr. Milne makes a monosyllable or a single word equal by sheer intensity three or four words in a preceding line. It is a device that compels correct reading of the lines, regardless of scansion. Look through the pages of these little books, *When We Were Very Young* and *Now We Are Six,* and notice the appearance of the verses on the page. The visible pattern they make in print shows you something of the intricacy and variety of Mr. Milne's verse forms, although their full flavor and fun are not evident until they are heard. Read them aloud and they fall upon the ear with such natural and easy perfection that they are memorized almost as soon as the words are familiar.

With all of these virtues, it is not surprising that some moderns have come to feel that Milne is the child's greatest poet, certainly their favorite poet. This enthusiasm would be harmless enough if it did not apparently curtail all further exploration on the part of some of Milne's admirers. Delightful as his verses are, they do not cover the full range either of the child's interests or of his capacity for enjoying poetry. Many poets achieve greater lyric beauty, more delicate imagery, and deeper feeling for the child's inner world. The child should know such poets as well as A. A. Milne.

But certainly we shall never encounter a writer who understands more completely the curious composite of gravity and gaiety, of supreme egotism and occasional whimsy that is the young child. A. A. Milne has written humorous verses for children, composed with deft craftsmanship and a sure knowledge of the little child's world, which should make them live as long as people live who love light-hearted English verse at its best. (pp. 93-4)

A. A. Milne's *Winnie-the-Pooh* and *The House at Pooh Corner* are different from anything that has preceded them. They seem to have grown as a natural sequence to the poems about Christopher Robin and Pooh, and they also developed, as the author says, from his small son's demands to hear a story for Pooh:

> "What sort of stories does he like?"
> "About himself. Because he's *that* sort of Bear."
> "Oh, I see." . . .
> So I tried.
>
> (p. 305)

The stories are unusual in that Christopher goes in and out of them on a familiar forest-dwelling level with the animals, but in the end he brings everything back to reality when he sets off up the stairs of his own house, headed for a bath, dragging Pooh by one leg. The stories are finished, Christopher is himself, and Pooh is Pooh. This is not only a tale about toys come to life but also a clever fantasy for the youngest, not too complicated, no fairies, just a little boy sharing make-believe adventures with his toys and the little creatures of the woods but knowing all the time that they *are* make-believe. It's a game of "let's pretend" put into story form, and children anywhere from five to nine or even ten enjoy both of these books. (p. 306)

> *May Hill Arbuthnot, "Verses in the Gay Tradition" and "New Magic," in her* Children and Books, *Scott, Foresman and Company, 1947, pp. 77-99 276-359.*

**Eleanor Graham**

A. A. Milne is dead, but has left us, warmly alive, his four Christopher Robin books. It is inevitable to call them that, for Christopher Robin had focussed his father's eyes on those moments of experience at very young level, had inspired his imagination, setting the mind in motion to create the verses and tales. The label also serves to distinguish them from those other books which had not the magic touch—*Once on a Time,* a story of which the author himself said that he had never known whether it was meant for children or adults, and no one else had ever been able to tell him; and *A Gallery of Children,* a huge out-size volume with coloured pictures by Willabeek le Mair, stories of princesses, magic and love, which stood about in unsold piles in many bookshops in the late '20's and early '30's.

It is the Christopher Robin books which place him beside the immortals—four little books, amounting to no more than 70,000 words in all (his figures), but preserving (even to the dry and sere) something of the unconscious joy and loveliness of childhood.

Twenty years ago people wrangled about them and made rude noises over **"Vespers,"** sympathising with the boy whose secret life had been thus thrown open to public view. If the work had been less good, it might have died under the angry criticism launched at it, but succeeding generations of children still take the verses to their hearts and remember them for life. Sensible people, trying them again in maturity, have to admit the perfection of form, and their genuine simplicity. Many have found their own memory recorders set in action by Milne's faithful mirroring of the moods and reactions which are part of every child's being.

These verses were almost as much inspired by Milne's own memories as by the daily contact with his son, though without Christopher Robin they would certainly never have been written. Somewhere he said that childhood's world is a very small place, intimately known, mapped out and labelled in every part, but soon forgotten until and unless some other child recalls it. It seems to have been so with himself, and the interaction of the two impressions, the one observed and the other experienced nearly forty years earlier, seems to have shown him the very essence of childhood when imagination and make-believe are only an extension of reality. Such material is delicate and spoiled as easily as one rubs the bloom off a hot-house grape; but Milne caught it dexterously, and transferred it to paper without damage or distortion. Had he been less detached, had he felt the situations more poignantly (as sentimental readers have often done), had he been less practised a maker of verses, the bloom would certainly have been lost.

Yet, to compare his work with that of Walter de la Mare, is to see at once that they lived in different worlds. De la Mare would never agree that childhood's world is small or easily explored to the limits. For him, it never faded, though young eyes have illuminated parts of it afresh for him too. In a sense, Milne was the journalist, seeing and getting what he had observed on to paper with all the skill at his command. He had not the magic in himself to transmute the things his eyes had seen into other shapes and forms by virtue of imagination. He had imagination, but was plainly not of those who can *live* in it.

He says he was never a child worshipper, and that he wrote his books "not as a poet becoming playful, nor a lover of children expressing his love, nor as a professional writer knocking together a few jingles for the little ones, but as a light verse writer taking his job seriously even in the nursery." No one will question his having taken the job seriously; the verse is so good. He had been learning his craft ever since his schooldays, purposefully, deliberately. He had great skill by the time he wrote his first verses for children, and he had acquired a mastery of the theory of verse which gave him great versatility. In *When We Were Very Young,* a volume of forty-four items, there can, for instance, be found a jingle, "**James, James, Morrison, Morrison;**" a nursery rhyme, "**The King's Breakfast;**" a rigmarole rhyme, "**Market Square,**" a cautionary tale, "**Teddy Bear;**" a nursery ballad, "**The Three Foxes;**" a ballad with refrain, "**The Dormouse and the Doctor;**" and a ballad with chorus, "**Bad Sir Brian Botany.**" He does not repeat himself, and there are no echoes of old favourites. There is hardly one which is not perfect in form.

He chose rhythms as carefully as he devised forms, and in "**Buckingham Palace,**" he used one which expressed exactly the to and fro pacing and stamping of the sentries. "**James, James,**" conveys admirably the often laboured pedalling on a tricycle of just such a three year-old as J.J.M.M.W.G. du P. The former also illustrated his dexterity in capturing moods. There is the first awe of the small child facing the great height and tremendous dignity of the soldier in red coat and busby, but so quickly brought to earth by Alice's matter-of-fact interpolations about such things as his socks. Nevertheless, there are verses in which he failed to appreciate the whole feeling of a situation. "**The Wrong House,**" for instance, misses the child's real shock at finding himself suddenly in unrecognisable surroundings.

Sometimes Milne remained wholly observer, and though the child might have made him look, what he saw he registered with his adult mind, and the verse then missed its proper relation to the very young. He knew that, and pointed it out in connection with "**The Mirror,**" though adding that even that would not have been written but for Christopher Robin. (pp. 51-5)

There is a feeling in *When We Were Very Young,* as of Milne being still a little surprised and incredulous at finding himself with a child in his house; but the Christopher Robin of the *Pooh* tales had become more of a reality, a partner. There is a comfortable familiarity in the relationship, and they are curiously identified with one another; as Milne was to his son, Christopher Robin was to Pooh and the others. Together they represent the intelligence, the authority, behind the simpler world inhabited by Pooh, Piglet and the rest, a world of mere being, doing, feeling. Christopher Robin has slipped out of the infantile state into the role of comforter, guide and friend, the one who knows everything, and can make everything right. He has gained experience. For instance, Pooh and Piglet are seen following their own tracks in the snow in half fearful speculation as to whose they can be. It takes Christopher Robin to show them the laughable truth.

Perhaps Milne's particular genius lay in recognising the little things which make up a child's daily round, lighting them up, not exploiting them for his own amusement. He brought his adult powers into a perspective in which they could function truly though in miniature. For him writing had to be fun, no one can read the *Pooh* tales without feeling that, without being aware of the lightness of his touch, the constant and spontaneous bubbling of fun and laughter, and most important of all in a child's book, of his unfailing benevolence. There is no jealousy, no unkindness, no trickery in his children's books—and it is interesting to find that he had thought a good deal about the subject. He knew that a child creates its own fairyland in its own terms, and that no matter how carefully the parents may try to keep away such dangerous communications, they cannot really deprive their children of the fruits of imagination. The milkman, for instance, in a conscientiously factual bedtime story, is immediately transformed into a legendary figure in the child's mind, and fairyland creeps in. Milne realised also the moral values which belong to the genuine fairy tales, truth, honesty, simplicity; and he saw that there was no place in them for sophistication or *worldly* wisdom.

Rabbit and Owl were his own creations, all the rest of the *Pooh* creatures were Christopher Robin's toys, worn by his handling to the shapes which Shepard made so familiar to us all. They were, in fact, drawn from his row of toys on the nursery shelf, in just the state of dilapidation they had reached. Mrs. Milne had given each his own voice, but their personalities were intrinsic in themselves. Eeyore's characteristic droop made him inevitably a person who looks on the gloomy side of things. Pooh, with that good-humoured rotundity, could not help being One of Very Little Brain, but also one who could contentedly sit on a log singing, **"Cottleston, Cottleston, Cottleston Pie."** It was an essential part of him that he should so love good things and be greedy in just that way which reflected clearly but indulgently nursery experience, and must have had many a child glance upwards to make sure no one was *meaning me*! Tigger's rolling eye, Kanga's maternal figure, Piglet's air of always trying to stand on tiptoe to make sure he was noticed, were all there, perfectly expressed in sagging stuffing and drooping ear.

Milne never seems to have been at a loss for a suitable small situation. He never faltered for the right word. He never, indeed, put a foot wrong in these books, and his care for the choice of the right word makes hay of the theories of limited vocabularies for young age groups. Only bad and careless writers really need such a discipline. Milne hands his five year-old readers such phrases as "hostile intent," "customary procedure," "expedition," "ambush." He extends their vocabulary and there is never any danger of dead spots arising from any failure in contact. He either uses his words so aptly that no further help is required, or drops in an explanation so cunningly that it seems neither intrusive nor educative.

Why did not Milne continue to write books in which he had achieved such near-perfection? Heaven knows that our queer world of children's books needs such people to bring to it those serious adult standards of work.

His own account of it is that . . . some tell you writing is an inspiration, others that it is simply a business like any other; others again that it is an agony. To him it was frankly fun, a thrill, the thrill of exploring. He had re-explored his little child's world, as he felt, from boundary to boundary. Was he to go making fair copies of what he believed he had done well? No, not A. A. Milne. (pp. 56-9)

> *Eleanor Graham, "A. A. Milne," in* The Junior Bookshelf, *Vol. 20, No. 3, March, 1956, pp. 51-9.*

### The New York Herald Tribune Book Review

"Let us think gratefully," said the French philosopher, Paul Hazard, "of those who through children and for children perform the miracle of springtime." Few have succeeded in this happy task to a greater extent than A. A. Milne. The two books of verses, **When We Were Very Young,** and **Now We Are Six,** and the two collections of stories, **Winnie the Pooh** and **The House at Pooh Corner,** have been received throughout the world "with an enthusiasm beyond all imagining." The verses about Christopher Robin, **"The King's Breakfast," "Disobedience,"** and the stories of Pooh, the Bear of Very Little Brain, gloomy Eeyore the donkey, eager Piglet, Tigger, Kanga and little Roo, Rabbit and Owl are beloved by children the world over. And for those older ones in a springtime mood, they hold forever glimpses of their own childhood, of universal childhood and of fleeting memories of children dear to them. A turn of phrase, a bit of imaginative play, and the child springs to life. **"Roundabout,"** for in-

stance, belongs absolutely to the three-year-old. The rapid change of character, the repetition in time to dizzy turns. Thousands have thought, as they read, "Why, that's my child." . . .

These are the qualities that enabled Mr. Milne to perform the miracle of springtime: delight in writing for its own sake: a vivid memory of a happy childhood renewed and sharpened by observation of his own child and his friends: long practice in light verse: the willingness to take great pains, and an unsentimental desire to draw a true picture of the inhabitants of the nursery in their artless grace and lack of moral quality. . . .

Here, indeed, were intimations of immortality. . . .

> *"Magic from Generation to Generation: Alan Alexander Milne, 1852-1956," in* New York Herald Tribune Book Review, *May 13, 1956, p. 8.*

### Barbara Novak

A. A. Milne's poems for children are at once lyrical, whimsical, and intimate. Lyrical, because in the truest sense of the word they are singable poems with a rhythmic structure which is delightful to the ear, and for this reason too, well-adapted to be read aloud to children. Whimsical, because they are filled with humor and fantasy, frequently using sound for the sake of sound in nonsense words, with a kind of freedom of thought which captures the gaiety of a child's mind and suggests a positive attitude to life and a fresh appreciation of the smallest things, which is too often lost in the experience of adult living.

They are intimate poems because in their phrasing and mode of expression they have a kind of inner whispering quality which imparts the feeling that the poem is a conspiracy between the child and the poet. If it is true that they were originally conceived in this way because of the personal relationship between the poet and his own child, they still transcend their specific purpose with universal qualities which make them meaningful to a much wider audience. Their intimacy derives from the poet's ability to establish a really strong relationship with the child's mind—to speak to him in his own language, and to anticipate and often mirror his thought processes, the way he would look at the world about him. Milne accomplishes this through the subjects or content he chooses to deal with, as well as through the actual formal structure of his poems.

The poetry of Milne delves into many sources for content, from profound themes such as **"Explained,"** in which the child asks to be told how God began, to humorous sound poems like **"Sneezles."** All have a magical blend of the proportion of the serious and the gay, the profound, and the humorous which is, for each, most appropriate to the relative situation in living experience.

It is a kind of content that is rooted in experience, and that displays incredible understanding of the child's own world of experience. It draws, therefore, on the things which to a child are real: the reality of the fantasy companion Winnie the Pooh is brought out in such poems as **"Us Two,"** as is the reality of the imaginary, only-to-be-seen-by-the-child Binker, in the poem of the same name. We are confronted here with a poetic vision which digs deep into the spiritual and imaginative resources of the child, and says for him what perhaps he would like to say himself:

> Binker—what I call him—is a secret of my own,
> And Binker is the reason why I never feel alone.

Indeed, we might almost say that Milne's poetic content falls into two broad categories: one in which the poet expresses something *for* the child, and one in which he expresses *to* the child.

In the former category, we may group such poems as **"Solitude,"** where the child himself, speaking in the first person, describes the house where he goes when he is seeking his own inner privacy, or **"Busy,"** where with joyous freedom of spirit he fantasizes about the many things he thinks he might be. There are, also, first person poems written as though by the child, which explore the specific pastimes of the child. **"The Engineer"** and **"Waiting At The Window"** tell us how he spends that perennially problematical rainy day, playing at trains, or finding names for the raindrops on the window pane. And too, there are poems which express the child's relation to others especially older people, such as **"Forgiven,"** where Nanny unknowingly lets Alexander Beetle out of the match-box, and the child, ultimately, is good-heartedly magnanimous about her very human error.

When dealing with the child's relation to older people, Milne manages beautifully to hit upon the very things that to a child being reared in a grown-up world are most universally meaningful in a psychological sense, or perhaps really, to state it more simply, most naturally and humanly true to his own feelings. In such poems as **"The Good Little Girl,"** in which the child is asked that ever constant grown-up question "Have you been a good girl?," or even in the tongue in cheek, written as though by a grown-up **"Rice Pudding,"** Milne manages with subtle humor to touch again upon the child's sense that grown-ups do not understand, even when in the simple matter of asserting his individual rights he prefers not to eat what he does not want to eat.

Here, I think, we may expect that the child will understand immediately what is the matter with Mary Jane, because he will probably recognize his own behavior on past occasions, even while the author-poet is professing bewilderment as the bewildered grown-up. This is the theme too, of the poem **"Independence,"** where the child states simply at the end:

> It's no good saying it. They don't understand.

But mostly, Milne's poems written in the "I" of the child deal with the child's life-experience in the activities of his day, with his imaginary friends, his imaginative games, his worlds of fantasy, and the sweet realities of his experiences in nature.

Always these poems for the child written as though by the child have an extraordinary inner-thought kind of quality, as in **"Down by the Pond,"** where the child, fishing, half aloud, half to himself, cautions people not to come near for the fish might hear. In **"Spring Morning,"** too, there is the blitheful sense of the unity of a child with nature; the child as a natural, free, unaffected being who can say:

> Where am I going? I don't quite know.
> What does it matter where people go?

And, in **"The Island"**:

> If I had a ship,
> I'd sail my ship,
> I'd sail my ship
> Through Eastern seas. . . .
> And I'd say to myself as I looked so lazily down
>     at the sea:
> "There's nobody else in the world, and the world
>     was made for me."

This poem alone could spark in itself a long consideration of Milne as a poet. Putting aside the lilting structure for the time being, there is here an incredible metamorphosis of fantasy into reality. The physical realities of the child's journey are graphically described. . . . (pp. 355-57)

[There] is a kind of poetic elaboration of detail which adds atmospheric reality to the fantasy of the mythical voyage to the distant isle. The child can climb, he can stagger, and stumble on his hands and knees, and hear the stones pattering down, and then finally, with ultimate satisfaction and a royal sense of achievement:

> And there would I rest and lie
> My chin in my hands, and gaze. . . .

Almost all of Milne's "I" poems have this immediate, true-to-the-child's-experience tone. Often too, they have the kind of nonsense whimsy which is too often lost in expression by and for adults. Thus, in **"Halfway Down,"** the child sits on a stair which really isn't anywhere but somewhere else instead. We are reminded here of E. E. Cummings' use of this sort of expression, though Milne's poetry differs in that it is not a sophisticated adult use of a child's manner of expression, but rather, the expression of a poet who has never lost the ability to think, feel, and express as a child.

In the category of poems in which he is expressing *to* the child, Milne himself appears for the most part in the clearly stated position of narrator, and again, establishes frequently what would seem to be a conspiratorial intimacy with his child listener. Many of these poems are distinct tales, often folk-lorish and adventurous in tone, and often, too, they deal with authoritative figures who are humanly appealing and not nearly as forbidding as their "positions" would lead us to suppose.

Thus, in **"King John's Christmas"** poor King John who was not a good man, yet had his hopes and fears, signed his Christmas wish not Johannes R. "but very humbly, Jack." It is interesting, too, that Milne phrases King John's Christmas wish in a child's terms: he wants some crackers and some candy, a box of chocolates would come in handy, oranges and nuts, a pocket knife that really cuts, but most of all, a big red India-rubber ball. This is, for all essential purposes, a story in rhyme, and the child can share King John's pleasure when he finally gets the BIG RED INDIA RUBBER BALL.

The same kind of lack of affectation in **"Important Peo-**

ple" occurs when Teddy Bear has an adventure in the poem of the same name. Here he meets **"His Majesty the King of France,"** who is not too important to bow stiffly, remove his hat, and even stop, handsome if a trifle fat, to talk carelessly of this and that.

To the child, all of these **"Important People"** must seem no more or less important than other grown-ups; and Milne, therefore, would seem to me to be using them very wonderfully, simply to demonstrate their humanity, and perhaps to enable the child to identify more easily with all grown-ups, who must seem important in their very role as grown-ups.

In the delightful **"King's Breakfast,"** after all, it is the cow, not the poor king, who has the final say, and though the king petulantly asks only for a little bit of butter for his bread, we feel distinctly that it is a child-like joy which prompts him to slide down the bannister in his glee at getting it.

In **"The Emperor's Rhyme,"** too, it is significant that the emperor had a rhyme which he used when he felt shy with strangers, or when someone asked him the time when his watch didn't go. These are the sorts of experiences a child would have, and yet, they deal also with human characteristics which extend from childhood to adulthood: shyness with strangers, embarrassment, self-consciousness, etc. And the Emperor's rhyme itself is a true child's rhyme, drawing for its humor on a child's arithmetic. The humor is probably even more apparent to the child at the end, when he reads that "eight eights are eighty-one, and nine nines are sixty-four." Such a poem draws not only on the areas of human behavior common to adult and child with which a child can identify (though on occasion one feels that only Milne's adults are so wonderfully fresh in spirit), but also on the child's innate love of nonsense sounds, rhymes that need actually make no real sense except, very properly, that "then it's time for tea."

Milne uses his content, too, in a half-nonsense way that is best characterized, perhaps, as meaningful understatement. In **"The Four Friends,"** for example, nothing really happens, and yet everything does. James was only a snail, who sat down on a brick. But there is, in this poem, a tone, sound, or mood, call it what we will, which is perhaps Milne's most meaningful mode of expression, and is contained actually in his manner of phrasing, and his method of statement, an integral expressive factor in the form of his poetry. It lies largely in his end line:

> But James was only a snail,

and in his pertinent repetitions of just this kind of understatement at the end of each stanza.

The simplicity, always, of his statements about James, after the more complex descriptions of the tempestuous activities and grand habitats of the other animals is extremely telling, telling of the simplicity of the snail itself, small, low-toned, humbly carrying his own house on his back, and no doubt the hero of the poem for the child.

It is difficult, of course, to submit to critical analysis the magic of Milne's sounds, and the unity of form and content in his poems defies the kind of dissection attempted

here. But his content becomes expressive, meaningful, magical, wonderful, because of the way he uses words, and the "how" of this seems certainly within the realm of our investigation.

The obvious love of word sounds and love of repetition of word sounds in his poetry would be, in itself, enough to endear his poems to the child, who shares very naturally this enchantment.

But Milne combines this with the above mentioned feeling for understatement and with a sensibility to phrased rhythms which derive impact and power through variation and a change of pace. In **"Buckingham Palace"**:

> They're changing guard at Buckingham Palace—
> Christopher Robin went down with Alice.
> Alice is marrying one of the guard.
> "A soldier's life is terrible hard,"
>                     Says Alice.

Here, after every stanza, it is the "Says Alice" which sets the tone, and by the very way in which it is spaced, off to the right like a signature, we know that this is somebody's statement, and almost, we feel, an aside.

The use, indeed, of parenthetical asides, is one of Milne's most delightful ways of introducing variation into his themes, adding an intimate aspect of direct conversation which should be most appealing to the child. In the poem **"Puppy and I"** there is this use of the parenthetical observation:

> "Where are you going to, Man?" I said
> (I said to the Man as he went by).

used wonderfully in conjunction with a kind of reverse wording re-statement technique, that operates as a counterpoint to the original question, and adds too, by its very nature, to the feeling of conspiratorial intimacy between reader or listener and narrator.

In addition, in such a poem, we find one of Milne's favorite modes of composing, a sort of repetition which is achieved by retaining the constancy of as many elements as possible, for the sake of rhythm and emphasis, as well as meaningfulness for the narrative:

> I met a man as I went walking
> We got talking
> Man and I. . . .
>
> I met a horse as I went walking
> We got talking
> Horse and I. . . .

These repetition poems, with adventures which carry from one stanza into another, are the kind that would lend themselves extremely well to singing or choral reading.

Such a poem is **"Disobedience,"** with the unforgettable James James Morrison Morrison Weatherby George Dupree, who must be so satisfying to the child's delight in interesting and appropriate names. In addition, there is the "to-be-shared" verse at the end, (Now then, very softly . . . ) which, with its lilting and melodious quality must impress itself simply and effectively, out of sheer joy

*Cotchford Farm, Sussex, from the garden.*

in sound and rhythm, on the child's inner store of literary riches.

There is in this poem, again, a thematic content which touches the experience of the child, here relegating to him the importance of the role normally played by the parent, and probably giving him great pleasure at the reversal. The same idea of grown-ups getting lost has been used more recently by Muriel Rukeyser in *Come Back Paul,* which also derives a large part of its charm from the expression of the child's exasperation with the irresponsibility of grown-ups.

Milne's poetry depends largely on the singing sounds of his rhythms, which are rooted in repetition and rhyme and are usually a lyrical combination of both. With Milne's poetry, too, humor and whimsy seem to set the tone more frequently than highly pictorial images. However, in some of his more serious nature poems, such as **"Spring Morning,"** he does capture through his choice of words, the atmospheric magic of the descriptive phrase which is capable of evoking strongly vivid images for his audience.

Perhaps because they are so musical, so singable, in their rhythms, and in the sounds created by their rhymes and repetitions, Milne's poems lend themselves extraordinari-

ly well to reading aloud. The original format of the poems in *When We Were Very Young* and *Now We Are Six* . . . indicates that Milne himself was strongly aware of the need for expressive and imaginative spacing, for variation of type, and for creative structuring of his words on the page, to help carry the mood of his poems, and as a guide for reading aloud, as well as silently.

He is extremely inventive in his use of italics: to indicate a change of tone and emphasis, to distinguish between speech and thought, or often too, to introduce his frequent asides, or inject the narrator's comments into a running narrative, as in **"Teddy Bear"**:

*And (think of it!) the man was fat!*

Or, in **"Vespers,"** where references to Christopher Robin's prayers are italicized, as well as the prayers themselves, while all of Christopher's irrelevant thoughts, such as, "If I open my fingers a little more, I can see Nanny's dressing-gown on the door . . . " are in regular type.

The richness of Milne's poetry lies in the extraordinary wealth of variety in both form and content. The content of his poems, the mood he wishes to express: the delight in nature, the tall tale that he spins of the Old Sailor, the child's fantasy that he will elaborate, the every-day world pointed up by poetic magic, the endearingly vivid characterizations of the King in the **"King's Breakfast"** or of Pooh and Christopher Robin, the humor, the fun, the joy in being, all create through their own meanings and substance, the formal structures in which he will present them.

The whimsical poems, filled with humor, will have light, bouncing rhythms as in **"Busy"**: "round about and round about and round about I go." The adventurous and narrative tales, very often, a ponderous note of the grandiose, as in **"Bad Sir Brian Botany,"** combined often, as here, with a hilarious sense of the ludicrous and a joyous love of descriptive sounds:

> I am Sir Brian          sper-lash
> I am Sir Brian          sper-losh

The nature-poems include a delight in water reflections as in **"The Mirror,"** where "silent trees stoop down to trees." There is, very appropriately in these poems, an air of quiet tranquillity, a kind of peace-with-the-world note which is conveyed by the soft even tempo of the words.

There are, too, occasional moments of sharp, poignant wistfulness, and echoes of human disillusionment, shared certainly by the child, that are strangely evoked by the singing rhymes that recall children's games, as in **"The Wrong House"** where the child expresses his dismay that the house "hasn't got a garden, a garden, a garden," and therefore isn't like a house at all.

We cannot exhaust Milne: the variety of his images or the richness of his vision. Nor should we hope to try. It would seem as though every phase of a child's experience is expressed and understood by a poetic form which is eminently suited in tone to its content. That Milne works with ideas and artistic forms which are universally appealing is perhaps best evidenced by the continued meaningfulness of his expression for a different generation of adults and children alike. Milne's poetic bequest may well serve as a fine example, in its honest freshness, and singing joy, for children's poets today and after today. (pp. 357-61)

> *Barbara Novak, "Milne's Poems: Form and Content," in* Elementary English, *Vol. XXXIV, No. 6, October, 1957, pp. 355-61.*

### Ronald Bryden

[In *The World of Christopher Robin*], Methuen have lumped together for Christmas the two verse-volumes, *When We Were Very Young* and *Now We are Six,* and once more a new generation of parents must wrestle in agonised reappraisal. No one else can decide for you, I can only marshal the evidence. Do you wish your child to know Christopher Robin? (p. 784)

[What] bothers me about Milne is the animal stuff. His class implications seem fairly harmless now: they still irritate my generation, but that privileged antediluvian infancy of muffins, hoops, nannies and miniature British Warms must seem as unreal and formally mythical to our Welfare State kids as to the fascinated little Muscovites. There's not much argument about his skill as a writer for children: no one else has understood so well children's

pleasure in the dawning powers of verbalisation, in choruses, puns, rhyme and rigmarole. One could even argue that childhood chanting of 'King John was not a good man' and 'I am Sir Brian—take *that*!' paves the way for appreciation of the use of sound by Hopkins, Joyce and Shakespeare; and the fact that many *Punch*-drunk parents dote whimsically on it all, without progressing farther, shouldn't, strictly, affect our judgment. No, the danger lies, I'm afraid, in Pooh himself: that stout, bow-legged figure bestriding the view through the nursery window on to the animal kingdom.

Of course, Pooh is beloved. Animals are children's only equals, the sharers of their instinctual life and secret freedom. But as Christopher Robin loses his freedom, Pooh, you'll notice, becomes increasingly his whipping-slave and scapegoat. It is Pooh who is greedy, dim-witted, timid and bad at sums: a failed child, a chimpanzee in trousers, Caliban. Here in embryo is the English attitude to animals: the patronage, the projection and rejection, which make up the cosy cults of pony-worship, dog-devotion, pussy-love. If you can't see what's corrupted by them, consider this. Our children may be the last generation to see the other kingdom in its autonomy and greatness. They may be able to fly and see the herds of Africa, the wild horses of the Rockies, the seal and caribou in their migrations and the brilliant water-world of the Barrier Reef. One of them may be the last man to see the last whale. It's difficult enough to achieve a pure response to familiar and human experiences. Do you want their first preparation for this vanishing one to be a parental whimsy about a child's fantasy about a manufacturer's caricatures of a pig, a donkey and a bear? (pp. 784-85)

> *Ronald Bryden, "That Little Gold Head," in* The Spectator, *Vol. 203, No. 6857, November 27, 1959, pp. 784-85.*

### Margery Fisher

A. A. Milne, in his stories of Pooh, uses some of his characters for satire. Owl and Kanga and, most of all, Eeyore, belong properly with all those animals, from Æsop's dog down to George Orwell's pig, who have given a devastating imitation of human temperaments. Lightly handled (they are toys, after all), Milne's little creatures can sometimes send a shiver down your spine. At the same time, Pooh and Piglet are facets of the child, and Pooh's house brings the same domestic pleasure to a child reader as a dolls' house does. So far, so good. The snag is that Milne, though he writes easily and with charm, does not seem to me entirely at home in the child's world.

Pooh belongs to the period of nannies and nurseries, when a parent was a parent, and, however friendly father and son may be, they are in two different worlds. This is emphasized by the bedtime-story framework ('Coming to see me have my bath?' 'I might,' I said. 'I didn't hurt him when I shot him, did I?' 'Not a bit.' and so on). The narrator is always there, occupying something of the position, physical and mental, of the Tramp in Čapek's *Insect Play,* and his asides and interpolations have an air of facetiousness which is uncongenial to some children of today. The interpolations, the free use of capital letters for comic emphasis ('Would you read a Sustaining Book, such as would help and comfort a Wedged Bear in Great Tightness?'), the lapses into sentimentality, are blemishes, to my mind, on a set of tales which, for their inventive energy, their verbal wit and their sheer exuberance have earned a permanent place on children's bookshelves. (p. 38)

> *Margery Fisher, "There and Back by Tricycle," in her* Intent Upon Reading: A Critical Appraisal of Modern Fiction for Children, *Brockhampton Press, 1961, pp. 36-49.*

### John Holmstrom

I was born only about 11 months after Winnie-the-Pooh, but by the time I could read, the Pooh books seemed as unshakeably classic as your Homer or your Virgil. Even now, so many disenchanted years later, it's hard to imagine our own fathers growing up in a Poohless world. Clearly it was necessary to invent him, and by 1927 the deficiency had been made good. Milne had created a hero to rank with [Kenneth Grahame's] Toad—though a remarkably unassertive one, a battered teddy-bear whose leading characteristic was mere vagueness, coupled with childish gluttony and a penchant for lyrical hums. Every middle-class child of the Thirties sucked in Milnian whimsy with, or shortly after, his mother's milk; our whole sense of humour must have been conditioned by it. . . . If Milne's grip had begun to weaken on kids of the Fifties and Sixties (a Latin translation of **Winnie-the-Pooh** and a parody compendium of Pooh criticism have latterly suggested that the cult is tending to recede into adult nostalgia rather than tap fresh minds), the new paperback edition of the two story-books, together with the two volumes of Milne's nursery poetry [all published by Methuen], presumably denote a counter-attack.

Rereading **Pooh** has its problems for the adult. Two things are immediately rebarbative: the arch use of capital letters for indicating Important Phrases as Used by Grownup Persons, and the elaborate Christopher Robin framework. Most fathers are fairly soppy about their firstborn, and no one would hold Milne's doting sentiments against him, but if doting gets immortalised for posterity, it can soon look rather sickly. The whimsical forewords to the books are exquisitely embarrassing already, and soppiness leaks through to the fictionalised projection of Christopher Robin ('He said "Silly old Bear" in such a loving voice that everyone felt quite hopeful again'). E. H. Shepard's illustrations present C. R. as an epicene bob-haired moppet of truly awful insipidity, and the temperature drops perceptibly at every entrance of the Little Master. We're told in the preamble to **When We Were Very Young** . . . that C. R. prefers to call himself Billy Moon: now, with a name like *that,* the kid might have gone far. I find that Shepard mirrors very faithfully the success or failure of Milne's characterisations. He doesn't quite bring Pooh off as an animated top-person, nor, oddly enough, does Milne, in spite of the Very Small Brain and the Hums and the Honey. The real successes in both media, it seems to me, are the more positive supporting characters like Piglet and Eeyore.

Piglet, the tiny bulb-shaped animal with the pointed head and 'excited ears', is a marvellously sympathetic creation, tremulously imaginative, longing for heroic exploits but prudently scared of them, aware that his intelligence is greater than Pooh's but not enough to compensate for his physical frailty. Piglet lives a life of high emotional intensity, his nerve-ends always ready to flutter with fear or hope—fear of Heffalumps, hope of a second glimpse of C. R.'s blue braces.

Piglet's antithesis is the hyper-depressive Eeyore, a drooping donkey who lives alone in a slough of self-pity. 'I suppose,' murmurs Eeyore on hearing of a party, 'they will be sending me down the odd bits which get trodden on.' He is maladjusted to Forest society, sarcastic and not easily helped. 'Thank you for happening to pass me,' he will sneer at an animal who has gone out of his way to be sociable. The story of Eeyore's Birthday is a brilliantly judged, almost Steptoish bit of pathetic comedy. And just as Eeyore's predictably miserable reactions give inexhaustible pleasure, Tigger's bounciness, Rabbit's bossiness, Owl's scholarly phoniness, lend themselves to a multitude of fruitful conflicts. Mr. Milne, for all the archness, was a master of humours.

I was amazed to learn that the two books of nursery poems have been reprinted even more often than the storybooks—over 100 times between them. And they really are hell. About a dozen have become nursery 'standards', and a few of these, however much one may deplore the upper-middling ethos, have lilt enough to capture any child's feet; 'James James Morrison Morrison Weatherby George Dupree' marches as swingingly as the *'Horst Wessel'* and probably more harmlessly. But apart from the sheer wetness of much of Milne's poetic whimsy, the aura of nannies and sou'westers is gruesomely pervasive, and there are occasional unguarded lapses into feudalism—or downright exploitation, as when the child staggeringly comments on a toy-making gardener:

> If you give him a smile,
> Only once in a while,
> *Then he never expects any money!*
>
> (p. 752)

> *John Holmstrom, "Whisper Who Dares," in* New Statesman, *Vol. LXX, No. 1809, November 12, 1965, pp. 752-53.*

### Stella Rodway

Since the twenties, the quirks of fashion (which have, incidentally, brought Christopher Robin's hair and gaiters back in) have never diminished the popularity with the under-sevens of the Pooh stories, and even of A. A. Milne's often gibed at but amazingly catchy poems, which are, in fact, less arch and sentimental than some space-age work. Not all children's classics have this instant appeal to children themselves, or such a subjective sense of those vagrant childhood moods of idleness, defiance, loneliness and inconsequence. (p. 631)

> *Stella Rodway, "Pooh in Paperback," in* The Spectator, *Vol. 215, No. 7168, November 12, 1965, pp. 631-32.*

### Roger Lancelyn Green

[**When We Were Very Young** and **Now We Are Six** contain] the best and most popular verses ever written for children: verse, very firmly, not poetry—but inspired verse that captures all our yesterdays in a prosaic and satisfying fashion, as even Stevenson had not succeeded in doing so completely and inevitably.

Adult critics may find much to condemn in Milne's verses, and occasional examples such as **'Vespers'** do stray perilously near the sentimental. But this is not a child's reaction: nearly all the verses in both volumes were loved, lingered over and learnt by heart by us children of the twenties—and my own children at the same age loved them almost as dearly in the fifties.

But Milne was to achieve something even greater. (p. 254)

After the slight archness of the 'frame' dialogue in the first chapter, **Winnie-the-Pooh** and **The House at Pooh Corner** spring to life on their own, dictate themselves to Milne and blow away every trace of the faults latent in his other works. The humour, with its touch of nonsense held in place by irresistible logic, and the sure and inevitable creation of character after character make **Pooh** the greatest work of its kind since *Alice*. Indeed, it is almost the only completely successful and original work of that kind, though the *Just So Stories* have many traits in common and certainly cannot be fitted into any other category or tradition.

The **Pooh** stories, wrote Kathleen Lines, 'are known and loved and quoted the world over', and in quotability at least they are only surpassed by *Alice,* though here again the *Just So Stories* run them a close second. Beatrix Potter had much of this quality, but her whole practical feminine outlook kept her from stepping over the boundary between fancy and fantasy. This was a boundary that Kenneth Grahame could cross, notably in 'The Reluctant Dragon', but it is only a momentary glimpse that he gives us before summoning us back to the deeper magic of *The Wind in the Willows.* (p. 256)

Pooh and his companions are the only immortal toys of fiction, and appear likely to remain so. . . . (p. 257)

> *Roger Lancelyn Green, "Kenneth Grahame and A. A. Milne," in his* Tellers of Tales, *revised edition, 1965. Reprint by Kaye & Ward. Ltd., 1969, pp. 249-57.*

**Vera Ohanian**

[What] is the true message conveyed to children [by **Winnie-the-Pooh**]? The real meaning is a denial of several great problems and pressures experienced in a parent-child relationships, in sibling and peer rivalry, and in accepting maleness and femaleness. The story events supporting this interpretation are explored below:

1. A denial of human problems is suggested through the major role played by animal characters. Nine of the ten characters, including the Heffalump and the Woozle, are animals. And it is they who carry out the plot. The one human character, Christopher Robin, is incidental to the story. He remains on the fringe, his feelings undepicted. He is important only to help the animals carry out the plot. Why, then, do the animals play the major role in **Winnie-the-Pooh**? Is it not to frustrate the possible occur-

rence of human problems? Certainly animals do not have social-emotional problems on the scale that humans do.

2. A further denial of human problems is achieved by employing one animal of a kind, with the exception of Kanga and Baby Roo. Each animal character lives alone in his own house and is independent and autonomous. Each animal character possesses unique abilities, strengths, and weaknesses. Kanga is big and powerful; no other animal competes in size. Piglet, fearful and small, manages feats impossible to Kanga. In such an arrangement the possibilities for conflict are mostly eliminated. There are also no parents to give orders to be obeyed, no siblings and peers to fight or compete with.

Further security is achieved through the inclusion of positive aspects of family life—togetherness, loyalty, and support. Though the animals live apart, they are readily available to help each other. The *one* human in the story, though a child, serves the role of a parent. Even in fantasy, it is too frightening to children to remove completely adult succor. Thus, Milne includes Christopher Robin, a giant among animals, used by them when needed.

3. Human problems are denied also through the simple and carefree life portrayed. Difficulties are readily solved. Recall how easily Eeyore's birthday gift is procured by Pooh-Bear—an empty, discarded, still sticky, honey jar belatedly offered. And that's all it takes to make Eeyore happy. Remember, too, how conveniently Owl's bell pull just turns out to be Eeyore's dropped tail! Even their expeditions are effortless and nothing more calamitous occurs than Baby Roo slipping into a stream. Their enemies, the Heffalump and the Woozle, turn out to be imaginary and non-existent.

4. Problems of sex are ignored. Early in the story Milne reveals his deliberate intent to conceal the sexes of the animals:

> When I first heard his name, I said, just as you are going to say, "But I thought he was a boy?" "So did I," said Christopher Robin.
> "Then you can't call him Winnie?"
> "I don't."
> "But you said—"
> "He's Winnie-the-Pooh. Don't you know what 'ther' means?"
> "Ah, yes, now I do," I said quickly; "and I hope you do too, because it is all the explanation you are going to get."

And so Milne closes this subject.

5. Problems associated with aging or with growing up are denied, too. Story characters remain undeveloped. They neither grow old nor die.

**Winnie-the-Pooh** has been described [by May Hill Arbuthnot] as "a clever fantasy for the youngest" and "a game of let's pretend put into story form." But *what* is to be pretended? The foregoing analysis provides the answer. The characters and story events deny the existence of the critical problems experienced by the young child in parent, sibling, and peer relationships, in accepting one's sex, and in growing up and old. The stories are built around fantasies which seem to say, "Let's pretend these problems do not exist. Don't let them bother you." Fundamentally, then, *Winnie-the-Pooh* deals with problems burdensome to the child between the ages of three to seven and offers a way of coping with them, through escape, and thus demonstrates mastery through denial. (pp. 950-51)

> *Vera Ohanian, "Cherished Books of Children: What Makes Them So?" in* Elementary English, *Vol. XLVII, No. 11, November, 1970, pp. 946-52.*

## Alison Lurie

Pooh is still a big culture hero. He means as much to the Now Generation as he did to us Back When.

My friends and I not only read Milne's books over and over as children; all through high school and college we went on speaking his language, seeing people and events in his terms. My husband lived his first term at Middlesex as Piglet, with friends who were Pooh and Eeyore, and the school grounds and surrounding country were remapped accordingly; at college, I knew girls who went by the names of Tigger and Roo. Even today, occasionally, I will go back and reread a favorite passage.

Writing about the Pooh books, on the other hand, has been awkward (if not impossible) since 1963, when Frederick C. Crews published *The Pooh Perplex*. It is not often that a satirical work achieves such success that it effectively destroys its object, but Crews almost managed it. He was not able to laugh into silence any of the dozen varieties of current literary criticism he so brilliantly parodied; but he did manage to stifle almost all critical comment on Winnie-the-Pooh for a decade. No one likes to imitate an imitation, and anyhow Crews had said most of what could be said about Pooh in one disguise or another. . . . (p. 11)

At first glance, Milne appears to be writing about his son, Christopher Robin, who was six when *Winnie-the-Pooh* appeared in 1926, and about his son's toys. But there are indications in the books that Milne was also thinking of his own childhood, and the people that surrounded him in the past.

[Milne] was the youngest of three sons of John Vine Milne, the headmaster of a small suburban London school for boys. At Henley House the three Milne children lived a half-private, half-public life, playing and eating with their father's pupils, and joining the classes as soon as they were old enough. The world of Pooh repeats this in many respects. It is a very old-fashioned, limited society, without economic competition or professional ambition. There are no cars, planes, radios, or telephones; war, crime, and serious violence are unknown. Aggression is limited to the mildest form of practical joke, and even that generally backfires. Except for Kanga and Roo, there are no family relationships. The principal occupations of the inhabitants are eating, exploration, visiting, and sports. The greatest excitement centers around the capture of strange animals or the rescue of friends in danger; but the danger is always from natural causes; accidents, floods, storms. Apart from occasional bad weather, it is a perfectly safe world.

The setting seems to suggest pre-1900 Essex and Kent, where Milne spent his holidays as a child, rather than the milder and more thickly-settled countryside of Sussex where he lived as an adult. The landscape is fairly bare and uncultivated, consisting mostly of heath and woods and marsh. There are many pine trees, and the most common plants seem to be gorse and thistles. Rain, wind, fog, and even snow are common.

Milne claimed in his *Autobiography* that he did not invent most of the characters in the Pooh books, but merely took over the toys which Christopher Robin happened to possess. . . . (pp. 11-12)

Nevertheless, there seem to be some echoes from Milne's own past in the dramatis personae. Milne's father, whom he describes in his *Autobiography* as "the best man I have ever known," was a serious, kindly schoolmaster, devoted to all his sons, as well as to the boys whose temporary guardian he was. Yet everyone recognized that Alan was his favorite child. The same situation occurs in the books, where Winnie-the-Pooh is the undisputed favorite of Christopher Robin. As a child Milne believed that his father "knew everythere there was to know"; but in fact he was pedantic rather than wise. ("Later on . . . I formed the opinion that, even if Father knew everything, he knew most of it wrong"). In this aspect, Milne senior may appear as Owl, the pompous schoolmaster ("If anyone knows anything about anything, it's Owl who knows something about something") who turns out to be nearly illiterate.

Milne's happy childhood centered around his father. As for his mother, he remarks:

> I don't think I ever really knew her . . . I neither experienced, nor felt the need of, that mother-love of which one reads so much . . . I gave my heart to my father.

He remembers his mother chiefly as a sensible, very efficient housekeeper ("She could do everything better than the people whom so reluctantly she came to employ: cook better than the cook, dust better than the parlour-maid . . . "). Like Rabbit, she lived in a state of preoccupation with small responsibilities and bossy concern for the duties of others. It is interesting that Rabbit, the officious organizer, and Owl, the solemn pedant, the characters most like caricatures of Milne's own parents, are also the only ones he claims to have invented himself, the live animals among the toys.

Next to his father, Milne's greatest attachment as a child was to his brother Ken, sixteen months older. Ken, he writes, was "kinder, . . . more lovable, more tolerant;" but Alan was brighter and quicker, though more timid. Like Pooh and Piglet, they were inseparable, so much so that they had hardly any use for other people. . . . (pp. 12-13)

Some of [the other characters] may also have real-life prototypes, either in Milne's childhood or that of his son. There is Kanga, the kind, fussy mother or nanny, with her continual "We'll see, dear," and lack of interest in anything except children and counting "how many pieces of soap there were left and the two clean spots in Tigger's feeder." Bouncy Tigger and little Roo are like many younger siblings, always pushing themselves forward in a noisy,

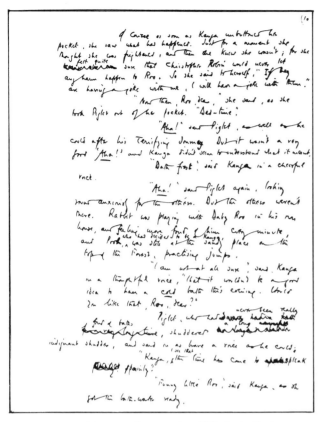

*A page of the original manuscript of* Winnie-the-Pooh.

simple-minded way, but no use in serious matters. Their arrival in the Forest, like the appearance of a younger brother or sister in early childhood, is sudden and unexplained:

> "Here—we—are— . . . And then, suddenly, we wake up one morning, and what do we find? We find a Strange Animal among us. An animal of whom we had never even heard before!"

Rabbit, Pooh, and Piglet form a plot to get rid of Roo, but as might be expected, it fails—like Tigger in the sequel, he must be accepted into the Forest.

Finally there is Eeyore, the complete pessimist . . . who is depressive with delusions of persecution where Tigger is manic with delusions of grandeur. ("Somebody must have taken it," he remarks when his tail is lost. "How Like Them.") Eeyore may date from a later period of Milne's life, the years 1906-14 when he worked on *Punch.* The Editor at that time was Owen Seaman, "a strange, unlucky man," always dissatisfied and suspicious, given to blaming his errors on extraneous circumstances: upon losing a golf match, Milne relates, "he threw down his putter and said 'That settles it. I'll never play in knickerbockers again.' "

Among all these characters seen from a child's viewpoint, Pooh is the child himself. The rest have virtues and faults particular to some adults and some children; Pooh, the hero, has the virtues and faults common to all children. He is simple, natural, and affectionate. But he is also a Bear of Very Little Brain, continually falling into ludi-

crous errors of judgment and comprehension; he is so greedy that he eats Eeyore's birthday jar of honey on his way to deliver it. But these faults are also endearing; all of us at birth were stupid and greedy, but no less lovable for that. As Milne himself has remarked, children combine endearing natural innocence and grace with a "brutal egotism."

> "Oh, Bear!" said Christopher Robin. "How I do love you!"
> "So do I," said Pooh.

But slow though he is, Pooh always comes through in an emergency. When Roo falls into the river, everyone behaves in a typical way. . . . But it is Pooh who rescues Roo, as he later rescues Piglet; it is Pooh who discovers the "North Pole."

If Pooh is the child as hero, Christopher Robin is the child as God. He is also the ideal parent. He is both creator and judge—the two divine functions shared by mortal parents. He does not participate in most of the adventures, but usually appears at the end of the chapter, sometimes descending with a machine (an umbrella, a popgun, etc.) to save the situation. In a way the positions of child and adult have been reversed—the people around Christopher Robin are merely animals and his old toys. (So Alice exclaims "Why, they're only a pack of cards!")

But the ironic view of the adult world and its pretensions is undercut by another sort of irony addressed to adults who might be reading the book aloud. These passages, which appear mostly at the beginning of ***Winnie-the-Pooh*** (there are none in the sequel) take the form of condescending conversations between the author and Christopher Robin.

> "Was that me?" said Christopher Robin in an awed voice, hardly daring to believe it.
> "That was you."
> Christopher Robin said nothing, but his eyes got larger and larger, and his face got pinker and pinker.

Behind the godlike child is another and more powerful deity: A. A. Milne, who has created both Christopher Robin and Pooh.

There are other hidden messages from the author to the adult or adolescent reader. The verbal hypocrisies of greed are mocked in Tigger, those of cowardice in Piglet, and those of polite etiquette in Rabbit. The most straightforward anti-establishment remarks, however, are reserved for Eeyore:

> "Clever!" said Eeyore scornfully . . . "Education!" said Eeyore bitterly . . . "What *is* Learning? . . . A thing *Rabbit* knows!"

A similar criticism may lie behind the frequent attempts of the characters to elaborate some error or misunderstanding into a system, as with Pooh's and Piglet's hunt for the Woozle. As soon as a real fact or observation is introduced, the system collapses, and the Woozle vanishes.

Milne's language, too, contains hidden messages. He pretends not to understand long words and makes fun of people who use them. He employs a special form of punctuation, capitalizing words usually written with a small letter, as is done now only in theatrical and film publicity. But in the Pooh books the effect is reversed: Milne capitalizes to show that though the character takes something seriously, the reader need not do so. When Pooh remarks "I have been Foolish and Deluded" the words are weakened by the capital letter; to have said that Pooh was foolish and deluded would have been much stronger.

A side effect of this is to weaken words that are conventionally capitalized, and by extension the things they stand for. Milne was aware of this; in an essay on his poem **"The King's Breakfast"** he makes a suggestion for reading aloud the lines:

> The King asked
> The Queen and
> The Queen asked
> The Dairymaid
>
> Don't be afraid of saying "and" at the end of the second line; the second and third words have the same value, and you need not be alarmed because one is a royal noun and the other is only a common conjunction.

When he uses a word it means what he tells it to mean; his Bears and Expeditions are of a very special kind. He makes the rules; he determines what things and emotions will be allowed into his books and on what terms.

In the same way, when Milne came to write his ***Autobiography*** he tended to remember selectively. His own childhood appears through a kind of golden haze. . . . As Milne himself once announced, "Art is not life, but an exaggeration of it." And an exaggerated, sentimental—and also sometimes rather condescending—tone sometimes appears in the ***Autobiography,*** especially when he speaks of his father. Describing his own departure for boarding school, he writes:

> Farewell, Papa, with your brave, shy heart and your funny little ways; with your humour and your wisdom and your never-failing goodness; . . . "Well," you will tell yourself, "it lasted until he was twelve; they grow up and resent our care for them, they form their own ideas, and think ours old-fashioned. It is natural. But oh, to have that little boy again, whom I used to throw up to the sky, his face laughing down into mine—"

This nostalgic theme recurs in the Pooh books, particularly in the final chapter of ***The House at Pooh Corner:***

> "Pooh, when I'm—*you* know . . . will you come up here
> sometimes?"
> "Just Me?"
> "Yes, Pooh."
> "Will you be here too?"
> "Yes, Pooh, I will be, really. I *promise* I will be, Pooh."
> "That's good," said Pooh.

This is also sentimentality, but a sentimentality which rises into pathos, via the pathetic fallacy. In fact, the world of childhood and the past, our discarded toys and land-

scapes, will not mourn us when we leave; the regret will be felt by our own imprisoned earlier selves. Milne ascribes to his father and to Pooh the passionate regret he feels for his own lost paradise.

It is no wonder that this particular lost paradise, this small, safe, happy place where individuality and privacy are respected, should appeal to people growing up into a world of telegrams, anger, wire-tapping, war, death, and taxes—especially to those who would rather not grow up. Milne's loosely-organized society of unemployed artists and eccentrics, each quietly doing his own thing, might have a special attraction for counter-culture types. For them, Pooh Corner would be both the ideal past and the ideal future—at once the golden rural childhood they probably never knew, and the perfect commune they are always seeking. (pp. 13-16)

> *Alison Lurie, "Back to Pooh Corner," in* Children's Literature: Annual of the Modern Language Association *Seminar on Children's Literature and The Children's Literature Association, Vol. 2, 1973, pp. 11-17.*

### Richard Adams

> [*The following excerpt is from an essay in which Adams recalls his childhood reading and its influence on his epic fantasy* Watership Down.]

My childhood—the 'twenties and early 'thirties—was the heyday of J. M. Barrie and of Christopher Robin, when children were seen by many people primarily as delicate, sensitive, small creatures, who ought properly to live in a world from which not only suffering, but to some extent reality, were excluded until they were older. This idea is not altogether false, of course, but at that time it was overdone. . . . (p. 92)

I personally felt resentful of this general atmosphere, which thwarted one's natural aggression while at the same time unfitting one for the rougher side of life, so that one felt—and hated knowing that one was justified in feeling—at a disadvantage. (pp. 92-3)

At that date you could not escape ***Pooh***—you were rolled in it by the grown-ups, who loved it. So did I, and I am ready to defend it now. The humour is often arch and falsely precocious. There is a cloying sentimentality in places. But one thing ***Pooh*** has, pressed down and running over. It has marvellous characters; clear, consistent, interacting upon each other, each talking like himself—as good as Jane Austen's in their own way. From ***Pooh*** I learned the vital importance, as protagonists, of a group of clearly-portrayed, contrasting but reciprocal characters—though I wouldn't claim that Hazel, Fiver and Co. come anywhere near Pooh and his friends. (p. 93)

> *Richard Adams, "Some Ingredients of 'Watership Down'," in* Children's Book Review, *Vol. IV, No. 3, Autumn, 1974, pp. 92-5.*

### Geoffrey Grigson

Once, oh once, did not the Public find its voice in the Poet? Once—but not now, O Apollo—weren't new poems sold, in the largest numbers? *Lalla Rookh,* and *Childe Harold,* and *Idylls of the King,* and *Poems and Ballads* (and *Proverbial Philosophy*)?

Then T. S. Eliot came; and poetry changed to modern; and did not sell.

As such facts are recited (often, if not quite so often as heretofore), how is it that no one remembers Alan Alexander Milne? How is it that no one is asked, in Advanced Level English, even in the Tripos, to estimate the influence upon 'Now I'm engaged to Miss Joan Hunter Dunn' of

> Hush! Hush! Whisper who dares!
> Christopher Robin is saying his prayers?

A. A. Milne was a poet—he wrote poems, shall I say, no less than John Betjeman, or Eliot; or William Empson. Undeniably *When We Were Very Young,* his most successful book, is filled with poems. Undeniably these poems have sold (and are selling still). Few other poems in English have sold so enormously. (p. 12)

This poet was born to a Scottish prep school master, in London, in 1882, six years before our Mr Eliot was born in St Louis, Missouri. He was educated (nothing 'wrong' about his education) at Westminster School and Trinity College, Cambridge; and soon enough, after editing the *Granta,* the undergraduates' magazine, he was helping to edit *Punch* in its least aggressive and most evasive days. This young man knew the electric fences of the interest in which he was now involved, his master J. M. Barrie, his editor R. C. Lehmann. (pp. 12-13)

With his own *curriculum vitae,* his own dye of the Poshocracy, in the Squeamish Age (in which St Loe Strachey, editor of the *Spectator,* led a deputation to the Home Secretary asking him to ban *Ann Veronica* by H. G. Wells), Milne's later poems of *When We Were Very Young* were in tune, precisely.

The nature of the best-seller has to do with the nature of a class, its prime interest is one of sociology, not literature; which is the fun of such books. The readers have mattered most of all, and it is not difficult to be sure of the readers who have found a voice in A. A. Milne, to be sure of the readership (and the sociological writership) to which he belonged. From the poems you need only to deduce the keepings of Christopher Robin, and Percy, and John, and Mary Jane, and Emmeline, and James James Morrison Morrison Weatherby George Dupree.

The poems intimate that these children are of good family—at least up to the Forstye standard. They have nannies and nurseries *(passim).* Maids are also in attendance—though not butlers (see **"The Wrong House"**).

Their homes, in London, are in the right squares, are not too grand and not too mean. Their families keep dogs, and are kind to uncles, aunts, and animals other than dogs; and display an embryo interest in bird-watching. Their daddies know about trout, mayfly, and expensive rods, their mamas about trugs and delphiniums. When they are not very ill, they are attended by frock-coated white-haired family doctors. They are Church of England—could a dissenting child or a Presbyterian child say 'Thank you, God, for my nice new braces'? They are accustomed,

with a full staff, to seaside holidays (I think in North Cornwall), in a rented house:

> When we got home, we had sand in the hair,
> In the eyes and the ears and everywhere.

Their world is Us, and the Other People. Those of the Other People who sell in shops or work with their hands (Jonathan Jo the gardener) are a little queer, and perhaps need washing (see **"Bad Sir Brian Botany"**), but they must be treated with consideration; which averts revolution. Bad Sir Brian blipped 'the villagers' on the head with his battle-axe and kicked them into the pond, and into the ditches, and under the waterfall. But observe that the treatment simply made Bad Sir Brian renounce his title, his battle-axe, and his spurred boots, which he threw into the fire; after which he 'goes about the village as B. Botany, Esquire'. He has become one of Us. The class structure is repaired, and improved.

Conclusions? We may now be sure that of these children the males are earmarked for the better schools, then the better colleges, high on the river *(mens mediocris in corpore sano),* at one of the 'two' universities; and that male and female they come of families comfortable, secure, self-certain, somewhat above the middle of the middle class.

Are the poems for other children of such homes? No, rather than yes. Children, in my experience, of every generation since and including the Twenties, have found the poems nauseating, and fascinating. In fact, they were poems by a parent for other parents, and for vice-parental nannies—for parents with a war to forget, a social (and literary) revolution to ignore, a childhood to recover. *When We—*We*—Were Very Young* the book is named, after all, indicating its aim; which, like the aim of all natural best-sellers, was not entirely explicit, one may assume, in the author's consciousness.

Here mamas of the middle way, and fathers, and nannies, those distorting reflectors of the parental ethos, could be sure of finding Innocence Up to Date. Little Lord Fauntleroy—here he was, stripped of frills and velvet (as we can tell by the splendid insipidity of the accompanying drawings) for modern, sensible clothes; heir, after all, to no peerage, but still the Eternal Child. No hint in these poems of children nasty, brutish and short, as *Struwelpeter* or Hilaire Belloc made them (or as they are being re-established in newspaper cartoons).

Are there ever tantrums, as these nice children say 'cos', and 'most', and 'nuffin'', and 'purfickly', and 'woffelly', in their nice accent?

> *What* is the matter with Mary Jane?
> She's perfectly well, and she hasn't a pain.

If there are tantrums, it is rice pudding again; but not the child psyche, not infant sexuality, not Freud, who had now entered the pure English world. (pp. 13-15)

The innocence of *When We Were Very Young*—of course it chimes with the last tinkle of a romantic innocence which by the Twenties had devolved to whimsy. Christopher Robin comes trailing the tattiest wisps of a glory soiled by expectation and acceptance. The clouds have gone grey. The Child, in spite of Westminster and Trinity, is all too much at last the Father of the Man. And whenever the Child's impresario allowed an entr'acte, it came in parallel modes of the expected and decayed—daffodowndillies and the last fairies (inherited from the more fanciful—and sinister—inventor of Peter Pan), Twinkletoes upon the apple leaves, the Lake King's daughter on the water-lilies, cave ancients tapping at golden slippers for dainty feet, bluebells, and blackbirds' yellow bills.

For some Poets Who Don't Sell, these poems for people towards the top with children beneath the age of literary consent have the qualities of rhythm, shape, economy, and games with words—good qualities, after all. Would it be too ponderous to say as well that they were poems for a class of middle to top people who had lost their intellectual and cultural nerve, who expected of right things which they had not earned, and who had scarcely looked a fact in the eye for fifty years? It might be too ponderous. But it would be true.

And sometimes out it comes in the charming sick, in the actual stuff, with an ironic unconsciousness. As Christopher Robin says, imagining himself on a desert island instead of his holiday coast of Cornwall, in the land of Betjeman:

> And I'd say to myself as I looked so lazily
> down at the sea:
> There's nobody else in the world, and the world
> was made for me.
>
> (pp. 15-16)

*Geoffrey Grigson, "The Mildly Monstrous," in his* The Contrary View: Glimpses of Fudge and Gold, *Macmillan, 1974, pp. 12-19.*

## Margaret Blount

Pooh [is] the most famous bear ever created. . . .

He is the first famous fictional bear and all the others owe him something; his size, his fondness for honey, ponderous *naiveté* and occasional flashes of brilliance have left their mark on other lesser bears, real or toy; and there is no question about Pooh's reality. His adventures in the Forest and Hundred Acre Wood spring as naturally from character as the happenings in any real life. (p. 178)

The solemn facetiousness and rather artful simplicity . . . and ponderous use of capitals may mar the stories for some. . . . But the individuality of Pooh, Piglet and friends is at times uncomfortably and sadly lifelike. Eeyore's sarcasm, made sharper because he is unlucky and unpopular—or thinks he is—is something unforgettable because one recognises it, as one does all the others; Owl, the pretentious scholar, his reputation resting on long words and a mythical ability to spell; Rabbit rushing here and there making lists, Army fashion, too annoyingly public spirited to leave anything alone; Tigger, brash and gaudy, the unclassifiable foreigner who doesn't know the rules; Kanga, Mother, Nanny who always knows best and squashes one's remarks with cast-iron illogicality as does Christopher Robin's Alice with her 'Sure to, dear, but it's time for tea.' (pp. 178-80)

*Margaret Blount, "Only Toys," in her* Animal Land: The Creatures of Children's Fiction, *William Morrow & Company, Inc., 1975, pp. 170-90.*

## Christopher Milne

[The] Christopher Robin who appears in so many of the poems is not always me. For this was where my name, so totally useless to me personally, came into its own: it was a wonderful name for writing poetry round. So sometimes my father is using it to describe something I did, and sometimes he is borrowing it to describe something he did as a child, and sometimes he is using it to describe something that any child might have done. **"At the Zoo"**, for example, is about me. **"The Engineer"** is not. **"Lines and Squares"** and **"Hoppity"** are games that every small child must have played. **"Buckingham Palace"** is half and half. Nanny and I certainly used to go and watch the changing of the guard, but I must—for a reason that will appear later—disown the conversation. On the whole it doesn't greatly matter which of the two of us did what: I'm happy to accept responsibility. But I must make two exceptions. The first is **"In the Dark"**.

There was one great difference between my father and myself when we were children. He had an elder brother; I had not. So he was never alone in the dark. Lying in bed with the lights out he could so easily be "talking to a dragon" and feeling brave, knowing that if the dragon suddenly turned fierce he had only to reach out a hand and there would be Ken in the next bed. But I could take no such risks. I had to keep reminding myself that the dragon was only a bedtime story one, not a real one. I had to keep reassuring myself that all was safe by staring at the little orange strip of light that ran along the bottom of the night nursery door, by straining my ears to hear the gentle but, oh, so comforting movements of Nanny in the next room. Sometimes she would call out. "I'm just going downstairs. I shan't be a minute.": and then I would wait anxiously for the sound of her returning footsteps. Once I waited and waited until I could wait no more. Something awful must have happened. I got out of bed, opened the night nursery door, crossed the deserted nursery to the door at the far end. And there was Nanny coming upstairs. "You naughty boy. What are you doing?" "O Nanny, you were such a long time; I didn't know what had happened to you." She was cross, but only a little bit, and I didn't mind. It was so lovely to have her back.

I continued to have night fears for a long time. When, later, I went to boarding school, this was my one consolation when the holidays came to an end: there were no dragons in dormitories.

Once—I can't put a date to it, but I think I must have been about ten—my father, when he came to say goodnight to me, asked me an odd question. "Which side do you usually go to sleep on?" he said. I thought for a bit. I didn't really know. So I made a guess. "My right, I think." He nodded. "That's supposed to be the best side," he said. "You're supposed to be more likely to have bad dreams if you sleep on your left, because then you're lying on your heart." Bad dreams! BAD DREAMS! I did have bad dreams, awful dreams about witches. Now I knew why. I had been going to sleep on my left side. . . . In those days I used to lie on my tummy with one hand tucked under the mattress and the other under the pillow. I would start facing one way. After a while I would feel restless and turn over to face the other way. Then over again, and so on until finally I was asleep. So I might end up on my right side, or I might equally well end up on my left. *I must never end up on my left side again!* Whenever I turned on to my left I must keep my eyes open, wide open, staring, however much I longed to shut them. Then I must turn back on to the other side as soon as ever I could. And every night from then on this became the way I had to go to sleep. For how long? For years, I believe.

> I'm lying on my left side . . .
> I'm lying on my right . . .
> I'll play a lot tomorrow
> I'll think a lot tomorrow
> I'll laugh a lot tomorrow . . .
> Good-night!

Before I come to the second poem that I must disown—and the reader may start guessing which one it will be—I must quote from something my father wrote in a "Preface to Parents" for a special edition of the verses and which he later reprinted in his autobiography.

> In real life very young children have an artless beauty, an innocent grace, an unstudied abandon of movement, which, taken together, make an appeal to our emotions similar in kind to that made by any other young and artless creatures: kittens, puppies, lambs: but greater in degree, for the reason that the beauty of childhood seems in some way to transcend the body. Heaven, that is, does really appear to lie about the child in its infancy, as it does not lie about even the most attractive kitten. But with this outstanding physical quality there is a natural lack of moral quality, which expresses itself, as Nature always insists on expressing herself, in an egotism entirely ruthless. . . . The mother of a little boy of three has disappeared, and is never seen again. The child's reaction to the total loss of his mother is given in these lines
>
> James James
> Morrison Morrison
> (Commonly known as Jim)
> Told his
> Other relations
> Not to go blaming *him.*
>
> And that is all. It is the truth about a child: children are, indeed, as heartless as that. . . .

Is it? Are they? Was I? I cannot pretend to know for sure how I felt about anything at the age of three. I can only guess that though I might not have missed my mother had she disappeared, and would certainly not have missed my father, I would have missed Nanny—most desolately. A young child's world is a small one and within it things may have odd values. A teddy bear may be worth more than a father. But the egotism with which (I will admit) a child is born, surely very quickly disappears as attachments are made and relationships established. When a child plays with his bear the bear comes alive and there is at once a child-bear relationship which tries to copy the Nanny-child relationship. Then the child gets inside his bear and

looks at it the other way round: that's how *bear* feels about it. And at once sympathy is born and egotism has died. A poem in which my father really does express what I feel is the truth about a child is **"Market Square"**, which ends up:

> So I'm sorry for the people who sell fine sauce-
>     pans,
> I'm sorry for the people who sell fresh mackerel,
> I'm sorry for the people who sell sweet lavender,
> 'Cos they haven't got a rabbit, not anywhere
>     there!

How well I remember this feeling of sympathy—totally misplaced, of course—yet agonisingly sincere!

Undoubtedly children can be selfish, but so, too, can adults. By accusing the young of heartless egotism are we perhaps subconsciously reassuring ourselves that, selfish though we still may be, there was once a time when we were worse. . . .

This brings me to the second poem I must disown—**"Vespers"**. It is one of my father's best known and one that has brought me over the years more toe-curling, fist-clenching, lip-biting embarrassment than any other. So let me, for the first time in my life, look it clearly in the eyes and see how things stand between us.

The general impression left by **"Vespers"**—especially with any one who has heard Vera Lynn singing it—is of a rather soppy poem about a good little boy who is saying his prayers. But if one reads it rather more carefully, one will see that it is nothing of the sort. It is a poem about a rather naughty little boy who is *not* saying his prayers. He is merely pretending; and to his and the author's surprise he has managed to fool a great many people. **"Vespers"**, then, is not a sentimental poem at all: it is a mildly cynical one. But even so, nothing to get worked up about. After all, everyone is naughty sometimes.

So you might think. But it is not quite what my father thought. Let us see what he had to say in that "Preface to Parents".

> Finally, let me refer to the poem which has been more sentimentalized over than any other in the book: **"Vespers"**. Well, if mothers and aunts and hard-headed reviewers have been sentimental over it, I am glad; for the spectacle in real life of a child of three at its prayers is one over which thousands have been sentimental. It is indeed calculated to bring a lump to the throat. But even so one must tell the truth about the matter. Not "God bless Mummy, because I love her so", but "God bless Mummy, I know that's right"; not "God bless Daddy, because he buys me food and clothes" but "God bless Daddy, I quite forgot"; not even the egotism of "God bless Me, because I'm the most important person in the house", but the super-egotism of feeling so impregnable that the blessing of this mysterious God for Oneself is the very last thing for which it would seem necessary to ask. And since this is the Truth about a Child, let us get all these things into the poem, and the further truth that prayer means nothing to a child of three, whose

thoughts are engaged with other, more exciting matters. . . .

**"Vespers",** it seems, is not just about what a certain little boy did on a certain occasion. It is the Truth (with a capital T) about a Child (with a capital C). And although I knew that this was my father's general feeling, I had entirely forgotten how uncompromisingly he had expressed himself.

It was at this point, while I was collecting my thoughts together, wondering how to go on, that I noticed the quotation from Wordsworth. It comes in the first of the two passages I have quoted:

> Heaven lies about us in our infancy

This is a line from Wordsworth's "Intimations of Immortality". At first glance it seemed at home in its context. But on looking closer I saw that this was far from the case. For the line had been given a new and altogether different meaning. Wordsworth had been saying that Heaven appeared *to the child* to lie around him. My father was saying that this was how it seemed to the *onlooker*. So then I read the whole poem. It is, of course, the Truth about a Child as Wordsworth sees it, and it is the complete reverse of my father's view. And at once it awakened an echo in my heart—as it must have awakened many another echo in many another heart.

> Those first affections,
> Those shadowy recollections,
> Which, be they what they may,
> Are yet the fountain light of all our day.

In those days of splendour and glory I certainly felt myself nearer to God—both the God that Nanny was telling me about who lived up in the sky and the God who painted the buttercups—than I do today. And so, asked to choose between these two views of childhood, I am bound to say that I'm for Wordsworth. Maybe he is just being sentimental. Maybe the infant William has fooled the middle-aged poet in the same way that the kneeling Christopher Robin fooled so many of his readers. Maybe my cynical father is right. But this is not how I feel about it. (pp. 24-30)

I don't really want to get too involved either with Poetry or with Religious Instruction, nor do I want to spend too long on my infant knees. Furthermore, in a world heavily overpopulated with sociologists, psychologists and research workers generally, I am reluctant to set up theories backed by nothing more than memory against the statistics and case histories of the opposition. However, this I must say. The Christopher Robin of that wretched poem is indeed me at the age of three. I retain the most vivid memories of saying my prayers as a child. They go back a long way, but I cannot date them. I well recall how I knelt, how Nanny sat, her hands round mine, and what we said aloud together. Did my thoughts wander? Were they engaged on other, more exciting things? The answer—and let me say it loudly and clearly—is NO. Would I agree that prayer meant nothing to a child of three? If the stress is on the last word, I must be careful: I may be thinking of a child of four. All I can accurately say is that I can recall no occasion when this was so.

At this point a picture floats uninvited into my mind. Nothing that ever happened, nothing to do with my parents, purely imaginary. Papa and Mama in church. Both kneeling. Mama's mind, disconnected from her ears, hovering around the Sunday lunch. Papa, squinting through his fingers, studying the hats in the pew in front. No, it's not only the three year old whose thoughts wander.

I said earlier that I was going to have things out with **"Vespers".** Partly, I must confess, I wanted to get my own back. But there was another reason. This seems the appropriate moment to give credit where credit was due.

And of course credit lies with my Nanny.

She had me when I was very young. I was all hers and remained all hers until the age of nine. Other people hovered around the edges, but they meant little. My total loyalty was to her. To the extent that I was a "good little boy", to the extent that my prayers had real meaning for me at a very early age and continued to have meaning for many years afterwards, and to the extent that all this was something acquired rather than inherited, this was Nanny's doing. Was she a brilliant teacher? Not specially. She was just a very good and very loving person; and when that has been said, no more need be added.

It will now be apparent why, earlier, I disowned the conversation in **"Buckingham Palace".** This poem, too, gets mentioned in the Parents Preface. " 'Do you think the king knows all about me?' Could egotism be more gross?" I'm prepared to let that go, but not the line that follows:

> Sure to, dear, but it's time for tea.

Listen to Alice saying that: the daily routine clearly far more important for her than the child's question. You find the same thing in the poem **"Brownie".** Here are the last two lines of each verse. The child is speaking:

> I think it is a Brownie but I'm not quite certain
> (Nanny isn't certain, too)

and

> They wriggle off at once because they're all so tickly
> (Nanny says they're tickly, too)

What Nanny actually says on both occasions—and you can hear her saying it, not even pausing in her sewing, not even bothering to look up—is "That's right, dear". Undoubtedly, this is the Truth about Some Nannies. But, as I hope I've now made quite clear, NOT MINE. (pp. 30-2)

Some people are good with children. Others are not. It is a gift. You either have it or you don't. My father didn't—not with children, that is. Later on it was different, very different. But I am thinking of nursery days.

It was difficult for him, of course. For there was Nanny always in the way, Nanny who claimed so much of my affection. And on the rare occasions when Nanny was out of the room, there was my mother in her place. On Nanny's day off there was Gertrude looking after me. Where did he fit in? Nowhere special. And now here was Soldier [the actor Louis Goodrich]. You could see how my eyes lit up at the very thought of Soldier, at the mere men-

*Milne with Christopher Robin and Pooh, 1926. This portrait by Howard Costner is called "the best known of all the photographs of Milne" by biographer Ann Thwaite.*

tion of his name. You could see (or you could be told) how he made me laugh, how I adored him. No, my father couldn't compete. Did this make him, I wonder, a little jealous, a little sad? Did he secretly envy those who had the gift? My poor father! All that was left to him were family visits to the London Zoo or family walks through the Sussex woods, and perhaps a few brief minutes of goodnight story.

People sometimes say to me today: "How lucky you were to have had such a wonderful father!" imagining that because he wrote about me with such affection and understanding, he must have played with me with equal affection and understanding. Can this really be so totally untrue? Isn't this most surprising?

No, it is not really surprising, not when you understand.

There are two sorts of writer. There is the writer who is basically a reporter and there is the creative writer. The one draws on his experiences, the other on his dreams. My father was a creative writer and so it was precisely because he was *not* able to play with his small son that his longings sought and found satisfaction in another direction. He wrote about him instead. (p. 36)

I must now introduce the toys.

Pooh was the oldest, only a year younger than I was, and my inseparable companion. As you find us in the poem **"Us Two"**, so we were in real life. Every child has his favourite toy, and every only-child has a special need for one. Pooh was mine, and probably, clasped in my arms, not really very different from the countless other bears clasped in the arms of countless other children. From time to time he went to the cleaners, and from time to time ears had to be sewn on again, lost eyes replaced and paws renewed.

Eeyore, too, was an early present. Perhaps in his younger days he had held his head higher, but by the time the stories came to be written his neck had gone like that and this had given him his gloomy disposition. Piglet was a present from a neighbour who lived over the way, a present for the small boy she so often used to meet out walking with his Nanny. They were the three round which the stories began, but more characters were needed and so two were invented: Owl and Rabbit. Owl was owlish from the start and always remained so. But Rabbit, I suspect, began by being just the owner of the hole in which Pooh got stuck and then, as the stories went on, became less rabbity and more Rabbity; for rabbits are not by nature good organizers. Both Kanga and Tigger were later arrivals, presents from my parents, carefully chosen, not just for the delight they might give to their new owner, but also for their literary possibilities.

So there they were, and to a certain extent their characters were theirs from birth. As my father said, making it all sound very simple, you only had to look at them to see at once that Eeyore was gloomy, Piglet squeaky, Tigger bouncy and so on. But of course there was much more to it than that. Take bears, for example.

A row of Teddy bears sitting in a toyshop, all one size, all one price. Yet how different each is from the next. Some look gay, some look sad. Some look stand-offish, some look lovable. And one in particular, that one over there, has a specially endearing expression. Yes, that is the one we would like, please.

The bear took his place in the nursery and gradually he began to come to life. It started in the nursery; it started with me. It could really start nowhere else, for the toys lived in the nursery and they were mine and I played with them. And as I played with them and talked to them and gave them voices to answer with, so they began to breathe. But alone I couldn't take them very far. I needed help. So my mother joined me and she and I and the toys played together, and gradually more life, more character flowed into them, until they reached a point at which my father could take over. Then, as the first stories were written, the cycle was repeated. The Pooh in my arms, the Pooh sitting opposite me at the breakfast table, was a Pooh who had climbed trees in search of honey, who had got stuck in a rabbit hole, who was "a bear of no brain at all." . . .

Then Shepard came along, looked at the toy Pooh, read the stories and started drawing; and the Pooh who had been developing under my father's pen began to develop under Shepard's pen as well. You notice this if you compare the early Poohs in *Winnie the Pooh* with the later Poohs in *The House at Pooh Corner.* What is it that gives Pooh his particularly Poohish look? It is the position of his eye. The eye that starts as quite an elaborate affair level with the top of Pooh's nose, gradually moves downwards and ends up as a mere dot level with his mouth. And in this dot the whole of Pooh's character can be read.

That was how it happened. And when at last the final story had been written, my father, looking back over the seven years of Pooh's life, wrote his dedication. It was to my mother.

> You gave me Christopher Robin, and then
> You breathed new life in Pooh.
> Whatever of each has left my pen
> Goes homing back to you.
> My book is ready, and comes to greet
> The mother it longs to see—
> It would be my present to you, my sweet,
> If it weren't your gift to me.

In the last chapter of *The House at Pooh Corner* our ways part. I go on to become a schoolboy. A child and his bear remain playing in the enchanted spot at the top of the forest. The toys are left behind, no longer wanted, in the nursery. So a glass case was made for them and it was fastened to the nursery wall in Mallord Street, [Chelsea,] and they climbed inside. And there they lived, sometimes glanced at, mostly forgotten, until the war came. Roo was missing. He had been lost years before, in the apple orchard up the lane. And Piglet's face was a funny shape where a dog had bitten him. During the war they went to America and there they have been ever since. . . .

If you saw them today, your immediate reaction would be: "How old and battered and lifeless they look." But of course they are old *and* battered *and* lifeless. They are only toys and you are mistaking them for the real animals who lived in the forest. Even in their prime they were no more than a first rough sketch, the merest hint of what they were to become, and they are now long past their prime. Eeyore is the most recognizable; Piglet the least. So, if I am asked "Aren't you sad that the animals are not in their glass case with you today?" I must answer "Not really," and hope that this doesn't seem too unkind. I like to have around me the things I like today, not the things I once liked many years ago. I don't want a house to be a museum. When I grew out of my old First Eleven blazer, it was thrown away, not lovingly preserved to remind me of the proud day I won it with a score of 13 not out. Every child has his Pooh, but one would think it odd if every man still kept his Pooh to remind him of his childhood. But my Pooh is different, you say: he is *the* Pooh. No, this only makes him different to you, not different to me. My toys were and are to me no more than yours were and are to you. I do not love them more because they are known to children in Australia or Japan. Fame has nothing to do with love.

I wouldn't like a glass case that said: "Here is fame"; and I don't need a glass case to remind me: "Here was love". (pp. 76-9)

Every year brings its new batch of readers, meeting Christopher Robin and Pooh for the first time, learning that maybe Christopher Robin is a real live person and expecting him still to look like his picture. Even if you are wise enough to realize that the books were written a long time ago and that real live people grow up, you may still find yourself judging them by today's standards. It is easy to see that some of the verses in *When We Were Very Young* are now rather out of date. Nannies in uniforms are now more or less extinct. But attitudes as well as people change. If today's reader detects an air of snobbishness and class consciousness here and there it would be unfair to blame the author for this. My father was writing in the 1920s about the 1920s to entertain people living in the 1920s and these were the attitudes current at the time. Yet if Christopher Robin seems a rather odd little boy, in one respect he is now less odd than he once was. Today his long hair and curious clothes are very much in fashion. But at the time, when other little boys had short hair, shirts and ties, they were decidedly unusual. Was this Shepard's idea, or my father's—or whose?

First let me say that it had nothing to do with Shepard. It is true that he used his imagination when he drew the animals, but me he drew from life. I did indeed look just like that. And the reason I looked like that had nothing whatever to do with the books either. What the reason was I can only now guess. At the time I accepted it as I accepted nursery food. It was just part of life. And I was that sort of child: the sort that accepts things without question. Later on, when I was older, I might perhaps have asked; but a tactful moment combined with a sufficient interest in learning the answer never presented itself. And it is not really until today that I have found myself wondering. Too late now to know for sure, and so I must just try to piece together such clues as survive.

When a child is small it is his mother who is mainly responsible for the way he is brought up. So it was with me. I belonged in those days to my mother rather than to my father. He was busy writing. It was she who gave the instructions to Nanny. And so it was she who found the patterns and provided the material (leaving Nanny to do the actual sewing). It was she who outlined the hair-style (leaving Nanny to do the actual scissor-work). This I know. All the same, there could well have been consultation and discussion in the drawing-room—while I was in bed and Nanny was busy with the ironing—before decisions were made and orders were given. This I don't know. But I suspect that the result appealed equally to both my parents—though for quite different reasons. I suspect that, with my golden tresses, I reminded my mother of the girl she had always wanted to have. And I would have reminded my father of the boy with long, flaxen hair he once had been. Each reason—as I hope to show—would have been in character. And the second provides the key that unlocks the secret of the Pooh books. (pp. 94-6)

Not long ago I came upon a photograph of my father taken when he was about 18 years old and showing him with his brothers, Barry and Ken. I had not seen a photograph of my father as a young man before; and as for my uncles, I had no idea at all what they looked like, either then or at any other time; for I never met them. I wouldn't have met Barry: my father never even spoke of him. And Ken had died when I was eight. I knew my aunts Connie and Maud well enough and I knew my cousins; but of my uncles I knew only what my father's autobiography told me: that he had disliked Barry (though it was never made clear exactly why), and that—for reasons all too obvious—he had adored Ken. And now, seventy years after it had been taken, here was this photograph of the three of them. It was, in its small, private way, a dramatic meeting. It would have been that in any case, however indifferent the photograph. But the photograph was very far from being indifferent. It was eloquent beyond anything I had ever seen. It was not content to show me three young men. It told me all about them.

In a single snapshot everything that I knew about the three brothers was confirmed and much that I didn't know became clear. There in the middle is brother Barry. But can he really be their brother? Is he really a Milne? He looks so different. Everything about him is different from the other two. His hair is black and curly and parted in the middle. Theirs is fair and straight and parted on the side. Ken and Alan are dressed alike in dark suits and stiff white collars. Barry is wearing a Norfolk jacket and knick-

erbockers. And since there is only one chair, it is of course Barry who is sitting in it, leaving the others to stand on either side. They are clearly posing for their photograph, thinking it all a bit of a lark. "All right then, here we are, the three Milnes. Fire away and don't blame us if it breaks the camera." And you can see at a glance that Barry is Mephistopheles and that inside himself he is chuckling "Ho, ho, ho!" And Ken is St. George and inside himself he is laughing "Ha, ha, ha!" You feel you know both Barry and Ken and that if you were an artist your fingers would itch to put it all down on paper. But Alan? Alan is different. Alan is difficult. He is clearly Ken's man, dressed like Ken, looking like Ken, on Ken's side and so on the side of the angels. But Alan doesn't wear his heart on his sleeve as the others do. Alan's heart is firmly buttoned up inside his jacket and only the merest hint of it can be seen dancing in his eyes, flickering in the corners of his mouth. You can see now why Alan has always been so difficult to draw.

Difficult to draw, yet easy to photograph. Artists failed. Photographers—even unskilled amateur photographers—succeeded. What about writers? What about an unskilled amateur writer? Well, I must just do my best. Luckily I shan't be attempting anything too ambitious, certainly not a full length study, just a collection of snapshots.

My father's heart remained buttoned up all through his life, and I wouldn't want now to attempt to unbutton it, to write about the things he never spoke about. All I hope to do is to catch some of the overflow that came bubbling out and get it on to the page before it runs to waste. No more than that. (pp. 101-03)

My father wrote *It's Too Late Now* in 1938 when he was fifty-six. It is subtitled "The Autobiography of a Writer" but it isn't really that at all. It is the story of a boy. A third of the book covers only the first eleven years of his life: half the book the first eighteen years. (p. 158)

He wrote his autobiography to please himself. He is not telling the reader how he became a great writer. He is not boasting of his successes. He does not give us a list of the famous people he rubbed shoulders with. The Pooh books occupy only eight rather unhappy pages. No, he wrote his autobiography because it gave him an opportunity to return to his boyhood—a boyhood from which all his inspiration sprang. It was in a sense his last visit: for I was now eighteen.

Let me explain.

*When We Were Very Young* and *Now We Are Six:* the titles trip from the tongue and we scarcely pause to ask ourselves who exactly is meant by "we". It is, of course, the obvious pronoun. "He" might have done instead but would have been a bit limiting. "They" is a bit condescending. "I" and "you" are clearly wrong. So only "we" remains. But that still leaves the question "Who is we?". Is it the "we" with which so many adults address the young? "And how are we today?" Heaven forbid! Is it then the universal "we": all of us—for whatever our age now we were all young once? Possibly this was how it was meant to seem. But I guess that in his heart my father intended it for just two people: himself and his son.

My father, who had derived such happiness from his childhood, found in me the companion with whom he could return there. But with Nanny in the way he could only take his dream son and return in imagination—to mend a train or keep a dormouse or go fishing. When I was three he was three. When I was six he was six. We grew up side by side and as we grew so the books were written. Then when I was nine and he was nine Nanny left. We could now do real things together: reality could in part replace the dream. For the next nine years we continued to grow up alongside each other. I was not aware of this, of course. I just saw him as my father. But he, I now suspect, saw me as a sort of twin brother, perhaps a sort of reincarnation of Ken. I—as I have already mentioned—needed him. He no less but for a different reason needed me. He needed me to escape from being fifty. (pp. 158-59)

> *Christopher Milne, in his* The Enchanted Places, *E. P. Dutton & Co., Inc., 1975, 169 p.*

## Sam Leaton Sebesta and William J. Iverson

The ingredients of [*Winnie-the-Pooh* and *The House at Pooh Corner*] are deceptively simple. The characters lose something (a tail, a house) or search for something (a strange animal, the North Pole) or misunderstand each other or try simple strategies that never quite work. *Winnie-the-Pooh* is climaxed by a flood and *The House at Pooh Corner* by a windstorm, but even these potential disasters have the gentle feel of the nursery. Milne knew (before psychologists noted it) that early childhood thrives on small dangers quickly defeated by the reassertion of security. He knew (before language development specialists noted it) that "big" words and word play are more intriguing to the child than controlled vocabulary. He never paused to explain what Hostile Animals with Hostile Intent might be up to, nor did he straighten out Pooh's confusion between an Ambush and a gorse-bush. He left Pooh wondering if Woozle is the plural of Wizzle or the other way around. He knew that small children can relish the type of humor in which the reader knows something the characters don't know, even when the understanding can only be derived by inference.

Above all, Milne presented childhood respectfully but without sentimentality. His autobiography makes clear his belief that the child is grossly egotistical. It is something of a surprise to discover again, after this observation, that he presented childhood with such tenderness.

Critics aren't all at ease with the Pooh books. . . . We place [Milne] here beside Nesbit, Grahame, and de la Mare without the slightest hesitation or apology. Surely most readers will know why. (pp. 191-92)

> *Sam Leaton Sebesta and William J. Iverson, "Fanciful Fiction; Color Portfolio of Picture Books, Folk Literature, and Fanciful Fiction," in their* Literature for Thursday's Child, *Science Research Associates, Inc., 1975, pp. 177-214.*

## Marcus Crouch

It will come as a surprise to no one to realise that Pooh is fifty years old this year. He was always middle aged, just as he was clearly middle class. He had the middle-aged muddled brain, as well as the middle-aged—and middle-class—knack of being useful in a crisis. His is the resourcefulness which appears, and often is, unpremeditated. Look how he discovered—more properly 'dicsovered'—that North Pole. . . . Pooh is part of the permanent literary landscape. Life without him is beyond imagining, and even those fortunates coming to him for the first time recognise him as an old friend. (p. 253)

*Pooh* and the two books of verse are often put with *Alice* and *The Wind in the Willows* among the books which began as the private experience of a particular audience and only afterwards found their way into the outside world. It is not quite true of Milne. The stories would not have taken quite this form if Christopher Robin had not owned a family of battered stuffed toys, just as Milne wrote 'Vespers' from the living model. But Milne, unlike Carroll and Grahame, was the complete professional writer. He probably shared Dr. Johnson's view of writers who write except for money. Most of the verses were written as a conscious exercise with book-production in mind, and if the Pooh stories were evolved at bedtime for a child's amusement there could have been little doubt about their ultimate destination. There is no sign in them of an improvisatory quality as in—say—Linklater's *Wind on the Moon*. A craftsman is always clearly at work, modelling, balancing, developing. The two books are episodic, as befits their bedtime-story origin and function, but each chapter can be taken entirely seriously—in critical terms—as a short story. They have the economy, the selectivity and the 'punch' of their peers in the world of 'adult' literature.

We have Milne's own evidence that this was not accidental. Writing, it is true, about the verse books, but the words are equally relevant to the stories, he says that they are "the work of a light-verse writer taking his job seriously even though he is taking it into the nursery. It seems that the nursery, more than any other room in the house, likes to be approached seriously". Here . . . is a fundamental statement of the proper role of the children's writer. Part of the reader's response to the Pooh stories is an unconscious reaction to perfection, to the exquisite balance of phrase and thought, character and action which marks the master. No child and few adults have ever said that they like Pooh for his style, but in both senses it is nevertheless true. There are other reasons. There is the observation. Milne says of the toys, "They were what they are for anyone to see; I described rather than invented them". This may be so, but it is the angle from which Milne observes them that makes them memorable. Then there is the humour which, like much of the author's work, is quite literally good enough for *Punch*. In one real sense the stories are not funny. No one of the characters laughs at another, and the reader is not encouraged to laugh either. There is no room here for either the belly laugh or the snigger. It is not the incident or even the word which is funny, but the concept, the philosophy of Pooh, and this produces not the laugh but the warm inner glow. When we laugh at characters it is usually because they are ridiculous and we feel superior. Christopher Robin calls Pooh "silly old Bear", but he knows, and we know, that Pooh is not silly at all.

Some of the appeal of the stories comes from the completeness of the enclosed world in which they are told. It would be as absurd to call this 'escapism' as to deplore the social privilege of the Pooh household. *We* are privileged to enter the forest where Piglet lives under the name of Trespassers W, to play pooh-sticks vicariously, and to share the perils of the flood. The stories speak irresistibly to the countryman struggling to get out of the most urban of children. (pp. 254-55)

Here's to Pooh, . . . obviously destined to go on living as long as words endure and children love fun and feel affection. Pooh lives! most definitely O.K. (p. 255)

> *Marcus Crouch, "Pooh Lives—O.K?" in* The Junior Bookshelf, *Vol. 40, No. 5, October, 1976, pp. 252-55.*

### Ellen Tremper

[In her essay "Now We Are Fifty,"] Alison Lurie points out that Eeyore is bitter about Education because he realizes, as does the reader who comes to the last chapter of **The House at Pooh Corner,** that it signals the end of Eden; for knowledge and education are the very things that will lure Christopher Robin out of the "enchanted place," the Forest. She writes: "No wonder many readers weep when they read the last chapter of this book. They know that they too have lost their childhood paradise." But her note of wistful nostalgia fails to account for an important aspect of the books . . .—their adult humor. It seems to me no accident that it should be Eeyore who opens the subject of education and knowledge, for witty Eeyore (who was *never* a child) is the most adultly humorous of the animals. We can extend the obvious theological metaphor of the loss of Eden by considering it from a more positive perspective; that is, viewing it as some theologians have, as "the fortunate fall." With our adult knowledge of what we missed in childhood through ignorance and inexperience, indeed, with our knowledge of what we would miss in our reading of the **Pooh** books if we were children again, we cannot regret our banishment from Paradise. Hindsight teaches us that our grown-up appreciation of Eeyore's wit and Pooh's artless artfulness—appreciation that comes only through knowledge—is the prize A. A. Milne awards us for having left, as our first Parents did, "[ . . . our] happy seat," to find "The World was all before [ . . . us]." (p. 44)

> *Ellen Tremper, "Instigorating 'Winnie the Pooh'," in* The Lion and the Unicorn, *Vol. 1, No. 1, 1977, pp. 33-46.*

### Roger Sale

[In his Babar stories, Jean de Brunhoff] allies child and adult so that each can arrive at the same place by a somewhat different route. With Dr. Seuss my adult pleasure is only a replica of my childhood pleasure; with de Brunhoff the two pleasures are somewhat different, since I do see more in his books than I did as a child, but they are never in conflict with each other.

With A. A. Milne, on the other hand, I really am not able to read as I once could. I loved the Christopher Robin books, but find only intermittent pleasure in them now,

and when they fail to cast their old magic spell, I am not just bored but offended. As a child listening to and staring at the Babar books, I trusted the relation I was enacting with the adult doing the reading, because the adult was not trying to ask me to respond any differently than I was. But the adult reader of Christopher Robin implicitly seeks more with the child being read to than that. The adult is explicitly put in the position of Milne himself, the child in the position of Christopher Robin: "you" and "I," the text says clearly. This might be all right, or even fun, except that Milne is always nudging Christopher Robin, instructing him, urging upon him good manners and good spelling and obedience, and this makes it hard on me as an adult reader. It may also explain why many children, after they become old enough to read to themselves, don't read these books, because so much in them depends on the relation of reader and read-to, adult and child.

Let me begin with a passage from **Winnie-the-Pooh** that shows Milne at close to his worst, being really quite offensive:

> "We are all going on an Expedition," said Christopher Robin, as he got up and brushed himself. "Thank you, Pooh."
>
> "Going on an Expotition?" said Pooh eagerly. "I don't think I've ever been on one of those. Where are we going to on this Expotition?"
>
> "Expedition, silly old Bear. It's got an 'x' in it."
>
> "Oh!" said Pooh, "I know." But he didn't really.
>
> "We're going to discover the North Pole."
>
> "Oh!" said Pooh again. "What *is* the North Pole?" he asked.
>
> "It's just a thing you discover," said Christopher Robin carelessly, not being quite sure himself.

Here, as all too often in Milne, the essential action is to construct a hierarchy, to calculate one's superiority to someone else and then worry about who is superior to oneself. Pooh can't say or spell "expedition"; he knows it and Christopher Robin knows it, so Pooh is a "silly old Bear." Christopher Robin can say the word, can hear the "x" in it, but can't spell it, just as he can know the North Pole exists, and that people discover it, but nothing else about it. Milne forces his child reader or listener into one of two uncomfortable positions. If the child isn't old enough to spot the defects in Christopher Robin's learning, he can at least laugh at Pooh, since even a young child can hear the difference between "expotition" and "expedition." If the child can spot the defects in Christopher Robin's learning he can laugh at him as well. In either case he must agree that it is important to know how to spell "expedition," which it isn't, and to know a lot about the North Pole, which it isn't either, and to rank boys and bears according to how much they know, which is not only not important but fraudulent and shallow snobbery.

But we don't have to try to defend this shallow snobbery by calling its putative fun innocent; there is a lot that is real fun in the Pooh books. Whenever I've taught them to university undergraduates we have fought a good deal, be-

*Christopher with his nanny Olive Rand and the original Piglet.*

cause the students really like Milne. When I state my objections to him, they are offended: who would want to unload such heavy machinery on such sweet books? When we sort matters out, two facts emerge: they like these books better at twenty-odd than they did as children, and what they enjoy are the parts of the books that are most relaxed, lazy, and cozy, that is, Pooh's hums, especially "The more it snows, tiddely pom" and "I could spend a happy morning seeing Roo"; Pooh when he is alone with Piglet, and Piglet any time; the jokes against Owl; Eeyore's gloominess; and Poohsticks. To isolate these parts of the books as what one cares about is to treat the Forest as Utopia, so that someone speaking harshly about the books is put in the position of one who is announcing it is time to leave Utopia.

What my students see is really there and is really what is best about the books, but the Forest is no Utopia. The books are essentially about the fact that Christopher Robin is now too old to play with toy bears. He is given a world over which he has complete power, and if he is not very attractive as a deus-ex-machina in story after story, if he is never as interesting as the Pooh and Piglet to whom he condescends, the pleasures of his power are clear enough. Christopher Robin is now going to school, doing sums, spelling, worrying about not getting things right; he takes his fear of ridicule and his need to fit into a hierarchy and his schoolboy facts and imposes them on the animals

in the Forest. Pooh is not, of course, a bear of very little brain, but Christopher Robin keeps putting him in situations where he will think he is, which is just what, one imagines, others are doing to Christopher Robin in his hours away from the Forest. Thus the alliance Milne seeks to create with Christopher Robin, whatever we may say of its entanglements otherwise, shrewdly seeks to console Christopher Robin for the pains of having had to leave the Forest. Children, certainly myself as a child, are much more interested than students of college age in learning about the ways it is sad, but all right, that we grow beyond early childhood, and even the snobbish Milne offers the assurance that we are growing toward something as well as growing away from something else.

Whatever of all this I may have understood as a child of Christopher Robin's age, I do know that Milne's most explicit statement of this theme, which comes in the closing sentences of *The House at Pooh Corner,* always moved me very much. It has come time for Christopher Robin to say good-bye to the Forest forever, and he takes Pooh up to the top of the Forest and dubs him Sir Pooh de Bear. Then:

> So they went off together. But wherever they go, and whatever happens to them on the way, in that enchanted place on the top of the Forest, a little boy and his Bear will always be playing.

I do not think it particularly sentimental of me that I still find it hard to say these words without beginning to cry, though I am aware that my tears are for the lost boy I was who also once wept over them. The lies they tell are known to be lies, and that saves everything. Pooh and Christopher Robin do not go away together, and we know it. The Forest is forever closed, except to the memory, and that is not a sentimental fact.

What I never saw as a child, but see in many places now, is that the Forest is becoming tainted long before it is closed by the alien values of Christopher Robin's and Milne's world. The animals are forever deferring and being asked to defer. Pooh and Piglet in clumsy ways, and Rabbit and Owl in more knowing and stupider ways, want to manage and control, to imitate Christopher Robin. That much is perhaps inevitable in most societies, but what makes it all painful is that Milne's view of schoolboy and adult life is so limited and empty, and his view of women, as seen in his digs at Kanga, is at the very least designed to foster the notion in Christopher Robin that one grows up by finding mothers silly and fussy. Even when Christopher Robin is at his best, as when he announces that the stick in Pooh's hand is the North Pole, he is still finding ways to control others by hiding his own ignorance. Candor is generally a fugitive and discardable virtue in the Forest, except, I must hasten to add, for Eeyore. He is, though not just for that reason, the one character I enjoy now even more than I did as a child, and his jibes at Rabbit at the end of the game of Poohsticks still make me want to clap, with surprise at Eeyore's sudden burst of healthy bad temper and with delight that the neofascist Rabbit is finally told off. But for the rest, the pleasures seem to me awfully thin, or else worse. (pp. 15-18)

*Roger Sale, in an introduction to his* Fairy

Tales and After: From Snow White to E. B. White, *Cambridge, Mass.: Harvard University Press, 1978, pp. 1-22.*

## Christopher Milne

What was the truth about my father? (p. 246)

The great scientist Sir Arthur Eddington once described man as "a kind of four-dimensional worm," meaning that he occupied a small volume of space but had considerable extension—seventy-odd years—in time. Elaborating a little on this picture, I see man as a kind of four-dimensional marine bristle worm—the sort that can unfurl a crown of long, waving, threadlike tentacles from the top of its head. The body of the worm is the factual truth about the man. Each thread as it touches someone becomes their personal truth. The tentacles that range on either side of the worm's body are those personal truths established during the man's lifetime. Those that stretch ahead are those truths that will be established after his death as people in the years ahead are touched by his life. Every child who, at some future date, reads about Pooh—whether in the original text or in translation or even in Disney's version—will be holding a personal truth about my father. Disney's Pooh may have little resemblance to the original Pooh, but this in no way affects the matter or makes this personal truth less truthful. Should it ever happen that the supporters of Shepard went to war with the supporters of Disney, this might be regrettable. People might die. But Truth would not. (pp. 247-48)

*Christopher Milne, in his* The Path through the Trees, *E. P. Dutton, 1979, 268 p.*

## Stephen Canham

[In *Winnie-the-Pooh,* it] is not difficult to recognize in Pooh a manifestation of the child's hunger, the incessant compulsion to check on the refrigerator just to see how it's doing, to see if there might be a little something in it that needs eating. He is more: I think he can be seen as a way of representing the child's body, the physical self to which the energy and excitement of the child is attached. Pooh is forever getting into tight places, into places where he doesn't fit, such as rabbit burrows and honey pots. Shepard's illustrations . . . capture the precarious balance of the bear body, the often awkward, often stumbling corporeal self. . . . [If *Winnie-the-Pooh*] does anything, it assures the child that this body, this hunger, is quite all right and perfectly normal, even wonderful and lovely. After all, we are asked, in order to make Pooh live, to love him in the same way that Christopher Robin loves him, to accept him in a bear hug that both recognizes and fulfills him, to acknowledge that his is a practical way to go about life. In the Introduction, Christopher Robin, finding that special cage in the zoo where you can experience the animals, not just watch them, rushes into the arms of one beloved bear with "a happy cry of 'Oh, Bear!' " This is what we too must do, what all children must learn, to accept and love the embrace of the body.

Pooh seems to move from a concern for himself and his forging toward a concern for others (such as Eeyore) and in the end is able to act decisively and intelligently to help his companions in the Hundred Acre Wood. The pattern is clear and constant: with Christopher Robin's loving reassurance, the bear of very little brain gradually moves toward an incredulous but proud recognition of his own capacities, a fuller sense of what he is and what he can do. In the next-to-last chapter, "Surrounded by Water," Christopher Robin does not need to rescue Pooh, for the paradigm can now be inverted, allowing Pooh to provide a clever means for the two of them to rescue Piglet. When we recall that he has already discovered a pole and saved Roo, his actions here seem even more significant. He is beginning to act, to think, to go beyond the fundamental, infantile "body first, all others after" premise of very young children and very immature adults. And notice too that at the end he is acting in consort with Christopher Robin, that together, at Pooh's instigation and idea, they sail off in the "Brain of Pooh."

Christopher Robin, of course, is more than the mental faculties of the child, just as Pooh is more than "the heavy bear who goes with me [, the first line of Delmore Schwartz's poem of the same name]." But Christopher Robin does show us the child's ability to sort things out, to make sense out of the world, and finally, crucially, to come into harmony with one's own body, to gain a sense of wonder at it, to love it and celebrate it. The eternal dichotomy of body and mind is here resolved quietly, beautifully, and with great sensitivity. Just as the child, for all of his or her occasional difficulty and frustration with the limitations of a developing form, can rise to moments of splendid grace and beauty, so does the book, for all of Pooh's misadventures, in the end go beyond them to a consoling and reassuring celebration of the bear within and around us. (pp. 26-7)

*Stephen Canham, "Reassuring Readers: 'Winnie-the-Pooh'," in* Children's Literature Association Quarterly, *Vol. 5, No. 3, Fall, 1980, pp. 1, 25-7.*

## Carol A. Stanger

What . . . is the appeal of the Pooh books for females? (p. 40)

The stories affirm female fantasies, attitudes, values, and sympathize in a comforting way with female anxieties. First, there is the powerful fantasy of the semiotic world, which, as Kristeva notes . . . , is tied up with the mother's body; of the possibility of resisting socialization into a male-centered culture and a masculine role which does not allow space or time "to do Nothing."

Second, the stories respect what is traditionally given low status in patriarchal society, nurturing and emotion. For example, in response to Eeyore's disillusionment with male knowledge—"What is Learning?". . . . "A thing Rabbit knows! Ha!"—Piglet gives Eeyore a bunch of violets because he thought "how sad it was to be an Animal who never had a bunch of violets picked for him".

Third, there is the attitude best represented by Pooh of accepting the physical side of oneself: whenever he feels a "little eleven o' clockish," he responds to his urges. Interestingly, that fact endears the character to the reader because Pooh's attitude is not to rank order the intellectual over the physical, a hierarchical state of mind that has a long history in androcentric culture. In spite of Milne's satirizing of Kanga's maternal acts, the stories basically accept physicality. Perhaps Milne was able to portray such acceptance despite his own discomfort (as suggested by his irritation with Tigger's lack of physical restraint), by making Christopher's defining trait his mind and Pooh's his physicality. In other words, instead of creating one round character—integrating the mind and the body—Milne draws two flat characters—splitting the mind from the body. The hidden function of this split in the stories may be to allow Christopher to be less earthy by projecting the animal aspects of human nature onto Pooh. One of the paradoxes of the Pooh characterization is that it celebrates the physical at the same time it devalues it: Pooh, the honey-eater, is the most loveable character in the books, but, nevertheless, a bear "of very little brain." Even as a poet, Pooh operates from the physical side, not from the intellectual: his hums, like baby talk, express the instinct to make noise.

Finally, the stories express the anxieties of the female reader. For both feminist and non-feminist women, the cost of living in a patriarchy as an inferior, as an "Other," is—at the very least—a great deal of anxiety. The Pooh stories help women escape these effects of sexism by raising the possibility of an eventual return to a kinder, more humanistic time. In his "Contradiction," the author assures us that "it isn't really Good-bye, because the Forest will always be there . . . and anybody who is Friendly with Bears can find it". In effect, the author is saying that the grown child can return to the semiotic world, the world of the mother.

But the structure of both books militates against ever freeing one's self from [what the French psychoanalyst Lacan calls] the Name-of-the-Father. After all, the author tries hard to control the interpretation of his literary work. For example, he made the artistic decision to narrate the stories himself and assimilate the maternal role. And he also takes great pains to remind Christopher and the reader of his authority as the author, his paternity of both text and protagonist, and of the unity he wants in his stories. . . . Milne, who despised the demands of realism that critics made on him, was probably unaware of the hidden ideology of male dominance, sexual ideology, that ties the Pooh stories together. Sexual ideology [, in the words of K. K. Rothven,] "operates by repressing what is repressible and displacing what is not, thus producing false resolutions of manifest contradictions in our society". In the Pooh stories, women are out of sight, and England, an ancient patriarchal society, is displaced by the Hundred Acre Wood. Milne creates, in effect, an all-male Eden, a pre-sexual and pre-literate world. Nonetheless, there is a great deal for women and girls to like in the Pooh stories, such as their respect for domesticity and close friendship, and Milne's empathy for the sadness of Christopher's initiation into the world of men. (pp.46-8)

> Carol A. Stanger, "'Winnie the Pooh' Through a Feminist Lens," in The Lion and the Unicorn, Vol. 11, 1987, pp. 34-50.

**Humphrey Carpenter**

[Milne] might well have become a professional mathema-

tician, like Lewis Carroll. . . . [As] with Carroll, Milne's humour is that of a mathematician. Each humorous situation in the Pooh books is reached by the logical pursuit of an idea to the point of absurdity. Pooh and Piglet, tracking a Woozle, are in fact following their own footprints round and round the same tree. They dig a trap for Heffalumps and therefore assume that a Heffalump must have been trapped in it. The North Pole is sought, and a pole is duly found, so it must be the right one. There is a mathematical simplicity in such stories very different from, say, the predominantly social comedy of Beatrix Potter's stories, or the humour deriving from the absurd psychology of Toad. Pooh's world is like Alice's in another respect too: people change their shape or their function somewhat unpredictably, and this is treated with an alarming coolness. In the very first story Pooh decides to turn himself into a cloud in order to obtain a honeycomb; later he becomes stuck in Rabbit's hole, and so Rabbit uses his legs as a convenient towel-horse; later still Eeyore's tail is discovered doing duty as Owl's bell-rope. Objects change their nature too, and just as disconcertingly. Eeyore's birthday presents—a pot of honey and a balloon—turn into an empty jar and a burst fragment, and are perfectly acceptable to Eeyore in this form. And there are Alice-like crises of identity: Piglet pretends to be Roo, and when the deception is discovered cannot get his own name back.

> 'There you are!' said Piglet. 'I told you so. I'm Piglet.'
>
> Christopher Robin shook his head again.
>
> 'Oh, you're not Piglet,' he said. 'I know Piglet well, and he's *quite* a different colour.'

Any plan embarked upon is likely to produce precisely the opposite consequences from those intended. Rabbit, Piglet, and Pooh set out to 'lose' Tigger in the forest, and as a result become lost themselves. The benevolent plan to build a house for Eeyore results in the destruction of the shelter he has just made for himself. This is not quite the world of Nonsense, but it is something very close. (pp. 192-93)

'Vespers' [from *When We Were Very Young*], with its refrain 'Christopher Robin is saying his prayers', is the last major appearance in English writing of the Beautiful Child, who by the 1920s had been dominating attitudes to children for nearly half a century. The poem appears at first to subscribe entirely to the Beautiful Child myth, with its description of the 'little gold head' drooping 'on the little hands'. But the Little Boy who 'kneels at the foot of the bed' is not quite so simple or late-Victorian a figure as that. The reader cannot be expected to know that Milne himself does not believe in the God to whom the child is praying—though of course that knowledge affects one's view of the poem. But the point of the poem is that Christopher Robin is *not* praying. He occasionally repeats one of the formulas he has been taught: '*God bless Mummy. I know that's right.*' But immediately he is distracted by something of real interest: '*Wasn't it fun in the bath tonight?*' The poem is in fact veiled ridicule of the whole business of formal prayers, the 'set phrases . . . words which reach no higher than a child's mind', against which Milne rails in his autobiography.

The prayers (suggests the poem) are meaningless to the child, compared to the real things in his life—hot baths, dressing-gowns, and the like. And the poem is also a negation of the very image around which it seems to be centred, the Beautiful Child. Christopher Robin may have a 'little gold head', but he is no angel. Milne does not believe that 'Heaven lies about us in our infancy'; the child in **'Vespers'**, far from having an unsullied perception of the divine, cannot turn his attention from the mundane to the spiritual.

Milne felt very strongly that the Wordsworthian view of childhood was completely wrong. He said so, eloquently and at length, in a 'Preface to Parents' appended to an edition of his children's verses. In this essay he accepts that 'very young children have an artless beauty' which leads adults to suppose that 'Heaven . . . does really . . . lie about the child'. But he argues that this 'outstanding physical quality' is accompanied by 'a natural lack of moral quality, which expresses itself, as Nature always insists on expressing herself, in an egotism entirely ruthless'. The penultimate verse of **'Vespers'** is intended to portray exactly this child-egotism:

> Oh! *Thank you, God, for a lovely day.*
> And what was the other I had to say?
> I said 'Bless Daddy,' so what can it be?
> Oh! Now I remember it. *God bless me.*

There was in a sense no need for 'Beachcomber' (J. B. Morton) to parody the poem, not long after it had first appeared ('Hush, hush, nobody cares, / Christopher Robin has fallen downstairs'). **'Vespers'** itself is intended to be an entirely ironic picture of childhood, a rather sarcastic nudge at adults who insist on viewing children as heavenly beings. In fact the irony was not generally perceived, and the poem was taken at face value as a sentimental portrayal of childhood. Milne's perceptions about childish egotism were not a little ahead of their time.

**'Vespers'** is the nearest Milne came to making a positive statement of belief or philosophy in his writings for children. Placed at the very beginning of them, it is a manifesto of what is to come. We will be shown children, and a childhood world, of considerable physical beauty, but this beauty will be a camouflage for ruthless egotism. To put it another way, children may be Arcadians in their physical appearance, but the Arcadia they inhabit is not an ideal world of fine feelings, not a dream-come-true land at all. It is distinguished by the naked selfishness of its inhabitants.

This is the theme that Milne worked out, first in his children's poems and then in the **Winnie-the-Pooh** stories.

The first collection of poems, **When We Were Very Young**, explores the theme tentatively. Its portrayal of childhood owes a lot to Robert Louis Stevenson's *Child's Garden of Verses,* and many of Milne's poems in the book are simply Stevensonian explorations of the childish imagination without any distinguishing mark of Milne other than his extraordinary facility with rhyme and metre, acquired from years of writing *Punch* verses. Several pieces even indulge the contemporary taste for fairy poetry, for example **'Twinkletoes',** which describes a fairy flitting from flower to flower. Nevertheless, the book also contains Milne's first sustained explorations of the 'ruthless egotism' of childhood.

The best known poem in it after **'Vespers'** is **'Buckingham Palace',** in which the two first lines of each verse are

> They're changing guard at Buckingham Palace—
> Christopher Robin went down with Alice.

The poem is an account of the child's perception of the adult world. This is filtered through Alice-the-nanny's own view of it, which is as remote from reality as is the boy's. Each of them, child and nanny, is concerned to find a place for himself or herself in the scheme of what they see. We are told at the outset that 'Alice is marrying one of the guard', and at the end Christopher Robin asks 'Do you think the King knows all about *me?*' The poem is framed by these two pieces of egotism; Alice and Christopher Robin are only interested in Buckingham Palace for what it can give *them.* In between, the poem is made up of the child's statements of what he has seen, with the nanny responding antiphonally. Ostensibly she is bringing him down to earth and is giving a more sophisticated view of things. In reality she is only replacing his childish view with hers:

> We saw a guard in a sentry-box.
> 'One of the sergeants looks after their socks,'
>                     Says Alice.
>
> We looked for the King, but he never came.
> 'Well, God take care of him, all the same,'
>                     Says Alice.
>
> They've great big parties inside the grounds.
> 'I wouldn't be King for a hundred pounds,'
>                     Says Alice.
>
> A face looked out, but it wasn't the King's.
> 'He's much too busy a-signing things,'
>                     Says Alice.

'Says Alice': the phrase carries echoes of the contemptuous 'Says you'. And, of course, the narrator's voice—Milne's own—is in the end rather contemptuous of Alice's spiritual short-sight. She has reduced the King and his court conveniently to her own level, and is even claiming a kind of responsibility for him (' "Well, God take care of him" '). To put it another way, the poem is taking a gently mocking look at the child's and nanny's universe, which appears to be a cosy hierarchy of (from the bottom upwards) Christopher Robin—Alice—the guards—the King—God. Christopher Robin and Alice have remade the King in their own image, just as Milne believed that all religion is man-made. The poem appears to be a celebration of security, just as **'Vespers'** appears to be a celebration of a child praying; both poems are in fact deeply mocking, and in **'Buckingham Palace'** the mockery is more obvious, for the poem ends with a ruthless assertion of egotism by both protagonists:

> 'Do you think the King knows all about *me?*'
> 'Sure to, dear, but it's time for tea,'
>                     Says Alice.

Alice panders to Christopher Robin's own egotism, then

obstinately reasserts her own world-view—'It's time for tea'.

Egotism is the predominant theme in all the best poems in the book. In **'Lines and Squares'** the child views the London pavements as existing solely for the possibility of offering him adventure: if he treads on the lines between the paving stones the bears will eat him. In **'Market Square'** he determines to buy a rabbit, and dismisses the entire market as valueless because it cannot provide one; finally, seeing rabbits all around him on the common, he expresses sheer pity for the market people, ' 'Cos they haven't got a rabbit, not anywhere there!' The Zoo is seen in similarly self-centred terms; the poem **'At the Zoo'** has the refrain 'But *I* gave buns to the elephant when *I* went down to the Zoo!' The marvellous comic narrative **'The King's Breakfast'** presents a childlike monarch who, just like a four-year-old, has his day ruined when he is denied the particular thing he wants to eat. (pp. 196-99)

And the most accomplished piece in **When We Were Very Young**, **'Disobedience'**, is both the sharpest and the funniest expression of Milne's belief in the 'ruthless egotism' of children.

A small boy—'James James / Morrison Morrison / Weatherby George Dupree'—has frequently warned his mother: 'You must never go down to the end of the town, if you don't go down with me.' She disobeys, and is never seen again. So far, the poem's comedy lies in the simple reversal of parent-child roles. But now we learn of the child's reaction—he 'Told his / Other relations / Not to go blaming *him*', and it is implied that he agrees with the King's view on the matter: ' "If people go down to the end of the town, well, what can *anyone* do?" ' In the 'Preface to Parents' in which he discusses the ruthlessness of children, Milne himself picks on this poem in particular as expressing what he is talking about, and says of it: 'It is the truth about a child: children are, indeed, as heartless as that.' Whether he was right must remain a matter for conjecture; Christopher Milne thought not, and wrote in his autobiography that, in circumstances such as James James Morrison Morrison's, at the age of three, he 'might not have missed my mother' and 'would certainly not have missed my father' (a nice backhander at the poem's author), but 'would have missed Nanny—most desolately'.

Right or wrong in its portrayal of childhood, **When We Were Very Young** caught the imagination of a public beginning to be sated with Peter Pan and the fairy-fashion, and the book was bought in quantities. It went through twelve printings in just over a year and brought Milne a fame which, despite all his apparent successes, had really deserted him up to that time.

He followed it with **Now We Are Six,** which explores the same theme with increased confidence but slightly less subtlety. The tone of the book is summed up by the last poem in it, which concludes:

> But now I am Six, I'm as clever as clever.
> So I think I'll be six now for ever and ever.

There are good things in **Now We Are Six**—among them the blackly comic **'King John's Christmas'**, in which (as in **'The King's Breakfast'**) an adult is portrayed as a selfish child, and **'The Knight Whose Armour Didn't Squeak'**, in which, again, an adult gets away with utterly selfish behaviour that would be condemned in the young. But the book has about it the air of a sequel, of writing to please an audience that knew what to expect. In fact, by the time it appeared Milne had already moved on from these comparatively simple examinations of 'ruthless egotism' to constructing a world peopled exclusively by egotists. . . .

[The] process of reliving childhood may have encouraged Milne to acquire, in 1925, a Sussex farmhouse for use as a weekend and holiday alternative to the family's London home. . . . To anyone of imagination, certainly to Christopher and his father, it was a true Enchanted Place.

And, being so idyllic, it provided the perfect ironic backdrop to the foolish, short-sighted goings on among the toys described in **Winnie-the-Pooh** and **The House at Pooh Corner.** As a setting it is as Arcadian as Grahame's River Bank and Barrie's Never Never Land, but the happenings it witnesses are much closer to those of Beatrix Potter's Sawrey. Milne, indeed, does not even allow his animal characters the breadth of personality that is to be found in the pages of Potter. Peter Rabbit, Tom Kitten, Tommy Brock, and Samuel Whiskers are each a composite of many (human) characteristics. Milne, writing about his son's toys, reverted to an older type of animal story, the fable as practised by Aesop and his many imitators. Milne claimed to be an admirer of *The Wind in the Willows,* but his use of animals (or toy animals) as representatives of human character could scarcely be more different from Grahame's. Pooh, Piglet, and Eeyore exist on a completely different plane from Rat, Mole, and Badger. Grahame's animals are subtle, many layered expressions of their author's ideals. The Pooh toys are as simple and predictable as Milne could make them. The narrative derives not as in Grahame from the characters' gradual discovery of each other's true nature, but from the conjunction and opposition of known quantities. No one, not even the comparatively imaginative Pooh, changes or develops as the story progresses. Christopher Robin gradually grows up, and will eventually leave them (thereby, one imagines, making their continued existence impossible), but this is something of which they remain blithely unaware. In a sense there is no 'story' as such, only a set of incidents which could be put in almost any order. One notes that Milne was brought up on *Uncle Remus;* he claimed not to have been influenced by it, but in construction his work has strong resemblances to Joel Chandler Harris's fable collection.

In 1964 there appeared Frederick C. Crews's book *The Pooh Perplex,* a collection of brilliant parodies of different schools of literary criticism, all taking **Winnie-the-Pooh** for their text. Crew's choice of Milne's work for this exercise was shrewd: trying to analyse the Pooh stories is really futile from the start, because they are almost entirely without layers of secondary meaning. They are exercises in the humorist's art, and almost nothing else. Yet (though to say it puts one in danger of seeming like one of the Crews parodies) there *is* a little more to them than this. They are, in fact, a continuing exposition of Milne's favourite themes: the selfishness or 'ruthless egotism' of childhood, and humanity's dependence on a God made in its own image.

Pooh, Piglet, and the other toys are really a family of children living their lives under the benevolently watchful eye of a parent-figure, Christopher Robin. This, of course, is exactly how real children treat their toys, exercising over them the domination that they themselves have to suffer from their parents. But, in the sense that the Pooh stories are about human character, Milne is not interested in portraying parental behaviour. All his satire is reserved for the 'children'—Pooh, Piglet, Eeyore, Rabbit, Owl, Kanga and baby Roo, and Tigger. Each of them personifies one characteristic, one type of selfishness. Pooh puts his appetite for honey before everything, and his chief interest in life is the possibility of obtaining 'a little something at eleven o'clock in the morning' (his clock at home is stuck at five minutes to eleven, like the pub clock in *Under Milk Wood,* which always shows opening time). Piglet is only concerned to save his own skin, and is prey to every possible fear: he does his best to get out of every Woozle-hunt or Heffalump-trapping on some paltry excuse. . . . Eeyore is self-pity taken to such an extent that it can provoke only ridicule: ' "And how are you?" said Winnie-the-Pooh. Eeyore shook his head from side to side. "Not very how," he said. "I don't seem to have felt at all how for a long time." ' Tigger is exuberance and *bonhomie* so unbridled that they become a kind of aggression towards other people; Rabbit is bossiness exercised for its own sake: 'It was going to be one of Rabbit's busy days. As soon as he woke up he felt important, as if everything depended on him.' Owl is self-respect for one's own (non-existent)

cleverness. . . . [All] the characters in the Pooh books are children in their ways of reacting to the world; only the motherly Kanga has predominantly adult characteristics, and she seems to have been included in the stories so that, in her company, the other apparently grown-up characters can be seen as the children they really are. . . . The only real adult in Pooh's world is Christopher Robin: a nicely ironic inversion which puts a neat frame round the stories. But his interventions in the narrative are not usually those of a parent sorting out unruly children: instead, Milne makes him step in as a *deus ex machina,* and appoints him not merely as adult in charge, but as God. On more than one occasion he observes Pooh's muddles *from high up*— sitting in a branch of a tree—and when he comes down, to make all well again, he does so chiefly through expressions of *love:*

> Then Piglet saw what a Foolish Piglet he had been, and he was so ashamed of himself that he ran straight off home and went to bed with a headache. But Christopher Robin and Pooh went home to breakfast together.
>
> 'Oh, Bear!' said Christopher Robin. 'How I do love you!'
>
> 'So do I,' said Pooh.

Note the ambiguity in Pooh's 'So do I.' Even at this moment of tenderness he seems to be expressing self-love, the old egotism.

Christopher Robin is, in other words, the God of Love. The toys know of no other power in their lives, and their feelings for him amount to worship:

*Christopher Robin's toys: Eeyore, Pooh, the second Piglet, Tigger, and Kanga; the original Piglet was destroyed by a dog and the original Roo lost in an orchard and never recovered.*

Piglet wasn't listening, he was so agog at the thought of seeing Christopher Robin's blue braces again. He had only seen them once before, when he was much younger, and, being a little over-excited by them, had had to go to bed half an hour earlier than usual; and he had always wondered since if they were *really* as blue and as bracing as he had thought them.

But Milne is mocking this worship, just as much as he is mocking all the toys' other characteristics. Christopher Robin has been presented to us at the beginning of *Winnie-the-Pooh* not as a god, but as a child (the author's son) listening to a story about himself and his toys. And at certain points in the story we are reminded of his real nature. The 'Expotition to the North Pole', which has something about it of a pilgrimage or crusade, is led by him; it is the only adventure which he himself initiates, and the reader knows that the supposed triumph (Pooh finding a pole which Christopher Robin decides *is* the North Pole) is really completely ridiculous. In 'Rabbit's Busy Day' in *The House at Pooh Corner,* Christopher Robin is entirely absent from the scene—learning to read. And in the final chapter in the second book, 'An Enchanted Place', he tries to explain to Pooh that he must soon leave him and go to school.

It is difficult to remain quite unmoved by this last chapter, in which a child tries to say his farewell to childhood, cannot find the words for it, and then laughingly gives up the attempt. Coming as it does at the end of Milne's writings for children—and so at what was effectively the end of a particular tradition and movement of English children's literature—one is inclined to regard it as a kind of *envoi,* a goodbye to an entire Golden Age. But it is a false effect, a piece of whimsy on Barrie lines rather than an organic part of Milne's creation. The plain fact is that Milne wishes to be rid of Pooh and the whole *opus,* and like Conan Doyle with Sherlock Holmes at the Reichenbach Falls he must do something dramatic. In fact it was too late: Milne had become irrevocably identified with Pooh, and lived the rest of his life resenting that the public identified him almost solely with his children's books, but failing to write anything else remotely as popular. Note the irony in the title of his autobiography, *It's Too Late Now.*

But in 1928 he did not know that it was too late to try to rid himself of Pooh and Christopher Robin, so he wrote this farewell scene, in which again we are reminded of Christopher Robin's role as God to the toys; for the setting—'an enchanted place on the very top of the Forest'—and the narrative tone has a vaguely religious connotation. Milne seems to be preparing us for some event not unlike Christ's ascension. On the other hand, he seems also to envisage a Peter-Pan-like state of perpetual continuation, in which Christopher Robin is trapped for ever within childhood:

> So they went off together. But wherever they go, and whatever happens to them on the way, in that enchanted place on the top of the Forest a little boy and his Bear will always be playing.

Quite apart from the faintly sinister implications of this—Christopher Robin as a boy who cannot grow up—there is also the inappropriateness of the statement that they 'will always be playing', for *play* is one thing that Pooh and Christopher Robin never do together in the stories. Everything that has happened to them both has been in deadly earnest.

So Milne has, at the end, lost confidence in his own creation. It is a pity, because otherwise *Winnie-the-Pooh* and *The House at Pooh Corner* are, on their own terms, more successful as works written for children than anything else produced during children's literature's Golden Age. *Alice, The Wind in the Willows, Peter Pan,* even the Beatrix Potter stories, all require some sort of adjustment before they can be taken in by young children: it is a matter partly of vocabulary but also of concept. One cannot escape the feeling with any of them that a full appreciation is only possible by adults. Milne is less ambitious than Carroll, Grahame, Barrie or even Potter: he sets out only to depict a very small fraction of human behaviour. But he manages to do so completely within a child's understanding; the Pooh books can be taken in fully by all but the smallest children, and the child reader is able to carry into adult life a perception of human character acquired from his readings of Milne. How many of us have, at one time or another, compared our friends or colleagues to Milne creations? Don't we all know an Eeyore, or a Tigger, or a Piglet? Don't we, indeed, recognise them in ourselves?

And yet they are not quite all of them mere types. Pooh transcends that, just a little. Certainly he is greedy. Certainly he is often a Bear of Very Little Brain. But he is also a poet, and in allowing him the dignity of being able to compose his 'Hums', Milne is allying him with [Kenneth Grahame's] Water Rat—is portraying him as someone whose vision of the world goes at least a little way beyond selfish short-sightedness:

> Pooh sat down on a large stone, and tried to think this out. It sounded to him like a riddle, and he was never much good at riddles, being a Bear of Very Little Brain. So he sang **"Cottleston Pie"** instead:
>
> Cottleston, Cottleston, Cottleston Pie.
> A fly can't bird, but a bird can fly.
> Ask me a riddle and I reply:
> 'Cottleston, Cottleston, Cottleston Pie.'
>
> . . . 'That's right,' said Eeyore. 'Sing. Umty-tiddly, umty-too. Here we go gathering Nuts and May. Enjoy yourself.'
>
> 'I am,' said Pooh.
>
> 'Some can,' said Eeyore.

None of Pooh's fellow-creatures has the faintest appreciation of his artistic gift. Their reaction is that of Mole to Rat's poetry, early in *The Wind in the Willows:* ' "I don't know that I think so *very* much of that little song." ' And at times, one must admit, Pooh's verses are almost as reprehensible as the boasting-songs of Toad:

> 3 Cheers for Pooh!
> *(For Who?)*
> For Pooh—
> *(Why what did he do?)*
> I thought you knew;

He saved his friend from a wetting:
3 Cheers for Bear!
*(For where?)*
For Bear . . .

But to put even this kind of thought into rhyme goes, one feels, beyond the total self-absorption which characterises the other inhabitants of the Hundred Acre Wood. Pooh has a little of the true visionary about him.

And of course he has humility. It is he, never others, who talks of himself as 'a Bear of No Brain at All' and 'a Bear of Very Little Brain'. Both Piglet and Eeyore are in a sense humble too, and appear to have no opinion of themselves. But with Piglet this is merely a manifestation of his timidity. He really regards himself as a person of some dignity and importance, taking the broken notice board next to his 'very grand house' with its mysterious inscription TRESPASSERS W as evidence that he had a distinguished grandfather named Trespassers William, and lecturing Pooh on the subject. . . . (pp. 200-07)

By contrast we are told at the start of **Winnie-the-Pooh** that Pooh 'lived in a forest all by himself under the name of Sanders', and E. H. Shepard's illustration shows him sitting outside a front door bearing the name-plate 'Mr Sanders'. This is never enlarged upon, but seems to suggest that Pooh has little self-centred concern with his own identity. By contrast, Owl is proud that he can spell his own name (and of course he spells it wrongly), and is in the habit of festooning his front door with importantseeming notices:

> PLES RING IF AN RNSWER IS REQUIRD
> PLEZ CNOKE IF AN RNSR IS NOT REQID

It begins to appear that *homes* are matters of particular importance to the characters. Eeyore's self-pity has made him an outcast, albeit by his own choice, so that he not only lives in the open air but occupies a patch of thistles faintly suggestive of the Waste Land. His plight does not escape the notice of Pooh, who as usual is the only one of the animals to perceive the needs of others:

> '*You* have a house, Piglet, and I have a house, and they are very good houses. And Christopher Robin has a house, and Owl and Kanga and Rabbit have houses, and even Rabbit's friends and relations have houses or somethings, but poor Eeyore has nothing. So what I've been thinking is: Let's build him a house.'

Though perceptive, he is still a Bear of Very Little Brain, which is why the plan to build the House at Pooh Corner goes a little awry. (The choice of those words for the title of the second Pooh volume is significant.) Similarly Pooh's greed, his only real fault of character, leads to a double disaster involving houses. He gets stuck in the front door of Rabbit's and so is unable to go home to his own. And the two episodes in which external forces (floods and gales) threaten the lives of those in the Hundred Acre Wood are seen entirely in terms of houses. Piglet and Pooh are marooned in theirs, and (after the great wind) Owl's is entirely destroyed. This last event leads Pooh to perform, in the penultimate chapter of **The House at Pooh Corner,** his greatest act of selflessness. Eeyore has found a 'new home'

for Owl, but everyone else knows that it is really Piglet's house, and an embarrassing situation arises. Is the truth to be told, Owl to be deprived of a roof over his head, and Eeyore's stupidity to be shown up? Even Christopher Robin is at a loss; he wonders 'whether to laugh or what'. And now comes the act of generosity, and it is not just Pooh who performs it, for by now Piglet (the Mole to Pooh's Water Rat) has acquired at least something of Pooh's lack of self-concern and perception of the needs of others. Piglet has grown up, and the selfish child, the ruthless egotist, has been replaced by a rather different figure:

> And then Piglet did a Noble Thing, and he did it in a sort of dream, while he was thinking of all the wonderful words Pooh had hummed about him.
>
> 'Yes, it's just the house for Owl,' he said grandly. 'And I hope he'll be very happy in it.' And then he gulped twice, because he had been very happy in it himself.
>
> 'What do *you* think, Christopher Robin?' asked Eeyore a little anxiously, feeling that something wasn't quite right.
>
> Christopher Robin had a question to ask first, and he was wondering how to ask it.
>
> 'Well,' he said at last, 'it's a very nice house, and if your own house is blown down, you *must* go somewhere else, mustn't you, Piglet? What would *you* do, if *your* house was blown down?'
>
> Before Piglet could think, Pooh answered for him.
>
> 'He'd come and live with me,' said Pooh, 'wouldn't you, Piglet?'
>
> Piglet squeezed his paw.
>
> 'Thank you, Pooh,' he said, 'I should love to.'

This is the real conclusion of the Pooh stories. The final chapter, 'In Which Christopher Robin and Pooh Come to an Enchanted Place, and we Leave Them There', is as we have seen a coda in a very different mode from the rest of the narrative. But is it quite fair to dismiss it as an unnecessary piece of whimsy, a regrettably sentimental lapse? Certainly the statement that 'in that enchanted place on the top of the Forest a little boy and his Bear will always be playing' is out of place when applied to the Pooh stories themselves. But perhaps Milne is half-consciously saying goodbye not so much to his own literary creation as to the whole image of the Enchanted Place, the Arcadia, the Never Never Land, the Secret Garden. He could not have foreseen that after him would come a very different era of children's books. But in concluding his writings for children, and so in effect ending his own career as an artist, he was undoubtedly saying goodbye to the childhood that he himself had been reliving alongside his own son Christopher. The farewell at the end of **The House at Pooh Corner** is a farewell to its author's own private Golden Age. And yet at the same time, in saying that Christopher Robin and Pooh can still be found 'in that enchanted place', Milne is reminding himself that the Secret Garden is always there for those who once knew it, and who can still find the door. As Christopher Milne has said in his own book, 'For us, to whom our childhood has meant so much, the journey back is short, the coming and going easy.' (pp. 207-09)

> *Humphrey Carpenter, "A. A. Milne and 'Win-nie-the-Pooh': Farewell to the Enchanted Places," in his* Secret Gardens: A Study of the Golden Age of Children's Literature, *Houghton Mifflin Company, 1985, pp. 188-209.*

## Chris Powling

[The] Pooh-books introduce us to what's already perfectly familiar, that's all. Well, almost all. The permanence of Pooh is certainly rooted in recognition-at-first sight, but it's the freshness built into every subsequent encounter by sheer literary craftsmanship which keeps us hooked. . . .

All the Pooh stories have [a] luminous what-did-I-tell-you quality. They're a celebration of the Obvious made suddenly less blinding. Yet, over and over again, the revelation is kept sharp by the author's verbal deftness.

Of course, as the years go by we have to work a little harder at the text. Time casts a stumbling-block or two into the passage of most books and Pooh is no exception. The biggest obstacle here, undeniably, is Christopher Robin.

Was there ever a more insufferable child than Christopher Robin?

Every inch of him exudes smugness—from the top of that curious, bobbed haircut to the tip of those tiny-tot sandals (and the smock and shorts in between are just as irritating). Okay, so we shouldn't take him at face value. Maybe there *is* deep irony in this twentieth-century version of the Victorian Beautiful Child. In Christopher Robin's case, however, we must certainly heed the wise advice of Oscar Wilde that it's only a superficial person who does *not* judge by appearances. With Milne's prose reinforced by E. H. Shepard's superb line-drawings, Christopher Robin must surely be just what he seems. And what he seems is a serious affront to anyone who believes children are simply people who haven't lived very long. (p. 6)

Christopher Robin nowadays is self-evidently a period-piece—part of a continuing costume drama of no greater handicap than the Eton collars and gobstoppers and dinner-gongs in the early William stories [by Richmal Crompton]. What still counts for youngsters, in my experience, is what should count for us: the toy-animals who are almost people. They're far more important than the twee human who is nowhere near a child.

And it's not hard to see why. That 'almost' is crucial. For Pooh and company are magnificently full-of-life only so far as *comedy* allows. They don't grow, for example. That's not their function. To grumble, as a recent critic has done, that 'the narrative derives . . . from the conjunction and opposition of known qualities. No one, not even the comparatively imaginative Pooh, changes or develops' is to miss the point by a mile. The known-qualities deployed by comedy are static because the pain of being otherwise would foul up the plot. Children are free to laugh at what happens to Eeyore precisely because they

recognise at once there's no need to feel sorry for him: he's so good at feeling sorry for himself. None better, in fact—just as Rabbit's bossiness can't be topped, nor Piglet's timidity, nor Tigger's bounce, nor Owl's pomposity.

Hence attention can be focussed right where Milne wants it—on a series of the most gentle come-uppances ever devised: 'There! What did I tell you?' The permanence of the Pooh-books, then, has nothing whatever to do with their psychological depth or the sharpness of their social comment or their status as morality. These don't matter a jot. What's important, through and through, is their success as storytelling. And this is a triumph. It survives shifts in fashion. It survives Christopher Robin. It even survives that odd tone-of-voice which, for all Milne's simple language, never quite settles for a child audience. The world Pooh creates is completely unique and utterly self-sustaining. Yes, it is a world that's very like ours . . . but much, much more like itself. (p. 7)

> *Chris Powling, "On the Permanence of Pooh," in* Books for Keeps, *No. 41, November, 1986, pp. 6-7.*

## John Rowe Townsend

Apart from any nostalgic pleasure, the adult returning to the Pooh books is bound to appreciate the sheer grace of craftsmanship. Milne was a most accomplished professional writer. He knew and accepted that he was a happy lightweight, and used to say merely that he had the good fortune to *be* like that. In children's as in adult literature, the lightweight of true quality is a rare and welcome phenomenon. The Pooh stories are as totally without hidden significance as anything ever written. . . . [For] all his rotundity Pooh—bless him—is one-dimensional. (p. 152)

> *John Rowe Townsend, "Fantasy Between the Wars," in his* Written for Children: An Outline of English-Language Children's Literature, *third revised edition, J. B. Lippincott, 1987, pp. 143-57.*

## Claudia Nelson

The most obvious characteristic of A. A. Milne's 1926 treatise on gender roles in middle-class English society, **Winnie-the-Pooh,** is its sheer emotional force. One of the most deeply angry writers of our angry century, Milne uses a mock-pastoral form to emphasize the raw brutality of the supposedly peaceful English country life, the undercurrents of passion and despair that twist and seethe beneath the placid surface of this ordered community. Here male and female inhabitants alike stand revealed as brute beasts. It is, in truth, a jungle out there—and Milne places the blame for society's sickness squarely on the shoulders of that symbol of the patriarchy, Christopher Robin, who, with devastating irony, alone retains human shape in the world that he has made bestial. The sexual malaise of the forest "animals," as Milne makes plain, results directly from Robin's subjection of the female element and exaltation of the male. Each animal feels the effects of this imbalance in a different way; thus each becomes an archetype to describe the effects of the patriarchy on the individual. (p. 17)

The fascination of the novel with obscured identities, with androgyny, and with "trying to pass" is constant, heartfelt, and only explicable biographically. . . . [This] mordantly bitter work is not, as has heretofore been assumed, the work of a man. For too long the coincidence of Mr. Milne's given names being Alan Alexander has deluded readers; but is it really reasonable to believe that this is the sort of work a man writes for his young son? No, "A. A. Milne" stands for just what it says it does: "A Milne" wrote this book—a Milne who, like Kanga, had seen her own identity swallowed up, through marriage, in that of an alien family of men. The author of this novel feels a close affinity for Pooh, the androgynous poet, and for Rabbit, the angry pseudoman. Writing, she knows because the patriarchy has told her so, is unfeminine (cf. Aphra Behn's wistful mention of "my masculine Part the Poet in me"); if she writes, can she be a real woman? And if she intends her story for her son, it is that her son may not become the monstrous—and, we hope, fictional—Christopher Robin, servant of the status quo. Like Charlotte Brontë, Milne takes a deliberately sexless nom de plume; like Zelda Fitzgerald, she allows her husband to pass off her art as his with a misleading dedication. The heartrending irony of this verse ("Say you're surprised? . . . Because it's yours—because we love you") is only too apparent. Milne cannot be surprised, either by the contents of her book or by her husband's blithe appropriation of them. Nor can she be surprised by the reason men give for their actions against women, the "because we love you" with which Robin also oppresses Pooh. But if she cannot be surprised, she can be—and is—dismayed, saddened, despairing. The deep personal tragedy of the "Pooh" books (their very name expressing the woman's helpless contempt for male society) can leave no reader unaffected in this marginally more enlightened age. (pp. 21-2)

> *Claudia Nelson, "The Beast Within: 'Winnie-the-Pooh' Reassessed," in* Children's literature in education, *Vol. 21, No. 1, March, 1990, pp. 17-22.*

**Richard Jenkyns**

A. A. Milne earns a book of more than 500 pages [Ann Thwaite's *A. A. Milne: The Man Behind Winnie-The-Pooh*] not for the bulk of his life's work, but for four small books for children written over a short period in the 1920s. . . . (p. 50)

Pooh's popularity is worldwide and looks set to last, with a fame among children's books surpassed, if at all, only by Alice. (p. 51)

What is the secret of Pooh's success? "Academic critics," Thwaite remarks, "have problems with children's literature. There is so little to say about it without sounding pretentious and absurd." This is especially true of the Pooh books; as John Rowe Townsend observes, they are "as totally without hidden significance as anything ever written." The silliest judgment cited by Thwaite comes from Humphrey Carpenter, who crashes straight into the heffalump trap. Milne's humor, he claims, is that of a mathematician: "Each humorous situation in the Pooh books is reached by the logical pursuit of an idea to the point of absurdity. . . . [Milne] handles words in the kind of de-

tached manner in which a mathematician deal with figures." That is what happens when a Critic of Very Large Brain feels he has to say something clever. It is an odd coincidence that Lewis Carroll and Milne should both have been mathematicians (Milne by education, Carroll by profession), but it is not more than that.

The contrast between the two writers is in fact revealing. Someone reading Alice and knowing nothing at all about its author would probably notice the donnish streak and the philosophical logician's cast of mind. Milne does not leave clues of that sort. People who met him found him charming, funny, and yet curiously aloof: you did not penetrate beyond the elegant surface. He is like that in the Pooh books too—friendly and humorous but giving very little away. He emerges from this biography as a man of high intelligence and an able controversialist. But in his children's books he seems as blithe and simple a soul as, say, P. G. Wodehouse.

And the Forest is a simple place; it is never frightening, like the Wild Wood in *The Wind in the Willows*. There is no fear or violence or villainy. We do not meet here Carroll's sense that grown-ups—metamorphosed into a Caterpillar, a Duchess, a Red Queen, or a Queen of Hearts—are alarming and unpredictable, or Beatrix Potter's awareness that her pretty watercolor animals are preying on one another, in the most literal sense, or Kenneth Grahame's social terror that dreadful lower-class weasels may be smashing up the manor house. Nor do the Pooh books offer any purchase for the fashionable notion that the best children's books are subversive.

Alison Lurie, who has popularized this idea, is cited by Thwaite for her suggestion that Milne's success is to have "created out of a few acres of Sussex countryside, a world that has the qualities both of the Golden Age of history and legend, and the lost paradise of childhood—two eras which, according to psychologists, are often one in the unconscious mind." In a way that idea seems plausible, and yet it somehow misses the point, for it describes an adventitious gratification that adults can draw from their reading of the books, not what is essentially there. Grahame chose *The Golden Age* as a title for one of his books about children (also illustrated by Shepard); nostalgic, allusive, and self-conscious, it shows what the Pooh books are not. Surely the charm of Milne's Pooh is that it is innocent of literary or symbolic resonances.

Only in the last chapter of ***The House at Pooh Corner,*** with its wistful scent of nostalgia and blue remembered hills, is there a subtext that is kept implicit. . . . In fact, Christopher Robin is about to go off to boarding school and realizing that he will have to grow out of his childhood toys. But this chapter apart, we seldom feel, as we do with most of the children's books that parents like best, that the grown-ups are talking to one another over our shoulders. That is a rarity in children's literature, and rarer than ever today. Even in so high a talent as Maurice Sendak a post-Freudian knowingness separates the adult from the child.

Part of Milne's success lies simply in his skill. Pooh and Eeyore are two of the most vivid and original characters in twentieth-century fiction. Richard Adams allows that for *Watership Down* he learned from the Pooh books "the vital importance, as protagonists, of a group of clearly portrayed, contrasting but reciprocal characters," but comparison between the two writers only brings out Milne's quality. Adams's teenage mutant boy scout hero rabbits are drawn with all the subtlety of Enid Blyton's school stories or *The Boys' Own Paper*. Milne's narrative, too, is beautifully controlled. He was a master of the light anecdote. . . .

But the Pooh books have also lasted because in a strange way they are real. Thwaite quotes the indignant protest of a small girl after watching Walt Disney's Pooh. "That's not true. . . . I *know* what happened. We read it. The book's true." It is certainly true that many adults are offended by the Disney travesty of Pooh as they are not by other cartoon vulgarizations of the classics. Partly this is because by the time they got their hands on Pooh the Disney studios had lost the creative vitality that redeems their earlier films, partly because their coarse draftsmanship insults Shepard's original vision. But not entirely: there is also a sense of falsehood. (pp. 51-2)

[In] a sense it is indeed true that Milne did not create Pooh. The toy was real, and it was his son who christened it. One of Thwaite's most interesting revelations is that Milne's bedtime stories were not about the toy animals, but about dragons and princesses and knights in armor—partly because he thought they were dull stuff that would send a little boy to sleep. What we get from the Pooh books is something quite different: the real life—almost—of Christopher Milne playing with his real nursery toys. Indeed some of Milne's critics have been repelled by just that: the feeling that a small boy's life has been exposed to public gaze.

Some people find Milne's style unbearably winsome: "It is that word 'hummy,' my darlings," Dorothy Parker wrote, "that marks the first place in *The House at Pooh Corner* at which Tonstant Weader fwowed up." But that is sloppy criticism. There is no baby language in the Pooh books. What we find is the bantering, affectionate tone in which adults address children, especially children they know well, and that is quite a different matter. Milne gives the impression of talking to his readers just as he talks to his son; in that respect *Winnie-the-Pooh* is one of the least patronizing of children's books. Christopher Milne has recalled that his father's "relationships were always between equals, however old or young, distinguished or undistinguished the other person."

The setting of the stories is real as well.

[Thwaite] says, "Part of the strength and charm of the stories comes from the juxtaposition of toy animal and forest." That too is real; it is the way things are within a child's make-believe. Milne's achievement is to get inside the childish imagination. It is a boy's world; none of the animals is female except for Kanga, and apparently Milne, uninstructed in marsupial biology, had supposed when he bought her that she too was male. And there are no adults in the Forest; instead Christopher Robin is, as Thwaite puts it, the "godlike child," serenely in command. . . .

"Pooh and Piglet are the children," Thwaite suggests, "and the boy takes on the role of the adult." The second half of that judgment is shrewd; the first part does not seem quite right. You love your teddy bear because he is both a humble listener, to whom you can tell things, and an avuncular presence whom you can cuddle for comfort ("Silly old bear!"). Pooh is less a child than a childlike uncle—a subtly different thing. (p. 52)

Pooh is immortal: "Wherever they go, and whatever happens to them on the way, in that enchanted place on the top of the Forest a little boy and his Bear will always be playing." Or will they? Like so many English literary figures, Pooh and his friends toured the United States, making money from personal appearances, and Milne eventually presented the animals to Dutton, his American publisher. They now reside in the New York Public Library: prisoners of Manhattan, they will never see the Forest again. (p. 53)

*Richard Jenkyns, "True Pooh," in* The New Republic, *Vol. 203, No. 16, October 15, 1990, pp. 50-3.*

**Janet Adam Smith**

Revisiting the children's books after reading [Ann Thwaite's *A. A. Milne: The Man Behind Winnie-the-Pooh*] is an odd experience, very different from reading them aloud to a child. I can still enjoy the funny rhymes like **"The King's Breakfast"** and **"The Dormouse and the Doc-**

*Milne with his wife Daphne in their sitting room at Cotchford Farm, 1950.*

tor," but those about Christopher Robin sound as soppy and embarrassing as ever, particularly the awful **"Vespers."** Ann Thwaite puts the case for its being ironic rather than sentimental, mocking the child who's thinking only of himself as he gabbles the words Nanny taught him. But if Milne meant to be ironic, his medium betrayed him. The effect—reinforced by the Shepard drawing—is to present a dear little innocent whose straying thoughts only make him the more quaint and lovable. One reaches for Belloc's *Bad Children* as an antidote.

Pooh is a different matter. Once one has gone beyond the dreadful dedication to Her ("Hand in hand we come / Christopher Robin and I / To lay this book in your lap") and the irritation of the occasional "Cos," and other baby talk, there are pleasures even for a granny. There is the fun of language—Eeyore "attached to his tail," threats from a gorse bush and an ambush, Owl's ponderous utterances, Eeyore's complaining tones. There is the reasonableness— it's important to know what you're looking for before you start looking for it; the possibility that Piglet's front door may have got thinner so though Pooh never gets fatter he may yet be stuck in it. There is the mad logic:

> "We mustn't stop now, or we
> shall be late."
> "Late for what?"
> "For whatever we want to be in
> time for."

As Humphrey Carpenter has pointed out, " Milne's humour is that of a mathematician. Each humorous situation . . . is reached by the logical pursuit of an idea to the point of absurdity."

In the books of verses, Milne is the outside observer, inventing what he thinks a child might think or feel. In the Pooh stories, as Ann Thwaite notes, he is remembering his own boyhood. Cotchford Farm, Ashdown Forest, Moon's toys, days with Ken—and his devotion to Kenneth Grahame's *Wind in the Willows*—all went to the making of the great good place. Behind the verses is a cozy ordered world of nannies and nurseries and walks in the park (maybe for children who know neither, nurseries and nannies are as romantic as castles and damsels in distress, their discipline as intriguing as the Code of Chivalry). But the world of the Pooh stories is wild and anarchic— though never violent and never really dangerous. There are no fixed routines, no nursery rules. Pooh gets up when he feels like it, eats whenever he fancies a little something, and enjoys Doing Nothing and also—when he feels like it—adventuring in search of the North Pole, without any grownup to say Don't, or Take Care, or Be Back by Teatime. And it all has to come to an end when Christopher Robin disappears into the disciplined, time-tabled world of school. (p. 6)

> *Janet Adam Smith, "Poohdom," in* The New York Review of Books, *Vol. 37, No. 14, September 27, 1990, pp. 3-4, 6.*

### Ann Thwaite

[Milne and his brother Ken were], by the standards of their time, extraordinarily free. 'Almost as babies,' Alan would recall, 'we were allowed to go walks by ourselves anywhere, in London or in the country.' They kept to the rules and their parents knew they could be trusted. It is peculiarly ironic that A. A. Milne should have been described by his fiercest critics as being metaphorically 'locked in the nursery'. . . . Milne's ideal of childhood has, in fact, little to do with nannies and nursery tea, much more to do with a love of adventuring. It is no wonder that there is no nanny or nursery in the Forest. The child is brave, godlike, omnipotent. And the toys, who are the real children, explore a world where they are not bound by nursery rules, where only friendship and hunger and a desire for adventure affect the pattern of their days. (p. 17)

[Alan's] early years had been full of affection, of freedom, independence and individuality. Much later these would be the wellsprings of his own books for children. (p. 75)

[Milne wanted the words in his children's verses] to have richness, flavour and bite, and he knew the power of the occasional unfamiliar word—just as Beatrix Potter did when she commented in *The Flopsy Bunnies* on the report that the effect of eating too much lettuce is 'soporific'. If one hears a small child refer to someone as 'well-intentioned' ('Ernest was an elephant and very well-intentioned') or to someone else 'wandering vaguely quite of her own accord', one knows one is in the presence of a Milne-listener. But most of the language in A. A. Milne's children's poems is, without being boring to an adult, easily understood by a three- or four-year-old, and that is a remarkable achievement. Milne wanted to make his position quite clear. He said of his first collection: it 'is not the work of a poet becoming playful, nor of a lover of children expressing his love, nor of a prose-writer knocking together a few jingles for the little ones, it is the work of a light-verse writer taking his job seriously, even though he is taking it into the nursery.' Milne's technical skill is admirable. It is his dextrous use of rhythm and rhyme that makes his children's poems lodge in the head, and this was what he most wanted. (p. 248)

[Milne realized], as he indicated in a letter to Irene Vanbrugh . . . , what a mixed collection the poems were.

> I am writing a book of children's verses. Like Stevenson, only better. No, not a bit like Stevenson really. More like Milne. But they are a curious collection; some *for* children, some *about* children, some by, with or from children.
>
> (p. 250)

In October E. V. Lucas seems to have been worried that Milne was playing too much golf. He thought Milne would be the better for a little more structure in his life and suggested that he should start writing regular prose again for *Punch*. Milne did not resent Lucas's advice about his 'literary career'. 'I have always been grateful to you for your interest in it', but he rejected the suggestion that he was idle—though he hesitated to mention that, for the moment, he really had no need to work, with money constantly flowing in from performances of the plays all over the place. A production of *The Truth about Blayds* by Liverpool Rep had been a particular success and earned Milne the best review (in the *Manchester Guardian* from C. E. Montague) that he said he had ever had in his life.

*Mr Pim Passes By* even ran for three months in Berlin in a German translation and accumulated 'a trifle of two thousand billion marks or so' at that time of runaway inflation\in Germany. *Mr Pim* was also put on in Vienna that year. Milne wrote to Lucas:

> I think my indolence is more apparent than real; or perhaps I should say that it is real, but I overcome it pretty well. I have written in the last five years: six full-length plays, four short plays, two novels, about a book and a half of essays and sketches, a book of verses, three short stories and various oddments: in addition, of course, to the more mechanical labour of seeing 9 books through the press, and rehearsing seven full-length plays, which is not too bad.

> Quite frankly I could not bear to write regularly for *Punch* again. I'm sorry, but there it is. It would make me miserable. And I suspect that what you really want is that 'Billy Book' you have been urging me to write; and you feel that, if I began a few chapters for *Punch,* I should be more likely to pull it off. Fear not. I will do it yet. I like writing; the sort of writing which doesn't come into plays; and I will do that book, or some other book, directly, which will make you say 'I always *said* he could write.'

> I will send you 20 or 30 of the poems next week, if you would like to see them—officially as Methuen's friend, or unofficially as mine. A mixed lot. So mixed that I think (hooray!) that they will require a prose introduction. (p. 251)

[Many have been nauseated], not by the rhymes themselves, but by the whole paraphernalia of nannies and afternoon walks and clean hands for nursery tea. 'It's that bloody nanny,' Roald Dahl said to me, admiring Milne enormously and regretting how his books have dated. In fact, the nanny (or 'Nurse') appears in only five of the forty-five poems in **When We Were Very Young** and in another four in the second collection **Now We Are Six**—and, of course, not at all in the Pooh books. . . . (p. 266)

[If ] one reads the poems objectively, ignoring the charming period illustrations (many of which, surprisingly, have *not* dated all that much—look at the boy putting on his raincoat) the main impression is of a number of entirely natural children, egotistical, highly imaginative, slightly rebellious, as children still are. Certainly, . . . Milne's own memories of childhood, which play such an important part in the poems, have little to do with nannies and nurseries, and a great deal to do with adventuring, without adults, with freedom and growing independence. The children in the poems are always wanting to break free from the constraints that are constantly being imposed on all children, from whatever social background. ('Don't do that?' 'Come here.') Milne's children want to get 'up the hills to roll and play', to watch the rabbits on the common, to ignore the boring injunctions to 'Take care, dear' and 'Hold my hand.' They want to go down to the wood where the bluebells grow or to travel to South America or to sail through Eastern seas.

It is not a bland world. The menaces and uncertainties of real life are there all right, but perfectly adjusted to a small child's understanding. There are the bears waiting to eat the sillies who tread on the lines of the street. There are the Brownies hovering behind the curtain. There is the constant worry of pet mice, and mothers, going missing—a fear, common in children, that the beloved animal may escape, that the person who goes out of the door may never come back. Bruno Bettelheim considers that the listening child can only enjoy the warning and has to repress the great anxiety that he will be permanently deserted. But the child in the poems is protected by his own egotism, is perfectly in control. Life goes on. ('If people go down to the end of the town, well, what can *anyone* do?') He would never be such an idiot as to tread on the lines; the bears are certainly not going to get him. There is a pleasurable thrill of danger, but ultimately a reinforced security.

The child answers politely all the endless grown-up questions (seething quietly inside) and thinks if only he were King of France he would not brush his hair for aunts. Indeed, if he were King of Greece, he would go so far as to push things off the mantelpiece. This seems to be a reasonable indication of three-year-old rebellion. The poems, in fact (and this is why they have lasted so long), are a true expression of the child psyche, as recognized by the child himself and as observed by his elders. They work both for children and for adults who can see through the class trappings to what is actually there. It helps too when one knows, as [critic Geoffrey] Grigson did not, that Milne did not come from a moneyed, smug background, or expect things which he had never earned. In fact, he was constantly worried by the established social order and the priorities of many of his readers. (pp. 266-67)

There have been critics who have found Christopher Robin, even in the **Pooh** books, a stumbling block to their full enjoyment. (p. 300)

[He] is seen in relation to Pooh and the other animals. Pooh and Piglet are the children and the boy himself takes on the role of the adult. The listening or reading child identifies with the superior strength and power he sometimes resents in the adults around him, however much he loves his parents. Christopher Robin is always resourceful and competent; he is the child as hero. In 'the world Pooh creates' it is Christopher Robin who reads sustaining books at moments of crisis, who comes to the rescue, who will make sure that no harm comes to the kidnapped Roo (whatever befell him in real life) and protects the animals from the teeth of fierce things. ('If Christopher Robin is coming, I don't mind anything.') He dries Eeyore's tail after its immersion in the river (having nailed it on on a previous occasion) and does all the comforting and useful things that parents do. The boy is brave and godlike to the toys, just as the loving parent is to a small child. It is absolutely beside the point to criticize him for being too good to be true.

Just occasionally, as any adult does too, Christopher Robin reveals his frailty, his feet of clay, and this surely adds to his appeal. He has forgotten what the North Pole looks like. ('I did know once . . .') It is Pooh who is childlike, egotistical, hungry, alternately boastful and self-deprecating, occasionally managing to be brave and un-selfish, accepting things without really understanding them, as children so often have to accept ununderstand-able explanations. The listening or reading child recognizes himself in Pooh and recognizes himself as he longs to be, as he thinks he *will* be, in Christopher Robin. He recognizes and enjoys the wit and tenderness of the books. (pp. 300-01)

Milne's animals have become part of the English language. It is taken for granted that people know what is meant by 'a particularly Eeyore-like tone' or 'behaving exactly like Tigger'. An editorial in an American newspaper even once went so far as to say that 'few people in responsible positions in society today have got to eminence without the influence of Pooh'.

All over the world, A. A. Milne's children's books are loved and cherished by children and parents together, and by a good many adults who are not parents. There are no better stories for sharing. There are no better stories for reading aloud and for finding one's way back to that childhood world where it is possible to do Nothing, or at least nothing that has anything to do with anything. (p. 486)

> *Ann Thwaite, in her* A. A. Milne: The Man Behind Winnie-the-Pooh, *Random House, 1990, 554 p.*

# Kit Pearson

## 1947-

Canadian author of fiction.

Major works include *The Daring Game* (1986), *A Handful of Time* (1987), *The Sky Is Falling* (1987).

Praised as a writer of realistic fiction for middle graders who uses traditional genres of children's literature such as the school story and the time travel adventure in a nontraditional manner, Pearson is especially respected for her insightful treatment of the maturation process of her young female protagonists as well as for her understanding of general human behavior. Her characters, preteens who are lonely and shy and are having difficulty fitting into their surroundings or with their parents or guardians, gain both acceptance and self-awareness by learning to cope with their circumstances. Pearson is often acknowledged for her sensitivity in representing the pain of children who feel like outsiders as well as for her successful delineation of the relationship between the present and the past. She is also well regarded for the beauty of her writing, the believability of her stories, and for her attention to detail, as well as for the evocative and moving effect of her books.

In her first novel, *The Daring Game,* Pearson creates a Canadian version of the English school story as she describes the world of a Vancouver boarding school in 1964. Adjusting to such elements of school life as homesickness, daily routines, and interpersonal relationships, eleven-year-old Eliza befriends Helen, the school rebel; when Helen suggests the "daring game" in which her dorm mates dare each other to break school rules, Eliza lies to cover for Helen when she leaves campus on a dare and jeopardizes her own standing at the school through her loyalty. Pearson's next work, *A Handful of Time,* injects elements of fantasy into a story which describes the relationships between two generations of mothers and daughters. When twelve-year-old Patricia is sent by her beautiful but cold mother to the family's lakeside cottage outside Edmonton while she divorces her husband, Patricia discovers an old watch which transports her back thirty-five years in time. Made invisible by the powers of the watch, Patricia observes her mother's miserable twelfth summer at the same site. Patricia, who is herself unhappy at the cottage, is able to help her mother; when she returns to the present, Patricia proves herself to her cousins and begins to develop a new understanding with her mother. Underscoring the main plot is the relationship of Patricia's mother and grandmother, a tense situation which parallels that of Patricia and her own mother. Pearson's most recent book, *The Sky Is Falling,* describes the evacuation of ten-year-old Norah and her five-year-old brother Gavin from England to Canada as "war guests" in 1940. Sent to live in a Toronto home with a wealthy widow, Mrs. Ogilvie, and her spinster daughter, Norah is ignored by the couple, who lavish all of their affection on Gavin. Norah runs away after clashing with Mrs. Ogilvie, but returns to re-

solve her problems and to develop an understanding with her host. The first book of a proposed trilogy, *The Sky Is Falling* was inspired by storyteller Alice Kane's memory of telling stories to evacuee children in Canada who, when hearing the tale of "Henny Penny," said that "the sky is falling back home, too." A former children's librarian as well as a teacher and reviewer of juvenile literature, Pearson fills her books with references to classic works of children's fiction; her characters are avid readers who often receive solace from their books, and Pearson has acknowledged such stories as Philippa Pearce's *Tom's Midnight Garden* and Frances Hodgson Burnett's *The Secret Garden* as direct influences on her works. The novels also reflect Pearson's personal background: for example, she includes some of her childhood experiences in *A Handful of Time* as well as her high school experiences in a Canadian boarding school in *The Daring Game*. Pearson received the Canadian Library Association's Book of the Year for Children Award in 1988 for *A Handful of Time.*

## AUTHOR'S COMMENTARY

*[The following excerpt is from an interview by Dave Jenkinson.]*

Born in Edmonton, Alberta on April 30, 1947, Kit moved to Vancouver with her family when she was nine. After four years, the Pearsons returned to Edmonton, but "then I was sent to Crofton House, a boarding school in Vancouver, for high school." (p. 66)

Regarding *The daring game*'s origins, Kit explains, "The reason I wanted to write about a boarding school was because I find it so intriguing that you can take an assortment of kids and put them in a situation where they're almost like a tribe. The adults have almost nothing to do with them; they're really on their own. When I was at Crofton House, there was a group of grade sevens who used to follow the grade twelves around. They seemed so lost, and I've never forgotten their vulnerability. They were all so far away from home."

Utilizing a familiar setting had its disadvantages though. "The old house that the school was in the book is exactly the same as the real school, but this got quite confusing. For example, when I first thought of the 'slipper express' as a way of passing messages, I thought I couldn't use it because there was a step in the *real* hall the slipper would fall off. It took me a while to realize that I was free to take out the step! I think that attachment to reality is common in a first book. I seem to be moving farther and farther away from my own life with each book. Someday I will do a sequel to *The daring game*. Eliza's going to go back for high school, but the story's going to be about Holly who's eight in the first book. It'll be set in the late Sixties, a much different time. That's about all that I know about it. It will be fun to do a sequel, especially because now the fictional school is more 'real' to me than the real school."

*A handful of time* was Kit's second book, but there was another manuscript between the two published titles. "I've had just one 'book' that didn't go anywhere. I think it happened because I wrote it too soon after *The daring game.* I started it immediately because I was terrified I wouldn't be able to write another book. I knew it was awful after about four chapters. It was so boring. It was about two kids who were trying to conceal the fact that their uncle had quit law school. I was having to go down to the library and do all this dull research about law school. It was so hard to stop that book because I knew I *could* write it. I'm stubborn enough that I can get through anything. I thought if I gave it up, maybe it meant I couldn't ever write another book."

Abandoning the "uncle" book, Kit turned to *A handful of time.* "I always knew I would write a book set on Alberta's lake Wabamun because I loved that place, but it meant so much to me I didn't know whether I was ready to do it. Then it was all I had left to do. I think I wanted to be a better writer before I attempted it. But then I just started it. The cottage in the book is our cottage. My family had a cabin on the lake until I was about 17 and then they sold it. Some of the book's incidents are from my childhood. For instance, the water bombing of the church

camp the older kids did one summer when I was little and I remember them talking about it." (pp. 66-7)

Reading her own books is something Kit finds difficult because she always finds things that she would like to change. "I think I would make more of the fact in *A handful of time* that Patricia was invisible. I had a lot of trouble with the invisibility. At one point I had Patricia going swimming. She takes all her clothes off, and she's really delighted, especially being so shy, that nobody can see her. I had this pile of clothes on the beach, and then I couldn't figure out whether you'd see the clothes when they were off her and whether they'd disappear when they touched her. I just left the whole scene out. Sometimes you have to leave things out if you can't figure them out."

"*The daring game* I still think doesn't have enough plot. I think it's got great details, and that's what kids have told me they love, but, if I wrote it again, I would make it a lot tighter. *Handful of time* had plenty of plot—too much plot—and the trouble was the characters. *Handful* I had to rewrite a lot more than *Daring.* My editor, David Kilgour, really helped me a lot. He didn't find Patricia's grandmother believable; he thought she was too nasty, and he wanted to know why. Now, *I* knew why, but I tend to know things in my head and forget to tell the reader. So I went through the manuscript and tried to give more reasons, such as her being unhappy because of her fiance's dying."

Fall of 1989 sees the publication of a third Pearson book, *The sky is falling.* (p. 67)

"The new book started a long time ago. Once I took a storytelling course from Alice Kane, and she told us about telling stories to the evacuated children at the University of Toronto—especially the story 'Alenoushka and her Brother,' the story which became the theme of my book. Then, when I was at Simmons and writing my thesis on Arthur Ransome, I was having fun one day wondering what happened to all his characters. I thought, 'When Bridget, the youngest was around ten, she would have been in England during the war. What if she had been evacuated?' Because I love books that are about characters from other books, I was going to write my own sequel to Arthur Ransome's books about Bridget and Titty being evacuated. Then I read a new book about Ransome and realized these characters were based on real people, so I didn't think I could do a sequel. Then I thought, 'Well, I just won't call them by the same names, but I'll know who they really are. As soon as I started the book, that whole idea got forgotten and the book has nothing to do with Arthur Ransome's characters—except that Norah discovers his books!"

"I have also heard about the war all my life from my parents. My mother used to tell me how 'adorable' the little English evacuees were. I got the feeling that some of these children were treated almost like little pets. Then I read the papers of the time and it was exactly like that. It's quite sickening how sentimental adults were about these 'splendid children who so bravely crossed the water and came to Canada.' "

"I did a lot of research for *The sky is falling.* I went to England to find a setting. I found quite a lot of books about evacuees in England but hardly anything about the ones coming over to Canada. I really relied on the papers, and they were incredibly helpful. Then Geoffrey Bilson's book, *The guest children,* came out after mine was finished. Much of what he had done, I had already found out—we were both doing the same research at the same time. I wish I'd been able to meet him before he died, to talk to him about it. His book is so good, and the only nonfiction one there is."

"I can't believe the British children weren't afraid, and that's what a lot of the book is about; Norah is afraid, but she can't admit it. I originally thought *The sky is falling* would cover the whole war, but when I finished it, it was only Christmas, 1940. I couldn't bear to leave Norah and Gavin stranded in Canada, and I could have just put in an 'Afterword' but I really didn't want to. I was itching to write more about them, and I suddenly decided one night that I would write two more books. They'd each be set two years apart and I'd cover the whole war, but that's all I knew. I know a little bit more about the second book now because I'm just starting it. Before I actually sit down to write, ideas are always floating up in my subconscious and I put them in my notebook. I now have two sections in my notebook—book two and book three, so it *will* be a trilogy! I know the last book is about Gavin, and he'll be 10 so I'll finally be writing about a boy as the main character. Norah will be 13 in the second book because I've always wanted to write about the trials of being 13—I have such strong memories of it, and I have to do it sometime."

As Kit has noted, to this point, her central characters have all been preteen girls. Kit explains, "That was my favorite age and still is. I think about age 11 and 12, just before adolescence, you have a kind of 'power', especially girls for some reason. You feel really confident, or at least I did. You're still very secure, but you're at the 'top' of childhood. You have all the freedoms of being a child but you have all the faculties of an adult. You can read as well as an adult; you can do things; you can go out by yourself. I think it's a wonderful age. I have such clear memories of being that age—and of the shock of it all ending at 13."

*The daring game*'s Eliza states quite emphatically, "I don't want to grow up." Says Kit, "Eliza is exactly the way I was. In fact, three friends and I made a pact when we were 12 that we would not grow up, and we really thought that we didn't have to. Patricia, because she wants to be a mother, is more willing to become a teen. I wish I'd emphasized this aspect more. I think Patricia's quite fascinated by her mother, Ruth, who obviously does want to grow up as fast as she can. Sometimes I worry because I don't want kids to think that they shouldn't *want* to grow up. It used to be more difficult for a girl. In the Fifties and Sixties, you were allowed to run free and do what you wanted and be a tomboy, and then, all of a sudden, you were supposed to wear nylons, lipstick and high heels. Girls don't have to go through that as much today. They are supposedly a lot freer, although I still have some little girls who come up and say, 'I feel just like that. I don't want to grow up.' What Eliza doesn't want to do, and I don't blame her,

is all the *artificial* stuff about growing up—being a 'feminine' teenager, being an object and all that stuff. Patricia won't have to go through that as much because she's a modern child."

A typical work day for Kit has the following pattern. "I try to get to my desk by nine. . . ." (p. 68)

"I don't plot before I write the first draft. I start with a situation, not really a plot. For example, I start with a girl going back to her mother's past. I know that much, and then I just write it. . . . I do the whole first draft from beginning to end and *then* I make an outline, which is really just leaving some blank pages in my notebook for each chapter. Then I read through the manuscript and put plot changes in the spaces for each chapter. Then I do the whole thing again from beginning to end. I always have to go through it again in order—I can't work on this bit and that bit. What I find the easiest is the dialogue, and it never really changes much. What I need to work on later are descriptions and character because I never get them exactly right the first time. I see places where I can develop character more and descriptive details I want to throw in, especially because I'm always obsessed with the setting."

"Characters do take over, and I've never known whether that's good or bad. In *The daring game,* for instance, I thought while I was writing it that Eliza and Helen wouldn't make friends until the end of the book, and lo and behold, they made friends at Christmas and I didn't know what to do about it. I'm very conscious of creating some characters. Miss Tavistock is supposed to be a mixture of Charlotte Bronte and Charlotte Yonge, two of my favorite Victorian authors—that's why she's named Charlotte. I very consciously did that, but Helen, for example, I don't know where she came from. She came so easily, full blown and complicated. I've sometimes thought about doing *The daring game* all over again from Helen's perspective. I could have done more with Helen, but I always find that in a book. There's so many strands you can follow, but you have to find a theme and stick to it."

One of the characteristics of Kit's writing is her inclusion of titles of books which her characters are reading. "I have to watch myself. I'm a former children's librarian, and I love children's books. I'm not trying to be didactic. But if the book's character loves reading, why not put the titles in? I remember reading Edward Eager as a child—that's how I learned about E. Nesbit because his characters were all reading her books. As soon as I read the Eager books, I rushed out and got the E. Nesbit books and read those and loved them." (pp. 68-9)

*Dave Jenkinson, "Kit Pearson: Boarding Schools, Beaches and Bombs," in* Emergency Librarian, *Vol. 17, No. 1, September-October, 1989, pp. 65-9.*

## TITLE COMMENTARY

### *The Daring Game* (1986)

As a librarian in a private all-girls school, I felt a certain familiarity with Kit Pearson's first novel. The setting for

*Pearson reading aloud from* The Daring Game *at its launching in 1986.*

this title is a boarding school for girls in Vancouver. Eliza, the main character, is anxious to attend a boarding school, to compare the real thing to what she has read in novels. When her family is transferring from Edmonton to Toronto for one year, it seems a perfect opportunity for her to enroll. Throughout the remainder of the story, we see Eliza involved in various typical situations, from getting used to living with four girls the same age, to adjusting to the daily routine of boarding school. In addition, she has to deal with the problems of pre-adolescence and homesickness, something new for her. One of the pastimes devised by the girls to relieve boredom, and also to test each other, is a game of dares, which get them into various types of mischief, some amusing and some very serious.

On one level, the story is an interesting look at life in a private school, with the almost military routine of daily activities, the necessary wearing of uniform clothes and shoes, and the distinct separation between boarders and daygirls. However, on a deeper level, we get a look at the loneliness of girls away from home for the first time, the feeling of rejection experienced by girls whose parents never visit, and the closeness that being in a similar situation can create.

A recommended title for any school library and of special interest to young people going to a new or private school. Pearson has shown remarkable insight into the emotional growth of young girls.

> *JoAnna Burns Patton, in a review of "The Daring Game," in* CM: Canadian Materials for Schools and Libraries, *Vol. XIV, No. 4, July, 1986, p. 167.*

This is not unlike many other girls' boarding school stories: the characters are well-defined, operate within a narrow framework, and are limited in their interests and development. This is an adequately structured first novel, weakened by stylistic lapses like "A coil of tightness inside her . . . sprung loose," and such fallacious concepts as having an expression in common usage in the U.S. treated as unknown: "Carrie giggled. 'What does that mean? You guys use such funny expressions.'" Carrie is American, the others are Canadian, and the expression is "Many happy returns of the day."

> *Zena Sutherland, in a review of "The Daring Game," in* Bulletin of the Center for Children's Books, *Vol. 40, No. 5, January, 1987, p. 95.*

I was reminded of the words which form the title of my review while reading from Kit Pearson's story about a Canadian boarding school for girls. The phrase is part of a description not of a group of high-spirited young boarders, but of an army regiment. Robert Ross, in Timothy Findley's 1977 novel, *The wars,* suddenly realizes that training camp in Lethbridge, Alberta, "was much like school: roll call and mess hall. Even the pranks were the same-apple-pie beds and water bombs". In *The daring game,* Pearson's main character, Eliza, makes the same discovery, while standing in the middle of a girl's dormitory: "It's like an army, thought Eliza. Ashdown had never seemed like this before. 'Let's apple-pie Bix's bed!' suggested Helen . . . ". In scores of boarding school novels girls and boys become hardened combatants in the eternal war against authority; headmistresses become barking generals, dormitories veritable bunkers. We are, in short, fascinated by the institutions which regiment our lives.

This long tradition of boarding-school fiction is predominantly British. Eliza first hits upon the idea of going to boarding school as a result of reading some books sent by an English grandmother, "books . . . with titles like *Fiona of the fifth* or *The turbulent term at St. Theresa's.* They depicted a dramatic world of odd rituals, ordered busyness and loyal friends. Of course, a Canadian boarding school might be different, but there must be some similarities". Here is Pearson's challenge set within the very text she is writing—to create a Canadian version of this well-known subgenre, the boarding-school novel.

Pre-adolescent girls would presumably form the potential audience for *The daring game.* Indeed, the novel opens with the familiar adolescent concern with appearance: "Eliza sat alone in the headmistress's study, trying to stop her knees from trembling. Tugging her dress over them, she wondered again if she should have worn her uniform". What better background, could there be for pre-adolescent appearance-consciousness than an institution where one wears a uniform, where an apparently democratic dress code merely serves to heighten the awareness of other physical and material attributes? Eliza mentally weighs the relative prettiness of her dorm mates; she is as painfully conscious of standards of beauty as she is of the fact that she is the only one of her mates who is not yet encased in a bra.

But the pre-adolescent fear which Pearson has best articulated and which many adults will have forgotten or ignored is the most basic: the fear of becoming an adolescent, a teenager. In fact, Eliza's desire to go to boarding school is born of more than her girlhood reading; we are told that "the prospect of attending the huge junior high school terrified her. Eliza didn't want to become a teenager". For Eliza, teenhood is synonymous with "movie stars," "backcombing," "dating", "dances", "lipstick," "nylons" and "invitations" and all of the above are decidedly anathema. By having Eliza form a friendship with an older girl, Madeleine (a puppy love relationship reminiscent of Rose's love for the older Coza in Alice Munro's *Who do you think you are?*), Pearson allows both Eliza and her young readers a link with this frightening world of teenhood—a comforting assurance that (the horrors of

dating and dances to the contrary) one may survive after all.

The most crucial link in *The daring game,* though, is one which Eliza forms with a peer and it is this relationship which is less surely drawn. Eliza befriends—much to everyone's surprise—the "problem" student, Helen—a girl whose boisterous and rebellious behaviour only thinly masks the insecurity of an unhappy home life. From this alliance grows the "daring game" of the title—a game which leads to Eliza's act of lying in order to protect Helen, who has gone outside the walls of the school on a dare. The ethical waters become truly muddied, but lest we are tempted to ponder the ethical perplexities of two wrongs occasionally making a right, the author whisks us away from the entire problem at rather short notice.

My sense of ethical unease is accompanied and intensified by a sense of political unease. Eliza's experience at Ashdown is clearly an upper-middle-class one; her father is an ophthalmologist who has just been invited to start an eye clinic at the Toronto General Hospital. How, then, is a reader to react to obvious bids for sympathy because of Eliza's relatively spare economic situation? "Eliza was fascinated. She'd never known anyone with servants before. Pam and Carrie must be as rich as some of the day-girls. You could tell by their clothes, and all the places they had been, that their families had more money than Jean's, Helen's and her own". One shudders to think of the living conditions of children of less-than-ophthalmological parentage.

Pearson's *The daring game* offers sensitive and valuable insights into the process of growing up. But the fears and challenges of growing up are always, to a degree, determined by social factors such as class. Writers should be aware of this fact and should write with it in their hearts and minds, for not all of the troubled Helens in our society can squeeze into Ashdown Academy and tell their stories. (pp. 79-81)

> *Lorraine M. York, in a review of "The Daring Game," in* Canadian Children's Literature, *No. 46, 1987, pp. 79-81.*

---

## A Handful of Time  (1987)

Patricia, a shy 12 year old upset by her parents' divorce-in-progress, is sent to spend the summer with cousins she's never met. While visiting them, she is miraculously transported back 35 years to when her mother, Ruth, was 12 years old and was also spending a miserable summer at the family cottage on a lake outside of Edmonton. Vancouver writer Kit Pearson's second novel for 10-13 year olds, *A Handful of Time* won't win any awards for originality of plot—too many children's books rely on the same device.

It might, however, win awards for writing. Pearson eschews gimmicks. When Patricia discovers an old pocket-watch and winds it up, time simply picks up where it left off—an elegant, logical, and not overly disturbing way to land Patricia in the past. Since the first time-shift doesn't take place until about page 50, it can't distract the reader from more important concerns, such as Patricia's feelings of inadequacy *vis-à-vis* her beautiful and famous mother, the host of a CBC television news show in Toronto. The time-shift sequences reveal how Ruth, a spirited, intelligent girl, had to fight to make a place for herself in a household where boys were favoured. Ironically, the grown-up Ruth stifles Patricia by giving her too much freedom.

Pearson opens with a quote from the Philippa Pearce classic, *Tom's Midnight Garden,* and that book's influence is apparent throughout. *A Handful of Time* offers a poignant look at the passing of time, and the extent to which adults retain their childhood selves.

There are many nice touches here. Patricia, invisible when visiting the past, sometimes gives the young Ruth a helping hand, but never enough to frighten her. And when at last Patricia gets the chance to prove herself to her cousins, she does it by quieting a baby and organizing a dinner—no high dramatics here! This is a subtle and memorable book with a Canadian context and universal appeal.

> *Annette Goldsmith, in a review of "A Handful of Time," in* Books for Young People, *Vol. 1, No. 2, April, 1987, p. 10.*

This sounds as if it should be a heartwarming story, but it isn't. The characters all share a certain sour selfishness that prevents the reader from enjoying and liking them. Patricia's parents are so absorbed in their own problems that they seem unbelievably indifferent to their daughter; her aunt and uncle, although kind, are so determined that everyone at the lake be happy that they are maddeningly oblivious to what is really going on in their family.

There are also undercurrents of intolerance and prejudice throughout the book, exemplified by some of the cottagers' attitudes toward the Indians on a nearby reserve. Patricia herself is not free of these imperfections. Her cousins are mean to her at first, but when they make overtures of friendship as the summer progresses she refuses to allow them to accept her. Instead she comes to prefer by far her trips to the past where she can observe the rebellious young Ruth.

Patricia's grandmother, Ruth's mother, is the unpleasant link between the two times. She is unhappy with her own life and Patricia sees her nag the 12-year-old Ruth relentlessly, trying to form her into her idea of a conventionally correct young lady. She applies a terrible double standard in her treatment of Ruth and of Ruth's two older brothers. In Patricia's own time, her grandmother comes to visit the family at the lake, arriving like a malevolent spirit. She tries to pry from Patricia details of her parents' marital problems, taking a thinly disguised spiteful pleasure in it all.

Although by the end of the story Patricia and her mother have determined to forgive all past grievances and start afresh, the reader is left with the uneasy feeling that the problems of this family are so deep that they will have no easy solutions. (p. 35)

> *Mary Ainslie Smith, "Living in the Past," in* Books in Canada, *Vol. 16, No. 5, June-July, 1987, pp. 35-7.*

This owes more than a nod to Pearce's *Tom's Midnight Garden* (acknowledged in the epigraph) although lacking that book's structural complexity, and the inevitable rapprochement with Mom and cousins is too obvious. What Pearson manages very well is the tension between family members who are supposed to like each other and don't, and the pain of a child who does not fit in. Simpler than most time fantasies, and written in a plain and gentle style, this is good wish-fulfillment reading for kids in the summer reading club who, like Patricia, would really prefer to be someplace else.

> *Roger Sutton, in a review of "A Handful of Time," in* Bulletin of the Center for Children's Books, *Vol. 41, No. 9, May, 1988, p. 186.*

Although [this] novel is about two generations of mother-daughter relationships, all readers see of the grown-up mothers, Ruth and Nan, is from the perspective of a child. Hence, both appear as wooden and flat characters. Although the watch device is a handy one to allow the girl a glimpse of the past, there is not much explanation as to how or why the watch possesses this power. Science fiction fans may be disappointed, but the book will show adolescents how relationships in the present are often locked into patterns of the past, and that a discovery of one's family often reveals much about oneself.

> *Yvonne A. Frey, in a review of "A Handful of Time," in* School Library Journal, *Vol. 35, No. 8, May, 1988, p. 100.*

Only "a handful of time" separates this new novel by Kit Pearson from her first, *The daring game,* but the differences in quality are appreciable. Again we meet an adolescent girl from Toronto who feels at odds with her new surroundings (in this case, the Alberta lake and cottage country rather than an exclusive girls' boarding school), and again this young girl's westward journey becomes a metaphor for her journey to confidence and emotional maturity. But several new elements enter Pearson's fiction with this newest novel, elements which make *A handful of time* a much more complex and self-aware piece of writing.

First of all, Pearson confronts head-on the relationship of her writing to the well-known "problem fiction" subgenre, a category of writing recently criticized by Michele Landsberg in her study of children's books. Pearson's Patricia *is* a young girl with a problem, but she is no candidate for the advice-pandering variety of children's fiction. When her father, whose main interests seem confined to word-processing, cuisinarts and sushi, tries to talk to his daughter about divorce, he sounds to Patricia "as if he were talking in a book, like the one her mother had just bought for her—*The boys' and girls' book about divorce*". Beware, yuppie parents, Pearson seems to be saying: this book is not a quick, easy substitute for parenting. Albertan cousins, put off by their citified relative, propose a separation pact of their own: "—so we have a solution," Patricia's cousin Kelly decides, "Every afternoon we'll pretend to go out together. Then we'll separate".

The marital separation, in fact, brings into focus an even more crucial separation in the novel: the separation between mother and daughter. Here we find both Pearson's strength and her weakness. The fantastic device of a trip back in time allows Patricia to comprehend why her mother appears so cold, so invulnerable; she has developed those qualities in response to the unfair gender-stereotyped treatment which she had received as an adolescent girl in a household of spoiled boys. Still, some of the negative aura surrounding the career-obsessed mother remains in the novel, in spite of Patricia's—and our—growing empathy. Late in the novel, Patricia is asked what she wants to do with her life. It quickly becomes obvious that she is going to eschew the upwardly-mobile road to fame which her mother, as a CBC television personality, has chosen: " 'Maybe I could run a restaurant . . . Or . . . Maybe I'll be a mother,' she said softly". In a novel which elsewhere manages to call into question the bourgeois assumptions of children's "problem" fiction, we find here what Betty Friedan christened "the feminine mystique" of the 1950s making a return visit. Must the "handful of time" during which women have turned bourgeois assumptions upside-down bring us, along with Patricia, back to the myths of the past? (pp. 53-4)

> Lorraine M. York, "A Journey to Confidence," in Canadian Children's Literature, No. 49, 1988, pp. 53-5.

---

### The Sky Is Falling (1989)

The Second World War setting of **The Sky Is Falling,** Vancouver writer Kit Pearson's third novel, is timely in that the book's release coincides with the 50th anniversary of that conflict. But this is more than just a book on a hot topic. As in Pearson's award-winning second novel, **A Handful of Time,** the central character must struggle to adapt to changing circumstances that suit her not at all. This is a theme with strong literary antecedents: Frances Hodgson Burnett's *The Secret Garden* comes to mind.

The year is 1940; France has fallen to Hitler and British children are being evacuated to other parts of the Commonwealth as the bombing intensifies. Ten-year-old Norah is outraged when told that she and her 5-year-old brother, Gavin, are going to Canada. She thinks it cowardly to flee and doesn't fancy taking care of Gavin. The two end up as rather unhappy "war guests" in a wealthy Toronto home, where Gavin is spoiled and Norah left to her own devices.

It is Pearson's attention to detail both funny and sad that makes this book so engaging. In the afterword she explains that her novel was inspired by storyteller Alice Kane's memory of telling stories such as Henny Penny to evacuee children and hearing from one child that the sky was indeed falling back home in England. The 9- to 12-year-old

readers of **The Sky Is Falling** will appreciate Norah's feelings of homesickness and isolation in a strange country and be cheered by her hard-won ability to cope.

> Annette Goldsmith, in a review of "The Sky Is Falling," in Quill and Quire, Vol. 55, No. 11, November, 1989, p. 14.

The Germans have begun bombing England, and Norah's parents decide to send their two children to Canada for safety. Norah is aghast at the idea and bitterly resists her parents' decision. Nevertheless, she and her five-year-old brother, Gavin, find themselves in Toronto with Mrs. Ogilvie, a wealthy widow. Norah, 10, reacts with a quiet rage that makes her a loner at school and keeps her distanced from Gavin, who is having his own difficulties. Compounding Norah's anger is the personality clash she has with Mrs. Ogilvie, who seems to prefer Gavin and doesn't hesitate to set rules that make no sense to Norah. She responds by covertly doing as she pleases, nurturing a forbidden friendship with a German boy whose mother is a cleaning woman. Though Norah eventually settles into her Canadian surroundings, it takes a major clash with Mrs. Ogilvie and an attempt to run away before Norah and her hostess finally begin to understand each other. Pearson's novel is a compelling, sensitive study of children traumatized by separation. Its strength is in its particularly well realized characterizations of not only Norah and her brother, but also secondary figures who bear on the children's lives.

> Denise Wilms, in a review of "The Sky Is Falling," in Booklist, Vol. 86, No. 18, May 15, 1990, p. 1805.

In contrast to most evacuation stories in which children retain balance despite their world being shattered, Norah's dissolution is realistic and moving. Minor characters are well drawn. Even the seemingly rigid widow is sympathetic and capable of change. Pearson uses the theme of the child as a pawn in an adult world gone wrong effectively. Her portraits of the well-meaning but shallow adults contrast strongly with the moving scene of the storytelling librarian whose rendition of the struggles of orphaned "Alenoushka and her brother," told without dramatics or even applause, holds the children spellbound. There is plenty of conflict and action to hold young readers' interest in Norah's struggles with her new family and school. Superior and compelling historical fiction for middle graders.

> Louise L. Sherman, in a review of "The Sky Is Falling," in School Library Journal, Vol. 36, No. 6, June, 1990, p. 125.

# Eleanor Spence

## 1928-

Australian author of fiction and nonfiction.

Major works include *The Green Laurel* (1963), *The Switherby Pilgrims* (1967), *The Nothing-Place* (1972), *The October Child* (1976; U. S. edition as *The Devil Hole*), *A Candle for Saint Antony* (1977).

One of Australia's most highly regarded writers for the middle grades through high school, Spence is considered a pioneer in the development of a distinctively Australian children's literature. Praised for creating both contemporary and historical fiction that treats a variety of social problems with characteristic understanding, she is acknowledged as among the first Australian writers to address topics such as alcohol and drug use, sexism and racism, deafness, autism, and materialism, and to show their effect on family and community in a balanced, low-key manner. Spence is also acknowledged for her portrayals of both child and adult characters and for her vivid detailing of Australian history and the Australian landscape. Setting her books in and around her hometown of Sydney, Spence delineates both the beauty and the ruggedness of Australia while exploring its social scene. She centers her stories around male and female protagonists who learn to cope with problems often connected to family life; frequently describing young outsiders who are ambitious, independent, and creative, Spence concentrates on the personal growth and maturation of her characters, who gain self-confidence by accepting responsibility for themselves. Despite the harshness of some of her topics, Spence underscores her works with optimism as well as such values as tolerance, loyalty, and equality.

A former teacher and librarian in both Australia and England, Spence was prompted to write for children when she recognized the paucity of juvenile literature set in Australia. Many of her works are closely aligned with Spence's personal background and interest in local history; her earliest works, adventure stories featuring female protagonists in mostly rural settings, are often inspired by her own experiences, while her more recent books reflect her work as a teacher of autistic children as well as the experiences of her family. These stories, which include mostly male protagonists and are set mainly in urban and suburban locales, are noted for their increased realism and believability. In addition to the many works she has set in present-day Australia, Spence has placed several of her books in the nineteenth and early twentieth centuries, backgrounds which she uses to reflect the growth of her country. Throughout her career, Spence has written several stories that observers consider especially notable. *The Green Laurel,* the story of how Lesley, the daughter of a nomadic family, finds security and self-appreciation in a housing settlement, is often placed among Spence's best books, while the works including handicapped characters, *The Nothing-Place,* which features Glen, a partially deaf pro-

tagonist, and *The October Child,* in which musically talented Douglas learns to accept his autistic younger brother, are noted for their sensitivity to their subjects without sensationalism. With *Me and Jeshua* (1984), Spence departs from her usual Australian settings to describe a nostalgic retrospective of the narrator's affectionate relationship with his cousin, Jesus. Spence won the Australian Book of the Year Award for *The Green Laurel* in 1964 and for *The October Child* in 1977, a work which was also placed on the International Board on Books for Young People (IBBY) Honour List in 1978; *The Left Overs* (1982) was highly commended for the Australian Book of the Year Award in 1983, an award for which *Me and Jeshua* was commended in 1985 and *Deezle Boy* (1987) was shortlisted in 1988.

(See also *Something about the Author,* Vol. 21; *Contemporary Authors New Revision Series,* Vol. 3; and *Contemporary Authors,* Vols. 49-52.)

---

## AUTHOR'S COMMENTARY

*Myself—the writer?* I've added the question-mark because, as I often try to explain to children and adults alike . . . , I'm always at a loss to separate the essential 'me' from the 'author' of a dozen or so novels. I don't believe it can be done; even works of fiction bear, written large or small, the imprint of the writer's personality, interests, and experience, though they are—and should be—in disguise.

The disguise can often wear thin. When asked by young readers (who seem to come up with more subtle questions every year) if any character in my books is actually *me,* I usually start mumbling and dodging, because I recall with a kind of guilt the number of literary, well-read, sensitive and imaginative heroes and heroines who emerge in so many of my books, to say nothing of the independent and ambitious ones like Harriet in **Lillipilly Hill** and Cassie in **Switherby Pilgrims** and **Jamberoo Road.**

I'm not saying I really *was* like that. Rather, these characters are romantic images of what I *sometimes* was. And they are the kinds of people I loved to read about in my own childhood. I think that as I grow older, becoming further removed in time from the days of my youth, I tend to recall some of the deeper, less obvious aspects of myself-as-child-and-teenager, and this has led to the creation of characters like Rowan in **Time to Go Home,** and Rudi in **A Candle for Saint Antony.** The fact that they are both boys, whereas earlier I tended to use girls as central figures, may have a significance in itself. To even things up, I've gone back to the female side in **The Seventh Pebble,** and make no apologies for calling my heroine 'Rachel', which is my own second name. . . .

Thus the answer to my young questioner, seeking to discover which person in my books is really me-in-disguise, would have to be: '*All* the central characters have something of me in them, not just me-as-a child. They also contain me-as-writer—and storyteller.' (p. 94)

I have always believed that every novel for young readers must have a story worth telling, on my side, and worth reading, on their side. The fact that many adults are dipping into children's fiction (either furtively or openly) suggests to me that they are as inevitably drawn to a 'good yarn' as their children. Yet it is this feature of the writer's task that has always given me the most trouble. My heart goes out to primary-school pupils who are expected to write a 'story' in the course of their 'Creative Language' lessons; I know exactly how hard it is to come up with a sound, believable, *original* plot. So often you think you have one, only to find that it breaks down miserably in the middle, or collapses before it reaches the finish-line. I rather tend to create characters first and foremost, and then hope they will obligingly suggest their own 'story', by doing things natural to their own personalities; this can be over-optimistic, and is by no means always successful. I would much prefer to be inspired right away by a brilliant plot-idea—or group of ideas—and build up my characters in the course of the action. I feel that must be the way a truly great story-teller works; he manipulates his 'people' according to his clearly thought-out plan, rather than letting the people manipulate *him.*

The problems I have with plots no doubt reflects the real-life difficulties I have with organising my own thinking. I invariably see two sides to every question, and try to fol-

low both at once. Or I start off to pursue a line of thought to its necessary conclusion, and become distracted by all kinds of fascinating little byways, and never get to the end at all. As a child, I spent hours day-dreaming; as an adult, I still do it, though I might appear to observers to be concentrating on the sheet of paper in my typewriter, boldly headed: 'Chapter Six'.

How much attention do I pay to the needs and wants and abilities of my young readers? This is the most vexed question of all, and one rightly asked by many librarians, teachers and parents, and sometimes the children themselves. I certainly don't work at my typewriter with, posed in the imagination in the middle distance, an 'average' boy or girl aged eleven and a half, with an IQ of 110 and a reading-age of twelve; that kind of limitation would rapidly stifle even the brightest flame of inspiration. Yet we must work within a certain framework of rules, and it is just this that, to my mind, makes writing for the young a more demanding job than writing for adults.

I did not set out with the intention of being a 'writer for children.' I *did* set out to be a writer. As a nine-year-old, I scribbled away at my own stories, unmoved by the fact that they were shamelessly derived from *Anne of Green Gables* or *Seven Little Australians.* I loved to read and write about families, and I was especially fascinated by orphans. I yearned to adopt neglected infants. As there were none available in our neighbourhood of small farms and orchards, where parents, though often hard-pressed financially, did a great job of bringing up their children, I had to settle for adopting stray kittens, or turning my assortment of dolls into orphanage-waifs. Because another dearly-loved book was Noel Streatfeild's *Ballet Shoes,* the foundlings usually graduated to brilliant futures.

Years later, when experience as a children's librarian gave me the idea of writing stories for children, I found it relatively easy to adopt a style suited to the theme—in this case, a straightforward adventure in the bush called *Patterson's Track.* I was *comfortable* using this means of expression, and time proved that young readers accepted and enjoyed it. I simply went on as I had begun.

The writer, like any other person, grows and alters and develops with time and circumstances. His or her books will inevitably reflect this pattern of growth, separated from the reality by distance, imagination, and much embroidery. Even my 'historical' stories, like **Lillipilly Hill** and **Switherby Pilgrims,** have their roots in a certain period of my own life when I was especially interested in local history, and the theme of **The Nothing Place** reflects the beginning of my concern for the handicapped and the 'disadvantaged' in the community.

My first consideration is to tell a story, not to pass on messages. At the same time, however, I do hope that the occasional reader might gain something positive from one or two of my books; after all, I am trying to share a particular experience with that person, who happens to be young. The gain, as I recall from my own childhood reading, is a moment of recognition, a glow of feeling shared with a character in a certain situation—a very special kind of joy. (pp. 95-6)

Eleanor Spence, "Notes by Eleanor Spence," in Innocence and Experience: Essays on Contemporary Australian Children's Writers by Walter McVitty, Thomas Nelson, 1981, pp. 94-6.

---

## GENERAL COMMENTARY

**Walter McVitty**

Given the quantity and frequency of her books, their acknowledged quality, their typographical elegance and the benefit of translations into various European languages, it is strange that Eleanor Spence has not yet shared the universal fame and adulation enjoyed by some of her Australian contemporaries. However, when one looks in retrospect at the total output of her two decades of writing, some explanations do suggest themselves. The subject matter of her books, while close to human concerns, is generally modest and unspectacular, while her style is always accomplished but mild and unobtrusive. Her stories, while always interesting, have usually been of no profound significance, so that one's involvement in them tends to be transitory, although enjoyable. Her characters generally have no aberrations and, until recently at least, suffer few traumas. She does offer diverting reading, of a quality which puts her in the first rank of writers for children, but the experience, in retrospect, is somewhat bland. Even though she has grown towards the modern realistic 'problem' novel, her quiet way has produced books which are so low-key that the easy impact which some others make by over-stating the case is never made by her. Eleanor Spence's writing is restrained, provoking no extreme responses but, rather, a quiet admiration. In spite of her focus on real characters and their problems, she remains suitably detached from them, always the omniscient author. She seldom intrudes on her own narrative, seldom comments except by inference and seldom even *describes* much—it's all no-nonsense, straightforward storytelling which never yields to any temptation to be 'literary'—there are no purple passages. (The closest she gets is at one point in *The Year of the Currawong* when she is moved to write: 'Next morning dawn came prettily with skirts of frost and scarves of mist'.) Metaphor and simile are rare indeed in her books, whose mood is much closer to austerity than extravagance. Such observations, seen together, might explain why such a gifted author has won sufficient minds, but fewer hearts, among her critical readership.

Eleanor Spence's first children's book *Patterson's Track* was well and truly within the established tradition of its day, the emphasis being strictly on adventure. The idea of commencing a story with a family of children going on summer holidays, with parents conveniently out of the way, and then proceeding to allow them to have Great Adventures in the Bush (including, of course, the obligatory bushfire) was quite conventional. And although there is the hint of ever-present danger, no reader is ever likely to doubt the safe and successful outcome of the *Patterson's Track* expedition. The bushfire is put out in a couple of paragraphs: the reader can tell that the episode is not going to end in disaster through the style itself: 'No sooner had one flame been laboriously conquered than another

leapt gleefully ahead of it'. Even when the reader is supposed to fear for Karen, trapped on a rock-face, the casualness of the writing assures us that all will be over safely within a page. (pp. 68-9)

*Patterson's Track* gets its impetus from a supposed piece of local history, a fact which indicates one of the author's special interests, one which leads her to write not only completely historical novels such as *The Switherby Pilgrims* but also to incorporate into her plots such details as Alex's investigation of historical records of the old mine in *The Year of the Currawong,* the children's planning for the Captain Cook Bi-Centenary celebrations in *The Nothing Place,* the uncovering of the old chapel in *A Candle for Saint Antony* or, in *The Summer in Between,* Faith Melville's writing of a play based on her romantic notions of the original inhabitants of the oldest house in the district. In *Patterson's Track* it is Karen's passionate desire to discover the real truth about an incident in 1820 which leads the children to go on the bush 'safari'. After being told the story of a convict named Simon Patterson, Karen becomes obsessed by an element of injustice which, she suspects, surrounds and discredits the memory of his name. While one can imagine a child being interested to hear the details of such a story, it is hard to believe that Karen could be so fired up as to convince a whole party of other children to set off (with adult approval) for a prolonged camping-hike into dense mountain country in search of they-know-not-what, on the strength of the germinal story for it comes across, *as the reader receives it,* as being of passing interest only. (p. 70)

The major theme of *Patterson's Track* (common also in Joan Phipson's work) and one which remains a constant preoccupation in Eleanor Spence's other books, is that of an individual's quest for identity, of the need to become a 'person' and to be accepted, to 'belong'. Karen, in *Patterson's Track,* is plain, untidy, self-conscious, poor at schoolwork and sport—a retiring, timid daydreamer—but she does change and grow by the end of the book, which is, in a sense, her personal drama of self-discovery.

Faith Melville, the subject of *The Summer in Between,* is, by contrast, already an accomplished leader among her peers in her small community of Kenilworth. . . . The arrival for summer holidays in Kenilworth of a rival, in the form of a similarly-commanding but less self-occupied and more perceptive Pauline, brings about a mild reversal for Faith Melville, whose leadership is now threatened. . . . Faith's capacity for growth, her ability to adjust to changed relationships and her successful reconciliation of her own personal conflicts, bring their own reward, the moral value of which is made clear by the author:

> A wonderful feeling of well-being took possession of her—a sense of belonging, and of being needed. It was not something she could put into words. So she sipped her milk and watched the currawongs, black and white shapes in the green shadows, and was extremely glad that she was Faith Melville of Kenilworth.
>
> (pp. 70-2)

Eleanor Spence returned to the historical novel for her third book, *Lillipilly Hill.* The main concern of its Victorian heroine Harriet Wilmot is to convince her family to remain in Australia rather than return to the ordered comforts of England, recently left behind. She already feels that she 'belongs', so her schemes are designed to make her family (and especially her studious brother Aidan) feel that way too. The main incident which leads to Aidan becoming accepted in the still-rough Australia of the book's pioneering setting is his role in a cricket match. Appropriately, it is the application of his acknowledged intelligence (a faculty which has made him vulnerable), rather than any sudden miraculous acquisition of sporting prowess, which leads to his success. The bush cricket match is an exciting and credible episode and has the value of bringing Aidan 'the knowledge that hereafter he would never lack for friends'. His relationship with a furtive runaway boy is even more important because this character, as much of an outcast as Aidan has felt himself to be, *has* succeeded in adapting, in coming to terms with the new wilderness and making it his own. *Lillipilly Hill* is a splendidly absorbing book.

The imperative need to 'belong', to put down roots and achieve an identity in relation to permanent surroundings, no matter how unpromising, and with troops of friends to sustain one, is the driving force for Lesley Somerville in *The Green Laurel. . . .* Lesley is the daughter of the proprietor of a miniature train used for pleasure rides at country fairs and carnivals: the Somerville family existence is thus a rootless, nomadic one, with neither permanent home nor regular friends. (pp. 72-4)

Mr Somerville's ill-health lands him in hospital, giving his family a period of respite from its travels and the chance to experience, for the time being at least, suburban life. During this period, Lesley visits what ought to be the 'dear perpetual place' of some affluent city acquaintances and discovers something important about material possessions and of the relation between having and being, for these people have not acquired the happiness and tranquillity which Lesley has believed middle-class life to guarantee. Lesley realises that, for a family, it's very much a matter of home-is-where-the-heart-is; it can be 'any sort of place'. . . . (p. 74)

*The Year of the Currawong* can be seen as another variation on the theme of belonging. In this book a history professor takes up a temporary appointment at a university college in rural New South Wales and his family, the Kendalls, move from Sydney to set up house at a place called Currawong Crossing. The whole family becomes so involved in their new life and environment, as the story develops, that nobody wants to leave at the end, just as in *Lillipilly Hill. The Year of the Currawong* is one of Eleanor Spence's happier and more satisfying children's books. The family is clearly delineated; the minor characters (for example, Mister Lee, the Chinaman—for whom the author is sensible enough to avoid trying to reproduce the peculiarities of speech) add variety and interest; the plot is neatly worked out, the mood is quietly joyous and the style is good. The warmth and competence of the writing, the strong sense of place and the careful unravelling of the mystery of the true ownership of an old mine make it a 'good read'. (p. 75)

After the first five books, which thematically form a group of their own, Eleanor Spence produced two related works of straight historical fiction, *The Switherby Pilgrims* and *Jamberoo Road.* Each book lacks the strong human-interest thematic focus of the earlier group and the concentration on one particular heroine with whom most young readers might happily identify. *The Switherby Pilgrims* tells of a Miss Arabella Braithwaite's emigration from England to Australia in the 1820s with a group of ten orphans in order to give them what she sees as a better chance in life. . . .

*Jamberoo Road* is a sequel in which Miss Braithwaite concentrates on planning for the future lives of the children.

*The Switherby Pilgrims* suffers through having to spread its interest over too many characters; its style is comparatively formal and the plot predictable, while certain aspects of it (for example, the role of Gracechurch as the dastardly villain) seem borrowed from music-hall melodrama. The literary potential of the hazardous sea trip, with innocent children sharing the vessel with convicts suffering near-intolerable privations, is rather glossed over—a promising opportunity missed. The details of life in the clearing which the Switherby party occupies in the Illawarra district might have been made more interesting and exciting if given the close day-to-day involvement of a Laura Ingalls Wilder, but the potential wealth of homely details of pioneer life is not really exploited. As far as they go, *The Switherby Pilgrims* and *Jamberoo Road* are interesting histories but one misses the richer saga they might together have become.

A change in the direction of Eleanor Spence's writing came suddenly with *The Nothing Place.* The uncomfortable reality of some aspects of everyday experience and the problems which seem to bedevil modern family life in materialist, urban societies, of which we were given the first signs of recognition in *The Green Laurel,* now became central issues as the author moved away from the more innocent rural world of her earlier books and into the realities of contemporary, urban experience.

At its simplest, one would say that *The Nothing Place* is about a partially-deaf boy, and that after the harmonious, intact and 'normal' families of *The Year of the Currawong* or *The Summer in Between* it was timely to introduce a variation, an alternative which might speak more genuinely about the human condition. . . . The notion of writing a book in which the hero had a handicap had precedents in Ivan Southall's *Let the Balloon Go* and Patricia Wrightson's *I Own the Racecourse!* But a handicapped hero, with his attendant worries and challenges, is no guarantee on his own that something 'meaningful' is being said to today's readers, for the casualties in life are not always the obvious ones like Glen Calder with his hearing problem. *The Nothing Place* and the books which follow present us with other ordinary people who sometimes seem to be making a bit of a mess of their lives and who can be seen to be 'crippled' in various ways. *The Nothing Place* title does not refer to Glen or to his deafness but to the spiritual emptiness of the barren new suburbs in which the only excitement seems to be the commercial kind offered by the central shopping centre. Glen might be handicapped by his deafness but other characters are handicapped, just as surely, by the stressful environment in which they live—and this is the theme which Eleanor Spence has been developing in her recent books.

*The Nothing Place* is the first of the Eleanor Spence novels which leave the reader feeling uncomfortable about the muddle of family life and the false aspirations of the new society. There's hardly a currawong or lillipilly in her books of experience. . . . There's no chance of a return to the innocent make-believe of *Patterson's Track* or *The Summer in Between.* The portrayal of family life in *The Nothing Place* is markedly different from that in, say, *The Year of the Currawong,* in which the father is a clever professor who walks about the house whistling 'Waly Waly', 'The Vicar of Bray' and 'The Earl of Moray'; Mummy paints pictures; little Chess wants to be an engineer and keeps asking frightfully intelligent questions at the age of eight about tree planting, soil conservation and timber-getting; Terry, a budding playwright, reads a *Classical Dictionary* while shelling peas; Alex, named after Alexander the Great, is likely to fall asleep reciting famous battle speeches of the ancients. I have never actually met such a family in real life although they do seem to exist in plenty of books. I do recognise, however, the evident reality of the 'warts-and-all' family life as presented in Eleanor Spence's more recent books.

There's nothing esoteric about the Calder family of *The Nothing Place.* Father is no mild-mannered professor, nor is he the laconic and benign teacher-farmer pipe-smoking dad of *The Summer in Between.* Instead, Mr Calder is a selfish boor . . . In the dreariness of the 'nothing place', families are no longer cosily intact. The sensitive Lyndall's parents have separated (a divorce is pending) and Shane's father is dead. Since Eleanor Spence is given to reporting (selectively, of course) rather than editorialising, any judgement upon the quality-of-life is only there by implication, so that many young readers would not recognise any intended irony in *The Nothing Place:* 'Some Mimosa Vale housewives spent an entire day [at the shopping centre]—between the school hours of nine and three—hunting for 'specials' in the supermarket, visiting the hairdresser, trying on shoes, or simply window-shopping and sipping coffee in the 'Boulevard' when their budgets were exhausted.'

Eleanor Spence's representation of childhood also underwent a change in her salutary journey away from the viewpoint of innocence. Her earlier heroines did have a besetting sin, the existence of which allowed personal conflict to arise at a certain point, adding to the drama, the resolution of which always had the effect of making that otherwise fine person into a better one. Terry, in *The Year of the Currawong,* had to learn to overcome her overweening pride and accept constructive criticism of her formerly unquestioned abilities as a budding writer, in order to grow from the experience. Faith's problem in *The Summer in Between* was similar, due to her unrealistic view of her own acting potential and an inflated self-image as an infallible leader of her peers. However, in *The Nothing Place* such matters would be of little consequence; such crises would merely be storms in very small teacups. The new

Spence children are more recognisable as the sort one meets every day in real life. The teenage Shelley is neither poet nor thespian—her interests centre on boys and fingernail polish: 'The neon lights of Southdale Court [the big shopping centre] had been dazzling her for at least twelve months'.

Shelley marks the beginning of this author's growing interest in the proper portrayal of behaviour in the teenage sub-culture. As the adolescent hero of *Time to Go Home,* Rowan Price is the character who must engage the reader's sympathy but, likeable as he is, there is more than one side to his portrayal. It probably only registers with the most careful of readers that, in the course of the book, this sixteen-year-old hero is often irritable, is capable of deliberate malingering and deceit, swears, gets drunk, forges a parent-teacher note, borrows money to buy cigarettes and steals from his sister. Another boy, Cliff, steals money so that he can go illegally to see restricted films; he also smokes pot. Rowan's sister Jill feuds with her friends, lies to her mother, is boy-mad, and can be as grumpy and vindictive as her brother. An otherwise kindly and controlled teacher is capable of reaching out and grabbing 'a handful of Rowan's hair, jerking his head back with a force that made Rowan's eyes water'. Rowan is from a one-parent family; his mother has to go out to work, so that she is sometimes irritable and short-tempered. Kippy's father is in gaol.

Singly or collectively, the above details of situation or behaviour, cited out of context, seem overstated—but in context they represent ordinary everyday occurrences and nothing more. I can imagine some adults wanting to reject *Time to Go Home* on the basis of such a description, yet some readers who know the book might doubt the veracity of this description and will want to check to see if all that really does happen, for Eleanor Spence's quiet method 'sensationalises' nothing.

*Time to Go Home* questions, by implication, the value of transitory sporting heroics and the hollowness of athletic achievement where this is pursued by individuals for the wrong reasons. Rowan wants to succeed at Rugby football because he thinks he is useless at everything else—success will gain him the attention and admiration of his peers. Luckily, the team's coach has a more balanced perspective. (His philosophical approach is perhaps too good to be true, but he plays a counselling role like many of his counterparts in children's literature everywhere.) Rowan's friendship with a young part-Aboriginal boy named Kippy, and his willingness to offer to coach this little boy's ragtag football team, is an example of his basic goodness. As the story progresses, Rowan experiences the usual conflicts of 'young adult' heroes: he wants to be liked by Kippy *and* his female admirer Andrea *and* his football peers but he also needs to *give* love and it would be true to say that the relationship with Kippy is not entirely selfless, while that with his mother is slightly Oedipal. That the story should end after Rowan has been beaten up brutally by his 'pot'-smoking rival, and is unable to play in the match for which all his efforts have been a culmination, is evidence of Eleanor Spence's determination to shirk no issues in her presentation of life—in which not all endings are happy.

With *The October Child* Eleanor Spence won her second Book of the Year Award and a renewed public attention. Family life is again the basic subject, genuine problems are introduced and the author's switch in interest from girls to boys is by now consolidated. *The October Child* is Carl, the fourth child in the Mariner family—and he is autistic. The family only gradually becomes aware that Carl is seriously handicapped but his behaviour proves to be so extremely disrupting to the formerly pleasant family life that the reader witnesses it breaking down as a result of the stresses Carl places on it. There is no sudden and magical cure for the general condition known as autism, even for an omnipotent author and, no matter how tolerant and patient, few households can long survive the rigours of life with a person so alarmingly handicapped. (pp. 76-82)

The portrayal of Glen Calder's father in *The Nothing Place* as a loveless and unlovable man was a contrast to the earlier representation of fathers as comfortable security-figures but Robert Mariner of *The October Child* is an entirely different picture again, one which I find exceptionally interesting. Although he is a respected and likeable person ('Robert Mariner was such a quiet and peaceable man that it was hard to imagine him quarrelling with anyone') there is an almost pathetic wistfulness about him. One feels that his retiring disposition ('He left most of the major family decisions to Beth') has brought him a placid existence at the expense of allowing the more adventurous life of his dreams to pass him by. He is thus something of a failure, which perhaps only Douglas is able to perceive, as he does while his family is moving in to the new home in Sydney: 'For the first time, Douglas saw him, not merely as a father, but as a tired, stooped, and perpetually worried middle-aged man'. . . . For this land-bound man—a mute, inglorious Walter Mitty—has always hankered for the sea, and it is interesting to note the little ways in which the author allows the reader to discover this fact, for she makes little of it. Joseph Conrad always believed that a writer should always hold back from his readers one aspect of a character, keeping it to himself—he felt that if a reader knows as much about a character as its creator does then the portrayal is bound to be flat and two-dimensional. Eleanor Spence is slightly more helpful. For instance, when Douglas is decorating his new bedroom (the one which Carl later wrecks) his father offers to give him some old prints which he happens to have, stored away somewhere: 'They're mostly sailing-ships, as I remember,' he says. His very name of Mariner is surely a nice little irony in itself. In a sense, the man is handicapped by his own reticence, just as his son is by his autism. It is a fine distinction which the author, characteristically, refrains from making herself.

And yet *The October Child* has little to do with the father and even his children Adrienne and Kenneth could be entirely dispensed with without seriously hurting the plot. The story doesn't need them, although their presence does fill out the picture of normal family life—the quality of which is, after all, the central interest in all this author's books. We take what we want from our reading and, for

me, the quiet portrayal of Mr Mariner seems one of the most subtle and interesting things Eleanor Spence has done. *The October Child* would be the poorer without this small insight into a particular character, but the book certainly doesn't belong to him—nor does it, in spite of its title, belong to Carl, for he is only the cause of the events on which the drama relies, for the main interest is in his effect on others in the family, his brother Douglas in particular. (pp. 83-5)

That *The October Child* is really about Douglas should be obvious from a study of the first chapter, which is germinal. The story is to be so much from his point of view that it even gives him cause to believe that *he* is the cause of his baby brother's abnormality. When *The October Child* starts, Carl's birth is imminent. We discover in the first lines that all is not well—Mrs Mariner is suddenly having a difficult time with the pregnancy. Even the weather is acting unseasonably, the hot wind is 'malevolent', and fair has become foul. (pp. 85-6)

Within a few paragraphs, Douglas has taken himself off to look for his older brother, assumed to be at a nearby lighthouse, the unusual weather having made the waves unsuitable for surfing. The lighthouse is on a peninsula which contains the 'Devil Hole' of the American title, a place at once fascinating yet terrifying to Douglas. . . . (pp. 86-7)

It is in these precincts that Douglas unexpectedly finds himself trapped between the devils of bushfire, dense fog and the deep blue sea (the Devil Hole). . . . (p. 87)

The essential drama in the early stages rests in the fact that, once rescued from his ordeal at the terrifying Devil Hole, Douglas finds his mother no longer at home—she has been taken unexpectedly to hospital for a premature birth, and it is suggested by his thoughtless brother that Douglas is to blame: 'She was real worried when you were missing in that fog, with fire and everything'. Guilt sets in immediately and pursues Douglas throughout the book, for he comes to feel that what turns out to be the baby's extreme abnormality may therefore have been his fault too. The weight of the world is truly on him: the reader is in no position to have any deep feelings about Carl, but Douglas is a character to stir the emotion of pity in each of us—yet one feels confident that he has enough maturity and resilience to survive.

Carl's condition, as described in *The October Child,* is obviously given authority through the author's experience as an aide at a centre for autistic children in Forestville in New South Wales. This book can in fact be read with interest simply as an informative account of autism, for the clinical indications are all there, as any reliable reference source will verify. This sort of information adds to one's range of understanding of people and problems, just as does the author's skill in representing family life while allowing for individual studies within it. Yet *The October Child* is more than mere documentary, and can take its place with the finest of children's literature, given its excellent style and structure.

The author's next book *A Candle for Saint Antony* is a most unusual one, presenting a situation new to Australian children's literature, for it deals with the mutual attraction of two adolescent schoolboys, one of whom confesses to being in love with the other, who is himself too confused either to recognise or admit his own feelings. Rudi is Austrian-born, poor, fatherless, industrious, artistic, intelligent, articulate, sensitive and pretty. Justin is affluent middle-class Australian, boorish, intelligent, handsome, 'macho'. (p. 88)

The two boys, so different in every respect, become friends, so much so that Justin's former cronies, now ignored, turn to innuendo to denigrate a friendship which they cannot understand. Probably the reversal in Justin's character and behaviour is far too sudden and complete to accept—he is a 'heavy' too soon made light—but the attraction is real and understandable.

The German teacher proposes a vacation visit to Austria for her class. Once it is determined that both boys are financially able to make the trip, the reader's interest in the first half of *A Candle for Saint Antony* is sustained through the excitement of following of the day-to-day build-up to the international flight itself (the days are counted, and then the hours). It takes thirty-eight pages of expectancy between the first mention of the excursion and the actual take-off, and the flight is described in the interested detail characteristic of such events, yet the return to Australia, at the end, occupies just one bathetic sentence: 'The flight home was just one long drag'.

In between is the lightness and exhilaration of a visitor's fascination with Vienna and the surrounding countryside, but *A Candle for Saint Antony* is no travelogue, for these events lead up to a sombre climax, in the ruins of an old chapel, where Rudi tells Justin that he loves him, and asks him to stay behind with him in Vienna. A jealous classmate overhears this proposal and in a showdown scene in the hostel recreation room spitefully forces Rudi into the position of having to explain, albeit briefly but by way of confession, his relationship with Justin, publicly before the whole group of boys. This scene has a tenseness not commonly found in children's literature (although it reads more like the denouement of a stage drama). Here is Justin, challenged to deny publicly his beautiful friend, who, for his own part, retains his dignity and human integrity to the end, in a moving and riveting scene, within its context:

> With the effort of his life, Justin took his hands from his face and spoke directly to Rudi.
>
> 'I was going to tell you, anyway. I have to go back—at least for now. All my family's there. Rudi—I'm sorry—'
>
> For the first time, Rudi's calm was ruptured.
>
> 'Sorry!' he repeated. 'Sorry—*for what?*'
>
> But Justin couldn't answer.
>
> Rudi glanced about him at the ring of alien faces, some jeering, some puzzled, some—like Simon's—distressed. And prayed that his voice would not tremble when he spoke.

> 'It was never the way you thought. It never would be.'
>
> He made himself walk slowly from the room. The others closed ranks behind him.

Apart from the central drama, *A Candle for Saint Antony* is notable, as usual, for the author's interesting portrayal of family life. Rudi's is simple and sombre and Justin's 'life-style' is the epitome of affluent, middle-class Sydney society—and again there is no value judgement made about it, other than by implication. Nevertheless, it might make interesting reading for the future student of what it was that middle Australia aspired to in the 1970s. Even Justin's given name is a typical middle-class pretension, and his education is purchased, of course, at a trendily innovative private (that is, non-government) school. (pp. 89-90)

In looking at Eleanor Spence's work as a whole, it is clear that there is at least one of her preoccupations which amounts to a sort of credo. She seems to regard busy work, especially of the creative kind, as having some sort of moral value. When such creative activity is pursued by individuals intent upon developing latent abilities, the rewards are shown to be even greater. The author looks favourably on industrious types who are also sensitive and sensible enough to know what motivates others and who go as far as nurturing and bringing out the best in them, too, as, for instance, Lyndall does in her dealings with Glen in *The Nothing Place.* Glen himself neglects school homework in order to work on ship models for the Captain Cook exhibition (itself a 'worthy' project):

> it was a task he had loved, so slow and painstaking but wonderfully creative. Best of all, it was something he could do all on his own, unhampered by deafness or the half-heard demands of teachers. For the first time since his arrival at Mimosa Vale, he was the centre of attention and approval from his fellows and that made his hours of loving toil amply worthwhile.
>
> (p. 91)

Eleanor Spence's didacticism is not simply a matter of promoting a Protestant work-ethic—she seems determined to pass on the adult writer's experience that busy, creative people are happy people and that to be bored and inactive is to waste opportunities for rewarding living and growth. Douglas, with his responsible attitudes to others and his musicianship, is assured of a worthwhile future while his brother Kenneth, being shiftless and self-centered, seems doomed to a miserable, parasitic life. I see nothing wrong in this sort of didacticism although it bothers some critics. The philosophy it expresses seems to me to be self-evidently true, and worth imparting.

As the depth and seriousness of the subject matter in Eleanor Spence's writing has increased, so too has it seen a corresponding and welcome infusion of levity, although subtle in nature. There is, for instance, much wry humour in *Time to Go Home,* as the author makes observations about her teenage hero but from an adult viewpoint. While on his way to school, pessimistically musing over the dismal state of his life, Rowan says aloud, 'Oh, hell!', and the author adds 'alarming two small Convent schoolgirls who were walking ahead of him'. (The comedy may be too adult-oriented—but at least it exists!) The English teacher is startled when Rowan asks a question about the meaning of a poem by Gerard Manley Hopkins: 'Good Lord! Are you serious?' is his response. Once he realises that the boy is genuinely interested, he approaches him with 'the caution of a hunter trying not to frighten a rabbit back into its burrow'. Sometimes the humour has a mildly surrealist quality:

> Two groups of First-formers, who unable to agree as to what season of the year it was, were using that part of the playground alternately as a cricket-pitch and a soccerfield. Rowan dodged between the wicket-keeper and the goalie, who were arguing fiercely as to whose territory was which.

In this setting, Rowan is having a discussion with a teacher: 'There was a lengthy pause, during which shrill cries of "Ow's 'at?" and "Goal!" assaulted his ears'. It's an incongruous scene which Spike Milligan or Jacques Tati could have invented, but Eleanor Spence makes little of such things, in a book full of cinematic 'sight-gags' and subtle throw-away lines which are a delight to encounter. (pp. 91-3)

The more closely one examines the novels of Eleanor Spence, the more highly one comes to regard them. Here is a writer who offers so many rewarding experiences uniquely her own as well as embodying the journey from innocence to experience which has transformed Australian children's literature. The word which most readily springs to mind in categorising her work is *refined,* but whereas for the earlier books this indicates a genteel quality, it is in the sense of elegant distillation of experience that it can be used for more recent work. Eleanor Spence is a writer with whose work increased familiarity breeds content—beyond the apparent blandness a richly rewarding experience awaits the reader who is prepared to give it the close attention it deserves. (p. 93)

> *Walter McVitty, "Eleanor Spence: Observer of Family Life," in his* Innocence and Experience: Essays on Contemporary Australian Children's Writers, *Thomas Nelson, 1981, pp. 67-93.*

**Ruth Grgurich**

When considering Mrs. Spence's total output to date, one is struck by the fact that there is a natural division in her works, in that the novels she wrote in the fifties and the sixties are different in many ways to those she wrote in the seventies. . . .

Her early fiction reflects her own childhood in the pre-war, pre-television days when the simple pleasures of picnics at the beach, shopping expeditions to the larger nearby town, prize nights at school, and church fetes were all part of family life; later she draws her inspiration from her own growing family and her work with handicapped children. (p. 31)

The themes in [her first two books, *Patterson's track* and *The Summer in between*] concerns self-realization and

leadership as well there is an historical sub-theme in each that acts as the pivot for the action in the stories.

Early Australian history provided the inspiration for three of the novels in this period, *Lillipilly Hill, The Switherby pilgrims* and its sequel, *Jamberoo Road.* (p. 32)

The characterization in these historical novels is excellent, Harriet and Cassie are memorable heroines, while Miss Arrabella Braithwaite deserves a book of her own. There is another delightful character in Dinny O'Brien in *Lillipilly Hill.* A fuller development of Marcie, she is independent and sharp-tongued and a fierce defender of anyone she calls a friend. Luke, who appears in both the pilgrimage books, is certainly not delightful, but he is an interesting character. He is the nearest Mrs. Spence comes in any of her books to a lost soul. His introspection, his rebellious nature and his sense of alienation that very nearly leads him into disaster, are convincingly treated.

Eleanor Spence's historical novels succeed I think in conveying to young people what it might have been like to be a pioneer, exiled in a remoteness that is impossible for us to appreciate now. (p. 33)

The striking thing about both these books is the business of the children. They take up projects with a singleness of mind that doesn't always seem consistent with their ages or character development. Terry, the central character in *The Year of the Currawong* organizes almost single-handed a historic "Back to the Crossing" parade and fete, which I feel would be a bit too much even for a precocious twelve year old.

I don't believe Mrs. Spence broke any new ground with this book; all the main ingredients appeared in earlier books. The plot, which revolves around a bit of local history, was used in two earlier books as well as there are too many theatrical props in the story—a ghost-ridden ruined pub, a mysterious tramp and a Chinese hermit—yet in spite of these the story is slow to develop. It lacks the conflict between the children that lifted *Patterson's track* above the ordinary and as well, it lacks the developing relationship between the children and parents that made *Lillipilly Hill* so absorbing.

Another aspect of Mrs. Spence's writing in the sixties was the development of her descriptive imagery. Interwoven into the stories is the beauty of the countryside. It is this loveliness that captures the hearts of Harriet and her father and makes them want to stay in this new country, and it comes across in a small boy's affinity with his environment:

> Chess ran across the grass with a fine sense of freedom . . . All the sensations of the countryside on a sunny early autumn afternoon came to him through the soles of his feet—the richness of rain-fed grass, the grittiness of yellow dust, the harshness of stone . . .

Eleanor Spence took a new direction in the seventies. All the positive aspects of her earlier books came together and she produced four novels which show great sensitivity and maturity. The central characters in all her earlier books had been girls and with the exception of *The Green laurel* all had rural settings. Now she turns her attention to boys in urban settings and possibly because of the settings I believe each of these books has a quality that transcends the locale. With a few minor adjustments the events could take place in any city, in any part of the world.

*The Nothing place* and *The October child* both concern children who are handicapped. Whichever way it is done, physical afflictions are difficult to handle fictionally without being tactless or tasteless. I think Mrs. Spence avoided both in these two books. Glen Calder in *The Nothing place* is partly deaf as a result of illness, but tries to hide the fact. As well as the central theme of coming to terms with reality, there is also an historical sub-theme which provides the impetus for the action in the story. This centres on a Captain Cook bicentenary exhibition which the neighbourhood children put on to raise money to buy Glen a hearing aid. Glen is so upset he runs away. It takes an old tramp, Reggie, to make Glen accept and come to terms with his disability.

Mrs. Spence looks at Glen from the inside, as it were, the reader is invited to feel what it is like to be deaf. This is possible because Glen has the normal intelligence of any twelve year old. However, when she made Carl Mariner in *The October child* autistic this wasn't possible since no one understands the minds of these unfortunate children, so here we see Carl from the outside, through the reactions of normal children and others, to what it is like to have a handicapped child as a perhaps embarrassing part of the family. (pp. 33-4)

The passage of time is skillfully handled through dialogue and the way the children change over the three years. The background of school, shopping, welfare centres and suburban streets are carefully integrated to give the reader a familiar setting. . . .

*Time to go home* and *A candle for St. Antony* have been labelled teenage problem novels, but I see them rather as very sensitive insights into the ways boys respond to the pressures of adolescence. (p. 34)

The noticably fewer characters in the four books which deal with contemporary city life gives them a tightness that adds to the sharp reality of their subject matter. Mrs. Spence makes some sharp social comments on the barrenness of suburban life as seen, for example, in shopping centres:

> Some Mimosa Vale housewives spend an entire day there—between school hours of nine and three—hunting for "specials" . . . or simply window shopping.

and on suburban family life:

> . . . his life (Mr. Calder's) appeared to revolve mostly about his work at the office and the leisure hours he spent at the Returned Servicemen's Club.

Eleanor Spence's last book, *The Seventh pebble* returns to a female protagonist and a country setting. Also she has turned once more to the past for her inspiration, but it is the not so distant past of pre-World War Two when some people, even in Australia, were worried by events taking place in Europe.

At the heart of the story is Rachel Blackwood, the eleven year old daughter of Hollybush Flat's only doctor. Her ordered and secure life is contrasted with Bridget Connell's casual hand-to-mouth existence. The Connells are newcomers to the small community and for the first time Rachel becomes aware of prejudice—the people she has known all her life reject the Connells. The fact that they are poor and there is no father is part of the answer, but the real reason lies in the fact they are Irish Catholics.

The ostracism of the Connells is subtly juxtaposed with wireless broadcasts of Hitler's campaign against the Jews in Germany. The Connell's courage, tenacity and family loyalty that enables them to withstand community disapproval is skillfully shown. In fact they dominate the book, although Rachel is the main protagonist she never at any time really involves the reader. Nevertheless, it is a thoughtful book that by implication suggests that behind our casual exterior Australians too, possess the seeds that could germinate into racial discrimination.

Once again Eleanor Spence has shown courage in tackling a difficult theme. The story is interesting enough but seems to lack the tight realism of the books in the seventies.

Discovering the themes and patterns in a writer's total work is the principal objective of a reader attempting a critical appreciation of an author's literary contribution. Reading all Eleanor Spence's adolescent novels it becomes apparent that a common theme appears in each of them, a theme that is relevant to today's adolescents and comes out regardless of period and setting. The author is concerned with self-discovery and the beginnings of accepted responsibility, not only to others, but for one's own actions. Her heroines and heroes find their way through the bewildering complexities of adolescence, each in their way, learning to distinguish between fancy and reality.

It is not the similarity of material that matters but the variety of treatment. Each of Mrs. Spence's novels is an individual work, presenting and solving its own problems. They are studies of the interaction of human beings and of the reaction of people to their environment and their times. She makes subtle observations, particularly in her later novels about such social problems as drugs and alcohol, sexism, racism and mateship, but she has never made them a focal part of her stories. She writes about them in such a detached way and they form such an intricate part of the story that they are frequently overlooked.

One flaw that I can see in Eleanor Spence's work is her characters never elicit from the reader a complete sense of identification. The main characters, for example, are not always as memorable as several of her minor characters, possibly because she uses the main character to act as observer of the actions of the other characters. This is not to say that the young reader cannot identify with her adolescent characters, but rarely, does a character totally capture both the interest and the emotions of the reader.

Eleanor Spence's settings are an integral part of her stories, they are never just the background for the action.

They help the reader to understand the characters' feelings, such as the sense of freedom that the countryside around Lillipilly Hill evoked in Harriet; create atmosphere; or provide a sense of the familiar for the reader when the theme may present difficulties, as in *The October child* and *A candle for St. Antony,* but whatever the setting one has the impression they form part of the author's own close association with her environment.

Eleanor Spence's consistency in producing books that are well written, eminently readable and touch the sensitive areas of adolescent life—sex, authority, school, drugs, relationships to parents and peers—play an important part in helping young people understand themselves and adult society. For these reasons I believe Eleanor Spence is one of this country's foremost writers for young people. (pp. 35-6)

> *Ruth Grgurich, "Eleanor Spence: A Critical Appreciation," in* ORANA, *Vol. 18, No. 1, February, 1982, pp. 31-6.*

## Helen Blenkiron

[While growing up] Eleanor Spence always had plenty of pets and playmates. Subsequently a theme of love and care flows through all her works to the reader. Reflected in her works is a natural understanding of the countryside and the simple life accompanying it, which children especially seem to enjoy. Also permeating her novels is the feeling that she has travelled a great deal. She began writing seriously for children due to the absence of children's books with Australian settings.

Throughout Mrs. Spence's novels there is a wide diversity of human problems which are sensitively and confidently handled by this perceptive author. Whether they be relationships, emotional distress or ill health, she displays innovative and unique techniques in portraying the individual struggling with the conflict of overcoming stereotypical patterns. In this sense she is remarkably and undeniably prophetic in her outlook on the human condition. Many of the problems she incorporates in her works such as divorce, emotional illness, physical hardships, that is to say the grim realities of life, have been so often denied in Australian children's literature. To write about them has taken both courage and insight, but it is always done in the context of family and community. Through this she has attempted to posit a dimension of tolerance and understanding in the young reader.

Mrs. Spence is interested in relationships and her works build to a crescendo with the publishing of *The October child* in 1976. In it we see germination of the earlier seeds sown, development and maturation of both contextual plot and writing style.

Her first series of five books, which thematically are in a category of their own, allude to the myth that life is easy. That is to say "schoolgirl" adventure, although there is a strong element of progressiveness even in them. They detail vividly Australian countryside and at the same time illustrate many facets of Australian pioneering history. They are only prototypal of the books she has matured to writing in the latter half of the 1970's.

She says herself of her transformed style:

> I progressed from stories of mostly secure and contented conventional families to tales of nomadic ones, single parent families, families with handicapped children, families in religious cultural conflict, foster families and so on.

Spence had distinguished herself for her prolific writing with an all embracing acceptance of people's hardships. Throughout her novels is a rich texture of sharing deep sensitivities touching latent and instrinsic responses in her readers. Integrating many aspects of problems which render growth through suffering, Spence brings to them understanding and presents many logical, tangible coping mechanisms. Brewing with an original progressive style she relates without undue didacticism how they are part of life to be faced with positivity and either accepted or overcome. Her wisdom and erudition instructs as to prejudice, fear, labels, and stigmas, which exacerbate crisis and inflict more pain where they already exist.

*Patterson's Track* is an historical adventure story set in the New South Wales bush. . . . The main theme is the reversal of Karen Winter from a reticent character, to become leader of the hike which had the aim of vindicating Patterson. So far so good, but the plot and overall characterizations are bland. It is the work of Spence, the novice. Her other early works: *The summer in between, The nothing place* and *Switherby Pilgrims* are all entwined or bound with bonds of friendship and care. However, they are truncated, in that they are confined to the social mechanics of the middle class. When they do mention or refer to other levels, such as poverty in *Switherby Pilgrims,* there is a paucity of the flow of rich language she matured to write in the late 70's and 80's. Being a philanthropist observer in her travelling, she gains more in insight and perception with each book she writes. She is endowed with a gift of the metaphysical which was in the gestation period until the late 70's.

The reverse of Karen Winter is experienced by Faith Melville in the *Summer in between.* She had to come to terms with the fact that she is an inferior actor to the less popular Colleen. This novel is also a study of solidarity borne out of confusion. By combining acting and writing talents a better production is made: unity erases dissension and discord. Often because of the power of the one failure latent talent is never allowed to surface and bloom. However the quality of writing still does not approach that of Spence's later works.

*The year of the currawong* is similar in theme and style to *The summer in between.* It deals with an individual discovering peace within. The protagonist, Elizabeth Kendall, is unsettled in the family situation after a move to the country. Elizabeth discovers that individuality and happiness depend upon disposition more than circumstance. In this novel Spence uses a special place, the old mine and the hill, the history behind them symbolizing the children's need to be able to escape parental overseeing in order to mature. The author uses a special retreat to symbolize the same idea in *A candle for St. Antony.* The chapel put together by Rudi and Justin is their private dwelling. In *The seventh pebble* the Connells and Rachel Blackwood experience many new and joyful experiences at their bush grotto.

There are too many characters in *Switherby pilgrims* for any of them to become convincing. They project as being bland and distant and although many causes are espoused, the novel fails to convince. Feminism is one underlying theme in this novel. Cassie is one girl who does not fit the stereotypical set for girls in the era. Sharply contrasted is Selina who enjoys sewing and embroidering. These activities were expected of girls at the time, and choosing any other was viewed as indelicate.

*The nothing place* is a lead up to *The October child.* The theme is the development and growth of Glenn who through illness has been left deaf. This novel transcends the style of the writer's earlier novels and exhibits a richness in character prototypes. One gains insight into the pain of being different, not to mention the allied suffering from people's awkward reactions. Glenn is justifiably angry when he learns the money he and his group of friends have raised from "The Museum": a group project to be used to buy him a hearing aid. Surreptitiously arranged, his peers have betrayed their motive of pity. He replies to Lyndall with all the dignity he can muster.

> Understand? Of course I do! What do you think I am—a half wit. You mean that all this time you and the others have been plotting to make a hand out to the poor deaf Calder kid, buy him a hearing aid so that he'll be more different from everyone else. What am I supposed to do—go down on my knees and thank you?

This is wonderful exposure for what happens to people with an obvious handicap. However it is not as succinct and does not have the subtle structural plot that interweaves the rich tapestry of character, plot, and language of *The October child.* Certainly Glenn can demonstrate how he feels, whereas Carl Mariner is autistic, and this offers a complex literary problem. Carl is viewed externally in the context of family with its ramifying problems.

Mrs. Spence is optimistic about resolutions in spite of revealing the horrendous problems to be overcome where an autistic child is concerned.

> Whilst I don't dare hint at miracles I am, I hope, suggesting that with the right sort of patient, consistent training, Carl might at best become acceptable as a family member, and at worst, achieve some degree of independence even within the limits of custodial care.

Narrated from the point of view of Douglas, and seemingly catastrophic for the Mariner family, it is through Carl's teacher Kerry, that hope emanates. Traits of patience, common sense, and determination are displayed, all of which add up to an impressive totality of faith, the antithesis of hopelessness. *The October child* is based on accurate case book medical history and succeeds magnificently as a novel. The difficulties confronting the Mariners are permanent and we see only one stage of the problem.

The open ending typifies an honest author who had to leave the future where it belongs: unknown. . . . [It] was the author's transcendentalism and lyrical efficacy of style,

not to mention experience and knowledge of the subject, autism, which gained for her the ["Children's Book of the Year"] award. It is interesting to note that in working with children on an appreciation of this novel their response was one of wonderment about what would happen to Carl and his family in the future.

Spence's early novels can be interpreted as being the embryonic stage of her latter works, nonetheless she was publishing novels containing elements of which her contemporaries were unaware. She was not alone in her progressiveness, Ruth Park, Nan Chauncy, Colin Thiele are just a few who come to mind who write high standard literature with overall appeal. However Spence's novels have been underestimated and overlooked for lighter literature which does not confront life's grim realities and remind us of its essence, divinity or spirituality. . . . [*Time to go home*] marks the culmination of one writing style, for there is the introduction of a new mode of writing with the inception of *The October child* continuing to the beautiful novel *A candle for St Antony.*

This last title presents a most unusual situation to Australian children's literature. It unveils the mutual affection between two boys, one of whom reveals he is in love with the other. We see the growth of this relationship between the two boys Rudi and Justin. The object is to describe something that is natural, yet misconstrued by observers. Subsequently the impact of this on the two boys aroused within them unnecessary guilt. By some people it is seen as a novel about homosexuality, but Spence intended it to be a book about a relationship that could have been homosexual, but not necessarily. In a general way, it was meant to be about the nature of friendship and love, but not in a specific sense, and not especially sexual. "It was a novel about love and not easy to write," says Spence. Rudi and Justin share a deep love and concern for each other. Whether it is sexual is up to the readers to discern for themselves. This novel succeeds *The October child* and delineates the maturation and development of this important author. Her issues are for everyone to ponder on, but somehow many would repudiate them and pretend they do not exist in their lives.

A book abounding with enriching experiences was written in 1980. *The seventh pebble* is a novel which re-embraces a particular era and although anachronistic to our present age, it concomitantly typifies deep prejudices and hatreds. It does this through profound friendships, religious antipathies and family loyalties pertinent to the human condition regardless of the period. Hitler's speeches can be picked up on the wireless, but the threat of war seems less momentous than the latest Shirley Temple film, the tap dance display, a birthday party, and the arrival of the large Connell family with a mysteriously absent father. Beautifully written, engendered with a loving humour it depicts poverty set against middle-class complacency. The main theme of the book is friendship and loyalty borne out of genuine acceptance, despite general or common opinion. Rachel becomes more and more attached to the impoverished Connells with their grandiloquent claims, social ineptness and mutual loyalty.

Spence's latest three works *The left overs, Me and Jeshua*

and *Miranda going home* define what is real for many children in our society, a predicament of not belonging to the mythical good family. These books enunciate a feeling of isolation and alienation many children experience in their family situation.

Spence herself says of her writing vocation:

> It is very much part of my job to discover what may entertain a new generation—or a handful of it. All of which keeps alive the child in me.

After some individual work with *The left overs,* one child's reaction was to embrace her appreciation for what she had vicariously experienced through a peer, who was in the foster home situation. The innate caring sense within this child thirsted for knowledge to relate and understand. She gained this after reading *The left overs.* This novel's theme is a sharp contrast to Spence's previous books in that these children felt left outside the pattern of the average family. It exudes Spence's experience and dimension for understanding people in a wide variety of real life situations. Under the guardianship of Auntie Bill, Drew, Jasmine, James and Straw reside at Barnfield. Barnfield is destined to close and so becomes a threat to the children's security. They endeavour to fend off the inevitability of their separation by some original ideas which add curry to the plot. Advertisements, an impromptu appearance on television, and constant changes to their appearances so that they will be wanted and kept together, are but a few of their contrivances. Spence has used beautiful merriment, juxtaposed with the desperate yearnings of children for love and care by their own parents, when in actual fact it is not humanly possible. Thus the title of the book is explained:

> Drew gave the chair a last whizzing spin.
> "Guess we're kind of like leftovers."
> "Left Overs", said Auntie Bill "make very good meals. As we all know in this house".

Of course the ending to the novel is that the children do not achieve what they would like—to be kept together. They either return to their parents or move on to suitable custodial care. This is a good and sensitive novel with a nice feel for the rather resigned, often to become the cynical, air of the unwanted child. It shows gently and clearly that there are no easy answers and that endings are more likely to be bitter sweet than happy.

Owing to the theme of *Me and Jeshua,* the young life of Jesus, Eleanor Spence had difficulty getting the book published. However a Christian firm, Dove Communications, finally published it and *Me and Jeshua* was commended in 1985. Accrediting her for her outstanding work, the Literature Board of the Australian Council granted her a Senior Writers' Fellowship for research. It was whilst on a trip to Israel that she gathered material for *Me and Jeshua* and *Miranda going home.*

Intrigue, juxtaposed with the episodic plot, surrounds Jeshua's parentage. The novel begins slowly and one is left confused as to the protagonists until the novel develops, abounding with adventure and philsophical dialogue between Jeshua and his cousin Jude. The novel is narrated through the medium of Jude. Jeshua demonstrates an element of transcendence as he seems omnipotent and pro-

phetic. Boyhood pastimes and mutual games between the two are related. The intricacies of family life are humourously written about and we are not spared life's grim realities. An appalling rendition of life cut down by soldiers slaughtering helpless victims is recounted honestly and without excuse to the young reader. Wisdom that a child could learn from is given incidentally with no didacticism and often by Jeshua. Jude has become lost whilst searching the market for a map. He finds himself terrified and alone in a cellar. His feelings are utter despair until he hears Jeshua's voice. When asked whether the map was worth the effort Jeshua assuredly replies:

> It's not foolish as long as it turns out all right.
> And it did turn out alright, didn't it Jude.

The era when Christ lived is embraced while simultaneously, the geographic details lend themselves to images that allow us to imagine what the child Jesus' life was like. The places blended and woven throughout the novel are the City of Branches, City of the Holy Mountain, Fountain of the Vineyard, Elijah's Mountain and the Great Temple.

In *Miranda going home* Spence amalgamates the identity crisis of both country and parentage. Miranda, an orphan, has arrived at her destination, her grandparents' home. She is different, an outsider, part Roman extraction although her orphan status may require some responsibility on the grandparents' behalf. Miranda accepts living with her strict intrusively questioning grandparents although she knows it will only be temporary. She returns to the Roman garrison to find proof of her heritage and rescues a baby whom she names Benjamin. Amid some dificult times she keeps Benjamin and eventually receives help from Miriam, Jeshua and Josef. However she voluntarily returns to her grandparents, enriched and more contented for her opportunity to experience independence and reciprocal love. The variety of sights and sounds and family relationships of the era are well captured. The setting and events are consequently credible and related in an uncomplicated way. Miranda can be seen as a strong-willed indomitable character who will find her own way in life by using the freedom she has to choose, by experience, than accept the inevitable. In *Miranda going home* it was returning to live with her grandparents, happier for her use of liberty which she independently chose. The inset map, possibly of the route Miranda took, is interesting for children to compare with the Holy Land—Nazareth (Town of Branches), Cana, and the Sea of Galilee. Unfortunately Bethlehem and Jerusalem are not marked but the map and novel are enough to arouse curiosity about the Holy Land. The novel has sublimity of style portraying the beauty of the English language. The lyrical free flowing style makes it a refreshing and informative work.

> Miranda came slowly down the outside stair controlling the tremor that, for a moment her grandfather's measured voice had aroused. It had the power to make her feel guilty all over again, and frightened, just as she had felt at the first sight of him, in the rain on the clock side of the journey from Gerasa.

Conveyed to us is the powerlessness Miranda felt, but had

to overcome when confronted by her grandfather. For children, here is a vicarious experience for them, as well as showing how to face such a situation with confidence and courage. One need not be daunted and overwhelmed by such threatening power to control as portrayed by adults. From beginning to end *Miranda going home* is written in this beautiful lyric style and the reader seems drawn back in time both historically and geographically, to identify with Miranda, her circumstances and life situation.

Eleanor Spence's book *Mary and Frances* was written in 1986. The prologue deals with poverty prevalent on the goldfields in the 1850's. The plot of the book tells how two women fulfil a dream, despite great adversity, to begin the first Australian religious order of nuns whose beginning was at Penola. Eleanor Spence is dealing with a purely Australian background, interwoven through what is a biography of the first Australian candidate for canonization, Mary McKillop, whose unique achievements began with a commitment to lifelong service to God's poor. Amidst obstacles which included unfounded accusations and excommunication, Mary is portrayed by Spence as clinging more tenaciously to her faith at these times. The prologue of the book gives us Frances Brady's background of living in poverty, motherless with several small brothers and sisters whom she was determined would not go to an orphanage. It despicts the life of the impoverished in Australia. We observe the far sighted dimension of perceiving life by this sensitive author. The Brady children talk about having relatives and realizing this to be wealth, even though not thought of as wealth by most people. We are given brief interludes of the history of Scotland, the background to the first Australian order, the Sisters of St. Joseph. She overcame excommunication and received papal approval for her order. When all seems lost and Mary's ally, Frances, seems daunted by the dispersion and expulsion of the order, Mary replies with precise advice for the impatience that ensues.

> They who wait for the Lord shall renew their strength,
> They shall mount up with wings like eagles.

Mary reveals her own security in her faith that they will achieve their dream in the end. The Sisters of St. Joseph can be located in all areas of greatest need throughout Australia and in some areas of New Zealand. Mary was rewarded with a journey to Rome and her homeland Scotland to receive papal approval and to recruit new novices. This is an interesting inspiratory biography with an abundance of understanding for the underprivileged viewing them as equals, with needs that can be rewardingly challenging for those working with them.

Spence writes with insight and a unique ability to convey to children concepts which are really above their understanding such as ex-communication and dedication to an ideal. In *Mary and Frances,* readers can gain an appreciation of the commitment that had to be started to alleviate the problems caused by the gold rush as well as the nineteenth century conditions of the poor. By combining two families at a personal realistic level, the novel has rendered accessible to children's understanding that which is ab-

stract to them. This last novel of Spence's is a continuation of the theme permeating all her novels, Christian ideals and how the living of their ideals can bring to the world harmony despite suffering and hardship.

In all her works Eleanor Spence offers many a panacea with a soupcon of humour, for seemingly insoluble problems. C. S. Lewis, a Christian writer, uses fantasy to illustrate Christian values, whereas Spence takes real life situations and sheds faith, hope and patience on them. These are the antitheses to hopelessness for problems and illustrate either acceptance of the inevitable or the overcoming of what may well be mastered. Spence has become a seasoned writer knowing well what ideas are capable of being grasped by children. (pp. 17-23)

> *Helen Blenkiron, "Eleanor Spence—A Woman Ahead of Her Time," in* Reading Time, *Vol. XXXI, No. IV, 1987, pp. 17-24.*

---

## TITLE COMMENTARY

### *Patterson's Track* (1958)

[How] valuable is the constant shift of loyalties in *Patterson's Track,* an excellent story by Eleanor Spence about three Sydney children, on a back-country visit, trekking through the bush with local friends. The story is memorable for its plot, which rests on the unravelling of a piece of local history, but still more on the behaviour of the children during their exacting journey. At the end of it, town-bred Barry has thought twice about the yokels and his sister has questioned his authority for the first time; none of the children is quite the same as before. These are cheerful, extroverted children; there is no dreary musing over emotions. All the same, you can watch the family pattern of town and country children changing and re-forming. This is a splendid study of character in action. (pp. 284-85)

> *Margery Fisher, " 'Little Birds in their Nests Agree': Family Stories," in her* Intent Upon Reading: A Critical Appraisal of Modern Fiction for Children, *Brockhampton Press, 1961, pp. 270-96.*

---

### *The Summer in Between* (1959)

[Marcia] Lane-Foster's design for the jacket of *The Summer In Between* is nearly conventional. Only a glow in its colour, an unusual vitality in the figures, distinguishes it from the covers of many tales of holiday adventure. The artist has in fact provided a comment on the story, for Miss Spence has written a conventional holiday story, without originality in invention or (except that this is Australia) in setting, but she has done it so well that the story glows with a light of its own. The plot might have been devised by anyone (and has indeed, frequently!). In Miss Spence's hands it becomes a live thing.

Faith, at twelve, has just left Junior School, where she has been the cleverest girl and the leader in all enterprises. The summer holidays, with Christmas as their centre-piece, lie ahead. It is a "summer in between" for afterwards she will go to Public School. In the eventful days that follow, she learns how to follow as well as how to lead and how to bear and grow through acquaintance with disappointment. A charming happy book, with neat sympathetic studies of many child characters.

> *A review of "The Summer in Between," in* The Junior Bookshelf, *Vol. 23, No. 5, November, 1959, pp. 296-97.*

From the very first sentence this book proclaims its Australian origin. 'It smells like Christmas,' the school girl heroine exclaims, 'I mean a sort of summery smell—all hot and dusty and smoky. It makes me think of picnics and swimming and eating Christmas dinner on a hot day.' Faith is twelve and this particular summer stretches between her last year at primary school and her first at high school. She is restless and unsettled, bored with her old life and a little apprehensive about what lies ahead, and into this abyss steps Pauline, a visitor from the city.

The lessons that Faith learns during this all-important summer are many and not least of them is the value of self-discipline. This is a book which girls of the right age—about ten to thirteen—should find absorbing reading and from which they should also unconsciously learn much that will be useful to them in the conduct of their own lives. (pp. 56, 59)

> *E. N. Bewick, in a review of "The Summer in Between," in* The School Librarian, *Vol. 10, No. 1, March, 1960, pp. 56, 59.*

### Lillypilly Hill (1960)

Eleanor Spence is one of those rare writers who by the sheer quality of her use of words manages to transport the reader to whatever scene she is writing about so convincingly that at once the world about us fades, and we are virtually living wherever Miss Spence chooses to take us. She paints the Australian scene as few other have done—the nearest approach would be perhaps Nan Chauncy for Tasmania.

In this story, the young reader will absorb an incredible amount of information relating to the wild life of the land, and the way in which the early settlers lived. The story centres around Harriet, the one member of the Lillypilly Hill family who, like her father, really loves the place and does not want to return to England. How she wins friends to help her persuade the other members of her family to settle there is the story of this book. (pp. 307-08)

> *A review of "Lillypilly Hill," in* The Junior Bookshelf, *Vol. 24, No. 5, November, 1960, pp. 307-08.*

### The Green Laurel (1963)

Eleanor Spence has great skill in creation of lively and attractive characters, she has a feeling for landscape and for social settings, she invents convincing episodes. She is less successful in the manipulation of a complex plot, and one gets the feeling, in her latest book, that here is the material for two books, neither of which she has developed ade-

quately. The first part promises well: the Somervilles on tour through Australia with their miniature train, with all the fun of the fair and friends lightly made in many towns, are delightful and colourful. When they meet the socially superior Brents in the easy democracy of a seaside resort the reader smells trouble, but when the trouble comes it is not of this kind at all. With their livelihood gone and their bread-winner in hospital the Somervilles go to live in an "outcasts" housing settlement. The second half of the book, with its picture of a major Australian social problem, makes a sharp contrast to the first, and the two parts are insufficiently integrated. One feels that the author has too little room to develop all her ideas: it might have been wiser to trim the fairground half and concentrate on the refugee camp, delving a little deeper into its complex characters. For all that a good book. . . .

> *A review of "The Green Laurel," in* The Junior Bookshelf, *Vol. 27, No. 4, October, 1963, p. 218.*

School crises, adjusting to a new way of life, a gang, and a new community bring the story to a climax almost too fast to be convincing after the long, slow beginning. This is good background material on life in Australia. The girls almost emerge as real personalities. Additional purchase.

> *Anne Izard, in a review of "The Green Laurel," in* School Library Journal, *Vol. 11, No. 9, May, 1965, p. 107.*

### The Year of the Currawong (1965)

Within the framework of an Australian adventure involving pinning down the disputed ownership of an old silver mine and the surrounding land, the author has managed to show off four very believable children as they develop both independently and within the family. Readers will probably sympathize most with the oldest, fourteen-year-old Elizabeth, who is at loose ends with apparently no particular interests or skills of her own, the only member of the family directed toward a special talent. But the others, from eight year old Chess on up have their own special appeal. Particularly notable is the fact that the children always maintain a realistic relationship with the adults of the story, and they are well drawn too—the parents, a swagman, an old Chinaman patiently devoting his life to a dream of finding more silver in a mine, and others. Despite some weaknesses (the process of discovering the missing deed to the land offers practically no suspense, and the story is slowed down by the author's wordy descriptions), readers will find this family warmly entertaining.

> *A review of "The Year of the Currawong," in* Virginia Kirkus' Service, *Vol. XXXIII, No. 21, November 1, 1965, p. 1118.*

This is fairly ordinary story. The Australian background is no longer novel to young readers. Perhaps the character of the Swagman might catch the imagination of some, but on the whole it is rather dull. The children and their parents are the stereotype characters that one meets in dozens of similar books. Mother is always baking or "doing the vegetables," while her mind is far away considering her next picture; she is an artist. While father is the traditional absent-minded professor of history, who hums, off-key, to denote his mood. Perhaps a 9-10 year-old might enjoy this book, but they certainly would not find it stimulating.

> *A review of "The Year of the Currawong," in* The Junior Bookshelf, *Vol. 29, No. 6, December, 1965, p. 375.*

---

### The Switherby Pilgrims (1967)

Eleanor Spence in **The Switherby Pilgrims,** . . . is both exciting and warm-hearted. Miss Arabella Braithwaite, faced with the problem of ten orphans in a village which has just been devastated by a typhus epidemic, decides very boldly to emigrate with them to New South Wales. The author skates rather lightly over their experiences on the five-month journey in a convict ship; too lightly perhaps for those who know something about conditions in sailing ships of the 1820s, and her story only becomes really gripping when they reach Australia. Here they are given a grant of land in the heart of the bush. They find themselves, after an exhausting journey, standing in a precipitous territory, all cliffs and ledges and lush undergrowth, and realize that out of this they have to carve not only a shelter for themselves but also a farm and cultivated fields. But they contrive it, Missabella, her ten children, the oldest of whom is only thirteen, and the convict who has been allotted to help them. There are no cheating *Swiss Family Robinson* strokes of good fortune but only grinding hard work, and in the end we see them securely established. The only flaw in the book is the episode of the evil father who tries to steal away one of the orphans. He comes to a violent end, but one that is not very convincingly narrated.

> *"Escapes from the Past," in* The Times Literary Supplement, *No. 3404, May 25, 1967, p. 461.*

A most unusual variant on the *Swiss Family Robinson* theme. After a Midlands typhus epidemic in the 1820's, "Missabella", a spinster daughter of the vicarage, emigrates to Australia to give ten destitute children a chance in life beyond the workhouse. The suspense of awaiting their passage, their disillusionment with the dark cramped cabin aboard a convict ship, and the colonists they meet are described vividly, and their taking possession of their plot of ground only to find it covered with trees. Their struggle for existence and gradual reclamation of the land changes to more terrifying adventure when they are held at gunpoint by an escaped convict, father to three of the children. Unfortunately Miss Spence jibs at making his ultimate fate clear, although she has already faced reality sufficiently to include a mentally handicapped boy crippled as a baby by the convict, and the Aborigine who becomes the eleventh orphan. The characters are beautifully differentiated, the intelligent tomboy and the feminine seamstress's daughter, the older boy expected to follow a grammar school education when his secret wish is to be a farmer, the gentle, hopeless convict allotted to them as a servant, and behind them all, "Missabella", bravely reso-

lute but almost overwhelmed by her responsibility, and the unfamiliar beauty of the Australian coast and hinterland permeating and shaping their lives. It is a rewarding book. . . .

> *A review of "The Switherby Pilgrims," in* The Junior Bookshelf, *Vol. 31, No. 3, June, 1967, p. 188.*

One middle-aged spinster shepherding ten orphans to New South Wales in 1825—unsuitable, intriguing but not ultimately satisfying. . . . The trouble is that it takes them too long (more than half the book) to arrive at their holding and to begin coping, which is what they (and we) have been waiting for from the start. Not to leave bad enough—isolation, inexperience, uncleared land—alone, there's a menace in the form of the escaped convict father of three of the children, and his downfall, rather than the success of their venture, provides the climax of the story. Missabella adjusting to circumstances is in the best British no-nonsense tradition, and so is the sharp style, making the contrived conclusion a particular disappointment. (pp. 1059-60)

> *A review of "The Switherby Pilgrims," in* Kirkus Service, *Vol. XXXV, No. 17, September 1, 1987, pp. 1059-60.*

---

### Jamberoo Road (1969)

Charlotte Yonge died in 1901. Even before her death the era of the bread-and-butter miss was over. In her late novels she lamented the fact herself; the disappearance of the earnest conscientious girl for whom most of her books catered, the fourteen to eighteen-year-old, no longer a child, not yet a woman, who in the quiet solitude of her schoolroom at home was preparing herself to meet the world.

But there are children's editors who will not recognize this. Still they turn out pleasant books for thoughtful girls, books about girls growing up, delicately spiced with romance; commendable books, written by authors who really care. They will certainly be bought by libraries, because they are made to look so good. But who is going to read them? They have not enough bite for the adult, they are too slow-moving for children, and whatever adolescents read nowadays—one moment *The Cat in the Hat*, the next *Lady Chatterley*—one can be fairly definite that it is not this sort of thing.

Eleanor Spence's **Jamberoo Road** is a sequel to her earlier **The Switherby Pilgrims.** It follows up the fortunes of the ten orphans from the village of Switherby who were taken by the vicar's sister, Miss Arabella Braithwaite, to begin a new life in Australia. Here we see them established on their farmstead in New South Wales. The early pioneering days, which gave the first book much of its interest, are over now, and Miss Arabella is trying to plan for the orphans' future. Cassie, with whom the book is chiefly concerned, goes as a governess to the daughter of a prosperous emigrant from Sussex. She could have married the son of the family, but prefers to return to Mount St. Matthew to marry the ex-convict who once worked for Miss Arabella. It is a kind and friendly book, with some fine descriptions of the Australian landscape—but there is not enough continuous incident to make a very gripping story.

> *"Yonge Misses," in* The Times Literary Supplement, *No. 3529, October 16, 1969, p. 1203.*

If you have read **The Switherby Pilgrims** then you will know what to expect. To my surprise **Jamberoo Road** is just as good, if not better. . . . The plot turns on Cassie's love for Eben, the freed convict who worked for 'Missabella'. But for me the important aspect of this novel and of its predecessor is the picture they give of an almost unknown period of our history. Thanks to Kipling most young readers know something about India in the nineteenth century, but very few know anything about Australia. Miss Spence has a deep understanding of young people though some of her adults are mere caricatures excepting of course 'Missabella'. Both boys and girls of eleven to fourteen should enjoy this book, especially those with an interest in history.

> *Joan Murphy, in a review of "Jamberoo Road," in* The School Librarian, *Vol. 17, No. 4, December, 1969, p. 402.*

We have met Miss Arabella Braithwaite and her ten orphans from Switherby before. Now they are firmly established at Mount Saint Matthew, their farm in Australia. . . .

These two books for they must be read together, give an excellent picture of life in Australia during the first half of the nineteenth century. It is not a political picture but a social one which is much more interesting for the average twelve to fourteen year old who will enjoy this book. The characters are real people with many of the all too familiar faults of real people but held together by a stronger sense of loyalty.

> *A review of "Jamberoo Road," in* The Junior Bookshelf, *Vol. 34, No. 1, February, 1970, p. 42.*

---

### The Nothing-Place (1972)

This book by Eleanor Spence, like her previous ones, embodies many of the best and most exciting trends in contemporary literature for children. To begin with, the reader's attention is held by the plot from the beginning—one races through the pages, anxious to find out what happens next. And what happens next is always interesting—and, perhaps more important, wholly convincing.

The descriptions of the 'nothing-place'—the Sydney suburb where all the events in the story take place, and of the Australian background in general, ring very true, and the characters are almost unnervingly recognisable as real people. There is Reggie, an old meths drinker who befriends the children about whom the story revolves, 'he was old, with sparse grey hair and whiskers, and his face had the roughened texture of bark that had been long shed'. The friendship between him and Glen, the partially deaf 'hero' of the story, is movingly but never sentimentally described. The relationship between Glen and his elder brother Graham, and between the boys and their parents,

is equally vividly conveyed. All the other characters are presented in the round—Lyndall, clever, plain, 'full of confident authority', whose parents, having lived apart for years, are arranging for a divorce; Shane, another of Glen's friends, whose hair sticks up spikily from his head and whose passion is cricket, and his older sister Shelley, pretty but selfish, interested only in boys in general and Graham in particular.

In many ways this is a strikingly original book, and should be enjoyed by anyone over eleven. The story stops on page 137, but one feels that the life of the characters goes on and one would like to know how. (pp. 79-80)

> *Barbara Sherrard-Smith, in a review of "The Nothing Place," in* Children's Book Review, *Vol. II, No. 3, June, 1972, pp. 79-80.*

Since the reading of fiction is a process of identification, books for children must present identifiable characters and problems for the young reader. To achieve this kind of identification the main character must usually function independently of parents and adult figures. This is especially true in "middle and older" books, and the reason is quite simple—children moving into adolescence need to define themselves as autonomous beings, independent of adults. In becoming independent they also become critical of the world adults have prepared for them to enter. For the writer working with such material there is a need to probe the tension between the adult behavior and the critical adolescent's understanding of the adult world. . . .

Eleanor Spence's **The Nothing Place,** set in dreary suburban Australia, is a good example of the "on their own" theme and the problems which somehow by the end of the book they must come to terms with. The main plot centers on Glen, a new kid in town who has recently suffered a hearing loss. As this loss becomes permanent the solution seems quite simple—buy the kid a hearing aid. But such a simple solution doesn't occur to Glen's parents, teachers or doctors.

In the hands of a less skillful author, **The Nothing Place** would be a boring story, but it is not. What saves it is the many characters and subplots that keep the reader's attention off the simple and easy solution to Glen's problems. But the flaw, and it's a major flaw, comes when one considers why the parents, not only Glen's but Lyndall's also, never do what is obvious. And one suspects it's not because the adults don't have time nor love but because Ms. Spence wants to keep spinning a story. She has placed her characters on their own, but she doesn't give us enough information to let us know why the adults failed to act. It is not enough to show mothers trying to keep pace with their housework and office schedules, or fathers hiding behind newspapers and television. That may keep the story going, but in the end Ms. Spence writes herself into a corner.

> *Ray Anthony Shepard, in a review of "The Nothing Place," in* Children's Literature: Annual of the Modern Language Association Seminar on Children's Literature and The Children's Literature Association, *Vol. 3, 1974, p. 229.*

A novel for children in which a character is deaf doubtless will be read by children in much the same way as any other, primarily for its entertainment value. Children often take little direct interest in the established literary integrity or worth of a book of fiction, as this is judged by the critics of such writings. Moreover, children and critics of children's literature are frequently at odds over the attractiveness of a piece of prose fiction. So much so that popular children's books are not necessarily the ones which win literary awards and vice versa.

While a child obviously is prepared to make judgments of the literary qualities of a piece of prose fiction in which a deaf child is portrayed, it is beyond his capacity to determine if the technical or psychological aspects of deafness found in such a novel are authentic. To take extreme examples, a poorly documented novel of this kind for children could badly mislead the child reader as to the realities of deafness; a child's book that carefully follows what is known from the studies of this affliction could greatly enlighten its readers.

Since the physical nature of childhood deafness usually has several psychological side effects, it is pertinent to inquire, then, if the available prose fiction for children treats the psychology of childhood deafness in an accurate manner. Beyond this, it is important to ask specifically of the fictional literature of these deaf characters: What are the emotional effects of deafness these characters portray? How does the fictional deaf character manage or control the psychological effects of his or her handicap? Is this portrayal the best one can expect, or could the depictions here of the psychology of childhood deafness be improved?

The relatively few books of prose fiction for children in which deaf children have roles provide the source for fairly complete answers to these questions. In 1962, Newton listed no books of prose fiction for children about deaf children in her bibliography *Books for Deaf Children*. The sum of deaf characters in children's novels since that time I can identify are Kumalik in *Child of the Arctic* by Hubert Woods (Follet, 1962), Hadrian in *Into the Forest* by Rosamund Essex (Coward-McCann, 1965), David in *David in Silence* by Veronica Robinson (Lippincott, 1966), Anna in *A Single Light* by Maia Wojciechowska (Harper & Row, 1968), Jeff in *Dead Before Docking* by Scott Corbett (Little, Brown, 1972) and Glen in *The Nothing Place* by Eleanor Spence.

It is apparent that the authors of the above books were convinced, most of all, that the degree of deafness a child suffers is directly related to the amount of psychological stress this impediment produces. (p. 196)

Jeff and Glen are relatively stable personalities. A medical operation has reduced Jeff's loss of hearing to 20 per cent. Glen's creator also handicaps him with only 'a certain degree of hearing loss'. Jeff's overriding fear is that his relatively slight handicap will be detected by those of the ship's company with whom he is travelling. He has previously gone to a 'special school' for the deaf, where he learned to lip-read accurately. And now, according to his uncle, Jeff 'can hear every word I say without even having

to watch my lips'. By the time Jeff solves the mystery of *Dead Before Docking* he 'is amazed at how little difference his deafness had made in anyone's attitude'. As for the children on board, 'the only thing that really interested them was his speechreading. They were already pestering him to teach them how!'

Since Glen, as well, lip-reads with unfailing precision there is little left of his tolerable deaf condition for Spence to exploit as plot material. However, for some insufficiently explained reason, Glen and his parents alike try to hide his deafness. Glen even resents an offer by his child friends (who know of his handicap) of money for a hearing aid. His mother, full of guilt over his deafness, does not tell his new school about his deafness even after learning Glen has been placed in the top section of his class. Of course, his teachers expect far too much of him, misjudge his abilities and behaviour, and fail him. Embarrassed by this he runs away (only a short distance) and innocently enters a closed store to hide out for the night. He is quickly caught and everything is forgiven. Glen agrees the cover-up of his deafness must now end.

Knowing that tragedies are seldom allowed in books of prose fiction for children, one could have predicted that deaf characters in such novels must successfully contend to some degree with their loss of hearing. And so it is. Even the fictional characters noted here who suffer the emotionally exhausting consequences of total deafness are given a ray of hope by their authors that the future will bring more intimate and mutually gratifying social relationships than they have so far experienced. (pp. 197-98)

Jeff and Glen, as previously noted, are given few problems of a psychological nature that cannot be managed, or in Glen's case, could not have been controlled if a modicum of simple common sense had been applied. Jeff, a marvellously independent child, actually puts his deafness to practical use. He lip-reads a man on the dock plotting over the phone to kill one of Jeff's fellow ship passengers. This advance notice is enough for Jeff to disarm the accomplishment of this evil deed.

By contrast with this, Glen's relatively slight problems with hearing are inflated by Spence beyond reasonable expectations. The prosaic nature of her novel is further in evidence as Glen and his parents are portrayed as ninnies all in a dither over whether Glen's slight degree of hearing loss will be found out and thereby disgrace the family. The weakness of this as plot material obviously requires Spence to fill up *The Nothing Place* with a potpourri of subplots extraneous to that which she creates for Glen. Each of these jostles the other for space in the narrative. Glen's minor problems, as could be expected, tend to lose their significance as they are submerged as part of this *mélange*. Thus the novel's ambitions (if they are so held) to be a significant commentary on how a deaf child manages deafness, are badly thwarted.

Criticising the quality of the depiction of the psychological nature of any fictional character is a heady undertaking. To decide if this portrayal is poorly or well done for fictional children deprived of their hearing is yet a stiffer task. For the latter analysis, obviously one must move behind the literary merits of these novels. (The quality of these books as literature is not an insignificant matter, of course, but a concern too large to deal with to any extent within the scope of the present discussion, nonetheless.) The merits of a fictional writer's accounts of the psychology of deafness in children will depend, then, on how well they conform to what the scholarly texts have to say on this subject.

With some of these academic resources in mind, it is safe to note that there is no attempt by their authors to avoid a description of the complete range of deaf behaviour for Kumalik, David and Hadrian. Their anti-social behaviour matches the description of this given by Rainer *et al.* to a significant degree. As they say, 'among the outstanding features of the deaf . . . are: a lack of understanding of, and regard for, the feelings of others (empathy) coupled with inadequate insight into the impact of their own behavior and its consequences in relation to others'. All three boys demonstrate the 'emotional immaturity' which Schlesinger and Meadow see as the most often-cited psychological handicap of the deaf: 'egocentricity, easy irritability, a lack of empathy, gross coercive dependency, impulsivity, and a lack of thoughtful introspection'. (pp. 199-200)

The depiction of Jeff and Glen, similar in the degree of their loss of hearing yet different in the manner in which they handle the psychological consequences of their handicaps, is not indefensible. First, it is proper, as the authors here imply, to assume that children with lesser hearing losses will experience less psychological trauma as a result of these losses than do profoundly deaf children. Then, as is shown with Jeff and Glen, different children with a similar degree of hearing loss will respond to this trauma in remarkably dissimilar ways. That Jeff is generally strongminded about his deafness, while Glen is usually weakwilled as to the resolution of its effects, represents the extremes of children's reactions which the handicap of deafness can trigger. . . .

In all the novels reviewed here the authors plot out a growing empathy, for the fictional deaf children they depict, from other characters in the narratives. Again, since tragedy has not been allowed in children's literature to any appreciable extent so far, the condition that a novel on deafness must end romantically is one authors have had to accept. The question remains, of course, as to whether the future novel of the deaf child might be permitted to end on a tragic note, so that the psychological problems of the deaf character remain less resolved at the plot's end than at its beginning. There is some sign from children's literature in general that more elements of tragedy may very well find their way into novels for children, and thus into those about the deaf. (p. 200)

> Patrick Groff, "Children's Fiction and the Psychology of Deafness," in The School Librarian, *Vol. 24, No. 3, September, 1976, pp. 196-202.*

---

**Time to Go Home** (1973)

**Time to Go Home** is a curious book which manages to dif-

fuse all its impact. Essentially, it concerns an Australian boy in mid-adolescence who lives at home with his mother and sister, goes to school, and whose chief interest is rugby. This isn't however, a book about sport, for although rugby is the focus of the main character's life, the book doesn't emphasise it; the real concern is with the every-day complexities of life during adolescence. But don't look here for a study in depth or textbook information in a literary guise. Adolescence is treated in a consciously off-hand way, details are observed but not stressed, simply noticed and passed over.

There are ample incidents to keep the reader interested, and enough sense of continuity to make one want to read on, but an overall purpose is lacking. The book exists as a fragment of a life similar to, but without the highly personal and sustained viewpoint of, a diary extract. There are good things here, but as there is no dramatic sweep, no concentration, we are not made to feel we have experienced anything unified. It is, in the end, a book without substance.

> Robert Bartier, in a review of "Time to Go Home," in Children's Book Review, *Vol. III, No. 5, October, 1973, p. 146.*

**Time to go home** is a low-keyed but incisive study of a lad of sixteen meeting adolescence in a way that is perfectly logical, given his circumstances and background. Eleanor Spence marks out certain areas of experience in which Australian Rowan Price has to make a choice—not that dramatic choice between crime or virtue which writers favour so often and so disastrously in junior fiction, but what amounts to a choice between quick notoriety or more lasting satisfaction. Rowan tries to believe that he can follow three paths at once—he can fight to win and keep a place in the top football team at school, he can please his parents by sitting for an advanced exam., and he can help half-aboriginal Kippy whom he has promised to coach with his many playmates in the rules of Rugby Union. Rowan is firmly centred in the book but if the adults are on the side line, they have a demonstrable existence of their own, and the contacts between the generations are of a properly two-way kind.

> Margery Fisher, in a review of "Time to Go Home," in Growing Point, *Vol. 12, No. 5, November, 1973, pp. 2260-61.*

Set in Sydney, Australia, this tale of a sixteen-year-old football fanatic, an intelligent lad caught in the net of an overwhelming passion for sport, is deftly handled both in plot and character. Rowan exhibits the self-satisfaction, the single-mindedness, the stupidities of many a boy talented enough to shine on the games field. It is to his credit that his failures consolidate his skill and help him to find a more satisfactory balance in personal relationships and non-sporting activities.

> G. Bott, in a review of "Time to Go Home," in The Junior Bookshelf, *Vol. 38, No. 1, February, 1974, p. 45.*

***The October Child*** (1976; U.S. edition as ***The Devil Hole***)

Eleanor Spence has made a courageous choice of subject for ***The October Child,*** a realistic and unsentimental novel about a retarded child and the stresses he produces on his parents and siblings. The Mariners are a united family, living in a small Australian coastal resort, until the keenly awaited birth of a fourth child, Carl Thomas. As a frenzied infant and raging toddler, he disrupts the household and tests, to their limits, its individual members.

The oldest boy, Kenneth, deeply resents the move to Sydney to be near a special school for Carl, but finds a substitute for seaside sports in a religious commune. Adrienne, at an age when television and friendships vie for attention, becomes sparing with her invitations home. Douglas is the sensitive, thoughtful child on whom his parents most depend for relief—his singing, after all, can quieten Carl's nighttime howls—but at least he has the consolation of his music studies in the city. Douglas's shedding of childish guilt and quiet acceptance of responsibility provide the small note of triumph on which the book ends.

Despite its theme, this is an enjoyable book, vivid with the sights and scents of Australia—sharks, kangaroos, frangipani blossoms—and salted with adventure.

> *Juliet Page, "Under Stress," in* The Times Literary Supplement, *No. 3879, July 16, 1976, p. 884.*

Here is a book clearly based on accurate case-book medical history, which succeeds magnificently as a novel. The Australian background helps in this. It is vividly created, and the reader can really understand what it must be like to have Christmas at mid-summer, with angels in Nativity plays sticky with perspiration, and the incongruity of carolling about snow on a hot sunshiny evening. The outdoor character of day-to-day life in a small seaside settlement also comes across beautifully, without any sense that Eleanor Spence is aware of her audience's possible ignorance. The family she creates is entirely believable, as are their differing reactions when the eagerly-awaited baby proves a disrupting autistic child who gradually wrecks the family's happiness, not least because, for his sake, they have to leave for Sydney where a suitable special school for Carl can be found. Father stays later and later at his new job, Mother becomes worn, old and despairing, Adrienne withdraws into a television world, and Kenneth, the frustrated athlete, rebelliously becomes utterly materially-minded and selfish, until he ends up with a kindly commune who, incidentally, are the only people with whom Carl seems at home. But it is Douglas, sensitive, musical and gentle, whose reactions we identify with closest. His singing is the first breakthrough into Carl's withdrawn world. The musical friend he makes helps him to a music school where he can forget the home situation temporarily, but there is no false happy ending, only an understanding that, though anything may still happen—Douglas' precious belongings may again be wrecked in Carl's moments of violence—patience should slowly bring about enough improvement for the family to come together again once more in peace. It is a moving, absorbing story,

with moments of humour as well as tangible frustration. (pp. 289-90)

> *M. Hobbs, in a review of "The October Child," in* The Junior Bookshelf, *Vol. 40, No. 5, October, 1976, pp. 289-90.*

Beware: the Devil Hole—a dread ravine on the Australian coast—is something of a booby trap; it takes on symbolic significance to Douglas because his delay there worries his mother and "could have started the baby"—but it's the baby born prematurely, autistic Carl, that's the focal point of a story patently about the damaging effects of such a youngster on a normally stress-prone family. . . . [The family moves to Sydney and Douglas has] a chance to attend the music school where his mentor, Daniel Mead, teaches. The solidly sympathetic young Meads, in turn, have a friend who teaches at Carl's school; and it is she who, in the last chapter, explains Carl's condition to Douglas—reminding him, the while, of his own incidental gain. We've learned with Douglas that living with an autistic child can be hell; but we haven't learned much—because he hasn't—about the methods of treating such children. A hopeless situation mistakable for an adventure is hard to accept as a work of fiction, however well-intended.

> *A review of "The Devil Hole," in* Kirkus Reviews, *Vol. XLV, No. 8, April 15, 1977, p. 437.*

This story presents an excellently drawn description of an autistic child and the pressure such a handicap puts on a family and its relationships with other people, but should it have been written for children? To those of an age not far removed from the fairy tale world of enchantments, Carl's behaviour might seem frightening, for rightly there is no happy ending—or even much improvement—nor is his handicap ever identified by name. That Douglas has gained in some measure from Carl's condition is due to his own talent which allows him to cope with the pressures of Carl. To a thoughtful young adolescent perhaps it does show a boy growing up into responsibilities and becoming aware of other people's feelings but despite the characterisation the book's theme makes it a novel to be learned from rather than enjoyed. (pp. 258, 261)

> *Margaret Payne, in a review of "The October Child," in* The School Librarian, *Vol. 25, No. 3, September, 1977, pp. 258, 261.*

A teacher of autistic children, this award-winning Australian author depicts the effects on a family when the fourth child proves to be autistic. Spence is neither didactic nor sentimental, although she gives an authentic and heart-wrenching portrayal of little Carl, and she avoids the case-study-fictionalized by focusing on Douglas, the second son of the Mariner family. . . . The ending, in which Douglas has a long talk with one of Carl's teachers, is sober and realistic in appraising the future, but it is weak in a literary sense. The story has great dramatic impact and, while it deals with a serious topic, provides enough action and development to have pace; the style, characterization, and dialogue are excellent.

> *Zena Sutherland, in a review of "The Devil*

*Hole,"* in Bulletin of the Center for Children's Books, *Vol. 31, No. 2, October, 1977, p. 37.*

---

### A Candle for St. Antony (1977)

Eleanor Spence has excelled herself with this book, it is one of the most moving stories I have read for a very long time. She has shown courage, even in these more enlightened times, of portraying a strong adolescent love, the homosexual inference of which is unstated but inherent.

The two teenage boys are Justin, an all Australian sport loving son of wealthy parents, and Rudi, the gentle music loving son of a Catholic immigrant from Austria. Rudi's father is now dead and he lives in a small flat with his mother and sister, clinging to their religion and music and yearning for their homeland. Justin attends an exclusive school because his parents can afford the fees, Rudi starts at the same school because he is determined to have the best education he can get and he works to find the money for it.

At first Justin hates Rudi and he and his friends set out to make life hell for him. But they can never overcome Rudi's gentle patience and understanding of them. A deep friendship develops between the two boys, excluding all the others, and a school holiday in Austria brings this friendship to a head.

Rudi has always had a great affinity to St. Antony, and when the boys discover a ruined chapel dedicated to the Saint they set out to restore it to some degree of order and beauty. Rudi's feeling for St. Antony, the Saint who resisted so much of the temptations of the world, is significant throughout the story. It is here at the chapel that he declares his love for Justin and is overheard by one of the other boys.

Naturally, the sniggers that have been mild until now, become more open, and Rudi goes off to stay with Austrian friends who understand and will care for him. The last meeting between the boys is traumatic—to Justin more than Rudi. Rudi is back where he belongs, he wanted Justin to stay with him but Justin's need is to return to his home and people. Each boy has to work out his own salvation in his own way, Rudi in Austria with people who understand him as he is and Justin back in Australia picking up the pieces of his old way of life with a new awareness of life and relationships.

This is a book which I shall remember for a very long time and one which I hope will not only help adolescents to understand themselves and their peers but also help adults to sympathise and not condemn.

> *M. R. H., in a review of "A Candle for St. Antony," in* The Junior Bookshelf, *Vol. 42, No. 1, February, 1978, p. 56.*

Two teenagers, unlike and inseparable—is it homosexuality? . . . The turnabout scene is a little sticky, and the mutual devotion of the two boys thereafter is even more so. Consequently, much as one admires Rudi and likes Justin for appreciating him, the pivotal episode—in which the relationship between the boys, back in Austria

on a class trip, suddenly totters on the nature of Rudi's intentions (proclaiming his love, he asks Justin to stay in Austria with him)—has an offputting sentimental ring. Of course Rudi didn't mean what Justin momentarily suspects and another boy, overhearing their conversation, assumes; and the book goes down, finally, on the sweetness and bitterness of their innocent love lost. (pp. 1005-06)

> *A review of "A Candle for Saint Antony," in* Kirkus Reviews, *Vol. XLVII, No. 17, September 1, 1979, pp. 1005-06.*

On the surface the novel pictures realistically and humorously Justin's affluent middle-class Australian milieu and the normal tensions of family life. Similarly, the vivid details of the flight from Australia to Austria become part of Justin's experiences leading to his appreciation of an older, more traditional way of life. But an undercurrent of the ambiguous emotions of adolescence runs through the story; and although Justin's schoolmates often indulge in innuendos, the narrative really poses questions about the nature of love and affection. The book, unlike *The Man Without a Face,* scarcely considers homosexuality. It deals with the relationship between a personal emotional crisis and its social context, and the author unfolds with insight and restraint a series of events that culminate in a shattering denouement. (p. 541)

> *Paul Heins, in a review of "A Candle for Saint Antony," in* The Horn Book Magazine, *Vol. LV, No. 5, October, 1979, pp. 540-41.*

---

### The Seventh Pebble (1980)

Rachel, daughter of the doctor in a run-down mining community, jogs along happily enough, disturbed by nothing more dramatic than a difficulty in distinguishing left and right feet in dancing class. But that is before the Connells come. The Connells are poor, scruffy, Roman Catholics and Irish. They stir up the sleepy village and no one will ever be quite the same again, least of all Rachel and her big brother Daniel. The summer of the Connells is a memorable one, culminating in a forest fire and a man-hunt. But before this Rachel has enjoyed much quiet pleasure, as well as more violent disturbances, sharing with the Connell children the making of a secret grotto. This life is too good to last. The Connells go as they came, and Rachel is left behind, grown-up beyond her years in the newly found knowledge that she, like the Connells, belongs to a minority—for her father is a German Jew and it is the year of Munich.

Within the compass of a small outback community Eleanor Spence handles big themes—birth and death, toleration and hatred, poverty—and handles them with confidence and humour. Her portraits are good as ever. She tells an excellent story with due regard to pace and climax. Above all she gives us the feeling of people in a society and of the obligations that this involves. A mature, relaxed piece of writing, full of unsentimental affection and clearsighted observation.

> *M. Crouch, in a review of "The Seventh Peb-*

*ble," in* The Junior Bookshelf, *Vol. 45, No. 4, August, 1981, p. 163.*

---

### The Left Overs (1982)

**The Left Overs** of the book by Eleanor Spence are four Australian foster children aged between eight and eleven who are threatened with seperation after a long time of living together almost like a "proper" family. They try to fight off the fateful happening and, as you might expect, they have lots of ups and downs. . . . This is a good and sensitive book, with a nice feel for the rather resigned—often later to become cynical—air of the "unwanted" child. It shows gently and clearly that there are no easy answers and that endings are more likely to be bitter-sweet than happy.

*Gerald Haigh, in a review of "The Left Overs," in* The Times Educational Supplement, *No. 3562, October 5, 1984, p. 29.*

---

### Me and Jeshua (1984)

An ambitious book from the Australian writer who has specialized in exploring the effect of a young outsider (seen as "different" by the world for a variety of reasons) on those around him. This is the simply told story of someone tracing childhood memories of his family and their history in a Middle Eastern country long ago, and of his deep friendship with a cousin who appears unexpectedly and whose past suggests a family mystery. But the cousin is Jesus, and the ordinariness of the narrative tone adds humour to an intriguing, thoughtful novel.

*Stephanie Nettell, "Paperbacks in Brief," in* The Times Literary Supplement, *No. 4278, March 29, 1985, p. 354.*

---

### Deezle Boy (1987)

I have always admired Eleanor Spence's ability to write about everyday social problems in a way which is easily understandable by young readers. In **Deezle boy** she has addressed the trauma of the natural mother who wishes to see her adopted child and has aimed the story to a slightly younger audience than usual.

Grant has a passion for trains particularly the XPT. When he is picked up after school by a strange lady she claims to be his mother's cousin. After travelling around the countryside staying at a refuge, a commune, and finally a hotel (during which time Grant discovers that Laurie is his true mother) he is reunited with his adoptive mother and grandfather. During their journey Grant learns much of the world around him, from which he has been protected.

As usual Eleanor Spence develops her characters with adroit skill. From a rather dreamy child Grant assumes a degree of leadership particularly when the group travel by train. Though his experiences may have been difficult he gains much from them. The gentle ending to the story

is a suitable resolution of the tale particularly for those readers who are in a similar situation to Grant. I am sure that **Deezle boy** will appeal to many young readers provoking thought and understanding. Recommended for 10+ year olds. (pp. 46-7)

*Laurie Copping, in a review of "Deezle Boy," in* Reading Time, *Vol. XXXI, No. IV, 1987, pp. 46-7.*

Eleanor Spence's work shows a steady progression in theme and craftsmanship. She has moved a long way from her essentially happy families of the late 1950s. In this new novel she has distanced herself from the intensity which was at the core of her Australian novels from **The October Child** onwards, and after two books set in Biblical times, she has returned to a contemporary story set in New South Wales. This book is possibly the sparest she has yet written but it carries as great a weight of implication as **A Candle for Saint Antony** and as deep a sense of responsibility as **The Left Overs** Eleanor Spence is a very fine writer and **Deezle Boy** is a perceptively crafted, carefully honed image for today. It is topical and compassionate but not trendy or sentimental. . . .

[The] issues do seem excessive, but Eleanor Spence knows what she is doing and is in control. Grant's one foray into fiction is *The Railway Children* (trains, obviously!) which "had a happy ending, with all the family coming together again, and no more worries. But it was an old-fashioned book. Anything with steam trains in it has to be out of date." Spence's book is as up-to-date as hair gel but movingly timeless in spirit. It will have more audience appeal even than **The Left Overs,** is a must for all primary and secondary school libraries, and is perfect for classroom sharing Year 5 and upward.

*Maurice Saxby, in a review of "Deezle Boy," in* Magpies, *Vol. 2, No. 5, November, 1987, p. 24.*

---

### The Family Book of Mary-Claire (1991)

The search for identity is . . . a subject in Eleanor Spence's **The Family Book of Mary-Claire.** In this a girl explores her antecedents as the generational saga of her family unfolds. This is a very different style of narrative from many we have seen in the older readers category. The interlocking stories of each generation are handled effectively and through their history, the changing nature of Australian society is revealed. Characters and setting are all carefully and effectively drawn.

*Margot Tyrell, in a review of "The Family Book of Mary-Claire," in* Magpies, *Vol. 6, No. 2, May, 1991, p. 22.*

While reading this book you will often turn to the two diagrams at the front. One charts the Whitby River Estuary on the north coast of N.S.W.; the second traces a family tree from Titus Cleveland (b. 1776) to Mary-Claire Hart (b. 1900). This is apt since the novel takes us from this family's early arrival in this region (they are escaping convicts shipwrecked in 1819) through nearly 100 years of settlement and development to Easter 1913, when a girl is writing in the family Bible: "My name is Mary-Claire Hart and mine is the last name on the family tree in the front of the book. So far".

Eleanor Spence very successfully focuses Mary-Claire's forbears by showing their youngest teenage years. We see Marius, who was born free into a family of felons one month after the shipwreck, between the ages of 10 and 13 (in 1832); then his daughter Miriam, whose kidnapping by a bushranger brings links with a darker branch of the family, also from 10 to 13 (in 1859); and then her son Marion at 11 and 12 (1882), when his musical talent becomes clear and he is witness to an act of vengeance by a mysterious woman in black. All three witness wreckage in others' lives. Yet essentially each has an instinct to preserve the truth of the past which has created them.

This symbolic riverland is subtly evocative. The river across which they travel and in which they drown is like time, says Marius, "It carries people's lives along like bits and pieces of floating stuff, sometimes fast and sometimes slow . . ."

It is a special book. In mapping the sources of Mary-Claire's identity, this wise prize-winning author brings to life some of the tensions in Australian culture (racism, materialism, an English-derived class prejudice); but she implies too that the resolution of such difficulties often lies in the attitudes of our children. Their resilience is our hope.

*Don Pemberton, in a review of "The Family Book of Mary-Claire," in* Magpies, *Vol. 6, No. 2, May, 1991, p. 32.*

# Jerry Spinelli

## 1941-

American author of fiction.

Major works include *Space Station Seventh Grade* (1982), *Who Put That Hair in My Toothbrush?* (1984), *Maniac Magee* (1990).

The creator of realistic fiction for middle graders and young adults that centers on their joys and sorrows in a manner both humorous and poignant, Spinelli is recognized for his understanding of preadolescents and adolescents, realistic delineation of both youthful and adult characters, accurate dialogue, and controversial reputation. Compared to Judy Blume for authentically portraying the often earthy speech and behavior of the young, Spinelli includes profanity, drinking, flatulence, and sexual references in his works as well as sexist, racist, and other prejudicial attitudes, elements which cause some observers to regard some of his books as crude and inappropriate for young readers. However, other reviewers maintain that his works reflect Spinelli's insight into contemporary youth and note the intelligence, sensitivity, and concern for others demonstrated by his characters despite their more questionable traits.

Spinelli, who writes from his own memories and from those of his seven children, is usually characterized as a writer of hilarious farces; however, he is also noted for addressing powerful themes in a mode accessible to young readers. For example, in *Space Station Seventh Grade* and its sequel *Jason and Marceline* (1986), Spinelli describes the maturing of Jason Herkimer while questioning society's attitude toward women as sex objects. Beginning as a self-absorbed seventh-grader with a macho attitude toward girls, Jason learns to accept his classmate Marceline McAllister as a whole person during their ninth-grade year; Marceline, an unconventional yet sensible young woman struggling to retain her identity and independence, rewards Jason with her friendship and respect. In *Who Put That Hair on My Toothbrush?*, Spinelli addresses both sibling rivalry and shared loyalty in a story filled with his characteristic humor. Spinelli moves into a new literary direction with the award-winning *Maniac Magee,* tackling the subject of racism. The book describes orphaned eleven-year-old Jeffrey Magee, called "Maniac" due to his sudden appearances and athletic skill, who spends a year traveling from the white West End of his town to the black East End in search of a permanent home. Forced to leave a supportive black family when he encounters reverse racism, Maniac touches the lives of people on both sides of town and gains the status of a folk hero. Among his other works, Spinelli is also the author of a young adult novel about the rescue of twenty-four beached whales by a group of six high school seniors and a vacation story for primary graders that introduces his first female protagonist. *Maniac Magee* won the *Boston Globe-Horn Book* Award in 1990 and the Newbery Medal in 1991.

(See also *Something about the Author,* Vol. 39; *Contemporary Authors New Revision Series,* Vol. 30; and *Contemporary Authors,* Vol. 111.)

---

## TITLE COMMENTARY

### *Space Station Seventh Grade* (1982)

Funny, close-to-the-source episodes from Jason's first year in junior high school, where his word for classroom is no longer hot, boring, or interesting, but safe—safe from the ninth graders who run the school and will pee on your sneaker if you're in their way at the urinal. Jason and his friend Richie have some ridiculous racial misconceptions; after gym showers, they conclude that blacks and Italians get pubic hair earlier than "we" (WASPs) do—and that classmate McGinnis, then, must be from northern Italy. Jason also has a macho attitude toward girls, and early on he becomes class hero for a night by chasing a "monster" in the woods—mostly to protect and impress the fluffy cheerleader he pines over through the book. But the girl he ends up relating to is Marceline McAllister, the skinny trombone player he insults with a moose call early on, then battles fiercely for second-to-last place among the track team's mile runners. When the moose call gets him suspended, Jason's stepfather takes the matter lightly, explaining to his mother that they will have a "new monster" to deal with as "the thirteen-year-old does not change from a worm to a butterfly. It changes from a butterfly to a worm." If so, though, Jason is a worm who turns, imperceptibly—learning from experiences with his Korean-American friend (Jason emphasizes the Korean origin, Peter the American present), an encounter in a black neighborhood, the death of Pete's little brother, and, especially, the staunch example of Marceline McAllister. This is not, then, as frivolous as it seems at first; but it is consistently zippy and bright—and all the better for not waving its colors prematurely. (pp. 1196-97)

*A review of "Space Station, Seventh Grade," in* Kirkus Reviews, *Vol. L, No. 21, November 1, 1982, pp. 1196-97.*

The format is interesting in this guide to adolescence—from Hayrides and Halloween to School and Snow, from Punishment and Pimples to Girls and Girl. The book is a series of essays which read like a novel. There is in Jason, whose ruminations we are reading, the spectrum of sincerity, sensitivity and callousness that are only human, but there is also a disturbing harshness. Jason's predicaments—loving The Cheerleader, hating his sister (and little brothers as a genre), his efforts at football, track, sandlot baseball—are universal experiences, indentifiable by young readers. But I wonder if they will be put off as much by the opening essay as I was.

Jason and his friend help an elderly, deaf woman carry her groceries home thinking she is a wealthy eccentric. When they arrive at her dumpy house and she gives them each a glass of ice water, they know the truth. She isn't rich. They aren't going to get paid. They wander through her house, looking into bedrooms and closets. Finally, they pass the old lady on the way out—she has dozed off in a living room rocker. I was appalled by this scene, this violation of a defenseless person's privacy.

There is, I suppose, little that is truly unique in the human growth process. It is comforting yet unsettling to realize our particular adolescent anguishes were par for the course. But it is this factor of the story that rankles. We are dealing with cliche experiences and Jason reacts predictably. The book reads a little too much like a sit-com and Jason remains two dimensional.

I know and have known seventh graders, some who have even gone through the annealing fire to become ninth graders—and have found much more genuine feeling and startling sparks of insight—wisdom as wise as it will ever be. This is not an unsettling or harmful book, it is disappointing. We skate on the surface of fabulous depths.

*Ann Jordan, in a review of "Space Station Seventh Grade," in* Best Sellers, *Vol. 42, No. 11, February, 1983, p. 448.*

Here, in the tradition of Judy Blume, is a boy's book which both sexes will enjoy. Spinelli describes one year in the life of Jason Herkimer, an archetypal thirteen-year-old. Important things in his life include the miniature space station he is building, sports, signs of puberty and a pretty cheerleader, Debbie Breen. Jason is often racist, sexist, crude in his speech and gross in his habits. He is also sometimes sensitive and always uproariously funny. The book is not really plotted; like most people's lives, it is a series of incidents, episodes and random thoughts strung together in a way that makes sense only much later. Jason, like many young adolescents, is almost totally self-absorbed. He reveals every nuance of his personality, but the other characters are flat and shadowy figures who move in and out of his awareness. Only his arch-enemy, Marceline McAllister, and for one heartrending moment, his friend Peter Kim, emerge from the background as real people. Jason, as he alternately gropes and hurtles toward maturity, will both exasperate and exhilarate his readers.

*Marilyn H. Karrenbrock, in a review of "Space Station Seventh Grade," in* The ALAN Review, *Vol. 12, No. 2, Winter, 1985, p. 35.*

---

## Who Put That Hair in My Toothbrush? (1984)

Greg, 15, put that hair in the toothbrush of sister Megin, age twelve. "Sibling rivalry," says Dad, a stubborn Pollyanna type. More like "sibling homicide," mutters their weary Mom, who has lately turned to spells of self-hypnosis in order to remove herself from the battlefront. And Spinelli, using Greg and Megin as alternating narrators, offers a breezy yet fierce, often slapsticky evocation of brother/sister hostilities here—while giving the two kids believable other concerns too. Greg calls Megin "Megamouth"; he's appalled by her filthy room, sure that she'll bring on an infestation of cockroaches. ("They're having the World's Fair for Bacteria in there.") But Greg's primary interest in life is beautiful Jennifer Wade, for whom he's redone his appearance (bodybuilding, "Sassooned" hair, etc.); and he blithely exploits the crush of not-so-pretty Sara to make contact with her elusive friend Jennifer, repenting later. Meanwhile, Megin calls Greg "El Grosso," incorrigibly plants a cockroach in *his* room, and provokes him into food-fights. Her affections belong instead to kiddie-brother Todd; to ice-hockey idol Wayne Gretzky; to a friendly Dunkin' Donuts waitress (who gives her freebies); to fellow tomboy Emilie, 89, a chance acquaintance whom Megin visits regularly in a nearby nursing home; and to classmates like ordinary Sue Ellen and extraordinary Zoe—a newcomer from California who fills a bra and wears green toenail polish. Will Greg and Megin eventually reach a genuine truce? Of course. But only after the warfare gets out of hand (violence on the ice)—and after Emilie's unexpected death brings Megin to the breaking-point . . . and Greg to the brotherly rescue. (As it happens, the quest for Megin's beloved, sunken hockey-stick winds up with sister saving brother.) As in *Space Station Seventh Grade,* then, Spinelli keeps things very light most of the way through, shading into more serious feelings—with considerable finesse—only at the end. So the upshot, if never really distinguished, is bright, personable, and reasonably lifelike—with nice average kids, unusually low-key/amusing parents, and a sure balance between farce and sentiment. (pp. 51-2)

*A review of "Who Put That Hair in My Tooth-*

brush?" in Kirkus Reviews, *Vol. LII, No. 9, May 1, 1984, pp. 51-2.*

He calls her Megamouth. She calls him El Grosso. Separated by two years in age and by decades in personality, Greg and Megin Tofer, sibling archrivals, jointly narrate the hilarious new book by the author of *Space Station Seventh Grade.* Chapters alternately labeled "Greg" or "Megin" are streaked with the same sort of raucous humor that characterized the first book, but the author has also shaded the narrative with quiet moments. Greg, smitten with love for one elusive girl and pursued by another, fills his chapters with accounts of amorous schemes and frustrations. On the other hand, Megin, the tomboy, writes mainly about sports, while also emphasizing her secret friendship with Emilie Bain—a lonely elderly resident of a nursing home. . . . With a sure ear for adolescent dialogue—especially for that of boys—the author has again succeeded in creating a lively, absorbing novel. (pp. 343-44)

*Karen Jameyson, in a review of "Who Put That Hair in My Toothbrush?" in* The Horn Book Magazine, *Vol. LX, No. 3, June, 1984, pp. 343-44.*

If you secretly snicker when your 12-year-old tells tales from the Totally Gross Jokes books, or if you have a young teen who's presently plowing through what we'll call the Grungy Stage, try Jerry Spinelli. As a father to six, Spinelli is Grade A Gross with seventh-grade sleaze, a master of those embarrassing, gloppy, painful and suddenly wonderful things that happen on the razor's edge between childhood and full-fledged adolescence.

In his second young-adult novel, **Who Put That Hair in My Toothbrush?,** he's toned down some of the more off-putting sleaze (pubic hair is out, green toenail polish is in) and tuned into his characters to produce a book most likely destined to become a junior high fave before the year is out.

*Deborah Churchman, "Tales of the Awkward Age," in* Book World—The Washington Post, *January 13, 1985, p. 8.*

### Night of the Whale (1985)

The crude—and crudely described—activities of a group of high-school seniors having an end-of-school fling at a beach house abruptly stop when they try to rescue two dozen beached whales. Spinelli exceeds the bathroom humor of *Space Station Seventh Grade* and *Who Put That Hair in My Toothbrush?* with his seemingly interminable string of descriptions of beer guzzling followed by flatulence, beer guzzling followed by vomiting, beer guzzling followed by urinating contests and beer guzzling followed by hangovers. These scenes are tempered by incidents involving a photo of the homecoming queen picking her nose and the wheelchair-bound but sexy newspaper editor having an epiphany on the beach. Many teens won't stay around until day five of this hedonistic week, when the revelers meet the whales and—flash!—grow up. Those who do will have a hard time buying it.

*David Gale, in a review of "Night of the Whale," in* School Library Journal, *Vol. 32, No. 5, January, 1986, p. 75.*

Mouse and his five friends whoop it up at a summer cottage during Senior Week. One night, stranded on the beach when their car breaks down, they discover several beached whales and try to help rescue them. The continual partying and subsequent rescue efforts are detailed in snappy, realistic dialogue that flows swiftly in the many hilarious scenes. The characters are likeable in spite of their zany "senioritis".

*Lionel Bender, in a review of "Night of the Whale," in* Children's Book Review Service, *Vol. 14, No. 8, March, 1986, p. 93.*

The description of the rescue of the suicidal mammals in the darkness of night is spellbindingly magical and written in a breezy, yet poetic, style. Unfortunately, the account of the whales doesn't begin until over half-way through the book. The first half, while undoubtedly ringing with truth, contains material inappropriate to the junior high audience the book appears to be aimed toward. References are made to beer farts, vomiting chocolate, erections, being "loaded," "tinkle" stories, and peeing records, and alcohol use as a means of proving manhood. While the whale plot is redeeming, other features render the book objectionable at the junior high level and questionable (although probably popular) at the senior high level. Spinelli needs to define his audience more carefully.

*Brook Dillon, in a review of "Night of the Whale," in* The Book Report, *Vol. 4, No. 5, March-April, 1986, p. 31.*

### Jason and Marceline (1986)

Jason Herkimer likes Marceline McAllister; can their relationship survive ninth grade and its overpowering social milieu? In this sequel to **Space Station Seventh Grade,** Marceline struggles to be herself and maintain her independence from a crowd mentality—even as she accepts Jason's friendship. He, meanwhile, is feeling slightly schizophrenic as he cherishes his relationship with Marceline but is caught up in the male social world that views women as bodies and nothing more. Spinelli plays this up to the hilt, liberally stirring in locker-room talk and adolescent crudities ("If a girl's balloons gain a millimeter overnight, your range-finder will pick it up. Let a whole summer go by, your fuses are blowing"). But the point of his story is to show Jason's fumbling efforts to treat Marceline as a whole person. Jason manages this at last, and ends up a little more sensitive to what's wrong with treating girls as sex objects. The crudeness here grates but is true to life, and the message is worthwhile. This will probably be popular with its intended audience, who might take comfort in the social struggles that are meaningfully depicted.

*Denise M. Wilms, in a review of "Jason and Marceline," in* Booklist, *Vol. 83, No. 9, January 1, 1987, p. 712.*

Spinelli has achieved a sort of reputation as a badboy of

*Spinelli in his office with his pet chinchilla and rat.*

juvenile letters, and here he moves into previously un-touched areas—lots of hickeys, sperm, and hormones. It's all done for laughs, and Spinelli can be very funny, if very crude. Some adults will shudder or sputter over this one, but YAs will love it. It's a quick, witty read, and even the print is big.

> Robert Unsworth, in a review of "Jason and Marceline," in School Library Journal, Vol. 33, No. 6, February, 1987, p. 95.

In the equally funny and often earthy sequel to *Space Station Seventh Grade,* the author again does not so much probe the teenage mind as rummage through it, uncovering a collage of small anxieties, the larger joys and bafflements of sex, the need for peer approval, and the often well-hidden earmarks of intelligence and decency. Marceline, a girl of good sense and even humor, nicely balances the ebullience and self-absorption of the prototypically adolescent hero. Jason, who tells the story, truly sounds like a teenager as he gets the nerve to kiss Marceline for the first time, a process he describes as being similar to docking two spacecraft. He brags about being " 'puhloooooootid' " on one-third of a can of beer and recounts in aching detail his misery when he and Marceline have a falling-out. His despairing parents, irked siblings, and, above all, Marceline watch Jason through the exuberant ascents and disastrous skids on the rock-strewn highway of his life,

seeming to realize that somewhere in him is a wonderful, funny, and loyal human being. Jason's alert life-saving and his gesture of sympathetic understanding toward a seventh-grade "nerd" earn him the reader's affection and the astonished approval of his cronies. He assures himself, too, of Marceline's love and, what is perhaps more important, regains her respect and friendship.

> Ethel R. Twichell, in a review of "Jason and Marceline," in The Horn Book Magazine, Vol. LXIII, No. 2, March-April, 1987, p. 217.

---

### Dump Days (1988)

J. D. and Duke are as lighthearted a pair of adolescents to have ever slapped a high five or to have dreamed of ways of earning money. As plan after plan is hatched during the hot days of June and July, their pockets remain empty thanks to the ingenuous generosity of Duke and plain bad luck. He forgets to charge the neighborhood youngsters for the fried scrapple and maple syrup he cooks up and loses in a flood the few dollars which he and J. D. have scraped together. Their entertaining and usually disastrous adventures are enacted in a colorful neighborhood boasting a nearby dump, which lures all with the promise of sighting rats and discovering discarded treasures; their busy street teems with swarms of small children and eccentric adults, all with arresting stories of their own. That the feckless boys, obsessed as they are on filling their stomachs with zeps—a kind of sub—and strawberry milks, should respond so sensitively to the violin playing of a new neighbor, Joy, may be a bit unlikely, but it is hard to resist J. D.'s guileless recounting of his confrontation with the bully Rhino Moast. As always, Spinelli has both his ears and eyes finely tuned to the whims and foibles of young and old. He neither judges nor berates but shakes everyone up in his own bag of tricks and watches to see what will spill out. A splendid concluding fiasco inevitably erupts in the boys' profitable street fair, leaving them bankrupt once more but richer in virtue as they replace Joy's violin, which has been broken in the melee. Despite all, they find that even without strawberry milks and zeps they have managed to have their perfect day.

> *Ethel R. Twichell, in a review of "Dump Days," in* The Horn Book Magazine, *Vol. LXIV, No. 3, May-June, 1988, p. 355.*

**Dump Days** presents a melange of thoroughly unlikable characters in seedy surroundings where the favorite pasttime is bashing a live rat with a baseball bat. . . . The handicapped boy is routinely ridiculed, as are both an elderly neighborhood woman and the town's mentally disturbed adult. These situations are played out without warmth or realization on the characters' parts that their actions are insensitive. Much of the text is comprised of the boys' conversations, which are stilted and tedious, with endless lines dedicated to sequences like "Yeah?" "Oh Yeah," "Yeah? Oh yeah," and an annoying stream-of-consciousness style made up of abrupt sentences. Spinelli's aim may have been to give readers a taste of a lazy small-town summer. If so, the flavor's about as appealing as the dead mole that J. D. keeps in his freezer.

> *Joanne Aswell, in a review of "Dump Days," in* School Library Journal, *Vol. 34, No. 11, August, 1988, p. 99.*

Despite a few glancing references to video games and a central plot episode involving a Vietnamese refugee, this innocent story could have taken place thirty years ago and overindulges in nostalgic glow. The boys' slang is squeaky clean, overdone, and dated. *Krymineez?* What saves this from the gee-whizzes are Spinelli's convincing portrait of a solid friendship and the freshly comic characterizations of the supporting cast: J. D.'s little sister Bertie, who tries to sell the boys a dead mole on layaway; Duke's big sister Doris, who guards "her" kitchen with evil zest. "I'll be back here in a minute. I don't wanna see a speck of *dust* out of place, *boy.*"

> *Roger Sutton, in a review of "Dump Days," in* Bulletin of the Center for Children's Books, *Vol. 42, No. 1, September, 1988, p. 21.*

---

### The Bathwater Gang (1990)

Eleven short chapters . . . develop a slight story about Bertie Kidd. She tells her energetic grandmother that she is bored on the second day of summer vacation, and her grandmother suggests that she start a gang. Fifty-nine girls gather for free pizza but only two show up at the first club meeting; the boys form a counter gang and mischief ensues. Finally, a free-for-all mud fight (with Granny improbably unrecognized under all that mud) convinces everyone that it is more fun to do things together. The title refers to the new gang's purpose: providing a mobile pet washing service. A book that's light, entertaining, and broadly limned for readers not quite ready for more substantial fare such as Janice Lee Smith's "Adam Joshua" stories or Ann Cameron's "Julian" series. (pp. 91-2)

> *Susan Hepler, in a review of "The Bathwater Gang," in* School Library Journal, *Vol. 36, No. 5, May, 1990, pp. 91-2.*

Jerry Spinelli's books portray an idyllic world in which plain speaking ("Boogie breath") and running amuck (literally, here, when it rains) comfortably coexist with cozy grandmas who clean up the mess. Bertie is bored, she starts a gang, havoc ensues. While the story is improbably plotted (it seems unlikely that no one would recognize Granny when she's covered with mud), it has enough action and arguments to ensure appeal.

> *Roger Sutton, in a review of "The Bathwater Gang," in* Bulletin of Center for Children's Books, *Vol. 44, No. 1, September, 1990, p. 16.*

---

### Maniac Magee (1990)

#### AUTHOR'S COMMENTARY

*[The following excerpt is from Spinelli's Boston Globe-Horn Book Award acceptance speech, originally delivered on October 1, 1990.]*

**Maniac Magee** is about, among other things, the kid as legendary hero. Several weeks ago my hometown librarian said, "Were you Maniac?"

You would think I'd have had a ready reply, but I didn't. It had not been necessary to answer that question, at least not consciously, in order to write the book.

So I thought about it.

I thought about the world that children inhabit. I don't know about you, but it's a world that, in many ways, I find indistinguishable from myth and legend.

Above the railroad tracks beyond the dead end of George Street in Norristown, Pennsylvania, where I used to live, there was a hummock of eraser-colored clay known as Red Hill. We believed it was the devil's home.

Next to Red Hill was a flat half-acre plain we called the spear field. It got its name from the weeds that grew there: tall—sometimes taller than us—and straight, with shafts about half an inch thick. And their roots were shallow and easy to pull out. One good yank—shake off the excess root dirt—and you had yourself a weapon.

We fought our wars in the afternoons. We hurled spears until everybody was dead, or until we heard the bell of the hokey-pokey man. We all went AWOL at once. Do you remember trying to run and fish in your pocket for a dime at the same time?

We would find the hokey-pokey man and his white cart at the dead end. He knew where to go for kids. He would flip the dishtowel off the block of ice, clack the ice shaver like a pair of castanets, and growl, "So who's up?"

I personally never wanted to be first. I wanted to be last, so I could have all the time I needed to marvel at the squad of bottles with their colored liquids—somehow reminding me of a barbershop—and to try to decide which flavor I wanted that day. It always turned out to be root beer.

I thought of other veterans of the hokey-pokey wars.

Jerry Fox, reverently known as The Pro because of his athletic skills, especially in street football. With the ball in his hands, he became slipperier than a squirrel. He would stand perfectly still, nonchalant even, waiting for you to reach, daring you; and when you did—*poof*—he was gone!

Buffalo Morris, whose name told you all you needed to know.

John Ribble, crewcut, swaggering, whose fastball you heard more than saw; passing you at the plate, it whispered *shhh* before thunking into the catcher's mitt.

Pickles Bordolino, whose status as the dirtiest kid in town was fame in its purest form. There was no judgment here, only wonder. And the excited question that dawned with each new day: How can he possibly show up any crummier than yesterday? He always did.

We never fought our wars over a woman. But if we had, she would have been Dovey Wilmoth. Platinum blonde in eighth grade, the world's most beautiful girl, she was the reason we pedaled, between wars, twenty times a day past her house on Haws Avenue.

When I think of those days, the sense of the remote and the timeless and the heroic is such that the spear field might as well have been the plains of Troy, and Dovey Wilmoth, Helen, the face that launched a hundred bikes.

And they remain there, *then,* as fixed in time as if painted on a Grecian urn.

Jerry Fox didn't really reach high school only to watch the football team play from the grandstand.

John Ribble didn't really lose his fastball and gain a pot-belly.

That's not really Pickles Bordolino, Esquire, sitting in a lawyer's office. Clean.

Dovey Wilmoth never grew up to become a nurse.

Growing up, getting a job, becoming ordinary, getting old—that's stuff for mortals.

Was I Maniac Magee?

I sure was.

Weren't we all? (pp. 40-1)

> *Jerry Spinelli, " 'Maniac Magee': Homer on George Street," in* The Horn Book Magazine, *Vol. LXVII, No. 1, January-February, 1991, pp. 40-1.*

An occasionally long-winded, but always affecting, parable-like story about racism and ignorance.

Jeffrey Magee is twice homeless—once involuntarily, at age three, when his parents plunge with a high-speed trolley off a bridge; the second time eight years later, when he voluntarily leaves the troubled home of his aunt and uncle. Jeffrey's subsequent yearlong flight generates a host of legends: his sudden appearances and astonishing athletic prowess earn him the name "Maniac," and his just-as-sudden disappearances ensure his fame. Innocently, he crosses between two strictly segregated parts of town, the white East End and the black West End, making friends and enemies in both camps and managing to soften the lines of segregation; later, he finds a new home in the West.

If this is sometimes a bit like a chalkboard lesson, it may be because racism is still a volatile subject that is more comfortably dealt with in parable form. The metaphorical style is a brave change from the realism of Spinelli's other books, while fans of his earlier, tongue-in-cheek, street-wise tone will find it also an integral part of this story—ballast for the mythic, shifting picture of Maniac's year on the run.

> *A review of "Maniac Magee," in* Kirkus Reviews, *Vol. 58, No. 9, May 1, 1990, p. 655.*

The author brightens the story with exaggeration, humor, and melodrama, but avoids the feverish hilarity of his earlier books. Despite Maniac's accomplishments and the author's clear message for racial harmony, the book avoids mawkishness through the good-natured characterization of people of both races and by the vigor and clamor of their speech and actions. The book becomes, in the end, a kind of twentieth-century morality play, with Maniac a larger-than-life leader and his rag-tag companions promising, if not totally redeemed, disciples.

> *Ethel R. Twichell, in a review of "Maniac Magee," in* The Horn Book Magazine, *Vol. LXVI, No. 3, May-June, 1990, p. 340.*

Warning: this interesting book is a mythical story about racism. It should not be read as reality. Legend springs up about Jeffrey "Maniac" Magee, a white boy who runs faster and hits balls farther than anyone, who lives on his own with amazing grace, and is innocent as to racial affairs. . . . Black, feisty Amanda Beale and her family lovingly open their home to Maniac, and tough, smart-talking "Mars Bar" Thompson and other characters are all, to varying degrees, full of prejudices and unaware of their own racism. Racial epithets are sprinkled throught the book; Mars Bar calls Maniac "fishbelly," and blacks are described by a white character as being "today's Indians." In the final, disjointed section of the book, Maniac confronts the hatred that perpetuates ignorance by bringing Mars Bar to meet the Pickwells—"the best the West End had to offer." In the feel-good ending, Mars and Maniac resolve their differences; Maniac gets a home and there is hope for at least improved racial relations. Unreal? Yes. It's a cop-out for Spinelli to have framed this story as a legend—it frees him from having to make it real, or even possible. Nevertheless, the book will stimulate thinking about racism, and it might help educate those readers who, like so many students, have no first-hand knowledge of people of other races. Pathos and compassion inform a short, relatively easy-to-read story with broad appeal, which suggests that to solve problems of racism, people must first know each other as individuals.

*Joel Shoemaker, in a review of "Maniac Magee," in* School Library Journal, *Vol. 36, No. 6, June, 1990, p. 138.*

Part tall tale and part contemporary realistic fiction, this unusual novel magically weaves timely issues of homelessness, racial prejudice, and illiteracy into a complicated story, rich in characters and details. . . .

A deep sense of story permeates this multiveined novel: Maniac runs (accomplishing fantastic athletic and superhero-type feats—bringing about both his folk hero image and nickname, "Maniac") and reads, although he never attends school. He changes others people's lives with books, either by reading from or by teaching the printed word. For instance, he entices Grayson to tell him baseball stories and later teaches the man to read. Furthermore, Maniac educates white families about black ones and black families about white ones, proving through his own actions the shared humanity of both groups.

As he jogs readers into analyzing what makes a home, Spinelli, in his best book to date, creates a provocative slice of life, showing graphically (and sometimes humorously) the pitfalls that face the homeless. Although this demands much concentration on the part of the reader, it is a unique effort, an energetic piece of writing that bursts with creativity, enthusiasm, and hope for the future; in short, it's a celebration of life. Good readers will thoroughly enjoy this, and teachers looking for interesting novels will find plumbing its depths rewarding.

*Deborah Abbott, in a review of "Maniac Magee," in* Booklist, *Vol. 86, No. 19, June 1, 1990, p. 1902.*

Spinelli writes humorously and bravely about a touchy subject that most children's authors and publishers tend to avoid. He's at his best when he's setting the scene, describing, for example, the first April day after a rainy night, when the streets are filled with kids and worms. As a white writer, the view of racism Spinelli presents, although politically correct, is still white. Readers may agree or disagree with his ideas and character portrayals. But at least Spinelli's made an attempt to bring racism out of the closet and to write about it in a way he sees relevant to school children's own experiences.

*Cathryn A. Camper, in a review of "Maniac Magee," in* The Five Owls, *Vol. 4, No. 6, July-August, 1990, p. 108.*

# Ellen Tarry

## 1906-

African American author of picture books and nonfiction.

Major works include *Hezekiah Horton* (1942), *My Dog Rinty* (1946), *The Runaway Elephant* (1950), *Young Jim: The Early Years of James Weldon Johnson* (1967).

Recognized as one of the first writers to use nonstereotypical black children as protagonists in juvenile literature, Tarry is noted for creating sensitive and satisfying stories about Harlem life for primary graders as well as informational books for young adults on influential historical and contemporary black figures. Writing from the hope that "one day all God's children will walk through the open door of opportunity in dignity," she is acknowledged for providing young readers with accurate portrayals of her characters, both black and white, in stories which have universal appeal and reflect her understanding of small boys and girls. Tarry is perhaps best known as the coauthor of *My Dog Rinty,* a picture book on which she collaborated with Marie Hall Ets that is illustrated with photographs by the husband and wife team of Alexander and Alexandra Alland. Considered an especially distinctive story of a boy and his dog that depicts the Harlem of the time in a semidocumentary style, *My Dog Rinty* describes how the misunderstood terrier Rinty, who lives with his young owner David and his family in a Harlem tenement, proves himself as a dog of special talents. Rinty, who is taken away from David after chewing holes in the living room rug and other instances of inappropriate behavior, is found to be a "born ratter and mouser," as a trainer describes the dog; the story ends with the reunited David and Rinty becoming celebrities after the terrier's success in pointing out rodent holes in city hotels, hospitals, and stores. *My Dog Rinty* is considered unique as a picture book for its matter-of-fact documentation of life in the urban black community, a fact which, underscored by its substantive story and promotion of racial tolerance, provided inspiration for subsequent authors and illustrators of children's literature about the black experience.

"Her unusual background," writes critic Sylvia G. L. Dannett, "has made [Tarry] the rare kind of person she is today." Born to a mulatto father and octoroon mother, Tarry knew from childhood that she would be a writer. She converted to Catholicism as a high school student, an experience that, along with the racism she encountered, greatly influenced both her philosophy and her literary subjects. After teaching grade school and adult education and writing a newspaper column on black heritage in Birmingham, Alabama, Tarry moved to New York. She joined the Negro Writers' Guild, where she met the poet and novelist Claude McKay, who introduced her to such figures as James Weldon Johnson, whose life and career she was later to profile. Through McKay, Tarry learned of the Writers' Laboratory that had been organized by the Bureau of Educational Experiments under the direction of

educator Lucy Sprague Mitchell; the lone African American member of the Writers' Lab, Tarry received a scholarship to attend the Cooperative School for Student Teachers, later to become Bank Street College, for two years. She also worked on the Federal Writers' project as a researcher for a book on the history of the Negro in New York. Introduced to Baroness Catherine de Hueck, the founder of the Catholic interracial center Friendship House in Harlem who had escaped from Russia during the Revolution, Tarry started a long association with Friendship House. Known as the "Story Lady" for the story hours she developed for neighborhood children, Tarry used her own tales with her listeners as well as those of other members of the Writers' Lab such as Margaret Wise Brown. Her first book for children, *Janie Belle* (1939) is a picture book about a black infant abandoned by her parents who is adopted by the head nurse of the hospital where she is taken; based on a true story, *Janie Belle* is the only one of Tarry's books to be written in a rhythmic style. Her next book, *Hezekiah Horton,* is the story of a small boy who has a fascination with automobiles. Ridiculed by the neighborhood boys for his Biblical name, Hezekiah becomes popular when a young white man in a long red convertible gives him and the other boys a ride. Called Mister

Ed in the story, the young man is journalist Eddie Doherty, a friend of Tarry's from Friendship House who also appears in the second of her books about Hezekiah, *The Runaway Elephant.* In this adventure, which is again based on a factual incident, Hezekiah makes a suggestion on how to capture an escaped circus elephant and gets his story in the paper. In addition to her biography of James Weldon Johnson, a work noted as the first biography of the poet, lyricist, lawyer, novelist, and NAACP leader for a young adult audience, Tarry has written biographies of Katherine Drexel, Martin de Porres, and Pierre Toussaint as well as an autobiography for adults. Among Tarry's other accomplishments are her cofounding of the Friendship House in Chicago, appointment to the Department of Housing and Urban Development, and work for the Archdiocese of New York.

(See also *Something about the Author,* Vol. 16 and *Contemporary Authors,* Vols. 73-76.)

---

## AUTHOR'S COMMENTARY

[The September that I was eleven] I started my last semester at Slater School and my new teacher inspired me to reach for the moon. We had only been in school a few days when she told us to write a composition on the most interesting experience we had during the summer. I could not write about raiding watermelon patches; blackberry hunting was tame. Until the night before the composition was to be turned in, I could not think of a subject. I just sat with my pencil and pad in my hands and looked out the window. Suddenly I noticed a calendar on the wall. On the calendar was a picture of an Indian camp scene. A wigwam stood among a cluster of russet-leaved trees with a thick forest in the background and a lake in front. Before the wigwam smoldered the embers of a campfire. A full moon shone on the lake and an Indian brave drifted downstream in a canoe—his oar raised. I thought about a camping trip we had planned, one that got rained out. I closed my eyes and rushed the Indian on about his business. Then I grouped my family about the fire and we told stories and sang songs until it was time to wrap up in our blankets.

The next day I turned in a descriptive composition on a camping trip outside Eutaw, Alabama. After the papers were corrected, the teacher picked my composition out and asked me to come to the front and read it to the class. I did and the other children were as quiet as could be. I could not understand why nobody said anything after I finished and I looked around at the teacher. Her plain, irregular-featured ebony face was beautiful with a glow that was new to me. Years later, I saw the same look on the face of a nurse who held a newborn baby in her hands. She left her desk and put one arm around my shoulders. For a moment I wondered if I had been caught in another "story."

"Someday," she said, ending my suspense, "someday Ellen is going to be a writer!" (pp. 20-1)

[Editor's note: After receiving a teaching degree, Tarry was appointed to teach the fourth grade at Slater School, her alma mater.] At the beginning of the next school year

I was assigned to a fifth grade. . . . During the first few days when they were still being eased back into classroom routine, I discovered that I had a group of exceptionally bright youngsters. Though they had little more conception of the world beyond than had the others, I heard a group of small girls talking about what they wanted to do when they grew up, and that was a step in the right direction. It was the boys who seemed less sure of themselves. I worried about them.

Among the Negroes I knew, there was an unwritten law which said girls had to be educated. Boys from large families were allowed to go to work after finishing high school. I knew of cases where these working brothers helped send their sisters through college. I also knew that this custom had produced a widening circle of young professional women who were perforce thrown in the company of unskilled laborers, and that many unstable marriages had resulted. It was frightening to think that the bright-eyed boys whose classroom lives were in my keeping might one day add to the human waste which was all around.

In search of a window through which my boys and girls might snatch glimpses of the world beyond Red Mountain, I scanned magazines, newspapers, and books for mention of any and all achievements by members of our race. I pin-pointed distant cities where Negroes had migrated to enjoy broader economic and cultural opportunities, and shared with my children whatever knowledge I had of a given community. I led my young charges afield by easy stages from the known to the unknown. (pp. 76-7)

Around this time, a Negro insurance company in Atlanta sent out a picture calendar called "Our Hall of Fame." Small photographs of Negroes who had made outstanding contributions to American culture adorned the top portion of the calendar. There were likenesses of such men as Crispus Attucks, Peter Salem, Benjamin Bannecker, Booker T. Washington, James Weldon Johnson, George Washington Carver, W. E. B. Du Bois, Benjamin Brawley, and John S. Hope. Miss Lizzie Thomas, who gave me the first book of poetry I ever owned, worked at the Booker T. Washington Branch Library with Mrs. Earline Driver and the two librarians spent many hours helping me find books containing biographical material about these men. Then I wrote my own version of their stories and told them to the children. (pp. 77-8)

The sketches of . . . famous Negro lives formed the basis for a series of lessons in reading, writing, spelling, and composition. With the help of one of my boys who was artistic, an attractive bulletin board was constructed on which the pupils' compositions were displayed. Though I had suspected that my principal was pleased with the project, I was sure of it when he started bringing visiting officials to my room. By the end of the year both teacher and pupils were convinced that Negroes could rise above the handicap of race. (p. 78)

I was still searching for a way to make my seventh grade teacher's prediction come true, that I would be a writer. I wanted to communicate with the world—to cry out against the outrage of racial discrimination and its attendant ills. But I knew it meant taking up another cross, and

I hesitated. I reread Booker T. Washington, and studied everything by and about James Weldon Johnson, Du Bois, and Brawley that I could find in our humble library. One of my chief sources of inspiration, I remember, was the folksy articles by Bruce Barton which appeared in Sunday supplements around the latter part of the 1920's.

The study of journalism, I thought, might be a stepping-stone, with books to come later. I dreamed of going to New York and enrolling at Columbia University's Pulitzer School of Journalism. But I had to start somewhere and a correspondence course was the first step. Then I went to a local editor and showed him the sketches I had written for my pupils.

Guillermo Talliferro, who edited *The Birmingham Truth,* read my stories and hired me. . . . From week to week my assignments grew and I became a combination reporter-columnist-editorial writer. Tally pushed me until I finally managed to sell ads, too.

One of the time-hallowed lacks which has handicapped my people has been the dearth of knowledge concerning our race in Africa and in the time shortly after we were brought to America. In a small way, "Negroes of Note," as my column was captioned, helped to fill this need. Years later I was criticized for having written "in defense of being a Negro," but at the time I was happy to do so. One of the peaks of this happiness was reached when my former principal suggested that other teachers might do well to use the material in my sketches for classroom work.

The published works of young Negro writers like Claude McKay, Countee Cullen, and Langston Hughes encouraged my awakening ambition. I regretted that more Negro women were not writing or being written about. There is no doubt this tiny spark was fanned when I read the life of Harriet Tubman, a runaway slave who went back into the land of bondage time and time again to lead loved ones to freedom. Harriet's exploits gave me courage to write the angry editorials about segregation and discrimination which appeared in the *Truth* under my byline. (pp. 79-80)

Bit by bit the small reforms I advocated in the *Truth* came to pass. . . . With each little victory, I became more aware of what I might be doing if only I were better prepared. I argued with myself; I prayed and thought of all that needed to be done. I could see and feel the lethargy which enslaved my people just as much as the unfair laws which gave them second-class citizenship. Even after I had sent for a catalogue and knew I could meet the requirements for admission to Columbia's Pulitzer School of Journalism, I was not sure how I would live if I left home. My only asset was a diamond ring which I could pawn, and I had a fear of being alone and hungry in a strange city.

The night I made the decision to leave Birmingham I was sitting on the front porch looking out over the lights of the city in the valley below. The moon was full and all the stars were out. The radio, just inside the window, was playing and Rudy Vallee was singing;

     . . . Look down, look down

that lonely road
Before you travel on. . . .

The magnitude of the heavens assured me and I decided that somewhere in such a vast and beautiful universe I would be sure to find my niche. (pp. 83-4)

[In New York, I was sponsored] for membership in the Negro Writers' Guild, a group of journalists and creative writers who gathered periodically in a Republican club house on West 136th Street. It was at one of these meetings that I first met Claude McKay, the Negro poet-novelist. . . . (p. 127)

[Claude] introduced me to James Weldon Johnson, Countee Cullen, Langston Hughes, Harold Jackman, Roberta Bosley, and many other important people in the literary world of that time. (p. 128)

Claude's place was furnished with rugs, stools, statues, tapestries, and paintings he had brought back from Morocco. It was here that we held our meetings and I was sitting on one of the tapestry-covered divans discussing the advantages of a writers' guild with one of the group when I heard Claude yell: "I'm Claude McKay, I don't want to write any *little* stories! Let Miss Tarry have it."

"What are you going to give Miss Tarry now?" I had learned to meet Claude's storms with calmness. "All she wants is a job."

"I'm going to get that, too," he said. "Jimmie has promised to straighten that out. But now he's telling me about some scholarship for a writer who wants to do stories for children. You go and take it. I write novels!"

"All right. I'll take it. Just tell me where to go. From here on, I'm not turning down anything."

"Good," he grinned and shooed his friend, whom he called Jimmie, in my direction. You tell *her* about it," Claude said. . . .

Jimmie [Baker, the husband of Augusta Baker, the Librarian in charge of children's work at the 135th Street branch library,] told me that the Bureau of Educational Experiments was setting up a Writers' Laboratory under the distinguished educator and writer, Lucy Sprague Mitchell. The Bureau was making an effort to have as many ethnic groups as possible represented. A scholarship was being offered to a Negro who was a writer and had teaching experience or vice versa. He instructed me to write Mrs. Mitchell at the Bank Street headquarters. . . .(pp. 133-34)

I like to remember my first impression of Lucy Sprague Mitchell. She was wearing a cotton dress and comfortable flat-heeled shoes, and a narrow black ribbon band kept her hair in place. From a cotton bag of the catch-all variety she extracted our correspondence. . . . I soon understood that the only thing Lucy Sprague Mitchell would ever expect from me was "books for children that children will read and enjoy." In a few weeks I was the lone Negro member of the Writers' Lab and two of the most important years in my life began. (p. 135)

I worked hard to show my gratitude for the opportunity

to learn how to tighten my fist and build a story. And there was much for me to learn.

My schedule also included classes at the Cooperative School for Student Teachers (now Bank Street College) and observation at the Harriet Johnson Nursery School and the Little Red Schoolhouse. (p. 136)

[I was later] granted a scholarship by the Bureau of Educational Experiments, which entitled me to study creative writing for children under Lucy Sprague Mitchell. (p. 137)

When the school year closed I had been granted a scholarship for another year. (p. 139)

[Editor's note: While in New York, Tarry was asked to join Friendship House, an interracial justice center in Harlem.] The long, happy hours at Friendship House fitted into my school work and gave me access to many of the books I needed for my research. The "B" [for "Baronness," the nickname of Friendship House director Catharine de Hueck] encouraged me to start a "story hour" for the children of the neighborhood. This gave me an excellent chance to try out my stories as well as the work of other members of the Writers' Lab on the audience for whom the stories were written. (p. 148)

As the school year closed I had finished two juvenile manuscripts and Myrtle Sheldon, an artist, dummied a picture book so I could peddle it. (p. 150)

On Christmas Eve I received my first check for *Janie Belle,* the foundling story that became my first book. It was scheduled for a late summer publication date. Janie Belle had come through just in time to play Santa Claus to a group of my most cherished story-hour children and I fought my way in and out of Macy's toy department that day to be sure that my boys and girls would be happy on the next. (p. 160)

Back at Friendship House [in 1940 after a trip from New York to New Orleans] I met Eddie Doherty. Eddie was a newspaper man and the "B" said he and Helen Worden, another writer, were gathering material for a series of articles on Harlem. (p. 173)

Eddie touched my life with a wand which produced a story for my second book. . . . We all like to remember the way the book happened because it was a happy bit of Harlem living.

In return for the help we had given with his story, Eddie gave a party at his home in Westchester and invited the Friendship House workers. He was to call for us in his new car and it was agreed that I would join the group in front of Madonna Flat. As soon as I crossed Lenox Avenue walking east I saw the crowd farther up 135th Street and wondered what the commotion was all about. The instant I saw tall, blond Eddie standing alongside a shiny red convertible full of wriggling, giggling brown urchins my story was started. As I drew closer I saw that Eddie was pushing a button on the dashboard which made the tan canvas top of the car go up and down. Each time it went up or down the boys squealed with delight and their eyes got bigger and bigger. (p. 174)

There was a lot of brilliant talk and music and good eats

[at the party], but my mind was busy with the tall, blond "Mister Ed" and his beautiful red automobile which had been full of little wriggling, giggling colored boys who squealed each time he made the tan canvas top go up and down. That night when I got home I made the first notes for *Hezekiah Horton,* as I called the little boy through whose eyes I saw the red car. (p. 175)

Grace Nail Johnson [the wife of James Weldon Johnson] had suggested that I show some of my manuscripts for children to the editor in the Junior Books department at Viking Press, publishers of many of her husband's works.

Following Mrs. Johnson's advice, I went to Viking, where I met May Massee, who had a wide reputation for publishing worthwhile juvenile books. So I became a Viking author. May Massee also understood my desire to have a Negro illustrate the little story of Hezekiah and the red automobile and was patient with my search for an artist whose sketches would meet her approval. We were both happy to select Oliver Harrington, whose cartoon, Bootsie, appearing in the Negro press, is an all-time favorite. (p. 182)

[Editor's note: Tarry then left New York for Chicago to become co-director of a Friendship House on the South Side.] Though authors were a penny a dozen in New York, it was different in Chicago. In 1942, this was especially true of Negro authors, and I had many requests to visit libraries and schools. Children who had read *Hezekiah Horton* always wanted to know about "Mr. Ed and his beautiful red automobile." When I was asked to speak at the Lincoln Center the librarian asked if I could bring Eddie along and he consented. The night before we were scheduled to speak at Lincoln Center there was a supper at Friendship House to which many of the civic leaders were invited. In the middle of the meal, Mildred Wiley brought me a telegram which read: "CANNOT JOIN YOU TOMORROW. AM OUT HUNTING AN ELEPHANT." The wire was signed: "EDDIE."

Sometime during the day I had heard that an elephant named Modoc had escaped from a circus in a nearby town and had wrought havoc wherever it wandered. There was great concern for property in the rural area where the big animal was roaming and even more concern for the elephant's life, as frost had already fallen. Eddie, I reasoned, had drawn an assignment to cover the elephant hunt.

"I've got it," I waved the telegram before the astonished group. "Mr. Ed and Hezekiah are going to hunt an elephant in the beautiful red car!"

[Ann Harrigan, co-director of the Chicago Friendship House with Tarry,] who had gotten used to my outbursts when a story idea was born, read the telegram to the gathering and explained that they had just witnessed the beginning of a new book for children. We all agreed that hunting an elephant in a red convertible should be an exciting literary adventure. It took eight years for my Hezekiah and "Mister Ed" to finish their adventure, but that, too, started at the Chicago Friendship House. (pp. 208-09)

May Massee of Viking Press wrote and asked me to meet with Marie Hall Ets, an author-illustrator who had suggested a juvenile which would depict the everyday lives of Negro boys and girls in an urban setting like Harlem. Marie and I met at the Viking offices on the same day New York was lashed by the August, 1944, hurricane and we made our first plans for the juvenile story which became *My Dog Rinty*. . . .

The housing shortage in Chicago became insignificant in comparison with the living conditions I found when I returned to New York in 1944. (p. 250)

The anguish caused by the housing shortage was forgotten when the child I had expected for Christmas came in November. Instead of the son I had prayed for, God sent me a daughter. (p. 251)

Except for colic, brought on by my dogged insistence in following a fixed feeding schedule as I had been instructed, Elizabeth was a healthy, happy baby. Fortunately, her colic struck at night. During the day, after bottles were washed, formula mixed, and clothes were on the line, I was with Marie Ets working at all the business which goes into making a book. The story was written, but we had to find a "typical" family and get permission to take pictures. Though it was hard finding a family to fit our needs, getting permission to take pictures in homes, places of business, public service centers, and churches in Harlem was an enormous task. My people's understandable suspicion of the white man and anything connected with the white man's world created situations which would have defeated the purpose of the book if I had not presumed upon many friendships. By the time Alexander and Alexandra Alland had taken the last picture for the book, I was immune to insult. (pp. 252-53)

In the juvenile field, when I started my teaching career, there were almost no books for young readers which showed the Negro as other than Uncle Remus or Little Black Sambo. Though Uncle Remus must be reckoned as an outstanding contribution to the folklore of the world and Sambo is universal, as a steady, exclusive reading diet such books would have given children a stereotyped idea of the Negro. Today, there are many beautifully illustrated juvenile books on library shelves which show Negroes in all walks of life. To have had a small part in adding to this list has been a privilege. Of such intangibles are the riches of an eventful life. (pp. 302-03)

> *Ellen Tarry, in her* The Third Door: The Autobiography of an American Negro Woman, *1955. Reprint by Negro Universities Press, 1971, 304 p.*

---

## GENERAL COMMENTARY

### Roi Ottley

Ellen Tarry is an artful creator of children's books which often pose a moral. Actually, she is more a missionary than a writer. Yet in both she has been successful, using her talents to present more effectively a message addressed to white and black alike.

> *Roi Ottley, "She Faces the Future with Faith,"*

*in* Chicago Sunday Tribune Magazine of Books, *May 22, 1955, p. 3.*

### Sylvia G. L. Dannett

Miss Tarry's devotion to her race does not manifest itself in distortions—neither in her fiction, nor in real life. The stories she writes include white people whom she remembers with affection from her Harlem days. She numbers many whites among her friends. "I guess I have no hate in me," she says, "because my white granddaddy and my colored grandmother loved each other so much. They are buried in separate cemeteries, but spirit can merge beyond the grave."

Her unusual background has made her the rare kind of person she is today. (p. 246)

> *Sylvia G. L. Dannett, "Ellen Tarry," in her* Profiles of Negro Womanhood: 20th Century, *Vol. II,* Educational Heritage, Inc., 1966, pp. 244-54.

---

## TITLE COMMENTARY

### *Hezekiah Horton* (1942)

Hezekiah was named out of the Bible and there must have been times when he wished his mother had known less of the Old Testament. The boys made his name the occasion of the sort of joke of which a small boy never tires, unless he owns the name. Partly for this reason he sat alone much of his time on the stoop of his apartment house on Lenox Avenue, Harlem; partly because from this position he could soak his mind in the sight of automobiles going past. For he was car-minded. His mother thought him touched in the head. He meant some day, when he was in long pants, to drive a car.

And then a long, low, red one with a canvas top that came down like magic and folded up stopped in front of the shop next door. The magic continued; the tall young man who drove asked him to go for a ride. The boys stood around, their eyes popping. "Are you Hezekiah's buddies?" the man called. They swarmed over the car, protesting that they certainly were. "Aren't we, Hezekiah?" "S-sort of," said the truthful child. So the car took more small boys than you would think unless you know how many can pack into a new red one, and by the time they had gone round the block the young man knew that Hezekiah was mad on motors. He said he would come back soon and take him for a ride all by himself, and when the boy stammered, "Will you just sort of let me feel the steering wheel?" told him to hurry and get to be eighteen and he'd teach him to drive. After that Hezekiah didn't care a hoot for any jokes. He was too busy getting to be eighteen. He was, as you may have inferred, a colored boy. It is to the credit of all concerned in making this slight but tender little book that this matter of color is not mentioned and that its many drawings [by Oliver Harrington] are not grotesque. A car has its charm for any little boy whose mind runs that way.

> *May Lamberton Becker, in a review of "Heze-*

*kiah Horton," in* New York Herald Tribune Books, *September 13, 1942, p. 9.*

Every car-minded small boy who can read at all will find this story exactly right. Its plot ingredients are so much the essence of his daily living and aspiration that it needs no oversimplified vocabulary. Recommended for all libraries.

> *Julia L. Sauer, in a review of "Hezekiah Horton," in* Library Journal, *Vol. LXVII, September 15, 1942, p. 797.*

This book is American; patently so in its text and more so in its illustrations. In America I believe it was extremely successful. Here, it may not appeal so strongly. It is an example of how little substance is required to make a book. Hezekiah is a negro boy who loves automobiles, all automobiles, and day-dreams about them. One day he and his bunch of young friends are given a ride in one and Hezekiah is promised another. And that is all there is in the story. On a second reading I am still wondering why so little substance makes so good a story. Perhaps it is that the author has succeeded in giving us an extremely neat and well-rounded vignette of a small boy's simple wishes and complete satisfaction at their attainment.

> *A review of "Hezekiah Horton," in* The Junior Bookshelf, *Vol. 9, No. 1, March, 1945, p. 25.*

---

## My Dog Rinty (with Marie Hall Ets, 1946)

The photographers whose skill and sympathy so beautifully presented last year the Springfield plan [Alexander and Alexandra Alland] now collaborates with the authors of this distinctive dog book so successfully that Harlem goes on record as well. For David, whose dog Rinty just would not behave, lived there and went to school. Rinty behaved worse than Mary's lamb: he not only followed to school, but would go in. When David scolded, he hung his head, but he was wagging behind. When tied up at home he chewed his rope in two, ate three shoes and a hat and chewed a hole in the rug. Indeed, he kept on digging holes, or trying to. He was the most energetic, loving and determined of dogs, and wherever he went he damaged things. It kept David busy trying to pay up. At last Rinty really had to go and a nice lady bought him. She even hired David to exercise him, so the two were not altogether separated. But as the dog chewed up Mrs. Moseley's beautiful apartment, she sent him once a week to dog school, and with David's help he learned to "mind and behave."

But he still dug holes, or tried to. The trainer said they mustn't even try to change that. Rinty was a "born ratter and mouser." So when the lady's landlord said all pets must go and she gave him back to David for keeps, something wonderful came of it. The newspaper put in a notice that Rinty could be hired to clear out mice. Never before had the mice been so nobly kept at bay. Besides, people began to realize that old tenements in Harlem have too many mice, and something important was done about that.

In these large photographs Harlem life moves before the spectator: Joe Louis's house, the shops on 125th Street, vegetable stands, story-telling at the library, the local newspaper office, home and school life, the nuns, the hospital. Through it all, mutual devotion of dog and boy maintains a glow.

> *A review of "My Dog Rinty," in* New York Herald Tribune Weekly Book Review, *Vol. 22, No. 39, May 19, 1946, p. 12.*

A very welcome and original dog and boy story of Rinty, who chewed rugs and behaved like a troublesome dog and kept his small master in constant trouble. This is the story of how Rinty became a socially desirable, extremely useful ratcatcher and precipitated his young owner, David, into Pied Piper fame. Substantial, well-written text—the Harlem background is treated as a matter-of-course—and every boy who has struggled to keep a dog against family and neighbor opposition will read this story with interest and sympathy.

> *A review of "My Dog Rinty," in* Virginia Kirkus' Bookshop Service, *Vol. XIV, No. 11, June 1, 1946, p. 252.*

This tale of a boy and his dog is compounded of old elements, but it has absolutely new magic, nor is this based entirely on the circumstances that Rinty and David live in Harlem, where wonders almost never cease.

A more important fact is Rinty himself, underrated and misunderstood and bandied about like a stepchild indeed, but finally discovered and appreciated for his special talents and true worth. . . .

The story of Rinty and David is told with great warmth and charm and illustrated by [Alexander and Alexandra Alland] with photographs that bring a vivid and recognizable Harlem to life.

> *Arna Bontemps, in a review of "My Dog Rinty," in* The New York Times Book Review, *June 16, 1946, p. 33.*

If there were no text to this book at all it would have great distinction. . . . There are many things that the people of Harlem need to make life better; but this book will convince everyone who looks at it that they have three dominating and infinitely precious assets—racial friendliness, tolerance, and laughter.

> *Mary Gould Davis, "Harlem Scene," in* The Saturday Review of Literature, *Vol. XXIX, No. 32, August 10, 1946, p. 31.*

[Stella Gentry Sharpe's] *Tobe* can be considered a catalog, [Jane Dabney Shackelford's] *My Happy Days* a catechism, but **My Dog Rinty** is a book—a piece of professional entertainment that has outlasted its purpose. Working with community groups on the South Side of Chicago, Marie Ets noticed the paucity of books about the black city child, and suggested the project; Ellen Tarry, an alumnus of the Bank Street Writers' Laboratory ("They wanted Claude McKay"—ET) and the author of two picturebooks, **Janie Belle** and **Hezekiah Horton,** was May Massee's natural choice as collaborator. A contest had been held in Harlem to choose the artist for **Hezekiah Horton** but this time ("Thank goodness") there was no need: Alexander Alland had just taken the photographs for *The Springfield Plan*, the record of a communitywide attack on racial and religious intolerance; he and his wife Alexandra were obviously qualified. . . .

Like many photographic books of the time, *The Springfield Plan* was conceived and constructed very like a documentary film—in this case knowingly: how wonderful it would be, says the jacket, if, inspired by one or another film, "we could take the pictures back with us, to study whenever we felt the need." ("Well, just that has been made possible in this book. . . .") Pare Lorentz's lyrical essays, the high-keyed March of Time reports, wartime evocations of bravery and sacrifice had all made their mark, and the semidocumentary—authenticity substantiating fiction—was in the offing. . . .

It is not too much to call *My Dog Rinty,* similarly shot 'on location,' a semidocumentary. Rinty is, yes, a bad dog who makes good and the story is wholly fabricated but it involves real places, public and private, and real people in their real-life roles—including the man reading picturebooks at the library (Spencer Shaw) and the 'story-lady' upstairs (Augusta Baker).

The realities of life in Harlem are broached too. Forever getting away and causing damage, Rinty is sent to obedience school and cured of every bad habit except making holes in people's carpets and trying to tear up their floors. He's a born ratter and mouser, the trainer explains, "worth a fortune." Fame instead comes to David and Rinty: "They were wanted at the hotel where dogs are not allowed. They were wanted at the hospital. They were wanted at the ten-cent store. They were wanted at the flower shop." Their picture is in the papers, they're the "Pied Pipers of Harlem." "But best of all, the owner of a block of old buildings where the poor people live in Harlem said: 'David and Rinty have shown me that my old buildings are full of holes. I'm going to tear them down and build new ones.' " There will be a big yard in the center and a welcome for well-behaved children and dogs—David and Rinty first.

Showing the social range in a community, any community, from hardship to decency to comfort to luxury (in Harlem from tenements to David's walk-up to a project, River House, to Sugar Hill "where the poor in old buildings live poorly; suggesting a concrete solution, that the buildings be replaced: all this was novel in a picturebook in 1946. Documenting life in a black community, intending that Harlem be seen like other places, the authors and photographers made it possible for other places to be seen like Harlem.

Of course *My Dog Rinty* lives for children for different reasons. A dog relinquished, then regained, everywhere shunned, then welcomed (the reiteration of "They were wanted . . .") is not to be denied. But without the brick-and-mortar development, authenticated by the photographs, one wouldn't hold to the thought that, honestly, there must be something to it, some boy and dog who caught rats and got their picture in the paper. See, they're right here, on the last page. (pp. 377-78)

*Barbara Bader, "Negro Identification, Black*

*Identity: 'My Dog Rinty',*" *in her* American Picturebooks from Noah's Ark to the Beast Within, *Macmillan Publishing Co., Inc., 1976, pp. 377-78.*

[*My Dog Rinty* is a] very simple story set in Harlem in the 1940s. . . . Like most stories illustrated with photographs, the plot seems contrived to fit the pictures. In addition, the clothes, cars, and situations belong to an earlier period and seem dated far more by the realism of the photographs than they might with some other sort of illustrations.

*Alethea K. Helbig and Agnes Regan Perkins, "Dictionary of American Children's Fiction, 1859-1959: 'My Dog Rinty',*" *in their* Dictionary of American Children's Fiction, 1859-1959: Books of Recognized Merit, *Greenwood Press, 1985, p. 365.*

---

### The Runaway Elephant    (1950)

Another jolly Hezekiah Horton adventure, this time with elephants. Hezekiah is again invited by his reporter friend in the big red automobile for a ride, and has a wonderful idea how to catch big Modoc, the run-away elephant, from the Dolly Brothers' Circus. In no time at all mysterious Mr. Smith is on his way to the wilds of Westchester armed with bread and peanuts. And Hezekiah sees the reunion of two friends, has a fine reward and a story in the papers and Mr. Ed gets his story. Based on an actual news story, this is a delightful, appealing story.

*A review of "The Runaway Elephant," in* Virginia Kirkus' Bookshop Service, *Vol. XVIII, No. 16, August 15, 1950, p. 465.*

We say that fact is stranger than fiction; nevertheless, it takes genius to find such a fact in the news as the escape of a bull elephant from the circus and turn it into a good story. That genius Ellen Tarry has, and she is ably abetted here by an irresistible artist [Oliver Harrington]. Together they created that lovable denizen of Harlem, "Hezekiah Horton," who appears again in this tale.

Hezekiah's newspaper friend, Mr. Ed, takes him along on the elephant hunt, into the "wilds of Westchester." Along the Bronx Parkway, Hezekiah thinks of just the man to help catch Modoc, and they go back for him. But we go on to a hilarious time with the circus people and the police, and their unhappy efforts at capture. They are considering the necessity of shooting Modoc, when along comes a siren-blowing motorcycle, escorting the red car. Who is the mysterious Mr. Smith? How does he manage the capture? Who was given the award? Any child from about six to eleven will love the solution.

*Louise S. Bechtel, in a review of "The Runaway Elephant," in* New York Herald Tribune Book Review, *October 8, 1950, p. 28.*

The story of the elephant hunt is one of rollicking fun. Reporters fly around, Hezekiah rides in the big red automobile, motorcycle cops clear roads, and Emmie and Julie, the other circus elephants, snort and trumpet as they aid in the search. . . . The story is based on an actual happening and young readers, experiencing all the thrills of Hezekiah's adventure, will wish they had been there too.

> *Agatha L. Shea, in a review of "The Runaway Elephant," in* Chicago Sunday Tribune Magazine of Books, *October 22, 1950, p. 15.*

---

### *Martin de Porres: Saint of the New World*   (1963)

There has been a renewed interest among adults in the life of St. Martin De Porres, the Dominican Negro of seventeenth century South America, since his canonization last May. In this delightful biography (Vision Book) boys and girls will come to know and admire the gentle St. Martin whose pleasant smile and kind words brought happiness to the lives he touched. The son of a Negro mother and a noble Spanish father, St. Martin's deep and abiding charity for all men was clearly evident even in his childhood. Ellen Tarry's description of St. Martin's miracles, his love of children, and his kindness to animals will help make **Martin De Porres** both a favorite Saint and a favorite book for young readers. (pp. 189-90)

> *A review of "Martin de Porres: Saint of the New World," in* Virginia Kirkus' Service, *Vol. XXXI, No. 4, February 15, 1963, pp. 189-90.*

---

### *Young Jim: The Early Years of James Weldon Johnson* (1967)

**Young Jim** is James Weldon Johnson and this is biographical fiction based on his boyhood in Jacksonville, his high school and college career at Atlanta University, his first regular job (as principal of the elementary school he had attended) and the moonlighting (as poet, lyricist, journalist) that betokened his later accomplishments. As a story it is slow, stiff and frequently stilted; as an account of the post-Reconstruction South (Johnson was born in 1871) it has episodes that exude poverty, humiliation and quiet determination: see especially Jim's stint as teacher in a school for rural Georgia Negroes. And there is a sense of the boy as father to the man who would win plaudits for his poetry, write the first of the "protest" novels, and become a leader in the NAACP—all referred to in an epilogue. This is not engrossing enough for a general audience, but it is the only full-length juvenile on Johnson and it has an old-fashioned honesty and dignity that merit consideration.

> *A review of "Young Jim," in* Kirkus Service, *Vol. XXXV, No. 11, June 1, 1967, p. 651.*

Young people who can be persuaded that James Weldon Johnson is worth their time and attention should enjoy **Young Jim** and learn from it. The chances are, however, that a parent, teacher or librarian will have to get them started, for the book concerns a long-ago subject—a Negro boy who grew up in Jacksonville, Florida, in the late 1800s. If readers can bridge that gap in their imagination, and if boys can forgive the author's naive handling of baseball, they can identify with the gifted, determined Jim Johnson who beat the odds and won in a white man's world. . . . Even though his poetry is somewhat out of date today, Johnson's story is inspiring.

> *A. L. Todd, in a review of "Young Jim: The Early Years of James Weldon Johnson," in* Book World—The Washington Post, *October 29, 1967, p. 20.*

[Johnson's] achievements are impressive; and his roles in Negro history, in entertainment, and in the world of letters need no embellishment to make a dramatic and inspiring story. His biography is not enhanced by a slight but persistent note of adulation; the writing style is a bit stiff: "As Jim approached the mound he stopped and picked up a handful of dirt, which he rubbed on the ball." or, " 'What is it?' Jim asked, noting the rapid rise and fall of the other boy's chest as he clutched the area around his heart."

> *Zena Sutherland, in a review of "Young Jim: The Early Years of James Weldon Johnson," in* Bulletin of the Center for Children's Books, *Vol. 21, No. 3, November, 1967, p. 50.*

This fictionalized biography succinctly describes Johnson's boyhood and youth which led to his amazing career as author, song writer, diplomat and public servant. Besides offering an inspiring life story, the book gives some penetrating insights into Negro life and problems at the turn of the century.

> *A review of "Young Jim," in* The New York Times Book Review, *January 21, 1968, p. 28.*

# Audrey Wood
## 1948-

# Don Wood
## 1945-

Audrey—American author and illustrator of picture books.

Don—American illustrator of picture books.

Major works include *The Napping House* (1984), *King Bidgood's in the Bathtub* (1985), *Heckedy Peg* (1987).

A husband and wife team who create picture books noted for their exuberance, rhythmic quality, and inventive, beautiful illustrations, the Woods structure their works around sleeping, baths, and other activities to which children can easily relate. Often setting their books in periods such as the Middle Ages, the Renaissance, and the early twentieth century, the team characteristically produce whimsical or playfully humorous stories, although they underscore their works with themes such as the fierce love of a mother for her children or the bond between a grandmother and her grandson. The works, which usually combine simple, spare texts with detailed double-page spreads, often feature adults as protagonists and include child characters who play pivotal roles. The collaborators are perhaps best known as the creators of two cumulative tales, *The Napping House* and *King Bidgood's in the Bathtub*. Told in verse, *The Napping House* describes how Grandma, napping in bed, is joined by her grandson, a dog, a cat, and a mouse; when a flea bites the mouse, each character is then roused in turn. In *King Bidgood's in the Bathtub*, the jovial king, who refuses to leave his bath, persuades each of the members of his court to join the fun; finally, a young page suggests pulling the plug to end the problem. The Woods's next book, *Heckedy Peg*, is noted for its timeless folktale quality. In this story, which is inspired by a sixteenth century game that is still played in England, a mother with seven children named for the days of the week goes off to the market to bring them each a special request. When the witch Heckedy Peg tricks the children and turns them into types of food for her banquet, she tells their mother that she can have her offspring returned to her if she can identify them; by coupling each of the children with their requests from the market, the mother defeats the witch and restores her brood to life.

The latest member of a family of artists that dates back to the fifteenth century, Audrey Wood is respected as the author and illustrator of several picture books that she created separately from her husband as well as for their collaborative works; she is also a sculptor and has taught art to children. Audrey, whose texts are often prompted by songs she hears inside herself as well as by the experiences of the couple's son, Bruce, often sings her texts to her sister, a musician, to hone their rhythmic qualities. Both Audrey and Don Wood have had experience in theatre, a background which Don notes as important to their current approach; "Picture books are about drama," he has said, and adds that "for us, the page is a stage." A former grade school art teacher who also contributes his works

to magazines, Don develops his illustrations simultaneously with his wife's texts so that word and picture will complement each other. Working most frequently in oils, he ranges in style from delicate, pale paintings done in shades of blue, green, lavender, and grey to robust and opulent canvases in rich, glowing colors that are filled with crowds of characters wearing broad expressions. Wood is often acknowledged for his use of light and shadow to show changes in time or mood as well as for his unusual treatment of perspective; his work has been exhibited at the Metropolitan Museum of Art in New York and has also appeared on the television program "Faerie Tale Theatre." With *Elbert's Bad Word* (1988), the story of a small boy who redeems himself after he catches an ugly word—a furry monster with a long tail—at an elegant adult party and says it aloud, the Woods collaborated for the first time on both text and illustration. *The Napping House* won the Golden Kite Award for illustration in 1984 and the Certificate of Merit from the Society of Illustrators in 1985, an award received by *King Bidgood's in the Bathtub* in the same year; the latter was also named a Caldecott Honor Book in 1986. In addition, these titles have received several other adult and child-selected awards and have been made into filmstrips.

(See also *Something about the Author,* Vols. 44, 50.)

---

## AUTHORS' COMMENTARY

DON WOOD: The picture book exists in a literary twilight zone: the spectacular child of the marriage of images and text. As such, it is probably as close to drama, or a thirty-two-page movie, as it is to either literature or art. For this reason the picture book makes unique demands on its creators.

AUDREY WOOD: Our methods of developing picture books have evolved to complement our individual styles and abilities. Since we are unique artists, working in a unique medium, we need a system of creating that will emphasize our strengths, de-emphasize our weaknesses, and perfectly complement our styles. No one can devise a system that will work for us. We must devise our own.

D: Where do picture book ideas come from? This question is usually belittled by creative people and answered evasively, if it is answered at all. You are inevitably left with the impression that the process of getting an idea is mystical, exclusive, beyond the reach of language and that anyone who even tries to discuss the subject will simply reveal his or her naiveté. We disagree. We think the question is quite reasonable, because we have an answer. Ideas come from cardboard boxes.

A: I keep two large cardboard boxes in my studio that I use for storing and generating ideas. Both boxes are full of hundreds of ideas—enough ideas to last several lifetimes. Why do I need so many ideas? Even after eight years of creating picture books, I still can't tell which ideas are the good ones. If I knew from the start which ideas were strong enough to survive the process of becoming a picture book, I would need only three ideas a year. But I don't; so I need as many ideas as I can get. I also never know what kind of idea I might need—humorous, educational, juvenile, young adult, easy reader—so I collect them all. There's nothing more difficult than sitting down and trying to come up with an original idea. It's easier to let ideas come to me. It's a way of sneaking up on the creative process.

At one time I believed ideas had to be written down on crisp, white pieces of paper of uniform size. Ideas were sacred gifts from the gods and had better be treated as such or I wouldn't be given any more. So I organized a three-ring binder with divisions for plots, themes, characters, and settings. Every piece of paper that went into my binder was accompanied by three little stick-on hole reinforcers, the kind used in high school. This would prevent any precious idea from escaping.

As my idea file grew, I began to encounter a problem. For instance, what should I do with the idea, "Tugford likes being a bad boy"? Does this idea belong under "theme"? Is it the beginning of a plot? Am I describing a character? Should I write this idea down three times and file it in three categories? Should I make a cross-reference? Eventually, the complexity of the system began to discourage me from writing down new ideas. I had to have a better system, one that suited my individual needs. That's when I threw away the categories and dumped my binder pages into cardboard boxes. There are no more crisp, white pieces of paper in my idea file. My boxes are full of jumbled-together notes scribbled on envelopes and bank deposit stubs, doodles drawn on place mats or while talking on the phone.

D: How do you generate enough ideas to fill two cardboard boxes? There's an old maxim that you shouldn't go shopping when you're hungry. If you do, you'll spend more, because you're in a state of mind receptive to food. Similarly, Audrey and I believe an artist must be idea hungry, that is, in a state of mind receptive to ideas. When you are idea hungry, you know you need ideas. This state is not necessarily natural, and it requires some self-discipline to attain. One method Audrey and I use is to pay attention to our emotions, especially our extreme emotions. Whenever we are amused, surprised, intrigued, or saddened, we ask why. We look to the root cause, the basic pattern of our reaction, and, inevitably, we find a strong idea. Soon this receptive state becomes second nature, and the idea boxes begin to fill.

A: Just what kinds of ideas go into the cardboard boxes? I call them *ideas,* but in truth they are bits and pieces of anything or everything that could suggest or contain ideas—snatches of childhood memories, life experiences, titles, names, proverbs, poems, single words, maps, magazine articles, and written and drawn character sketches.

How do I create picture books from these bits and pieces of ideas? I begin by sitting down in front of the cardboard boxes and reading through the ideas playfully. I allow the ideas to lead me here and there. Sometimes they combine into groups; sometimes I shuffle them together and deal them out like cards. Character sketches and doodles are stacked on titles; themes are paired with plots; and life experiences are matched with dreams and fantasies. This process usually takes several days.

At last, an idea steps out in front of all the rest, an idea that excites me deeply. It has density. I test the idea, asking myself questions. Is the idea simple? Will it be suitable for a picture book? Does it have substance? Does it evoke strong visual images? If all the answers are yes, this may be the magic moment when a book is born. I say "may be" because only one idea in many that reaches this stage actually becomes a completed project.

D: The best way to demonstrate how an idea leads to a completed project is with concrete examples. Here are bits and pieces from the idea boxes that led to some books. (pp. 556-58)

[One] book grew as a composite of a theme idea and a character sketch. The theme concerns the power of a child's imagination. One evening at dusk, when our son Bruce was three years old, he, Audrey, and I were walking out in our backyard, which is surrounded with foliage. We were all holding hands, and Audrey, on a whim, made a silly noise, "Whooo." Quick as a flash, Bruce ran back inside the house. Audrey and I retrieved him and explained that she had made the noise and that she hadn't meant to scare him. Then we all three took hands and walked out into the backyard again.

This time, probably more as an experiment than as a whim, Audrey said "Whooo" again. Exactly the same thing happened. Again we retrieved Bruce from the house, and Audrey explained the noise explicitly. She asked him to look at her mouth, and she made the noise several times. She explained we were going to go outside and that she would make the noise again. Bruce was quite pleased with the idea. We took hands and walked out into the backyard. Audrey said, "Here I go, Whooo." Bruce's eyes popped open, and back into the house he ran. As first-time parents this was a revelation to us. Bruce seemed like a rational little being, and yet, in his mind, the line between reality and imagination was obviously very thin.

Audrey noted this occurrence in the idea box, and eventually combined it with character drawings of our spooky kitten who spent half of her kittenhood puffed up and walking on tiptoe. These two elements inspired *Scaredy Cats.*

A: As a young child, our son Bruce quickly outgrew his desire for naps. Don and I had absolutely no luck in putting him down. We soon learned, however, that if we sent him off to his granny's cozy, relaxing house, with her wonderful, quiet bedroom, he would rest in the afternoon. I began calling my mother's house "the napping house." A note with these three words inspired *The Napping House.* (pp. 559-60)

D: [The] . . . methods we have described are playful and whimsical. There's a simple reason for that; we make playful and whimsical picture books. These methods work for us because they complement our goals.

People constantly say to us, "I've got a great idea for a children's book." What interests us is the fact that these people are usually right; they do have a great idea for a children's book. When I first met our British publisher, he told me, "You can make a story out of anything." At that time I thought he was exaggerating wildly. The longer I work, the more I agree with him. There are many great ideas for picture books. If someone says, "I've got a great idea for a picture book," the proper response is, "So what are you going to do with it?"

A: Once I've got that "great idea" I must put some meat on the bones. I would like to have an exciting concept with a beginning, a middle, and—what is often so difficult to achieve in picture books—a strong end. Usually, however, all I've got is a strong concept. Putting meat on the bones is the toughest step in the whole process. It's quite abstract, and the best way to demonstrate it is to discuss the process that I went through with *King Bidgood's in the Bathtub.* Though the process sounds simple, the time involved with writing and developing the text covered many weeks and resulted in dozens of versions.

*King Bidgood's in the Bathtub* began with a false start. I put two weeks of concentrated work into a project titled "Nightmare Pie." I wanted to create a pair of folklike heros, larger-than-life Paul Bunyan types, the difference being that these two characters, Mr. and Mrs. Bidgood, were of grandparent age and lived on a typical suburban block. Everything that happened in the Bidgoods' household, no matter how trivial, strongly affected the entire neighborhood. For instance, if there were a heat wave, all the neighbors knew that Mrs. Bidgood had left her oven door open. The fun was supposed to happen when Mr. Bidgood coaxed Mrs. Bidgood into making one of her famous nightmare pies for his birthday. Although the story seemed to have endless possibilities, the plot was too complex for a picture book. The concept wasn't focused; the conflict wasn't clear; and there was no ending in sight.

The weeks I spent on "Nightmare Pie" were the longest time I'd ever spent on an idea that went nowhere. The only excuse I have is that I fell madly in love with Mr. Bidgood, a stout, mischievous, red-bearded fellow who captured my heart and led me astray. When it became obvious that the story wasn't working and the character was, I put Mr. Bidgood back into the box and let him stew awhile. Meanwhile, I began sifting through the cardboard boxes again. Eventually this note caught my eye: "the sultan's bath, a magical place, a fantastic bath experience where anything could happen." An interesting idea, but as usual no beginning, middle, or end—no problem, conflict, or resolution. I began to search for a problem. If the sultan were in this wonderful bath, why would he ever want to get out? That's the problem: the sultan's in the bath, and he won't get out. Now just what kind of a character should this sultan be?

I could almost see Mr. Bidgood peeking over the edge of my cardboard box and grinning broadly. Of course! Mr. Bidgood would be perfect. But, since a red-bearded sultan seemed unlikely, I made him a king. King Bidgood's in the bathtub, and he won't get out! That really excited me. Now I had a strong character with a problem. How would the conflict work? If King Bidgood's in the bathtub and he won't get out, who wants him out? And how do they try to get him out? That's when I added the king's court. Every time a member of the king's court tried to coax the king out of the tub, he or she ended up in the tub with the king.

All good things, no matter how much fun, must come to an end. How was I going to get the king out of the tub? Finding the right ending took many days. Although the solution was maddeningly simple, it proved to be elusive, until at last I recalled the gesture that had never failed to get my own son out of the tub. You pull the plug. Now I had a complete idea.

D: The nature of the idea indicates how we proceed. In many of Audrey's books the text serves only as a sound track for a thirty-two-page movie. Often the text is all dialogue with no narration. The art, consequently, is very important. Books of this nature are worked up from the very first stage in dummy form: the art and text develop together, simultaneously, all the way through. The first step is a very rough dummy, thirty-two pages all drawn out on one large sheet of paper. Vague art notes, stick figures, and plot developments are indicated on each page. This way you can see your book as an entirety—and see the rhythm of it. One distinct advantage of the art and text developing together is that the art has an opportunity to modify the text.

How does art modify text? In one of the earlier versions

*From* King Bidgood's in the Bathtub, *written by Audrey Wood. Illustrated by Don Wood.*

of *The Napping House,* Audrey had a snoring granny, a dreaming child, a dozing dog, a snoozing cat, a slumbering mouse, and a wakeful flea, all on a cozy bed in the napping house. It read beautifully. I began to work with the art, and it was dull. We discussed the problem, and Audrey revised the text so that the wakeful flea was on the slumbering mouse, who was on the snoozing cat. The characters were now all piled one on top of the other, instead of just scattered on the bed. The art was lively, and the text had been greatly improved.

A: Some of my books are created without dummies. These usually fall into categories of poems or songlike texts. In this process I often sing the story as I write it. For instance, after writing the text for *The Napping House,* rather than going directly into dummy form, I sat down with my sister who is a musician, and we composed a melody to accompany the text. By putting the text into musical form I discovered revisions to improve the rhythmic quality of the writing. When the new text was ready, I handed it to Don, and he began work on the dummy. As mentioned earlier, more modifications occurred. First the music revised the text; then the art revised the text.

D: Audrey and I are strong believers in letting a project rest. Experimentation has taught us that three days is a beneficial rest period. Perhaps a one-day rest will work for certain phases of certain projects. All that matters is that when you return to the project, everything seems new. Awkward sentences or incorrect perspectives that were once invisible are now painfully obvious. Learning to use

even this rudimentary technique required experience and discipline. It required experience to know when a project needs to rest, and discipline, because we never wanted to put our work aside.

A: Polishing can make the difference between a good and a great text. Because so few words are used in a picture book, each one must be perfect. I always check my manuscript word by word, line by line, evaluating every sentence for excitement, visual impact, sensory input, rhythm, variety, and colorful word usage. What can be eliminated? What can be substituted? While polishing the text, I may produce up to twenty separate versions. With so many versions I always maintain a master of the original. The polishing process often takes several weeks, and it also can produce surprising revisions, which lead to even further polishing.

D: There is one last valuable phase in our process. We use an informal network of friends, relatives, and their children to review our work before submission. Some of the adults have a literary background; some do not. Their opinions are extremely valuable to us and often result in significant revisions in our dummies. Their children's opinions are important, too, but in a different way. As a general rule, you can't really trust what a child tells you about your efforts. If they like you, they will almost always like your work. So we watch as the dummy is being read to children, preferably by someone who has never seen the book. Are they visibly excited? If so, is the excitement generated by the important elements of the story or just incidental details? It is also valuable to go through the manuscript with them afterward, questioning them to make sure they understood each line.

A: After adding still further revisions, we now have a final dummy ready for submission. This method of creating usually takes months. The creation of the method took years, and it continues to evolve as we progress from book to book. In the story of Bruce's walk into our backyard Don spoke of the thin line between the child's imagination and reality. In that incident the rational information I gave Bruce was overwhelmed by the evocative power of the strange sound I made. The incident reminds me of a game I used to play with my younger sister when I was six and she was four. Though my role sounds cruel, I remember we both enjoyed the game. My sister and I loved to look through my parents' encyclopedia of wildlife. My favorite section was the reptiles and amphibians. That's where I could make up stories about the pictures—stories, which to my sister's distress, caused the snakes and lizards to come alive for her and crawl off the page. This is the power of picture books—stories that come to life for young listeners and readers whose imaginations are so strong that they, as yet, have no boundaries. Of course, this power can be used irresponsibly to make snakes crawl off the page, but it can also be used responsibly. If you do your work well, you can lead your readers into new worlds, worlds of delight and truth, humor and magic, worlds that are as real to your readers as this one. That is the joy of creating the picture book. (pp. 560-65)

> *Don and Audrey Wood, "The Artist at Work: Where Ideas Come From," in* The Horn Book Magazine, *Vol. LXII, No. 5, September-October, 1986, pp. 556-65.*

---

## GENERAL COMMENTARY

### Lisa See

Audrey and Don Wood have created 20 children's books between them. Some have been written and illustrated by Audrey alone: *Balloonia, Tugford Wanted to Be Bad* and *Detective Valentine.* They coauthored *The Big Hungry Bear,* which Don then illustrated. But their most successful works have been those written by Audrey and illustrated by Don. Their three top sellers are *Heckedy Peg* (69,000 copies in print), *The Napping House* (in its seventh printing with 127,000 copies), and *King Bidgood's in the Bathtub* (a Caldecott Honor Book; 100,000 copies).

Although the Woods's work celebrates the lives of average children, their own childhoods were anything but ordinary. "I was introverted and an outsider," Audrey Wood recalls. "I was an observer. I always felt I was biding time until I found the people I was looking for." One of her earliest memories is of her artist father repainting murals for the Ringling Brothers Circus. The tallest man in the world bounced Audrey on his knee, the fat lady held her, the little people babysat. When she was a toddler, her family moved to Mexico, where she learned to read before she was three. By the time she was in first grade, she had decided to become an artist. Later she realized she could meld art and storytelling in children's books.

Says her husband: "Audrey remembers what it's like to be a child, remembers the state of mind, how it felt to be excluded. The solution for *King Bidgood* came from Audrey's memories of how to get our child out of the bathtub—pull the plug. The child almost always thinks through the problem." (p. 211)

[*Elbert's Bad Word* marks a] deviation for the Woods. Audrey wrote the text and crafted the line drawings, which took Don another six months to execute. This collaboration emerged from Audrey's habit of doodling on scraps of paper while on the phone, and Don's compulsion to amplify her simple sketches. "Seeing his modeling gave me the knowledge that I could use that style of shading and modeling in my own work," Audrey says. "I feel that I have absorbed that osmotically into my art style."

"Audrey draws expressionistically which I, as a realist, can't do," adds Don. "Her work is more psychological, where I spend a lot of time planning and plotting. So for me to have access to her work was wonderfully exhilarating."

Their collaboration begins with a concept, which often comes from an idea box to which they both contribute; they estimate it contains about 2000 entries. "The sultan's bath is a fantastic place," for example, was one such idea that eventually evolved into *King Bidgood.* It's practically impossible to break down the magical process of collaboration except in the most basic terms. When Audrey writes, she writes as an author/illustrator. While the text is in progress, Don has the opportunity to make comments as the future illustrator. "I'm a control artist," says Don. "I use oil, a medium that takes four days to dry. I can sand back down to the gesso, if I don't like what's happening. So I would have to say that I love the 'wild men'—James Marshall, Ralph Steadman, Audrey Wood—the artists who draw quickly and compulsively."

For Audrey, writing children's picture books is akin to writing poetry or song lyrics—a constant process of refinement, of whittling down, to make the five minutes it takes to read the book a full experience. Each story undergoes up to 20 revisions over a six-month period. She experiments in five or six different forms—picture book, story book, different endings, different points of view, a text entirely in dialogue or entirely in narrative. "Even though Audrey eventually rejects these other ideas," Don explains, "she retains little nuggets that have come out of the process. The result is layering and depth."

Generally, Audrey works on four stories simultaneously at various levels of completion—writing, revising, illustrating, gestating in a drawer. She usually has another four stories in what she calls the "memory house" in her head. It's a concept she has borrowed from the early Greeks, who used this vizualization technique to retain oral stories. *Elbert's Bad Word* rattled around in her memory house for eight years after her own son provided the inspiration.

It takes Don up to two years—working seven days a week, 12- to 14-hour days, to do the paintings for a book.

The stories dictate to Don the style in which the book will

be rendered. *The Napping House* was "homey," while the character of King Bidgood was so overblown that it appealed to Don as an opera—with full Renaissance costumes, dramatic emotions, and "everyone talking big." For the realistic rendering in *Heckedy Peg,* Don researched the lighting and style of late 16th-century Flemish genre painters, especially the work of Franz Hals and Adrien Brauer (one of Audrey's ancestors).

Before he sets brush to canvas, Don and Audrey have made tough producer/director decisions. They cast their friends, editors, relatives, neighbors, and very often their son, Bruce, as the models for the illustrations. Audrey designs the costumes—sometimes gathering vast quantities of "stuff at a local thrift shop, sometimes drawing a specific costume and having it made. Then there's an elaborate staged reading, with all the actors costumed and made up. The photographs and live sketches from this event become Don's reference material.

"If Don gets stuck, I might put on a costume and sit for him," Audrey confesses. She was the mother in *Heckedy Peg,* and when they didn't want to ask any of their friends to play the part of the witch, Don painted himself in the role. Their son has been featured in *King Bidgood, The Napping House* and *Quick as a Cricket. . . .*

Any two people who collaborate must answer the inevitable question: Do you fight? "Yes, we fight," Audrey answers, "but we fight creatively. By now we can even tactlessly say what we think. And with *Elbert's Bad Word* the chemistry was extremely exciting. A third artist emerged." Very clearly the most important aspects of collaboration are trust and respect. Since their schedules are so hectic, they make appointments with each other and prepare diligently for the critiquing process. Audrey serves as Don's art editor, accepting and rejecting his work on dummies. He serves as her editor. "We each have tremendous creative control and keep absolute veto power," Don says.

The Woods began writing children's books in what they refer to as "the Dark Times" in children's publishing. "With the baby boom, we're in a renaissance," explains Don. "Children's bookstores are a phenomenon. They're hot. It's quite a ride we've jumped onto." The climate has changed so much since the early days of their careers that they already have the next two years' book signings, speaking engagements and visits to schools roughly mapped out.

Don voices their enthusiasm for doing picture books for children who enjoy them at the age when "their 'reality editor' has no boundaries. It's wonderful to be able to communicate with such startling beings who have the ability to completely and totally submerge themselves in a book. What they're looking at has more reality than anything else in the room." (p. 212)

> *Lisa See, "Audrey and Don Wood," in* Publishers Weekly, *Vol. 234, No. 5, July 29, 1988, pp. 211-12.*

## TITLE COMMENTARY

### *Moonflute* (1980)

One night when the moon is full, Firen cannot sleep, so she goes out into the night to get her sleep back from the Moon. The Moon responds with a magic Moonflute which, when Firen plays on it, transports her on an incredible trip through the night world and finally back to her own bed. It's all as boring as you might expect. This is the type of children's book that appeals to adults—trendy adults, at that. The imagery is tired, the vocabulary much too advanced for any child willing to be seen reading a picture book. (Playing the flute "Firen could hear waltzes of billowing clouds, minuets of migrating birds, rhapsodies of blooming flowers, and ballads of people far, far away.") The color illustrations are overblown, albeit striking, but again, are not designed with children in mind. The black-and-white illustrations are muddy and indistinct. The whole thing is a pretentious waste of time.

> *Elaine Fort Weischedel, in a review of "Moonflute," in* School Library Journal, *Vol. 27, No. 1, September, 1980, p. 65.*

*[The following excerpts are from reviews of the revised edition published in 1986.]*

Previously published in 1980, "this has been redesigned with a revised text," according to the publishers. One wonders if the effort was worthwhile, despite the Woods' previous and much more successful *Napping House* and *King Bidgood's in the Bathtub.* The story is one of those overwritten, idyllic fantasies that adults nostalgically associate with the state of childhood. A little girl named Firen demands to know what the Moon has done with her sleep. The Moon sends her a flute that magics her away on an airy search over town, country, sea, jungle, and back to bed, where her parents appear to tuck her in after her dream. The narrative relies heavily on description and will have more than Firen yawning. The drawings are delicate and spidery; the paintings, dominated by blues and greens, are slick in style, with some awkward insets of scenes depicted from a different perspective. Not the Woods at their sprightliest.

> *Betsy Hearne, in a review of "Moonflute," in* Bulletin of the Center for Children's Books, *Vol. 40, No. 8, April, 1987, p. 159.*

This is a fanciful story in which the reader ceases to care about the quest, becoming absorbed in the wonder of the places Firen visits. The ending is a bit contrived to bring Firen home, but one's imagination is well satisfied. Illustrations by Don Wood, done in eerie shades of blue-like moonlight, are perfect for the text.

> *Elizabeth Sachs, in a review of "Moonflute," in* New Directions for Women, *Vol. 16, No. 4, July-August, 1987, p. 14.*

### *The Napping House* (1984)

Don Wood's paintings endow Audrey's familiar plot with beauty and newness, conveying atmosphere as well as illustrating the story. It's told in the round, starting with

Granny napping in her bed. Her grandson, dog, cat and a mouse pile up on Granny and a flea attaches itself to the mouse. The flea nips the mouse; the cumulative effects end with everyone startled awake, up and about. During the sleeping time, pale lavender and hazy grays in the pictures, like the murmurous rain slanting across the house, pervade the scenes with a stillness emphasized by luminous highlights that add mystique to recognizable humans and objects. With the sun shining again and action resumed, a burst of golden-yellow invigorates the company. A child's swing, a treehouse, a flower-laden fence and many extra touches speak volumes about Granny's home and the bond between her and her grandson.

> *A review of "The Napping House," in* Publishers Weekly, *Vol. 225, No. 17, April 27, 1984, p. 86.*

This cumulative tale has the distinction of some wonderfully inventive artwork, giving a panache that many other books of the same type lack. Here, the story starts on a rainy, dreary day, just the sort of day that's perfect for napping, which is in fact what the household is doing. On a cozy bed sleeps a nightcapped granny. A somnambulant child piles in the bed, and he's followed by a dozing dog, a snoozing cat, and a slumbering mouse, who unfortunately is bitten by a wakeful flea, causing a chain of events that awakens the whole house to what is now a beautiful, sunny day. Wood's artwork, with its unusual yet highly defined shapes, shadings, and perspectives, will hold as much appeal for adults as it does for children. Wood also does wonderful, almost imperceptible things with light; as the rain slowly ends and the sun begins to break through, the blue bedroom is transfigured until the last spread shows a glorious rainbowed day. An appealing, stylish book that is perfect for story hours.

> *Ilene Cooper, in a review of "The Napping House," in* Booklist, *Vol. 80, No. 18, May 15, 1984, p. 1350.*

The illustrations, full-color oil paintings, are confined, except for the first and last, to the bedroom. Interest springs from the contortionist poses of the sleeping people (in a bed too small—though it bows obligingly—even for granny) in the first half, and the riotous awakening (dog chasing cat chasing mouse) in the second. As the mound of sleepers on the bed grows, interest is heightened as the perspective continually changes to a higher plane, then down again for the denouement. For cumulative suspense and the power of cause-and-effect, *Mr. Gumpy's Outing* (Holt, 1970) by John Burningham is better, but the humor here will tickle many preschoolers.

> *Patricia Dooley, in a review of "The Napping House," in* School Library Journal, *Vol. 30, No. 10, August, 1984, p. 67.*

Cool, somnolent paintings that have a quiet humor illustrate an engaging cumulative tale. . . . The cool blues and greens are superseded by warm colors and bursts of action as each sleeper wakes, ending in an eruption of color and energy as naptime ends. A deft matching of text and pictures adds to the appeal of cumulation and to the

silliness of the mound of sleepers—just the right kind of humor for the lap audience.

> *Zena Sutherland, in a review of "The Napping House," in* Bulletin of the Center for Children's Books, *Vol. 38, No. 1, September, 1984, p. 18.*

---

### King Bidgood's in the Bathtub   (1985)

The Woods' last effort was the exceptionally well-wrought **Napping House.** No less clever is this story of a stubborn king who refuses to leave his bathtub. The court is in an uproar when the page brings the news of the king's watery dalliance. The mustachioed knight thinks he can budge him by telling him it's time to battle, but the king says "today we battle in the tub," and an elaborate two-page spread shows him amid toy soldiers, boats, and bubbles. The queen, the duke, and others try to persuade him to dry off, but in the end it is the young page who solves the problem—he pulls the plug! Wood's glorious pictures must be seen to be appreciated. The realistic figures are executed in glowing colors, and the rich detailing both in costumes and settings brings the Renaissance court to life. As he did in **The Napping House,** Don Wood delineates the passage of time through the use of subtly changing light that enriches the pictures with magnificent hues. Beauty aside, this also has a panache and sly wit that will please children and their parents, who will be called on to peruse the book again and again.

> *Ilene Cooper, in a review of "King Bidgood's in the Bathtub," in* Booklist, *Vol. 82, No. 3, October 1, 1985, p. 272.*

Audrey and Don Wood seem to enjoy their work. In their book **The Napping House** and in this latest creation they express an exuberance that is quite infectious. **King Bidgood's in the Bathtub** is a short farce about a Renaissance King who one day refuses to leave his bathtub. Members of his royal staff (including the Queen) attempt to persuade him to perform his kingly duties. One by one they fail. As this dilemma builds to a tumultuous and bubbly climax, a clever Page, in a surprise gesture, finds an apt solution.

The nicely designed jacket serves as a prologue—the illustration shows the delighted king peeking through his bath curtain. Telltale bubbles and steam drift over the courtiers' heads as the title starts the story: "King Bidgood's in the Bathtub." Opening the cover, the jacket flap copy announces " . . . and he won't get out!"

The painting on the title page (the illustrations are all oil paintings) shows us an exterior view of the king's castle, densely packed with turrets and stone walkways. Turn the page and there is a double-page spread of the castle's interior, showing endless stairs up which the straining Page is carrying water to our hydropathist.

These outside and inside views are a good example of rhythm and pacing, core elements of a picture book. The book builds in a series of double-page illustrations. Views of the royal staff members outside the bath alternate with

*From* Heckedy Peg. *written by Audrey Wood. Illustrated by Don Wood.*

scenes of their attempted persuasion inside, culminating with the entire court immersed with the King.

The confusion near the end reminds me of the magnificent scene in "A Night at the Opera," the Marx Brothers movie, in which what appear to be dozens of people congregate in a tiny cabin aboard an ocean liner. Just when it seems that not one more person can fit, another appears, poised to enter. The door is slowly opened and a tidal wave of people pours out in a great gush. It's startling, explosive and hilarious.

Unfortunately there is no similarly funny resolution in the Woods' book. Throughout, the bathtub scenes are clearly the most fun, so that when the Page, as hero, puts an end to the merriment (and does it in a rather lackluster manner)—we're disappointed. Instead of cheering the Page for his resourcefulness, we resent him.

Another element disturbed me. All the characters are painted to look as if they are overacting. In a farce, even a broad farce, such elaboration is deadly. Combined with language like "glub, glub, glub" or "yum, yum, yum" one senses a failure to be truthful to the lighthearted nature of the story. This false ring has a quality of condescension which I don't believe was the author's intention. In truth, even pure entertainment for young children can be vibrant and personal, ultimately lasting, without being overdone.

> *Arthur Yorinks, in a review of "King Bidgood's in the Bathtub," in* The New York Times Book Review, *October 13, 1985, p. 37.*

In this humorously original tale, various members of the Court, all clothed in elaborate Elizabethan dress, try to dislodge the King from his bubbly tub. . . . Much of the delight is in Don Wood's meticulous oil paintings, which juxtapose the starched, overdressed, "shocked" demeanor of the Court with the King's twinkling, sensual, even lascivious manner. Minute details in the paintings emphasize this contrast; the red-haired naked King frolics while the fully-clothed courtiers emerge dripping from the bath with literally all their starch taken out. A voluptuous book whose rich range of colors and tones reflect the passing hours of the day. As in the Woods' **Napping House,** the few simple words of text per large, well-designed page invite storytelling—but keep the group very small, so the children can be close enough to pore over the brilliant, robust illustrations.

> *Susan Patron, in a review of "King Bidgood's in the Bathtub," in* School Library Journal, *Vol. 32, No. 3, November, 1985, p. 79.*

### Heckedy Peg (1987)

**Heckedy Peg** is a story fashioned and inspired by a 16th-century game that has lasted through the ages. Audrey Wood's nicely bare-boned tale begins: "Down the dusty roads and far away, a poor mother once lived with her seven children named Monday, Tuesday, Wednesday, Thursday, Friday, Saturday, and Sunday." There is a sense of the past in this book, a feel of a familiar tale told at the fire to old and young alike, a timeless quality to this mother's unconditional and steadfast love for her children. There is also a truly rotten witch, Heckedy Peg, who challenges the lighthearted innocence of the children, though one Don Wood picture suggests that her evil may be complicated. Any witch who wears a feather boa can't be all bad.

Mr. Wood's lush full-color oil paintings have the depth and textures of old masters, but at times they seem a bit crowded, like too many fine paintings hung in a gallery. They fit well with the ancient story, and there is a fascinating use of light that tells us more than words can about the the family's joyfulness. These children, each with a face so individual that you begin to know him or her, actually care for one another. Their mother loves and knows them best, however, and in the end she protects them as only a parent can. The conclusion, I am glad to say, has not been softened for the faint of heart; it fits the time and setting, and any adult who may object should remember G. K. Chesterton's words: "Children are innocent and love justice while most of us are wicked and naturally prefer mercy."

> *Patricia MacLachlan, "Magic Good, Bad and Rotten," in* The New York Times Book Review, *November 8, 1987, p. 50.*

With heady artistic and textual momentum, the Woods have collaborated on an exuberant new picture book production. Seven children named after the days of the week each request something special from the market as their mother sets out, warning them against admitting strangers or touching fire. Along comes witch Heckedy Peg, who convinces them to light her pipe and then turns them into food, which she plans to eat back at her hovel. In the end, the mother finds them but must guess which child is which to break the spell, and she does so by matching up the food on the table with the children's requests ("Bread wants butter. That's Monday"). There's nothing more gripping than a kidnapping-rescue tale, and these large-scale illustrations play up the drama with throbbing color contrasts and swirling lines of action. Dark tones dominate the danger, while the opening and closing idylls glow with golden green. The page design is compellingly varied. The realistic portraits are well drafted; though individualized, each child is radiant with trust, their mother unfailing in strength, the witch eerily grotesque. Occasionally, the effects are slick, but this has a rhythmic vitality characteristic of the Woods' best work.

> *Betsy Hearne, in a review of "Heckedy Peg," in* Bulletin of the Center for Children's Books, *Vol. 41, No. 4, December, 1987, p. 80.*

Although the dust jacket claims that the story was "inspired by a sixteenth-century game still played by children today," the narrative depends not on prototypical characters in universal folkloric situations but upon artificiality and clichés. . . . Contrived though the story is, the artwork—albeit technically adroit—is even more disturbing. Don Wood employs a grandiose baroque style to illustrate a text that attempts to emulate the pattern and structure of a childlike, straightforward folk tale. Specifically, the pages display a kind of rampant eclecticism with pretentious visual echoes of painters from Rubens to Sendak. Presuming to create atmosphere, the artist has given the book a slick, superficial glamour, expending a great deal of oil paint in elaborate illustrations that are heavy with color, with irrelevant detail—a super abundance of drapery, for example—and with an excess of overwrought emotion. (pp. 197-98)

> *Ethel L. Heins, in a review of "Heckedy Peg," in* The Horn Book Magazine, *Vol. LXIV, No. 2, March-April, 1988, pp. 197-98.*

---

### Elbert's Bad Word　(1988)

As the only child at an elegant party, Elbert hears a strange word. "The word floated by like a small storm cloud. It was ugly and covered with dark, bristly hairs. With a swift flick of his wrist, Elbert snatched the word from the air and stuffed it into his back pocket." Soon the word flies into his mouth "like a little gnat." When Elbert is upset a moment later, out comes the word. "Everyone at the party was shocked. They couldn't believe their ears." Enter a friendly wizard gardener, who shows Elbert how other words, uttered with enthusiasm, are more satisfying than the little monster. The next time he needs to let off some steam, Elbert emits *Thunder and Lightning!* and *Blistering Hoptoads!* and the act brings him cheers from fellow party-goers. The slapstick events of the party will engage readers from the start; the image of the word as a little monster frees the story from didacticism while making clear that bad words are not necessary, given a few creative substitutions. A comic but sensible book on the topic.

> *A review of "Elbert's Bad Word," in* Publishers Weekly, *Vol. 234, No. 11, September 9, 1988, p. 133.*

This single-idea cautionary tale has lively, absurdist pictures of tiara-crowned, formally dressed adults recoiling in horror or cavorting with glee when Elbert, the only child at the party, speaks a word. The transformation of a word into a visible, furry creature, makes its point clearly, but the long words offered as replacement (MY STARS! . . . RATS AND BLUE BLAZES! . . . ZOUNDS AND GADZOOKS!) are as alien to a modern child as the adult garden party with its butler and titled guests. The book may offer a way for adults to tackle the thorny problem of bad language, but good-boy Elbert, with his bow tie and soaped mouth, is unlikely to be a child's favorite story character.

> *Shirley Wilton, in a review of "Elbert's Bad Word," in* School Library Journal, *Vol. 35, No. 2, October, 1988, p. 130.*

In a spoof as lighthearted as the Woods' ***King Bidgood's in the Bathtub,*** a small boy at a stuffy garden party encounters a truly reprehensible word.

The story is made funnier by its quiet understatement. The collaborative illustrations are less pretentious than some of Don Wood's work, and more polished than his wife's: well designed, satirical (the crowd of adult guests all wear black and supercilious, complacent expressions), and full of action. The bad word waxes and wanes, a wonderfully comic manifestation. A delightfully imaginative book.

> *A review of "Elbert's Bad Word," in* Kirkus

Reviews, *Vol. LVI, No. 19, October 1, 1988,* p. *1476.*

# CUMULATIVE INDEX TO AUTHORS

This index lists all author entries in *Children's Literature Review* and includes cross-references to them in other Gale sources. References in the index are identified as follows:

**AAYA:** *Authors & Artists for Young Adults* Volumes 1-6
**CA:** *Contemporary Authors* (original series), Volumes 1-133
**CANR:** *Contemporary Authors New Revision Series,* Volumes 1-33
**CAP:** *Contemporary Authors Permanent Series,* Volumes 1-2
**CA-R:** *Contemporary Authors* (revised editions), Volumes 1-44
**CDALB:** *Concise Dictionary of American Literary Biography,* Volumes 1-6
**CLC:** *Contemporary Literary Criticism,* Volumes 1-68
**CLR:** *Children's Literature Review,* Volumes 1-26
**DLB:** *Dictionary of Literary Biography,* Volumes 1-107
**DLB-DS:** *Dictionary of Literary Biography Documentary Series,* Volumes 1-8
**DLB-Y:** *Dictionary of Literary Biography Yearbook,* Volumes 1980-1989
**LC:** *Literature Criticism from 1400 to 1800,* Volumes 1-17
**NCLC:** *Nineteenth-Century Literature Criticism,* Volumes 1-33
**SAAS:** *Something about the Author Autobiography Series,* Volumes 1-12
**SATA:** *Something about the Author,* Volumes 1-65
**TCLC:** *Twentieth-Century Literary Criticism,* Volumes 1-43
**YABC:** *Yesterday's Authors of Books for Children,* Volumes 1-2

Author Index

# CUMULATIVE INDEX TO NATIONALITIES

Hamilton, Virginia  **1, 11**
Hansen, Joyce  **21**
Haskins, James  **3**
Hautzig, Esther R.  **22**
Haywood, Carolyn  **22**
Henkes, Kevin  **23**
Henry, Marguerite  **4**
Hentoff, Nat  **1**
Highwater, Jamake  **17**
Hinton, S. E.  **3, 23**
Hoban, Russell  **3**
Hoban, Tana  **13**
Hoberman, Mary Ann  **22**
Hogrogian, Nonny  **2**
Howe, James  **9**
Hughes, Langston  **17**
Hunt, Irene  **1**
Hunter, Kristin  **3**
Hurmence, Belinda  **25**
Hyde, Margaret O.  **23**
Isadora, Rachel  **7**
Jarrell, Randall  **6**
Jonas, Ann  **12**
Jordan, June  **10**
Joyce, William  **26**
Keats, Ezra Jack  **1**
Kellogg, Steven  **6**
Kherdian, David  **24**
Klein, Norma  **2, 19**
Konigsburg, E. L.  **1**
Kotzwinkle, William  **6**
Krementz, Jill  **5**
Kuskin, Karla  **4**
Langstaff, John  **3**
Lasky, Kathryn  **11**
Lauber, Patricia  **16**
Lawson, Robert  **2**
Le Guin, Ursula K.  **3**
Leaf, Munro  **25**
L'Engle, Madeleine  **1, 14**
Lenski, Lois  **26**
LeShan, Eda J.  **6**
Lester, Julius  **2**
Lionni, Leo  **7**
Lipsyte, Robert  **23**
Livingston, Myra Cohn  **7**
Lobel, Arnold  **5**
Locker, Thomas  **14**
Lowry, Lois  **6**
MacLachlan, Patricia  **14**
Manley, Seon  **3**
Marshall, James  **21**
Mathis, Sharon Bell  **3**
Mayer, Mercer  **11**
Mazer, Harry  **16**
Mazer, Norma Fox  **23**
McCloskey, Robert  **7**
McClung, Robert M.  **11**
McCord, David  **9**
McDermott, Gerald  **9**
McHargue, Georgess  **2**
McKinley, Robin  **10**
McKissack, Patricia C.  **23**
Meltzer, Milton  **13**
Merriam, Eve  **14**
Milne, Lorus J.  **22**
Milne, Margery J.  **22**
Mohr, Nicholasa  **22**
Monjo, F. N.  **2**
Moore, Lilian  **15**
Mukerji, Dhan Gopal  **10**
Munsch, Robert N.  **19**

Myers, Walter Dean  **4, 16**
Naylor, Phyllis Reynolds  **17**
Ness, Evaline  **6**
Nixon, Joan Lowery  **24**
O'Brien, Robert C.  **2**
O'Dell, Scott  **1, 16**
Oneal, Zibby  **13**
Parish, Peggy  **22**
Pascal, Francine  **25**
Patent, Dorothy Hinshaw  **19**
Paterson, Katherine  **7**
Paulsen, Gary  **19**
Peck, Richard  **15**
Peet, Bill  **12**
Petersham, Maud  **24**
Petersham, Miska  **24**
Petry, Ann  **12**
Pfeffer, Susan Beth  **11**
Pierce, Meredith Ann  **20**
Pinkwater, D. Manus  **4**
Prelutsky, Jack  **13**
Pringle, Laurence  **4**
Provensen, Alice  **11**
Provensen, Martin  **11**
Pyle, Howard  **22**
Raskin, Ellen  **1, 12**
Rau, Margaret  **8**
Reiss, Johanna  **19**
Rey, H. A.  **5**
Rey, Margret  **5**
Rockwell, Thomas  **6**
Rodgers, Mary  **20**
Rylant, Cynthia  **15**
Sachs, Marilyn  **2**
Salinger, J. D.  **18**
Sanchez, Sonia  **18**
Sattler, Helen Roney  **24**
Say, Allen  **22**
Scarry, Richard  **3**
Schwartz, Alvin  **3**
Schwartz, Amy  **25**
Scott, Jack Denton  **20**
Sebestyen, Ouida  **17**
Selden, George  **8**
Selsam, Millicent E.  **1**
Sendak, Maurice  **1, 17**
Seredy, Kate  **10**
Seuss, Dr.  **9**
Showers, Paul  **6**
Shulevitz, Uri  **5**
Silverstein, Alvin  **25**
Silverstein, Shel  **5**
Silverstein, Virginia B.  **25**
Simon, Seymour  **9**
Singer, Isaac Bashevis  **1**
Slote, Alfred  **4**
Smucker, Barbara  **10**
Sneve, Virginia Driving Hawk  **2**
Sobol, Donald J.  **4**
Speare, Elizabeth George  **8**
Spier, Peter  **5**
Spinelli, Jerry  **26**
Steig, William  **2, 15**
Steptoe, John  **2, 12**
Sterling, Dorothy  **1**
Stevenson, James  **17**
Strasser, Todd  **11**
Suhl, Yuri  **2**
Tarry, Ellen  **26**
Taylor, Mildred D.  **9**
Thomas, Ianthe  **8**
Thomas, Joyce Carol  **19**

Thompson, Julian F.  **24**
Thompson, Kay  **22**
Tobias, Tobi  **4**
Tudor, Tasha  **13**
Tunis, Edwin  **2**
Uchida, Yoshiko  **6**
Van Allsburg, Chris  **5, 13**
Viorst, Judith  **3**
Voigt, Cynthia  **13**
Walter, Mildred Pitts  **15**
Watson, Clyde  **3**
Weiss, Harvey  **4**
Wells, Rosemary  **16**
Wersba, Barbara  **3**
White, E. B.  **1, 21**
White, Robb  **3**
Wibberley, Leonard  **3**
Wilder, Laura Ingalls  **2**
Wilkinson, Brenda  **20**
Willard, Nancy  **5**
Williams, Jay  **8**
Williams, Vera B.  **9**
Wojciechowska, Maia  **1**
Wood, Audrey  **26**
Wood, Don  **26**
Worth, Valerie  **21**
Yashima, Taro  **4**
Yep, Laurence  **3, 17**
Yolen, Jane  **4**
Yorinks, Arthur  **20**
Zim, Herbert S.  **2**
Zindel, Paul  **3**
Zolotow, Charlotte  **2**

**AUSTRALIAN**
Base, Graeme  **22**
Chauncy, Nan  **6**
Fox, Mem  **23**
Hilton, Nette  **25**
Klein, Robin  **21**
Lindsay, Norman  **8**
Mattingley, Christobel  **24**
Ormerod, Jan  **20**
Ottley, Reginald  **16**
Phipson, Joan  **5**
Southall, Ivan  **2**
Spence, Eleanor  **26**
Travers, P. L.  **2**
Wrightson, Patricia  **4, 14**

**AUSTRIAN**
Bemelmans, Ludwig  **6**
Nostlinger, Christine  **12**

**BELGIAN**
Herge  **6**
Vincent, Gabrielle  **13**

**CANADIAN**
Blades, Ann  **15**
Burnford, Sheila  **2**
Cleaver, Elizabeth  **13**
Cox, Palmer  **24**
Doyle, Brian  **22**
Houston, James  **3**
Hughes, Monica  **9**
Korman, Gordon  **25**
Kurelek, William  **2**
Lee, Dennis  **3**
Little, Jean  **4**
Lunn, Janet  **18**
Major, Kevin  **11**

# CUMULATIVE INDEX TO TITLES

Title Index

**Title Index**

Title Index

**Title Index**

*Title Index*

Title Index

ISBN 0-8103-4863-2